MI & SOU...

ACCESS

Orientation

While anyone who reads newspapers today knows that **South Florida** is not always paradise, it still comes close, especially for visitors escaping from northern winters. From **Key West** to the old-money world of **Palm Beach**, from the "River of Grass" known as the **Everglades** to the pristine beaches along the **Gulf of Mexico**, South Florida lures vacationers with its magical blend of water, sand, and palms.

Nature still dominates life in the region. Compared with other metropolitan areas, South Florida's air is virtually pollution-free. Trade winds sweep away city grime, and the cities that have sprung up here on the edge of the Everglades are, for the most part, sparkling clean. Tourists and locals alike look to the sea for comfort and pleasure, experiencing it at a distance from chaise lounges or up close in Hobie Cats, Jet Skis, and ocean kayaks available for hire. From French-influenced **Hollywood** (popular with Canadians in the winter) to **South Beach** (the trendiest spot in South Florida), water sports of all kinds provide hours of entertainment on the Atlantic. And on the kinder, gentler Gulf of Mexico, the beaches on **Sanibel** and **Marco Islands** are world famous for their abundance of seashells.

While nature has been good to the region, it also has cursed it. On 24 August 1992, South Floridians—especially those in **South Dade County**—experienced nature's fury with the arrival of Hurricane Andrew. Most of the building damage has been repaired, and many things look even better than they did before the storm. The trees and foliage have recovered in most places, but toppled trees, stripped palms, and lopsided regrowth of Norfolk Island pines are still evident on **Key Biscayne** and around **Homestead.**

A more benign but still dramatic gesture of nature is the South Florida sunset. In Key West this event is celebrated amid jugglers, T-shirt vendors, and mellow hippies. The western sky turns pink, crimson, violet, and blue until the sun sinks into the water. That fiery ball is an endless source of energy—and income—for South Florida.

When you visit makes a difference. Miami bustles year-round, and the tourist season is long in the **Florida Keys.** On the other hand, such destinations as **Naples**, Palm Beach, and **Ft. Lauderdale** are quieter (and less expensive) during the hot summer. June through November is hurricane season, when afternoon showers are a daily event.

But you can always count on the sun. And as you settle in after a day at the beach, you'll find that years of worry lines have disappeared. Daylight slips away, and the neon lights start buzzing. It's time to change the pace. Start with a cocktail or a fresh-squeezed lemonade, topped off with an ocean view. Hungry? Seafood is always the best bet. And no matter where you are, never hesitate to ask about the fresh catch of the day. Grouper, dolphin (the fish, not the porpoise), shrimp, and stone crab— all hauled in from local waters—are certifiably delicious.

How To Read This Guide

Miami & South Florida ACCESS® is arranged by neighborhood so you can see at a glance where you are and what is around you. The numbers next to the entries in the following chapters correspond to the numbers on the maps. The text is color-coded according to the kind of place described:

Restaurants/Clubs: Red   Hotels: Blue

Shops/♦ Outdoors: Green   Sights/Culture: Black

    ♿ **Wheelchair accessible**

Wheelchair Accessibility

An establishment (except a restaurant) is considered wheelchair accessible when a person in a wheelchair can easily enter a building (i.e., no steps, a ramp, a wide-enough door) without assistance. Restaurants are deemed wheelchair accessible *only* if the above applies *and* if the rest rooms are on the same floor as the dining area and their entrances and stalls are wide enough to accommodate a wheelchair.

Rating the Restaurants and Hotels

The restaurant ratings take into account the quality, service, atmosphere, and uniqueness of the restaurant. An expensive restaurant doesn't necessarily ensure an enjoyable evening; however, a small, relatively unknown spot may have good food, professional service, and a lovely atmosphere. Therefore, on a purely subjective basis, stars are used to judge the overall dining value (see the star ratings at right). Keep in mind that chefs and owners often change, which sometimes drastically affects the quality of a restaurant. The ratings in this guidebook are based on information available at press time.

The price ratings, as categorized at right, apply to restaurants and hotels. These figures reflect the general price range of establishments in the area.

The restaurant price ratings are based on the average cost of an entrée for one person, excluding tax and tip. Hotel price ratings reflect the base price of a standard room for two people for one night during the peak season.

Restaurants

★ Good	
★★ Very Good	
★★★ Excellent	
★★★★ An Extraordinary Experience	
$ The Price Is Right	(less than $8)
$$ Reasonable	($8-$14)
$$$ Expensive	($14-$20)
$$$$ Big Bucks	($20 and up)

Hotels

$ The Price Is Right	(less than $100)
$$ Reasonable	($100-$175)
$$$ Expensive	($175-$250)
$$$$ Big Bucks	($250 and up)

Map Key

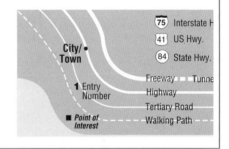

Getting to South Florida

South Florida is easily accessible by all forms of transportation. Airline travel to **Miami** is direct and swift from almost any place in the US, and Miami is the major entry point for air traffic from Latin America. Miami is also the site of the world's largest cruise port—with **Ft. Lauderdale's Port Everglades** running a close second. The **Gulf Coast** boasts an ultramodern international airport near **Ft. Myers,** with a growing number of flights. **Interstates 95** and **75** offer direct routes by car, although you may be surprised at how long it takes to drive here from North Florida—it's a good eight-hour journey from the Florida-Georgia border. As for other surface transport, **Amtrak, Greyhound,** and even car-pool rides advertised in local classifieds will get you to South Florida.

FYI

Accommodations

Hotel reservations are highly recommended throughout South Florida, particularly during the winter. Directories of accommodations are available free from each area's convention and visitors' bureau. The **Florida Accommodations Directory,** an annual compilation of 800 to 850 member hotels of Florida's major hotel association, is available from the **Florida Hotel/Motel Association** (200 W College Ave, Tallahassee FL 32301, 904/224.2888). Send $2 (for international requests, send $4); only mail requests will be honored.

Climate

Florida's designation as the Sunshine State is not just some starry-eyed copywriter's fanciful ad copy. Expect brief thunderstorms during the summer rainy season, especially in the afternoon. Bring a sweater or long-sleeved overshirt even in summer, as hotel air-conditioning can be chilly. Hurricane season runs from June through November. If a hurricane watch is declared, stay tuned to local media for information.

Months	Average Temperature (°F)
January-March	69
April-June	78
July-September	82
October-December	73

Drinking
The legal drinking age in Florida is 21. Alcoholic beverages are verboten on beaches and in parks, and it's no longer legal to carry open cans and bottles in cars. Some cities in Florida ban alcohol sales on Sunday mornings. Bar hours vary by municipality and by county.

Fishing Licenses
Required in Florida for people over 16 years old (senior citizens excluded), saltwater fishing licenses are available at bait and diving shops, sporting goods stores, marinas, and tax collectors' offices. For more information, call the **Florida Marine Patrol** (800/342.5367).

Seat Belts and Child Restraint Seats
Florida law requires that front-seat passengers wear seat belts. Children under five years old or weighing less than 40 pounds must travel in car seats throughout the state.

Smoking
Smoking is prohibited in most places in South Florida, including malls, public buildings, and offices. Some large restaurants set aside smoking sections.

Taxes
Florida's statewide sales tax is six percent, to which most counties tack on additional tariffs. Additionally, on car rental bills, the entire state charges a $2.05 daily tax. And some cities levy an additional tax on accommodations and restaurant meals.

Telephone
The area code for Dade County (Miami), Broward County (Ft. Lauderdale), and Monroe County (the Keys) is 305 (you may have to prefix the 305 with "1" before some local numbers); for Palm Beach County, it's 407; and for Gulf Coast cities such as Naples and Ft. Myers, it's 941. Dial "1" before toll calls and long-distance numbers. At pay phones, local calls cost 25¢; credit card and collect calls have a $1 surcharge.

Time Zone
South Florida is on Eastern time.

Tipping
Some establishments tack a tip onto a restaurant check, especially for groups of five or more. A standard gratuity is 15 to 20 percent.

Visitors' Information Centers
Florida has a well-developed information network for visitors. The **Florida Vacation Guide** is available free from the **Florida Department of Commerce, Division of Tourism, Visitor Inquiry** (126 W Van Buren St, Tallahassee FL 32399-2000, 904/487.1462). For information on attractions, contact the **Florida Attractions Association** (PO Box 10295, Tallahassee FL 32302, 904/222.2885). Camping information is available from the **Florida Campground Association** (1638 N Plaza Dr, Tallahassee FL 32308-5364, 904/656.8878); for a copy of the *Florida State Parks Guide,* call 904/488.9872. For sports brochures and schedules, contact the **Florida Sports Foundation** (107 W Gaines St, Tallahassee FL 32399-2000, 904/488.8347). In addition, each area has local visitors' and convention bureaus that provide free guides to the area, accommodations directories, and other information.

The Main Events

Whether it's dancing in a conga line that stretches as far as the eye can see or cheering talented athletes toward victory, folks in South Florida need no excuse for celebration, especially in the winter, when the weather is pleasantly cool. Here are some of the year's major events—call ahead for specific dates. All phone numbers are in the 305 area code unless otherwise noted.

January

Orange Bowl Classic and Festival Culminating with one of college football's biggest games on **New Year's Day**, the **Orange Bowl Festival** in **Miami** runs from mid-December through mid-January, with parades, pageants, and sports contests. In 1996, the game will move from its namesake venue, the **Orange Bowl**, to **Joe Robbie Stadium**. Call 471.4600 for more information. The day after the game, the **Carquest Bowl** between the Southeastern and Big East conferences takes place (call 564.5000).

Art Deco Weekend Few places in the nation celebrate their architectural heritage with a street party, but **South Beach** goes all out to mark the rebirth of the world's interest in Art Deco buildings. Call 672.2014 for information.

Taste of the Grove Restaurants in Miami's **Coconut Grove** neighborhood show off their most popular dishes to a hungry crowd (call 444.7270). If you're in the mood for more, stop by the **South Florida International Wine and Food Festival** in **Miami Beach** the following weekend (call 531.4851).

February

Miami Film Festival Foreign films, US premieres, and the best from Cannes are screened at various locations; call 377.3456 for information.

Irish Fest Set in **Ft. Lauderdale**'s **Bubier Park,** this music, dance, and food festival shows that South Florida's range of ethnicities extends well beyond Latin America and the Caribbean (call 800/882.ERIN).

Coconut Grove Arts Festival One of the nation's largest arts festivals unfolds here on **Presidents' Day** weekend, when 300 artisans come from all over to sell original posters, sculpture, and other works of art on the streets of this central neighborhood. More than 50 chefs prepare culinary samples (call 447.0401).

Canadafest Long a favorite haven for snowbirds from Quebec, **Hollywood Beach** hosts this celebration, giving visitors a chance to hear lilting French or sample *poutine* (french fries with cheese sauce). For information, call 921.3399.

Doral-Ryder Open This major **Professional Golf Association (PGA)** tournament brings together the top names in the sport to battle for dominance at the **Doral Golf Resort & Spa** in **West Miami,** competing for $1.4 million in prizes. Call 422.4653 for more information.

March

Annual Sanibel Shell Fair The **Gulf Coast** community of **Sanibel Island,** one of the best areas in the US to collect seashells, hosts this cornucopia of treasures from the deep. For information, call 941/472.2155.

Lipton Championships Tennis players from around the world compete at this two-week tournament at the **International Tennis Center** on **Key Biscayne,** a quiet island overlooking downtown Miami. For information, call 446.2200.

Carnaval Miami/Calle Ocho Join the longest conga line in the world, taste Cuban delicacies and vats of paella, and dance the merengue almost anywhere along this 23-block celebration of Miami's Hispanic heritage in **Little Havana,** where Latin stars entertain. For information, call 644.8888.

Seven-Mile Bridge Run Not just for recreational joggers, this jog across the **Seven-Mile Bridge** in the **Florida Keys** attracts top athletes. The setting is breathtaking, with the **Gulf of Mexico** on one side and the **Atlantic Ocean** on the other. For information, call 743.8513.

SunFest Downtown **West Palm Beach** hosts one of the world's largest jazz festivals for three days, during which not only music—but also arts and crafts, food, and water sports—keeps visitors entertained (call 407/659.5992).

May

Naples Tropicool Fest Canoe races, art exhibits, and concerts highlight this outdoor festival at various locations around **Naples** on the Gulf Coast (call 941/262.6141).

June

Goombay Street Festival Highlighting Miami's links to the Bahamas and Africa, this Coconut Grove fest celebrates with food, a parade, and other entertainment (call 372.9966).

July

Ft. Lauderdale Fourth of July Sandblast Before the castles melt into the sea, glimpse the spectacular sand sculptures at this sand castle contest on **Ft. Lauderdale Beach;** the event culminates in an elaborate fireworks display. Call 761.5363 for information.

August

Miami Reggae Festival Two days of reggae music played in **Bicentennial Park** in downtown Miami will make you feel as if you've journeyed to Jamaica. For information, call 891.2944.

October

Columbus Day Regatta Although this is officially a sailboat race from Key Biscayne to an offshore island, many revelers in South Florida's largest yachting event find time to toss water balloons at each other and catch all-over tans. From shore, the sight of colorful spinnakers poised against the blue waters of **Biscayne Bay** is stunning. Call 593.3065 for information.

November

Miami Book Fair International One of the largest fairs of its type in the nation, this week-long festival for bibliophiles draws publishers from all over the world, writers, and hundreds of street vendors to downtown Miami. For more information, call 237.3258.

Festival of Trees What happens when professional designers and artists create Christmas displays? The results are on exhibit at the **Museum of Art** in Ft. Lauderdale. Call 525.5500 for more information.

December

Winterfest Boat Parade The parade of yachts and sailboats laden with twinkling Christmas lights is a South Florida tradition, and this one on the **Intracoastal Waterway** in Ft. Lauderdale is the biggest of them all. People line the shore to watch this nocturnal celebration of holiday magic. Call 767.0686 for more information.

Miami/Dade County

Once known solely for its sandy beaches, posh hotels, and lush tropical landscape, Miami has in the past 35 years become a vibrant international community; in fact, it's sometimes referred to as the capital of Latin America. Thanks to massive migration, dollar flight, and investment from the Caribbean and Latin America, the city is a base for all kinds of commerce and industry, as evidenced by its skyline of towering banks and office buildings that cater to global trade.

Miami's development as a major metropolis is echoed by the flowering of a world-class arts and entertainment community, including two symphony orchestras, a professional ballet company, and an annual international book fair. The ambience of **South Beach**, once a declining neighborhood, has been compared to that of the French Riviera, with its European-style sidewalk cafes, elegant dining spots, and a glittering clientele to match. (All told, Dade County comprises 28 municipalities, among them **Miami**

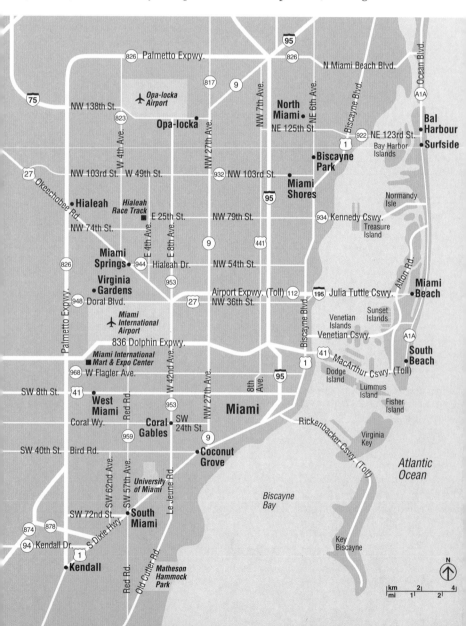

Beach, **Coral Gables,** and **Aventura,** and a plethora of neighborhoods, including **Little Havana** and **Little Haiti.**) In addition, families can enjoy **Metrozoo, Parrot Jungle and Gardens, Fairchild Tropical Gardens,** the **Miami Seaquarium,** and **Villa Vizcaya,** an Italianate mansion overlooking **Biscayne Bay.**

Miami's international ties were born with the area's first tourist, most likely the Spaniard Ponce de León, who explored Biscayne Bay in 1513. Europeans settled the region half a century later with the establishment of the Spanish Jesuit mission **Tequesta.** Pioneers came later, and industry slowly took hold.

In the early 19th century, fierce wars raged between the native Seminole and the settlers. **Fort Dallas,** an army outpost established in the 1840s to protect settlers, is generally considered the first "town" in Dade County and the precursor of Miami. The settlers and the Seminole eventually made peace as the town grew into an important trade center. But Miami remained little more than an outpost until 1896, when Henry M. Flagler extended his **Florida East Coast Railroad** to Biscayne Bay. He was enticed by a group of Miamians led by Julia Tuttle, who knew Flagler was dismayed that his chances of luring northern tourists south had dimmed after the disastrous freeze of 1894-95, which had extended nearly to Palm Beach. Tuttle sent Flagler a branch of orange blossoms to prove that Miami remained balmy and unaffected by the disaster.

Once persuaded, Flagler settled in Miami, financing the building of hotels, the dredging of Biscayne Bay, and other civic improvements. But the city's growth was still limited by the **Everglades,** an enormous marshland that began near what is now **Northwest 27th Avenue.** Private dredging of the vast area began in 1909; by the 1920s, a real estate boom had taken hold. In the late 1920s, however, the city was hit by the Great Depression, a terrible hurricane, and a capsized ship that blocked **Government Cut,** Miami's principal pathway to the ocean. During World War II, the military established training bases in South Florida. After the war, many men who had trained as soldiers returned as civilians, and a new population boom began.

Fidel Castro seized power in Cuba in 1959, touching off an exodus that would permanently alter Miami's demographics. Thousands of Cubans arrived in the so-called Freedom Flights of the 1960s, many of them successful entrepreneurs whose businesses and properties had been confiscated.

Less than 20 years later, political unrest in Haiti led to another addition to Miami's so-called melting pot, as thousands of Haitians moved into what would become Little Haiti, north of downtown. Today, the city is a tropical melange of cultures, offering a richness of languages and customs, foods and festivals, attitudes and traditions.

Miami has certainly had its share of ups and downs, and Dade County is plagued with complex ethnic tensions with nary a solution in sight. But despite those problems, people come to Miami to flee oppression in other countries—and to escape boredom and homogeneity in other states. Played out against the tropical landscape, all this human drama only adds to the city's intriguing complexity.

Area code 305 unless otherwise indicated.

Getting to Miami/Dade County

Airports

Miami International Airport (MIA) is the seventh-largest in the nation in total passenger volume and the second-busiest in international traffic. (More than 30 million travelers came through **MIA** in 1994, more than half of them international passengers.) Located eight miles west of downtown, the airport has its own police and fire stations, a huge cargo terminal, 34 shops, 48 restaurants, and a 24-hour multilingual information service (in front of **Concourse E**). **MIA** is in the middle of an expansion project that will double the terminal space and roughly double the number of gates, among other changes. To contact the police, use one of the special phones labeled "Airport Tourist Police."

Airport Services

Airport Emergencies	911
Currency Exchange	876.0040
Customs	869.2800
Immigration	536.5741
Information	876.7000, 876.7515
Interpreters	876.7515
Lost and Found	876.7515
Parking	876.7515
Police	876.7373

Airlines

Aeroflot	577.8500, 800/867.8774
Aerolineas Argentinas	530.9926, 800/333.0276
Aeroméxico	441.0090, 800/237.6639
AeroPerú	594.0022, 800/777.7717
Air Aruba	551.1100, 800/882.7822
Air Canada	800/363.5440, 800/776.3000 in FL
Air France	374.2626, 800/237.2747
Air Jamaica	358.3222, 800/523.5585
Alitalia	526.6815, 539.0593, 800/223.5730
ALM Antillean	477.0955, 800/327.7230
American	800/433.7300
Avensa	381.8001, 800/4AVENSA
Avianca	883.5151, 800/AVIANCA
Aviateca Aerolineas de Guatemala	871.1587, 800/327.9832
Bahamas Air	800/222.4262
British Airways	526.7800, 800/247.9297
BWIA	371.2942, 800/327.7401
Cayman Airways	266.4141, 800/422.9626
Chalk's International	371.8628, 800/4CHALKS
Continental	871.1400, 800/525.0280
COPA	477.7333, 800/FLYCOPA
Delta	448.7000, 800/221.1212
Ecuatoriana	800/328.2367
El Al	532.5441, 800/223.6700
Faucett	591.0610, 800/334.3356, 800/432.0468 in FL
Guyana Airways	871.8480, 800/327.8680
Haiti Trans Air	590.1200, 800/394.5313
Hispaniola Airways	591.1704, 800/570.3806
Iberia	800/772.4642
LAB	374.4600, 800/327.7407

Miami International Airport

F   E   D

■ Main Information Counter (Level 2)

G   C

H   B

Gate Locations for Major Airlines

Concourse B
Air France
Virgin Atlantic

Concourse C
American

Concourse D
American
American Eagle

Concourse E
British Airways
BWIA
El Al
Lufthansa
Tower Air

Concourse F
Avianca
Carnival
Iberia
United
Viasa

Concourse G
Air Canada
Air South
Bahamasair
Northwest/KLM
Paradise Island

Concourse H
America West
Continental/SAS
Delta
TWA
USAir

LACSA	800/225.2272
LADECO Chilean	670.6705, 800/825.2332
LAN Chile	670.9933, 800/735.5526
Lufthansa	526.8936, 800/645.3880
Mexicana	526.6214, 800/531.7921
Nicaraguense	223.0312, 800/831.6422
Northwest	441.1096, 800/225.2525
SAETA	477.2104, 800/82SAETA
SAHSA	526.4330, 800/327.1225
Surinam Airways	262.9792, 800/432.1230
TACA International	800/535.8780
Trans-Brasil	591.8322, 800/872.3153
TWA	371.7471, 800/221.2000
United domestic travel	800/241.6522

international travel	800/538.2929
USAir	358.3396, 800/428.4322
Varig Brazilian	358.3935, 800/468.2744
VIASA	358.3900, 374.5000, 800/GOVIASA
Virgin Atlantic	445.9940, 800/862.8621, 800/VSSALES in FL
Zuliana	597.8780, 800/223.8780

In addition, **Opa-locka Airport** (953.1300), the area's largest general aviation airport, is seven miles north of **MIA** and five miles from **Joe Robbie Stadium.** In a recent 12-month period, there were about 224,000 takeoffs and landings here. **Kendall-Tamiami Executive Airport** (238.6093), the state's second-busiest general aviation airport, is 25 miles southwest of downtown Miami. It sees about 225,000 takeoffs and landings a year.

Getting to and from Miami International Airport

By Bus MIA is served by **Metrobus** (638.6700), the county bus system. The bus terminal—where passengers are picked up and dropped off—is outside, opposite **Concourse E.** Buses run daily from 6AM to midnight; the fare is $1.25, and exact change is required.

By Car The airport is about a 15-minute drive from downtown, except during peak traffic periods (generally, weekdays from 8AM to 9:30AM and from 3PM to 6PM), when the trip can take 30 minutes or more. To get to downtown Miami from **MIA,** take **Le Jeune Road (NW 42nd Ave)** south to connect with **Route 836,** and drive east. To get to the airport from downtown, take Route 836 west to Le Jeune Road; drive north until you see signs for the airport. Long- and short-term parking lots are within walking distance of the main terminal. A moving sidewalk connects the terminal to parking garages, which have entry points on the fourth floors.

The following rental car companies have 24-hour counters at the airport:

Avis	637.4900, 800/331.1212
Budget	871.3053, 800/527.0700
Dollar	887.6000, 800/800.4000, 800/822.1181 in FL
Hertz	871.0300, 800/654.3131
National	638.1026, 800/328.4567
Value	871.6761, 800/327.2501

By Limousine Limos serve the airport by prior arrangement only. **Cars of the Rich & Famous Limousine Service** (945.2737, 800/343.0513) charges from $55 to $70 for a ride to the airport from downtown Miami and vice versa; **City Limousine Service** (944.5466, 800/819.5466) charges $65. Rates do not include gratuities.

By Shuttle Bright blue-and-yellow **SuperShuttle** vans (871.2000) provide door-to-door service to and from **MIA.** Look for the shuttle stations at the van/limo booths on the ground level outside the baggage claim area. Pickup from the airport takes from 15 to 20 minutes.

By Taxi There are numerous stands outside the baggage claim area. Approximate fares from the airport: to downtown, $15; to Miami Beach, $25; and to Northeast Dade, $30. The airport also is served by blue cabs, which take passengers only to nearby hotels and other addresses within special zones for a flat rate up to $14; the cost varies by zone.

By Train There's no feasible way to get from the airport to downtown Miami by train.

Bus Station (Long-Distance) Greyhound serves Miami at three terminals. The downtown depot (700 Biscayne Blvd, at NW Seventh St, 374.6160) is open daily from 7AM to 10PM; the airport-area terminal (4111 NW 27th St, at NW 41st Ave, 871.1810) is open 24 hours a day; and the **Homestead** station (5 NE Third Rd/Murray Dr, at US 1, 247.2040) is open Mondays through Saturdays from 8:30AM to 1PM and from 3PM to about 5:30PM.

Train Station (Long-Distance) Amtrak trains arrive at, and depart from, 8303 Northwest 37th Avenue (north of NW 79th St) near **Hialeah;** for information, call 835.1221 or 800/872.7245. The station is open Mondays, Wednesdays, Fridays, and Sundays from 6AM to midnight; Tuesdays, Thursdays, and Saturdays from 6AM to 7PM. Many trains serve the station.

Getting around Miami/Dade County

Navigating Miami and Dade County is confusing, if only because the city of Miami is a tiny part of a nearly 2,000-square-mile area comprising nearly 30 municipalities. And that doesn't even include "unincorporated Dade County," another 1,813 square miles that include such well-known neighborhoods as **Kendall** and **Aventura.**

Bicycles Heavy traffic and self-absorbed (or just plain rude) drivers make biking in most parts of Dade County dangerous. Bicycling *is* feasible—and even pleasurable (with a helmet, of course)—in **Key Biscayne, Miami Springs,** some agricultural sections of **South Dade,** and parts of the **Everglades.** Among the many companies that rent wheels, a few of the best are **Cycles on the Beach** (713 Fifth St, between Meridian and Euclid Aves, South Beach, 673.2055); **Gary's Megacycle** (18151 NE 19th Ave, at NE 181st St, North Miami, 940.2912); and **Mangrove Cycles** (260 Crandon Blvd, Key Biscayne, 361.5555).

Buses Getting around Greater Miami by bus is not recommended. Bus service, provided by **Metro-Dade County** under the name **Metrobus** (638.6700), is notoriously undependable. Bus routes do extend to some popular tourist areas such as **Miami Beach,** and they connect to **Metrorail,** the excellent elevated rail transit system. **Metrobus** fare is $1.25, in coins or in combination with a dollar bill. Buses run from 6AM to midnight.

Driving The best way to get around Dade County is by car; in fact, without one, you won't be able to see much of the area. But beware of exiting **State Routes 112** and **836** into the central city between the airport and **Biscayne Bay,** for criminal gangs have singled out motorists for attack in these areas. Following several brutal attacks on tourists in the early 1990s, Miami police established a visitor information center at the exit ramp from State Route 112 at **Northwest 27th Avenue.** Other trouble spots are expressway ramps near downtown, where robbers have been known to smash windows and grab belongings from cars stopped at traffic lights. To avoid such incidents, leave maneuvering space between your car and the cars around you; if threatened, proceed through stop lights after checking for traffic. While police have reduced the incidence of crimes against visitors significantly, it pays to be aware of your surroundings and of suspicious characters at all times. (For other tips on how to navigate Miami, see "Street Plan," on page 11.)

Ferries or Boats A Ft. Lauderdale–based company called **Water Taxi** (565.5507) serves Miami's tourist areas with motorboats. These Coast Guard–certified craft seat from 25 to 125 passengers and depart from hotels, restaurants, and many other attractions. They run daily from 10AM to around midnight (often later). The one-way cost is $7; an all-day pass is $14.

Jitneys Private operators run "jitneys" (vans) along bus routes for $1. These small buses are controversial, however, because some lack insurance coverage and are not closely regulated by authorities.

Parking Except for a few areas, parking on the street or in merchant lots is no problem in Dade County. In

South Beach, parking is such a nightmare that most restaurants, clubs, and hotels use valet service to park cars. Parking spaces on the street in South Beach are sometimes available during the day, but not at night. Valet service is also offered at popular locations in **Coconut Grove.** In downtown Miami, metered parking is available on **Biscayne Boulevard;** if metered parking spaces are full, parking garages are well marked and easy to find on nearly every block. Note that along Biscayne Boulevard and in parts of downtown near the **Miami Arena,** entrepreneurial vagrants stake out parking meters and demand spare change to "watch your car." It's not a bad investment.

Taxis Since it's virtually impossible to hail a taxi on the street, you should call for a cab. Additionally, taxi stands are usually located outside hotels, at major tourist attractions, and at the airport. Cab drivers are required to undergo courtesy training to receive and keep their licenses. Other cities have adopted this "Miami Nice" program, which has trained thousands of cabbies in Miami. However, you will still encounter many taxi drivers who don't speak English very well. **Metro Taxi** (888.8888) and **Yellow Cab** (444.4444) are two reliable companies.

Tours Sight-seeing excursions are plentiful throughout Miami. Operators with long track records are **American Connections** (420 Lincoln Rd, between Washington and Drexel Aves, 531.6070); **American Sightseeing Tours** (11077 NW 36th Ave, at NW 110th St, 688.7700); **A-1 Bus Lines/Gray Line of Miami** (1642 NW 21st Terr, at NW 16th Ave, 358.1000); and **Flamingo Tours** (16251 Collins Ave, at NW 162nd St, 948.3822). These operators and many others offer multilingual, individual, and group tours. Reservations are required in most cases.

Trains Instead of a subway, Miami has the **Metrorail** (638.6700), an elevated rail transit system that runs from downtown Miami south to Kendall and north to Hialeah. In addition, the **Metromover** (638.6700) has computerized cars that loop the central business district, the **Brickell Banking District,** and the **Omni** shopping area. They connect to each other and to **Metrobus** routes.

Metrorail fare is $1.25, in coins only and in exact change. Tokens are also available at the stations. Trains operate daily from 6AM to midnight; the frequency varies. Service is usually extended for special events, such as the annual **Orange Bowl Parade** and events at the **Miami Arena. Metromover** cars run daily from 6AM to midnight, and the fare is 25 cents (exact change is required).

In addition, **Tri-Rail** (800/TRIRAIL) is a commuter train with 15 stations linking Miami with Ft. Lauderdale and **Palm Beach County,** and it connects to **Metrorail.** Trains run daily except Thanksgiving and Christmas.

Walking Walking is a good way to explore certain sections of Miami, especially downtown, South Beach, **Coral Gables,** Coconut Grove, **South Miami, Homestead,** and the Brickell Banking District.

FYI

Money Banks are open weekdays from 9AM to 5PM. Automatic teller machines (ATMs) are widely available, especially at banks and outside **Publix** grocery stores, and at some malls and convenience stores. Currency exchange is offered at most large banks in downtown **Miami,** in the **Brickell Banking District,** in **Coral Gables,** and at the **Miami International Airport.**

Personal Safety In the early 1990s, bands of criminals preyed on tourists, particularly in the area around the airport and near expressways leading to the beaches. After several tourists were murdered, Miami officials formed tourist police units, posted clearer highway signs, and ran sting operations to catch criminals in the act. Stickers were banned from rental cars so visitors would be harder to identify. Since then, crime has dropped. However, it pays to be watchful at all times. If lost after dark, do not exit expressways except in busy, well-lighted neighborhoods. Get help from a fast-food restaurant or convenience store if you can't find a fire station or police station. Never leave briefcases, purses, or other belongings unattended, even in hotel lobbies. If your car is bumped or someone suspicious tries to stop you, drive immediately to a safe area and get help from authorities.

Publications The *Miami Herald* is **Dade County**'s main daily newspaper, with entertainment listings on Friday. Other regional papers are the *Miami Daily Business Review* (a tabloid issued five days a week), the *South Florida Business Journal* (a weekly), *New Times* (an arts and entertainment weekly), and *Miami Today* (a news weekly). Turning to magazines, *South Florida* is a monthly that features listings of events of interest to visitors.

Restaurants Reservations are recommended for many restaurants in **South Beach, Miami Beach,** Coral Gables, and other areas popular with visitors, particularly during the winter tourist season. A few restaurants offer "early-bird" specials or other discounted meals in the late afternoon. Jackets and/or ties are usually not required of men except in very formal dining spots.

Shopping Miami's best-known shopping areas are **Bal Harbour** (for upscale designer clothing), South Beach and the **Lincoln Road** pedestrian mall (for eclectic boutiques offering clothes and art), **Miracle Mile** in Coral Gables (for shoe stores, bridal shops, jewelry stores, and art galleries), **Flagler Street** in downtown Miami (for electronics, luggage, and discount clothing), and the **Dadeland Mall** in **Kendall** (for clothing, furniture, shoes, and designer goods).

Street Plan Most streets in Dade County are laid out on a grid, whose axes are **Miami Avenue** (running north-south through downtown Miami) and Flagler Street (running east-west). In general, avenues run north-south; streets, east-west. Most thoroughfares are numbered according to a quadrant system, meaning that, for example, 7200 Northwest 36th Street is 72 blocks west of Miami Avenue and 36 blocks north of Flagler Street. But exceptions abound: Streets in such areas as Miami Beach, Coral Gables, **Key Biscayne, Hialeah,** and **Miami Springs** follow no such plan, so carry a map. To add to the confusion, many major highways carry multiple names. The **Palmetto Expressway** also goes by the name **State Route 826; Route 836** is often called the **Dolphin Expressway;** and **Highway 1** is known as **US 1, Dixie Highway,** and, in some sections, **Biscayne Boulevard. Red Road** is also known as **57th Avenue** and **Curtiss Parkway.** The **Airport Expressway** is also known as **State Route 112,** and the **Don Shula Expressway** is the same as **State Route 874.** Other major thoroughfares are **I-95, I-75,** and **Florida's Turnpike.**

Taxes Miami's sales tax is 6.5 percent, and its total accommodations tax is 12.5 percent (6.5 sales tax plus 6 percent bed tax). There's an additional tax on restaurant meals that varies depending on municipality, size of the restaurant, and whether it's located in a hotel.

Tickets You can use a charge card when dealing with **Ticketmaster** (358.5885), which handles tickets for most theatrical and sporting events and concerts. Note that all transactions take place over the phone, as the agency has no offices open to the ticket-buying public.

Visitors' Information Center The **Greater Miami Convention and Visitors Bureau** (701 Brickell Ave, at SW Seventh St, Suite 2700, 539.3088; fax 539.3113) is open Mondays through Fridays.

Phone Book

Emergencies

AAA Emergency Road Service 800/222.4357

Ambulance/Fire/Police 911

Dental Emergency 800/733.6337

Hospitals
    Jackson Memorial Hospital, Miami 585.7200
    Mercy Hospital, Coconut Grove 854.4400
    Baptist Hospital of Miami, Kendall 591.3445

Locksmith 274.8000

Pharmacy (24-hour)
    Eckerd Drugs 274.6776, 932.5740

Poison Control 800/282.3171

Police (non-emergency) 595.6263

Visitors' Information

Amtrak 800/872.7245

Better Business Bureau 625.0307

Convention and Visitors Bureau 539.3088

Disabled Visitors' Information 574.5444

Greyhound Bus........274.2040, 379.7403, 871.1810

Metro Transit (Metrobus, Metromover, and
Metrorail) 638.6700

Road Conditions......................................470.2510

Time 324.8811

US Customs 869.2600

US Passport Office 536.5395

Weather 324.8811

Downtown Miami/ Key Biscayne

Today, on the eve of its centennial, Miami is the number one city in Florida. Yet its development is tied more intimately to that of Latin America and the Caribbean than it is to the rest of the state—indeed, Miami is looked upon by Central and North Floridians as exotic, if not downright outré.

Nowadays, downtown Miami is astir with dozens of stores that lure South American tourists looking for duty-free electronics. The prices here are seldom lower than in suburban areas, but the sense of a Caribbean marketplace is intoxicating. When the business day is over, however, much of the city center closes and becomes unsafe. (One exception is **Bayside Marketplace**, which is near a few of the city's best hotels.)

So don't let the trappings of paradise fool you into letting down your guard, especially in your car, and beware of "bump-and-rob" and "smash-and-grab" thefts while you're sitting in traffic. (The **Metromover**, recently extended to the **Omni International Mall** and Brickell Avenue, offers a relatively safe, convenient way to travel around downtown for 25¢ a ride.) If you do drive, you should know that Miami's road system was laid out on a quadrant grid, with the intersection of **Flagler Street** and **Miami Avenue** the city's center. Flagler Street separates north from south; Miami Avenue, east from west. Throughout the city, avenues run north-south, and streets run east-west.

Near downtown's bargain emporia is the busy **Port of Miami**, the nation's largest cruise port. With as many as eight giant ships and 14,000 passengers in port on some days, the industry pumps $2.5 billion into South Florida's economy every year.

Other, less bustling activity takes place downtown at the **Metro-Dade Cultural Center Plaza,** which comprises a fine arts center, a museum, and a public library—each of which can easily keep a visitor occupied for hours. Gastronomically speaking, downtown has focused for the most part on quick bites for busy execs, from excellent pasta at **Greenwich Village** near the **Brickell Banking District** to informal **Smitty's Restaurant** (though some notable exceptions do come to mind, such as the elegant **Hotel Inter-Continental Miami**'s Le Pavillon restaurant).

Just across the **Rickenbacker Causeway** is the island community of **Key Biscayne.** Although located just 10 minutes from downtown, Key Biscayne has the feel of a tropical resort. Sandy Atlantic ocean beaches stretch from **Crandon Park** to the **Bill Baggs Cape Florida State Recreation Area**, while the **Sonesta Beach Resort Key Biscayne** offers premier accommodations for visitors. In 1992 Hurricane Andrew badly damaged the island's parks, resorts, and businesses, particularly **Bill Baggs Cape Florida**, which was stripped of its tall pine trees. But replanting and rebuilding efforts are slowly restoring much of the island's casually elegant atmosphere.

Area code 305 unless otherwise indicated.

1 Smitty's Restaurant ★$$ Breakfast pancakes made from scratch, old-fashioned burgers cooked to order at lunch, and a popular dessert called "chocolate mess" are all reasonably priced and quickly served. In a neighborhood filled with fast-food joints, this eatery is a ray of hope for real food on the run. ◆ American ◆ M-Sa breakfast and lunch. 3195 NE Second Ave (at NE 32nd St). 576.3397 ⚹

2 Bakehouse Art Complex Constructed in 1920 as a bakery, this building today provides studio space to the largest working colony of artists (more than 200) in South Florida. The complex, which comprises 60 studios, holds a free open-house showing every second Sunday of the month from 1PM to 5PM. ◆ For tour and exhibition information, call Tu-F 10AM-4PM. 561 NW 32nd St (at NW Fifth Ave). 576.2828 ⚹

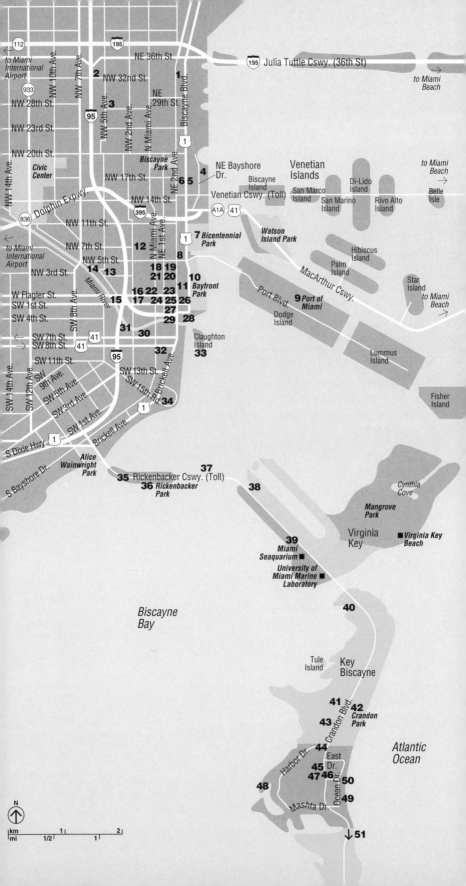

3 Miami Fashion District Though seldom publicized, Miami is headquarters to several hundred manufacturers and wholesale dealers of clothing from Latin America and the Caribbean. Throughout this loose collection of shops, their goods are available to retail customers at dramatically reduced prices. ♦ M-Sa. NW Fifth Ave (from NE 25th to NE 29th Sts)

4 1800 Club ★$$ With its dark, funky decor and eccentric servers, this restaurant could have been pulled straight from *The Front Page.* A longtime favorite of journalists, the friendly bar and dining room serve well-prepared food that makes up in value what it lacks in excitement. The fish dishes tend to be overcooked, but the steaks are great, and the onion rings are tops. ♦ American ♦ M-Sa lunch and dinner. 1800 N Bayshore Dr (at NW 18th St). 373.1093 ♿

5 Les Violins Though it was founded in 1962, this place recalls the America of the 1940s, or Cuba as it was in the 1950s: a supper club in the grand old style, still favored by a largely Hispanic clientele. The food is certainly adequate, though hardly inventive; beef dishes predominate. What really draws crowds here is the Las Vegas–style show of the sort that most people thought left town when Jackie Gleason went off the air. The name, by the way, comes from the strolling violinists who compete with singing waiters when the 30 or more dancers aren't on stage. There's nothing else in town like it. Valet parking is available. ♦ Cover. Shows: W-Su. Reservations recommended. 751 Biscayne Blvd (at NE 17th St). 371.8668 ♿

CROWNE PLAZA®

HOTELS · RESORTS

5 Crowne Plaza Miami $$$$ Formerly **The Omni,** this remains one of downtown Miami's premier hotels. The exterior—generic urban hotel—is nothing to write home about, but the hotel's large ballrooms and catering staff make it especially popular with conventioneer types. The 530 comfortable guest rooms (all recently renovated) begin on the fifth floor and continue up 15 stories (the lower floors are occupied by a shopping complex; see below). The few amenities include a heated pool, and valet parking. ♦ 1601 Biscayne Blvd (at NE 16th St). 374.0000, 800/843.6664; fax 374.0020 ♿

Within the Crowne Plaza Miami:

Fish Market ★★★$$$$ One of Miami's most appealing downtown dining options, this also happens to be one of the inexplicably few upscale seafood restaurants. Recommended dishes—all expensive but delectable—include ravioli of smoked shrimp and fennel, Florida lobster with truffles and mushrooms, and snapper with cilantro. The service and wine list are first-rate, and valet parking is available. ♦ Seafood ♦ M-F lunch and dinner; Sa dinner. Reservations recommended. 374.4399 ♿

Omni International Mall This three-level plaza was downtown's main shopping destination before the advent of **Bayside Marketplace** (see below). Aside from **J.C. Penney,** most of the 90 or so shops are small, moderately upscale boutiques struggling for a chic urban identity. Of special interest are such emporia as **Sunglass Hut** and **Wolf Cameras** (for photo gear and one-hour processing). In the **Omni** are the only movie theaters in the downtown area: one, four-screen; the other, six. Kids line up to ride the Italian carousel on the first level. ♦ 1601 Biscayne Blvd (at NE 16th St). 374.6664 ♿

Marriott Biscayne Bay Hotel & Marina $$$$ In addition to a small shopping arcade, this hotel has an excellent pool and its own marina on the bay. A 31-story high-rise, the property contains 605 elegantly decorated rooms, including 23 units on a luxury-level concierge floor. The views of Biscayne Bay and Miami's skyline are superb. Business-people will appreciate the plentiful meeting spaces. Valet parking is available. ♦ 1633 N Bayshore Dr (between NE 15th and NE 17th Sts). 374.3900, 800/228.9290; fax 375.0597 ♿

Within the Marriott Biscayne Bay Hotel & Marina:

Bay View Restaurant ★$$$ The weekday lunch buffets at this cozy, casual eatery have different themes, ranging from Caribbean to seafood. But it's really the spectacular view of Biscayne Bay that draws all those office workers from the area. ♦ American ♦ Daily breakfast, lunch, and dinner. 536.6414 ♿

6 S&S Restaurant ★★$ Customers queue up at the entrance to this family-run eatery for its down-home fare, including wonderfully prepared meat loaf, stew, pot roast, and mashed potatoes. Dating from the early 1940s, it's one of the oldest restaurants in Dade County. ♦ American ♦ M-Sa breakfast, lunch, and dinner. 1757 NE Second Ave (at NE 17th St). 373.4291 ♿

7 Bicentennial Park One of Miami's most controversial green spaces, it covers 35 acres of prime waterfront land. Among the park's faults: There's no provision for parking; a mound in the park blocks the view of Biscayne Bay; few structures in the park attract the general public; and—worst of all—it's considered unsafe (though occasional festivals and concerts do transform it into a busy, raucous place). Hordes of homeless people have set up house here, some putting up waterfront shacks that the city periodically dismantles. ♦ 1075 Biscayne Blvd (north of NE Sixth St). 575.5256

8 Freedom Tower This monument to the strengths and weaknesses of downtown Miami (illustrated at right) was built in 1925 by architects **Schultze & Weaver.** Inspired by the 13th-century Giralda (Bell Tower) in Seville, Spain (as was the **Biltmore Hotel** in Coral Gables), its distinctive three-component design comprises a wide base, a narrow tower, and a two-story cupola. It originally housed the now defunct *Miami News,* a paper that moved out in 1957. The building stood vacant until 1959, when the US Government used it as a processing center for Cuban refugees (ergo the name). The tower was added to the National Registry of Historic Places in 1979, but it nonetheless was allowed to deteriorate. In 1990, more than $25 million was raised for its renovation, which involved the addition of carved oak doors, intricate stonework, paintings, and Oriental carpets. But the developer failed to attract tenants, and today the tower is shuttered. ♦ 600 Biscayne Blvd (at NE Sixth St). 374.1060

9 Port of Miami/Dodge Island Miami is the largest cruise ship port in the world, with more than a third of the so-called free world's cruise ships docking here in a year. Most ships leave twice a week for three- and four-day jaunts to the Bahamas and back or seven-day cruises around the Caribbean. The most popular departure days are Friday and Sunday, when an impressive parade of megaships—sometimes extending as far as one and a half miles along the dock—can be seen.

10 Bayside Marketplace This is a prime example of the type of waterfront shopping/ dining complex that the Rouse Company of Columbia, Maryland, does so well. Instead of trendy designer boutiques, most of the shops here are mid-priced, utilitarian outlets for national and regional chains: **Victoria's Secret, The Sharper Image,** and **The Gap** all cater to a young, urban clientele, with several casual restaurants thrown in for good measure. Avoid the huge, undistinguished fast-food arcade, which is crowded with push cart vendors who, ironically, provide the mall's only link to the traditional concept of a marketplace. Impromptu concerts are held

along Biscayne Bay, and there are plenty of places to walk. ♦ M-Th 10AM-10PM; F-Sa 10AM-11PM; Su 11AM-9PM. 401 Biscayne Blvd (at NE Fourth St). 577.3344 &

Within Bayside Marketplace:

Los Ranchos ★★$$$ Miami's most famous Nicaraguan restaurant is based in the western community of Sweetwater, but this urban outpost mimics it well. The food is incredibly flavorful: The Nicaraguan *churrasco* (grilled flank steak) is a must, and the *pargo* (red snapper) with a sweet-and-sour sauce of tomatoes and onions is excellent. On the wine list are some splendid (and reasonably priced) South American choices. It's a distinct change of pace for **Bayside.** ♦ Nicaraguan ♦ Daily lunch and dinner. 375.8188 &. Also at: 125 SW 107th Ave (at SW First St), Sweetwater. 221.9367 &; Los Ranchos/Town & Country Shopping Center, 8505 Mills Dr (at SW 117th Ave), Kendall. 596.5353; and the Falls Shopping Center, 8888 SW 136th St (at US 1). 238.6867

Las Tapas ★★★$$$ A local favorite for authentic Spanish cuisine, this place offers fantastic tapas (small hot or cold appetizers). Begin with two traditional Iberian treats: thin Spanish sausages and a Spanish omelette. Also highly recommended are the paella, brimming with lobster, shrimp, and scallops, and other seafood dishes. Large windows overlook the hustle and bustle of **Bayside Marketplace,** making this a good people watching spot. The rustic decor, tiled floors, and hams hanging from the ceiling evoke the ambience of a Spanish bistro. ♦ Spanish ♦ Daily lunch and dinner. 372.2737 &

Hard Rock Cafe ★$$ This is the place to indulge in rock 'n' roll memorabilia, not the rather pedestrian burgers-and-chicken menu. Guitars once belonging to Keith Richards, Eric Clapton, and Jimi Hendrix hang on the walls. Also on display: Janis Joplin's hat, Madonna's jacket, and Gloria Estefan's bustier. It's great fun if you don't mind crowds and noise. The on-premises souvenir shop sells rock T-shirts. ♦ American ♦ Daily lunch and dinner. 377.3110 &

Restaurants/Clubs: Red   **Hotels:** Blue
Shops/❦ Outdoors: Green   **Sights/Culture:** Black

10 Claude and Mildred Pepper Bayfront Park Though known simply as "Bayfront Park," this spot salutes the late Claude Pepper, Florida's longtime congressman and champion of senior-related issues, and his wife. Pepper is also commemorated here by a fountain (which, because of the expense, the city turns on for only four hours a day). Noted Japanese sculptor Isamu Noguchi redesigned the park in 1989, just before his death. In the park is a memorial to the *Challenger* astronauts and an amphitheater frequently used for free pop and symphony concerts. ♦ 301 Biscayne Blvd (between NE Third and NE Fourth Sts)

11 Hotel Inter-Continental Miami $$$$ From the outside, the most impressive aspect of this hotel is its 34-story height; inside, it's *The Spindle,* the massive Henry Moore sculpture that dominates the lobby. Exploiting Miami's assets, a huge skylight bathes the five-story atrium with sunshine, and the triangular design of the building provides each of the hotel's 645 rooms with a splendid view of the city. The hotel has a heated pool and valet parking. ♦ 100 Chopin Plaza (at Biscayne Blvd). 577.1000, 800/327.3005; fax 577.0384 ♿

Within the Hotel Inter-Continental Miami:

Le Pavillon ★★★★$$$$ In addition to being the finest restaurant downtown, this is also the most sedate: Lush banquettes, mirrors, chandeliers, low lighting, and a deep, rich decor all underscore an air of elegance. The service is efficient and low-key, but the cuisine is full-throttle: Potato and apple *tartine* and shrimp with risotto are good starters; among the entrées, order the smoked lamb chops or grilled swordfish. ♦ Continental ♦ M-Sa lunch and dinner. Reservations required; jacket required. 577.1000 ♿

12 Miami Arena This is the home of the **Miami Heat National Basketball Association** franchise. It's also the stage for other sporting events and touring spectaculars, ranging from annual visits by the **Ringling Brothers and Barnum & Bailey Circus** to concerts by opera star Luciano Pavarotti. ♦ 701 Arena Blvd (at NW Seventh St). 530.4400 ♿

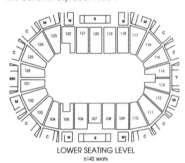

LOWER SEATING LEVEL
6142 seats

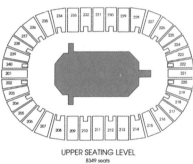

UPPER SEATING LEVEL
8349 seats

Small-Fry in South Florida: Ten Terrific Things for Kids

Count the palm trees while riding the **Metromover** elevated train through downtown **Miami.** Hands down, it's the best view of the city.

Start a shell collection on **Sanibel Island.** When you get home, make crafts with your shells for family presents.

If you're 12 or older, learn to water-ski without a boat at **Quiet Waters Park** in **Ft. Lauderdale.** A cable pulls skiers.

Get splashed by Lolita the Killer Whale during a show at the **Miami Seaquarium** on **Key Biscayne.** Be sure to visit the shark tank and play ball with the dolphins between shows.

Snorkel at **John Pennekamp Coral Reef State Park** or **Harry Harris County Park** in the beautiful **Florida Keys.**

Pick up some creepy souvenirs at **La Casa de Los Trucos** in **Little Havana.** Blow your allowance on next year's Halloween costume.

Go in-line skating in **Coconut Grove,** on the **Broadwalk** in **Hollywood,** on **Ocean Drive** in **South Beach,** or on the **Riverwalk** in Ft. Lauderdale.

Ride an elephant at **Caribbean Gardens** in **Naples.** Take the boat cruise to see the monkeys up close on their private islands. Help other kids hold up a seven-foot boa constrictor—it's heavy!

Inspect the see-through house at the **Museum of Discovery and Science** in Ft. Lauderdale. Pet a snake when the handlers bring them out. And don't miss an IMAX movie at the **Blockbuster IMAX Theater.**

Cradle a macaw at **Parrot Jungle and Gardens** in **South Dade.** But don't touch the alligator!

13 Scottish Rite Temple Inspired by the historic opening of King Tutankhamen's tomb, architects **Kiehnel & Elliott** adorned this small but magnificent building with Egyptian motifs. On the Classical facade, four massive columns support the roof, topped by two-headed eagles. Dating from 1922, this temple is one of the earliest examples of Art Deco in the US, predating even Miami Beach's Art Deco District. ◆ 471 NW Third St (at NW North River Dr). 374.4700 &

13 Fort Dallas Barracks Pioneer William English constructed this building in 1849 at the mouth of the Miami River, originally using it as slave quarters. Later, during the Seminole Wars, it served as an Army barracks. Julia Tuttle bought the entire plantation property in 1891 and lived there for several years. In 1925, the Daughters of the American Revolution (DAR) moved this building—the only structure remaining of the original fort at the time—to its present location in **Lummus Park.** The city fenced it off in the late 1980s, when the homeless began building shacks around the property; plans to reopen the site to the public have been delayed since 1992. ◆ 404 NW Third St (at NW Fourth Ave). 579.6935

14 Joe's Seafood ★★$$$ With outdoor tables overlooking a dingy, commercial stretch of the Miami River, this restaurant-cum–fish market serves myriad seafood dishes—as well as beef entrées and salads—with a Latin touch. The crab cakes are superb; everything comes with crackers and a tasty smoked fish spread. The charming setting reveals a different side of Miami, as commercial fishing boats, freighters, and huge yachts alike putter up the river. ◆ Seafood ◆ Daily lunch and dinner. 400 NW North River Dr (at NW Fourth St). 374.5637 &

14 Garcia's ★★$ The consistently fresh and well-seasoned food offered at this new riverfront seafood house is starting to attract attention. Try the grouper chowder or the lemon-pepper grilled grouper. ◆ Seafood ◆ Daily lunch and dinner. 398 NW North River Dr (at NW Fourth St). 375.0765 &

15 East Coast Fisheries ★★$$ You'd expect a long menu at a restaurant that maintains its own fishing fleet, but nothing prepares first-time visitors for the more than 150 offerings at this commercial-looking, two-story riverside building. The company supplies fish to many other area restaurants as well, but the sense of freshness is truly palpable here. Though the number of options can be overwhelming, the fish is incomparable. The service is lackadaisical. Oenophiles should take note that the wine list is limited (and you can't bring your own). ◆ Seafood ◆ Daily lunch and dinner. 360 W Flagler St (at NW North River Dr). 373.5516 &

16 Metro-Dade Cultural Center Plaza Three important cultural institutions share a one-square-block plot of land near the middle of the downtown area. **Philip Johnson,** master of the Postmodern style, brought a strong Spanish influence to bear, giving all the buildings a sand-and-adobe appearance. In the center he placed a large plaza, which frequently serves as a setting for outdoor events. ◆ 101 W Flagler St (between NW First and NW Second Aves)

Within the Metro-Dade Cultural Center Plaza:

Center for the Fine Arts (CFA)
Controversial in some circles for its failure to implement an acquisitions policy, the center has no permanent collection. But even its critics concede that it does bring in important exhibitions from the world's great museums on a regular basis, and it stages many other worthy programs, including a fine chamber music series and educational offerings. ◆ Admission. Tu-Su; Th until 9PM. 375.1700 &

Historical Museum of Southern Florida
The erratic development of South Florida is traced here through participatory exhibits that go back long before Ponce de León set forth on his early Caribbean cruise. From prehistory to "Miami Vice," from the Seminole Wars to the Mariel boatlift, the area's past, present, and future are portrayed with graphics and artifacts, including Indian ceramics, clothing, and utensils, and a streetcar from the 1920s. An important living resource of the museum is historian Paul George, who leads trips and walking tours through many of the city's neighborhoods. Participation, for a fee, may be arranged through the museum. ◆ Admission. M-Sa; Th until 9PM; Su noon-5PM. 375.1492 &

Miami-Dade Public Library The main branch of the county library system has 700,000 volumes cataloged on a sophisticated computer system and one of the most complete genealogy collections in Florida, including Census records from all over the nation. Art exhibitions are mounted in the auditorium and second-floor lobby. The rotunda contains a mural by Edward Ruscha that visualizes Shakespeare's maxim "Words without thoughts never to heaven go." ◆ M-Sa; Th until 9PM; Su afternoon Oct-May. 375.2665 &

17 Top Hat Cafe ★★★$ Located in the **Museum Tower** office building, this is the perfect place to get out of the heat for a light salad or a hearty three-cheese steak. You'll be surrounded by neon lights and Art Deco styling, not to mention lawyers, bankers, and brokers. ◆ American ◆ M-F lunch. 150 W Flagler St (at NW First Ave). 381.6337 &

18 US Federal Courthouse The principal architect of Coral Gables, **Phineas Paist,** worked on this building in 1931 with another Gables powerhouse, designer Denman Fink.

Fink supplied a striking mural for the central second-floor courtroom: *Law Guides Florida Progress* depicts the evolution of Miami from wilderness to cosmopolitan urban center. The building uses many native materials, including oolitic limestone (known as Key stone) for the exterior and marble and coral rock for interior walls. The inner courtyard provides a welcome respite from street crowds. The building also served as Miami's principal post office until 1978, as evidenced by the brass postal fixtures visible in the lobby. This is where the US tried Panama strongman Manuel Noriega, the only prisoner of war currently behind bars in the US. ♦ M-F. 300 NE First Ave (between NE Third and NE Fourth Sts). 536.4548 &

19 Miami-Dade Community College, Wolfson Campus The largest community college in the US has several campuses, but this is the largest and most interesting. In it is the **Francis Wolfson Art Gallery,** which specializes in contemporary art. Miami Book Fair International, one of the largest in the country, takes place here every November, turning the campus and surrounding streets into a bibliophile's mecca. Especially interesting is the fair's **Antiquarian Annex,** with rare and unusual manuscripts. ♦ M-F. 300 NE Second Ave (at NE Third St). 237.3000, art gallery 237.3696 &

20 Gesu Church Miami's first Roman Catholic congregation was established in 1876. This church (pictured below), home to the city's oldest parish, was built in 1925 on a site that Henry Flagler had donated in 1897. It is notable for its stained-glass windows and altar of Italian marble. ♦ 118 NE Second St (at NE First Ave). 379.1424 &

21 Dade Federal Savings Building & Arcade During Miami's early years, a high water table, material shortages, and other limitations conspired to keep building heights restricted to only one or two stories. With the boom years of the 1920s, however, structures stretched taller, materials became more varied, and design grew more adventurous. One product of the loosening of architectural strictures was this 1925 **Pfeiffer & O'Reilly** building. It's one of Miami's few remaining examples of the interior arcade, a style of construction popular for retail outlets. The exterior facade has eight arches, each a storefront, though there is only one entrance into the building and the arcade. Inlaid into the floor near the elevators is a beautifully stylized mosaic. ♦ 122 NE First St (at NE First Ave) &

21 SunBank International Center In 1912 this became Miami's first federal building; for many years, it contained the city's post office and courthouse. In designing it, **Oscar Wenderoth** basically adhered to the Neo-Classic Revival style popular for federal

offices, but he incorporated some unique tropical touches: recessed windows and a roof with an extended overhang to minimize exposure to sun, rain, and heat. The ornate clocks inside are beautifully preserved. Dr. William H. Walker bought the building in 1937 as headquarters for the First Federal Savings and Loan of Miami, which later became AmeriFirst. It is no longer in business, and the building now houses SunBank and the United Way. ♦ 100 NE First Ave (at NE First St) &

22 Metrofare Dining Complex Located in the **Government Center** skyscraper, this food court offers a wide array of quick meals. It's a handy place to stop for lunch on the run if you happen to be here while changing trains. ♦ M-F breakfast, lunch, and dinner. 111 NW First Ave (at NW First St) &

Within the Metrofare Dining Complex:

Granny Feelgood's ★$ "Granny" is actually Irving Field, a shrewd restaurateur who saw a market in catering to urban workers reeling from heavy business lunches. Several restaurants use the name, but only these at the food court are under the original ownership. The menu is limited to health-conscious cuisine, including vegetarian pasta, a variety of salads, and some wickedly healthful desserts, such as carrot cake and apple crumb cake. At press time **Cafe Feelgood**; offering cappuccino, espresso, panini (sandwiches) and pastries, is due to open in the **Metrofare Dining Complex**. ♦ Health food ♦ 579.2104 &

Granny's Island ★$ This branch of **Granny Feelgood's** (see above) offers salads and fruit juices of all kinds. ♦ American &

Mi Habana ★$ Such Cuban staples as black beans and rice and pastries are the order of the day here. ♦ Cuban ♦ 577.3496 &

Metro Grille ★$ For traditional favorites such as chili, burgers, and fries, this spot is a good choice. ♦ American ♦ 372.3778 &

Chinese Gourmet Cafe ★$ You'll find the sweet-and-sour chicken, egg rolls, and wonton soup here a nice change from Miami's preponderance of Cuban *croquetas* (croquettes) and *media noches* (sandwiches). ♦ Chinese ♦ 579.0055 &

22 Dade County Courthouse When it replaced the original 1904 courthouse in 1928, this 360-foot-high structure was the tallest building in the US south of Washington, DC. Perhaps reflecting South Florida's fascination with Italian architecture, the courthouse is faced with terra-cotta, though architect **A. Ten Eyck Brown** also drew on Greek and Roman elements, placing Doric columns on the lower floors and a Greek temple–style peak at the top. The elevator doors and mosaics in the lobby display an early state seal that shows a Plains Indian; rumor has it that the seal was originally designed for a western state, ended up in Florida by default, and was later discarded. ♦ 73 W Flagler St (at NW First Ave) &

23 Alfred I. duPont Building This is a classic example of the conservative Depression Moderne style of architecture: solid and blocklike on the outside, with most of the ornamentation hidden in the interior. The second-floor bank lobby has a good deal of adornment, including a painted ceiling that depicts Florida's history. Many architectural and design elements, including elevator doors and teller screens, have been spectacularly preserved. ♦ 169 E Flagler St (at NE Second Ave) &

23 Floridita Bar Restaurant $ It requires a bit of exploring to find your way downstairs to this unusual Cuban bar/restaurant, but for many downtown businesspeople, it's the only place for a quick lunch or drink. It is the direct descendant of a restaurant and bar still operating in Havana that claims to be the birthplace of the daiquiri. Whatever the drink's lineage, this restaurant makes a fine rendition of it and provides solid Cuban food to accompany it. ♦ Cuban ♦ M-Sa lunch and dinner. 145 E Flagler St (between NE First and NE Second Aves). 358.1556

23 Seybold Building John Seybold built this arcade-style building in 1921 to contain his soda fountain and bakery. Today, the enlarged building retains its historic character but houses 10 floors of gem merchants. This is the place to comparison shop and haggle over jewelry, gold, and silver. ♦ M-Sa. 39 E Flagler St (between NE Miami and NE First Aves) &

23 McCrory's This seemingly commonplace five-and-dime made the history books in the 1960s when blacks, demanding to be served, staged a sit-in at the then whites-only store. ♦ Daily. 23 E Flagler St (at NE Second Ave). 371.1361 &

24 Burdines Founded in 1898, just two years after Miami was incorporated, this department store has grown with the city. William Burdine's first store had two employees and resembled a frontier shop. Shortly after his death in 1911, the store expanded to a five-

story building, which was remodeled and enlarged to its present size in 1936. In 1947, another building was added across the street, the two connected by a bridge over South Miami Avenue. Most of the store's business today is conducted at suburban branches, which have longer hours and more convenient parking. Owned by the national Federated department store conglomerate, it remains one of the most influential stores in South Florida. ♦ M-Sa; Su afternoon. 22 E Flagler St (at S Miami Ave). 835.5151 &. Also at: Cutler Ridge Mall, 20507 S Dixie Hwy (at SW 205th St). 252.5200 &; Dadeland Mall, 7535 SW 88th St (between S Dixie Hwy and Palmetto Expwy). 662.3400 &; and Miami International Mall, 1455 NW 107th Ave (at NW 14th St). 835.5151 &

GUSMAN CENTER

25 Maurice Gusman Center for the Performing Arts This structure was designed in 1925 by **John Eberson.** Originally called the **Olympia,** it was a Paramount Enterprises' theater and the first air-condi-tioned building in Dade County. At the time, Paramount was one of the major theater owners in the US, and the elegant Romanesque decor of its buildings was famous. Behind the theater's ornate sidewalk ticket booth (still in use), the 10-story structure was originally used for vaudeville shows, then for films. Its orchestra pit still occasionally accommodates an ensemble that plays for silent films, though it is more often filled with an orchestra that accompanies dance troupes. The elaborate lobby only hints at the theater's unique decor. Inside, it resembles a walled Italian garden with secondary walls projecting out from the actual theater walls. Plaster statues and details decorate the balconies, and 264 lights twinkle behind holes in the ceiling to create the effect of a starry night.

Beyond its visual beauty, the 1,700-seat theater is famous for its acoustics, which put it in great demand as a venue for concerts and other theatrical presentations. Broadway shows need more stage space than this building provides (they head for **TOPA** on Miami Beach), but it hosts many of the area's top events, including performances by the **Florida Philharmonic Orchestra,** the **New World Symphony Orchestra,** and, each February, the Miami International Film Festival.

The theater was purchased in 1972 by pharmaceutical king Maurice Gusman, who renovated it and donated it to the city of Miami in 1975. ♦ 174 E Flagler St (at NE Second Ave). 374.2444, concert listings 374.8762 &

26 Ingraham Building At one point, several developers were determined to make Second

Avenue the city's principal shopping street—the "Fifth Avenue of Miami," according to developer Frederick Rand. The 1926 real estate bust crushed those dreams, but the avenue remained fashionable, as this elaborate structure attests. Architects **Schultze & Weaver** (who also built New York City's Waldorf-Astoria hotel) had gained considerable fame in Miami for their **Freedom Tower** (see above) and Coral Gables's **Biltmore Hotel,** both designed in the Spanish style. In this 1927 office building, originally home of the real estate division of Henry Flagler's **Florida East Coast Railroad,** they turned to Neoclassic Revival and some of the Italian Renaissance flavor of the **Villa Vizcaya** in Coconut Grove, as evident in the double-arched windows. The lobby's vaulted ceiling is particularly noteworthy. The building is named after James Ingraham, the first president of Flagler's Model Land Company. Today, the office building is especially popular with law firms. ◆ 25 SE Second Ave (at SE First St) ᴄ

26 **Walgreens** Looking for all the world as if it were transplanted from Miami Beach's Art Deco District, this 1936 Streamline Moderne structure occupies a site donated by Henry Flagler to the Married Ladies Afternoon Club, which later became the Miami Women's Club. The present building, designed by the firm of **Zimmerman, Saxe & MacBride, Ehmann,** today houses a full-service drugstore. ◆ Daily. 200 E Flagler St (at NE Second Ave). 373.8401 ᴄ

27 **International Plaza** Despite the collapse of CenTrust, the financial institution that erected this monument to itself and then foundered during the savings and loan crash of the 1980s, this building remains the most striking bit of modern architecture in Miami. Designed by world-famous architect **I.M. Pei** and completed in 1983, the 47-story tower is divided into several levels but is uniformly lit through a computerized system that bathes the entire structure in light. Though the "everyday color" is brilliant white, it frequently changes hues for various events. When the **University of Miami Hurricanes** football team has a major game or victory, for example, the building glows aqua and orange. ◆ 100 SE First St (at SE First Ave) ᴄ

28 **First Union Financial Center** Formerly known as the **Southeast Financial Center** and now home to First Union Bank, this office building, with its two million square feet of space, towers 55 stories above Biscayne Boulevard. It's the tallest building in Florida, if not the entire southeast US. The tower was designed in the mid-1980s by **Charles E. Bassett** and the award-winning architectural firm of **Skidmore, Owings & Merrill.** ◆ 201 Biscayne Blvd (at NE Second St) ᴄ

29 **Occidental Plaza Hotel** $$$ Tucked behind the **James L. Knight Center** (a convention hall that doubles as a concert venue for rock groups and shows) on the Miami River, this all-suites hotel (129 of them) is comfortable and reasonably priced. Be forewarned: It can be difficult to find on downtown Miami's one-way streets. ◆ 100 SE Fourth St (at SE First Ave). 374.5100, 800/521.5100; fax 381.9826 ᴄ

Within the Occidental Plaza Hotel:

Florencia Restaurant ★★$$$$ This is one of the chain of restaurants found in every **Occidental Plaza Hotel** around the world. A peach-and-white decor sets a formal tone for gourmet interpretations of the food of Spain. A favorite dish is the skillfully prepared cod. ◆ Spanish ◆ M-F lunch and dinner; Sa dinner. 579.8651 ᴄ

Bijan's Fort Dallas ★$$ Good seafood—especially local grouper and snapper—is the big draw at this riverside restaurant, where the service can be curt but the food is great. The kitchen adds a Caribbean touch to straight-forward techniques like broiling and grilling. The conch fritters are a must. ◆ Seafood ◆ M-Sa lunch and dinner. 64 SE Fourth St (at SE First Ave). 381.7778 ᴄ

Flagler Palm Cottage Made of Dade County pine in 1897, this is the last of the several houses that Henry Flagler built in anticipation of an influx of new Miami residents. He put up 14 cottages on 14th Street (now SW Second St) between First and Second Avenues, renting them for $15 to $22 a month. The City of Miami moved this cottage, which is closed to the public, to its present location in 1980 to save it from being demolished to make way for a parking garage. ◆ 66 SE Fourth St (at SE First Ave)

Hyatt Regency Hotel $$$$ The principal attraction of this property is its adjacency to the banking district and to the **James L. Knight Center.** In addition to 615 regular rooms, there are 54 units on the luxury **Regency Club** level, plus two restaurants and two lounges. At press time, the hotel was undergoing renovation. Valet parking is available. ◆ 400 SE Second Ave (at the Miami River). 358.1234, 800/233.1234 ᴄ

A hammock (derived from the native Arawak word for "jungle") is a dense hardwood forest. Few are left in South Florida, but at one time their proliferation made the area, especially around Coconut Grove, nearly impenetrable. Early on, many South Florida pioneers recognized the beauty and value of hammocks and took steps to preserve them. One of the finest examples is at Matheson Hammock Park in South Dade.

Restaurants/Clubs: Red **Hotels:** Blue
Shops/ 🍴 Outdoors: Green **Sights/Culture:** Black

30 Tobacco Road ★★$$ Miami's veteran late-night jazz and blues joint is as comfortable as an old shoe. The club obtained the city's first liquor license in 1912—thus making it Miami's oldest bar—and it became a speakeasy during Prohibition. The secret closet upstairs where liquor and roulette wheels were once stashed is now part of the club. While the simple, casual menu is not extensive, the food is very good. ◆ Cover. Sa-Su. M-F lunch and dinner; Sa-Su dinner until 5AM. 626 S Miami Ave (at SE Seventh St). 374.1198 &

Fishbone Grille ★★$$ Delicious food abounds in this whimsical restaurant where the menus mimic magazines and none of the plates match—in fact, some even carry logos from other restaurants. ◆ Seafood ◆ M-Sa lunch and dinner. Reservations recommended. 650 S Miami Ave (at SW Seventh St). 530.1915 &

31 The Miami Line In a city that devotes a substantial part of local construction money to art in public places, Rockne Krebs's sculpture remains unique: a multicolored, 3,600-foot stretch of neon attached to the **Metrorail** bridge spanning the lower downtown area. From twilight to dawn, the striking, light-filled work is visible from I-95 as a glowing reminder of Miami's inspiring light, which has attracted artists and photographers for decades. ◆ Metrorail bridge over the Miami River, parallel to I-95 between exits for Biscayne Blvd and SW Eighth St

32 Greenwich Village ★★$$$ The owners—an Italian with long experience in the cruise business and an Austrian chef—originally intended to entice the banking crowd with solid American cooking. But when the occasional pasta special proved more successful than the meat loaf, the menu metamorphosed into an amalgam of Italian conception and South Florida ingredients. The fish dishes, grilled meats, and sublime pasta are the best bets, and the homemade napoleon is the perfect end to a meal. It's crowded at lunch and a bargain at dinner. ◆ Italian ◆ Daily lunch and dinner. Reservations recommended. 1001 S Miami Ave (at SE 10th St). 372.1716 &

33 Brasserie Brickell Key ★★$$$ Even though it has a French name, this restaurant serves wonderful Italian dishes, such as tortellini and spaghetti carbonara. If you're in the mood for a quiet picnic on the Biscayne Bay seawall, the owners will pack a box lunch for you. ◆ Italian ◆ Daily lunch and dinner. 601 Brickell Key (at Claughton Island, two blocks east of Brickell Ave). 577.0907 &

34 Brickell Banking District More international banks are clustered in this short stretch than in any other location in the country. As the parade of high-rise banks trails off, a colorful array of condominiums takes over. The architecture here is boisterous. This is where **Arquitectonica** first created a stir with the **Atlantis** condominium (2025 Brickell Ave, at SW 20th Rd). A five-story rectangular block was cut from the center of the multihued building, only to be embedded as a ground-level sculpture. In the space where the block was cut is a whimsical red spiral staircase and a single palm tree, which can be seen for miles around (and in the opening sequence of the television series "Miami Vice"). **Arquitectonica** also designed several other condos in the area, including the **Palace** (1541 Brickell Ave at SW 15th Rd), the **Imperial** (1627 Brickell Ave between SW 15th and SW 17th Rds), and **Villa Regina** (1581 Brickell Ave at SW 15th Rd). The latter is a striking waterfront building, given a rainbow paint job by Israeli artist Yacov Agam. ◆ Brickell Ave from the Miami River to the Rickenbacker Cswy

Within the Brickell Banking District:

Brickell Emporium ★$ The best breakfast bet in the Brickell area, this convivial deli is known for its friendly service and dependably good food. The bagels are first-rate; another good choice is the corned beef and eggs. The sandwiches are huge, the salads fresh. It does get crowded, so be prepared to share a table with other diners. ◆ American ◆ Daily breakfast, lunch, and dinner. 1100 Brickell Plaza (at S Miami Ave). 377.3354 &

Brickell Club ★★★$$$$ Crowning a statuesque 26-story tower, this restaurant, designed by architect **Charles Treister,** has wrap around windows affording panoramic views of the bay and the downtown skyline. It retains the exclusive mien of a private club (which it used to be), making it the place Miamians go when they want to impress and enjoy sumptuous food amid Old World elegance. Valet parking is available. ◆ American ◆ Tu-Sa dinner. 1221 Brickell Ave (at SE 12th Terr), 27th Floor. 536.9000 &

35 Rickenbacker Causeway The first bridge linking Key Biscayne with the mainland was built in 1947, and a section of it about a mile east of the toll gate still is used as a fishing pier. Key Biscayne is the third and largest of the three islands connected by the chain of bridges called the Rickenbacker Causeway. In crossing from downtown Miami to Key Biscayne, you pass over Hobie Island (also called Windsurfer Beach) and Virginia Key. The bridge's tallest span rises 75 feet above the water, commanding an arresting view of Biscayne Bay (if you want to enjoy it at leisure, you must park at the fishing pier and walk back; stopping on the bridge is verboten). Once it reaches Key Biscayne, the causeway becomes Crandon Boulevard, the island's main drag. Along its entire length runs a wide bicycle lane and a fitness path. ◆ Toll. Off Brickell Ave (one block east of S Miami Ave)

36 Rickenbacker Park This narrow strip of land is on Hobie Island, along the causeway linking the mainland to Virginia Key. In the park is an excellent bayside beach and an outpost of **Sailboards Miami,** which rents equipment for windsurfing and other water activities. It's one of the few places in Miami where you can park your car and walk a few steps into the water. ◆ Hobie Island (also called Windsurfer Beach). 361.7245

37 Rusty Pelican $$$ This restaurant is frequently touted by locals who have learned to ignore the ho-hum food in favor of one of the best views in Miami. Perched on one end of Virginia Key, the second-story dining room affords an extraordinary panoramic view of the city skyline and Key Biscayne. It's well worth the price of a drink at the bar. ◆ American ◆ Daily lunch and dinner. 3201 Rickenbacker Cswy, Virginia Key. 361.3818 &

38 Bayside Seafood ★$$ Adjacent to the hurricane-damaged **Miami Marine Stadium,** this small and friendly restaurant appeals to a hardy band of regulars—no one else thinks to look for it. It's their loss, for they're missing good food served in a laid-back climate. ◆ Seafood ◆ Daily lunch and dinner. 3501 Rickenbacker Cswy, Virginia Key. 361.0808 &

Miami Seaquarium®

39 Miami Seaquarium One of Florida's five most popular attractions, this park draws more than one million visitors a year. Among the several shows are ones starring dolphins, manatees, and Lolita, a killer whale. The cycle of shows is repeated every two hours. Other attractions include exhibitions on Florida's aquatic geography, close-up looks at life beneath the surface of tropical waters, and a coral reef. On the grounds are shops and concessions; a monorail provides a quick overview. ◆ Admission. Daily. 4400 Rickenbacker Cswy, Virginia Key. 361.5705 &

40 Sunday's on the Bay ★$$$ As tropical as a restaurant gets, this place has a huge terrace for outdoor dining and an equally spacious indoor eating area. The menu leans toward fairly conservative seafood recipes. A band and deejays enliven the deservedly popular Sunday brunch buffet. ◆ Seafood ◆ Daily dinner; M-Sa lunch; Su brunch. Reservations

recommended. 5420 Crandon Blvd, Key Biscayne. 361.6777 &

41 International Tennis Center Home of the **Lipton Championships** tennis tournament, this center features a new 7,500-seat stadium that expands to 14,000 seats during the annual event (in March). Open year-round to the playing (and paying) public, the center has 16 hard courts, eight clay courts, and two grass courts. ◆ Court fees. Daily. 6800 Crandon Blvd (across from Crandon Park), Key Biscayne. 365.2300 &

42 Crandon Park This county park facing the Atlantic Ocean is one of the area's most popular beaches. Notwithstanding the crowds—which can reach 40,000, causing a major parking and traffic crunch along Crandon Boulevard—the beach remains a strong draw. The three-mile-plus shoreline drops gradually, and the white-sand beach is wide. The park provides many picnic tables and grills, as well as seven large picnic shelters available for rent to larger groups. There are also more than a hundred cabanas (with showers and chairs) for rent, each accommodating up to five people. Lifeguards are on duty, and boats can be rented. ◆ 4000 Crandon Blvd, Key Biscayne. 361.5421, marina 361.1281

43 Links at Key Biscayne Golf Course Designed by Von Hagge and Devlin and built in 1972, this impressive layout overlooks Biscayne Bay and is surrounded by lush mangroves. It hosts the annual **Royal Caribbean Classic** and features a complete spectrum of golf services for the entire family. ◆ Greens fees. Daily from 7AM. 6700 Crandon Blvd, Key Biscayne. 361.9139 &

44 Oasis $ From 6:30AM until well after dark, this is a regular stop for residents of Key Biscayne Village, passing bikers, and joggers who want a shot of *café cubano,* a Cuban pastry, or a *media noche.* Pick up the fixings for a Latin-style picnic here before heading to the beach. ◆ Cuban ◆ Daily breakfast, lunch, and dinner. 19 Harbour Dr (at Crandon Blvd), Key Biscayne. 361.5709 &

44 Stefano's ★$$$$ This place enjoys a great reputation, in part because of its longevity and late hours. Whatever culinary excellence it once had has worn over time, but the regulars keep it packed. The pasta is very good—it has to be, to keep islanders coming back at these prices. The fresh seafood is also tasty, but service is erratic. A jazz trio plays Coltrane on weekends. ◆ Italian ◆ Daily lunch and dinner. 24 Crandon Blvd (at Harbor Dr), Key Biscayne. 361.7007 &

45 Mangrove Cycles This shop helps visitors travel the island's many well-marked bike trails. Close to **Crandon Park** (see above) and **Bill Baggs Cape Florida State Recreation Area** (see below), it sells and rents a variety of bicycles for children and adults. ◆ Tu-Su. 260 Crandon Blvd, Key Biscayne. 361.5555 &

46 Key Colony Condominium Though there are many private homes on Key Biscayne, some of the island's most luxurious residences are found among the 1,200 units of this four-building complex. The buildings are notable for their steep-sloping walls, which give each unit's balcony a sense of space and seclusion. ♦ 101-251 Crandon Blvd, Key Biscayne

Within Key Colony Condominium:

Pat's at Key Colony ★★$ Hidden inside the condominium compound is a tiny restaurant run by Pat Molinari, whose chief business is catering. Her lunch specials have a South Florida flair, like the grilled dolphin "Neptune Burger." Sip an iced tea with a piece of Pat's carrot cake and you'll wonder why her place remains undiscovered. ♦ American ♦ M-F lunch. 235 Crandon Blvd, Key Biscayne. 361.6010 ♿

47 Linda B. ★★★$$$ Unlike traditional steak houses, this restaurant has a light, airy decor. But the porterhouse, sirloin, and prime ribs are definitely on the heavy side. The service is excellent. If you're looking for a "prime"-time dining experience on Key Biscayne, this is the place. ♦ Steak house ♦ Daily dinner; Su brunch. 320 Crandon Blvd, Key Biscayne. 361.1111 ♿

47 Art Gallery Center Along with some fast-food restaurants, this center houses three galleries on the second floor: the **Commenoz Gallery, M. Gutierrez Fine Arts,** and the **Sandy Wallin Art Decor Gallery.** ♦ Daily. 328 Crandon Blvd, Key Biscayne. 361.7052 ♿

Within the Art Gallery Center:

La Boulangerie ★$ Gourmet sandwiches on fresh-baked croissants are the draws at this quaint French bakery/cafe. The seating is crowded, and the service can be slow, but the food is worth the wait. Try one of the natural juices—they make a healthy accompaniment to the homemade pastries. ♦ French ♦ M-Sa lunch and dinner. 361.0281 ♿

48 President Nixon's House Many visitors first heard of then-quiet Key Biscayne when President Richard Nixon established a vacation home on the island. Little is left of the "Florida White House"—a later owner enlarged the residence substantially, though the huge helicopter pad remains on the waterfront—but the address still attracts the curious. It's a private residence, and visitors are not allowed. ♦ 485 W Matheson Dr (at Harbor Dr), Key Biscayne

Sonesta Beach Resort Key Biscayne

49 Sonesta Beach Resort Key Biscayne $$$$ Each of the 300 contemporary rooms at this 10-acre oceanfront resort has a private balcony overlooking the ocean. The resort appeals to conventioneers and families alike: Supervised activities for children and many resort amenities are offered. The pool is long enough to swim laps, and there are tennis courts, an exercise room, and an immaculate beach. The restaurant (see below) is one of Key Biscayne's best. ♦ 350 Ocean Dr (between East and E Heather Drs), Key Biscayne. 361.2021, 800/SONESTA; fax 365.2096 ♿

Within the Sonesta Beach Resort Key Biscayne:

Two Dragons ★★$$$ While it might seem odd to find a Chinese restaurant the focal point of a tropical resort, the **Sonesta** does a first-rate job here. The seafood selection is exten-sive, with the menu sampling several cuisines rather than focusing on a single region. The food is elegantly prepared and served. ♦ Chinese ♦ Daily dinner. 361.2021 ♿

50 Silver Sands Motel $$$ This 56-room hotel has none of the amenities offered at nearby resorts, nor does it charge their prices—it's simple, clean, and has as handy a beach location as any other lodging on Key Biscayne. There's a restaurant . ♦ 301 Ocean Dr, Key Biscayne. 361.5441 ♿

51 Bill Baggs Cape Florida State Recreation Area This once heavily wooded park and beach area covering 406 acres at the southernmost tip of Key Biscayne is still recovering from Hurricane Andrew's devastation. New plantings are gradually restoring the shade, and the beaches are as inviting as ever. The park is named for the *Miami News* editor who pushed and cajoled the state to create the park, which was home to many rare native plants until the hurricane's storm tide extinguished them with saltwater. ♦ 1200 S Crandon Blvd, Key Biscayne. 361.5811

51 Cape Florida Lighthouse Built in 1825, this 95-foot-high brick tower is the oldest original structure in South Florida still standing. The lighthouse served a dual purpose in the early 19th century, not only warning ships of the treacherous reefs along the Florida Keys but serving as a haven for settlers fleeing Indian attacks. In 1836 Seminole Indians sacked the lighthouse and killed the lightkeeper's assistant. Pioneers persevered, however, and the colony grew. The lighthouse is located next to a small stone pier at the very tip of Key Biscayne, where the beach gives way to the seawall. ♦ Admission. Daily. Southern tip of Key Biscayne. 361.5811 ♿

Little Havana/Points West

The 30-block area along Miami's **Southwest Eighth Street** called **Little Havana** (extending roughly from **I-95** west to **SW 37th Ave**) has been known by that name for nearly 35 years. Over time, however, the neighborhood has welcomed not only Cubans fleeing oppression but immigrants from Central and South America as well. As a result, Nicaraguan, Honduran, and Salvadoran influences are beginning to overwhelm the once-dominant Cuban flavor. In an effort to reflect this broader mix of cultures, part of Little Havana has officially been named the **Latin Quarter** (generally, SW Eighth St between **SW 27th** and **SW 12th Aves**). Nowadays, most Cuban immigrants settle in the thriving industrial city of **Hialeah**, where more jobs are available and commerce is more vibrant.

The section of Southwest Eighth Street known in Spanish as **Calle Ocho** remains relatively untouched by American franchise stores. There is only one gringo-style supermarket, for most people shop at their corner *bodega,* where they can find foods reminiscent of "home," such as yuca, papaya, and *coquito,* a coconut candy made all over the Caribbean. You'll find one **McDonalds** and one **Dunkin' Donuts,** but locals are more likely to patronize the tiny *cafeterías* (carry-out or mini-restaurants) that serve hearty creole stews in their small dining rooms and dispatch *café cubano* from counter windows along the street. In fact, you can buy just about anything in the small stores along Calle Ocho—from men's shirts to children's toys—without leaving the neighborhood. Being able to speak Spanish helps, of course, but the people are friendly and sign language is universally understood.

Also along Calle Ocho are a few of the best Cuban restaurants in town, including many that, recalling the elegance of pre-Castro Havana, insist they are really Spanish (some are, but many are not). With its nightclubs, theaters, cigar factories, and churches, this pulsing street is almost a city unto itself. (*Drivers beware:* This traffic-burdened street is one way heading east. The best way to experience it is on foot, proceeding west from downtown.)

Area code 305 unless otherwise indicated.

1 José Martí Park Located in the heart of Little Havana, this park includes a softball field, racquetball and basketball courts, a pool, a river walkway, a small outdoor amphitheater, and open picnic areas. Since the park opened in 1984, its design—by John Fernsler and Ignacio Bunster of the nationally recognized firm of Wallace, Roberts, and Todd—has won the Florida Association of Housing and Redevelopment Official Highest Honors Award in 1985 and the American Society of Landscape Architects Award in 1988. ♦ 351 SW Fourth St (at SW Third Ave). 579.6958

2 Taquería el Mexicano ★$ With all its mirrors, bright green and orange walls, and music, this restaurant looks at first like a fun house. But don't be deceived by appearances, for it offers some of the best authentic Mexican food in Little Havana. Menu items range from the popular enchiladas and *tortas* (sandwiches on crusty rolls) to the lesser-known *lengua en salsa* (beef tongue) and *pozole* (hominy). The owners take special pride in making every *amigo* feel welcome. ♦ Mexican ♦ Daily breakfast, lunch, and dinner. 521 SW Eighth St (at SW Fifth Ave). 858.1160.

♦ Also at: 1945 SW Eighth St (between SW 19th and SW 20th Aves). 649.9150

3 Casa Prieto The windows of this classic Cuban *dulcería* (bakery) are filled with grandly decorated cakes to celebrate any occasion. It offers Cuban pastries and cookies, too. ♦ Daily. 745 SW Eighth St (between SW Seventh and SW Eighth Aves). 854.8000 ♦

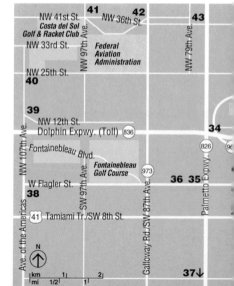

3 Malaga ★$$ Despite its decidedly Cuban menu, this is one of those restaurants that claims to be Spanish. The food is so good that it doesn't matter—if you don't mind the slightly shopworn look of the place. Wooden tables are set up in the courtyard, with small dining areas off to the side. The excellent seafood paella is served Cuban style (slightly moist). The seafood tends to be overcooked, but the meat dishes are good: The pot roast, the garlic-smeared Cuban steak called *palomilla*, and the spicy fried veal are all recommended. The service is erratic. ♦ Cuban ♦ Daily lunch and dinner. Reservations recommended. 740 SW Eighth St (between SW Seventh and SW Eighth Aves). 858.4224 ৬

4 La Esquina de Tejas ★$ This is the most talked about, if not the best, Cuban restaurant in Miami. Ever since then-President Ronald Reagan wooed Hispanic voters by stopping here, it has been mobbed by the curious as well as the hungry—in fact, Southwest 12th Avenue has been renamed Ronald Reagan Avenue. The food *is* good, especially the classic sandwiches of pork, ham, and cheese on Cuban bread. ♦ Cuban ♦ Daily breakfast, lunch, and dinner. 101 SW 12th Ave (at SW First St). 545.5341 ৬

5 Brigade 2506 Memorial An eternal flame atop a simple stone monument commemorates the ill-fated 1961 Bay of Pigs invasion of Cuba by an army of Cuban exiles funded and trained by the US. Other monuments stand south of the flame on a block-long, tree-shaded *prado* where the bungalow-style homes of Miami's early settlers still are visible. ♦ SW Eighth St (at SW 13th Ave)

5 Cuban Museum of Art and Culture Although plagued by erratic funding, this museum struggles on in its effort to preserve and interpret the heritage of pre-Castro Cuba. Several heated debates have broken out over whether to admit the works of artists who have exhibited in post-revolutionary Cuba. A recent exhibition featured art by the *balseros* (refugees who fled Cuba in 1994 on flimsy rafts, only to be intercepted by the US Coast Guard and detained at Guantánamo Bay Naval Base). ♦ Donation. W-Su 1-5PM. 1300 SW 12th Ave (at SW 13th St). 858.8006 ৬

La Casa de Los Trucos
(THE HOUSE OF COSTUMES)

6 La Casa de Los Trucos It's Halloween every day in this shop, where a notice on the front door warns: "We remind you that you enter at your own risk. We demonstrate items that explode, shock, jump out. And squirt water." Frankenstein costumes, Easter bunny outfits, exploding pens, psychedelic yellow wigs, and plastic vomit are its stock-in-trade. Original costumes are made in the back room. The store puts on magic shows during the two tourist seasons: January through March for Northerners and June through August for Latin Americans. ♦ M-Sa; daily in October. 1343 SW Eighth St (between SW 12th and SW 13th Aves). 858.5029. ৬ Also at: 8590 SW 40th St (between SW 85th and SW 86th Aves). 553.3553

7 Casa Panza ★★$$ With just 13 tables, a small counter, and Spanish sausages and hams hanging from the ceiling, this is a cozy spot for an authentic Spanish (not Cuban) meal. Recommended are the Valencian-style paella and the *tortilla de patatas* (potato omelette). Carmita López cooks all the food (she and her husband, owner Jesús, hail from Madrid), which adds to the feeling of dining in a friend's home—a home in Spain, that is. On Tuesdays and Thursdays, Spanish guitarist and singer Paco Fonta performs. Other Spanish musical entertainment, including flamenco dancing, is offered Fridays through Sundays. ♦ Spanish ♦ Daily lunch and dinner. 1620 SW Eighth St (at SW 16th Ave). 643.5343 ৬

8 España You might at first mistake this import shop for a mausoleum: Much of the showroom is filled with religious statues, some six feet tall. Shrines are popular with many Cubans, who revere St. Lazarus in particular because he endured poverty and pain. The most colorful and delicate of the statues, intended for display indoors, are made of sawdust and plaster. T. Pla, the genial proprietor, will gladly explain the differences between his statues and show off his guitars and other objects, all imported from Spain. ◆ M-Sa. 1615 SW Eighth St (at SW 17th Ave). 856.4844 ᕱ

9 Alpha 66 Headquarters A military-training operation founded in the early 1960s just after the Bay of Pigs invasion, this organization is dedicated to the overthrow of Fidel Castro. Though the US government frowns on some of its activities, its storefront headquarters is open to the public. Photographs of the organization's heroes and training camps in the Everglades, the Florida Keys, and South and Central America lend it a museumlike air. It is a testament to the Cuban exiles' devotion to *la causa* ("the cause"), even 35 years after Castro came to power. The organization, which actively plans incursions into Cuba, claims about 200,000 members worldwide, mostly in the US. ◆ Daily. 1714 W Flagler St (near SW 17th Ave). 541.5433 ᕱ

10 Plaza de la Cubanidad The memorial fountain here is dedicated to José Martí, a leader in Cuba's fight for independence from Spain. Red brick sidewalks frame the monument, which contains a quotation from Martí, *"Las palmas son novias que esperan"* (The palm trees are girlfriends who wait), in which the trees represent mourners for the loss of the homeland who await the return of the Cuban diaspora. ◆ SW corner of W Flagler St and SW 17th Ave

ANTELO CIGARS

11 Antelo Cigars One of the last of the authentic Cuban cigar factories, this tiny workshop employs a handful of cigar makers trained in Honduras, the Dominican Republic, and Cuba. In one day, it produces up to a thousand cigars made of Mexican and Dominican tobacco. Owner Arnaldo Laurencio sells to stores in Miami, New York, New Jersey, and California. ◆ M-F; Sa until noon. 437 SW 17th Ave (near SW Fourth St). 642.8911 ᕱ

La Casa de las Piñatas

12 Casa de las Piñatas In Latin America, no child's birthday party is complete without a piñata, that colorful receptacle of toys, candy, and confetti. The 200 unique creations here draw buyers from all over the US and Latin America, according to owner/piñata maker Diego Rodríguez, who has been in the business for 20 years. Unlike Mexican and Central American piñatas, which burst open when blindfolded children pummel them with sticks, the Cuban versions yield treats when children pull the ribbons at the bottom. Made of paper and wood, most have fanciful figures on top, such as the Lion King, Snow White and the Seven Dwarfs, and Power Rangers. Also available are Mexican piñatas, other children's toys, and imaginative party supplies. ◆ M-Sa; closed the last two weeks of December. 1756 SW Eighth St (near SW 17th Ave). 649.4711

El Camino

Flowers

13 Botánica El Camino *Botánicas* are Cuban herb shops that sell, among other things, items used in the Santería religion, an Afro-Cuban tradition that borrows from Catholicism. This shop displays carnations, chrysanthemums, and baby's breath along with shelves of love potions, "money house-blessing" air freshener, "jinx-removing deodorant air spray," "road openers" (to help open new life paths), colored candles in the shape of naked persons, rams' horns, and rusted metal stakes, the last possibly for use in religious rituals. If you have no need for any of the above, there are also used Spanish-language dime novels. ◆ Daily. 1896 SW Eighth St (at SW 19th Ave). 643.9135

14 Guayacan Restaurant ★$$ For simple Nicaraguan cooking, this is a good starting point. Seating is limited to a counter and 20 tables, but the service is friendly. Try *salpicón* (a marinated beef dish) or tripe with vegetables. *Pargo tipitapa* is a Nicaraguan classic of deep-fried snapper with a zesty pepper-and-onion sauce. There are also many hearty soups. ◆ Nicaraguan ◆ Daily lunch and dinner.

1933 SW Eighth St (at SW 19th Ave).
649.2015 &

15 Centro Vasco ★$$$ Cuban food with a
Basque touch is the somewhat diffuse focus
of the menu here. The paella and seafood
dishes are especially tasty. It is a comfortable
spot to linger over Cuban coffee and flan.
♦ Cuban/Spanish ♦ Daily lunch and dinner.
Reservations recommended Saturday and
Sunday. 2235 SW Eighth St (at SW 22nd
Ave). 643.9606 &

16 Casa Juancho ★$$$$ This is Miami's
gastronomic version of Disneyland, from
beginning to end. Waiting diners stand by
the smoked hams hanging from the ceiling,
then parade to their tables past cases filled
with fresh meat and seafood. The mostly
Galician cooking is fairly authentic, with
dishes such as a layered potato torte and
an excellent *caldo gallego* (white-bean soup
with sausage and pork). The entrées tend
to be overcooked; the one clear winner is
the exceptional *crema catalán* dessert. It's
worth coming here for the experience—but
remember, the experience far outclasses the
food. ♦ Spanish ♦ Daily lunch and dinner.
Reservations recommended. 2436 SW
Eighth St (at SW 24th Ave). 642.2452 &

17 Gaucho's Cafe ★★★$$$ A real find,
this authentic Argentine restaurant offers
an intimate dining experience and culinary
delights cooked to order. Many Argentine

favorites, such as chicken *mariscada*
(with seafood) and seafood with rice and
creole sauce, aren't even on the menu.
Other delicacies available are *panqueque de
manzana* (apple crepe) and *posilipo* (shrimp,
mussels, and clams over linguine in a
Provençale or *pomodoro*—tomato—sauce).
Everything about the place contributes to the
genuine Argentine ambience, down to the
handmade red-and-black gaucho costume
on display. On Saturday nights, live folkloric
and tango music is performed. ♦ Argentine
♦ Daily lunch and dinner. 2901 SW Eighth St
(near SW 29th Ave). 649.9494 &

18 Islas Canarias ★$$ Many Cubans swear
this is the best restaurant in Miami. The
menu is no different from that at a dozen
other Cuban restaurants, but subtle nuances
give everything a slight edge over the
competition. Specialties include *picadillo*
(ground beef cooked with olives and spices)
over rice and *palomilla,* a garlic-smeared
steak. ♦ Cuban ♦ Daily breakfast, lunch, and
dinner. 285 NW 27th Ave (at NW Second
St). 649.0440

19 La Tasca ★$$ Cuban food is the staple
here, with different specials every day.
The usual pork dishes, black beans and rice,
and roast chicken are served with panache.
Local patrons of the arts often dine here after
attending operatic or theatrical performances
at nearby **Dade County Auditorium** (see
below). ♦ Cuban ♦ Daily breakfast, lunch,
and dinner. 2741 W Flagler St (at NW 27th
Ave). 642.3762 &

20 Dade County Auditorium For many
years this has been a stopgap theater, taking
on shows too big for the **Maurice Gusman
Center for the Performing Arts** downtown
and too small for the **Jackie Gleason
Theater** in Miami Beach. The stage is large
enough to suit the **Florida Grand Opera,**
which stages several performances (out
of five productions annually) here. The
auditorium is home to the **Miami City Ballet,**
and many visiting ensembles perform here
as well, utilizing the stage and seating
capacity of nearly 2,500. Extensive parking
is available for a fee. ♦ 2901 W Flagler St
(at NW 29th Ave). 547.5414 &

Restaurants/Clubs: Red   **Hotels:** Blue
Shops/ Outdoors: Green   **Sights/Culture:** Black

21 Versailles ★$$ The most famous Cuban restaurant in town also gives the impression of being the oldest (it's not). Ceiling-to-floor mirrors cover the walls, much to the delight of children. The huge menu embraces every Cuban dish known to the connoisseur. For the adventuresome diner looking for the real thing, this is a good stop. ♦ Cuban ♦ Daily breakfast, lunch, and dinner. 3555 SW Eighth St (at SW 36th Ave). 445.7614 &

3632 S.W. 8TH ST.
MIAMI, FL. 33135

22 La Carreta ★$ Named for a bull-drawn cart used to transport sugarcane from the fields, this restaurant is a Miami institution, known for good, cheap Cuban food and the sugarcane plants that grow on the front lawn. Don't miss the photos of pre-Castro Cuba, including the capitol in Havana, the birthplace of José Martí, and the Hotel Internacional on Varadero Beach. Portions tend to be large, but if you're in the mood for just a *café con leche,* a pastry, or a glass of *guarapo* (sugarcane juice), you can get it at the *cafetería* in back. ♦ Cuban ♦ Daily breakfast, lunch, and dinner. 3632 SW Eighth St (near SW 36th Ave). 447.0184. & Also at: 11740 Kendall Dr (near the Florida Turnpike). 596.5973; 8650 SW 40th St/Bird Rd (near SW 86th Ave). 553.8383; 5350 W 16th Ave, Hialeah (near Westland Mall). 823.5200

23 Phoenecia ★★$ This friendly Lebanese restaurant serves excellent food at bargain prices. There's a wide range of first courses to sample, including the best hummus in town and excellent stuffed grape and cabbage leaves. The stuffed eggplant is a good entrée, as is the *kibbeh nayeh,* Lebanon's version of steak tartare. ♦ Lebanese ♦ Daily lunch and dinner. 2841 Coral Way (between SW 28th and SW 29th Aves). 443.1426 &

24 Latin American ★$ With just 30 or so chairs grouped around a circular counter, this restaurant is a Miami favorite. The small kitchen is in the middle, so you can see your meal being prepared as you wait. Freshness has its price, though: The smell of the smoke coming from the grill tends to cling to your clothes. The house specialty is sandwiches, but other typical Cuban dishes—*frijoles negros* (black beans) and *vaca frita* (flank steak)—also are served. The mamey shake (a tropical fruit drink) is particularly good. ♦ Cuban ♦ Daily breakfast, lunch, and dinner. 2940 Coral Way (between SW 29th and SW 30th Aves). 448.6809 &

25 Miracle Center Since its completion in 1989, no one can decide if this structure is modern art or the result of an earthquake. The New Wave architects at **Arquitectonica** took a huge, rectangular block of concrete, painted it blue, and covered it with panels that resemble cracked walls. Toss in a few shops and an inconvenient parking garage with hair-raisingly steep ramps, and you have the most controversial shopping complex in Miami. On the fringe of Coral Gables, the center has no national anchor to act as a draw, though it does feature a spectacular 10-screen movie theater and a few sportswear chains, including **The Limited, The Gap,** and **Structures.** ♦ M-Sa; Su afternoon. 3301 Coral Way (between SW 32nd and SW 34th Aves). 444.8890 &

26 El Cid Campeador ★$$$ From its castlelike facade to its antique furniture and bronze dinnerware, this Spanish restaurant is a tribute to medieval history. Local patrons swear the *zarzuela valenciana* (shrimp, mussels, scallops, lobster, clams, and grouper in a tomato sauce) is the best in town. The service is slow, so while you wait, take a tour of this interesting place. Valet parking is available. ♦ Spanish ♦ Daily lunch and dinner. Reservations recommended. 117 SW 42nd Ave (at W Flagler St). 643.3917

27 Airport Regency $$ This modest, six-story hotel has 176 small and neat rooms, many with balconies, plus a pool, and a restaurant. ♦ 1000 NW Le Jeune Rd (at NW 10th St). 441.1600, 800/432.1192 in FL, 800/367.1039; fax 443.0766 &

28 Marriott Miami Airport $$ One of the largest in Dade County, this hotel has 782 rooms distributed among six buildings. Convenient for both conventioneers and families, it offers plenty of conference space, free airport transportation, a restaurant, tennis courts, and exercise rooms. At press time, the complex was slated to split into a Marriott hotel, a Fairfield Inn property, and a Courtyard hotel, and offer a range of low to mid-level prices. ♦ 1201 NW Le Jeune Rd (at NW 12th St). 649.5000, 800/228.9290; fax 642.3369 &

29 Sheraton River House $$$ This hostelry offers considerable convenience, with its location opposite the **Hertz** drop-off terminal, a half-mile from the airport on a major approach. The lobby is strictly hotel standard, but the 408 rooms are comfortable; amenities include a pool, a tennis court, a dining room, and numer-ous convention facilities. ♦ 3900 NW 21st St (between NW 42nd Ave and NW Douglas Rd). 871.3800, 800/325.3535; fax 871.0447 &

Choice Cuban Cuisine

Almost every locale lays claim to a celebrated regional concoction, from Philly's cheese steak to California's health cuisine. **Miami Beach** was once known for its cheesecake and is still famous for Key lime pie, but thanks to recent immigration, it is delicious Latin American and Caribbean cuisine that you'll find in abundance here. And there's a proliferation of wonderful Cuban restaurants—from **La Esquina de Tejas** to **Versailles**—that dish up the ferociously caloric and savory fare that is the city's favorite.

The Cuban variation of daily bread, *pan,* ranks up there with the greats of Italy, France, and the Middle East. The rest of the menu revolves around nutritious rice and beans. Fish and meat dishes are often prepared in a sumptuous sauce known as *sofrito,* made of peppers, onions, garlic, tomatoes, and ~cumin. Sure hits are *arroz con pollo* (baked chicken with saffron rice), *bistec palomilla* (thin steak heaped with minced onions and garnished with parsley), and *masas de puerco* (pork chunks). Plantains (similar to bananas) are served with most entrées; choose either the *maduros* (soft and sweet plantains) or *verdes* (fried green plantains). And

save room for *flan* (custard) or *tres leches* (a terrifically rich and sweet Nicaraguan dessert).

In a hurry? Grab a bowl of *caldo gallego,* a white bean soup with *chorizo* sausage and pork, or *tamal en cazuela,* a cornmeal porridge. Or indulge in a Cuban sandwich, which is served warm on grill-pressed Cuban bread and comes in many varieties—the popular *media noche* is filled with ham, pork, and cheese.

Batidos (tropical fruit shakes) are made from such exotic fruits as mamey, mango, and *guanabana.* A bottle of nonalcoholic *malta* (malt soft drink) is worth a swig. Or try a rum-based drink—a *mojito* (garnished with mint) or a daiquiri. Both were favored by Ernest Hemingway during the years he spent in Cuba.

The classic finale is coffee. Many Miamians can't live without a periodic demitasse of *café cubano,* also referred to as a *cafecito,* which will give you a legal rush unequaled in the States and bring you to your senses no matter how much you've feasted. At breakfast, sip a *café con leche* (coffee with steamed milk). For more clues on deciphering a Cuban menu, see "Fare with Flair" on page 31.

---

30 Miami International Airport (MIA)
Eight miles west of downtown, this is a hub for flights from around the US and the world and the second-busiest airport in the country in international passenger volume. ♦ 876.7000 &

Within Miami International Airport:

Hotel MIA $$ You can't get accommodations any closer to the airport than this, for the hotel is actually located inside the terminal. It has 260 rooms, ranging from singles to suites. Amenities are few (mostly restricted airport concessions), but the convenience makes it ideal for business travelers. There's also a restaurant. ♦ Concourse E. 871.4100, 800/327.1276; fax 871.0800 &

31 Hilton Airport and Marina $$$ Right around the corner from the airport, this hotel is a popular venue for modest-size conventions. The 500 rooms (83 of them suites) are pleasantly furnished, and on the

grounds are a tennis court, exercise equipment, and two restaurants. The hotel is on Blue Lagoon, a small body of water where you can rent Jet Skis, paddleboats, and other water sports equipment. **The Towers** is a three-story luxury complex with 128 units and 16 suites at slightly higher rates. Valet parking and free transportation to the airport and downtown are available. ♦ 5101 Blue Lagoon Dr (at Red Rd). 262.1000, 800/445.8667; fax 267.0038 &

32 Hotel Sofitel $$ Part of the international French-owned chain, this place fosters an image of European cultivation and, to a large extent, succeeds. The 281 rooms (plus 25 suites) are tasteful and spacious. Recreational facilities (Jet Skis, paddleboats, and the like) on nearby Blue Lagoon, lighted tennis courts, and an exercise room make this place a good value. ♦ 5800 Blue Lagoon Dr (at Red Rd). 264.4888, 800/258.4888; fax 262.9049 &

Within Hotel Sofitel:

Le Cafe Royal ★★★$$$$ The kitchen at Miami's most elegant nouvelle French restaurant doesn't miss a step when it comes to updating the classics. Appetizers include marinated salmon in virgin olive oil with vinaigrette potatoes, and *mesclun* salad with five kinds of greens. Among the entrées are fresh monkfish baked in phyllo pastry and served with sautéed mushrooms; sautéed medaillons of lamb flavored with thyme; and roast duck in a mushroom-tomato sauce. You'll have a hard time trying to save room for the crème brûlée with vanilla sauce or the Cointreau soufflé, but they're both well worth it. ♦ French ♦ M-F lunch and dinner; Sa dinner; Su brunch. Reservations required. 264.4888 ♿

33 Pizza Loft ★$$ It may not cater to the trendsetters, but on those days when there's nothing like a good pizza, this is the place to go. No fancy doughs or exotic dried vegetable toppings, just a thin crust, good tomato sauce, and fresh ingredients. Eat in or take out. ♦ Italian ♦ Daily lunch and dinner. 6917 W Flagler St (at NW 69th Ave). 266.5111 ♿

34 The Spirit ★★$$$ Airlines have always been an important part of Miami's development, and at this restaurant, plane buffs can luxuriate in airline memorabilia, mostly items rescued from now-defunct **Eastern** and **Pan American.** Not surprisingly, the place is a favorite with airline people, especially those who worked for the two late, lamented carriers. The tabletops are decorated with glass-covered collages of airline tags, and the "chairs" are old airplane seats (though diners are not scrunched up against their neighbors here). Miniature planes hover overhead, and historical pictures and travel posters adorn the wall. Thankfully, the fare has little in common with the real thing (airline food, that is). Steaks are grilled over real wood (not chips), fish can be made to order, and pasta is a favorite. ♦ American ♦ M-F lunch and dinner; Sa dinner. 7250 NW 11th Street (just off the Milam Dairy exit of the Dolphin Expwy/Rte 836). 262.9500 ♿

35 Mall of the Americas This regional mall gets points for its grandiose name alone, but its big draw has nothing to do with an international view. This is a discount mall in which many stores—including **Home Depot, Marshall's, Luria's,** and **T.J. Maxx**—sell at off-price. ♦ Daily. 7795 W Flagler St (at Palmetto Expwy/Hwy 826). 261.8772 ♿

36 Shilla ★★$$ Clean, intimate, and authentically delicious, this is the ultimate Korean restaurant. Korean barbecue at your table is featured, along with casseroles,

dumplings, and a few interesting Chinese dishes. The service is excellent, and prices are reasonable. ♦ Korean ♦ M-Tu, Th-Su lunch and dinner. Reservations recommended. 7917 NW Second St (at NW 79th Ave). 267.0011 ♿

36 Casa Larios ★★$$$ An oddball in central Miami, this cafe looks like a delicatessen, but its food is worthy of an elegant restaurant. Despite its simple appearance, it is one of the most authentic Cuban restaurants in town. Gloria Estefan loved it so much that she encouraged the owners to launch **Lario's on the Beach** with her in trendy South Beach. The seafood is particularly noteworthy, especially the rice with squid. And the meat dishes—fried beef, *picadillo* (a ground beef dish), and pork morsels—are all worth savoring. ♦ Cuban ♦ Daily breakfast, lunch, and dinner. 7929 NW Second St (at NW 79th Ave). 266.5494 ♿

大利飯店
Tropical Chinese Restaurant
MIAMI

37 Tropical Chinese Restaurant ★★★★$$$ This award-winning restaurant offers the best dim sum in South Florida. The steamed whole snapper and pine seed lobster "song" (a mousse of ground lobster seasoned with the smokey flavor of dry Chinese sausage, served on iceberg lettuce, then folded like a taco) are superb. On weekends, the place is jammed with Chinese families, an indication of how good the food is. The only thing ordinary about this place is its location in a strip shopping center. ♦ Chinese ♦ Daily lunch and dinner. 7991 SW 40th St/Bird Rd (near SW 79th Ave just west of the Palmetto Expwy/Hwy 826). 262.1552, 262.7576 ♿

38 Los Ranchos ★★$$$ Located in Sweetwater, a community sometimes dubbed "Little Managua," this is the original—and the best—Nicaraguan restaurant in the Miami area. The *pargo tipitapa* (deep-fried snapper) and the house specialty, *churrasco* (grilled flank steak), are sure winners. ♦ Nicaraguan ♦ Daily lunch and dinner. 125 SW 107th Ave (at SW First St), Sweetwater. 221.9367. ♿ Also at: Bayside Marketplace, 401 Biscayne Blvd (at NE Fourth St), Miami. 375.8188; Los Ranchos/Town & Country Shopping Center, 8505 Mills Dr (at SW 117th Ave), Kendall. 596.5353; and the Falls Shopping Center, 8888 SW 136th St (at US 1). 238.6867

39 Miami International Mall The only international aspect of this mall is its food court. But, with two **Burdines, J.C. Penney, Mervyn's,** and **Mayor's Jewelers,** it satisfies the needs of the most demanding shoppers. ♦ Daily. 1455 NW 107th Ave (at NW 14th St). 593.1775 ♿

40 Miami Free Zone Most people purchase duty-free goods only at airports, but at this international wholesale trade center, you can buy them for export or pay duty on goods released for the domestic market. US Customs supervises the exhibition and sales areas, where more than a hundred companies sell everything from cosmetics to computers. ♦ M-F. 2305 NW 107th Ave (at NW 25th St). 591.4300 ⑤

41 Mrs. Mendoza's Tacos al Carbon ★★$
Fresh beef burritos, vegetarian tacos, and pork fajitas served with screaming hot salsa attract locals and tourists to this counter-style fast-food Mexican restaurant, located in a shopping center. There is nothing fancy about the place—bare walls, plain tile floors, and small tables with stools—just good, simple food and a great beer selection. You'll probably have to wait in line for lunch, but the food is worth it. ♦ Mexican ♦ M-Sa lunch and dinner. Doral Plaza Shopping Center, 9739 NW 41st St (at NW 97th Ave). 477.5119 ⑤

42 Doral Golf Resort & Spa $$$$ The most extravagant resort in Dade County features something for everyone. The **Spa at Doral** is an ultra-deluxe health facility that offers a full regimen of exercise and diet control. The "Blue Monster" is the famous **PGA** championship golf course, one of four on the resort's 650-acre "campus." There are also putting greens, 15 tennis courts, five restaurants, valet parking, and numerous other amenities.

Fare with Flair

For those venturing into a Cuban restaurant for the first time, the following glossary should help in deciphering the menu.

Boniato: A tuber similar to a sweet potato.

Café con leche: Espresso-strength coffee diluted with steamed milk. Ask for it strong, or it will be diluted about two to one. Remember, Cuban coffee is served very sweet; specify no sugar ("*sin azúcar*") if you want it unsweetened.

Caldo gallego: A thick, hearty Spanish soup made with white beans and ham.

Cerveza: This oft-heard word means beer.

Ceviche: A popular dish of raw seafood that is "cooked" by being marinated in citrus juice with onions and peppers.

Chimichurri: Often served with grilled meat, this Nicaraguan sauce consists of oil, garlic, and herbs.

Chorizo: This fatty Spanish garlic sausage is intensely flavored.

Churrasco: Nicaraguan-style marinated and grilled flank steak.

Churros: Long Cuban "doughnuts" often sold at coffee stands.

Flan: This custard resembles crème caramel.

Maduros: Sweet, ripe plantains usually sliced at an angle or mashed and then fried.

Masas de puerco: Chunks of fried pork served with onions and lime.

Mojo: Similar to *chimichurri,* this meat marinade is made from oil, garlic, and herbs.

Moros y Cristianos: The name means Moors and Christians, but on the menu it stands for black beans with white rice.

Palomilla: Beefsteak, usually flank, rubbed with oil, garlic, and lime and then grilled.

Pargo: Red snapper, cooked in a variety of ways.

Plátanos: Plantains (cooking bananas) can be sliced or mashed when still a little green and then fried.

Queso: Cheese, usually a bland jack cheese.

Ropa vieja: Literally translated as "old clothes," this dish contains shredded cooked beef in a tomato-based sauce.

Tres leches: Although it means "three milks," this dish is quite solid, more like a very sweet cake.

Yuca: Ubiquitous in Cuban cooking, this tuber is often cut in chunks for stews or cooked, sliced, and fried like french fries.

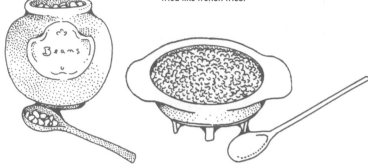

Lights, Camera, Action: The South Florida Screen Scene

Call it Hollywood Southeast. Once an occasional movie prop, **South Florida** has stolen the show, serving as a backdrop for—and sometimes even as the subject of—some of the nation's most memorable films. Top-notch directors and TV producers in the past decade or so have rediscovered this area's sunny beaches, climate, and convenience. The following is a select listing of films shot in South Florida:

Heart and Soul (1917) Exotic silent-film vamp Theda Bara (née Theodosia Goodman, of Chillicothe, Ohio) was one of the first performers to appear in a film shot in **Ft. Lauderdale.**

The Idol Dancer (1919) For this classic film, D.W. Griffith chose Ft. Lauderdale's palm-lined **New River** to re-create a Thanksgiving dance, complete with five-piece jazz ensemble.

Miami (1924) This film, about the hedonistic, Gatsby-esque rich of the Jazz Age, was a favorite at the time.

Key Largo (1948) Shot on **Key Largo,** this may be the quintessential South Florida movie. Gangster Edward G. Robinson and his alcoholic companion, expertly played by Claire Trevor, hold as captives a refugee from life seeking a new start (Humphrey Bogart) and a lonely widow (Lauren Bacall).

The Miami Story (1954) Barry Sullivan plays an ex-con in director Fred Sears's film about crime in the golden city.

The Rose Tattoo (1955) Anna Magnani, who won an Oscar for her performance, co-stars with Burt Lancaster in producer Hal Wallis's film adaptation of the Tennessee Williams play—which spawned a tattoo craze among **Key West** teens.

A Hole in the Head (1959) Directed by Frank Capra, this movie stars Frank Sinatra and Eddie Hodges as, respectively, father and son. It also features the Oscar-winning song "High Hopes."

Operation Petticoat (1959) Starring Cary Grant and Tony Curtis, this Blake Edwards spoof about escapades in the Navy was shot on a pink submarine in **Miami.**

Where the Boys Are (1960) Spring Break in Ft. Lauderdale: This is where it all began. The otherwise forgettable flick features Connie Francis singing the eponymous song.

All Fall Down (1962) Featuring scenes shot in Key West, this film about a dysfunctional family stars Eva Marie Saint, Karl Malden, Angela Lansbury, and Warren Beatty (in one of his first roles).

P.T. 109 (1963) Cliff Robertson plays a young John F. Kennedy during World War II in this movie made in Key West.

92 in the Shade (1975) Key West writer Thomas McGuane directed Peter Fonda, Warren Oates, and Margot Kidder in this adaptation of his novel about rival fishing boat captains.

Caddyshack (1980) This goofy-but-hilarious spoof of golf and country-club living stars Chevy Chase, Bill Murray, Rodney Dangerfield, and a memorable mechanical gopher.

Absence of Malice (1981) Sally Field and Paul Newman star in this drama about a criminal investigation gone awry and the newspaper exposé that fuels it.

Body Heat (1981) Filmed in **Palm Beach,** this erotic drama—a homage to Billy Wilder's quintessential film noir *Double Indemnity*—is about a love affair that leads to self-destruction and murder. Kathleen Turner assays the role originated by Barbara Stanwyck, and William Hurt takes on Fred MacMurray's part as an insurance investigator. Hot, hot, hot!

Scarface (1983) Al Pacino plays a brutal Cuban cocaine-peddling gangster in this unremittingly violent remake of the 1932 original; Michelle Pfeiffer and Steven Bauer also star.

Miami Blues (1990) Alec Baldwin plays Junior, a psychopathic criminal who meets his match in Miami detective Hoke Moseley, the character created by the late mystery novelist Charles Willeford of Miami. Jennifer Jason Leigh also stars.

Ace Ventura—Pet Detective (1993) This twisted comedy, which launched the film career of elastic-faced Jim Carrey, was shot in Miami.

Miami Rhapsody (1994) Sarah Jessica Parker confronts her fear of marriage in this romantic comedy, which also stars Antonio Banderas and Mia Farrow. It was shot in Miami and directed by David Frankel.

The Specialist (1994) Sharon Stone seeks the aid of Sylvester Stallone, an explosives specialist, in this action thriller shot in Miami and Ft. Lauderdale.

True Lies (1994) Filmed in Miami and Key West, this comedy thriller, which stars Arnold Schwarzenegger and Jamie Lee Curtis, is about a secret agent whose two worlds collide.

Just Cause (1995) This mystery thriller about a man on Death Row and a trusting journalist stars Sean Connery and Kate Capshaw; it was shot in **Miami Beach** and Ft. Lauderdale.

The entire resort has 670 rooms and suites, many with private patios or balconies. ♦ 4400 NW 87th Ave (at NW 41st St). 592.2000, 800/223.6725; fax 594.4682 &

43 Fairfield Inn $ With its 135 rooms and heated pool, this three-story hotel is not only cozy but very economical. Continental breakfast (there's no restaurant) and added security on the third floor are available at no extra cost. ♦ 3959 NW 79th Ave (at NW 36th St). 599.5200, 800/228.2800 &

44 Cisco's Cafe ★$$ A cheerful crowd convenes here almost every night, so expect a wait. Recommended are the *pollo fundido* (burnt chicken) and Cisco's chimichanga (shredded beef served in a crispy tortilla with ranchero sauce, guacamole, and sour cream). Top it all off with deep-fried ice cream and Mexican coffee. ♦ Mexican ♦ Daily lunch and dinner. Reservations

required for six or more. 5911 NW 36th St (at NW 57th Ave). 871.2764 &

45 Fair Havens Center Located in the wooded village of Miami Springs, this pueblo-style building is a designated landmark and a good example of the Southwestern architectural style that characterizes older homes in this quaint, quiet town. Constructed in 1926 by aviation pioneer Glenn Curtiss, it has operated through the years as a luxurious hotel, a botanical garden, a physical rehabilitation center, a spa named for the Kelloggs of cereal fame, and, currently, a nursing home. ♦ 201 Curtiss Pkwy (two blocks from Miami Springs Circle). 887.1565 &

Bests

Cristina Saralegui
Host, The Cristina Talk Show

Miami's Cuban quarter—**Little Havana**—is one of my favorite places in town, and when we talk about Little Havana, Miami, Florida, USA, we are talking about a small strip of street blocks in the center of Miami, considered the emotional home of Cubans who live in the US.

Cutting right down its center, you will find **Calle Ocho** (Southwest Eighth Street), the street where it all happens in Little Havana. The food, the fun, and the feeling of nostalgia for the old country—that's what keeps us Cubans coming back to Calle Ocho, even if it's to savor a single cup of *café cubano,* the very strong and sugary demitasse that fuels Cubans into gear. It's something we honestly can't do without. My favorite place for *café cubano* is **Versailles** restaurant. The cafeteria adjacent to the restaurant is where people stand elbow to elbow and holler their orders to the two or three attendants who are always on hand to serve Cuban delicacies. Try a *cortadito,* which is the same demitasse mixed or "cut" with hot milk.

Dining along Calle Ocho is one of the most satisfying experiences. This is a place with some of the best Cuban and Spanish restaurants in the world. My favorite is **Centro Vasco.** This is because I am Cuban, of Basque descent. My family originally comes from the north of Spain, the Basque country, and **Centro Vasco** has the best northern Spanish cuisine in Miami. The restaurant has been here since

1962. It was founded in Havana, Cuba, in 1940 by Juanito Saizarbitoria, one of my grandfather's best friends from the old country. Two favorite dishes: *arroz a la Vasco* (yellow rice with meat) and *porrsalda* (chicken broth with potatoes and leeks). I also like **Casa Juancho** (Spanish cuisine) and **Malaga** (Cuban and Spanish cuisine).

All along Calle Ocho, you can find small *cafeterías* where you meet interesting local characters. You can taste all kinds of pastries made with tropical fruits like guava or coconut. They're absolutely delicious and, of course, very high, calorically speaking. In the *cafeterías,* Cuban men buy their cigars and come to talk about politics and all of the latest developments back on "The Island." One of the hot Cuban *cafeterías* is **La Carreta.**

Call it Rio à la Mode. For an entire week in mid-March every year, Miami celebrates with a big bang called Carnival Miami. From beauty pageants and galas to parades to the Calle Ocho Street Festival, it's the biggest block party in America. Estimated attendance is about one million. The party extends the length of Southwest Eighth Street from Fourth Avenue to the corner of 27th Avenue, with every block along the way offering sights, sounds, and tasty delights. The live music goes on nonstop with some of the biggest names in Latin entertainment. Food is, of course, a big part of the celebration. You can taste in one day all of the typical cuisines from around Latin America—from black beans and rice to the world's largest paella, cooked on site by master chefs.

Coconut Grove

Coconut Grove is a zesty, lively place where locals and tourists congregate day and night. Any given weekend will find one festival or another spilling out from **Peacock Park** into the streets; among them are food tastings, the Coconut Grove Bed Race, and the world-renowned Coconut Grove Arts Festival. Fun lovers are drawn to the open-air shopping and dining of **CocoWalk** and **Mayfair**, the sidewalk cafes that offer people watching, the eclectic mix of boutiques, and the allure of the posh **Grand Bay Hotel** and **Mayfair House.**

Although its nightlife is what makes people take notice, Coconut Grove also boasts some of Miami's most beautiful waterfront, which can be viewed from the public parks that dot the village. **David Kennedy Park, Alice Wainwright Park, Kenneth Meyers Park,** and **Peacock Park** are favorite places for bikers, joggers, in-line skaters, and sun worshipers. The waterfront also draws the rich and famous. Sylvester Stallone and Madonna have purchased homes on the waterfront not far from the splendid architectural treasure **Villa Vizcaya.**

As early as the mid-1800s, anglers and seafarers were attracted to salvage opportunities off the coast. Ralph Middleton Munroe, a Staten Islander, built small boats, which easily negotiated shoals and reefs, and tested them here during the winter; he later moved to the area. In addition to designing boats, he was a skilled homebuilder (his first home, **The Barnacle,** is now a museum) and a persuasive spokesperson for the area. Others followed, including Charles and Isabella Peacock, who constructed South Florida's first hotel in 1882, and industrialist James Deering, who came in 1914 to build **Villa Vizcaya.**

Coconut Grove is home to a special breed of Miamians, who fight fiercely to preserve the area's beauty and history. Any plan that calls for cutting down trees is sure to draw immediate fire. Some lament that architectural good taste has succumbed to marketing showmanship. Though many historic buildings remain, much has disappeared in the rush to cater to the tourist trade.

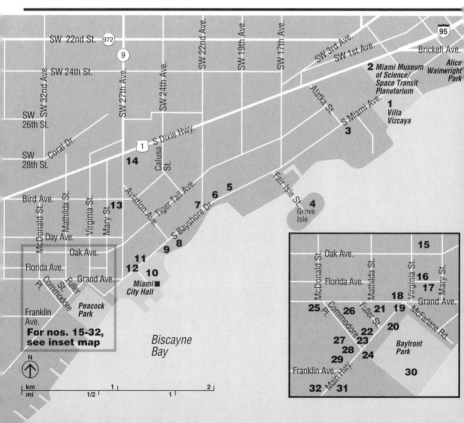

1 Vizcaya Museum and Gardens (Villa Vizcaya)

"Venice in the tropics" is one description of **Villa Vizcaya,** James Deering's winter home, built in 1916 by **F. Burrall Hoffman Jr.** Deering, co-founder of International Harvester, was a tireless art collector who wanted a winter home. What started as a retreat became the epitome of America's emulation of European elegance. It took nearly three years to build and even longer to finish what ended up as a small village with extensively landscaped grounds, gondolas, waterways, housing for support staff, and gardens to feed them. Not all of this was at Deering's insistence; much of the grandiose ornamentation came from his decorator, Paul Chalfin, who was a curator at the Boston Museum of Fine Arts when he met Deering.

In 1912 they traveled together to Italy, and, as Deering described his vision, Chalfin indulged in the fantasy of creating his own museum. They went to Italian villas and bought entire rooms; they purchased Roman sarcophagi and turned them into fountains and brought back a fireplace from Catherine de Medici's château. When they completed their travels, they sent architect **Hoffman** to Europe to see the sights that inspired them; when he returned in 1914, construction began.

Deering took the name of his estate from a Basque word meaning "elevated place." He envisioned a house of 76 rooms, each of which would open onto the bay or a garden. He spent winters in the house from 1916 until his death in 1925. The house and grounds were privately maintained for another 25 years, though 130 acres of the estate were sold to the Catholic church and later became the site of a church and Mercy Hospital. By 1952, when Dade County purchased the property from the Deering family, only 35 of the original 180 acres remained. Today, the house is maintained as a museum and serves as a splendid site for concerts and receptions. It is widely considered the finest example of Italian-Renaissance architecture in Florida. The grandeur of this estate was never duplicated, but Deering's legacy continued in another way. The artisans he brought to Florida to fulfill his dream stayed and created many other structures as well. (Though not in the same league as **Vizcaya,** another example of the Deering vision is the **Charles Deering Estate,** built by John's brother on Biscayne Bay in South Dade.)The staff at **Vizcaya** gives frequent tours of the first floor of the house and its 34 rooms of antique furnishings. Visitors are free to walk through the second floor, the peaceful gardens, or into the dense hammock, which gives a good sense of what Coconut Grove was like in its infancy. Inside, there are extensive tapestries and fine examples of Italian furniture. The **Music Room** and the **Renaissance Room,** with its plaster ceiling from Venice, are particularly notable. Outside, walk down the long gravel pathway to the water where Deering built a stone barge. It was constructed as a breakwater but makes a striking visual statement as well. ♦ Admission. Daily. 3251 S Miami Ave (at 32nd Rd). 250.9133 ⴠ

2 Miami Museum of Science and Space Transit Planetarium

This 45-year-old museum and more modern planetarium are separate entities housed in one complex. Sections of both have been renovated (a Mediterranean facade, fresh paint, and new carpeting and tile), and a 25,000-square-foot addition brings the museum's total square footage to 53,000—and growing. Kids love the exhibits, including hands-on insect and reptile displays and a collection of fossils and artifacts. The science museum also houses a **Birds of Prey Center and Hospital** and has a bald eagle on display. Whenever possible, birds treated at the center are released back into the wild. Frequent traveling exhibitions are shown—including animated dinosaur shows—to supplement the museum's 140 permanent exhibits. Plans call for construction of a three-story wing that will double or triple the existing space. (Construction is expected in 1997.)The planetarium is right next door, its entrance marked by an enormous world globe that once decorated the lobby of the **Pan Am Clipper Terminal** two miles away. Daily star shows are presented inside, and laser displays projected on a 65-foot dome spin fantasies of space travel and cosmic evolution.

While on the grounds, visitors can walk through **Vizcaya Village,** a parklike setting containing a series of small buildings that were originally part of the mansion's support operation. It's easily accessed by walking across the street from the **Vizcaya Metrorail** station. Separate admission to museum and planetarium. Daily. 3280 S Miami Ave (at SW 32nd Rd). Museum 854.4247; planetarium 854.2222 ⴠ

3 Ermita de la Caridad

This conical shrine to Our Lady of Charity is built on part of the bayfront land purchased from **Vizcaya** by the Catholic church. The shrine is 90 feet high and 80 feet in diameter at its base, giving it the look of a beacon. It is arranged so that worshipers, most of whom are Cuban, are facing Cuba, and above the altar is a mural depicting Cuba's history. ♦ Daily 9AM-9PM. 3609 S Miami Ave (at Alatka St). 854.2404 ⴠ

4 Grove Isle Club & Resort $$$$ Part of a residential complex that includes three tony high-rise condominium buildings, this 49-room resort is just off the beaten path on a 20-acre island. Each tropically decorated guest room has a private balcony and ocean view. The grounds are lushly landscaped, and there is a large swimming pool with a poolside bar for drinks or light fare. Amenities include an 85-slip marina, the casual outdoor **Ship's Deck Restaurant,** the more formal **Bistro Restaurant** (see below), and a center with 12 tennis courts. The resort was taken over recently by HMG/Courtland Properties, which sank millions into renovations; long-range plans include the addition of a spa. Although the prices are higher than in the past, the place is extremely popular, attracting a mix of businesspeople and families. ♦ 4 Grove Isle Dr (at Fair Isle St). 858.8300; fax 858.5908 ♿

Within the Grove Isle Club & Resort:

Bistro Restaurant ★★★$$$$ In charge of the hotel's two restaurants and catering, new French-trained chef Alain Verbeiren (from the acclaimed **Grand Bay Hotel;** see below) uses fresh ingredients in new ways, with seafood the specialty. In an airy, tropical setting, the restaurant is open only to club members and hotel guests. ♦ Mediterranean/Italian ♦ Daily breakfast, lunch, and dinner. 858.8300 ♿

5 Silver Bluff It is easy to pass by this white outcropping, but it shouldn't be overlooked. The bluff glitters in the sunlight along South Bayshore Drive on the grounds of **Ransom Everglades Middle School.** A rocky cliff of oolitic limestone (coral rock), it was formed by wave action when the sea level stood several feet higher than it does today. Once extending more than two miles along the bay, it has been eroded by nature and commercial development. In 1911, the area around **Silver Bluff** was a subdivision, which was incorporated as a town in 1921, only to be annexed by Miami in 1925. ♦ North side of S Bayshore Dr (between Crystal View and Emalthia Sts)

6 Villa Woodbine Built during the Depression for paper manufacturer Charles S. Boyd, this estate has an optimistic, forward-looking design. **Walter de Garmo,** the first registered architect in Florida and a longtime resident of Coconut Grove, was a strong proponent of the Mediterranean Revival style also popular in Coral Gables. The house and grounds are often used for receptions and other private gatherings. ♦ 2167 S Bayshore Dr (at SW 22nd Ave). 858.6660; fax 285.1362

7 Rock Reef Kentuckian Thomas Means Culbertson commissioned **Walter de Garmo** to construct this house in 1926. Basking in sunlight rather than emphasizing the area's unusual flora, the house sits on a slight ridge above Biscayne Bay to take advantage of the ocean breeze. Its exposure is underscored by entryways onto two streets. The Calusa Street side was the rear of the house when Culbertson lived here. Today, the home is a private residence. ♦ Entries at 2401 S Bayshore Dr and 3231 Calusa St

8 Monty's Stone Crab ★★★$$$ If you drop in here during the week, you'll very likely catch sight of the local movers and shakers, especially at lunchtime. A big, open airy space with a wonderful view of Coconut Grove and the waterfront, the restaurant is named for Monty Trainor, one of Miami's most influential citizens, who originally owned it and several other restaurants, all called **Monty's.** (In 1986, he sold this spot to Terremark, a corporation that demolished the original, quaint restaurant to build **Monty's Marketplace**—a modern multiuse building that now houses the seafood house. Ownership changed again a couple of years ago, and it's now owned by Steve Kneappler.) The menu features dependable seafood and steak dishes, and true to its name, in season, the stone crabs are a delight. ♦ American ♦ Daily lunch and dinner. 2550 S Bayshore Dr (at Aviation Ave). 858.1431 ♿

Behind Monty's Stone Crab:

Monty's Raw Bar ★$$ This huge outdoor raw bar has varnished picnic tables set under chikee huts (umbrella-like palm-thatch huts open on all sides), a large bar, and big-screen TV for sports events. The drinks are good, the bartenders are friendly, and the food is fine. Try the tasty grilled chicken sandwich or one of the large, fresh salads. This is a fun place to hang out in the evenings or on a weekend afternoon after walking in the Grove. There's

---

Restaurants/Clubs: Red **Hotels:** Blue
Shops/ Outdoors: Green **Sights/Culture:** Black

live entertainment nightly. ◆ Seafood ◆ Daily lunch and dinner. 856.3992 ᕪ

9 Chart House ★★$$$ You can't beat this restaurant on Sailboat Bay for a romantic evening on the water. It's set behind one of the marinas that dot the shoreline in the Grove, so the views at twilight are spectacular. And the food's good, too: Specialties include steak, prime rib, and seafood. ◆ American ◆ Daily dinner. 51 Chart House Dr (at S Bayshore Dr). 856.9741 ᕪ

10 Pan American Terminal Building Dinner Key was an island until 1917 when it was attached to the mainland as part of the construction of a naval aviation facility. Today, the Key includes a marina and this terminal building. The terminal itself was once home to the **Pan American Airways** clipper fleet, planes that traveled the globe and took off and landed on open water. Coconut Grove was a terminus for flights to and from Havana and other routes as well. In the late 1930s, it was the largest port of entry for foreign air travelers coming to the US. Tens of thousands of spectators came to watch crews roll out the "flying boats" from the nearby hangars, slide them into the bay, and then remove their wheels, reversing the process when they landed. The hangars are now used by nearby boatyards. The building, with an elegant futuristic design, is now **Miami City Hall.** ◆ 3500 Pan American Dr (between Aviation Ave and S Bayshore Dr). 250.5300 ᕪ

11 Doubletree at Coconut Grove $$$ After undergoing a $1-million renovation, this older hotel now has 192 rooms (including 19 suites) and a warm tropical decor. Its primary clientele is business travelers, but it welcomes families. The casual restaurant **Cafe Brasserie** overlooks a large swimming pool and offers American cuisine. Just across the street from the **Pan American Terminal Building,** the hotel has great views of Sailboat Bay. It's also near the Grove business and restaurant district and the **Grand Bay Hotel** (see below). ◆ 2649 S Bayshore Dr (at Darwin St). 858.2896 ᕪ

12 Grand Bay Hotel $$$$
A European aesthetic pervades this first-rate hotel; popular among celebrities, it's one of Miami's finest. A recent multi-million-dollar renovation has made it even more luxurious, replacing cool elegance with a sophisticated Florida decor. The 181 rooms are done in soft greens and beiges; staircases provide interest-

ing architectural accents; and a giant red metal sculpture by Alexander Lieberman and beautifully manicured grounds round out the picture. The lobby is the setting for afternoon tea and caviar and champagne tastings accompanied by classical piano music. In fact, everything about the hotel stresses the "Grand" in **Grand Bay** and definitely pushes it a cut above the competition. There's a 24-hour state-of-the-art health club with trainers available upon request, and the second-story pool has a lovely view of the bay. For corporate types, there's a business center complete with fax machines, computers, and 24-hour room service from the hotel's excellent kitchen. This is also *the* poshest place in town for family breakfasts, power lunches, evening chatter, and late nightcaps. ◆ 2669 S Bayshore Dr (at 27th Ave). 858.9600, 800/327.2788; fax 859.2026 ᕪ

Within the Grand Bay Hotel:

GRAND
CAFE

Grand Cafe ★★★★$$$$ Chef Pascal Oudin, who previously worked at the well-known **Alexander Hotel** on Miami Beach and at the **Colonnade** in Coral Gables, has added his special touch to the established favorites at this fine restaurant. The food remains regional American—albeit an unusual combination of French cooking with Florida ingredients. Highly recommended are the delicious Florida crab cakes with wasabi sauce and the potato-wrapped black grouper with tamarind sauce. ◆ American ◆ Daily breakfast, lunch, and dinner. Reservations recommended. 858.0009 ᕪ

13 E-Z Kwik Kountry Store It hardly has landmark status, but this is one of the busiest social spots in Coconut Grove. In a run-down setting made shabbier by neglect, the market offers a sizable selection of wines, sells both half and quarter kegs, and has a very active deli counter. It's popular with sailors anchored in nearby Sailboat Bay. ◆ Daily 5:30AM-2AM. 2988 SW 27th Ave (at Bird Ave). 444.2093 ᕪ

If you look closely when traveling on McFarlane Road, you'll see the grave of Eva Munroe, first wife of Coconut Grove pioneer Ralph Munroe. The young Mrs. Munroe died of tuberculosis and was originally buried on the north bank of the Miami River. Her body was moved to its present location beside the Coconut Grove Branch Library when Munroe bought property in what is now the Grove. He had planned to be buried next to Eva, but his second wife had him buried in New England.

14 Crook & Crook Bait and Tackle A great selection of fishing equipment and boat merchandise combined with friendly service makes this an angler's delight. ♦ M-F 7AM-9PM; Sa 6AM-9PM, Su 6AM-5PM. 2795 SW 27th Ave (at S Dixie Hwy). 854.0005; fax 854.2474 &

15 Miami Tennis Sports Owner Rob Weinberg looks more like a bodybuilder than an agile tennis star, but he knows his business and his shop has everything for players of all levels. If you need to try out those new shoes or rackets, there's a public court across the street next to the Grove Fire Station. Now you know how all those firefighters keep in shape. ♦ M-Sa. 3300 Rice St (at Oak Ave). 443.1288 &

16 Tula Ristorante ★★$$$ This restaurant combines several styles, from a Venetian flair for seafood (the chef is from Italy) to an extravagant Genoese way with pasta (the owner hails from San Remo). Don't miss the *piccatina*, which is similar to veal scallopini with lemon and artichokes. The fish dishes, too, are recommended. The small wine list is moderately priced. ♦ Italian ♦ Daily dinner. Reservations recommended. 2957 Florida Ave (at Virginia St). 441.1818; fax 446.6159 &

17 Mayfair Shops in the Grove Under one name (architect **Kenneth Treister** originally called the complex **The World of Mayfair**), there are three distinct buildings and an ever-changing panorama of chic shops. The first building completed was **Mayfair East,** the section bordered by Grand Avenue and Mary Street. It was several years before the completion of the second phase of the project, bordered by Virginia Street and called **Mayfair West.** There is another **Mayfair** building across Florida Avenue, but it never developed a stable retail clientele. The complex has been controversial since it was built in the early 1980s, called by some a horrifying

interpretation of **Gaudí** and by others, an inspired and individual creation. **Treister** used an astonishing array of materials, among them stone, wood, stained glass, statuary, metal etchings, fountains, wrought iron, and hammered metal. He wanted carved concrete in some areas, but there was no technology for doing it, so construction was halted while he invented one. The complex is as tropical in its engineering as it is in design: For example, like early Grove bungalows, the public areas are cooled by breezes instead of air-conditioning. Much of the interior is still open to the air and light, and visitors have the illusion of walking in a tiled jungle filled with plants, pathways, and fountains. Hard-hit by the recession and the collapse in the late 1980s of the Latin American economies, **Mayfair** was further hurt by the opening of **CocoWalk** (see below), but now seems rejuvenated with the addition of 10 theaters and an eclectic mix of shops. Recently sold, the complex is being completely renovated. ♦ Mayfair East: 3390 Mary St; Mayfair West: 3340 Virginia St. 448.1700 &

Within Mayfair East:

Planet Hollywood ★★$$ Actor Sylvester Stallone—who recently bought a home in the Grove—is a partner in the snazziest new restaurant in town, along with Arnold Schwarzenegger, Bruce Willis, Demi Moore, film producer Keith Baris, and restaurateur Robert Earl. It's *the* place for film buffs—a life-size replica of Stallone in the cyber chamber from the movie *Demolition Man* is hanging from the ceiling and the car he drove in the movie *Cobra* is on display. The restaurant has an extensive collection of memorabilia, which includes the golden idol from *Raiders of the Lost Ark,* Marilyn Monroe's jumpsuit from *The Asphalt Jungle,* and many other items from movies past and present. Diners watch trailers from soon-to-be-released films or custom videos. The menu features unusual pastas, exotic salads, gourmet pizzas, turkey burgers, and a range of huge desserts including an apple strudel made from a recipe from Schwarzenegger's mom. The burgers are tasty, as is the Mexican shrimp salad. Service is Disney-friendly and efficient. All in all, the restaurant is fun, the food is good, and the portions are large. ♦ Californian ♦ Daily lunch and dinner. 445.7277; fax 445.9550 ♿

Stephane Kelian Snappy boutiques have come a long way. This shoe store sells only a single line—women's shoes designed by Frenchman Stephane Kelian. ♦ M-Sa. 856.1400 ♿

Baby Baby Boutique Resembling the closet of a Victorian grandmother, this shop is replete with lace and frills and exquisite gifts for both mom and newborn. ♦ M-Sa 10AM-8PM. 445.7890 ♿

Within Mayfair West:

Chiyo ★★$$ By far the best Japanese food in the area is served here. The menu, available at tables or at the sushi bar, features the usual cast of raw delicacies and some unusual innovations. Tiger's Eye is salmon wrapped in seaweed, then wrapped again in squid before it's grilled and sliced. The Chiyo Roll (cooked white fish, eel, and scallions wrapped in rice) is equally good. The tempura and other specialties are also imaginative. ♦ Japanese ♦ Daily lunch and dinner. 445.0865 ♿

Planet Hollywood Boutique This free-standing retail store offers a full line of **Planet Hollywood** clothing and merchandise, such as swimsuits, sweatshirts, beach bags, and towels emblazoned with the restaurant's logo. Be sure to check out the celebrity handprints wall. ♦ M-Th 11AM-11PM; F-Su 11AM-12AM. 3399 Virginia St (at Grand Ave). 445.7277 ♿

Mayfair House $$$$ A top-notch hotel in a shopping mall is odd enough, but this exotic building designed by **Kenneth Treister** adds a few extras to make a visit even more unusual. Among the most noticeable: A white limousine is available for pickup and delivery from **Miami International Airport,** guests receive a glass of champagne on arrival, and each of the 182 suites features a different design and a private terrace. Everything about the hotel is Coconut Grove to the max. The suites, all charming, fall into nine distinct categories based on size and amenities. The hotel, which was recently sold along with the **Mayfair** shops, has been redecorated with new carpeting and furnishings. ♦ 3000 Florida Ave (at Virginia St). 441.0000, 800/433.4555; fax 447.9173 ♿

Within Mayfair House:

Mayfair Grill ★★★$$$ As with the hotel, change is in the wind for this restaurant. Chef Allen Susser of **Chef Allen's** in North Miami has been brought in to consult with Chef Rolando Cruz-Taura, but though the two are planning to make menu changes, the cuisine is expected to remain a meld of Florida produce and spices with Caribbean and Latin influences, typified by such dishes as plantain-crusted snapper with dark rum butter sauce and passion-fruit crème brûlée. ♦ Floridian/Caribbean ♦ Daily breakfast, lunch, and dinner. 441.0000 ♿

18 CocoWalk Imagine a shopping mall in the shape of an outdoor promenade with touches of Mission architecture. Place it at the Grove's biggest intersection and you have a recipe for immediate success, interminable parking queues, and major pedestrian congestion. At its heart is a high-tech 16-theater complex built by AMC, but the mall continues to jump late into the night thanks to covered outdoor bars and restaurants that revel in South Florida's climate. Many of the shops, like **Banana Republic** and **B. Dalton Bookseller,** are neither upscale nor down but somewhere in between. Visitors come for the atmosphere more than the shopping. ♦ 3000 Grand Ave (between Main Hwy and Virginia St). 444.0777 ♿

Within CocoWalk:

Cafe Med ★$$ Tucked away on the first floor, this restaurant caters to the artsy citizens who favor the Grove. The wine list is a tad expensive, but the food is moderately priced and a good value. The pasta dishes are highly recommended. ♦ Italian ♦ Daily lunch and dinner. 443.1770 ♿

Hooters ★$ This is one in a chain of restaurants cashing in on dressing the waitresses in tight T-shirts and short shorts. A fraternity atmosphere prevails; try the chicken wings. ♦ American ♦ Daily lunch and dinner. 442.6004 ♿. Also at: 3805 N University Dr (at NW 38th St), Sunrise. 748.1000 ♿; 5975 N Federal Hwy (north of Commercial Blvd), Ft. Lauderdale. 928.1825

Dan Marino's American Sports Bar and Grill ★★★$$ Miami Dolphins sensation Dan Marino owns this unique sports bar. The football memorabilia on the walls might be coveted by the Hall of Fame. The restaurant also has a game room and two virtual reality machines, plus billiard tables. The food is reliable and runs toward burgers and sandwiches; it's the sports ambience that makes this the place to be. ♦ American ♦ Daily lunch and dinner. 442.2544 &

Cheesecake Factory ★★★$$ This recently opened restaurant is getting rave reviews. Reasonably priced—although the seafood and steak dishes are slightly more pricey—the menu has more than 200 items, including a dozen chicken dishes, ranging from chicken fajitas to grilled double breast lime chicken. The portions are so enormous that doggie bags are de rigueur. Of course, the desserts are cheesecakes, 30 of them, including white chocolate raspberry truffle, Craig's crazy carrot cheesecake, and chocolate chip cookie dough cheesecake. ♦ American ♦ Daily lunch and dinner; Su brunch. 447.9898 &

Rocky Mountain Chocolate Factory A sinfully rich whiff of chocolate greets you at the door. Dieters take heart: There are many chocolates that are sugar free, some even salt free. This franchise of the Colorado-based chain makes many of its goods on site. A big seller is the semisweet fudge, which is merely out of this world. ♦ Daily. 443.7366 &

McFarlane Road is named for the first female homesteader in Coconut Grove. She was the founder of the Housekeepers Club (now the Coconut Grove Women's Club) and the Grove's first schoolteacher. She originally came to Coconut Grove to be a companion to Ralph Munroe's mother.

The first gathering place in Coconut Grove was the Peacock Inn (originally known as the Bayview Inn), which was built where Peacock Park now overlooks Biscayne Bay.

MARCUS ANIMATION GALLERY

Marcus Animation Gallery Cartoon lovers rejoice: Here's where you'll find Disney characters cavorting with Looney Tunes creatures from Warner Brothers. It is the only Florida gallery authorized to carry animation art from all the major studios. Note also the store's collection of funky clocks. ♦ Daily. 441.2357 &

Baja Beach Club One of the hottest nightclubs in Florida, this popular spot offers two always-hopping dance floors stoked to a high pitch by energetic DJs. A generous buffet is a Friday night favorite. ♦ Cover. W-Th, Su 9PM-5AM; F-Sa 6PM-5AM. 3015 Grand Ave (at Main Hwy). 445.0278 &

Cafe Tu Tu Tango ★★$$ Long on concept, short on execution, this place was modeled on an artist's loft in Barcelona, Spain. Easels are set up around the restaurant, and while you nibble on New World tapas, you can watch artists painting and dancing. The tapas, which come in appetizer portions, are very imaginative, so go as a group and share several. ♦ Mediterranean ♦ Daily lunch and dinner. 529.2222 &

Fat Tuesday For the best frozen daiquiris around, visit this bar on the second floor of **CocoWalk**. If you have a designated driver, try a real alcoholic right-hook: the top-selling 190 Octane. Happy Hour Monday through Friday. ♦ Daily. 441.2992 &

Señor Frog's Mexican Grill ★$$ Though hardly a definitive exploration of Mexican food, this slightly grubby hole-in-the-wall has a 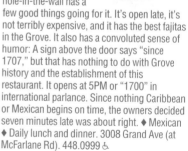 few good things going for it. It's open late, it's not terribly expensive, and it has the best fajitas in the Grove. It also has a convoluted sense of humor: A sign above the door says "since 1707," but that has nothing to do with Grove history and the establishment of this restaurant. It opens at 5PM or "1700" in international parlance. Since nothing Caribbean or Mexican begins on time, the owners decided seven minutes late was about right. ♦ Mexican ♦ Daily lunch and dinner. 3008 Grand Ave (at McFarlane Rd). 448.0999 &

Maya Hatcha The owner of this eclectic boutique, Vivian Jordan, is of Maya descent, and the selection of natural fabric products reflects her heritage. She offers imported goods from around the world, including a wide variety of African art, clothing, and textiles at modest prices. The shop's logo (pictured above) depicts a stylized Maya hatchet in the shape of a head. ♦ M-Sa; Su afternoon. 3058 Grand Ave (at Main Hwy). 443.9040 ♿

Johnny Rockets ★★★$ Take a trip back to the 1950s in this old-fashioned hamburger shop. The waiters are extra-friendly, and the apple pie is great. Play the Aretha Franklin song "Respect" on one of the many mini-juke boxes and watch the waiters and cooks stop to dance. ♦ American ♦ Daily lunch and dinner. 3036 Grand Ave (at McFarlane Rd). 444.1000 ♿

Mandarin Garden ★★★$$ This is considered one of the better Chinese restaurants in Miami. It serves Szechuan, Hunan, and Mandarin dishes, and the staff is friendly and competent. ♦ Chinese ♦ Daily lunch and dinner. 3268 Grand Ave (at McFarlane Rd). 442.1234 ♿

19 Cafe Sci-Sci ★★$$$ It's pronounced "she-she," and once you've been here you'll know why. The Grove's most aggressive sidewalk cafe teeters on the edge of pretentiousness, but the food is good. Try the *taglioni al radicchio* (ribbon-shaped pasta with vegetables, parmesan, and cream sauce) or the popular risotto. The seafood is highly recommended, as is the filet mignon. ♦ Italian ♦ Daily lunch and dinner. 3043 Grand Ave (at McFarlane Rd). 446.5104 ♿

20 Ritchie Swimwear Whether you need something for swimming or for sunning, this stylish shop has it covered or uncovered depending on your selection. The sales staff is particularly helpful, though oriented to the tourist trade. ♦ M-Th; F-Su until 8PM. 3401 Main Hwy (at Fuller St). 443.7919; fax 687.0537 ♿

21 Grove Book Worm Owner Sterling Grace seems to have a (literally) encyclopedic memory concerning the 30,000-plus titles on his shelves. He can't have read them all, but you feel he must have. Browsers are welcome to linger. ♦ Daily. 3025 Fuller St (between Grand Ave and Main Hwy). 443.6411 ♿

22 Kidz In addition to Guess? for kids, there's an extensive selection of other clothes for trendy tykes. Prices are high, but the selection is irresistible. ♦ M-F until 11PM; Sa until midnight; Su noon-10PM. 3436 Main Hwy (between Fuller St and Commodore Plaza). 443.5884; fax 448.1162 ♿

23 Joffrey's Coffee & Tea Co. This new coffee and pastry shop offers outdoor seating for people watching and popular desserts such as tiramisù. The specially roasted coffee is imported from South America and Africa. If you like specialty coffees, try the Captain's Blend or the cappuccino. ♦ American ♦ Su-Th until midnight; F-Sa until 2AM. 3434 Main Hwy (between Fuller St and Commodore Plaza). 448.0848 ♿

24 Sharkey's ★$$ On the corner of Main Highway, this popular sidewalk spot is very busy on the weekends, serving seafood along with views of Grove-ites on parade. Try the combination chicken and shrimp Caesar salad or the fried shrimp dinner. In season the stone crabs are good and reasonably priced. ♦ Seafood ♦ Daily lunch and dinner. 3105 Commodore Plaza (at Main Hwy). 448.2768 ♿

Restaurants/Clubs: Red   **Hotels:** Blue
Shops/ 🌳 Outdoors: Green   **Sights/Culture:** Black

25 Farmers' Market Informality is the key to this Saturday market, held in a vacant lot where fresh produce, fish, and homemade goods from around the county are sold. It's crowded, so go early, but stick around since there are sure to be impromptu barbecue stands for brunch. ◆ Sa until 3PM. Corner of Grand Ave and Margaret St ♿

26 Cafe Europa ★$$$ This pricey restaurant has an outdoor dining area so covered and fenced you'll feel as if you're indoors. Much of the food—especially the bouillabaisse—is good, if not exciting. ◆ French ◆ Daily lunch and dinner. 3159 Commodore Plaza (between Grand Ave and Main Hwy). 448.5723 ♿

27 Nostalgia by Anna You'll take home sweet memories thanks to Polish-born owner Anna Gluski, a woman of European sensibilities, international charm, and South Florida savvy. All items in the shop are antiques, among them vintage clothing for women and children dating back to the turn of the century. ◆ M-Sa; until 9PM December-April. 3112 Commodore Plaza (at Main Hwy). 448.8883 ♿

27 Kaleidoscope ★★$$$ With its second-floor terrace, this restaurant has the best view of any in the downtown area. It's great for people watching and reasonably good for dining. Portions are decent, the food is satisfying if not imaginative, and the European cafe ambience is perfect for a warm Florida night. Try the snapper with bananas for an unusual treat. ◆ American ◆ Daily lunch and dinner. Reservations recommended. 3112 Commodore Plaza (at Main Hwy). 446.5010 ♿

28 La Boulangerie ★★$ This cafe offers fresh-baked French-style gourmet sandwiches, a fine selection of health foods, and delicious croissants. Friendly service in a quaint atmosphere adds to the delight. ◆ French ◆ Daily breakfast and lunch. 3425 Main Hwy (at Commodore Plaza). 443.0776 ♿

29 Coconut Grove Playhouse When it opened in 1927, the playhouse (illustrated above) was a movie theater. It flourished for 25 years, but eventually closed as more modern theaters opened. In 1956, a local developer, George Engel, bought the building and had it lovingly restored. Its great impact on the Grove, however, wasn't so much architectural as commercial. It was the site of the American premiere of *Waiting for Godot* and many other productions, establishing itself and Coconut Grove as an important center of American theater. Since 1985, when Arnold Mittelman was hired as artistic director, the theater has bounced from acclaim to brickbats, but it has never been accused of being dull. The company sponsors eight to 10 productions a year in the main theater (1,100 seats) and stages additional shows in the 140-seat **Encore Room.** ◆ 3500 Main Hwy (at Charles Ave). 442.4000 ♿

29 Taurus ★★$$ Coconut Grove is famous for its many sidewalk cafes, and this one has been in business longer than any other restaurant in the Grove. In 1919, Grove pioneer Commodore Ralph Middleton Munroe and his son Wirth designed and built a place called the **Tea Chest** especially for the Commodore's daughter Patty, who wanted a business of her own. For many years she ran a small tea shop, serving sandwiches and other accoutrements of civilized afternoon teas. Today, the original structure is the front section of this larger restaurant.

Under the new ownership of Tom and Bruce Wilson, this remains one of Coconut Grove's most popular hangouts for Happy Hour. It has always had a greater reputation as a place to be seen in than as a place to eat. The menu remains basically the same, with red meat and fish being the major staples. But fresh salads and pastas are being added to the mix, and the patio is open for outdoor dining. Long-time Chef Al Wells has stayed on so the roast beef remains a good bet and the Florida lobster is a treat. What makes this place so popular? The terrace, where the **Tea Chest** once served patrons, overlooks the most scenic stretch of Main Highway and is a great place for people watching, a favorite Grove hobby. ◆ American ◆ Daily lunch and dinner. Reservations recommended. 3540 Main Hwy (between Charles and Franklin Aves). 448.0633 ♿

30 The Barnacle In addition to his skill as a boatbuilder, Coconut Grove pioneer Ralph Middleton Munroe was adept at designing and building houses. The original structure on this property was a 1908 bungalow that showed Munroe's appreciation of natural surroundings. He sank a termite-treated pine foundation deep into the ground to protect the building against hurricanes. For beams and supports, he used lumber salvaged from shipwrecks that he cut to size in his own mill and bolted to the foundation. The house is named for the small tower at the top that clings to the roof like a barnacle to a ship's hull. This barnacle is useful, however: It has skylights that open by ropes and pulleys to aid circulation and force warm air out of the house.

Munroe later raised the original, single-floor house and built a new first story under it. At the same time, he carried out an extensive renovation of the roof and added new rooms. He died in 1933, but his family lived in the house until 1973, when it was purchased by the state of Florida. In 1992, Hurricane Andrew spared the house but severely damaged a boathouse, which has since been repaired. Munroe's yacht, the *Micco,* was a total loss.

Today, the house is operated as a state historic site and museum. In response to popular demand, the state has opened it to the public three days a week and also offers special lectures on the lawn once a month. ♦ Admission. F-Su until 4PM; four tours each day. 3485 Main Hwy (at Munroe Dr). 448.9445 &

31 The Pagoda One of the earliest extant structures in Coconut Grove, this is part administration building and part museum for **Ransom Everglades School,** which was opened in 1903 by Paul Ransom, a New York attorney seeking a southern outpost for the **Adirondack-Florida School.** It was the first in a series of two-campus educational institutions that shuttled students south in the winter. The school closed during World War II but was opened again in 1947 and renamed for its founder. Now a year-round educational institution (there is a middle school on a separate campus), it is one of the most admired private schools in the region.**The Pagoda,** named for its distinctive layered construction, is amazingly well suited to the tropics, given its design by architects in Buffalo, New York. Its durability is due partly to design and partly to native materials—coral rock and Dade County pine. Everything about the design and placement works toward comfort: Built high on a ridge overlooking Biscayne Bay, its many windows and high ceiling capture cool ocean breezes. A less heralded aspect of its construction is the ability to survive hurricanes. Today, it serves as the office of the school's headmaster and is open by appointment only. ♦ 3575 Main Hwy (at Royal Rd). 460.8847; fax 441.7603

32 Plymouth Congregational Church Few buildings have played so prominent a part in Coconut Grove's development as this church (pictured below) whose congregation organized in 1897 (two chapels preceded the present building). The impressive stonework is the effort of a single Spanish mason who laid it all by hand. Workers at the church take delight in pointing out the spot at the lower right of the main entrance where a hole was cut to allow cats free passage to the sanctuary, where they kept mice under control. The hand-carved, oak-backed walnut front door is from a monastery in France and is thought to be several hundred years old. In 1954, the two transepts and a new chancel were added to the original structure. Just beyond the church building is **Plymouth Hall,** built in 1926 as the pastor's residence. It now serves as classrooms. ♦ 3400 Devon Rd (at Main Hwy). 444.6521 &

Plymouth Congregational Church

Coral Gables

When it was founded in the 1920s, Coral Gables was promoted as "The City Beautiful," a microcosm of Florida's booming growth and tropical design. Today, it works hard at preserving the buildings that once made it one of the most progressive cities in America. Yet Coral Gables is by no means an architectural mausoleum: As it attracts more and more multinational corporations and rides the crest of the emerging global economy, the city

continues to grow—and to reinvent itself. For example, **Miracle Mile**, a major downtown thoroughfare, is enjoying a renaissance, with a pedestrian-friendly sidewalk promenade, a new **Luria's** specialty department store, and the renovation of other establishments. Its revival was sparked by a return to the downtown area of shoppers, some of them among the 35,000 employees who work in nearby office buildings.

The contemporary architecture in Coral Gables retains a sense of history. Take the **Colonnade Building**, the turret-topped structure that originally contained the offices of city founder George Merrick. Today, the sturdy, Classical rotunda that impressed prospective landowners in the 1920s is the gleaming entryway to a stately but modern hotel. Four blocks north on historic **Ponce de Leon Boulevard**, a classic 1926 building is preserved as another hostelry, the antiques-filled **Hotel Place St. Michel.**

Innovations in Coral Gables now often lean toward the culinary. The city boasts many of the region's finest restaurants, ranging from **Yuca**, the trailblazing New Wave–Cuban venture, to **Christy's**, an established spot famous for its Caesar salad. There also are more than a dozen great Italian restaurants, such as the elegant and traditional **La Bussola** and the trendy **Caffe Abbracci.** Culturally speaking, the city is home to the **Ring Theatre**, which offers professional and high-quality amateur productions at the **University of Miami.** Also on campus are the **Gusman Concert Hall**, a superb venue for chamber music and small theater productions, and the low-key but influential **Lowe Art Museum.**

In his dream of "The City Beautiful," George Merrick envisioned a place where the Old World met the new, and Coral Gables was designed with an international flavor: Gondolas plied canals connecting the **Venetian Pool** with **Tahiti Beach** on **Biscayne Bay**, the architecture and many of the street names were Spanish, and the city was referred to as Miami's Riviera. Merrick's influence is particularly palpable on parts of **Coral Way**—the broad boulevard that travels the width of Coral Gables—especially the section of it just west of **City Hall**, which is lined with a string of Spanish Renaissance houses.

Besides Merrick, two other figures were important to the city's architectural development: Denman Fink, Merrick's uncle, was the city's art director, and **Phineas Paist** was the supervising architect of Coral Gables. **Paist** established an architectural board of review whose approval was required for any new construction or remodeling—a system still followed today. As a result, Coral Gables, though only 10 minutes from **Miami International Airport**, has remained unblighted by the high-rise developments, freeway overpasses, and other trappings of modern urban life so common to most US cities.

Area code 305 unless otherwise indicated.

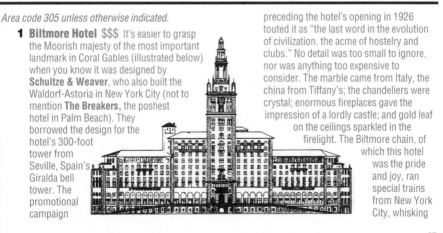

1 Biltmore Hotel $$$ It's easier to grasp the Moorish majesty of the most important landmark in Coral Gables (illustrated below) when you know it was designed by **Schultze & Weaver**, who also built the Waldorf-Astoria in New York City (not to mention **The Breakers**, the poshest hotel in Palm Beach). They borrowed the design for the hotel's 300-foot tower from Seville, Spain's Giralda bell tower. The promotional campaign preceding the hotel's opening in 1926 touted it as "the last word in the evolution of civilization, the acme of hostelry and clubs." No detail was too small to ignore, nor was anything too expensive to consider. The marble came from Italy, the china from Tiffany's; the chandeliers were crystal; enormous fireplaces gave the impression of a lordly castle; and gold leaf on the ceilings sparkled in the firelight. The Biltmore chain, of which this hotel was the pride and joy, ran special trains from New York City, whisking passengers to the tropics in less than 40 hours. On the 155-acre grounds was a waterway where gondolas were poled between the hotel and Tahiti Beach, two golf courses, tennis courts, a bridle path, and one of the largest swimming pools in the world. It was in this pool that the hotel's swimming instructor broke his first world record. His name? Johnny Weissmuller.

For all its offerings to the wealthy, even the richest were unable to support the enormous cost of the hotel. Sold numerous times, it was eventually bought by the government for use as a VA hospital, at which point many of the building's artifacts were destroyed to clear the way for remodeling and the installation of fluorescent lights. In 1973 the property was turned over to the city, and in 1985, after $52 million in renovations, it reopened as a luxury hotel. The renaissance was short-lived, however, as financial pressures closed the hotel in 1990. But the **Biltmore** threw open its doors again in 1992 under the management of Westin Hotels, which refurbished the health club and spa and recently spruced up sections of the lobby and the country club facility. Today, the property has 277 rooms; the two golf courses, tennis courts, bridle path, enormous pool, and waterway have survived the hotel's many changes of ownership, to the advantage of its modern-day guests. ♦ 1200 Anastasia Ave (at De Soto Blvd). 445.1926, 800/727.1926; fax 442.9496 ♿

Within the Biltmore Hotel:

The Cafe ★★$$ When the hotel closed a couple of years ago, patrons sadly mourned the loss of this restaurant's Sunday brunch, which was always packed. Today it's once again a popular attraction. Overseen by the chef, Calvin Hollingsworth, the buffet is loaded with waffles, pancakes, granola, eggs, muffins, and other popular breakfast fare. Lunch and dinner are fairly pedestrian; it's really the atmosphere that remains the draw. ♦ American ♦ Daily breakfast, lunch, and dinner. 445.1926 ♿

Il Ristorante ★★$$$ Dining here is an intimate experience, thanks to chef Donna Wynter. The colors are muted, the lighting is low, and everything, including the food, is elegant, in keeping with the charm of one of Florida's landmark hotels. The fare is Italian, with lots of pasta entrées as well as fish, lamb, and chicken dishes. ♦ Italian ♦ Daily dinner. Reservations recommended. 445.1926 ♿

2 Coral Gables Congregational Church George Merrick's father, Solomon, was a Congregationalist minister, so it's not surprising that his son built this, the first church in Coral Gables (illustrated below). In trying to reconcile a New England Protestant aesthetic with a Spanish Catholic design theme, the church's architects opted for Mediterranean Revival, a modified Spanish style that later was used widely in the area. Characteristic of that vernacular is the bell tower, which mirrors that of the **Biltmore Hotel** (see above) across the street. Inside the church is a fine collection of 16th-century wooden furniture, by some accounts recovered from shipwrecks and donated anonymously. The collection also includes sconces and other furnishings Merrick bought on a trip to Spain and donated to the church. In the 1960s protesting students from the **University of Miami** published the school's first underground newspaper in the church's tower. Today, the church sponsors an excellent series of chamber concerts each summer and other arts events throughout the

Coral Gables Congregational Church

year. ♦ 3010 De Soto Blvd (at Anastasia Ave). 448.7421 Ꮺ

3 De Soto Plaza and Fountain George Merrick's spacious town plan called for 14 plazas strategically placed around the city. This European-style traffic circle is one of the most picturesque. The fountain at the center is raised two steps above the intersection of three thoroughfares. Water streams out of the mouths of carved faces into the fountain's large stone basin, and next to each face is an image of a three-masted ship—a possible allusion to Columbus's voyage to the New World. ♦ Intersection of Sevilla Ave, De Soto Blvd, and Granada Blvd

4 Venetian Pool The distinctive limestone called coral rock used in many early Coral Gables homes came from a quarry on this site. When construction moved too close to this quarry, Denman Fink and **Phineas Paist** hit on the idea of disguising the ugly quarry. The result was this pool, with limestone outcroppings for diving platforms, Venetian lampposts, and a small bridge connecting an island to a casino on the "mainland." William Jennings Bryan, the famous orator, used to give speeches at the pool extolling the virtues of Coral Gables. The observation tower was once a popular site for parties, and occasionally the pool was drained to form an amphitheater. By design, the unfiltered pool was drained nightly and refilled each morning with 800,000 gallons of artesian well water— a practice abandoned in 1986 because of water shortages. Today, the public is welcome to swim in the pool, for a fee. ♦ Admission. Tu-F 10AM-4:30PM, 11AM-7:30PM December-March; Sa-Su 10AM-4:30PM. 2701 De Soto Blvd (at Sevilla Ave). 460.5356 Ꮺ

5 Casa Azul A private residence, this house is named for its roof of blue glazed tile. Its architect, **H. George Fink,** who was George Merrick's cousin (and the son of designer Denman Fink), was especially active in Miami Beach before joining Merrick in 1921. When this stone house was completed, the two cousins went to Spain on an architectural study trip, only to discover that they were celebrities: Citing Fink for "interpreting the Spanish arts in America," King Alfonso XIII made him a don, the equivalent of a knight. ♦ 1254 Coral Way (between Columbus and Madrid Sts)

Free guided tours of many major art galleries in Coral Gables are offered the first Friday of each month. Patrons are ferried about on trams, and the galleries arrange to have their openings take place in conjunction with gallery nights. Get information from any participating gallery, or call the Virginia Miller Art Gallery (444.9844).

6 Doc Dammers House If George Merrick brought the Old World to Coral Gables, Edward "Doc" Dammers brought the new. He's best remembered as the wheeler-dealer property salesman who stood, literally, on a soapbox and auctioned off muddy lots as the land of dreams. To make the dreams tangible, he used photographs of his own house in sales pitches; customers came in droves. Those colorful anecdotes aside, Dammers's lasting legacy is not land sales but his quieter work as the first mayor of Coral Gables. The house is a private residence. ♦ 1141 Coral Way (at Columbus St)

7 Greely House Its design alone tells the viewer that this large house was a latecomer to the neighborhood. Unlike the dark coral rock homes nearby, this has light, stuccoed walls and a Modernist design. In creating the house, **L. Murray Dixon** used curved lines and geometric shapes and added barrel tiles to the roof, all elements of the style that became fashionable in the 1930s. A private home, the property is closed to the public. ♦ 1140 Coral Way (at Columbus St)

8 Ponce de Leon Plaza This was the first plaza Merrick built, and it was in its shadow that the first land sales were held in Coral Gables—events that remain the stuff of South Florida legend. To gather prospects, Merrick ran special buses and trains that shuttled potential buyers south from New York City and other points north. ♦ Coral Way (at Granada Blvd)

9 Poinciana Place George Merrick was nearly 30 when he married, and, as things go in the backwoods, it was a royal affair. Just as he was a rising star in Coral Gables, his bride, Eunice Peacock, came from an important Coconut Grove pioneer family. The home Merrick built for his wife and himself predates most of the houses that went up with development, and it has less of the Spanish influence he deemed essential in the 1920s. With a long overhanging roof and dark stone walls, the house looks somewhat forbidding, but when the Merricks lived here, it was filled with the congenial chatter of parties and the excitement of planning sessions for the new city. Eunice was a leading figure in South Florida until 1989, when she died at the age of 93. Today, the house is a private residence. ♦ 937 Coral Way (at Granada Blvd)

9 Coral Gables House Fourteen-year-old George Merrick helped his father build the first house on this lot in 1900. Six years later it was replaced by this stone beauty, built by George Merrick, from which he took the name of the city he envisioned. At the turn of the century, the Merrick family plot consisted of 160 acres. Today, the yard is a good deal smaller, and the house is a treasure of a museum. The years have done nothing to detract from its striking simplicity, and the coral-tiled and gabled roof that started everything is kept in tip-top shape. A Merrick concept ahead of its time, the house reveals a Postmodernistic jumble of influences, from the tropical wrap-around veranda to the classic portico and Palladian second-floor window. The house was constructed primarily of coral rock and native Dade County pine, prized for its resistance to termites. The museum's hours are quirky, but it's worth a visit nonetheless. ♦ Nominal admission. W, Su 1-4PM. 907 Coral Way (at Toledo St). 460.5361 ♿

10 **Pape House** The Mediterranean Revival style of varying roof lines and multiple outside walls is beautifully embodied in this striking house, designed by **Frank Wyatt Woods.** The roof is especially interesting: George Merrick imported tiles from Spain and Cuba to give it—and other homes—an authentic look. It is now a private home. ♦ 900 Coral Way (at Toledo St)

11 **Merrick House** Partly to interest prospective homeowners in Coral Gables, George Merrick had his cousin **H. George Fink** design a house that would fill an entire block, on the former site of an old packing plant. Coral rock and stucco give the exterior a rough, asymmetric look. The house and servants' section are enclosed by a wall with an unusual roofed gate. A private residence, the house has been renovated and remains in pristine condition. ♦ 832 S Greenway Dr (at Castile St)

12 **David William Hotel** $$ Purchased in 1991 by Juan Calderoni of Argentina, this hotel was undergoing changes at press time. It remains a bargain for anyone who wants to stay near the Gables business district. There are 71 regular rooms, with 50 more set aside as one-bedroom suites with kitchens; there's also a restaurant. Renovated a couple of years ago, the hotel retains a traditional elegant look, with dark wood paneling. Plans include a new banquet facility accommodating 150 guests. ♦ 700 Biltmore Way (at Cardenas St). 445.7821, 800/232.8770 ♿

13 **550 Biltmore Way** When he built this office building, **Thomas Spain**, a professor of architecture at the **University of Miami,** used large, monolithic blocks to construct the facade, and traditional Spanish elements—such as stone lions in the front, deep-set rectangular windows, and marble interior floors—to ensure that the building melded with the Spanish-influenced designs so prevalent in the surrounding neighborhood. ♦ 550 Biltmore Way (between Segovia and Hernando Sts) ♿

Within 550 Biltmore Way:

Cafe Cappuccino $ A good place to stop for a quick morning cup of its namesake cappuccino or an on-the-run business lunch, this actually is more a lobby bar than a sit-down restaurant. Its marble floors, polished brass, and abundance of ferns lend a feeling of informality. The menu is light, with muffins and croissants with morning coffee, and salads, sandwiches, and the like for lunch. ♦ American ♦ M-F breakfast and lunch. 441.2959 ♿

Allure This boutique specializes in casual womenswear from Paris with an upscale feel but down-home prices. ♦ M-F. 444.5252 ♿

14 **Kilims** A former tenant of South Dade's **Dadeland** (a major mall), this shop recently moved to Coral Gables. It offers all sorts of items for the home and office, including wallpaper and furniture. The array of vases, candleholders, picture frames, and mirrors will catch your attention. ♦ M-Sa. 504 Biltmore Way (at Hernando St). 446.5058 ♿

15 **Door Store** This nationwide chain sells furniture that epitomizes upscale informality. It looks a bit out of place in the heart of Coral Gables's historic district, but the bargains remain unchanged: Kitchen chairs, bar stools, desks, and office furnishings are all available at reasonable prices. ♦ M-Sa; Su afternoon. 490 Biltmore Way (at Hernando St). 445.1421 ♿

16 **Coral Gables City Hall** Financed by a municipal bond offering and built in only four months for $200,000, **City Hall** (illustrated on page 49) was completed in 1928. **Harold Steward** worked closely with George Merrick on this and several other municipal buildings. Now listed on the National Registry of Historic Places, the building perfectly embodies Merrick's Spanish Renaissance design philosophy.

The structure's semicircular eastern end looks out over Coral Way, in the city's central business district. Twelve columns support a stone cornice, in whose center is the coat of

arms Denman Fink designed for the city. Clearly influenced by Spain's official coat of arms, it features a shield divided into quarters, one depicting a castle, one a pelican, another a crocodile, and the fourth a lion. Fink also included figures representing Art and Labor gazing at each other over the shield. Current versions of the city's coat of arms show the Muse of Art fully clad, but on this original design, Fink rendered her topless. Directly beneath the coat of arms, at ground level, is a fountain in the shape of a contorted face, a motif carried over to the fountain at **De Soto Plaza** (see above). On the walls of the building, a number of haphazardly archived but readable documents chronicle the development of Coral Gables. The structure is crowned by a tri-level bell tower that contains a clock, a 500-pound bell, and a striking mural of the four seasons painted by Fink and restored in 1957. ♦ Free. M-F. 405 Biltmore Way (at Le Jeune Rd). 442.6400 ♿

Within Coral Gables City Hall:

Coral Gables Department of Historic Preservation This small office has a large store of information and a helpful staff. Ensconced here are the city archives, which are available to anyone curious about Coral Gables's history. ♦ M-F. 460.5216 ♿

Coral Gables Farmers' Market It's fun to visit this small European-style green market early on a Saturday morning during the growing season, which runs from mid-January to mid-March. The city-sponsored market, which sets up in the park across the street from **City Hall,** has blossomed since its inception in the early 1990s. Shoppers are likely to find luscious baked goods to munch while checking out the produce. ♦ Sa 8AM-1PM mid-January–mid-March. 460.5311 ♿

17 Le Provençal ★★$$$ This informal restaurant offers the opportunity to have dinner with André—or two Andrés, as it were: André Mazoyer, the manager, and André Guibert, the chef. Together, they have combined casual (even a touch seedy) Left Bank ambience with high-quality Right Bank food to come up with one of the city's most engaging French restaurants. As you'd expect in a place claiming Provençal heritage, the bouillabaisse is rich, and the other fish dishes are imaginative. The staff is friendly. ♦ French ♦ M-Sa lunch and dinner. 382 Miracle Mile (at Le Jeune Rd). 448.8984 ♿

PRESTON SCOTT
DESIGN WITH FLOWERS

17 Preston Scott This lovely little shop is a joy. The interior changes seasonally, but everything has a floral theme. A full-service florist, it also offers beautiful Christmas ornaments during the season and unique accents for the garden in springtime. Gift items like stationery, handblown glass, and silk flowers also can be had here. ♦ M-Sa. 380 Miracle Mile (at Le Jeune Rd). 443.0671 ♿

Coral Gables City Hall

MICHAEL BLUM

17 Franco B The clothes Franco Burani stocks are conservative, but they are made to exacting specifications. You won't see the latest European fashions on the racks here, but whatever you do find is guaranteed not to go out of style anytime soon. ♦ M-Sa. 350 Miracle Mile (at Le Jeune Rd). 444.7318 &

17 J. Bolado Heading to a polo match? Then this is the shop for you. The leisurewear selection is excellent but conservative, and the service is unfailingly polite. ♦ M-Sa. 336 Miracle Mile (between Le Jeune Rd and Salzedo St). 448.2507 &

18 Carroll's There's no Carroll on the premises— this luxury jewelry store is managed by Stephen Moorman, whose brother Robert runs another store on Ft. Lauderdale's version of Miracle Mile, Las Olas Boulevard. With Rolex watches, Waterford crystal, and Lenox china, the selection here is as traditional as the store is solid. ♦ M-Sa. 365 Miracle Mile (at Le Jeune Rd). 446.1611 &. Also at: 915 E Las Olas Blvd (between SE Ninth and SE 10th Aves), Ft. Lauderdale. 463.3711 &

18 Leather World The facade is 1950s retro, and the name is terribly passé, but the selection inside is top-notch. Leading brands such as Hartmann are sold at a slight discount. House brands of luggage, purses, wallets, and desk appointments—all equal in quality to the name labels—are easier on the budget. ♦ M-Sa. 339 Miracle Mile (between Le Jeune Rd and Salzedo St). 446.7888 &

18 Cinderella Boutique Gilda Olaniel stocks clothes and shoes for all ages, from infant to preteen, but her clothes for toddlers have the greatest allure. ♦ M-Sa. 329 Miracle Mile (between Le Jeune Rd and Salzedo St). 442.0379 &

J. VINCENT

18 J. Vincent There's not a hair out of place in this sleek shop, which sells metal furnishings. The store custom crafts furniture, but its inventory has expanded to include a large array of accessories as well as an eclectic mix of furniture styles, ranging from Chinese antique to modern. ♦ M-Sa. 323 Miracle Mile (at Le Jeune Rd). 445.8381 &

18 Thai Orchid ★★$$ At first glance, this restaurant seems to have a greenhouse instead of a kitchen: The owner grows exquisite orchids, which adorn the dining area and grace every table. There also is a natural microbrewery on the premises. The menu is thorough in its evocation of Thailand's flavorful cuisine. Try one of the curries or any of the fish dishes, such as deep-fried snapper with ginger sauce. Duck entrées are good, as is the garlic pork. The kitchen spices to your specifications and also offers a macrobiotic menu. It is notable, too, for being one of the rare Coral Gables restaurants to serve lunch on the weekend. ♦ Thai ♦ Daily lunch and dinner. 317 Miracle Mile (at Salzedo St). 443.6364. & Also at: 9565 SW 72nd St (between SW 95th and SW 96th Aves). 279.8583

18 Daisy Tarsi Shop This is a good place to find that special dress for garden and cocktail parties—or even the perfect gown for a second wedding. New owner Maryellen Fonte enlisted couturier Digna Yero to create outfits exclusively for the shop, and she plans to sign up other designers as well. ♦ M-Sa. 311 Miracle Mile (at Salzedo St). 854.5557 &

18 Caffe Abbracci ★★★$$$; Restaurateur Nino Pernetti is a Coral Gables legend: He started as manager of one restaurant, became a partner in running **Caffe Baci** (*baci* is Italian for kisses), and then, in keeping with his theme, opened this establishment (*abbracci* means hugs). He recently sold his stake in **Baci** to concentrate on this place, which has garnered accolades as the best Italian restaurant in a city that abounds in them. All the pastas are exquisite, but manager Alex Portela recommends the pounded veal chop with tricolor pasta, topped with salad. ♦ Italian ♦ M-F lunch and dinner; Sa-Su dinner. Reservations recommended. 318 Aragon Ave (at Salzedo St). 441.0700 &

19 Rivoli Devoted exclusively to handbags and accessories, this shop carries merchandise from top designers. ♦ M-Sa. 266 Miracle Mile (at Salzedo St). 446.2680 &

Restaurants/Clubs: Red	**Hotels:** Blue
Shops/ ☂ Outdoors: Green	**Sights/Culture:** Black

20 Books & Books Since 1982, this has been Coral Gables's—and Miami's—best bookstore. Mitchell Kaplan, the genial proprietor, has assembled a staff of helpful bookworms as eager to dig up a rare used book or poetry collection as they are to hook you on the latest John Grisham thriller. Browsers can while away hours exploring nooks and crannies. Upstairs is an extensive selection of used books and a gallery where photos are often exhibited; there's also a children's-book corner. The bookstore occupies the former **John M. Stabile Building,** which, dating from 1924, is one of the oldest commercial buildings in Coral Gables. A loving rendering of the Mediterranean Revival style, it has a balcony, an ornamented doorway, awnings, and the original tiled roof. ♦ M-Sa; Su afternoon. 296 Aragon Ave (at Salzedo St). 442.4408. ♿ Also at: 933 Lincoln Rd (in the Lincoln Rd pedestrian shopping area), Miami Beach. 532.3222

21 285 Aragon Avenue Although built after the first surge of expansion in Coral Gables, the old **Police and Fire Building** is a classic example of the use of coral rock in so many structures in the area. **Phineas Paist,** who designed many of the town's early buildings, here modified the Mediterranean Revival style with the straight lines and large masses favored during the Depression. The WPA built the structure in 1939 as a public safety headquarters. The three arched bays on the west side held fire trucks. Above the bays are the sculpted heads of two firefighters and the families they protect; at the base of the stone pillars are two pairs of iron firemen's boots. The tower on the northwest corner was constructed not only for aesthetic purposes but to hold a water tank used in training exercises for firefighters. The building was used as a police and fire station until 1975; since 1981, it has been the headquarters of the Junior League of Miami. ♦ 285 Aragon Ave (at Salzedo St) ♿

22 Cendy's Too genteel to call itself a liquidator, this store styles itself as a discounter of name-brand women's shoes. Whatever its label, the shop often has incredible bargains on discontinued lines of designer footwear. ♦ M-Sa. 281 Miracle Mile (at Salzedo St). 444.1010 ♿

22 JohnMartin's ★★★$$ This classic Irish restaurant has become more casual since its recent renovation, which reduced the size of the formal **Waterford Room.** The prices were reduced as well, but the menu, good food, and nice atmosphere haven't changed a bit. The restaurant's name comes from its owners: John Clarke, who used to cook at the **Biltmore Hotel** and now oversees the kitchen here, and Martin Lynch, a longtime restaurateur. Their experience is evident in the quick, efficient service and in the menu, which goes far beyond potatoes and stew. Fresh poached or grilled salmon, jumbo shrimp with mustard butter, and steak with whiskey and mushroom sauce are standouts. This is an especially

George Merrick's Blueprint for Paradise

The roots of Florida's first planned community go back to 1899, when Solomon Merrick, a Congregational minister from New England, moved to Florida and invested $1,100 in a backcountry homestead. By 1903, Solomon and his young son, George, were established enough to build a home, which was called the **Coral Gables House** after its coral-colored tiled and gabled roof.

When Solomon died in 1911, George was called home from college to manage the family's plantation. He eventually met Eunice Peacock, whom he married, and together they gathered a circle of Florida visionaries to plan a new community that would emphasize both beauty and utility. Merrick called on his uncle, the artist Denman Fink, to translate into American terms the Mediterranean style he admired so much. Landscape architect **Frank Button** was charged with designing the gardens, parks, and plazas that Merrick regarded as essential to the high quality of life he envisioned. By 1921 the grapefruit groves were cleared, and the streets, sidewalks, plazas, fountains, and arched entrances that would grace **Coral Gables** had been laid out.

By the time Coral Gables was incorporated in 1925, Merrick had spent $100 million on improvements and $5 million on advertising. The city grew rapidly, especially after the ultra-chic **Biltmore Hotel** (see page 45) opened in early 1926. But later that year, a ferocious hurricane destroyed many of the buildings as well as much of South Florida's economy, dimming the optimism engendered by the great land boom.

With the Depression, banks foreclosed on much of the property, and Merrick's dream faded. People still came to South Florida, especially after World War II, but their tastes had changed. Mediterranean Revival architecture was no longer fashionable, and many of Merrick's design elements were repainted, covered, or bulldozed. True to history, revisionist excess prompted another backlash: Coral Gables today is closer to Merrick's vision than ever before.

good value at lunch. ◆ Irish ◆ Daily lunch and dinner. 253 Miracle Mile (between Salzedo St and Ponce de Leon Blvd). 445.3777 &

Within JohnMartin's:

JohnMartin's Pub ★$$ A spin-off of the restaurant, the tavern has decent pub grub, complemented by Harp lager on tap and Irish music—all much to the delight of sons of Eire. The bar itself, carved in mahogany by local artisans, is a beauty. It's the Happy Hour hot spot for the business crowd. ◆ Daily lunch and dinner. 445.3777 &

22 Tiskets 'N Taskets Owner Connie Dahms has gathered an interesting assortment in this delightful gift shop, sometimes described as specializing in "Country French." No matter how the store is categorized, it's plain fun just to browse. The selection ranges from beautifully topped walking canes to gourmet coffees and cocoas, from glassware to children's toys. ◆ M-Sa. 241 Miracle Mile (between Salzedo St and Ponce de Leon Blvd). 443.4806 &

22 Lily's Many stores sell cosmetics, but few have a selection as carefully chosen as that found in this boutique. Several perfumes and men's fragrances are imported exclusively from the manufacturers. The service is particularly thoughtful. ◆ M-Sa. 239 Miracle Mile (at Ponce de Leon Blvd). 442.4533 &

22 Perfumania The atmosphere and high-pressure sales tactics scream *discount,* but if you know what you want and don't mind the hectic style, you're likely to save 30 percent or more. ◆ M-Sa. 223 Miracle Mile (at Ponce de Leon Blvd). 529.0114 &

22 Suzanne Ltd. This shop caters primarily to women who like eveningwear in bright colors with sequins, ruffles, layers, and pleats. It's expensive, but the selection is good. ◆ M-Sa. 207 Miracle Mile (at Ponce de Leon Blvd). 442.1552 &

23 Giorgio's On often-staid Miracle Mile, Jorge Miranda raises a welcome contemporary voice. He stocks trendy, well-selected men's designer clothing, some loud, some (relatively) subdued, all of high quality. Of special interest is the incredible array of socks and ties, most in unique patterns. ◆ M-Sa. 208 Miracle Mile (at Ponce de Leon Blvd). 448.4302 &

24 Holiday Inn Coral Gables $ Nothing fancy or historic distinguishes this motor inn, but there's no denying its handiness and family orientation. Most of the 168 rooms have king-size beds, children stay for free, and a comfortable restaurant (see below) provides room service. ◆ 2051 Le Jeune Rd (at Navarre Ave). 443.2301, 800/HOLIDAY &

Within the Holiday Inn Coral Gables:

Greenstreet's $$ Its standard hotel restaurant menu does nothing to set this restaurant apart in a city known for fine dining, but it does have the advantage of convenience. The kitchen provides room service for the hotel's guests. ◆ American ◆ Daily breakfast, lunch, and dinner. 445.2131 &

25 La Bussola ★★★$$$ The name means "the compass," but it doesn't connote a nautical motif. Instead, it is a tribute to a famous Roman restaurant of the same name. Owner Claudio Giordano shows an enlightened respect for culinary custom in his menu, which includes a creative balance of traditional items and local ingredients. The pastas are particularly fine, especially the pumpkin-filled ravioli, and the wine list is extensive. When it comes to preparing special requests, there's no more accommodating staff in town. ◆ Italian ◆ M-F lunch and dinner; Sa-Su dinner. Reservations recommended. 270 Giralda Ave (at Salzedo St). 445.8783 &

Le Festival ★★$$$ This is heaven to Americans who learned about classic cooking in the 1960s, when sauces were heavy and so were the chefs who concocted them. Owner Ramón Rodríguez believes in French tradition, and his staff serves it to a packed house every night. House pâté, a knockout cheese soufflé, and duck à l'orange all reflect the house style. Lighter dishes have been added, such as red snapper with wine sauce and crushed onions. ◆ French ◆ M-F lunch and dinner; Sa dinner. Reservations required. 2120 Salzedo St (at Alcazar Ave). 442.8545 &

26 Casa Rolandi ★★★$$$$ Designer Sam Robin is responsible for the striking contemporary look of this restaurant, weaving tropical blues with Italian terra-cotta and Mexican adobe. The menu features fresh fish tinged with mountain herbs, pasta with truffles, and meat cooked in a brick oven. Try the whole fish cooked in rock salt, seafood pizza fresh from the brick oven, or a pasta sampler, including black ravioli stuffed with shrimp and tortellini with veal and white truffles. New owner Giorgio Santerini and Gilberto Barrera, the chef, have overhauled sections of the menu, leaving the always inventive and ever satisfying favorites intact. ◆ Italian ◆ M-F lunch and dinner; Sa-Su dinner. Reservations required. 1930 Ponce de Leon Blvd (between Navarre and Majorca Aves). 444.2187 &

27 Coral Gables School Education figured prominently in George Merrick's advertising of the virtues of his new community. In designing its first public school, **Richard Kiehnel** drew heavily on the Mediterranean Revival style, especially in the arched, open-air walkways and two large outdoor courts. The building continues in its original function as an elementary school. ♦ 105 Minorca Ave (at Galiano St). 448.1731 &

28 La Palma Building This was originally the **Cla-Reina Hotel,** a graceful lodging place for early visitors to Coral Gables; later it became the **La Palma Hotel.** Interior designer Lynn Wilson bought the building, moved in, and rented space to other designers and doctors. The facade still has a Mediterranean charm about it. ♦ 116 Alhambra Circle (at Galiano St) &

Within the La Palma Building:

La Palma Ristorante ★★$$$ Paolo Montecchi, founder and former owner of **Greenwich Village** on Brickell Avenue, opened this beautiful spot in 1994. Large windows overlook a courtyard with 40 outside tables and tiny lights twinkling in the trees. Eating in the courtyard gives you the feeling of hanging out at an outdoor cafe in Europe. The pasta is homemade and cooked fresh, as is the fish. Try the *agnolotti del vindante* (a homemade pasta stuffed with porcini mushrooms in a delightful sage sauce)—it gets rave reviews. ♦ Continental/Mediterranean ♦ M-F lunch and dinner; Sa-Su dinner. 445.8777 &

29 Hotel Place St. Michel $$ If any hotel ever represented George Merrick's vision of Coral Gables as European-Floridian, this is it. Designed by **Anthony Zink** as an office building, it opened in 1926 and was converted to the **Sevilla Hotel** a short time later. Extensively restored in 1979, it is now owned by Stuart Bornstein, who also owns hotels and restaurants in Miami Beach. The 27 antiques-furnished rooms have been painstakingly decorated to reflect a European aesthetic, and each is unique in design and layout. Hallways showcase period pieces, and each room has an Art Nouveau glass transom. Continental breakfast is included. ♦ 162 Alcazar Ave (at Ponce de Leon Blvd). 444.1666, 800/258.1103 &

Within Hotel Place St. Michel:

Restaurant Place St. Michel ★★$$$ This restaurant's atmosphere benefits from the lavish care given its parent hotel. Sunday brunch here has been called glorious; a jazz pianist entertains while patrons partake of an endless buffet. The ambience is romantic, quiet, and casual, so diners feel comfortable rather than overwhelmed by pretentiousness. ♦ American ♦ Daily breakfast, lunch, and dinner; Su brunch. 446.6572 &

30 Hyatt Regency Coral Gables $$ The architectural firm **Nichols Partnership** and interior designer Jeffrey Howard did a superb job of integrating a large hotel and office complex with the traditional architectural style associated with Coral Gables, which emphasizes small buildings. Of these two towers, one is devoted to offices, the other to 14 stories of hotel rooms and suites. The 242 rooms are spacious, comfortable, and neat, if not opulent. The large interior spaces are intended to re-create the feel of the Alhambra, the castle after which the street is named. Much of the interior detail is of stone, and many rooms are named after parts of the original Alhambra. The hotel is especially popular with business groups in need of large meeting spaces. Five floors above street level is an excellent pool, and valet parking is available. ♦ 50 Alhambra Plaza (between Galiano St and Douglas Rd). 441.1234, 800/233.1234; fax 443.7702 &

Within the Hyatt Regency Coral Gables:

Two Sisters ★★$$$ Nearly large enough to accommodate an army, this restaurant takes its name from the main dining area of the Moorish Alhambra. The food is reliable; at night, the menu focuses on tapas, paella, and wok–stir fry beef. ♦ Pacific Rim/Spanish ♦ Daily breakfast, lunch, and dinner. Reservations recommended. 441.1234 &

Alcazaba This nightclub is striking, thanks in part to the black and silver decor and the brilliant costumes worn by the serving staff. There's a snack buffet at Happy Hour; otherwise no food is offered. Music is provided by a DJ. ♦ Cover. Entertainment: W, F-Sa. 441.1234 &

31 Jones Meats & Deli The meat at this butcher/deli is available to go or to consume on the premises from a limited sandwich menu, though the tiny chairs and tables are far from comfortable. The shop adds a surprising note of informality to the neighborhood. ♦ M-Sa. 127-129 Giralda Ave (at Merrick Way). 444.6183 &

31 Country by Nature Rustic isn't a word that comes to mind when touring the shops in Coral Gables, so this shop is unusual. A furniture store with all the trimmings from pillows to pictures, it sells beautifully handcrafted copies of American antique furniture. Like the cost of the originals, prices can be high. ♦ M-Sa; Su afternoon. 100 Giralda Ave (at Galiano St). 442.1660. & Also at: 628 S Miami Ave (between SW Sixth and SW Seventh Sts). 577.0844

uca

32 Yuca ★★★$$$ This popular and innovative Cuban restaurant has a new chef, Guerilla Veloso. The urbane managing partner, Efraín Vega, keeps things running smoothly. The menu reflects the change but retains some favorites, such as plantain stuffed with dried cured beef dressed in a sour cream and green sauce. It also features plantain-coated dolphin with tamarind tartar sauce and plantain puree. Desserts are notable, especially the pumpkin flan on a gingersnap crust. ♦ Nouvelle Cuban ♦ M-Sa lunch and dinner; Su dinner. Reservations recommended. 177 Giralda Ave (at Ponce de Leon Blvd). 444.4448 &

32 Le Glacier ★★$$ One of the quiet treasures of Coral Gables, this low-key eatery features unpretentious food and friendly, efficient service. The menu has been expanded to include fish, veal, poultry, soups, and salads, with terrific ice-cream concoctions (as the name implies) to round out the meal. ♦ Continental ♦ M-Sa lunch and dinner. 166 Giralda Ave (at Ponce de Leon Blvd). 447.9667 &

32 Bangkok, Bangkok ★★$$ Traditional Thai food is the focus here, but in dressed-up dishes. "Little Big Man" is a whole stir-fried red snapper; "Roasted Duck Darling" is an extra crispy version. The satay and *phad thai* (a noodle dish) are delectable, as are several seafood dishes and curries. ♦ Thai ♦ Daily lunch and dinner. Reservations recommended. 157 Giralda Ave (at Ponce de Leon Blvd). 444.2397 &

32 Las Puertas ★★★$$$ This restaurant takes Mexican food to heights of elegance. The tasteful decor includes the fiery colors of Mexico. Service is warm and friendly. Sample anything—duck fajitas, *gorditas* (corn cakes stuffed with meat), or flour tortillas—for the quality is good throughout. Note that it can be difficult to get a seat for dinner. ♦ Mexican ♦ M-Sa lunch and dinner; Su dinner. Reservations recommended. 148 Giralda Ave (at Ponce de Leon Blvd). 442.0708 &

32 Justa Pasta ★★★$$$ A mix of Northern Italian and Cajun fare characterizes the menu here, with felicitous results. The pastas are spectacular—especially the shrimp and scallops on angel hair pasta in a dijon sauce. Also good are the veal Marsala and veal piccata. Desserts are sinfully rich: The tiramisù is celebrated, and the mousse cakes are popular as well. The 70-seat restaurant, formerly located at Ponce Circle, has a tropical decor with lots of greenery. ♦ Northern Italian ♦ M-F lunch and dinner; Sa-Su dinner. Reservations recommended. 139 Giralda Ave (at Ponce de Leon Blvd). 567.9555 &

32 Darbar ★★★$$$ The secret here is in the 15 spices mixed together to create wonderful chicken, shrimp, lamb, rice, and vegetable dishes. Serving tandoori and other dishes in an urbane setting has helped make this restaurant a success. On the menu is English-made Indian beer and, for those who can take the heat, vandal curry. ♦ Indian ♦ Daily lunch and dinner. Reservations recommended. 276 Alhambra Circle (at Ponce de Leon Blvd). 448.9691 &

32 Luminaire Even if you're not in the market for new furniture, this store can be approached as a gallery of innovative design. Its contemporary European furniture is created by world-renowned architects and designers. You'll find everything for the home, including accessories and fabrics. ♦ M-Sa. 2331 Ponce de Leon Blvd (at Aragon Ave). 448.7367 &

33 Paper Emporium Everything here is truly letter perfect: pens in an array of colors, all sizes and types of paper, postcards, and every imaginable gadget to aid the accomplished or would-be letter writer. The only thing this convivial shop lacks is organization, but browsers will be in heaven. ♦ M-Sa. 2347 Galiano St (at Aragon Ave). 445.7090 &

34 JJ's American Diner ★$$ Have a blast from the past at this nostalgic restaurant, where servers wear 1950s costumes, the tunes are oldies, and the menu items are straight out of "Happy Days." Breakfast is the most popular meal (the pancakes are great, the omelettes so-so), but lunch and dinner have their adherents. The food is greasy enough to win a frown from the American Heart Association, and the portions are enormous (an order of onion rings is as big as a football). The restaurant makes up in atmosphere what it lacks in culinary invention, presenting a strong case for a hearty weekend bite. ♦ American ♦ Daily breakfast, lunch, and dinner. 2320 Galiano St (at Aragon Ave). 448.6886 ♿

35 Gallery of the Eccentric Claire Savitt has gathered an intriguingly eclectic group of American folk artists whose work includes ceramics, furniture, and more. All her pieces are whimsical and full of color; many are in the Grandma Moses vein. Of the 30 artists Savitt shows, half live in Florida. The prices are moderate. ♦ Tu-Sa. 233 Aragon Ave (at Ponce de Leon Blvd). 446.5550 ♿

36 Colonnade Building As development in Coral Gables boomed, city founder George Merrick constructed this grand building as his sales headquarters in 1926. The design is Spanish and Baroque, with some liberal borrowing from Hadrian's Mausoleum in Rome. Renovated in the late 1980s, the structure retains all the original design elements, including a columned facade supporting a covered sidewalk, ornamented archways, and a 75-foot-high rotunda. After Merrick's organization closed, the building housed many businesses, including a movie company and, during World War II, a training center for pilots, who used the rotunda as a basketball court. The Florida National Bank operated here in the 1950s. Intercap Investments renovated the building in the 1980s, connecting it to the then-new hotel complex behind it (see below). ♦ 169 Miracle Mile (at Ponce de Leon Blvd) ♿

36 Omni Colonnade Hotel $$$$ Original plans for this luxury hotel called for the rotunda of the **Colonnade Building** to be filled with shops. That hasn't happened yet, but the rest of the development is striking in its adherence to the **Colonnade**'s exterior design. Seamlessly attached to that building is this superb hotel, which is affiliated with the Omni chain. At press time, planned renovations included the refurbishing of all 157 rooms (including 19 suites). The cautiously opulent feeling of an earlier era, emphasized in public areas with marble floors, polished dark mahogany, and the burnished leather of an English library, isn't expected to change dramatically. The amenities, including 24-hour room service and valet parking, are tops. In keeping with the restrained decor and space limitations in the heart of the city, the heated pool is on the 10th floor. The hotel is accessible from Miracle Mile but has a vehicular entrance on Aragon Avenue. ♦ 180 Aragon Ave (at Ponce de Leon Blvd). 441.2600, 800/533.1337; fax 445.3939 ♿

Within the Omni Colonnade Hotel:

Aragon Cafe ★★$$$$ The atmosphere is Coral Gables Spanish; the food, American continental. Chef Mark Dekrines and a new maître d' have changed the menu somewhat and added alfresco dining. The menu includes lamb, poultry, and duck as well as seafood. The piano bar is a romantic setting for a preprandial cocktail. ♦ American ♦ Tu-Sa dinner. Reservations required. 441.2600 ♿

Doc Dammers, the first mayor of Coral Gables, was also a high pressure salesman for George Merrick. He joined Merrick in selling Coral Gables after being promised the job of mayor.

Restaurants/Clubs: Red	**Hotels:** Blue
Shops/ ♟ Outdoors: Green	**Sights/Culture:** Black

Doc Dammers ★$$ The casual saloon decor doesn't quite fit into the single huge room devoted to this informal and often noisy restaurant, but it's one of the few spots in Coral Gables open nearly around the clock. Best for breakfast, it's so-so later in the day, with uninspired burgers, pizza, and pasta. Good bets include meat loaf, salad Niçoise, and the couscous-seafood combination. The outdoor cafe is great for lazy weekend lunches. There's live entertainment Tuesday through Saturday. ♦ American ♦ Daily breakfast, lunch, and dinner. 441.2600 ♿

Biscayne Miracle Mile ★★$ Home cooking is served with a broad smile here. Trademark dishes are fried chicken, roast turkey, turnip greens, and broiled fish. Nothing is too fancy, and nothing costs much more than $4. ♦ American ♦ Daily lunch and dinner. 147 Miracle Mile (at Ponce de Leon Blvd). 444.9005 ♿

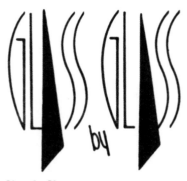

Glass by Glass Devoted to glass objects and collectibles, Renato Glass's new store has the look and feel of an art gallery. One piece on display is the striking *Balancing Rocks* by Rosin Loredano. Most items are functional as well as beautiful. ♦ M-Sa. 141 Miracle Mile (at Ponce de Leon Blvd). 444.3600 ♿

37 Chic Parisienne Prospective brides come hundreds of miles to explore the selection at this small, exclusive boutique, generally considered the best of the several bridal shops in the neighborhood. Even if you're not engaged, it's a fun place to browse. ♦ M-Sa. 118 Miracle Mile (at Galiano St). 448.5756 ♿

37 Royal Linen This shop is a tribute to the wonders of linens. Handmade tablecloths, napkins, and pillowcases are among the lacy confections chosen by owner Lenore Rosenberg. On display are handmade lacy blouses, beautiful parasols, placemats, runners, and table toppers. The work is exquisite. ♦ M-Sa. 86 Miracle Mile (between Ponce de Leon Blvd and Galiano St). 443.8393 ♿

38 Melody Inn ★★★$$ The menu here proves that Switzerland's cuisine is just as varied as its languages. Proprietor Hans Burri weds Italian, German, and French elements, with harmonious results. Try his morels on toast, luscious Wiener schnitzel with mushrooms, pork with mustard, or fish with herbs and stock. Several Swiss wines are available. The desserts are suitably decadent and suitably Swiss—don't miss the vanilla ice cream topped with seven kinds of chocolate. ♦ Swiss ♦ Tu-Su lunch and dinner. Reservations recommended. 83 Andalusia Ave (at Galiano St). 448.0022 ♿

39 Estate Wines & Gourmet Foods ★★$ New owner Hans Viertl has a three-fold vision of his tiny shop/restaurant. The wine store stocks hard-to-find wines and Champagnes; the gourmet store imports cheeses and pâtés from Europe and sells sandwiches made on fresh baguettes; and the catering business focuses on upscale office parties and meetings. Once a month, Viertl hosts wine tastings and lectures, during which winery representatives discuss their products. ♦ Continental ♦ M-Sa lunch. 92 Miracle Mile (between Galiano St and Douglas Rd). 442.9915 ♿

39 Packaging Store Whether your dilemma is having too many things to carry back home or fulfilling shopping requests for out-of-town friends, this store eases the shipping blues. They pack and ship everything from oranges to furniture. And if you need a quick gift, there's a good selection of fruit. ♦ M-Sa. 44 Miracle Mile (at Douglas Rd). 441.9565 ♿

39 Wedding Cake Gallery With all the bridal stores along Miracle Mile, it's not so unusual that this specialized bakery is here as well. The sight of multiple, multitiered cakes in the window is breathtaking. If you thought all wedding cakes were the same, try a free sample of one of these. ♦ M-Sa. 30 Miracle Mile (at Douglas Rd). 444.6772 ♿

40 Rex Art For anyone with a creative bent, this art supply store is the one to visit. The selection is huge, from chalks and oils to paper, drafting tables, fine pens and pencils, and an excellent collection of books and art magazines. Saturday mornings are a madhouse, but the rest of the week service is efficient and friendly. ♦ M-Sa. 2263 SW 37th Ave (between Andalusia and Valencia Aves). 445.1413 ♿

41 Vatapá ★★★$$ Walking into this authentic Brazilian restaurant is like entering a tropical rain forest. The decor is exotic and romantic. The owner, Remi Martini, is also the executive chef, and her husband, John, manages the place, which has been called the best South American restaurant in Miami. The menu includes char-grilled Angus sirloin steak, pasta, and salads. ♦ Brazilian ♦ Daily lunch and dinner. 2415 Ponce de Leon Blvd (between Miracle Mile and Andalusia Ave). 461.5669 ♿

42 Bugatti ★★$$ Originally, this simple storefront was to be a pasta shop, with a small restaurant on the side. Later, owner Klaus Frisch decided to move the pasta factory elsewhere and devote the place to dining. So he cut the stools down to chair height, added some marble-topped tables, and ended up with one of the best pasta restaurants in town. The menu is limited, and the atmosphere is decidedly cool, but the service is as efficient as it comes. The tortellini with porcini is excellent, the four-cheese pizza is heavenly, and the coffee is hands-down the best in Coral Gables. At these prices, the food's a steal. ♦ Italian ♦ M-Sa lunch and dinner; Su dinner. 2504 Ponce de Leon Blvd (at Andalusia Ave). 441.2545 ♿

42 Caffe Baci ★★★$$$ With a metallic domed ceiling, this trendy spot tends to be somewhat noisy, but that doesn't detract from the food, which is consistently interesting and often exciting—thanks to new owner Federica Rossi and chef Fabrizio Donadi. The pastas are very good, and the appetizers are intricate. A good bet is the spinach linguine with vegetables or the bouillabaisse. Fish dishes are also worthwhile. And don't miss the mango tart—it's out of this world. ♦ Italian ♦ M-F lunch and dinner; Sa-Su dinner. Reservations recommended. 2522 Ponce de Leon Blvd (at Valencia Ave). 442.0600 ♿

42 Didier's ★★★★$$$ When this restaurant originally opened at another address, it had 14 tables and long lines. At its new location, the number of tables has increased to about 40, but the place is just as popular, and the food remains first-rate. The intimate atmosphere is enhanced by the sheer white curtains on the windows. Born in Burgundy, French-trained chef/owner Didier Collangette brings his Gallic expertise to these shores in this French restaurant, one of the best in Miami. From the bouillabaisse to the tuna with mango sauce, from the fresh basil soup to the rack of lamb with fresh mint sauce, this is a culinary treat. And the service is great. ♦ French ♦ M-F lunch and dinner; Sa-Su dinner. Reservations recommended. 2530 Ponce de Leon Blvd (at Valencia Ave). 567.2444 ♿

43 Andalusia Bake Shop Customers here are divided between bankers in three-piece suits buying a Danish before a board meeting and students grabbing a muffin on the run. Unusual for a commercial bakery, the desserts have a homemade look and taste. A number of area restaurants buy their bread here. ♦ M-Sa from 6AM. 248 Andalusia Ave (between Ponce de Leon Blvd and Salzedo St). 445.8696 ♿

44 The Bistro ★★★$$$ This is not a large place, but it's wonderful. Long a popular hangout for locals, it provides a great business lunch and a leisurely dinner. The service is friendly and knowledgeable, and the food is terrific. Try the rack of lamb, or the salmon served with celery mousse and a burgundy wine sauce. ♦ French/Continental ♦ Tu-F lunch and dinner; Sa dinner. Reservations recommended. 2611 Ponce de Leon Blvd (at Sevilla Ave). 442.9671 ♿

45 Charade ★★$$$ Originally set aside by George Merrick as a showroom for furniture makers from Cuba, this building was turned over to the **University of Miami** after World War II; it was sold and converted to a restaurant in 1960. Today it is a beautiful space, with high beamed ceilings and lush flower arrangements. In back is a skylighted sunroom; in front, much of the original wood furnishing has been kept. The food, service, and atmosphere all are excellent. Recommended are the lobster thermidor and the veal dishes. ♦ French/Continental. ♦ Daily lunch and dinner. Reservations recommended. 2900 Ponce de Leon Blvd (at Palermo Ave). 448.6077 ♿

46 Christy's ★★★$$$$ George Bush eats here when visiting his son, as do steak lovers from all over. Offering superb prime ribs, this place has earned its reputation as one of the best beef restaurants in town. A rich filet mignon is served with teriyaki sauce. The setting is English club. Power brokers are always dining here, but so are June and Ward Cleaver types. ♦ Steak house ♦ M-F lunch and dinner; Sa-Su dinner. Reservations recommended. 3101 Ponce de Leon Blvd (at Malaga Ave). 446.1400 ♿

47 French Normandy Village This is one of **Coral Gables's International Villages.** While founder George Merrick envisioned Coral Gables as a city inspired by Spanish and Mediterranean architecture, he also thought some diversity was required in its design. To that end, he laid out "foreign villages" throughout the city. He planned on more than a dozen, but the 1926 hurricane and the decline of the land boom halted development at seven, all constructed between 1925 and 1926. Villages planned but never realized included Swedish, Moorish, English, and Persian. The ones actually built (see below) remain in splendid condition and illustrate Merrick's intention that Coral Gables offer homes for every income level.

The 11 town houses in the **French Normandy Village** are built on a short, U-shaped street that lends privacy and emphasizes shared architectural elements: Gingerbread, peaked roofs, and timber beams are all borrowed from Norman architecture in France and England. Today, they house families as the original plan intended, but in the 1930s and 1940s, they were used by fraternities from the **University of Miami** and even as billets during World War II. ♦ 400 block of Vizcaya Ave (at Le Jeune Rd)

48 Italian Village Although George Merrick was almost as strongly influenced by Italy as by Spain, this is the least known of all his international villages. Architect **Frank Wyatt Woods** so seamlessly integrated these five houses that it's hard to see where the village begins and ends. All have entrances fronting the street, with stairs leading to the doorway from street level and walled gardens on one side. ♦ Altara Ave (between Monserrate and Palmarito Sts)

49 Colonial Village Designed by **John** and **Coulton Skinner,** the architects who created the **French Normandy Village,** these houses are a hybrid of Georgian and antebellum Southern architecture, with touches of Greek Revival. All the homes back onto the **Riviera Golf Course.** Inside, they have considerable open space with large rooms and high vaulted ceilings. ♦ Santa Maria St (at the Riviera Golf Course)

Trattoria & Bakery

50 Tutti's ★★★$$ Who would imagine that a city of 40,000 people could support yet another Italian restaurant? This is one of the most popular in town, and with gourmet pasta at sensible prices, it has caused a sensation since its opening in 1993. The inventive Tuscan lasagna layers grilled vegetables and chicken instead of pasta, and the rigatoni with tomato sauce is laced with pesto. The downside to this always-hopping restaurant is the number of customers and the noise they make. ♦ Italian ♦ M-F lunch and dinner; Sa-Su dinner. 4612 Le Jeune Rd (at Hwy 1). 663.0077 ♿

51 Chinese Village All eight homes in this village, designed by **Henry Killam Murphy,** share bright trim and painted roofs. Red is a popular color for door frames and grillwork, and the sloping yellow roofs are particularly striking. A communal Chinese style is further evoked by wood carvings, ceramic animal symbols for good luck, and decorative gates. ♦ Riviera Dr (between Sansovino, Maggiore, Castania, and Menendez Aves)

52 University of Miami George Merrick envisioned a comprehensive education plan as the heart of his design for a new city. Within that plan, the creation of a university was crucial. There had been discussion of establishing a **Pan American University** in the greater Miami area before Merrick entered the debate. But he had something no one else had offered: money and a site large enough to contain the facility. In donating the land and a matching grant of $5 million, Merrick ensured that the university would be built in Coral Gables. It still occupies the 160-acre site he specified, bounded by Campo Sano Avenue on the north, San Amaro Drive on the west, Highway 1 on the south, and University Drive on the east. The architecture of the school, however, does not follow Merrick's original plans for a Mediterranean Revival campus. A major drawback to visiting the university is the lack of viable parking for nonstudents. Those willing to brave the traffic, however, will find some of Coral Gables's treasures on the campus. ♦ 1306 Stanford Dr. 284.5500 ♿

Within the University of Miami:

Ring Theatre The "ring" refers to the polygonal design of the university's first classroom building, which the Department of Drama used for performances until this 300-seat facility was completed. Scheduled to reopen at press time; performances are staged throughout the year by both student and professional companies. ♦ 1380 Miller Dr. 284.3355 ♿

Gusman Concert Hall Not to be confused with the **Maurice Gusman Center for the Performing Arts** in downtown Miami, this intimate (600-seat) and acoustically fine theater is ideal for chamber performances. Graduate recitals are open to the public, and many visiting ensembles perform here as well. Miami's Friends of Chamber Music sponsor an extensive series that brings world-class chamber groups to the stage throughout the year. ♦ 1314 Miller Dr. 284.6477 ♿

Restaurants/Clubs: Red   **Hotels:** Blue
Shops/ ♟ Outdoors: Green   **Sights/Culture:** Black

Lowe Art Museum

Lowe Art Museum Miami's first professional art exhibition space today houses one of the most interesting and unsung collections in South Florida. The initial funding came from Joe and Emily Lowe (he was president of Popsicle Corporation), who also donated a portion of their substantial collection of works by New York artists to the museum in 1952. The most heralded section of the museum today is the Samuel H. Kress Collection, which includes outstanding examples of Renaissance and Baroque art, including works by Correggio, Tintoretto, and Andrea Della Robbia. Less well known but also interesting is a series of paintings by Washington Allston, the fine Barton Collection of American Indian Art, and the extensive collections of Latin, Asian, and American art. There also is a Native American wing. Also represented are El Greco, Chagall, Rembrandt, and Botero. ◆ Admission. Tu-Sa; Su afternoon. 1301 Stanford Dr. 284.3535 ᕴ

53 **French City Village** Architect **Mott B. Schmidt** patterned these residences after 18th-century French town houses, including courtyards and gardens off the kitchens. The rooms tend to be small, but the detail is exceptional. The village is only one block long; the houses on the east and west ends are alike, as are the next in from each end, a pattern that culminates with the unique center residence. Strict building codes in Coral Gables ensure that any renovation or new construction will adhere to the pattern, right down to the shade of yellow used to paint the houses. ◆ 1000 block of Hardee Rd (between Leonardo and Cellini Sts)

54 **French Country Village** A sense of pastoral space still pervades the large backyards of these homes. There are two exterior styles: farm-type houses and rustic dwellings. Inside, they share the same basic elements, including four bedrooms, two rooms for servants, wrought-iron balconies, and high ceilings. This was to be one of the largest villages, but the hurricane of 1926 put an end to most construction. Several of the houses were finished later using the original plans. A good example of the rustic dwelling is at 517 Hardee Road; at the west end of the block at 536 Hardee Road is a splendid, turreted château-style house. ◆ 500 block of Hardee Rd (between San Vicente and Maggiore Sts)

55 **Dutch South African Village** What immediately distinguishes these houses are the twisted coil chimneys and the filigree detail on their peaked roofs. Inside, they all are L- or U-shaped, with small rooms and a tidy look. **Marion Syms Wyeth,** the first registered female architect in Florida, also designed a **Persian Village,** which was never completed, and many buildings in Palm Beach. ◆ Maya Ave (at San Vicente St)

56 **Bagel Emporium** ★★$ No one else in town makes better bagels than these folks, who provide a slice of New York City in Coral Gables. The sandwiches are fresh, and the tuna on a bagel is a treat, as is the matzo ball soup. The surroundings have been freshly renovated. Beer and wine are on the menu, if you're looking for more than just bagels. Take out or eat in—they deliver, too. ◆ Deli ◆ Daily breakfast, lunch, and dinner. 1238 S Dixie Hwy (at Mariposa Ct). 666.7417 ᕴ

Bests

Bob Hosmon

Restaurant Critic/Wine Columnist/Assistant Dean, University of Miami

South Beach—Lunch at the **Booking Table Cafe** and dinner at **Bang.**

Coconut Grove—The new Miami at **Cafe Tu Tu Tango**.

Best restaurant in the Sunshine State—**Mark's Place** in **North Miami.**

For understanding the Hispanic influence in South Florida—**Yuca** in **Coral Gables; Versailles** and **Casa Blanca** in **Miami.**

Native Miami—**East Coast Fisheries** in Miami, **Joe's Stone Crab Restaurant** in **South Miami Beach, Cap's Place** at **Lighthouse Point.**

Theater—**Acme Acting Company** at the **Area Stage.**

Museums—The **Museum of Art** in **Ft. Lauderdale, Norton Gallery of Art, Center for the Fine Arts,** and the **Lowe Art Museum.**

Symphony—**Florida Philharmonic Orchestra,** the **New World Symphony Orchestra**.

Best-kept secret in South Florida—The cultural program **"Cultural del Lobo"** at the **Wolfson Campus** of **Miami-Dade Community College.**

Best cultural happening—Miami Book Fair International.

Best place to look for books and culture—**Books & Books,** in Coral Gables and **Miami Beach.**

South Miami/ South Dade County

Driving south from downtown **Miami**, suburban development eventually gives way to farms and open spaces. The town of South Miami, with its vibrant, small-town shopping district, adjoins sprawling suburban **Kendall**—land of the mall and the commuter. But farther south in the **Homestead/Florida City** area, farms replace tract homes and building restrictions protect environmentally sensitive areas.

As its name implies, Homestead was once a pioneer town. Founded as the headquarters for railway crews extending track to **Key West**, Homestead and Florida City developed an important industry: farming. Locally grown vegetables and exotic fruits can be found in stores and roadside markets; much of it is shipped around the nation. Homestead is also a popular gateway to many South Florida attractions, including **Everglades National Park**, **Biscayne National Park**, and the **Florida Keys.** On weekends, parts of **South Dade** teem with bicyclists, hikers, boaters, and other outdoor types.

South Dade was virtually swept away by Hurricane Andrew, which tore through the region on 24 August 1992. The worst natural disaster in US history, Andrew flattened much of the cities of Homestead and Florida City, as well as many suburban developments. Thousands were left homeless, and one of the area's economic engines, Homestead Air Force Base, was destroyed. Other long-time South Florida attractions, including **Metrozoo** and **Monkey Jungle**, suffered major damage.

For nos. 33-43, see pg. 66

Happily most of the area is back to—and in some ways better than—its pre-Andrew days. New shopping centers, hotels, and restaurants have risen along **Highway 1** and other major thoroughfares, giving much of South Dade a "brand-new" look (in fact, whole housing subdivisions today sport new roofs and new paint jobs, and a few have benefited from the so-called Jacuzzi effect, in which homeowners use their insurance money to make major improvements). Downtown Homestead's historic business district, with shops dating to the 1920s, is recovering. But scattered abandoned buildings covered with spray-paint—some missing windows or roofs—can still be seen throughout the region. Andrew's legacy still lives in the trees, which were stripped by the winds and are growing back in sometimes ungainly fashion.

Area code 305 unless otherwise indicated.

1 Laesch/Bartram House This two-story wood-frame house is a good example of pioneer Florida architecture. It was built around 1905 by the Laesch family, who moved to Florida in 1898 and founded a company to can locally grown fruit (the company closed in 1953). In 1927 the house was remodeled by **H. George Fink,** who worked closely with George Merrick in developing Coral Gables. **Fink**'s renovation is in the Gables' Mediterranean Revival style. He added an elegant front entry and doorway framed by Corinthian pillars. In 1979 the private residence was purchased by the Miami Friends, who named it **Bartram House** after a fellow Quaker, John Bartram. It remains a private home. ◆ 1205 Sunset Dr (at Schoolhouse Rd), South Miami

1 Coco Plum Women's Club In 1912 the pioneer women of the area established a club for "literary, educational, and community service," and in 1914 they built a wood-frame clubhouse. When developer George Merrick began buying land to build Coral Gables in the 1920s, he tried to acquire the club's five-acre plot but was turned down. Then, the ladies had an idea: They would sell Merrick four of their five acres if he would, in return, build them a spacious new clubhouse. Both sides got what they wanted: Merrick got land he never really needed, and the club got this splendid Mediterranean-style building that continues to serve as its headquarters. ◆ 1375 Sunset Dr (at SW 53rd Ave), South Miami

2 Whip 'n Dip Ice Cream Shoppe ★$$ Forget the silly retro name for a moment and step in the door. It even *looks* like a 1950s soda fountain, except for the signs proclaiming "light ice cream, frozen yogurt, and no-cholesterol desserts." There is, thank goodness, real ice cream, too, and it's fabulous. ◆ M-Th 11AM-10:30PM; F-Sa until 11:30PM; Su 1-10:30PM. 1407 Sunset Dr (at Yumuri St), South Miami. 665.2565 ♿

3 Tropical Audubon House Built in 1932 by **Robert Fitch Smith,** this house shows the pride with which early Miami settlers approached the details of their homes. The chimney is cut from native coral rock (oolitic limestone), and there is considerable detail in the extensive woodwork of the house, which is currently a private residence. ◆ 5530 Sunset Dr (at SW 55th Ave), South Miami

3 Sunset Stores In a city as young as South Miami, legends are scarce, but this drugstore (illustrated above) is part of the town's culture. In addition to serving as a pharmacy, there's a candy counter, a card shop, and other gift items. ◆ M-Sa 8AM-9:30PM; Su 9AM-7PM. 5640 Sunset Dr (at Red Rd), South Miami. 667.7577 ♿

3 Fancy's ★★$ This well-priced Italian treat makes carbo-loading fun and delicious. The homemade pasta is especially good. Try the *puttanesca,* made with hot Italian sausage, or the primavera for noodles with crunch. The menu sports nearly a thousand wines. Takeout is available, too. ◆ Italian ◆ Daily lunch and dinner. 7384 SW 56th Ave (at SW 74th St), South Miami. 661.3981 ♿

Bookworks

4 Bookworks This small bookstore isn't part of a chain. The staff is knowledgeable about the store's selections, which are particularly good in fiction and travel. ◆ M-Th until 9:30PM; F-Sa until 10:30PM; Su 11AM-7PM. 6935 Red Rd (at Sunset Dr), South Miami. 661.5080 ♿

4 Crown Wine Merchants A large, modern store with an outstanding selection of fine wines, this shop has a well-informed staff, led by wine authority Chip Cassidy. ♦ M-Sa until 8PM. 6751 Red Rd (at San Ignacio Ave), South Miami. 669.0225 &

4 Cafe Kolibri ★★$$ If you're trying to eat healthy, try an organic carrot-beet juice with a soya burger. Or maybe you're in the mood for oven-roasted game hen or duck *capriccio* (roasted to a golden crisp). This trendy newcomer to the South Miami scene draws crowds with unusual menu offerings, rich desserts, an international assortment of beers and wines, and a deli take-out section. ♦ Continental ♦ Daily breakfast, lunch, and dinner. 6901 Red Rd (at San Remo Ave), South Miami. 665.2421 &

5 Bakery Centre Now considered a white elephant, this building replaced the **Holsum Bakery,** which dated to 1926. It was renovated in 1986 as a shopping mall, but the design rendered the retail and commercial areas unworkable. Ever since, there has been discussion about a complete overhaul. In the meantime, the major draws are the AMC multiplex movie theater and a fine children's museum. ♦ 5701 Sunset Dr (at Red Rd), South Miami &

Within Bakery Centre:

Miami Youth Museum Exhibits here change every few months and generally involve participatory viewing, suitable for children of all ages. The museum rents *Ed-U-Kits,* hands-on materials teaching children about art, the environment, and Florida history. Prearranged tours (some outside regular hours) are available. At press time, the museum was planning a move to Kendall Drive (at Florida's Turnpike). ♦ Admission. Daily 10AM-5PM. 661.3046 &

El Manara ★★$$ Nothing about the decor in this cozy restaurant speaks of the Middle East, and a diner may wonder if there's anything authentic here. Rest assured, the hummus, *baba ganooj* (an eggplant dish), stuffed vine leaves, and lamb kabobs are right out of the original Bible belt. On Saturday night, dinner can be a crowded affair. ♦ Middle Eastern ♦ Daily lunch and dinner. Reservations recommended. 5811 SW 72nd St (between SW 58th Ave and S Dixie Hwy), South Miami. 665.3374 &

Restaurants/Clubs: Red   Hotels: Blue
Shops/ ♦ Outdoors: Green   Sights/Culture: Black

6 A Likely Story A good bookstore is hard to find, but this one specializes in books and toys for children, and does a splendid job of it. The staff knows the stock and understands kids as well. ♦ M-Sa. 5740 Sunset Dr (between SW 57th and SW 58th Aves), South Miami. 667.3730 &

6 CD Solution This musical melting pot, located in a small shopping center, sells more than 10,000 mint-condition used CDs at surprisingly low prices. College students seeking alternative rock, classical music lovers, and country-western truckers jostle for space to see what's new in the bins. If you don't like your purchase, the store will buy it back for $5. ♦ 1590 S Dixie Hwy (at SW 57th Ave), Coral Gables. 662.7100 &

7 Hotel Vila $$ A favorite with Miami's many Brazilian visitors, this new, rather ordinary-looking place is within walking distance of South Miami's retail district and a **Metrorail** station. The 128-room hotel prides itself on its Brazilian cuisine, central courtyard, and multilingual staff. ♦ 5959 SW 71st St (between SW 59th and SW 60th Aves), South Miami. 667.6664 &

7 Mack Cycle One of Miami's premier bicycle stores, it offers mountain and road bikes, as well as accessories. The staff also can tell you all about the best cycling routes through South Dade. Unfortunately, there are no bike rentals available, but visiting cyclists can get biking gear and good advice. ♦ M-Sa, Su 11AM-4PM. 5995 SW 72nd St (between SW 59th and SW 60th Aves), South Miami. 661.8363 &

8 Dorn Buildings Robert and Harold Dorn came to Florida in 1910 to grow mangoes and avocados and ended up erecting this group of buildings at the corner of Sunset Drive and South Dixie Highway. Their Mediterranean Revival style may be unimpressive by today's standards, but these small structures played a big part in South Miami history: 5904 South Dixie was the **South Miami Post Office,** and 5900 Sunset Drive was one of the area's first drugstores. ♦ 5904 S Dixie Hwy and 5900 Sunset Dr (intersection of S Dixie Hwy and Sunset Dr), South Miami ♿

8 Alices Day-Off Located in one of the **Dorn Buildings,** this shop would shock early settlers with its trendy, neon-tinged bikinis. Choose from an extensive selection of swimwear that will encourage everyone to hit the beach. ♦ Daily; M-Sa until 8PM. 5900 Sunset Dr (at S Dixie Hwy), South Miami. 284.0301 ♿

9 Norman Brothers Locals who discover this place never go anywhere else for herbs, lettuce, and other vegetables, much of it brought in fresh daily from nearby Homestead. There's also a good bakery, and the meat counter offers an excellent selection and low prices. ♦ Daily. 7621 SW 87th Ave (between Sunset and Kendall Drs), South Miami. 274.9363 ♿

10 Foremost Sunset Corners One of the best wine shops in South Florida, offering an extensive selection of fine vintages. Manager Mike Bittell's cousin Larry Soloman oversees the spirits end of the business, including an excellent selection of single-malt Scotches and cognacs. A small deli section offers coffees, cheese, and other light fare. ♦ M-W until 9PM; Th-Sa until 9:45PM. 8701 Sunset Dr (at Galloway Rd), South Miami. 271.8492 ♿

11 Thai Orchid ★★$$ Lodged in an unassuming shopping center, this establishment packs in locals looking for moderately spiced Thai food in pleasant surroundings. The atmosphere is enhanced by the orchids on every table—the owner grows them and shares the harvest daily. The owner also paints the flowered plates but leaves the cooking to others who clearly know what they're doing: The food is first-rate. Curries are good, the whole fried fish is excellent, and any of the several duck dishes are delectable. The kitchen spices to your specifications and also offers a macrobiotic menu on request. ♦ Thai ♦ Daily lunch and dinner. 9565 SW 72nd St (between SW 95th and SW 96th Aves), Miami. 279.8583 ♿

12 Shibui ★★$$ The upstairs sushi bar here is marvelous, with several areas for traditional seating on floor mats; there are also tables downstairs. The sushi is the freshest in town, and the cooked dishes—tempura, teriyaki, *katsu* (breaded, fried pork or chicken), sukiyaki—are all on a par with the best in South Florida. Though it's squirreled away in a quiet neighborhood, this restaurant is filled every night. ♦ Japanese ♦ M, W-Su dinner. 10139 SW 72nd St (at SW 102nd Ave), Miami. 274.5578 ♿

13 Wellesley Inn at Kendall $$ This friendly suburban motel with 106 rooms is situated on a small lake near several shopping centers. Children under 18 stay free with their parents. ♦ 11750 Mills Dr (at SW 117th Ave), Kendall. 270.0359, 800/444.8888; fax 270.1334 ♿

14 Punjab Palace ★$$ An immaculate Indian restaurant with a tandoor oven and a chef who knows how to use it. The tandoori chicken is excellent. Other recommended dishes include *rogan josh* (lamb), any of the curries, and the appetizer pastries. ♦ Indian ♦ Daily lunch and dinner. 11780 SW 88th St (at SW 117th Ave), Kendall. 274.1300 ♿

15 Dadeland Mall One of the first regional malls in South Dade, it still makes a big impact in the marketplace with such heavy-duty anchors as **Burdines, Lord & Taylor,** and **Saks.** Along Kendall Drive, it's designed in the "mall sprawl" system and, following recent enlargements, can be very exhausting to navigate. There are more than 200 stores in the center. Among them, don't miss **Arango,** a hot spot for what's new in decorative arts, home furnishings, and useful design. Judith Arango is a highly regarded design authority whose store windows alone are reason enough to brave mall crowds. ♦ Daily. 7535 SW 88th St (between S Dixie Hwy and Palmetto Expwy), Miami. 665.6226 ♿

16 Siam Lotus Room ★★$$ The atmosphere is dark and romantic, but it's the excellent Thai food that keeps this restaurant busy. The whole fried snapper is terrific, especially with a white-hot chili sauce. *Phad thai,* the national noodle dish, is another winner. ♦ Thai ♦ Daily lunch and dinner. 6388 S Dixie Hwy (at SW 62nd Ave), Miami. 666.8134 ♿

Lychees, carambolas, and the "monstera," an edible philodendron, are among the 500 varieties of exotic fruit, herbs, spices, and nuts found at the Fruit & Spice Park.

Barnes & Noble
Booksellers • Since 1873

17 Barnes & Noble Bookstore It's 10PM on a Saturday night and you don't want another video. Instead, you head for this bookstore (formerly **Bookstop**) in the **Greenery Mall,** to pick up an insightful guide to the film industry. Or maybe you just want the latest romance or science fiction novel. Early birds and night owls flock to the giant store, which includes a coffee bar and a full schedule of literary events for kids and grownups. ♦ Daily until 11PM. 7710 SW 88th St/Kendall Dr (at SW 77th Ave), Kendall. 598.7292. ♿ Also at: 18711 Biscayne Blvd (at NW 187 St). 935.9770

18 Marriott-Dadeland $$ Although impersonal from the outside, this hotel is well located; nearby is **Dadeland Mall** and adjacent neighborhood office complexes. Its 302 rooms are good size and well furnished. There's also a small health club and pool in the hotel. Free transportation to and from the airport is available. ♦ 9090 S Dadeland Blvd (between Kendall Dr and S Dixie Hwy), Miami. 663.1035; fax 666.7124 ♿

18 Shorty's Bar-B-Q ★$ Long ago, when Miami was still a southern town, this was the best barbecue joint in town. Today most barbecue places have given way to Cuban *cafeterías,* but this eatery still gets top marks for good food and quick service. The dining area is like a barn with picnic tables. You may have to share table space, but in an atmosphere this friendly, it seems perfectly natural. Barbecued pork and chicken are tops, the beans are heavenly, and the slightly sweet secret barbecue sauce is for sale at the cash register. ♦ Barbecue ♦ Daily lunch and dinner. 9200 S Dixie Hwy (at Dadeland Blvd), Miami. 665.5732 ♿

BORDERS
B O O K   S H O P°

18 Borders Book Shop This national chain opened its southernmost store across from the **Dadeland South Metrorail** station in 1994. Within days, it was filled with children, poetry lovers, fiction enthusiasts, and just about everyone else who loves books. The mammoth store sells newspapers and magazines, and

has a popular espresso bar with pastries. It's also become a social center, with folk music, author appearances, children's book corners, and even a chess club. ♦ M-Sa until 11PM; Su 11AM-8PM. 9205 S Dixie Hwy (at SW 72nd Ave), Kendall. 665.8800 ♿

19 Captain's Tavern ★★$$ For two decades, this restaurant has amazed locals with its combination of fresh seafood and an astonishing wine list that includes some of the world's greatest reds at bargain prices. Red wine with fish is a favorite of Bill Bowers, who captains this restaurant with passionate eccentricity. The menu ranges from steamed mussels to swordfish and such favorites as grilled fresh tuna and salmon. The crowd is largest on Tuesday, lobster night, though Bowers turns away from 100 to 150 people Friday and Saturday nights as well. ♦ Seafood ♦ Daily lunch and dinner. 9621 S Dixie Hwy (at SW 96th St), Miami. 666.5979 ♿

20 Matheson Hammock Park Named after the pioneering Matheson family (which once owned Key Biscayne), this was the first public beach in Dade County. The land was donated to the city by William Matheson in 1930, and his initial grant of 84 acres has been increased to 520 acres of prime beachfront and hammock. The park, including trails in the wooded area, was extensively developed under the Roosevelt administration's Economic Recovery Act. In 1936 the Civilian Conservation Corps developed the area further. Although damaged in several hurricanes (most recently by Andrew), it continues to be one of South Florida's environmental and recreational treasures. ♦ Admission for cars and boats. 9610 Old Cutler Rd (between SW 93rd and SW 101st Sts), Miami. 666.6979

FAIRCHILD
TROPICAL
GARDEN

20 Fairchild Tropical Garden Within 83 acres, these extraordinary gardens contain more tropical plants than any other garden in the mainland US. The founder, well-known horticulturist Dr. David Fairchild, worked closely with landscape architect William Lyman Phillips in 1937 to design a facility that was attractive to visitors and useful to scientists. In addition to the miles of paths, the garden includes a nursery and research center. Much of the lushness was stripped away during Hurricane Andrew, but a massive volunteer effort performed triage on the garden immediately after the storm, and plants are growing back beautifully. ♦ Nominal admission. 10901 Old Cutler Rd (between SW 93rd and SW 101st Sts), Miami. 667.1651

21 Parrot Jungle and Gardens

This surprisingly exciting park is designed to look like a jungle. The Flamingo Lake is familiar to anyone who watched the opening scenes of "Miami Vice," but visitors come primarily for the exotic flora and hundreds of parrots, toucans, macaws, and other birds from around the world. The cactus garden is particularly interesting, and other types of unusual vegetation are well labeled. The parrot shows, given several times daily and featuring the birds riding bicycles on a tightrope, are a must-see attraction. Most of the birds are allowed to fly freely in and out of the 29-acre park; they remain voluntarily, as they have since the preserve was established by Francis Scheer in 1936. ◆ Admission. Daily. 11000 SW 57th Ave (at SW 112th St), Miami. 666.7834

22 Charles Deering Estate

This 350-acre public estate remains closed indefinitely because it suffered extensive damage during Hurricane Andrew. Charles Deering was the brother of James Deering, who created **Villa Vizcaya**. Both men built expansive homes on Biscayne Bay, but in very different styles. Where **Vizcaya** is all Venetian elegance, this estate reflects its South Florida location. ◆ 16701 SW 72nd Ave (between SW 152nd and SW 168th Sts), Miami. 235.1668 ⓑ

23 Quality Inn South

$ The 100 rooms at this simple but neat motel are among the best lodging values in South Dade. The rates vary seasonally but are always reasonable. A few units have kitchens, and there's a heated pool. ◆ 14501 S Dixie Hwy (at SW 144th St), Miami. 251.2000, 800/221.2222 ⓑ

24 The Falls

Looking like a cross between a Hawaiian film set and a Caribbean restaurant, this tropical mall is made up of stores that open onto a central area with cascading fountains, a huge pond, rough-hewn wood, and hanging plants. **Bloomingdale's** is the anchor, and there's a sprinkling of upscale chain stores such as **Banana Republic, Victoria's Secret, Polo,** and **Ann Taylor.** A large movie theater complex is located here as well. ◆ Daily. 8888 SW 136th St (at S Dixie Hwy), Miami. 255.4570 ⓑ

25 Metrozoo

Considered among the finest zoos in the country, this sprawling 300 acre park boasts a natural habitat allowing over 260 species of birds, reptiles, and mammals to roam freely on land surrounded by moats. Hard hit after Hurricane Andrew in 1992, nearly 85 percent of the exhibits are now open to the public including its famous aviary, the Asian elephant and koala displays. Also available are guided tram tours, a children's petting zoo, and daily shows at the **Amphitheater** and the **Ecology Theater**. ◆ Admission. Daily. 12400 SW 152nd St (at SW 124th Ave), Miami. 251.0400

26 Gold Coast Railroad Museum

A passionate endeavor by a group of South Florida rail enthusiasts, this outdoor museum includes not only memorabilia but several restored railcars. Among them is a domed observation car built in 1949 and the *Ferdinand Magellan,* the only Pullman car constructed expressly for US presidents. It was used by Franklin Roosevelt, Truman, Eisenhower, and Reagan. Still under reconstruction after Hurricane Andrew, the museum and its train rides are open only on weekends. ◆ Admission. Sa-Su 11AM-4PM. 12450 SW 152nd St (at SW 124th Ave), Miami. 253.0063 ⓑ

27 Weeks Air Museum

In its infancy, Miami was a major aviation hub, and **Tamiami Airport** was a bustling center. Today, the airport is used primarily for private air-craft, but one hangar is devoted to a fond recollection of its history, with more than 30 aircraft on display. Champion acrobatic pilot Kermit Weeks opened the museum in 1987. ◆ Admission. Daily. 14710 SW 128th St (at Tamiami Airport), Miami. 233.5197 ⓑ

28 Cauley Square

A cluster of wooden buildings was built here in the early 1900s for workers on the Key West rail line. A splendid pocket of South Florida pioneer architecture, they were lovingly restored to house antique shops, ceramic studios, a confectionery, and a general store. Unfortunately, Hurricane Andrew ripped the buildings apart. Business owners hope to rebuild, but only a handful of shops are open, including the **Christmas Store.** ◆ 22400 S Dixie Hwy (at SW 224th St), Goulds. 258.3543 ⓑ

29 Lee's Bakery

If you're looking for the best Key lime pie in Miami, you'll find it here. Inside the wooden display case at Bert Wexelbaum's tiny 1950s-era shop sit dozens of pies topped with toasted swirls of meringue. Each morning Bert, a local character in his own right, picks up

65

a load of pies cooked according to his special secret recipe at a local bakery, and then opens his shop. Both full and half pies are available. When the 80 or so pies are gone, he closes the door and goes home, so it's best to stop in before noon. ♦ Tu-Su 10AM-4PM. 23135 S Dixie Hwy (at SW 232 St), Goulds. No phone ₺

30 Monkey Jungle The trainers and exhibits here provide an eye-opening experience for everyone who grew up thinking Tarzan's sidekick Cheetah would make a cuddly pet. The park's claim that it is "the place where humans are caged and monkeys run wild" is only slightly exaggerated—fences had to be installed around the 20-acre park to keep the simian inhabitants from devouring nearby farm produce. Guides introduce the numerous types of monkeys in residence, and visitors have many opportunities to see the animals in a natural setting. ♦ Admission. Daily. 14805 SW 216th St (at SW 147th Ave), Miami. 235.1611

31 Knaus Berry Farm The outer reaches of Homestead, called "The Redland" after the area's rich, red soil, are an unlikely location for a bakery, but city dwellers beat a path to this small and unusual operation, run by a family of German Baptists. Its pecan rolls and fruit pies are treasured commodities on Miami tables. Also produced here are luscious breads, wonderful fruit milk shakes, and an extraordinarily intense strawberry jam. ♦ M-Sa December-April. 15980 SW 248th St (between SW 157th and SW 167th Aves), Homestead. 247.0668 ₺

SOUTH MIAMI

For nos. 1-32, see pg. 60

FRUIT & SPICE PARK

32 Fruit & Spice Park Even in tropical Miami, this is an exotic attraction: a 20-acre park established in 1944 to showcase the range of tropical fruits and vegetables that can be grown in South Florida. About half of the trees were lost to Hurricane Andrew, but visitors can still see a variety of fruits, vegetables, and nuts, including many kinds of bananas. The now ubiquitous carambola (star fruit) was developed here, along with many other fruits. Guided tours may be arranged by calling a week in advance. The park's shop sells books, exotic seeds, and canned fruit and vegetables. ♦ Free. Daily. No credit cards. 24801 SW 187th Ave (at SW 248th St), Homestead. 247.5727

33 Coral Castle of Florida Latvian immigrant Edward Leedskalnin built this oddity between 1920 and 1940, and to this day no one knows how he did it. With a self-devised system of pulleys and ropes, he single-handedly constructed a three-acre castle with a nine-ton gate, all out of native coral rock. He also built a coral rock telescope that remains fixed on the North Star. Legend has it that he built the castle as a memorial to a woman who spurned his love. ♦ Admission. Daily. 28655 S Dixie Hwy (between SW 288th St and Newton Rd), Homestead. 248.6344 ♿

34 Tiffany's ★$ Reflecting the area's country hours, this eatery is open only for breakfast and lunch. The elaborate breakfast menu includes eggs Benedict; omelettes with cheese, mushrooms, and artichokes; and corn bread. Lunch is simpler, with club sandwiches, burgers, and a range of salads. The establishment is notable for its fresh ingredients and cheerful atmosphere. ♦ American ♦ Daily breakfast and lunch. 22 NE 15th St/King's Hwy (at Krome Ave), Homestead. 246.0022 ♿

35 Chez Jean-Claude ★$$ This charming house-turned-restaurant brings European flair to Homestead's predominantly American dining scene with dishes such as Alsatian roast duck with red cabbage, shrimp with garlic and shallots, snapper with fresh herbs, and Provençal lamb stew. The audience seems to love it. ♦ French ♦ Tu-Su dinner. 1235 N Krome Ave (at NW 12th St), Homestead. 248.4671 ♿

36 Florida Pioneer Museum This small but informative museum is a good place to learn something of Florida's past. It exhibits artifacts from the pioneer days of the early 1900s as well as Indian objects and other memorabilia, including a railroad caboose. ♦ Admission. Daily October-May; M-Sa, Su afternoon June-September. 826 N Krome Ave (at NW Eighth St), Homestead. 246.9531 ♿

37 Cooper's ★★$ Cay and Jean Cooper's country restaurant is right on the corner of one of Homestead's busiest intersections, making it a favorite stop for both locals and visitors. Try a deli sandwich for lunch, fried catfish for dinner, or a slice of homemade pie anytime. ♦ American ♦ Daily breakfast, lunch, and dinner. 1090 N Homestead Blvd (at SW 308th St), Homestead. 242.8740 ♿

38 Howard Johnson Lodge $ This motor lodge was nicknamed "Hojo Hospital" in the aftermath of 1992's Hurricane Andrew, when it served as a sort of M★A★S★H unit for disaster relief officials. Today the remodeled 50-room hotel welcomes tourists. The location is convenient to the Keys and South Dade retail areas, and there's a restaurant—not a **Howard Johnson's**—on site. ♦ 1020 N Homestead Blvd (at S Dixie Hwy), Homestead. 248.2121 ♿

Five Things You'll Wish You Had Packed

1 A raincoat. **South Florida** gets more than 3,000 hours of sunshine a year, but when it rains, it pours—40 to 65 inches of rain a year, most of it in summertime.

2 A sweater. Sure it's hot, but air-conditioning in hotels and many restaurants is sometimes over-efficient.

3 A Spanish-English dictionary—especially handy in **Miami**.

4 A hat. Even with sunscreen, it's wise to shade the face, head, and neck.

5 A second swimsuit. Who likes putting on a damp bathing suit?

39 Super 8 Motel $ Located only a few blocks off high-density South Dixie Highway, this clean and (for the genre) spacious 52-room motel is a world apart. It's quiet and close to several decent restaurants. There's also a park across the street. ♦ 1202 N Krome Ave (at NW 12th St), Florida City. 245.0311 &

40 Capri Restaurant $ Seems like everything but the kitchen sink is served at this popular restaurant. Caesar salad, lasagna, steaks, and stuffed peppers are among the items on the menu. ♦ Italian/American ♦ M-Sa lunch and dinner. 935 Krome Ave (at Lucy St), Florida City. 247.1542 &

41 Robert Is Here Don't miss the Key lime milk shakes or the farm-fresh strawberry shakes at this open-air market, which also stocks mango, carambola (star fruit), and other exotic fruits and vegetables straight from Florida farmlands. Your winter tomatoes likely come from this fertile region or a hundred miles north in Palm Beach County. ♦ Daily until 7PM. 19200 SW 344th St (at SW 192nd Ave), Florida City. 246.1592 &

42 Farmers' Market Restaurant $ Inside the farmers' market for this fertile region, this restaurant serves a basket of fries and coleslaw along with the daily special. Fare includes fish sandwiches, submarine sandwiches, and steaks. ♦ American ♦ Daily breakfast and lunch; M-Sa dinner. 300 N Krome Ave (at Palm Dr), Florida City. 242.0008 &

43 Comfort Inn $ This is a pleasant, strategically located place to sleep before striking out for **Everglades National Park** to the west, the pricey Florida Keys to the south, or **Biscayne National Park** to the east. The 65 rooms fill up quickly in winter, so reserve early. Free continental breakfast is included. ♦ 333 SE First Ave (S Dixie Hwy/Hwy 1, .5 miles south of the terminus of Florida's Turnpike), Florida City. 248.4009, 800/221.2222 &

Agriculture is Dade County's second largest industry. About 1,650 farms and nurseries produce winter vegetables, ornamental plants, limes, and other tropical fruit.

44 Hurricane Andrew Motor Inn $ This rebuilt 160-room hotel (formerly the **Park Royal Inn**) resembles the chain hotels along Highway 1 in Florida City—except for its tacky moniker. Naming a hotel after the region's worst natural disaster may show incredibly bad taste, but the place gets noticed. Visitors headed for the Keys regularly pull over just to take photos of the big sign, and tell their friends back home another story about wacky South Florida. ♦ 100 Hwy 1 (south of SW 344 St), Florida City. 247.3200, 800/521.6004 &

44 Hampton Inn $ Your stay in tiny Florida City probably will be your cheapest night's sleep before heading into **Everglades National Park** or the Florida Keys, unless you plan to camp. This inn has 122 rooms, cable TV, and movies. ♦ 124 E Palm Dr (at Hwy 1, .5 miles south of Florida's Turnpike terminus), Florida City. 247.8833, 800/426.7866 &

45 Florida Keys Factory Shops Before saying goodbye to the Miami area on your way to the Keys, here is one last opportunity to go shopping. This discount center, which opened in 1994, sells off-price clothing, shoes, sporting goods, books, and perfume. Unlike many outlet malls, it is nicely landscaped, with a food court and play area for the kids. ♦ M-Sa until 9PM; Su 11AM-6PM. 250 SW 344th St/E Palm Dr (at Hwy 1), Florida City. 248.4727 &

Restaurants/Clubs: Red   **Hotels:** Blue
Shops/ ♣ Outdoors: Green   **Sights/Culture:** Black

46 Biscayne National Park Though it remains easily accessible by land, this park is unusual in that 95 percent of it is underwater. Stretching from Key Biscayne to Key Largo, it consists of 181,000 acres of prime marine habitat, including the beginnings of the long coral reef that flanks the Florida Keys for 200 miles. This is where Spanish explorers and pirates sailed—and sank. Many of the land areas bordering the park are covered with mangrove trees, which provide important nutrients to marine life. Because they form dense thickets with high roots and tangled branches, mangroves give shelter to many waterfowl, including pelicans, herons, ibis, and other wading birds.

Underwater, the park is a treasure trove for divers and snorkelers. Explore the intricate mangrove channels, colorful coral reefs, and shipwrecks. For those less inclined to submerge themselves, the beauties of the park are accessible

through glass-bottom–boat tours (reservations required; call **Biscayne Aqua Center,** 247.2400). Camping is permitted on Elliot Key and Boca Chita Key, with access by boat only.

The route into the park is well marked, and just outside park headquarters is a **Visitors' Center** with audiovisual presentations about the park as well as recreational opportunities in the surrounding area. ◆ SW 328th St (N Canal Dr at Biscayne Bay), Homestead. 247.7275

46 Homestead Sports Complex This new 6,500-seat baseball stadium was built to attract a major league team for spring training, but so far there have been no takers. With six diamonds, the complex does, however, offer a year-round schedule of children's baseball programs, training camps, and semi-pro games. ◆ 1601 SE 28th Ave (south of SW 312th St), Homestead. 246.8721 &

46 Homestead Motorsports Complex Next door to the baseball stadium, the city of Homestead is erecting a 60,000-seat auto racing track. Ralph Sanchez, the man behind the **Miami Grand Prix,** plans to bring that world-famous race to Homestead sometime in the late 1990s. In the meantime, this 1.5-mile oval track was scheduled to play host to NASCAR stock car drivers as we went to press. ◆ 1707 SE 43rd Ave/SW 152nd Ave (north of SW 336th St), Homestead. 379.5660 &

Bests

Tony Goldman
Owner, The Goldman Properties Company

If you arrive in **Miami** during the daytime, go directly to **South Beach** and breathe the fresh air. If you arrive at night, go directly to South Beach and breathe the fresh air. Enter **Miami Beach** by **Route 395,** the **MacArthur Causeway;** you'll pass the cruise ships on your right, and the Miami skyline will be behind you.

Stay at one of the small, authentic Art Deco hotels on **Ocean Drive:** the **Imperial, Colony, Century, Cavalier, Waldorf, Avalon,** or, best of all, the **Park Central.** While at the Park Central try **Barocco Beach** for the best pasta in Miami. The stone crab at **Joe's Stone Crab Restaurant** is an absolute must. Order the fried chicken and mashed potatoes at **Lulu's. Mark's Place** in **North Miami Beach** serves the finest and most creative food in Miami and ranks with the top five in the country, in my judgment.

You must people watch and sip a cappuccino at the

News Cafe on Ocean Drive, a few steps away from Gloria Estefan's wonderful **Lario's on the Beach,** a fun and value-packed Cuban-American cafe. Don't miss **Toni's Sushi** and **Maiko.**

For the best five-dollar gourmet pizza in the world, go to the **Riviera Kitchen and Bar** on Ocean Drive. They offer 40 wines by the glass, eight draft beers, and beautiful people, too.

Actually, everybody in South Beach is beautiful. There are fashion photo shoots everywhere you look. Yes, South Beach is also the center of the fashion photography industry on the East Coast.

Wonderful moments: a drink at sunset at the **Rusty Pelican** on Key Biscayne; a candlelight dinner at the **Century** cafe; the experience of the **Rascal House** in Sunny Isles; lunch at the tucked away **S&S Diner,** an original Art Deco diner with original German counter waitresses—uniforms, accents, and all; and **The Spot** and **Rebar** for *hot* late-night dance bars.

The Busby Berkeley pool at the **Raleigh Hotel,** and the postage-stamp-size pool at the **Park Central Hotel.**

South Beach/ Mid–Miami Beach

South Beach ("SoBe") is Miami's Soho, the American Riviera, an international tourist destination, and the city's favorite playground all rolled into one. It's packed with trendy restaurants, nightclubs, funky shops, and artists' studios. The area has also become a stomping ground for the international fashion, media, and entertainment crowd, which hangs out at restaurants like **Bang**, overseen by culinary star Robbin Haas, and beautiful historic hotels like the **Raleigh** and the **Marlin.**

All this activity is set against the candy-colored background of the historic **Art Deco District** (see sidebar), a square mile encompassing more than 800 buildings that reflect the Art Deco architecture of the 1930s as well as the Mediterranean Revival style. Most of the structures are within a few hundred yards of the beach, and the brilliant azure sky makes the white exteriors with their pink, aqua, and green trim seem to shimmer in the bright sun.

On the fringe of the Art Deco District, the atmosphere is more institutional: The area's only accredited museum, the **Bass Museum of Art,** sits cheek by jowl with two concert halls and a mammoth convention center. Farther north, out of the historic district, Deco charm gives way to luxury. The broad, sandy stretch of Mid–Miami Beach (also known as **Mid-Beach**) harbors some of the most famous hotels in the state, such as the **Fontainebleau Hilton Resort and Spa** and the **Doral Ocean Beach Resort.**

Most of Miami Beach's interesting sights and activities can be found along its north-south axis, with a few important cross streets tying everything together. In South Beach, much of the action is concentrated right on the water along **Ocean Drive,** and **Washington Avenue** has become the center of commerce and restaurants. When you reach Mid–Miami Beach, Ocean Drive disappears and **Collins Avenue** takes over as the main thoroughfare for hotels, but restaurants are few and far between. Not coincidentally, the three busiest cross streets are tied to the three causeways linking the beach to the mainland across **Biscayne Bay,** beginning with the **MacArthur Causeway** (which becomes **Fifth St** at the southern end of the island). In the middle, the picturesque **Venetian Causeway** (there's a toll here) merges with **17th Street** and **Lincoln Road Mall** and, at the northern boundary of Mid-Beach, is the **Julia Tuttle Causeway** (which becomes **Arthur Godfrey Rd** at 41st St). The best way to explore SoBe is on foot, though parking is exceedingly difficult and, when found, expensive. But if you don't splurge for valet parking, you may end up with a ticket from the beach's eagle-eyed parking-enforcement bureau.

Area code 305 unless otherwise indicated.

1 South Pointe Park Miami Beach is an island that begins at this small but convivial park. Its **Sunshine Pier** is the best place to watch the action in and around the **Port of Miami,** the busiest cruise port in the world and one of the most active deep-water container ports in the country. Most ships arrive and depart on Friday and Sunday. Concerts are occasionally given in the park's band shell. ◆ Daily dawn to dusk. 1 Washington Ave (at Biscayne St)

2 Joe's Stone Crab Restaurant ★$$ South Beach's most famous restaurant is not its best, but for stone crabs—one of the area's unique treats—it's tops. Joe Weiss opened a sandwich shop on the beach in

1913, but it was another 10 years before he served stone crabs, a crustacean whose thick, porcelainlike claws contain meat that is sweeter than lobster. Today, the restaurant, still owned by the Weiss family, has its own crabbing fleet to guarantee a good supply of claws (when stone crabs are out of season— late May to late September—the place is closed). Other restaurants tout their stone crabs, but none can compare. The garlic creamed spinach and hash browns are also legendary, and the Key lime pie is a beach benchmark. Most of the other menu items, however, are run-of-the-mill.

Nearly as famous as the stone crabs is the wait for a table here—no reservations are accepted, and the method of *persuading* the

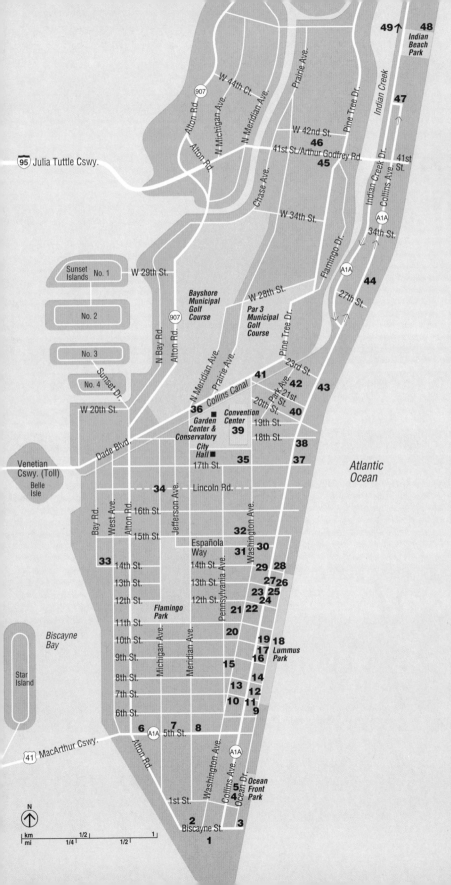

maître d' to speed things up is a mystery to all but insiders. If you don't have time to wait, go early or try lunch: It's the same menu and just as good. They'll also prepare a tasty take-out order, ideal for a picnic on the beach. Valet parking is available. ◆ Seafood ◆ Daily dinner; Tu-Sa lunch; closed late May to October. 227 Biscayne St (between Washington Ave and Alton Rd). 673.0365 &

3 Penrod's Beach Club $$ Mostly for the younger set, this restaurant has a bar, cafe, swimming pool, and private beach with volleyball and other sports. The fare is simple but adequate for a day at the beach; the grill stays open with louder music until the wee hours. American ◆ Daily lunch and dinner; M-Th until midnight; F-Su until 2:30AM. 1 Ocean Dr (at Biscayne St). 538.1111 &

4 Century ★★★$$ The elegant and airy indoor/outdoor design of this restaurant, on the quiet southern end of Ocean Drive, is as good a reason to stop in as the food. Try grilled tuna with purple anise sauce, or steamed clams with lemongrass and green curry. The Sunday brunch is wonderful. ◆ American ◆ M-Sa breakfast, lunch, and dinner; Su brunch and dinner. Reservations recommended. 140 Ocean Dr (between First and Second Sts). 674.8855 &

Miami Beach was a deserted barrier island until the 1880s, when Henry Lum started a coconut farm here (his business eventually went broke). Other visionaries followed, including John Collins, an investor in Henry Flagler's railroad, but the island developed slowly because of its isolation. Collins found a better farming site than Lum's and, at age 70, began growing avocados. Interest in Miami Beach continued to grow as entrepreneurs from Miami, across Biscayne Bay, kept an eye on Collins's and other successful developments. A ferry service was eventually set up, canals were dug, and parts of the bay were dredged. In 1921 Collins built a bridge linking the mainland at downtown Miami to Miami Beach (his financing came from Carl Fisher, who had made a fortune inventing the auto headlight). The span extended for 2.5 miles, making it the longest wooden bridge in the world. Other bridges and causeways followed, and the island now has six links to the mainland.

5 Amnesia This French-owned disco draws huge crowds of Miami night crawlers and trendy Europeans. The big open-air dance floor can be magical, but be prepared for lots of attitude at the door. ◆ Cover. W-Su 11PM-5AM. 136 Collins Ave (at Second St). 531.5535 &

6 Coco Bongo This high-tech club programs disco on Fridays, and Latin music with some of the biggest names in salsa and merengue on Saturdays, pulling in a young, good-looking, and hard-dancing Latino crowd. ◆ Cover. Th, Sa 10PM-4:30AM. 1045 Fifth St (at Lenox Ave). 534.4999 &

7 Tap Tap ★★$ Named for Haiti's colorful buses (there's one parked in the alley outside), this lively and charming restaurant is a gathering place for Miami's Haitian community. Haitian artists painted the incredibly detailed, brilliantly colored wall murals, Haitian musicians play every weekend, and there are shows of Haitian art. The food is generic Caribbean but good. Try a Barbancourt rum at the bar. ◆ Haitian ◆ Daily lunch and dinner. 819 Fifth St (between Jefferson and Meridian Aves). 672.2898 &

8 Cycles on the Beach One of the best ways to tour the Art Deco District is by bike. There are wheels here for toddlers (comfy trikes), seniors (larger three-wheelers), and everyone in between. For visitors, the shop offers hotel pick-up and drop-off service. There's also a good selection of hand-painted T-shirts and biking paraphernalia. ◆ Daily until 7PM. 713 Fifth St (between Meridian and Euclid Aves). 673.2055 &

9 Park Central Hotel $$ New York entrepreneur Tony Goldman refurbished this Art Deco beauty, built in 1937 by **Henry Hohauser.** Deco historians admire its size (seven stories) and details (a fluted eave and octagonal windows). The 75 rooms are neat and well appointed. At various times, Goldman has tried to turn the lobby into an art exhibition space, a wine bar, and a casual jazz lounge, but none of these efforts has tempered its basic coldness. There are two restaurants, and valet parking is available. ♦ 640 Ocean Dr (between Sixth and Seventh Sts). 538.1611, 800/727.5236; fax 534.7520 &

9 Casablanca ★$$ This tiny place has less room inside than out, on the pleasant porch—a surprisingly serene spot for hectic Ocean Drive. The food ranges from European to Caribbean; try the pizzas, pastas, and delicious desserts. ♦ Eclectic ♦ Daily breakfast, lunch, and dinner. 650 Ocean Dr (at Seventh St). 534.9463

10 Bash The coolest club on a block packed with clubs and bars (among them **Jessie's Dollhouse,** the **Union Bar,** and **Lucy's**), this place has jamming dance music inside and jamming Caribbean/world-beat music on the leafy back patio. Celebrity owners Sean Penn and Mick Hucknall stop by when they're in town. ♦ Cover; free Wednesday and Sunday. W-Su 10PM-5AM. 655 Washington Ave (at Sixth St). 538.2274 &

10 The Strand ★$$ This large, popular restaurant, with a bar to match, draws crowds from every facet of SoBe life. The food is good, solid Americana, Miami-style: meat loaf, black-bean soup, seafood, salads, and sinfully rich desserts that get snatched up by pub crawlers in the late hours. Valet parking is available. ♦ American ♦ Daily dinner until 11:45PM. 671 Washington Ave (between Sixth and Seventh Sts). 532.2340 &

10 WPA ★$ With its great 1930s-style mural and enormous platters of food, this is the place to satisfy those late-night hunger pangs.

The hamburgers and salads are good, but it's the setting that you'll remember. ♦ Eclectic ♦ Daily lunch and dinner; M-Th, Su noon-midnight; F-Sa noon-3AM. 685 Washington Ave (at Seventh St). 534.1684 &

11 Puerto Sagua ★$ A Miami Beach mainstay, this Cuban eatery has been here forever (as have some of the waiters), and it has one of those inimitably humorous murals by the Scull sisters, painters of folk art–style scenes of Cuba. The Cuban food is as good and solid as you'll find anywhere. Try *picadillo* (spicy beef hash), *palomilla steak* (grilled steak with lime and raw onions), or Cuban sandwiches (crusty baguettes with ham and cheese served warm). ♦ Cuban ♦ Daily breakfast, lunch, and dinner. 700 Collins Ave (at Seventh St). 673.1115 &

ΛVΛLON

12 Avalon Hotel $$ Opened in 1941 as the **St. Charles Hotel,** this classic example of the Streamline style of architecture was designed by **Albert Anis,** who also did the 40-room **Majestic Hotel** across Seventh Street. Today, the two hotels are managed by the same firm, featuring a total of 106 small but neat rooms and a restaurant in an excellent, though sometimes noisy, location. ♦ 700 Ocean Dr (at Seventh St). 538.0133 &

12 Beacon $ Built in 1936 by **H.O. Nelson,** this beautifully maintained hotel, with its horizontal lines, Deco stucco relief, and stepped parapet, has the look of living history. The 81 rooms are small, but it's a friendly place, especially popular with European visitors. There is a restaurant on site. ♦ 720 Ocean Dr (at Seventh St). 531.5891 &

12 Booking Table Cafe ★$ Fresh fish is the way to go here. And don't miss the rich desserts and wonderful varieties of coffee. ♦ Cafe ♦ Daily breakfast, lunch, and dinner. 728 Ocean Dr (between Seventh and Eighth Sts). 672.3476 &

12 A/X Fashion designer Giorgio Armani brings his casualwear to SoBe. From T-shirts and shorts to blue jeans and sporty dresses, Armani offers classic and affordable designs. ♦ M-Sa until 9PM; Su 11AM-7PM. 760 Collins Ave (at Eighth St). 531.5900 &

13 Gallery of the Unknown Artists Locals love to hang out at this eclectic gallery, which has constantly changing shows of local artists and occasional special events. ♦ Call for hours. 735 Washington Ave (at Seventh St). 532.2265 &

Restaurants/Clubs: Red	**Hotels:** Blue
Shops/ Outdoors: Green	**Sights/Culture:** Black

13 Rose's Bar & Lounge A favorite on the beach, this place has a great music bar—with live rock, jazz, and blues—and pool tables. ♦ No cover. Daily 5PM-5AM. 754 Washington Ave (at Seventh St). 532.0228 Ꮭ

13 Versace The Italian designer's inimitable and expensive jeans, as well as Miami Beach–inspired shirts, bags, and jewelry, are all featured here. The store anchors a sort of couture corner, which includes designer and other upscale shops (**Stephane Kelian, Magazine, Hola, Betsey Johnson,** and **Hugo Boss**) all gathered around the corner of Eighth and Washington. ♦ M-Sa 11AM-7PM. 755 Washington Ave (at Eighth St). 532.5993 Ꮭ

14 News Cafe ★$ This is the closest thing to a bistro on the beach and one of the best places to watch the fashion models. It's more comfortable indoors, but the sizable clientele usually spills out onto the sidewalk. The menu is simple—soups and sandwiches—but very good. The newsstand is well stocked, a plus if you're dining alone. ♦ American ♦ Daily 24 hours for breakfast, lunch, and dinner. 800 Ocean Dr (at Eighth St). 538.6397 Ꮭ

14 Lario's on the Beach ★$$ For Cuban food cafe-style, this is the place to go. The traditional dishes are all reliable, but the shrimp Creole stands out. Gloria Estefan is an owner of this gorgeous Deco diner. ♦ Cuban ♦ Daily breakfast, lunch, and dinner. 820 Ocean Dr (at Eighth St). 532.9577 Ꮭ

14 Caffe Milano ★★$$ Simple yet elegant, this restaurant serves terrific pasta and abundant salads. Sit indoors—the outdoor seating can be cramped and crowded. ♦ Italian ♦ Daily lunch and dinner. 850 Ocean Dr (at Ninth St). 532.0707 Ꮭ

14 Mango's Tropical Cafe Though they serve food here, the reason to come to this leafy, balconied club is the great live Cuban music by Miguel Cruz's band. Half tropical rumba dance hall, half collegiate cruise bar, it offers a great, sweaty dancing good time. ♦ Cover. Daily noon-from 2AM to 5AM. 900 Ocean Dr (at Ninth St). 673.4422 Ꮭ

FELLINI
R E S T A U R A N T • B A R

15 Fellini ★★$$ This tiny, ornate yet cozy restaurant serves delicious Italian food without attitude. Try salmon carpaccio, crab-filled agnolotti pasta, or beef medallions with porcini mushrooms. ♦ Italian ♦ Daily dinner. 860 Washington Ave (at Eighth St). 532.8984 Ꮭ

15 Thai Toni ★★$$$ The decor is distinct—Deco Thai, with sconce lighting, skirted chairs, and chopsticks. Elegant and traditional Thai food is enhanced by a tropical touch, as in duck with pineapple, beef curry with avocado, and lobster with ginger. ♦ Thai ♦ Daily dinner. Reservations recommended. 890 Washington Ave (at Ninth St). 538.8424 Ꮭ

16 Mermaid Guest House $$ There may be no dining room, and no phones in the rooms of this tiny Caribbean-style rooming house, but its funky, laid-back charm, courtyard garden, and friendly atmosphere bring lots of Europeans and artists to stay in its 10 rooms (a few with kitchenettes). ♦ 909 Collins Ave (at Ninth St). 538.5324; fax 672.6559 Ꮭ

17 Breakwater Hotel $$ Designed by **Anton Skislewiczs,** this quintessential Streamline-style hotel was enhanced by a restoration that added etched windows to the largest porch on Ocean Drive. With 60 rooms, the hotel puts guests right in the middle of South Beach action; it's also home to an excellent restaurant. ♦ 940 Ocean Dr (between Ninth and 10th Sts). 532.1220 Ꮭ

Within the Breakwater Hotel:

Paparazzi ★$$$$ This restaurant is popular for people watching (especially in the outdoor bar), though the food is less impressive than the decor. The pasta is good, and the meat dishes are better than the fish, especially the veal chop with arugula and the osso buco. Another traditional Tuscan dish, cold veal with tuna sauce, is an excellent starter. Valet parking is available. ♦ Italian ♦ Daily lunch and dinner. Reservations recommended. 531.3500 Ꮭ

17 Edison $$$ With five stories and 64 rooms, **Henry Hohauser**'s Mediterranean Revival hotel is one of the largest and most popular on Ocean Drive. The rooms are generally small and simple (oceanfront accommodations are more spacious). Although not visible from the street, a lighted pool links this hotel with the **Breakwater Hotel** next door (see above). There is a restaurant, and the large outdoor patio with a bar is open during the day for guests only. ♦ 960 Ocean Dr (at 10th St). 531.2744 Ꮭ

18 Art Deco Welcome Center/Oceanfront Auditorium Inside the auditorium are the offices of the Miami Design Preservation League (MDPL). Founded in 1976 by Barbara Baer Capitman, a tireless promoter of an Art Deco district, the MDPL blossomed into the country's first Art Deco society and an important educational vehicle. The league sponsors many activities in the Deco District, the best-known of which is the weekly walking tour (it leaves Saturday at 10:30AM from MDPL; fee). It also sponsors a weekly bike tour (departing Sunday at 10:30AM from **Cycles on the Beach,** see above; fee and bike rental charge). The offices include the **Art Deco Welcome Center** (open daily until 10PM; 672.2014), a visitors' aid center with maps and brochures, and a shop specializing in Deco knockoffs, T-shirts, posters, and other fund-raising art. This is a must-stop for anyone visiting South Beach.

Still operating after many years, the auditorium itself is the venue for dances and senior citizen programs. But the young have converted the outdoor dance floor into a roller rink. With music blaring, in-line skaters of all ages come to practice and show off their stunts. Skate rentals are available.

Behind the auditorium, the historic Beach Patrol Station includes such Deco design elements as porthole windows and a ship's railing around the top. Facing Ocean Drive, the huge date and temperature indicators are popular props for photographs.
♦ 1001 Ocean Dr (at 10th St). 673.7739 ♿

19 Clevelander Bar ★$ The outdoor bar at this venerable hangout is still packing them in. The food is okay (sandwiches, salads, and finger food), but most people come here for the lively scene and for live music, ranging from reggae to R&B. On the second floor is the **Clevelander Gym.** ♦ American ♦ Daily breakfast, lunch, and dinner. 1020 Ocean Dr (between 10th and 11th Sts). 531.3485 ♿

20 Wolfsonian Foundation Mitchell Wolfson Jr. purchased this building (originally home to the Washington Storage Company) to house his extensive decorative arts collection and then turned it into a study center for visiting scholars. A small gallery open to the public features a sampling of his collection, which dates from 1885 to 1945. In an extensive renovation, architect **Mark Hampton** preserved many of the building's most interesting features, such as the Spanish-Baroque relief on the outer walls.
♦ Nominal admission. M-F afternoon. 1001 Washington Ave (at 10th St). 531.1001 ♿

20 Park Washington Hotel $ Definitive Deco architect **Henry Hohauser** designed this graceful 30-room hotel. The proprietor, who also owns the nearby **Kenmore Hotel** (see below), has landscaped the entire block, using trees and decorative walls to create a refuge from the noise of Washington Avenue. There's no restaurant on the property. The neighboring **Bel Aire** (with the same owner) rents kitchenette apartments by the week or month. ♦ 1020 Washington Ave (at 10th St). 532.1930; fax 672.6706 ♿

The Rise, Fall, and Rise Again of Art Deco

Although the term "Art Deco" wasn't coined until the 1960s, the style itself was firmly fixed in the wake of the *Paris International Exposition of Decorative Arts* in 1925. That fair fused many styles, which American designers further interpreted by incorporating influences as diverse as Egyptian and Aztec. The American version also strove to be modern and forward-looking.

When a sunbathing craze swept the US in the 1920s, architects and designers added sun motifs to their work; fountains were also popular. By the 1930s, a few whimsical elements had slipped in: Flamingos were etched in window glass, and architects wrapped "racing stripes" around buildings to give an impression of speed and motion. Add to this mix the influx of European immigrants through-out the 1930s, and a fertile design community was firmly rooted.

What is now called the **Art Deco District** (see page 79) was developed mainly after the devastating hurricane of 1926 leveled much of **Miami Beach.** Although the disaster was a tragedy in many respects, it provided an opportunity to rebuild and create a uniform architectural style for this large area. Architects **L. Murray Dixon, Russell T. Pancoast,** and **Henry Hohauser** were among those who reshaped not only Miami

Beach, but American design in general. The style that years later was dubbed "Art Deco" combined classical design features with the dictates of a tropical climate—bands of windows took advantage of natural light, canopies provided shade, and porthole windows reflected the area's reliance on the shipping and cruise industries. In addition, American designers altered the European Art Nouveau style, leaning toward pastels and what they called "gemological" colors: shades of emerald, ruby, and sapphire.

Many of the buildings were taken for granted in later years, and it was only in the 1970s that an Art Deco revival sparked the interest of a new generation. After a long and bitter fight with prodevelopment forces, the Florida Architectural Board of Review designated 20 blocks of **South Beach** the **Miami Beach Architectural Historic District.** That success spurred more interest, eventually allowing locally authorized districts to control development and provide design guidelines. By the 1980s, museum exhibitions, photographic essays, and TV programs celebrating Art Deco had piqued the public's imagination. The media attention in turn attracted the world's leading fashion photographers and models, making Art Deco a popular backdrop to thousands of magazine and catalog spreads.

20 Kenmore Hotel $ Architect **Anton Skislewiczs** is responsible for the sweeping interior neon in the large, graceful lobby here. The 60 rooms are similar to those in its sister property, the **Park Washington Hotel** (see above), and there's a restaurant and a swimming pool. This is a good deal in the heart of the district. ♦ 1050 Washington Ave (at 11th St). 674.1930; fax 534.6591 ♿

20 Lulu's ★$ This small storefront serves big helpings of down-home Southern cooking: The chicken-fried steak, strip steaks, pork chops, and corn and okra fritters are to die for. But it is best known for its second-floor **Elvis Room,** whose every detail pays tribute to "the King." ♦ Southern ♦ Daily lunch and dinner. 1053 Washington Ave (between 10th and 11th Sts). 532.6147 ♿

20 11th Street Diner ★$ Built in 1948 by the Paramount Dining Car Company of Haledon, New Jersey, this Art Deco diner was transported to Wilkes-Barre, Pennsylvania, where it opened that same year. After 44 years in business, it was dismantled and moved to its present SoBe location, where it was restored. The food is good, and the servings are hearty. Save room for dessert. ♦ American ♦ Daily breakfast, lunch, and dinner. 1065 Washington Ave (at 11th St). 534.6373 ♿

21 Old City Hall The nine-story tower of this Mediterranean-style masterpiece designed by **Martin Luther Hampton** is a South Beach landmark. Its compass windows, barrel-tiled roof, and rich detail make the building a Deco-era showplace (see illustration below). ♦ 1130 Washington Ave (between 11th and 12th Sts)

CHRIS MIDDOUR

22 Details Walking along Washington Avenue, you can't help but be lured in by the enticing window display in this small storefront. Inside are objets d'art—furniture and home accessories—imported from around the world, as well as unique clothing. ♦ Daily until 8PM. 1149 Washington Ave (between 11th and 12th Sts). 672.0175 ♿

22 Muffin Man ★$ This tiny eatery offers fresh, nutritious homemade food—salads, sandwiches, and, of course, muffins—plus games, art, photos, magazines, books, and a relaxed atmosphere in which to enjoy them. ♦ Californian ♦ M-Sa breakfast and lunch. 232 12th St (between Washington and Collins Aves). 538.6833 ♿

23 Meet Me in Miami Designer Debbie Ohanian has made her mark with this funky department store. Whether you're looking for the latest SoBe fashions or for retro designs, this is the place to shop. The store also offers a full beauty salon, a wig section, and a small boutique selling sexy lingerie. ♦ M-Th until 10PM; F-Sa until 11PM; Su 2-8PM. 1201 Washington Ave (at 12th St). 538.8780 ♿

23 Findings Mayra Gonzalez showcases innovative local designers in this elegant jewel box of a store that sells women's eveningwear and casualwear, along with vintage clothing. ♦ M-W 1-9PM; Th-Sa 1-11PM. 1218 Washington Ave (between 12th and 13th Sts). 672.9692 ♿

23 Glam Slam With clubs in Minneapolis and Los Angeles, the artist formerly known as Prince opened this sister establishment in a giant 1930s Art Deco movie palace. There's good music and an interesting crowd. Thursdays are "Erotic City," Fridays get funky, and Sunday is reserved for retro disco. The door policy varies. ♦ Cover. Th-Su 10PM to dawn. 1235 Washington Ave (between 12th and 13th Sts). 672.2770 ♿

24 Marlin Hotel $$$ Owned by Chris Blackwell, founder of Island Records, this is SoBe's most popular hotel among celebrities. The 12 suites are elaborately decorated in a mixture of styles, but every aspect—from fixtures to furniture—is artistically designed. The full-scale recording studio in the lobby attracts some of the biggest names in the music industry. Valet parking is available. ♦ 1200 Collins Ave (at 12th St). 673.8770; fax 673.9609 ♿

Within the Marlin Hotel:

Sha Been ★$$ This is the only restaurant in SoBe that serves authentic Jamaican food. The best bets are the spicy jerk chicken and the seafood specials. Also try the mouthwatering conch fritters. If the food isn't enough to draw you in, the decor will. ♦ Jamaican ♦ Daily lunch and dinner. 673.8373 ♿

25 Hotel Leslie $$ This small, classic example of South Beach Art Deco style was recently taken over by Chris Blackwell, owner of Island Records and of the nearby **Marlin Hotel** (see above). Designer Barbara Hulanicki has redone the hotel inside and out in a brilliant mix of tropical colors, and the 44 rooms now feature a variety of decors and extras, such as radio/CD/cassette players. There is a restaurant as well. ♦ 1244 Ocean Dr (at 12th St). 534.2138; fax 531.5543 ♿

26 Cardozo $$ Now owned by singer/ entrepreneur Gloria Estefan, this hotel—one of SoBe's Deco gems—has had a checkered history of renovation. Featured as a set in Frank Sinatra's 1959 film *A Hole in the Head*, it faded badly in the 1960s and 1970s, but was the first to be renovated (by Barbara Capitman's son Andrew) during South Beach's revival in the 1980s. The exterior now features a dizzying color scheme, but the 56 rooms have been beautifully redone. ♦ 1300 Ocean Dr (at 13th St). 535.6500, 800/782.6500; fax 532.3563 ♿

Within the Cardozo:

Allioli Restaurant ★★$$ Visually, this restaurant lives up to the hotel's gorgeous sweeping interior. Its innovative and delectable Euro-Mediterranean food also gets high marks: There's a plentiful assortment of tapas, plus roasted *piquillo* peppers stuffed with *bacalao* (salt cod) mousse, any of several paellas, and almond-and-black-pepper–crusted salmon with ratatouille flan. ♦ Mediterranean/continental ♦ Daily lunch and dinner. 538.0553 ♿

Restaurants/Clubs: Red   Hotels: Blue
Shops/ ♦ Outdoors: Green   **Sights/Culture: Black**

26 Cavalier Hotel $$ Sister establishment to the **Hotel Leslie** (see above), this hotel provides similar comforts and services, but the 46 rooms are decorated in a Jamaican, island style. There is no restaurant. ♦ 1320 Ocean Dr (at 13th St). 531.8800, 800/688.7678; fax 531.5543 ⅊

27 Sushi Rock ★★$$ The sushi here is exquisitely fresh, creative, and varied. All the menus are actual 1960s and 1970s album covers (hence the name). ♦ Japanese ♦ Daily lunch and dinner. 1351 Collins Ave (between 13th and 14th Sts). 532.2133 ⅊

Race Relations

Ethnic and racial tensions have led to some of the ugliest moments in **Miami**'s history, particularly the race riots of the 1980s. The roots of these problems go back many years. After Fidel Castro took power in Cuba in the 1960s, people fled that country and poured into Miami, then a typical Southern city emerging from segregation. The Cubans, many of them professionals who arrived with nothing but the clothes on their backs and didn't speak English, took hotel jobs and other labor-intensive employment, thus displacing African-Americans. Cuban refugees also benefited from federal assistance programs that African-Americans felt should be available to them.

Over the years, Cuban-Americans established businesses, hiring Spanish speakers who continued to emigrate in waves from Cuba (and, later, Central America). The Latins soon dominated, transforming Miami into the vibrant international business center it is today. **Little Havana** paved the way for **Little Managua, Little Haiti,** and other minicities for refugees from all over the Latin and Caribbean world.

Anglos (the Miami term for white non-Hispanics) had long controlled business and government here, but they sat back as tensions mounted. Many Anglos moved in "white flight" to Northern Florida or to other parts of South Florida, such as **Ft. Lauderdale** and **Boca Raton.**

During the 1980s, several black Americans were killed or injured by Hispanic or Anglo cops, who juries subsequently cleared of wrongdoing. These events led to several incidents of rioting and looting in African-American communities. Meanwhile, the newest arrivals, struggling Haitians, though also of African descent, further antagonized black Americans with their separate language, customs, and work ethic.

Civil disturbances, crack cocaine, and the recession of the early 1990s have led to continued economic decay in Miami's black community. Today, African-Americans remain the most economically disadvantaged group in Miami, while thousands of immigrants are making their way here in search of the American Dream.

28 Penguin Hotel $ Along the last stretch of Ocean Drive to be refurbished, this classic 1930s hotel has 44 rooms, including several suites, decorated with Deco period pieces. It's sparkling and quiet, although some guests have complained that the staff isn't always very helpful, and there is no restaurant. ♦ 1418 Ocean Dr (at 14th St). 534.9334 ⅊

29 Club Deuce "The Deuce" (as locals call it) has been hanging in there since long before South Beach became SoBe, and it's still a real neighborhood bar. It may be seedy, but everyone from transvestites, trendies, and yuppies to construction workers drinks here. It has a pool table and a great jukebox, but no food is served. ♦ Free. Daily 8AM-5AM. 222 14th St (between Washington and Collins Aves). 531.6200 ⅊

29 Tattoos by Lou Get yer tattoos here! Models, club kids, and Harley riders come to Lou's, called the best tattoo studio in Miami (it's safe and clean, too). Pick from an enormous number of designs, or bring your own. ♦ M-Sa noon-midnight; Su afternoon. 231 14th St (between Washington and Collins Aves). 532.7300 ⅊

30 Grillfish ★$ A dramatic mural and high ceilings make this a pleasant place to eat simple, reasonably priced, and impeccably fresh seafood. In fact, there's none fresher. ♦ Seafood ♦ Daily dinner. 1444 Collins Ave (at Española Way). 538.9908 ⅊

30 Wings of Steel SoBe wouldn't be complete without a place to purchase or merely gawk at a Harley-Davidson motorcycle. For those who can't afford a Harley, this store offers the accessories to make you look as if you do. ♦ Daily 10AM-midnight Nov-May; M-Th 10AM-10PM, F-Sa 10AM-11PM, Su noon-10PM June-Oct. 280 Española Way (at Washington Ave). 672.4294 ⅊

30 Osteria del Teatro ★★$$$ Housed in a streamlined wing of the old **Cameo Theater,** this place successfully combines traditional Italian ideas with Florida ingredients. Stone crab shows up in pasta dishes, and the fish entrées, especially the mixed grill, are excellent. The desserts—which are more French than Italian—are very good.

♦ Italian ♦ M, W-Su dinner. Reservations recommended. 1443 Washington Ave (at Española Way). 538.7850 ♿

31 Española Way Spanish Village Between Washington and Drexel Avenues, Española Way gives way to this shopping area, with its picture-pretty building fronts and recently refurbished sidewalks and landscaping. Home to small boutiques, clubs, and the **Española Way Artist's Center,** it's one of the beach's busiest nightlife areas. ♦ Española Way (between Washington and Drexel Aves)

31 Clay International Youth Hostel $ With its wrought-iron balconies, this hostel has an Alpine look. There are separate dormitories for men and women, and kitchen facilities are available. ♦ 406 Española Way (at 1438 Washington Ave). 534.2988 ♿

BANG
R E S T A U R A N T

32 Bang ★★★$$$ When it first opened, this restaurant was instantly *the* fashionable place to go, but then the party atmosphere began to affect the food and service. New chef Robbin Haas (called one of the top 10 in America by *Esquire*) has revamped the service and the menu, and his sophisticated dishes are nothing less than exquisite. Try oak-roasted portobello mushrooms with sweet corn polenta, whole snapper with Thai noodles and roasted vegetables, or double-cut pork chop with truffles and peppercorn–red wine sauce. The wine list is the most extensive on South Beach, and the desserts are wonderful. Valet parking is available. ♦ Eclectic ♦ Daily dinner. American Express or cash only. Reservations recommended. 1518 Washington Ave (between 15th and 16th Sts). 531.2361 ♿

33 Starfish ★★★$$$ Local social diva/designer Debbie Ohanian turned **Gatti's,** once a hangout for the likes of Al Capone and Jackie Gleason, into a stylish cream-and-white wedding cake of a restaurant; with a lovely garden where herbs are grown for the kitchen. The food is an eclectic Florida-Caribbean-nouvelle mix. This is also a SoBe nightlife social center; the Saturday drag queen performances are a hoot. ♦ Eclectic ♦ Tu-Su dinner. Reservations recommended. 1427 West Ave (at 14th St). 673.1717 ♿

34 Lincoln Road Mall Lincoln Road was built by developer Carl Fisher, who intended it as the first commercial area in fledgling Miami Beach. He ran it east-west to link the beach and its hotels with the waterfront homes he was selling on Biscayne Bay. One of the area's great visionaries, Fisher staked his claim in a mangrove swamp and dredged sand from the bay's bottom to raise the center of Miami Beach above sea level. He envisioned Lincoln Road, named after Abraham Lincoln, as the Fifth Avenue of the South, expanding the original dirt trail to four paved lanes, building wide sidewalks, and planting royal palms (he removed the coconut palms and their inconvenient tendency to drop fruit on passing customers).

Seeking to redesign the area, the city in 1960 hired architect **Morris Lapidus,** who drastically changed the landscaping and closed the road to motor traffic—which slowed its revitalization. Nevertheless, it has finally blossomed into a busy walkway full of cafes, restaurants, galleries, boutiques, and artists' studios. And the absence of cars gives it a blessedly peaceful atmosphere next to the hustle of Ocean Drive. Recently the city gave the mall another major face-lift, adding trees and lighting. Now it's filled with strollers day and night, particularly during the very popular **Gallery Walk,** held the second Saturday of every month. ♦ Between Alton Rd and Washington Ave

Within Lincoln Road Mall:

Colony Theatre Notable among architects for its zigzag parapet, this was one of five movie theaters on Lincoln Road in its earlier heyday. Now all are either gone or serve other purposes, but this one remains an intimate venue especially popular with dance troupes and chamber music ensembles. ♦ 1040 Lincoln Rd (at Lenox Ave). 674.1026 ♿

Art Deco District

This one-square-mile section of Miami Beach—bounded by Sixth Street, Ocean Drive, 23rd Street, and Lenox Avenue—is the country's youngest officially designated historic district. It encompasses more than 800 buildings that beautifully preserve not only the Art Deco designs of the 1930s but many related styles, including Mediterranean Revival. In addition to its architectural elements, one of the most striking Art Deco aspects preserved on **South Beach** is the brilliant palette of colors.

Although the Art Deco style never disappeared, it did fade for a time, and the historic district today enjoys a renewed emphasis on restoration. Zoning regulations encourage a return to original design features and colors. Visitors can easily see splendid examples of Art Deco not only in residential and commercial facades, but in interior furnishings as well.

Pioneering Miami Beach developer Carl Fisher built the seven-story Van Dyke Building, with Miami's first elevator, in 1924 so prospective buyers could scan potential oceanfront lots with a telescope.

The Frieze ★$ In the South Beach heat, most locals stop here to cool off. The large assortment of homemade ice cream beats every other outlet for miles around. ♦ Ice cream ♦ M-Th; F-Sa until 1AM; Su until midnight. 1626 Michigan Ave (at Lincoln Rd). 538.0207 ♿

Sterling Building Alexander Lewis built this structure in 1928, strongly rooting it in the Mediterranean style. It featured two smaller buildings facing each other across a small courtyard. In 1941 architect **V.H. Nellenbogen** linked the two buildings at the second floor but kept the courtyard open to Lincoln Road. The linked upper half is done in glass block, illuminated at night by blue neon lights. It is now owned by philanthropist Mitchell Wolfson Jr., one of the country's leading collectors of decorative arts (part of his collection is on view at the **Wolfsonian Foundation,** at 1001 Washington Ave), who has carefully restored many of the fine details. During the Deco period, the building housed a Packard dealership; now, it contains a private women's club and several shops. ♦ 927 Lincoln Rd (between Michigan and Jefferson Aves) ♿

Within the Sterling Building:

Books & Books Smaller than the original store in Coral Gables, this branch has the same eclectic collection of books, personal service, and attention to detail. There are frequent poetry readings and literary discussions in the evenings. ♦ M-Th until 9PM; F-Sa until midnight; Su noon-5PM. 532.3222 ♿

Alliance for Media Arts South Beach's only movie theater is a tiny place that shows independent, foreign, and art films. It has a gallery for local artists as well. ♦ 531.8504 ♿

Italian designer Gianni Versace's palatial home on Ocean Drive was built in 1930 as a replica of Christopher Columbus's son's palace, Alcazar de Colón, in Santo Domingo. Originally called Casa Casuarina (House of the Pine, for the Australian pines growing on the site), it was rechristened the Amsterdam Palace in 1935, when George Amsterdam purchased it.

Restaurants/Clubs: Red **Hotels:** Blue
Shops/♟ **Outdoors:** Green **Sights/Culture:** Black

FLOWERS & FLOWERS

Flowers & Flowers This shop provides wonderfully unusual arrangements assembled with loving attention to detail. Specialties include baskets (with everything from chocolates to erotic scents) and a selection of "celebrity" arrangements named after SoBe notables. They deliver. ♦ M-Th until 10PM; F-Sa until midnight; Su 1PM-5PM. 534.1633, 800/274.1633 ♿

34 South Florida Art Center (SFAC) This is an umbrella organization for 85 artists' studios in five buildings on Lincoln Road. The many activities that take place here—monthly gallery walks, tours, events, performances, and classes—are largely responsible for the revitalization of the Lincoln Road area. ♦ Spaces at 1632 Pennsylvania Ave, 1655 Lenox Ave, and 800, 810, 841, and 1035 Lincoln Rd; main offices and gallery at 924 Lincoln Rd (between Michigan and Jefferson Aves). 674.8278 ♿

34 Pacific Time ★★★$$$ Hung with unusual artwork, this big, airy space is a notable addition to Lincoln Road. Chef Jonathan Eismann's Asian–Pacific Rim cuisine is both subtle and original, a blend of Japanese, Chinese, and Thai influences. Highlights of its mostly seafood menu include grilled local offshore dolphin and wok-sautéed yellowfin tuna, but the oven-roasted rack of lamb is excellent, too. ♦ Asian ♦ Daily dinner. Reservations recommended. 915 Lincoln Rd (between Michigan and Jefferson Aves). 534.5979 ♿

34 Miami City Ballet One little-known pleasure on Lincoln Road is standing outside the big glass windows of the ballet's studios and watching this young, vibrant, world-class company rehearse. It performs often throughout South Florida, but you can get a free sneak preview here before buying tickets. ♦ 905 Lincoln Rd (between Michigan and Jefferson Aves). 532.4880 ♿

34 Van Dyke ★★$$ This recently opened counterpart to the very popular **News Cafe** (see above) is the new hot spot for people watching and socializing on Lincoln Road. The cafe-style food is good, and there's a jazz bar on the second floor. The seven-story Mediterranean building in which the restaurant is located was built in 1924 by pioneer Miami Beach developer Carl Fisher, who used to bring prospective property buyers to the top floor to scout their sites. At press time, the upper floors were being converted into luxury loft-style hotel suites. ♦ American ♦ Daily breakfast, lunch, and dinner. 1641 Jefferson Ave (at Lincoln Rd). 534.3600 ♿

34 Gertrudes ★★$ There are more coffees and teas here than you can imagine, from decaf chocolate orange cappuccino to espresso, plus desserts and other cafe fare. It was named one of the top 10 coffee shops in the nation by *Bon Appetit*. You can sit here for hours talking, reading the many magazines and papers, or just watching the world go by. ♦ American ♦ Daily breakfast, lunch, and dinner. 826 Lincoln Rd (between Jefferson and Meridian Aves). 538.6929 ♿

34 World Resources Cafe ★★$ This laid-back, mostly outdoor cafe is a center for Miami's world-beat music and arts scene,

with Haitian, Cuban, and a multitude of other drummers and musicians jamming almost every night by the Lincoln Road fountain, in front of the cafe's sidewalk tables. There also are periodic special events. Inside, the restaurant is decorated with furniture and art objects from around the world—from a canopied Balinese bed to handmade glass beads. The Thai food is fresh and flavorful—try the sweet, strong Thai iced coffee. ♦ Thai ♦ Daily dinner until midnight. 719 Lincoln Rd (between Meridian and Euclid Aves). 534.9095 ♿

34 Lyon Frères ★★$$ Miami Beach's answer to New York's **Dean & Deluca,** this is a combination gourmet deli, cafe, and wine bar, with tables inside and out. It's expensive but worth it. The choices are staggering: There are 15 kinds of sandwiches, plus dozens of other selections, such as chicken curry, smoked whitefish salad, poached salmon salad, hummus, tabbouleh, fennel salad with parmesan cheese, quiche, and more. ♦ Eclectic ♦ Daily breakfast, lunch, and dinner until midnight. 600 Lincoln Rd (at Pennsylvania Ave). 534.0600 ♿

The Rebirth of Swank South Beach

After the 1950s and 1960s, when such stars as Ed Sullivan and Jackie Gleason gave it a swank reputation, **Miami Beach** became the laughingstock of the resort world. By the 1970s, **South Miami Beach** was in decay, its buildings run-down and filled mostly with senior citizens cowering at rising crime. Its tag line was "God's waiting room."

But the Miami Design Preservation League—founded by visionary Barbara Baer Capitman—saw the beauty in those aging buildings. In 1976 the league succeeded in having a square-mile area of South Miami Beach dotted with Art Deco–era buildings placed on the National Registry of Historic Places, making them the first structures from this century to receive such recognition.

It was artist Leonard Horowitz who added color to the district, when he painted the old Deco buildings wonderful candy colors of pink and lemon, turquoise and lavender. Those outrageous colors attracted the producers of the hit 1980s TV series "Miami Vice." The show's popularity gave Miami glamour appeal and created international awareness

of Miami Beach's unique look. The fashion industry (with photographer Bruce Weber and German catalogs notable early examples) started to take advantage of the tropical weather and picturesque locations. Promoter Louis Canales brought in New York personalities and press. In the late 1980s artists and developers, dreamers and hustlers, moved in, opening nightclubs, restaurants, and model agencies, renovating hotels, and staging art events.

Now **South Beach** is a destination for international tourists, the fashion world, the media, and film and music stars. It's packed with fashion models and nightclubbers, trend-setters and wannabes, with what may arguably be the largest percentage of beautiful people in any square mile, anywhere. After appearing in almost every magazine imaginable, South Beach is beginning to suffer a fashion backlash, no longer on the cutting edge. But while it may have already been "discovered," South Beach is still a vibrant neighborhood, a playground for Miami and the world.

34 Lincoln Theatre When it was a movie house, this theater drew enormous crowds for major South Florida premieres. Like many buildings on Lincoln Road, it went through an extended period of disuse. It was renovated in 1989 as home to the **New World Symphony Orchestra,** the country's only national training orchestra. Under the leadership of artistic advisor Michael Tilson Thomas, the orchestra quickly gained wide recognition as an outstanding ensemble. It gives several performances each of nearly a dozen subscription concerts, as well as chamber programs and other recitals that draw on the theater's superb acoustics. ◆ 555 Lincoln Rd (at Pennsylvania Ave). 673.3330, box office 673.3331 ♿

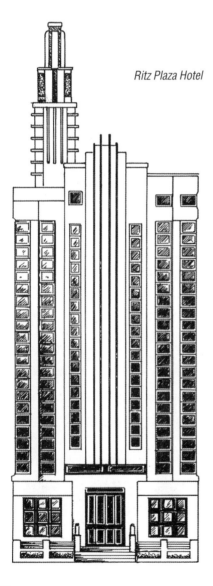

Ritz Plaza Hotel

35 Jackie Gleason Theater of the Performing Arts (TOPA) Cagey publicist Hank Meyer had the idea of drawing attention to Miami Beach by inviting comedian Jackie Gleason to originate his 1960s TV program from the city. Gleason accepted, using this theater as his broadcast site until the show went off the air. The 3,000-seat hall was long considered too large and poorly designed to be an effective facility for many arts events. After an extensive renovation in 1990, however, many producers were surprised to learn otherwise, and today it is a popular venue for touring Broadway shows and concerts by visiting orchestras. In front is a large sculpture by Roy Lichtenstein called *Mermaid.* Valet parking is available. ◆ 1700 Washington Ave (at 17th St). Box office 673.7300 ♿

36 Holocaust Memorial Miami has one of the largest Holocaust survivor populations in the US, and this memorial is its moving and thought-provoking monument to victims of the Holocaust. Conceived in 1984, it took four years to build and was finally dedicated in 1990 by Elie Wiesel. Sculptor Kenneth Treister's giant hand reaching out of a pool symbolizes human pain; a walkway leads past a memorial wall of victims' names. ◆ Free. Daily. Corner of Dade Blvd and Meridian Ave. 538.1663 ♿

37 Ritz Plaza Hotel $$ On the outer fringe of the Art Deco District, this 132-room hotel (pictured at left) has a strong, late-Deco feeling, thanks to the roof's multilevel spire and the rounded corners on projecting walls around the long swimming pool. The rooms were spruced up during an extensive modernization. There is a restaurant on site. ◆ 1701 Collins Ave (between 17th and 18th Sts). 534.3500, 800/522.6400; fax 531.6928 ♿

38 Raleigh Hotel $$ Designed in 1940 by **L. Murray Dixon,** this is a more full-service hotel than most of those on Ocean Drive, and it caters heavily to the New York fashion and media crowd. The elaborate pool, once considered the most beautiful in Florida, has been renovated to its former glory. The 107 rooms feature bedside remote controls, VCRs, fax services, multiple telephones, and elegant modern wrought-iron furnishings. There's a bar and a restaurant, as well as a coffee bar. ◆ 1775 Collins Ave (between 17th and 18th Sts). 534.6300, 800/223.5652; fax 538.8140 ♿

Barbara Baer Capitman (1920-90), the "First Lady of Art Deco," moved to Miami Beach in the 1970s and founded the Miami Design Preservation League, which kicked off the city's architectural restoration crusade.

39 Miami Beach Convention Center Long known as a destination for conventioneers as well as tourists, Miami Beach began to lose ground in the 1970s to newer areas with larger convention facilities. In 1988 this center was reopened with 1.1 million square feet of exhibition space—double its original size. It also gained a striking new facade that has been both criticized and praised as a compendium of Art Deco styles. ♦ 1901 Convention Center Dr (between 17th and 19th Sts and Washington Ave). 673.7311 &

40 Wolfies $$ Contrary to legend, the food at Miami Beach's most famous delicatessen isn't the best in town; it's just memorialized by tradition. But the atmosphere is unpretentious, and no one complains if you linger over the newspaper with a cup of strong coffee or a toasted bagel. ♦ Deli ♦ Daily 24 hours. 2038 Collins Ave (at 21st St). 538.6626 &

41 Governor Park $$ This masterpiece of the Art Deco Streamline style is situated where you'd least expect it—tucked away on a side street off the ocean. **Henry Hohauser**'s hotel (see illustration below) has been restored with great flair to the luster it had when it opened in 1939. Much of the original decor—checkerboard floor tiles, a stainless-steel marquee, and glass panels etched with flamingos and palm trees—remains, serving as a textbook example of Deco style. The 125 rooms are neat and comfortable, there's a restaurant, and the location is grand. ♦ 435 21st St (at Washington Ave). 532.2100, 800/542.0444; fax 532.9139 &

42 Bass Museum of Art Designed in 1930 by **Russell T. Pancoast** as the **Miami Beach Library and Art Center,** this was the first public building in Miami Beach with an exhibition space for fine art. It was the centerpiece of a nine-acre park donated to the city by pioneer John Collins (grandfather of the architect), and its carefully manicured gardens provided a graceful pathway two blocks east to the ocean. The art center opened in 1935 with an exhibition curated by Gustav Bohland, who also sculpted the bas-relief on the building's facade.

Some of the original land was later given over to development, and in 1963 Miami Beach built a larger library in front of the earlier building. At that point philanthropists John and Johanna Bass donated money for renovation and a multimillion-dollar art collection to be housed inside. In addition to the museum's

Governor Park

CHRIS MIDDOUR

permanent collections, touring exhibitions are frequently on view. Of special note are *The Holy Family* by Rubens, a pair of enormous Belgian tapestries, and works by Dürer and Toulouse-Lautrec. ♦ Admission. Tu, Th-Sa; W afternoon until 9PM; Su afternoon. 2121 Park Ave (at 21st St). 673.7530 &

43 Holiday Inn Oceanside Convention Center $$ Although converted not long ago to a **Holiday Inn,** this hotel has been in constant use since the beach was first developed. Originally it had one of the first swimming pools (called the Roman Pools) built on the beach, and it was visible for miles because of its trademark windmill. The 353-room hotel provides basic services, including a restaurant, at reasonable rates, and the oceanfront location remains superb, close to South Beach but away from the hustle and bustle of Ocean Drive. ♦ 2201 Collins Ave (between 22nd and 23rd Sts). 534.1511, 800/HOLIDAY; fax 532.1403 &

44 Seville Beach $$ Smaller than some of the more extravagant beachfront establishments, this hotel offers 322 rooms. It's nothing fancy, but it boasts a good location and a restaurant, and it's popular with families. ♦ 2901 Collins Ave (at 29th St). 532.2511, 800/327.1641; fax 531.6461 &

45 The Forge ★★$$$$ Although famous for its food, this restaurant is best known for one of the country's largest and most fairly priced wine collections. Owner Alvin Malnik is also an ardent collector of Tiffany glass and period furniture, much of which finds its way into his ornate, multichambered restaurant. The food is more interesting than inventive, with the most popular and best dishes concentrating on beef and seafood. The heavily sauced hobo steak, a vanilla duck, and brick-oven–baked tuna are all dependable. The tasty desserts are as rococo as the decor. Valet parking is available. ♦ American ♦ M-Sa dinner. Reservations required. 432 41st St (between Royal Palm and Sheridan Aves). 534.4536 &

Miami Ink

The following is a list of books that will give you a better understanding of this warm and vibrant city and its environs.

Bay of Pigs: The Untold Story by Peter Wyden (1979; Simon & Schuster)

The Big One: Hurricane Andrew by the *Miami Herald* staff and photographers (1992; Andrews and McMeel)

Billion-Dollar Sandbar: A Biography of Miami Beach by Polly Redford (1970; E.P. Dutton)

Castro's Final Hour by Andres Oppenheimer (1992; Simon & Schuster)

Deco Delights by Barbara Baer Capitman and Stephen Brooke (1988; E.P. Dutton)

The Everglades: A River of Grass by Marjory Stoneman Douglas (1990; Pickering Press)

Going to Miami: Exiles, Tourists and Refugees in the New America by David Rieff (1987; Little, Brown and Company)

Guerrilla Prince: The Untold Story of Fidel Castro by Georgie Anne Geyer (1991; Little, Brown and Company)

Hialeah Park by John Crittenden (1989; Pickering Press)

Marjory Stoneman Douglas: Voice of the River by John Rothchild (1987; Pineapple Press)

Miami by Joan Didion (1987; Pocket Books, Simon & Schuster)

Miami, City of the Future by T.D. Allman (1987; Atlantic Monthly Press)

Miami, Hot & Cool by Laura Cerwinske and Stephen Brooke (1990; Clarkson N. Potter)

Miami: The Sophisticated Tropics by Morton Beebe (1991; Chronicle Books)

Miami: The Way We Were by Howard Kleinberg (1989; Surfside Publishing)

Miami, U.S.A. by Helen Muir (1953; second edition, 1990; Pickering Press)

The Rainy Season: Haiti since Duvalier by Amy Wilentz (1989; Simon & Schuster)

46 Arnie and Richie's ★$ Surprisingly, this is one of the very few delicatessens in one of Miami Beach's biggest hotel districts, which is fine, because it's good enough to fill the gap. The brusque service is typical of delis, but the food is fresh and dependable. ♦ Deli ♦ Daily breakfast, lunch, and dinner. 525 41st St (at Royal Palm Ave). 531.7691 ♿

47 Fontainebleau Hilton Resort and Spa $$$$ Built by **Morris Lapidus** during the heyday of Miami Beach's rediscovery as a vacation destination, this grande dame (pronounced foun-tain-*blue*) was the quintessential ocean resort, with sports and spa facilities, children's activities, and an entire shopping arcade in the basement. The beachfront was built to include a heated lagoon, saltwater pool, rock garden, and boardwalk. Since Hilton took over management of the hotel, it is less gaudy—but also a little less fun. The 1,206 rooms, while tidy, fall short of luxurious. There are six restaurants, and valet parking is available. ♦ 4441 Collins Ave (north of 41st St). 538.2000, 800/HILTONS; fax: 534.7821 ♿

At the Fontainebleau Hilton Resort and Spa:

Robert Haas Mural On the southernmost wall of the hotel, artist Robert Haas's mural appears to be a direct view of the ocean. It's Deco trompe l'oeil, though, and a crafty way of preserving some of the street's atmosphere where it takes a jog away from the ocean.

48 Doral Ocean Beach Resort $$$$ A popular spot for conventions, this 422-room hotel will please some with its high-energy pace and discourage others. It only becomes a resort for relaxation when you take the rear exit and head for the large, well-maintained beachfront. There are many family amenities, such as a wading pool and supervised children's activities. Valet parking is available. ♦ 4833 Collins Ave (at 48th St). 532.3600, 800/327.6334; fax 534.7409 ♿

Within the Doral Ocean Beach Resort:

L'Originale Alfredo di Roma $$$$ This place is original only because it's an offshoot of the Italian *ristorante* in Rome where fettuccine Alfredo was created. That claim to fame nonetheless fails to justify the restaurant's high prices, for much of the food on the menu is mediocre. The dining room is packed with patrons, most of them tourists; serious diners eat here once and don't return. ♦ Italian ♦ Daily dinner. Reservations recommended. 532.3600 ♿

49 The Alexander $$$$ The elegant and restrained atmosphere in the lobby of this hotel/condominium is far removed from the hustle and bustle of many of Miami Beach's convention-oriented hostelries. The 170 suites are large and elegantly furnished. The beach is excellent, and there are two pools for those who don't care for saltwater. Valet parking is available. ♦ 5225 Collins Ave (at 52nd St). 865.6500, 800/327.6121; fax 864.8525 ♿

Within The Alexander:

Dominique's ★★$$$$ Dominique d'Ermo made his mark in Washington, DC, where his restaurant is famous for such offbeat offerings as rattlesnake, alligator, and all other manner of game. He primarily duplicates the menus of other similar restaurants, but does it better. The game for which the restaurant is famous is not as well prepared as the seafood entrées, especially the delicately flavored lobster fricassee and salmon in parchment with shredded vegetables, lime, and ginger. ♦ French ♦ Daily breakfast, lunch, and dinner; Su brunch. Reservations recommended; jacket required. 861.5252 ♿

In the 1960s city fathers pushed to expand the narrow natural beach on Ocean Drive to today's extra-wide expanse, in anticipation of the need for a wide beach to balance the towering casino hotels they then hoped would be built.

Alina Interián
Executive Director, Miami Book Fair International

Miami's a real multicultural city, in the sense that you can find cuisines and neighborhoods true to the spirit of other countries—Cuba and Haiti, for example. The neighborhood of **Little Havana,** of course, is the heart of the Cuban experience, but you can find other equally authentic examples throughout the city—in **Coral Gables** and **Miami Beach.**

RESTAURANTS

North Dade

Unicorn Village Restaurant: If someone loves vegetarian food, I always tell them to go to **Unicorn Village.** They have an award-winning vegetarian restaurant, with pasta, fish (coconut-crusted grouper), and fantastic salads. You can also have wine with your meal, which isn't always possible in a vegetarian restaurant.

Coral Gables

JJ's American Diner: It's good to know that in a kind of chi-chi town like **Coral Gables,** it's possible to get good, solid diner fare. I like their sandwiches in particular: the blackened chicken, turkey melt, Reuben. Plus they have all that fattening and irresistible dessert stuff. And it's inexpensive.

Restaurant Place St. Michel: There are lots of good restaurants in **South Dade,** but what makes this restaurant special is its romantic atmosphere. Great for preserving or sparking a relationship; just make sure one of you can afford the bill! I think it's worth it, though. The menu changes according to the seasons and features meat and seafood that are transformed by yummy tropical touches.

Yuca: The crème de la crème of Cuban fare with a New World twist. If I have guests in town who have never tried Cuban food and they have an adventurous palate, this is the place I take them. They never forget it. Some of my favorites: the sweet plantain stuffed with cured dried beef and the skirt steak.

Miami Beach (South Beach)

Lario's on the Beach (owned by Gloria Estefan): If you're looking for Cuban food and fate has brought you to **Ocean Drive,** this is the place to go. Not as upscale as **Yuca** in **Coral Gables,** but definitely a pleasant place to hang out and enjoy traditional, well-prepared Cuban food. Recommended: pork loin, shrimp creole, Spanish omelette, mamey flan.

Pacific Time: This restaurant is both elegant and low-key. The food is consistently fine—New World cuisine with a Pacific Rim twist; try the grouper with sake and ginger. The logical fine dining choice if you're exploring **Lincoln Road Mall.**

Tap Tap: This **South Beach** restaurant/gallery serves spicy, authentic Haitian food in a colorful, painted setting. Local musicians gather for spontaneous jam sessions in the restaurant and exhibition space (currently housing a Gede exhibit on *voudou* art);

come around 8PM or 9PM for dinner. Soup, grilled goat, fresh fish, vegetarian entrées, and tropical fruit sorbets are all favorites—and reasonably priced.

COFFEE BARS/WINE BARS/HANG-OUT SPOTS

Coconut Grove

Cafe Tu Tu Tango: For a late-night snack or afternoon glass of wine, this tapas bar fits the bill. Everything is served in small, appetizer-size portions, and the atmosphere is fun and lively. Don't miss the pizza or the plantain and boniato chips with salsa.

Miami Beach

Gertrudes: Named after you-know-who, this **Lincoln Road** coffeehouse features great flavored coffees (try the Cappuccino Gertrude, with hazelnut syrup), Italian sodas, and desserts in a relaxed setting. Indoor-outdoor seating permits plenty of people watching, or a good hour-long read.

News Cafe: One of the oldest establishments on **Ocean Drive,** this casual sidewalk cafe features surprisingly good salads, sandwiches, and Middle Eastern specialties.

The Restaurant at Van Dome: For a quick salad, glass of wine, or French bread and brie, I like to stop by this popular **Lincoln Road** destination. The upstairs lounge stays open late and accommodates large groups, with nightly entertainment that usually permits conversation. A comfey spot.

NIGHTCLUBS/BARS/MUSIC SPOTS

Centro Vasco: Right now, this is one of the hottest places in town for Cuban music. Thursdays at 10PM, there's a Cuban Jam Session. Friday through Sunday, the famed Cuban singer Albita takes to the mike at 10PM. You can't visit **Miami** without seeing Albita!

Stephen Talkhouse: Good music (rock, blues, alternative), full bar, relaxed atmosphere.

Tobacco Road: Originally a 1920s speakeasy, Miami's oldest bar features great rhythm and blues. A full bar upstairs and down. Very late night. If you're in Miami and you want to hear music, this and the **Talkhouse** are the first places to check.

Cameo Theater Disco Night: Sunday is disco night, still going strong after three years. Lots of young kids dancing to music they don't even remember, but the classic tunes remain solid.

Bash: A good place for late-night dancing; the crowd ranges from early 20s to graying at the temples. Hip, fun, and not overly self-conscious.

Louis Canales
Publicist/Promoter/Club Owner

South Beach offers ample opportunities for displays of firm flesh and truly decadent behavior. The raw energy of the place has a vulgarity that seduces all who visit. This city, silly at times but never, never boring, has the highest number of portable phones, vanity license plates, Rolex watches, and personal in-line skating instructors per capita in the nation.

Truly Felliniesque in its makeup, its inhabitants are a delicious mix of Euro-trash, Hollywood celebrities, New York debutantes on the lam, artsy trendoids, Latin American magnates, and a local fauna that just happens to be the most exotic this side of Pago Pago. The pace is tropical slow and the hours kept are continental, with the favored hour for dining never before 10PM and the night's rounds of entertainment and follies never starting before the bewitching hour. If not overcome by all the apparent fluff, the visitor to this area, also known as the Billion Dollar Sandbar, can come away feeling well satisfied by real substance and a taste of the future.

1) **Raleigh Hotel** on Collins Avenue: At the bar, master barman John De Luca makes the best martinis on the Eastern seaboard. Chef Mark Lippmann's restaurant is the power lunchroom of the city with great and affordable food, the beach club boasts the most beautiful pool in Florida, where you can get a glimpse of everyone from Calvin Klein to Johnny Depp and Kate Moss. The gym has one of the best trainers in town, Chris Berchiatti.

2) Sunday Gospel Brunch with vocalist extraordinaire Maryel Epps at the **WPA** restaurant.

3) Upstairs at the **Van Dyke** on Lincoln Road: Elegant, intimate, sophisticated, with Toni Bishop and her combo providing the perfect mellow jazz groove.

4) **Pacific Time** restaurant: Chef Jonathan Eismann's tribute to Asian cuisine with a delicious and provocative American twist.

5) **Century:** Elegant, high concept but casual. The food, a perfect balance. Paloma Picasso favors dining alfresco on the terrace. French designer Thierry Mugler and Madonna prefer inside seating.

6) **Max's on the Beach:** Chef Kerry Simon (formerly of the Plaza Hotel in New York) offers his unmistakable touch in a setting any true sophisticate can feel at home in.

7) **Sports Cafe:** Best home-style Italian restaurant on the beach. The very likeable and well-liked Erinn Cosby (comedian Bill's daughter) works her magic hosting the room.

8) **World Resources Cafe:** Steve Rhodes offers excellent Thai food in a gallery setting replete with Third World objets d'art and live world-beat entertainment.

9) Stone Crabs: They run from September through April and are found only in the surrounding waters. Since you only eat this crustacean's claws, which are incredibly sweet and succulent, fishermen just detach the large claw, leaving the smaller one for self-defense, and throw the crabs back into the ocean, where they will grow it back again over the following year.

10) The tropical splendors of the sunrises and sunsets. The well-deserved, famous, full moons.

11) **ORIBE Salon** on Collins Avenue: While it's impossible to book an appointment with this hairstyling wunderkind at his salon in New York City,

in **Miami Beach** he might just be able to fit you in between Sylvester Stallone and best-selling romance novelist Pat Booth.

12) A portrait seating with photographers Alexis Rodriguez-Duarte, Iran Issa-Kahn, or David Vance. What Scavullo did for Martha Mitchell in New York City a generation ago, these kids can do for you today in Miami.

13) Miami Film Festival (February): Nat Chediak, the creative director of the festival, introduced Spanish genius film director Pedro Almodovar to American audiences through this event. You get the picture.

14) Miami Light Project (year-round): Janine Gross and Caren Rabbino's multidisciplined performance series. The best in the country outside of the Brooklyn Academy of Music.

15) Miami Book Fair International (November): The premier literary event of the nation. A gargantuan feast for the mind, with hundreds of authors participating in lectures, conferences, and symposiums. Free and open to the public.

16) **Miami City Ballet** (winter season): Artistic Director Edward Villella has kept Balanchine's genius alive and well and thus positioned the company to take its rightful place center stage in the 21st century.

17) White Party at **Vizcaya** (Sunday after Thanksgiving): A fundraiser to benefit Health Crisis Network, South Florida's longest-established agency helping the HIV-positive community and people living with AIDS. It's set in **Vizcaya,** the magnificent Italian palace built for James Deering and now a museum. The event is the jewel in the crown of the gay party circuit and attracts thousands from around the world.

If you are lucky or well connected:

18) Getting invited to any of Chris Blackwell's rooftop parties at the **Marlin Hotel.** The entertainment mogul's soirees attract everyone from supermodel Naomi Campbell to the rock group U-2.

19) Getting invited to lunch at designer Gianni Versace's magnificent family enclave, **Casa Casuarina.** Royalty of every variety in attendance.

20) Getting invited to Craig Robins's dinner parties. The young developer, a partner in DACRA Companies, has managed to brilliantly craft impressive guest lists which headily combine power brokers and luminaries in the fields of art and commerce on an international level.

21) Getting invited to any of author Brian Antoni's parties. Wonderful and unexpected combinations of creative types. From George Plimpton, Stephen King, and Brett Easton Ellis to meditation gurus and high-art drag queens doing swan dives into the pool, fully clothed.

22) Getting invited to brunch at fashion photography great Bruce Weber's beachfront spread on Ocean Beach. Every variety of human physical perfection, dazzling brains, and mega style-setters, plus the company of the friendliest and prettiest Labrador retrievers (the host's pets) in the world.

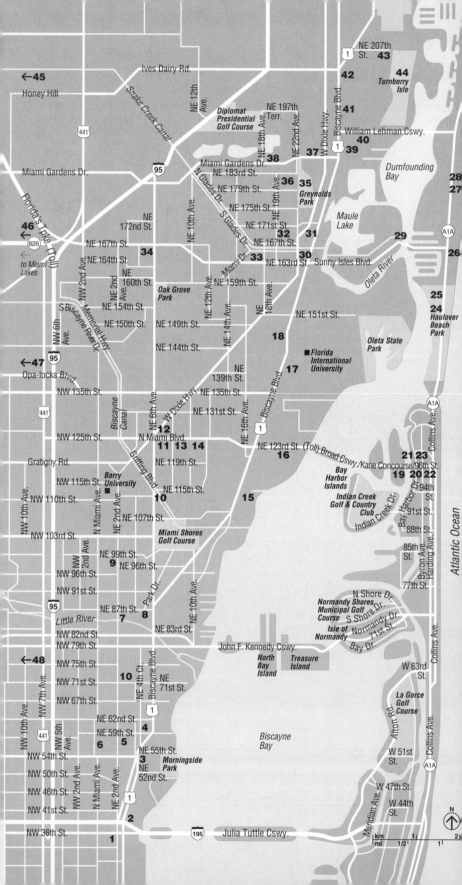

North Miami/ North Dade County

To the casual motorist driving along **Interstate 95**, North Dade County, which extends north from Miami to Ft. Lauderdale, may seem nothing more than an unbroken urban stretch. However, anyone with a little extra time to explore will discover that this area harbors a gold mine of lovingly preserved historic villages and interesting new communities. You'll find the city of **Opa-locka**; the **Miami Lakes** area; the **Morningside** neighborhood; **El Portal Archaeological Zone**; quaint **North Bay Village**; and **Aventura**, a high-style shopping, dining, and residential area.

Miami's huge population boom over the past three decades has spawned the development of residential areas and their corollary—the inevitable shopping center—in all directions. This rapid, seemingly haphazard growth has left much of northwestern Dade County without a common architectural or historical theme—with the notable exception of developments along **Biscayne Boulevard** on the mainland and **Collins Avenue** on Miami Beach. Biscayne Boulevard began as a principal thoroughfare linking Miami and its port with **Miami Shores** and its large pineapple plantations. Collins Avenue connected South Florida's many oceanfront developments, especially the downtown area, with **North Miami Beach,** which was originally planned as an elegant resort called **Fulford-by-the-Sea.**

Today, both Biscayne Boulevard and Collins Avenue are filled with glitzy shopping districts and historic homes. They also boast numerous family restaurants of good quality, but not many of the "hot," publicity-attracting establishments that populate Coral Gables and Coconut Grove. The few culinary trendsetters that North Miami *can* claim, however, are true standouts: At **Mark's Place**, impresario Mark Militello turns out world-class continental cooking, and Allen Susser at **Chef Allen's** is an innovator intent on developing a cuisine unique to Florida.

As the megalopolis that is South Florida continues to flourish, increasingly more businesses and their clientele are relocating to the northern part of Dade County to be equidistant from Miami and Ft. Lauderdale. From ocean resorts to light industry and high-tech housing, this is one of the fastest-growing parts of South Florida.

Area code 305 unless otherwise indicated.

1 Miami Design District Spanning several blocks just off Biscayne Boulevard, this area is sometimes called "Decorators' Row" because its denizens cater in large part to the wholesale trade, specifically interior decorators and clothing designers. While some stores may open their doors to the lay public by appointment only, others permit browsers, and a few will even sell directly to individuals who can come up with some form of company identification or affiliation to at least preserve the illusion of a sale to the trade. Even if you don't buy, it's ideal for window shopping: This is where the latest designs come first. Times have been tough lately for the design district, with many of its occupants abandoning shop and heading to Davie and its decorators' mall, **Design Center of the Americas (DCOTA).** ♦ NE Second Ave (between NE 35th and NE 40th Sts)

Vinnie Tartaglia teaches ambitious young men to box at the Allen Park/DeLeonardis Youth Center gymnasium in North Miami Beach, where Muhammad Ali once trained and still occasionally visits.

The industrial town of Medley brings in so much tax revenue from business that it offers its 862 residents (at last count) a staggering number of services: free lunch at the city dining room, city-subsidized rent, free bus service to schools, grocery stores, and beauty parlors, a free health club, and free home health care and cleaning services for the bedridden.

Restaurants/Clubs: Red   **Hotels:** Blue
Shops/ ♀ Outdoors: Green   **Sights/Culture:** Black

American Police Hall of Fame & Police Museum

CHRIS MIDDOUR

2 American Police Hall of Fame & Police Museum With a police cruiser appearing to be racing up its plain concrete facade (see illustration above), this otherwise undistinguished building is impossible to overlook. The collection of law enforcement–related memorabilia—presented with an emphasis more on mild sensationalism than on scholarly archivism—stretches the traditional definition of a museum. The police car from the futuristic film *Blade Runner* is on display, and advertisements depict a retired electric chair dubbed "Old Sparky." Visitors can have their photos snapped while behind bars, or play Sherlock Holmes while puzzling out a solve-it-yourself crime scene. ♦ Admission. Daily. 3801 Biscayne Blvd (at NE 38th St). 891.1700 &

3 Morningside Among the several neighborhoods that went up along Biscayne Boulevard in the 1920s, this one has best retained its architectural integrity. As with most developments planned in the early part of this century, its components were all built in the same style, in this case Mediterranean Revival. A strong association of local homeowners has worked hard to have a section of the neighborhood designated a historic zone, meaning that strict guidelines now apply to renovations and restorations. Despite the deterioration of the area west of Biscayne Boulevard, this neighborhood's saga exemplifies the power of focused civic strength. The installation of barricades blocking entrance to the neighborhood along much of Biscayne Boulevard has reduced dramatically traffic flow in the area. ♦ Bordered by Biscayne Blvd, Biscayne Bay, NE 50th St, and NE 60th St

Within Morningside:

John Nunnally Home The wealthy candy manufacturer who built this house drew heavily on local materials, such as termite-resistant Dade County pine. Still a private residence, the house is a classic example of the Mediterranean Revival style so typical of the district. ♦ 5731 NE Sixth Ave (between NE 57th and NE 58th Sts)

5940 NE Sixth Court One of the first homes built in Morningside, this Mission-style house deviates slightly from the neighborhood's signature Mediterranean Revival style. Its architect took full advantage of the location, incorporating a second-floor balcony that embraces cool breezes wafting off the bay. It still is a private residence. ♦ 5940 NE Sixth Ct (between NE 59th and NE 60th Sts)

4 Cushman School This institution was built by **Russell T. Pancoast** in 1926. Operating continuously ever since, the private elementary school today has nearly 300 students in nursery school through sixth grade. Dr. Laura Cushman, from whom the school took its name, had an enormous influence on Miami's educational system, from the first class she taught in 1924 on the front porch of her house. In addition to her teaching duties, Dr. Cushman was the school's principal for 50 years, remaining active here until her death in 1986. The V-shaped facility was laid out to take advantage of breezes off the nearby bay. The bell above the main entrance came from **Villa Vizcaya.** ♦ 592 NE 60th St (at NE Sixth Ave). 757.1966 &

5 Little Haiti This ethnic enclave is more concept than reality for visitors, who will be hard-pressed to sense the sort of cultural ambience so palpable in nearby Little Havana. Sprawling along Northeast Second Avenue, the area is decidedly residential rather than commercial. Few signs of any Haitian presence are evident, beyond the one- and two-table restaurants that open and then close down with alarming rapidity and shops with French names. ♦ NE Second Ave (between NE 55th and NE 70th Sts)

6 Villa Paula Back in the 1920s, this was one of the most elaborate homes in Northeast Dade County. It originally housed the Cuban Consulate, hence the Neo-Classical details—

such as the columns—so popular in Cuban architecture. Its name refers to the wife of the first Cuban consul, who died in the house under mysterious circumstances. Legend has it that her ghost still roams the building. It is a private residence. ♦ 5811 N Miami Ave (at NE 58th St)

7 Sherwood Forest House A private residence, this English Tudor gem stands out in striking contrast to the other homes in the neighborhood. It is the sole realization of a dream held by land developer D.C. Clarke, who in 1925 began construction of Sherwood Forest, which he envisioned as Miami's most beautiful and picturesque subdivision. The area, which had been heavily planted by an earlier owner, botanist Ferney McVeigh, held great promise as a residential enclave until the land boom went bust. ♦ 301 NE 86th St (at NE Third Ave)

8 El Portal Archaeological Zone and Burial Mound Designated a public park in 1920, this zone is one of the few remnants of 1,800 years of occupation of the area by a thriving native population. The site, which has been preserved by the county, includes a prehistoric village and burial mound, a 19th-century pioneer homestead, and a coontie mill used for processing starch from a native tuber. ♦ Along the Little River (at 500 NE 87th St). 751.2406

9 Miami Shores Theater Paramount Pictures commissioned Miami architect **Harold P. Steward** to design this theater, but World War II held up its construction. By 1946, when it finally was completed, the theater could lay claim to the dubious distinction of being one of the last structures built in South Florida in the Art Deco style. Today, the active performing arts theater offers classes, and productions for adults and children alike. ♦ Admission. 9806 NE Second Ave (at NE 98th St). 751.0562 ♿

10 Biscayne Park Village Hall This classic example of the log cabin was built from a kit by artists commissioned by the Depression-era Works Progress Administration (WPA). **Biscayne Park** was laid out in 1919, incorporated in 1931, and designated a bird sanctuary shortly thereafter. Today, the village hall is used by the city government. ♦ 640 NE 114th St (at NE Sixth Ave)

SHIROI HANA

11 Shiroi Hana ★$$ Imagine a comfortable neighborhood tavern that serves sushi, and you'll see why this convivial restaurant is such a hit with locals. The sushi is impeccably

fresh, the teriyaki well prepared and delicately seasoned, and the fried fish cutlets sublime. The menu isn't broad, but what is on it is good. ♦ Japanese ♦ M-F lunch and dinner; Sa-Su dinner. 12460 NE Seventh Ave (at NE 123rd St). 891.5160 ♿

Biscayne Wine Merchants

& Bistro

12 Biscayne Wine Merchants & Bistro ★★★$$ This is the place for those with Champagne tastes but beer pocketbooks. French food is served in a casual, if crowded, setting—smack in the middle of a wine and beer store. Browse the racks to select your dinner vintage. ♦ French ♦ M-Sa lunch and dinner. 738 NE 125th St (between NE Seventh and NE Eighth Aves). 899.1997 ♿

13 Center of Contemporary Art Dade County's first collecting art museum in 40 years, this 23,000-square-foot complex was scheduled to open as we went to press. Also in the works: a gift shop with books, and space for film, dance, and music festivals. Special events will include tours of architecturally interesting neighborhoods. ♦ Admission. Call for information. 12340 NE Eighth Ave (between NE 123rd and NE 124th Sts). 893.6211 ♿

14 William Jennings Bryan Elementary School Architect **E.L. Robertson** was very active in Miami Beach's Art Deco District, but this building has a strong Mediterranean Revival style. Of particular note are the arched windows and openings and the interior courtyard and arcade. The school is named for the famous orator, who moved to Miami early in this century to help sell real estate for George Merrick, founder of Coral Gables. The facility is still in use. ♦ 1200 NE 125th St (at NE 12th Ave) ♿

The Golden Glades Interchange, that motorist's nightmare, was originally a peaceful pineapple plantation.

North Miami Beach was the site of the first auto-racing track in Dade County. Constructed of wood, it was destroyed in a hurricane in the late 1920s and never rebuilt.

15 La Paloma ★★★★$$$ Owners Werner and Maria Staub have been perfecting the art of tempting diners for over 20 years, and the result is exquisite cuisine that rivals Europe's finest. Favorite dishes include a seafood combination in Champagne sauce; Mediterranean bouillabaisse; and veal steak Sabrina (served with Port wine sauce and kiwifruit). For dessert, try the Swiss chocolate basket, filled with fresh berries, or the Grand Marnier parfait cake. Impeccable presentation and service are the hallmarks here, and the ambience is elegant and intimate. The list of wines and Champagnes is extensive. ♦ Continental ♦ Tu-Su lunch and dinner. Reservations recommended. 10999 Biscayne Blvd (at NE 110th St). 891.0505 ♿

16 Mark's Place ★★★★$$$$ A star in South Florida's culinary constellation, Mark Militello is acclaimed for cutting-edge cuisine that marries New World ingredients with classic techniques. By many estimations, this is the best restaurant in South Florida. It is engaging but hectic: Expect to wait, even with a reservation. Once seated, however, you'll find the food inspired, with one new concept following another in rapid succession. You can't go wrong with the braised grouper with leek and saffron lobster sauce, yellowtail with tangerine-fennel butter, oak-roasted salmon, or roasted pork loin stuffed with chestnut pesto and sun-dried tomatoes. The (admittedly pricey) wine list has a broad selection. Valet parking is available. ♦ American ♦ M-F lunch and dinner; Sa-Su dinner. Reservations required. 2286 NE 123rd St (at NE 23rd Ave). 893.6888 ♿

17 Gourmet Diner ★$$ Jean-Pierre Lejeune, who owns this bistro, has a deceptively clever idea about food—keep it simple and good, and the customers will line up. They've done so here, where meals are served informally, and at reasonable prices. The handwritten menu, which changes daily, follows the lead of the market, but there are some standards, including beef Burgundy, duck with apples, salad niçoise, and many fish specials. ♦ French ♦ Daily breakfast, lunch, and dinner. No credit cards accepted. 13951 Biscayne Blvd (at NE 139th St). 947.2255 ♿

18 Miami Ice Arena Ice skating in Florida? When this $2-million rink opened, thousands of Miamians flocked here for some northern exposure. Skate rentals are available, so visitors can show their stuff, too. ♦ Tu-Su. 14770 Biscayne Blvd (at NW 147th St). 940.8222 ♿

19 Barbara Scott Gallery You'll find mostly contemporary art at this gallery, which specializes in top New York artists. ♦ Tu-Sa. 1055 Kane Concourse (between Bay Harbor Terr and E Bay Harbor Dr), Bay Harbor Islands. 865.9393; fax 865.9395 ♿

20 Renato's Bay Harbor ★★★★$$$$ Originally home to the highly acclaimed **Cafe Chauveron,** this restaurant has continued a tradition of excellent dining that some describe as magical. Although continental, the à la carte menu has an Italian accent. Start with the sautéed shrimp wrapped in prosciutto or the signature cold antipasto of grilled vegetables. The veal scallopini with exotic mushrooms and golden raisins is a popular entrée. The Grand Marnier soufflé, which made **Cafe Chauveron** famous, is still on the menu. The decor—Italian tile, coquina shell arches, and blue-fabric–covered walls—lives up to the elegance of the menu. Diners can sip cocktails by moonlight on the patio, which overlooks the Intracoastal. ♦ Italian/Continental ♦ Daily dinner Oct-June; Tu-Su dinner June-Aug. Reservations recommended; jacket and tie not required, though the ambience suggests dressy attire. 9561 E Bay Harbor Dr (at Indian Creek), Bay Harbor Islands. 866.8779 ♿

21 The Palm ★★$$$$ This quintessentially American steak house offers huge portions of high-quality beef at astronomical prices. The lobster is notable too. ♦ Steak house ♦ Daily dinner. Reservations required. 9650 E Bay Harbor Dr (at 96th St), Bay Harbor Islands. 868.7256 ♿

22 Surfside This small village is a little oasis in time as well as space, a recollection of 1930s Miami Beach in the center of the city's most fashionable area. Its heart is a two-block stretch of Harding Avenue adjacent to the upscale and trendy **Bal Harbour Shops**

(see below). ♦ Harding Ave (between 88th and 96th Sts)

23 Bal Harbour Village This chic but tiny village comprises palatial high-rise and single-family homes, resort hotels, and the internationally famous **Bal Harbour Shops** (see below). Tourism is its number one industry. Bounded by 96th St, Bal Bay Dr, the Atlantic Ocean, and the Intracoastal Waterway

Within Bal Harbour Village:

BAL HARBOUR

Sheraton Bal Harbour $$$$ Sure it's expensive, but if you want proximity to the beach and shopping—plus first-rate amenities—this is a perfect choice. The concierge, multilingual staff, shopping arcade, tennis courts, and spa facilities are all part of the 668-room hotel's resort approach. The lobby, with its large atrium, is truly beautiful. The hotel offers three restaurants, including a cafe and the pricey **Bal Harbour Bar and Grill**, which is open daily for dinner. ♦ 9701 Collins Ave (at 96th St). 865.7511, 800/334.8484; fax 864.2601 &

Bal Harbour Shops South Florida's answer to Rodeo Drive has become even trendier since jet-setters discovered South Beach. Shops on two levels of an open, plant-festooned structure draw the rich from around the world. **Saks** and **Neiman Marcus** anchor either end, but the true glitz in the lineup of designer luminaries in between: **Gucci, Versace, Tiffany & Co., Charles Jourdan, Chanel, Bulgari Jewelers, Mark Cross, Louis Vuitton,** and **Fendi** all have exclusive boutiques. The shopping here caters to everybody, not just the clothes-horse: Also on hand are a large **Williams-Sonoma**

and a well-stocked **FAO Schwarz** for kids. ♦ M, Th-F 10AM-9PM; Tu-W, Sa 10AM-6PM; Su noon-5PM. 9700 Collins Ave (at 96th St). 866.0311 &

23 Seaview Hotel $$$ With 120 rooms, this hotel has long been a mainstay among snowbird regulars. It has a subtle and quiet Caribbean charm that most other lodgings in the area lack. The staff is warm and courteous, and the poolside cafe is particularly good. Valet parking is available. ♦ 9909 Collins Ave (at 99th St). 866.4441, 800/447.1010; fax 866.1898 &

24 Haulover Beach Park This mile-long stretch of unbroken sand is an odd sight along Miami Beach's heavily built up shoreline. The park got its name in the early part of the century when residents had to haul their boats over the surrounding swamps to reach the ocean. ♦ 10800 Collins Ave (at 108th St), Sunny Isles. 947.3525

Within Haulover Beach Park:

Nikko Gold Coast Cruises One of the best ways to see South Florida is from the water, and a trip on any of this company's three ships, each carrying 150 people, provides lots of exciting views. Several seven-hour itineraries are available, with ships traveling the Intracoastal Waterway to Ft. Lauderdale and down to Biscayne Bay, taking in **Bayside Marketplace,** the **Everglades, Villa Vizcaya,** an Indian village, and other sites. ♦ Fee. Daily. Haulover Beach Park Marina. 945.5461 &

Skyward Kites Originally located on South Beach, this kiosk offers a new approach to the traditional hobby of kite flying, with space-age materials, bright colors, and unusual shapes. Lessons are available. ♦ Daily, weather permitting. 945.1681 &

FINE SEAFOOD RESTAURANT

25 Salty's $$ Good food is served by barely clothed waitresses in a boatyard setting. The seafood is fresh and the burgers hearty, but it's the view that makes a visit worthwhile. Dockside dining and dancing are part of the fun. ♦ American ♦ Daily lunch and dinner; Su brunch. Reservations recommended. 10880 Collins Ave (at 109th St), Sunny Isles. 945.5115 &

Miami Hot and Cool

Miami, which has gone in and out of fashion several times in its brief history, has been hot since the late 1980s, when fashion models, photographers, and club-hoppers rediscovered **Miami Beach,** and celebrities followed.

One of the first of this superstar breed, Madonna purchased a $6-million mansion overlooking **Biscayne Bay.** Sylvester Stallone bought a house nearby in 1994 and, along with Bruce Willis, Arnold Schwarzenegger, and Demi Moore, invested in **Planet Hollywood,** a restaurant in **Coconut Grove.** Among the international jet set owning property in Miami are fashion designers Gianni Versace and Paloma Picasso.

Another group of Miami-bred celebs came home, including singer/entrepreneur Gloria Estefan, singer Jon Secada, actors Andy Garcia, Steven Bauer, and Mickey Rourke, and ball player Jose Canseco.

Then there are the stars who bought into Miami's glitzy image before it became quite so glitzy. They include Julio Iglesias, Whitney Houston, Roy Lichtenstein, and Anne Rice.

Other celebs have come and gone (rather quickly) over the past few years, including guitarist Jimmy Page of Led Zeppelin fame. Melanie Griffith and Don Johnson left, but Johnson's sidekick on "Miami Vice," Philip Michael Thomas, is still here.

26 Holiday Inn Newport Pier Resort $$$ This 12-story hotel has many of the amenities of an oceanside resort, including two restaurants, freshwater pools, and activities for children. The hotel is adjacent to a public fishing pier, where snapper is a popular catch. The 350 rooms are medium-size and comfortable. Valet parking is available. ♦ 16701 Collins Ave (between Sunny Isles Blvd and NE 170 St), Sunny Isles. 949.1300, 800/HOLIDAY; fax 956.2733 &

27 Riu Pan American Ocean Resort $$$ Full resort amenities are a big draw at this renovated hotel on the ocean. Many of the 146 rooms look out over the ocean, but be sure to ask, as several offer only the slightest view. Free transportation to area sights and shopping is available, and there's a good continental cafe with friendly service. Valet parking is available. ♦ 17875 Collins Ave (at 178th St), Sunny Isles. 932.1100, 800/327.5678 &

28 Suez $$ Flamboyantly decorated by even Miami Beach standards, this 197-room, two-story motel is popular with families for its location (away from the frantic scene farther south on the beach) and reasonable rates. A third of the rooms have kitchens (there's a dining room on the premises). Adults can indulge in tennis; kids have a wading pool, a playground, and supervised activities. ♦ 18215 Collins Ave (at 182nd St), Sunny Isles. 932.0661, 800/327.0691; fax 937.0058 &

29 Shooters $$ This is a waterfront bar/restaurant gone suburban, with a relaxing view of the Intracoastal for those enjoying cocktails or dinner from the light menu of burgers, salads, and tidbits. The cooking isn't revolutionary, but this place is hard to beat for a relaxed meal this close to the city. ♦ American ♦ Daily breakfast, lunch, and dinner. 3501 NE 163rd St (at the Intracoastal Waterway). 949.2855 &. Also at: 3033 NE 32nd Ave (at Oakland Park Blvd), Ft. Lauderdale. 566.2855 &

30 Laurenzo's Italian Market A genuine Italian-American market on a grand scale, this is the best place in town to get Italian cheeses and baked goods. There's a full-service butcher counter and a wine shop famous for its selection of Italian and American vintages. Next door is a farmers' market with fresh herbs and produce. ♦ M-Sa 7AM-7PM; Su 7AM-6PM. 16385 W Dixie Hwy (at NE 163rd St). 945.6381 &

BERMUDA BAR

30 Bermuda Bar ★★$$ An island getaway in the middle of a suburban mall, this restaurant has a wide, open-style kitchen that serves Caribbean fare and fancy pizza. An added surprise is the sushi bar. Popular with locals for its music and bright lights, the restaurant doubles as a nightclub. ◆ Eclectic ◆ Daily until 5AM. 3509 NE 163rd St (at the Sunny Isles Bridge), Sunny Isles. 945.0196 ♿

30 Artichokes ★★★$$ This all-natural, no-red-meat restaurant caters to the health-conscious. Chicken and seafood dishes are available for those not ready to commit to vegetarianism. Fat-free dishes are on the menu, too. ◆ Natural food ◆ Daily dinner. 3055 NE 163rd St (between Biscayne Blvd and NE 25th Ave). 945.7576 ♿

31 Cloisters of the Monastery of St. Bernard de Clairvaux The oldest structure in South Florida wasn't built here but was brought to the US from Spain by newspaper magnate William Randolph Hearst. He so admired the 12th-century monastery in its native Segovia that he bought it for $500,000, disassembled it stone by stone, crated it, and shipped it home. An outbreak of hoof-and-mouth disease prompted customs officials to quarantine the straw-packed stones. When customs agents burned the straw, they neglected to put the stones back in numbered order, so the entire shipment remained packed in crates for three decades. They finally were purchased by two Florida entrepreneurs looking for a new tourist attraction. It took 19 months to assemble the architectural jigsaw puzzle, and in 1954, when it was finished, not everything found a place: Some stones were left over, and some objects seen today—such as the corbels—are not original to the cloisters (they came from Hearst's private collection).

In 1964 the Episcopal church purchased the cloisters, and today it is a functioning house of worship as well as a museum. Among the displays are a cabinet belonging to Pope Urban VII, several ancient books, a 16th-century cabinet, and an extensive garden. ◆ Daily 10AM-4PM. 16711 W Dixie Hwy (at NE 167th St). 945.1462 ♿

32 North Miami Beach Cultural Center This gymnasium-turned-theater showcases drama, music, and dance performances, all enhanced by state-of-the-art acoustics. Formerly the **North Miami Beach Performing Arts Center,** it also functions as a community gathering place. ◆ 17011 NE 19th Ave (at NE 171st St). 948.2990 ♿

33 Worldwide News Behind the unassuming exterior of this strip mall shop is the area's largest, most diverse collection of magazines and newspapers. ◆ M-F 8AM-9PM; Sa 8AM-6PM; Su 8AM-4PM. 1699 NE 163rd St (at NE 17th Ave). 940.4090 ♿

34 Ham & Eggery ★$ The name is pure kitsch, as is the sign below the giant chicken out front: "Welcome to Cholesterol Heaven." Actually, a number of low-cholesterol options are available. Breakfast is served around the clock, with a few homey items like meat loaf and fried chicken added at night. Service can be slow, but hotcakes and hash browns shouldn't be consumed in a hurry. ◆ American ◆ Daily 24 hours. 530 NE 167th St (at NE Fifth Ave). 947.1430 ♿

35 Greynolds Park Of the city's many parks, this is one of the most popular and accessible. It was created during the Depression by the Civilian Conservation Corps (CCC) and named for the original landowner, A.O. Greynolds, who operated a rock-mining company. When Greynolds abandoned the property, he left behind piles of refuse, including railroad ties and a steam engine. The CCC bulldozed the trash, covered it with sand and rock, and topped the resulting 42-foot-high junk heap with an observation tower—which still stands today. The CCC also transformed the quarries that Greynolds's workers had dug into a lake and lagoon, where paddleboats may be rented. The park also has extensive bicycle paths, exercise stations for joggers, a playground, bird walks, and one of the city's finest golf courses. ◆ Nominal admission for vehicles. 17530 W Dixie Hwy (at NE 175th St). 945.3425 ♿

36 Gary's Megacycle This is the best place in the area to get outfitted for a local ride or a tour of the popular 7.5-mile trail that runs through nearby **Greynolds Park.** In addition to a wide range of adult bikes, the shop rents bike trailers for children. ◆ M-F 8:30AM-8PM; Sa 9AM-6PM; Su 10AM-4PM. 18151 NE 19th Ave (at NE 181st St). 940.2912 ♿

37 Neal's ★★★$$$ Owner/chef Neal Cooper created a masterful menu with a delightful Asian touch at this often-crowded restaurant, which seats 70 diners. The creative pizza tidbits that are passed around help whet the appetite for the main course, which is invariably worth the wait. The artworks on the wall, which are rotated to keep the decor distinctive, are for sale. ◆ Bistro ◆ M-Sa dinner. 2570 NE Miami Gardens Dr (at W Dixie Hwy). 936.8333 ♿

Restaurants/Clubs: Red	**Hotels:** Blue
Shops/ Outdoors: Green	**Sights/Culture:** Black

38 Bagel Bar ★★$ A New York tradition comes alive at this noshery spanning three generations. Expect to wait a few minutes before being seated at this popular place; crowds come from miles around to sample fine smoked fish, appetizing baked goods, and, of course, bagels. ♦ Deli ♦ Daily breakfast, lunch, and dinner. 18515 NE 18th Ave (north of NE 183rd St). 932.3314 ♿

39 Loehmann's Fashion Island Since its renovation and expansion, this shopping and entertainment complex features the 16-screen **AMC Fashion Island Theatre,** a **Barnes & Noble** bookstore, **The Gap** clothing store, a **Publix** superstore, and **Prezzo,** a **Dennis Max** restaurant. The anchor store is **Loehmman's,** the famous New York women's clothing discount house, where designer clothes and accessories entice frenzied crowds to compete for the best bargain. ♦ Daily. 18703 Biscayne Blvd (at NE 187th St). 932.0520 ♿

Within Loehmann's Fashion Island:

LOEHMANN'S

Mick's ★★$$ Southern cooking from Atlanta's Peasant Company comes to North Dade. Recommended are the fried green tomatoes and meat loaf. The portions are large, the cooking home-style. ♦ American ♦ Daily lunch and dinner. 932.0006 ♿

North Miami is the home of Florida's first working film studio—the still-active Ivan Tors Studio (where the TV series "Flipper" was filmed).

Restaurants/Clubs: Red   **Hotels:** Blue
Shops/ ⊤ Outdoors: Green   **Sights/Culture:** Black

39 International Jewelers Exchange Fifty jewelry stores combine under one roof to offer a mind-boggling selection of baubles. Don't miss **The Vault,**  which has an awesome array of diamonds and estate jewelry. Repairs are available, and there are watches aplenty. ♦ M-Sa. 940.2052 ♿

40 Chef Allen's ★★★★$$$$ Allen Susser has such disarmingly friendly manners that customers forget he's one of the most important chefs in the region—until the food arrives. His cooking combines a classic purity with a commitment to using local ingredients. Start with Key lime pasta with crab and mustard, or the lobster and crab cake with strawberry-ginger chutney. For the main event, go for the extra thick veal chop with mustard and mushrooms, tuna with mango salsa, or mango chicken with Jamaican scotch bonnet peppers. The wine list, featuring American classics, is extensive and reasonable, and the desserts are stellar. ♦ American ♦ Daily dinner. Reservations required. 19088 NE 29th Ave (near NE 190th St and Biscayne Blvd). 935.2900 ♿

ᐃVENTURA MALL

41 Aventura Mall This upscale shoppers' paradise has a well-planned variety of merchandise for every taste and budget. The big draws here are **Macy's, Lord & Taylor, J.C. Penney,** and **Sears;** plans are in the works to add outposts of **Bloomingdale's** and **Burdines** as well. ♦ M-Sa; Su afternoon. 19501 Biscayne Blvd (at NE 197th St). 935.1110 ♿

CO-ED

42 Olympia Fitness Centers Work off those calories at this state-of-the-art coed gym. Daily, weekly, and seasonal memberships are available. Massage therapy is offered, too.♦ M-F 5AM-10PM; Sa 8AM-7PM; Su 9AM-5PM. 20335 Biscayne Blvd (in the **Promenade Shops**). 932.3500 ♿. Also at: 14736 NE Sixth Ave (between NE 144th and NE 149th Sts). 944.0736

43 Waterways When demand for waterfront living increased dramatically in the mid-1980s, Coscan, a Canadian developer,

built an enormous bayfront development of condo-miniums anchored by this collection of 35 charming shops and restaurants.
♦ 3565 NE 207th St (east of Biscayne Blvd), Aventura. 935.3201 &

Within Waterways:

Kampai! ★★$$$ The name is Japanese for *Cheers!*—which perfectly describes the ebullient atmosphere at one of the best Japanese restaurants in the Miami area (there's another in South Miami). The menu is enormous by even classic Japanese standards, encompassing not only the usual sushi and sashimi (served at a lacquered bar with a splendid harbor view), but many sautéed, stir-fried, and grilled dishes. The lengthy appetizer list includes a number of unusual temptations, such as spicy conch, pickled abalone, and excellent fried eggplant.
♦ Japanese ♦ M-Sa lunch and dinner; Su dinner. 931.6410 &

Unicorn Village Restaurant and Market ★$$ The signs say "health food," but read that as excellent cooking with nutritious ingredients. The complex comprises a large health food store, an excellent wine shop, and a fine restaurant, where the fish dishes and pasta are particularly good, and the salads are top-notch. The wine list, drawn from the store's own extensive stock, is excellent.♦ Health food ♦ Daily lunch and dinner. 933.8829 &

Bruzzi ★★$$ Inventive and relaxed, this restaurant represents a little touch of California. A typical Aventura crowd—read upscale and well-dressed—and a new slant on various popular dishes make this an excellent stop in North Dade. Dine indoors or overlooking the water. A jazz band and vocalist perform on weekends. ♦ Italian ♦ Daily lunch and dinner. Reservations recommended Saturday and Sunday. 937.2400 &

Sher Galleries Diverse original editions of masters and future masters are on display at this gallery, which inspires connoisseurs, collectors, and the art-loving public.
♦ M-Sa until 9PM. 921.9920 &

A RAFAEL HOTEL

44 Turnberry Isle Resort & Club $$$$
This is an island by design only: It is the tip of a tiny peninsula slightly cut away from the mainland and connected by a small bridge. In the midst of Aventura's yuppified crowds, the resort is unique in every way. Though a relatively new property, it's done in the grand old style, with 340 large, tastefully appointed rooms and suites divided among five elegant buildings, including the small **Marina Hotel** and the larger **Country Club Hotel.** A sizable portion of the resort's 300 acres is given over to two Robert Trent Jones Jr. golf courses and a 24-court tennis facility. Among the 11 cafes and eateries is a world-class restaurant (see below). Baby-sitting and children's activities are available, along with 24-hour room service. There's a private beach for guests, a fully equipped spa and health club, and four swimming pools. Valet parking is available. ♦ 19735 Turnberry Way (between Aventura Blvd and NE 197th St). 932.6200, 800/327.7028; fax 933.3811 &

Within Turnberry Isle Resort & Club:

The Veranda ★★★$$$$ Chef Todd Weisz is rapidly making a name for himself as an artiste of New World cuisine. Fresh native produce—such as mangoes and Key limes—and seafood are prominent in his menu, and his homemade desserts are daring. The wine list and service are first-rate. ♦ American ♦ M-Sa breakfast, lunch, and dinner. 932.6200 &

HOME OF THE MIAMI DOLPHINS
HOME OF THE FLORIDA MARLINS

45 Joe Robbie Stadium Since it opened in 1987, this has truly been South Florida's major major-league facility. The $115-million, 75,000-seat stadium is home to the **NFL's Miami Dolphins** and the **Florida Marlins** baseball team. Concerts, shows, and exhibitions are also held here. An infusion of finances and energy from owner H. Wayne Huizenga, of Blockbuster Video fame, has helped push South Florida into the big leagues of sports and entertainment alike. Beginning in 1997, the college football classic **Orange Bowl** will be played here. ♦ 2269 NW 199th St (at NW 27th Ave). 623.6100 &

46 Main Street Shops The crowning glory of the small, affluent planned community known as Miami Lakes, this open-air shopping street is dotted with dozens of tiny stores, a 10-screen theater, **Sam Goody's, The Wearhouse,** and several quaint cafes. The style is Mayberry-meets-the-Caribbean, with red-brick streets, recalling a simpler time before enclosed supermalls and insipid Muzak characterized the shopping experience. ♦ M-Sa; Su afternoon. 6810 Main St (at NW 67th Ave), Miami Lakes. 821.1130 &

HOTEL & GOLF CLUB

46 Don Shula's Hotel & Golf Club $$$ Owned by the winningest coach in football, the **Miami Dolphins'** Don Shula, this 201-room hotel and country club complex has fantastic golf facilities. You'll often catch team members working out at the nearby athletic club, which is one of the best. While some critics lament that the place has slipped of late, the property still ranks high among golfers and other sports-minded types. ♦ Hotel, Main St, Miami Lakes; golf club, nearby, at NW 154th St and Palmetto Expwy. 821.1150 &

Within Don Shula's Hotel:

Don Shula's All Star Cafe ★★$$$ A practically nonstop parade of famous faces and a decor celebrating sports add to the excitement of this restaurant. In fact, they pretty much overshadow the food—mostly burgers, sandwiches, and light fare. A high-tech video and sound system broadcasts sports events. ♦ American ♦ Daily breakfast, lunch, and dinner. 821.1150 &

Within Don Shula's Golf Club:

Shula's ★★$$$ Considered one of Florida's best, this steak house has a country club atmosphere enlivened by **Dolphins** memorabilia. The portions could satisfy even football-player-sized appetites. The Angus beef comes from the Graham farms of Georgia—no small coincidence, since it was the Graham family that developed the country club and the entire community of Miami Lakes in the first place. Valet parking is available. ♦ Steak house ♦ M-F lunch and dinner; Sa-Su dinner. 822.2324 &

47 Opa-locka Located a few miles west of North Miami, this is one of South Florida's least-known treasures, and, like George Merrick's dream city of Coral Gables, it was the creation of a real estate genius. When Glenn Curtiss, who made his initial fortune with the invention of the *Curtiss Jennie* and other World War I–era aircraft, and his partner James Bright divided their 100,000-acre ranch in 1925, they built **Opa-locka,** "created" the town of Hialeah by building a horse-racing track in the wasteland west of Miami, and founded the Pueblo-style town of Miami Springs.

Opa-locka is a contraction of the Indian word *Opatishawockalocka,* whose unpronounce-ability Curtiss feared would discourage land sales. Shortened to "Opa-locka," his development was, he claimed, the "Baghdad of Dade County," a tropical recreation of the *1001 Tales from the Arabian Nights.* In the 1920s the country was in a swoon over Rudolph Valentino's *Sheik* films, and Curtiss played to the fad by designating Ali Baba Avenue and Sharazad Boulevard the main thoroughfares of this cattle pasture on its way to being a city.

The land bust and other financial problems spoiled most of Curtiss's dreams. His buildings crumbled, and the area became a ghetto. Ironically, the city developed by the aviation pioneer is best known today for its large airport, catering mostly to private planes and air shows. In recent years, the city renovated several buildings. Unfortunately, the area remains dangerous at night, with a high crime rate and a proliferation of drugs.

Within Opa-locka:

Opa-locka City Hall Of all the buildings in town, **Bernard Muller's City Hall** is the most dazzling. It's extraordinary in size and design, with minarets, blue-and-white domes, and striped, sand-colored outside walls. In a tragic case of poor timing, the building was completed only weeks before the disastrous 1926 hurricane destroyed not only structures but the entire Florida land boom as well. After its restoration, the building was designated a Thematic Resource on the National Registry of Historic Places. ◆ M-F. 777 Sharazad Blvd (at Ali Baba Ave). 688.4611 ♿

48 Hialeah Park Developed by **Opa-locka** founder Glenn Curtiss, Hialeah has become heavily Cuban in population over the years. It used to be famous for this racetrack, built for thoroughbred racing on 228 acres of prime land. The original park included a roller coaster, a Miccosukee Indian Village, and a jai alai court. All that remains is the racetrack, which has had a series of ups and downs as regulating officials have tried to coordinate its schedule with those of other regional racetracks. Through good times and bad, however, the park, which is on the National Registry of Historic Places, remains home to a flock of 400 flamingos. ◆ Free. M-F. 2200 E Fourth Ave (at E 22nd St). 885.8000 ♿

The Oleta River has been designated an "urban wilderness river." In practice that means you may feel far removed from civilization while paddling down the waterway, but in reality you're floating through a very commercial area. Rent boats at Greynolds Park in North Dade.

The first radio station erected in South Florida was in North Dade County. WGBU had a 50-foot tower, and its signal reached all the way to England—quite an accomplishment, considering it took place in 1924.

Bests

Jenni Person
Director of Programming, South Florida Art Center

As far as I'm concerned, the place to be in the Miami area is **Lincoln Road** in **South Beach**. In fact, it's probably the best place to be in the world. Lincoln Road is Utopia by virtue of the fact that it is a place where an incredible mix of communities truly coexist. It is Utopia also because between the **South Florida Art Center,** the **New World Symphony Orchestra,** the **Miami City Ballet, Area Stage,** the **Colony Theatre,** and the **Alliance for Media Arts,** there are probably as many as 400 working artists based on Lincoln Road. And you can be a part of the process (visit artists' studios at the **Art Center** or witness rehearsals at the **Ballet**), which gives the Road a constant sense of buzz and progress. Artists have definitely made their mark here, quite literally in some cases, such as Carlos Alves's recycled ceramic fountain, and then by continuing to be a vital voice through the recent redevelopment initiative, spurring both dialogue and arts projects. It's an interesting study in the partnership between commerce and culture . . . in fact, that's its mission of late.

A pedestrian mall known as the "Fifth Avenue of the South" in its heyday, the Road is also home to boutique shops (as a result of the gentrification spurred by the artists who rediscovered it as dilapidated territory 10 years ago, of course, like everywhere else in this country) and some really wonderful restaurants and cafes, including the world-class **Pacific Time, Lyon Frères,** and **World Resources,** set inside as well as outside on the Road surrounding a fountain. **World Resources** is a really easy place to hang out and run into everyone you know or need to talk to for whatever reason. You'll sit sipping a selection from a wide variety of beers and wines from all over the planet figuring out how to instill, broaden, and maintain the habit of arts patronage in your generation (proudly 20-whatever/ Gen X), while people at the next table talk about global trade (of the commodity, spiritual, or conceptual variety) on Internet with the owner of the restaurant who hosts a 'net server. **World Resources** also hosts entertainment around its sensuous fountain, generally of live world music. One of its most popular events is the monthly Full Moon Party, featuring performances and drumming circles, which are often hosted by local personalities such as favorite rocker Nil Lara, an amazing artist who fuses good old American guitar rock with tropical rhythms and traditions.

You can do some really interesting consuming on the Road. For example, the other day, I went from getting my bleach done in what is the funkiest yet most luxurious salon on earth, **Some Like It Hot** (appropriately named, given my addiction to having a fully peroxided head); into **Debris,** the store owned by the guys who run the **Lincoln Road Antique & Collectible Market,** to let them know that the red cushioned velvet and chintz headboard they sold me was working out just fine; to a juice bar for a wheatgrass, aloe, banana, strawberry, or whatever shake; to another shop to buy a couple of feather boas as holiday gifts; to **Books & Books,** the perfect community bookstore, to pick up a book they'd graciously ordered for me one day when I went in obsessing over an author, deciding I needed to own every single piece of text Ann Beattie had ever published; and back to my office. This trip would have been impossible without stopping to greet people who are a real part of my life. These people are artists, merchants, businesspeople, politicians, and drag queens. They're people with all different generational, geographical, cultural, historical, and sexual identities.

One time, I brought a cousin visiting from New York to Lincoln Road. Halfway through the tour and stunned by the number of people who had greeted us, he said, "What are you? The Mayor?" Fact is, that's just the Road. You too can be the Mayor of Lincoln Road, just spend three days here . . . chances are you'll want to.

Ft. Lauderdale/ Broward County

To the uninitiated, Broward County (aka Greater Ft. Lauderdale) is simply *Where the Boys Are*, the almost-forgettable 1960 flick that made Spring Break a national rite. Yet this county, which sits two dozen miles north of Miami, offers much more than fun in the sun. Broward has 4,200 restaurants—reputedly more per capita than anywhere else in the US—plus rows of swank art galleries and antiques shops and a dozen major shopping malls. There's nightlife that walks on the wild side, day cruises to the Bahamas, major-league baseball training in the spring, horse tracks, dog racing, and jai alai.

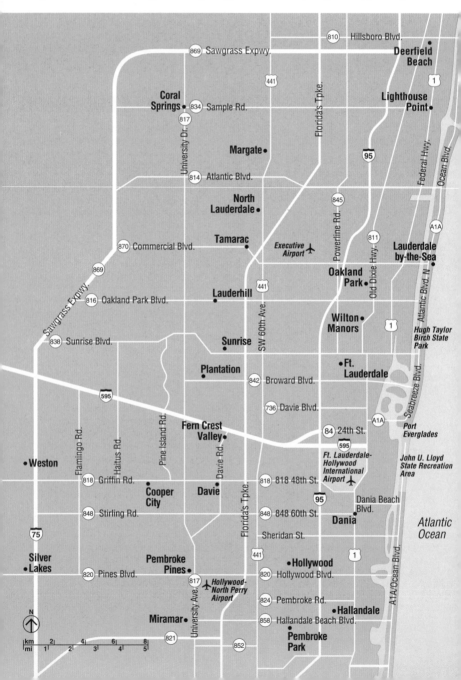

And yes, there are 23 miles of beaches, lots of water sports, and plenty of beer bashes.

Broward County was named after Napoleon Bonaparte Broward, a Florida governor who crisscrossed the **Everglades** with canals and drained the "River of Grass" so it could be used for farming and development. Since its 1915 incorporation, the population of Broward has grown to 1.2 million residents, and some four million visitors travel here each year. Today it's a vibrant, cosmopolitan county that still has some small-town charm. And its proud residents are always eager to make improvements, funding such ambitious projects as a riverfront pedestrian promenade, a performing arts center, and a museum.

Finally, don't forget that, for many, Broward is vacation land—a place where visitors look forward to lazing away the day poolside, slathered in sunscreen; lounging on the beach; and shopping, seeing the sights, and savoring world-class meals. And in all but the most formal establishments, the dress code is strictly casual. Only one rule seems to apply: No shirt, no shoes. . . no service.

Area code 305 unless otherwise indicated.

Getting to Ft. Lauderdale/ Broward County

Airports

Ft. Lauderdale–Hollywood International Airport (FLL), the county's main airport, is three miles south of downtown **Ft. Lauderdale.** It's generally less hectic than **Miami International Airport,** but it's still busy: The airport handles more than 400 flights a day; in 1994, 10.5 million passengers took to the skies here. It offers direct flights to Europe, in addition to cities throughout the the the US, Canada, the Caribbean, and South America.

Airport Services

Airport Emergencies......................359.1244 or 911

Business Service Center.............................359.7610

Currency Exchange 359.7610

Customs, Immigration, and Interpreters

Use courtesy phone on first level of all terminals (push button for **Broward County Aviation Information**), or call information at 359.1200

Ground Transportation

Yellow Cab 565.5400,
shared limo ride 561.8888,

Yellow Cab for disabled persons 565.2800

Lost and Found 359.1217

Parking...359.0200

Police...359.1244

Airlines

Air Canada ....baggage 523.2003,
....800/422.6232

Air Sunshine......................434.8900, 800/432.1744

Airways International ....airport desk 359.4737,
....reservations 526.2000

American...800/433.7300

Canadian 359.2906, 800/426.7000

Canadian Holidays.............920.9426, 800/282.4751

Carnival..............................359.7886, 800/222.7466

Chalk's International..........359.7980, 800/424.2557

ComAir...800/354.9822

Continental.......................525.4126, 800/231.0856

Delta..................................763.2211, 800/221.1212

Icelandair 359.2735, 800/223.5500

Island Express...359.0380

Laker Airways
(charters to Princess Casino) 359.7728,
.................................800/422.7466, 800/545.1300

Midwest Express 359.0244, 800/452.2022

Northwest...........air cargo 359.2960, 800/225.2525

Paradise Island.................359.8043, 800/432.8807

TWA....................................522.1100, 800/221.2000

United 800/241.6522

USAir/USAir Express.........462.5420, 800/428.4322

Walker's International 359.1405, 800/WALKERS

In addition, the **Executive Airport** (1401 W Commercial Blvd west of I-95, Ft. Lauderdale, 938.4966) handles airplane, helicopter, and hot-air-balloon charters. **North Perry Airport** (7750 Pines Blvd at University Dr, Pembroke Pines, 964.0220) offers charters and flight instruction. And **Pompano Beach Air Park** (1001 NE 10th St, west of Hwy 1, Pompano Beach, 786.4135) is the base for the **Goodyear Blimp,** as well as a center for charters and instruction.

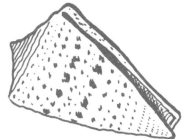

Ft. Lauderdale-Hollywood International Airport

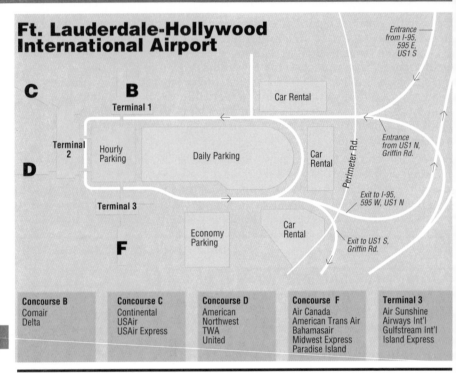

Concourse B	Concourse C	Concourse D	Concourse F	Terminal 3
Comair	Continental	American	Air Canada	Air Sunshine
Delta	USAir	Northwest	American Trans Air	Airways Int'l
	USAir Express	TWA	Bahamasair	Gulfstream Int'l
		United	Midwest Express	Island Express
			Paradise Island	

Getting to and from Ft. Lauderdale–Hollywood International Airport

By Bus A bus is not the most convenient mode of transportation here, but the price is right. A bus ride costs 85¢, and a transfer costs 10¢ more; exact change is required. A public **Broward County Transit** bus (357.8400) stops every 20 minutes at the north and south ends of the airport's upper terminal. Take the "No. 1 Ft. Lauderdale" bus to go north (downtown) or the "No. 1 Aventura" bus to go south (to **Hollywood** or other points south). Buses run daily from 5:30AM to 10PM.

By Car The airport is a five-to-10-minute drive from downtown **Ft. Lauderdale**, except during peak traffic periods (weekdays from 8AM to 9:30AM and 4:30PM to 6PM), when the trip can take up to 20 minutes. To get downtown from the airport, drive north on **Highway 1**, turn left (west) at **Broward Boulevard,** then left again (south) at **Southeast Third Avenue.** To get to Ft. Lauderdale's oceanfront hostelries, drive north on Highway 1, then turn east on the **17th Street Causeway.** To get to Hollywood, **Hallandale,** and **Dania,** follow Highway 1 south; for **West Broward,** take **I-595** west. To reach **North Broward,** take I-595 west, then exit north to **I-95** or exit on **Florida's Turnpike.** And for the cruise-ship center, take I-595 east or go north on Highway 1, then east on **State Road 84.**

To get to the airport from downtown Ft. Lauderdale, drive south on Highway 1 to the airport entrance on the right (past State Rd 84). Well-marked green airport signs designate the way. To get to the airport from Ft. Lauderdale's oceanfront hostelries, head west on the 17th Street Causeway, then turn south on Highway 1 to the airport entrance. From Hollywood, Hallandale, and Dania, follow Highway 1 north to the airport entrance (south of State Road 84). Short-term parking lots are within easy walking distance of the main terminal; a shuttle bus serves the long-term lot. During peak tourism periods, parking lots fill up quickly, and car rentals can be hard to come by.

The following rental car companies have counters, courtesy phones, or shuttle buses at the airport (not all offer 24-hour service):

Alamo	525.4713, 800/327.9633
Avis	359.3250, 800/331.1212
Budget	359.4700, 800/527.0700
Dollar	359.7800, 800/421.6868
Hertz	359.5281, 800/654.3131
National	359.8303, 800/227.7368
Payless	529.9129, 800/729.5377
Rent Rite	763.2666, 800/327.9025
Sears	359.4770, 800/527.0770
Thrifty	525.4355, 800/367.2277
Value	923.4141, 800/468.2583

By Limousine Waiting for two or three strangers to show up to share a limousine with you sometimes can take a while, depending on the time of ay and the popularity of your destination. But if ou hit it right, a shared limo can be a bargain-riced luxury. Rushed? You may prefer a private mo. **Gray Line** (561.8888) is located outside the aggage claim area; it costs $6 to downtown for a hared ride, $24 for a private ride. Private, direct ervice to downtown via **Broward Limousine and irport Service** (791.3000, 979.3800) costs $24.

y Shuttle The **SuperShuttle** (764.1700) ansports passengers to and from the airport. Reservations are required for trips to the airport, ut they are not necessary for rides from the irport. To get from downtown to the airport osts $12.

y Taxi The taxi stand is located near the baggage laim area at the terminal's lower level. Fares, vhich are metered, are $2.45 the first mile and 1.75 each additional mile. A 10-minute ride owntown will run about $10.

y Train You'd have to be a public transportation iehard to consider using the local rail system, but it's certainly possible. At **Terminal 1** or **Terminal 3,** lower level, east end, a **Tri-Rail** shuttle bus (800/TRIRAIL) will take you to the **Tri-Rail** train station. There are 15 train (and shuttle) departures weekdays, with fewer on weekends.

Bus Station (Long-Distance) Greyhound
(515 NE Third St at NE Fifth Ave, 764.6551, 764.6621) provides long-distance bus service.

Train Station (Long-Distance) Ft. Lauderdale
has a small **Amtrak** station (200 SW 21st Terr, west of I-95 and south of Broward Blvd; follow signs for **Tri-Rail;** 587.6692, 800/872.7245). It's open daily from 6:45AM to 6:45PM. Two northbound and two southbound trains depart from here daily; taxis wait outside the station.

In addition, **Tri-Rail** trains (800/TRIRAIL) carry passengers from Broward County north to points in Palm Beach County and south to points in Dade. (For addresses of the six **Tri-Rail** stations in Broward County, see "Trains" under **Getting around Ft. Lauderdale/Broward County**).

Getting around Ft. Lauderdale/Broward County

Unless you don't mind frittering away hours of valuable time waiting for public transportation, a ar here is a must. Most of the county's metropolitan reas hug the **Atlantic** shoreline, with easy access off our north-south routes: **Florida's Turnpike, I-95, ederal Highway,** and **Route A1A. I-595** funnels notorists into **Davie, Plantation, Sunrise,** the **verglades,** and points west, eventually hooking p with **I-75.** (For other tips on how to navigate roward, see "Street Plan," below.)

icycles In general, South Florida drivers are otorious for their lack of respect for bicyclists and pedestrians, so try to stick to parks instead f roughing it on the streets. **Ft. Lauderdale**'s **nyder Park** (3299 SW Fourth Ave at Perimeter Rd, 68.1585) is popular with cyclists, and **Brian Piccolo ark** (9501 Sheridan St, between Palm Ave and Douglas Rd, Cooper City, 437.2600) offers a elodrome. Rent bikes at the **International Bicycle hop** (1900 E Sunrise Blvd at Hwy 1, 764.8800) or at **arsity Cycle Center** (2601 N Federal Hwy between Dakland Park and Sunrise Blvds, 561.2236), both in t. Lauderdale.

uses Broward County Transit (357.8400) has fleet of air-conditioned public buses that tool long 36 routes, stopping at most of Greater Ft. auderdale's major points of interest. The main outes are Route 40 (downtown Ft. Lauderdale and he beach), Route 30 (downtown, the **Broward Mall, awgrass Mills** shopping center, and other points vest), Route 2 (cross-county from the **Hollywood ashion Center** to **Coral Springs**), and Route 1 downtown, the international airport, **Hollywood, Aventura Mall** in Dade County, and the **Metro-Dade** us system). Buses run daily from 5:30AM to 10PM. ickups are 15 to 90 minutes apart, with the longest vaits on weekends and holidays. Exact change (85¢) s required; transfers (10¢) are available only with the irst fare and expire within two hours of purchase.

You can buy weekly passes at county libraries, chambers of commerce, and in the **Central Terminal** (Broward Blvd and NW First Ave, Ft. Lauderdale).

Driving Driving is by far the best way to negotiate Broward's thoroughfares. But with its wildly looping interchanges, nonstop road construction, and interminable traffic jams in some areas, the county can seem downright perilous. Always be prepared for the unexpected, such as drivers making left turns from far-right lanes ("the New York turn," in local parlance) or cars stopping dead in the road, then lurching into reverse. Remember, millions of tourists lurk on Broward's roadways, many of them behind the wheels of rental cars. So drive defensively. (Also consult "Street Plan," below.)

Ferries or Boats About a dozen Water Taxis ferry passengers across Ft. Lauderdale's extensive canal system, plying the **Intracoastal Waterway** and **New River** and picking up fares at marinas, motels, restaurants, bars, and movie theaters near the water. Run by a company aptly named **Water Taxi** (565.5507), the taxis sport green-and-yellow awnings and side curtains. One-way fares are reasonable ($7); the all-day rate ($14) is a real bargain. Water Taxis also can be rented for parties or by the hour, and pub crawls, mansion and marina sight-seeing excursions, and historic tours can be arranged for groups of 15 or more. The Water Taxis run daily from 10AM to about 1:30AM.

Parking Street parking is feasible in most cities, but watch for signs indicating tow-away zones. Downtown and beach parking often is metered (some meters are monitored 24 hours). There are a few parking garages in and around downtown Ft. Lauderdale, among them two city-owned lots. The **Performance Arts Center Parking Lot** (**PACA** to insiders) is at the northwest corner of the intersection of **Southwest Second Street** and **Southwest Fifth Avenue.** The **City Parking Garage**

103

(CPG) is on the northeast corner of the intersection of **Southeast Second Street** and **Southeast First Avenue** (across from the library). Both have the same telephone number (486.1601).

Taxis The airport has taxi stands, but elsewhere most taxi companies require that you call for pickup. Major cab companies include **Central** (564.0700); **Friendly Checker** (923.9999); and **Yellow Cab** (565.5400).

Tours Ninety-minute trips aboard *Carrie B* (768.9920), a yacht, offer a glimpse of **Millionaire's Row,** navy ships, and the yachts of the rich and famous. The yacht departs daily at 11AM, 1PM, and 3PM from the corner of Southeast Fifth Avenue and Las Olas Boulevard in Ft. Lauderdale. No reservations are necessary, and live narration is included in the rate.

A vaudeville show and all-you-can-eat ribs are the trademarks of a three-hour riverboat-style dinner tour of the Intracoastal Waterway aboard the *Jungle Queen* (462.5596). Shorter tours of homes on Millionaire's Row are offered, too. Sight-seeing cruises depart daily at 10AM, 1PM, and 7PM from the **Radisson Bahia Mar Marina** on A1A, just south of the **Radisson Bahia Mar Beach Resort** (south of Las Olas Blvd) in Ft. Lauderdale.

Day and evening trips can usually be reserved just a day in advance on the *Discovery I* and the *Scandinavian Dawn,* ships that offer gambling casinos, enormous dining buffets, Las Vegas–style entertainment, and discos. Cabins that provide a respite from the crowds are available for a small charge. For reservations, call **SeaEscape Ltd.** (379.0000, 800/432.0900 in FL, 800/327.7400) or **Discovery Cruises** (800/937.4477).

Dr. Paul George leads historic tours of a Ft. Lauderdale cemetery and other local points of interest. For information, call **Miami**'s **Historical Museum of South Florida** (375.1625). And **Las Olas Horse and Carriage** (SE Eighth Ave and E Las Olas Blvd, 763.7393, beeper 357.1950) offers carriage rides through the city nightly except Monday. One reliable area tour operator is **Florida Network Tours** (621 W Hallandale Beach Blvd near W Dixie Hwy, Hallandale, 947.9300).

Trains Tri-Rail commuter trains (800/TRIRAIL) run between **West Palm Beach** and Miami, with many stops throughout Broward County. Most trains run during rush hours, with two or three midday trains traveling in each direction. There are six stations in Broward: in Hollywood (3001 Hollywood Blvd, west of I-95); at the **Ft. Lauderdale–Hollywood International Airport** (275 Tigertail Blvd, exit I-95 at Griffin Rd, go west to Ravenswood, turn south on Ravenswood and continue for a quarter mile to Tigertail Blvd, and head east one block); in Ft. Lauderdale (200 SW 21st Terr, west of I-95 and south of Broward Blvd); at **Cypress Creek** (6151 N Andrews Way, exit I-95 at Cypress Creek Rd and head west to Andrews Ave, and follow signs; park at Cypress Creek Bowl, 6000 N Andrews Ave at Cypress Creek Rd, walk across Andrews Ave, and pass the AT&T building to reach the train station); in **Pompano Beach** (3491 NW Eighth Ave, exit I-95 at Sample Rd and head west, and follow signs); and in **Deerfield Beach** (1300 W Hillsboro Blvd, west of I-95).

Trolleys Anyone can climb aboard the free downtown trolleys run by the city of Ft. Lauderdale (463.6574), which help to ease weekday rush-hour congestion. Two trolleys circle downtown: The Broward/Las Olas Boulevard route runs Monday through Friday from 11:30AM to 2:30PM; the Downtown/Courthouse shuttle operates Monday through Friday from 7:30AM to 5:30PM. Look for blue-green "trolley stop" signs, located at the intersection of Southeast Second Street and Andrews Avenue and at Southeast Third Avenue and Broward Boulevard, among other stops.

Walking You can stroll Ft. Lauderdale's beach from **Las Olas** to **Sunrise Boulevards,** take in the **Arts and Science** and **Historic Districts** on Southwest Second Street (from SW Seventh to SW Second Ave), or stop for a drink while window shopping on Las Olas Boulevard (from SE Sixth to SE 12th Aves). Farther north, try the **Galt Ocean Mile Shoppes** (NE 32nd St, just north of Oakland Park Blvd on the west side of A1A). Southward, head to Hollywood's **Young Circle** (Hwy 1 at Hollywood Blvd), a popular open-air park and free-concert venue.

FYI

Money Most banks are open weekdays from 9AM to 5PM. Automatic teller machines (ATMs) are easy to find, especially in banks, outside most **Publix** grocery stores, and in some malls and big office buildings. Foreign currency exchange is available at many commercial banks, at **Thomas Cook Foreign Exchange** (3526 N Ocean Blvd, north of Oakland Park Blvd, Ft. Lauderdale, 566.2666), and at **Tele-trip Business Service Center** (100 Terminal Dr, Ft. Lauderdale–Hollywood International Airport, second level of the Delta Terminal next to the bookstore, 359.7610).

Personal Safety While generally safe, Broward County does have its share of crime. Keep your belongings safe, and avoid neighborhoods where you sense trouble. Lock your car doors and keep the windows rolled up. Leave plenty of escape room between your car and the one in front when stopped at a light. If bumped from behind and unsure of the other driver's intentions, motion the driver to follow you to a police station, fire station, or 24-hour store.

Publications The two local dailies are the *Sun-Sentinel,* published in Ft. Lauderdale, and *The Herald,* the Broward edition of Miami's leading paper. Entertainment listings are published on Fridays in both papers. Free weeklies include *XS* and *New Times,* both published Wednesday. They appear in boxes around the county (in downtown Ft. Lauderdale, go to the post office at 330 SW Second St, just west of SW Second Ave). *South Florida* magazine is published monthly and sold in grocery stores and at newsstands.

Restaurants Reservations are usually necessary only at upper-crust eateries, and some exclusive restaurants require men to wear jackets and ties. In most cases, it's best to call ahead.

Shopping Shopping is most rewarding at **Sawgrass Mills Mall** (a mile-long bargain mecca of books, shoes, clothes, household goods, and more); Ft. Lauderdale's **Galleria Mall; Hallandale's Fashion Row** (a magnet with 60-odd discount fashion stores); and **Pembroke Lakes Mall** (the county's newest, featuring a 17th-century Italian gazebo). Antiquers head to the 150 stores along **Dania's Antique Row.**

Street Plan Broward County is laid out in quadrants—northeast, northwest, southeast, and southwest—but most main highways are known by names or state or federal highway designations. To confuse matters further, many housing developers assigned streets numbers that don't correspond to the countywide grid and named roads after flora, fauna, or whatever else caught their fancy. **Hollywood,** for example, features streets named after US presidents—in order of when they held office.

Remember that the ocean is to the east, and **I-95** runs along the east coast. Other major north-south routes are **Florida's Turnpike, US 1 (Hwy 1), US 441 (State Rd 7),** and **Route A1A.** Florida's Turnpike (with a toll charged by the mile) cuts a high-speed swath on the west and provides easy access to all major cities. About four miles east of the turnpike, I-95 is free of charge but hectic. A more sluggish route is **Federal Highway** (also known as US 1, **Rte 1,** and Hwy 1). And the slowest route is sometimes-picturesque, ocean-hugging Route A1A, but its frequent stoplights, scenery gawkers, and slow drivers likely will send you seeking faster options. Those heading east-west should take advantage of **I-595,** which joins up with **I-75** to provide access to spots west of **Miami.**

Taxes Broward County levies a 6 percent sales tax and a 3 percent bed tax, meaning that a $100 hotel room will really cost $109. The tax on restaurant meals is 6 percent.

Tickets Call **Ticketmaster** (523.3309). Note that all transactions take place over the phone, as the agency has no offices open to the ticket-buying public.

Visitors' Information Center The **Greater Ft. Lauderdale Convention and Visitors Bureau** (200 E Las Olas Blvd, between SE First and SE Second Aves, Suite 1500, 765.4466, 800/356.1662; fax 765.4467), which handles tourist information, is open Mondays through Fridays from 8:30AM to 5PM.

Phone Book

Emergencies
AAA Emergency Road Service 749.5400

Ambulance/Fire/Police 911

Dental Emergency .....Referral service 800/733.6337

Hospitals
  Broward General Medical Center,
  Ft. Lauderdale 355.4400

  Cleveland Clinic Hospital,
  Ft. Lauderdale 568.1000

  Holy Cross Hospital,
  Ft. Lauderdale 771.8000

  Joe DiMaggio Children's Hospital at Memorial,
  Hollywood 987.2000

  Northwest Regional Hospital,
  Margate 974.0400

Locksmith (24-hour)
  Night Owl 748.0666,
  Southport Hardware 522.5033

Pharmacies (24-hour)
  Eckerd Drugs 525.8173
  Walgreens 981.1104, 772.4206

Poison Control 800/282.3171

Police (non-emergency)
  Ft. Lauderdale 761.5700
  Hollywood 967.HELP
  Broward Sheriff's Office 765.4321

Visitors' Information
American Youth Hostels
  Youth hostel house 462.0631,
  Youth hostel international house 568.1615

Amtrak 587.6692, 800/872.7245

Arts and Entertainment Hotline..................357.5700

Beach Conditions 468.1597

Better Business Bureau...............In Miami 625.0307

Broward Transit 357.8400

Convention and Visitors Bureau 765.4466
  ....800/356.1662

Greyhound Bus 764.6551
  ....800/231.2222

  Lost and Found 761.5450
  on buses 357.8400

Time and Temperature 748.4444

US Customs 356.7239, 356.7241

US Passport Office 765.4575

Weather 661.5065

Ft. Lauderdale

Around the turn of the century, Ft. Lauderdale was little more than a town with a post office where a few homesteaders fished and manufactured starch from the coontie plant. Today, that small crossroads, now the government seat of **Broward County**, is a bustling business center with a burgeoning historic and arts district and a revitalized downtown, dotted with internationally acclaimed modern architecture.

The city's success was a long time in coming. Spanish explorers arrived in the area in the early 1600s, and though they settled for a while by Río Nuevo

"New River"), they were just passing through. The name **New River** stuck, however, as did that of Major William Lauderdale, whose detachment of Tennessee army volunteers built a fort along the waterway in 1838 to quell an Indian uprising. Before the turn of the century, three Fort Lauderdales had been built, yet none survived; the army and most would-be settlers, under frequent Indian attack, weren't very interested in persevering in the mosquito-infested swamp.

Few remnants of Ft. Lauderdale's early settlers have survived, except for an Indian reservation in the western reaches of the county and the restored **Himmarshee Village** homestead along the New River, both of which are open to visitors. Today, Seminole Indians operate a bingo hall, hawking trinkets and tax-free cigarettes, while some wrestle alligators for tourists and guide airboat tours of the **Everglades.** As for the military element introduced by Major Lauderdale more than a century ago, naval ships under the flags of many nations still regularly stop at Broward's busy **Port Everglades**.

In the Roaring Twenties, real estate speculators dredged the city's canals to create what they called the "Venice of America." Today, 85 miles of navigable canals and rivers meander through Ft. Lauderdale, making the city a popular port for sailors and yachters. In fact, the **Whitbread Round the World Race**, a grueling ocean journey by sailboat, made Ft. Lauderdale its first US port of call in 1990 and returned in 1994. At many oceanside homes, you'll see a car in the driveway and a boat tied up at the dock in the backyard. Some residents even rent their docks to visitors.

Known for its strong civic pride, Ft. Lauderdale is determined to become an all-around tourist destination, and it is spending big bucks to accomplish its goal, as evidenced by the science and entertainment complex along the New River and the gleaming office towers that were built in the late 1980s and early 1990s to light up the downtown skyline. Also in the early 1990s, **Ft. Lauderdale Beach** was spruced up, with a new sidewalk promenade and a neon-lit, wave-shaped wall.

And even more development plans are on the drawing board: **Beach Place**, a $40-million beachside entertainment, dining, and retail complex, was scheduled to open in the next couple of years as we went to press. Downtown, visitors will eventually be able to saunter through **Brickell Station**—yet another fun complex, with outdoor cafes, shops, 460 feet of navigable water frontage, and an AMC theater expected to have 24 screens, the most under any one roof in the US.

Area code 305 unless otherwise indicated.

1 Don Arturo ★★$$ Broward County boasts few Cuban restaurants, but this one rivals Miami's best. Its Mediterranean decor is traditional in the manner of Little Havana restaurants, while its menu offers authentic dishes containing pork, black beans, rice, and plantains. ♦ Cuban ♦ M-Sa lunch and dinner; Su dinner. 1198 SW 27th Ave (at SW 12th St). 584.7966 &

1 Secret Woods This 55-acre park is so beautiful that the local poets' society meets here. A boardwalk and wood-chip nature trail lend access, and there also is an amphitheater. ♦ M-F. 2701 W State Rd 84 (at SW 25th Terr). 791.1030

2 Snyder Park Wedged against the north side of the main airport, this 73-acre park is a hidden but wonderful surprise. Underground springs feed two lakes, one for swimming, the other for bass fishing. Popular with cyclists and in-line skaters, the park also features nature trails, picnic spots, boating facilities, and volleyball courts. ♦ 3299 SW Fourth Ave (between SW 28th and SW 34th Sts). 468.1585

3 Lester's Diner ★★$ Popular for breakfast and post-barhopping, this casual eatery is a classic in the truck-stop mode, particularly well known for serving a famous 14-ounce cup of java. ♦ American ♦ Daily 24 hours. 250 E State Rd 84 (between SE Fourth and S Andrews Aves). 525.5641 &. Also at: 4701 Coconut Creek Pkwy (one block east of US 441), Margate. 979.4722

4 Sailorman This shop claims to be the world's largest new and used marine emporium, and it may very well be. An enormous hodgepodge of nautical equipment and fishing gear is sold here, and it is particularly noted for its used-but-in-good-condition hardware for sailboats and dinghies. Phone orders are accepted. ♦ M-Sa. 350 E State Rd 84 (at S Federal Hwy). 522.6716, 800/523.0772 in FL; fax 760.7686 &

5 Alex's Flamingo Groves Not too many of these citrus shops are left, but they're pure Florida. This one sells fresh-squeezed orange and grapefruit juice and has a gift shop. Ship your purchase home or take it with you. ♦ Daily. 2323 S Federal Hwy (at E State Rd 84). 525.2913 &

6 Tina's Spaghetti House ★$ Established in 1952, this is not a fancy place, but its longevity can be attributed to certain basics—like good lasagna and, of course, spaghetti. ♦ Italian ♦ M-F lunch and dinner; Su dinner. 2110 S Federal Hwy (south of SE 20th St). 522.9943 &

7 Ernie's Bar-B-Q ★★$ Inside this local treasure, the walls are scrawled with libertarian philosophizing, but most folks concentrate on the food. Feast on conch chowder (doctor it with the sherry on your table), thick barbecue sandwiches on slices of soft Bimini bread, spicy conch salad, and cold draft beer. The rooftop patio, overlooking busy Federal Highway, represents pure urban charm. ♦ Caribbean/barbecue ♦ Daily lunch and dinner. 1843 S Federal Hwy (at SE 18th St). 523.8636 &

8 Bob's News & Book Store If you need to know the latest news in Miami or anywhere else in the world, stop by here to pick up foreign and stateside newspapers and magazines. It's a great place for browsing. ♦ Daily until 9PM. 1515 S Andrews Ave (at SW 16th St). 524.4731 &

9 Brownie's Bar and Package Store This popular neighborhood watering hole claims to be the oldest bar in Ft. Lauderdale, with its musical roots in a jazz club founded by Brownie Robertson in the 1930s. ♦ M-F; Sa until 3AM; Su until 2AM. 1411 S Andrews Ave (between SW 14th and SW 15th Sts). 522.6697 &

10 Downtowner Saloon and Steak House A Gay Nineties decor and a young crowd make this bar a popular gathering place. ♦ Daily until 2AM. 10 S New River Dr E (between SE Third and S Andrews Aves). 463.9800 &

10 Squeeze This may be a progressive club, but you'll find more than a few yuppies partying here. ♦ Tu-F until 2AM; Sa until 3AM. 2 S New River Dr W (between SE Third and S Andrews Aves). 522.2068 &

11 Shirttail Charlie's ★★★$$ Named after a local character who wandered the streets in the 1920s wearing a long Seminole tunic, this popular restaurant is famous for its seafood. On the menu: alligator, conch chowder, clam chowder, blackened fish, and chicken. Dine indoors or out. Thanks to a great view of the developing Arts and Science District across the New River, it may be even more satisfying for an after-theater drink. Guitarists play Friday and Saturday; Sunday is reggae night. ♦ American ♦ Daily lunch and dinner. 400 SW Third Ave (at SW Fourth St). 463.3474 &

12 Broward Center for the Performing Arts Conceived as a unique public-private effort, this $55-million performing arts center is at the heart of the Arts and Science District, which has been under development since the early 1990s. The multiuse complex of theaters, designed by **Benjamin Thompson**, overlooks Sailboat Bend, a hairpin curve on the New River. Take a Water Taxi to the shows, and ask about public tours. There's a parking garage across the street. ♦ 201 SW Fifth Ave (at SW Second St). 522.5334, box office 462.0222 &

13 Riverwalk This unique public project, which is beginning to spark private development along the New River and downtown, invites pedestrians to stroll along the river. At its heart is **Linear Park,** which runs for a mile along the north bank and a half mile on the south side, linking 10 acres of public parks. The walk itself is a broad path through a landscaped setting, punctuated with 3,000 bricks engraved with the names of people who paid $35 or more to own a piece of it. It starts on the west at **Cooley's Landing Park** (SW Seventh Ave) in a historic neighborhood called Sailboat Bend (Tequesta Indians lived here as early as 1450 BC; nearby is the site of the 1863 Cooley Massacre, which drove settlers away for decades afterward). The walk continues to about Southeast Fifth Avenue, stretching through the six-block Arts and Science District.

Planned additions include boat slips, an upgraded boat ramp, and a comfort station with laundry facilities and restrooms. Though the entire project is not yet completed, its essence is already palpable. It's a fun place to stroll or just relax on a bench. Take in the scenery via a telescope stationed in a gazebo, or visit one of the several outdoor educational stations in the shadow of the **Broward Center for the Performing Arts.** SW Second St (at SW Seventh Ave)

Within Riverwalk:

Esplanade In this two-acre park are an outdoor classroom, an entertainment pavilion with a stage, and interactive science exhibits (including telescopes). Whisper "I love you" into a giant, yellow satellite dish and watch the expression of a friend standing at the other dish. Some 1920s-era structures that had been here were demolished after a campaign to move them out of the park failed. ♦ SW Second St (between SW Fourth and SW Fifth Aves)

14 Museum of Discovery and Science/ Blockbuster IMAX Theater An arched atrium canopy and flying buttresses accent this $32-million complex, which was designed by **E. Verner Johnson.** Of note are the 30,000 square feet of science exhibits, plus the area's only interactive IMAX theater, a high-tech, five-story movie screen with a 14,000-watt sound system. ♦ Admission. M-F; Sa 10AM-8:30PM; Su noon-5PM. 401 SW Second St (at SW Fourth Ave). 467.MODS &

15 Old Ft. Lauderdale Historical Complex Take a one-block-long journey into the past. This complex is being developed into a downtown center of "living history" as part of a $3.5-million Historical Society campaign. A pretty park overlooking the New River stands at the south end of the complex. Metered parking is available. ♦ SW Second Ave/Moffat Ave (south of SW Second St). 463.4431 &

Within the Old Ft. Lauderdale Historical Complex:

Ft. Lauderdale Historical Society Lectures, tours, special events, and other programs for both kids and adults are offered by this history museum. The exhibits change periodically; recently featured was **Panorama of the Past,** a chronological look at the county's history. It is also home to the society's research archives, with more than 250,000 historical photos and countless documents. ♦ Admission. Tu-F until 4PM. 219 SW Second Ave (south of SW Second St). 463.4431 &

Restaurants/Clubs: Red	Hotels: Blue
Shops/ ⏚ Outdoors: Green	Sights/Culture: Black

Philemon Bryan House The Broward chapter of the American Institute of Architects occupies this historic concrete-block home (built circa 1905). It originally belonged to Philemon Bryan, patriarch of one of the city's important early families and owner of the area's first hotel (see below). At press time, the house was undergoing renovation; when reopened, it will be used for administrative purposes and will be closed to the public. ◆ 227 SW Second Ave (south of SW Second St). 463.4431

New River Inn The county's oldest surviving hotel building, this 1905 creation was built by **Edwin T. King** for Philemon Bryan (see above), and it was the first in Broward to make the National Registry of Historic Places. **King** held a patent on its hollow concrete-block design. The former 40-room inn sparked many intriguing stories: In the 1970s, rumor had it that someone had hidden President Warren G. Harding's golf clubs at the inn, but it turned out to be a hoax. ◆ 231 SW Second Ave (south of SW Second St). 463.4431 &

King-Cromartie House Architect **Edwin T. King** built this fascinating house (illustrated below) in 1907. **King,** his wife, Susan, and their four children lit their house with acetylene gas before electricity was installed in 1915—four years after their first telephone was put in. The house—which was constructed of Dade County pine—originally sat at 520 Southeast New River Drive. Today, the structure houses a museum filled with period antiques that depict the life of a local pioneer family. Behind the building is a replica of the area's earliest school, where Ivy Cromartie Stranahan, the county's first teacher, taught nine students in 1899; the original school was destroyed by a hurricane. ◆ Admission. Call for appointment. 229 SW Second Ave (south of SW Second St). 463.4431

Chart House ★★★$$$ Originally a pair of homes built in 1904 by pioneer Philemon Bryan for his two sons, this restaurant remains of historic interest to visitors because of its wooden floors and ceilings. Both the upstairs and the downstairs afford views of the river. The seafood is as good as the setting, and prime rib and steak are popular favorites. Don't miss the mud pie. ◆ American ◆ Daily dinner. 301 SW Third Ave (south of SW Second St). 523.0177 &

THE JUICE EXTRACTOR
NATURAL ORGANIC RESTAURANT

15 Juice Extractor ★$$ Stop for a glass of fresh carrot-and-beet juice (and maybe a plate of steamed bison steak) after a day at the nearby museum. Everything is low-fat or fat-free at this natural organic restaurant—good news for string-bikini wearers. ◆ Organic ◆ F-Su breakfast, lunch, and dinner (occasionally open other days). 320 SW Second St (at SW Third Ave). 524.6935; fax 525.7452 &

King-Cromartie House

15 Good Planet ★★$$ Modern artwork covers the walls, and rock music videos flash on several TVs stacked atop one another in this funky, casual restaurant. Don't miss the *pozole,* a Mexican corn soup normally reserved for weddings but served here every day. Tasty fare includes Mexican, chicken, and vegetarian dishes. The desserts are fabulous. ♦ Eclectic ♦ M-F lunch and dinner; Sa dinner. 214 SW Second St (at SW Second Ave). 527.GOOD &

16 Olde Towne Chop House ★★$$$ Great steaks are served here in a handsomely appointed building that dates back to the 1920s. Buffalo is included on the unusual menu, which also lists terrific beef and seafood choices. It's within walking distance of the **Broward Center for the Performing Arts,** so you can stop here for a pre-show dinner. There's also a piano bar. ♦ American ♦ Daily lunch and dinner. 201 SW Second St (at SW Second Ave). 522.1253 &

16 Broward County Historical Commission The changing exhibits here emphasize local history. In the archives are photos, cassette tapes, microfilmed newspaper records, maps, and documents. ♦ Free. M-F. 151 SW Second St (at SW 2nd Ave). 765.4670 &

16 Riverwalk Brewery ★★$$ Be sure to visit Ft. Lauderdale's first brewery and try home-brewed Riverwalk Red, Blackbeard's Gold, Marlins Light, Dark Special, or such Brewmaster's Specials as fruit beers. Then watch to see how they're all made; the open-view stainless-steel vats are not just a gimmick. The food is surprisingly good; the "shashlik of steer"—slices of marinated, grilled beef with peppers, mushrooms, onions, and tomatoes—is the best bet. ♦ Eclectic ♦ Daily lunch and dinner. 111 SW Second Ave (between W Broward Blvd and SW Second St). 764.8448; fax 767.0591 &

17 The Edge Black attire seems to be de rigueur at this alternative and progressive rock/dance club. Go to catch the national acts or to mingle with a twentysomething crowd. ♦ Cover. Daily until 4AM. 200 W Broward Blvd (at SW Second Ave). 525.9333 &

18 Broward Central Bus Terminal Op art goes tropical here in a way that only the world-famous **Arquitectonica** team can do it. You don't need to ride the bus to enjoy the architecture of what must be the most unusual bus terminal in the nation. ♦ N Andrews Ave (at W Broward Blvd). 357.8400 &

19 One River Plaza Built in 1926 as Ft. Lauderdale's first "skyscraper," this nine-story building was used in World War II as an observation post for sighting enemy planes (none was ever spotted). Renovated in 1988 by KRV Company, it is used as an office building today. ♦ 305 S Andrews Ave (off Las Olas Blvd) &

20 Bubier Park Named for a former city mayor, this 2.5-acre park has become downtown's major festival site. ♦ E Las Olas Blvd (at S Andrews Ave)

21 New River Center Home of the Ft. Lauderdale *Sun-Sentinel,* Sunbeam-Oster, and other companies, this 1990 **Cooper Carey & Associates** building marries Art Deco influences with Postmodern sentiments. ♦ 200 E Las Olas Blvd (between SE Second and SE Third Aves). 525.0002 &

22 Blockbuster Entertainment Headquarters This skyscraper was the world headquarters of Blockbuster Video, founded by H. Wayne Huizenga. Huizenga also owns the **Joe Robbie Stadium,** where the **Miami Dolphins** play, as well as two athletic organizations: the **Florida Marlins,** South Florida's major-league baseball team, and the **Panthers** hockey team. Blockbuster Entertainment Corp. was merged into Viacom in 1994, but it maintains a significant presence here. ♦ 1 Blockbuster Plaza (at S Andrews Ave). 524.8200 &

22 Museum of Art An internationally known architectural landmark—in fact, one of the first elements in the revitalization of downtown Ft. Lauderdale—now houses this institution. Private sources contributed about $8 million to build the Postmodern 63,000-square-foot building, designed by **Edward Larabee Barnes** and completed in 1986; it is considered a work of art in itself. Its fittingly monumental exhibition spaces were created to house permanently the largest gathering of works in the Americas from the **CoBrA** collection (artists from Copenhagen, Brussels, and Amsterdam) and the country's biggest William Glackens collection, among other exhibits. Works by Frank Stella, Larry Rivers, and Andy Warhol are on display as well. ♦ Admission. Tu 11AM-9PM; W-Sa 10AM-5PM;

Su noon-5PM. 1 E Las Olas Blvd (at S Andrews Ave). 525.5500, 763.6464 &

23 SunBank Center A campanile and decorative bridge connect this 17-story office tower, completed in 1991, to a low-rise building. ♦ 501 E Las Olas Blvd (just west of Hwy 1/S Federal Hwy) &

24 Broward County Main Library This building boasts lots of angled glass and a sweeping six-story atrium. Head to the third floor for your favorite periodicals or examine the extensive film and video collection on the sixth floor. You can read or just relax in the outdoor plaza. Adjacent to the library is the **City Park Municipal Garage,** designed by **Donald Singer.** ♦ M-Th 9AM-9PM; F-Sa 9AM-5PM; Su noon-5:30PM. 100 S Andrews Ave (at SE First St). 357.7444 &

Within the Broward County Main Library:

Charcuterie Too! ★$ The word "charcuterie" is French for a pork-butcher shop (hence the pig symbol), but chicken, not pork, seems to be the popular option in this Euro-style cafe, which serves salads, pasta, sandwiches, and fresh-baked breads. Try the delicious, chunky chicken-salad sandwich or the *torte rustica* (a pastry crust filled with artichokes and ham). ♦ Continental ♦ M-Sa breakfast and lunch. Second floor. 463.9578 &

25 First Union Center Made of "red dragon granite" with limestone accents, this 21-story glass landmark was designed by **RTKL & Associates.** It's home to the First Union National Bank and Ruden, Barnett, a prominent law firm. ♦ SW corner of E Broward Blvd and SE Third Ave. 760.4848 &

26 Left Bank ★★★$$$$ The countrified European atmosphere here is conducive to fine dining—and romance. Chef Jean-Pierre Brehier is the star of the "Sunshine Cuisine" TV show, and his menu—which ranges from baked dolphin and seafood to veal and filet mignon—reflects an amalgam of Florida flavors and French sensibilities. ♦ Eclectic ♦ Daily dinner. Reservations recommended. 214 S Federal Hwy (at SE Second St). 462.5376 &

Restaurants/Clubs: Red Hotels: Blue
Shops/♟ Outdoors: Green Sights/Culture: Black

27 Henry E. Kinney Tunnel Named after a *Miami Herald* bureau chief, Florida's only highway tunnel was built in 1960 after traffic got so bad that it was described as the "worst bottleneck on Highway 1 from Maine to Florida." Cars travel through the tunnel from south of Southeast Second Street and then under the New River. ♦ Federal Hwy (south of E Broward Blvd)

28 Stranahan House The city's first trading post, dating back to 1901, is Broward County's oldest building (illustrated above). It also was the home of Ivy Cromartie Stranahan, the county's first teacher, and her husband, Frank. The wood-frame building was carefully restored in 1984. Nearby is the spot where Frank began running a ferry across the New River in 1893. Tours are available. ♦ Admission. W-Sa 10AM-4PM; Su 1-4PM. 335 SE Sixth Ave (at E Las Olas Blvd). 524.4736 &

29 Las Olas Boulevard Where settlers once traded with Indians, this shopping district (illustrated on page 115) today draws an upscale crowd interested in tiny art galleries, sidewalk cafes, antiques shops, fancy boutiques, and bridal salons. Developed in the 1940s by merchants envious of the success of Palm Beach's tony Worth Avenue, Ft. Lauderdale's "street of dreams" stretches for six blocks between Southeast Sixth and 12th Avenues and beyond. In the early 1980s, the then-new **Galleria Mall** (see page 117) threatened to divert much business from Las Olas Boulevard, but the district has since been spruced up and seems to sprout more shops as time goes by. The ambience is pleasant, the two-story buildings appealing. Las Olas means "the waves" in Spanish, and the boulevard was so named because in 1917 it led to the first bridge connecting Ft. Lauderdale with the ocean. Parking spaces are available on side streets. Many stores are closed on Sunday, but some are open as late as midnight on weekends as this area increasingly secures its position as the place to see and be seen.

On Las Olas Boulevard:

Flowers & Found Objects This quaint, pretty shop sells flowers, lamps, baskets, and knickknacks. ♦ M-F 7:30AM-5:30PM; Sa

7:30AM-2PM. 521 E Las Olas Blvd (between SE Sixth and SE Seventh Aves). 523.4155 &

Santa Lucia ★★★$$$ Owner Angelo Ciampa has created an intimate yet minimalist restaurant (it has only two employees) that declares its independence from mediocrity with interesting pasta and seafood dishes. One of the more unusual offerings is penne served with fresh peaches or mangoes; also recommended are the whole grilled yellowtail snapper and the huge grilled veal chop. ♦ Italian ♦ M-Sa dinner. Reservations required. 602 E Las Olas Blvd (between SE Sixth and SE Seventh Aves). 525.9530 &

Shades of Light You'll gape at the one-of-a-kind "Ulla" lamps that look something like Tiffanys. Made by Ulla Darni—the owner of this shop—these stunning creations are reverse-painted and fired in deep, rich hues. It's a great place for window-shoppers. ♦ Tu-Th 11AM-6PM; F-Sa 11AM-10PM. 613 E Las Olas Blvd (between SE Sixth and SE Seventh Aves). 766.2671 &

Lois Collection Talk about eclectic: This shop has everything from fine gifts to furniture. ♦ M-Th; Sa noon-5PM. 619 E Las Olas Blvd (between SE Sixth and SE Seventh Aves). 763.2543 &

Riverside Hotel $$ The former **Hotel Champ Carr** retains a garden atmosphere in an urban setting—even with a fireplace burning on some 80-degree days. Paddle fans, tile floors, wicker, and coral-rock fireplaces in the lobby recall another era. The 108 rooms, which have refinished oak furniture (no carbon-copy decor here), over-look either the river, the boutiques, or the city. At one time or another Frankie Avalon, Ralph Nader, and Ronald Reagan have all slept here. ♦ 620 E Las Olas Blvd (between SE Sixth and SE Seventh Aves). 467.0671 &

Within the Riverside Hotel:

Cafe International ★★$$$ Steak, chops, veal, and seafood are served in a dining room that is rich in traditional mahogany and exudes intimacy and importance. ♦ Continental ♦ Daily lunch and dinner. Reservations recommended. 467.0671 &

Six Twenty ★$ Pale pinks and greens adorn this busy coffee shop, which serves salads and sandwiches to the well-heeled denizens of, and visitors to, this neighborhood. ♦ Coffee shop ♦ Daily breakfast and lunch. 467.0671 &

Galleria G'Vanni ★★$$$ Experience unconventional Italian food in an Art Moderne setting. The salmon piccata is great, as is the pasta. The desserts are fabulous. ♦ Italian ♦ Daily lunch and dinner. 625 E Las Olas Blvd (between SE Sixth and SE Seventh Aves). 524.5246 &

Aldo International Men's Boutique An ultra-special menswear store, it carries designer suits and formalwear. Its clients are said to include Jerry Lewis and Lee Majors. ♦ M-Th 10:30AM-6:30PM; F-Sa 10:30AM-8PM, 9PM-midnight. 700 E Las Olas Blvd (between SE Seventh and SE Eighth Aves). 462.7110 &

Apropos Gallery Just a few blocks from the federal courthouse where 2 Live Crew was prosecuted on obscenity charges, this location formerly housed the nation's only "totally erotic art gallery." The sex theme no longer sells here; instead, you'll find modern paintings and sculptures. ♦ M-W 10AM-7PM; Th 10AM-9PM; F-Sa 10AM-11PM; Su 1-9PM. 701 E Las Olas Blvd (between SE Seventh and SE Eighth Aves). 524.2100 &

Needlepoint Originals Needlepoint is ubiquitous in this shop, right down to the "Open/Closed" sign hanging on the front door. But there's more: Folkloric and Haitian art lines the walls as well. ♦ M-Th 10AM-6PM; F-Sa 10AM-10PM. 702 E Las Olas Blvd (between SE Seventh and SE Eighth Aves). 463.1900 &

Lounge Lizards If you're very hip, you'll enjoy lounging around in the clothes and accessories sold here. ♦ M-Th 10AM-5:30PM; F-Sa 10AM-5:30PM, 9PM-midnight. 703 E Las Olas Blvd (between SE Seventh and SE Eighth Aves). 522.8661

De Ligny Art Galleries Life-size statues, Leon Axelrod sculpture, and Ramon Orrit paintings are just some of the works sold at

Las Olas Boulevard Shops

this museumlike store. ♦ M-Sa 10:30AM-5:30PM; open nights in Jan. 709 E Las Olas Blvd (between SE Seventh and SE Eighth Aves). 467.9303 &

Amartin South Florida's oldest furrier is so exclusive that idle browsers are not welcome. Antiques also are sold here. ♦ M-Sa 10AM-5PM. 713 E Las Olas Blvd (between SE Seventh and SE Eighth Aves). 462.7697 &

Flora Ottimer A (young) grandmother's dream: cute and bright clothing for children, from newborn through age 14. ♦ M-Th 10AM-6PM; F-Sa 10AM-9PM. 713B E Las Olas Blvd (between SE Seventh and SE Eighth Aves). 463.2292 &

Le Cafe de Paris ★★★$$$ The Chaîne des Rotisseurs, the prestigious gourmet society, once met for dinner at this romantic restaurant. The staff is attentive, and the menu has all the standards, including *chicken cordon bleu,* filet mignon, and rack of lamb. Owner Monsieur Flematti also runs the **French Quarter** (see below). ♦ French ♦ M-Sa lunch and dinner; Su dinner. 715 E Las Olas Blvd (between SE Seventh and SE Eighth Aves). 467.2900 &

Sue Gordon's Bridal Salon/Suite Suzanne One side of this sprawling shop is dedicated to lingerie and bath products; the other to wedding necessities. You'll also find lots of lace, pillows, potpourri sachets, candles, and evening purses. ♦ Sue Gordon's: M-W, F-Sa 10AM-5:30PM; Th 1-8PM. Suite Suzanne: M-W 10AM-5:30PM; Th 10AM-8PM; F-Sa 10AM-5:30PM, 8PM-midnight; Su 4PM-10PM. 717 and 721 E Las Olas Blvd (between SE Seventh and SE Eighth Aves). 522.8200 for both &

China Yung ★$ Every neighborhood has to have a Chinese restaurant, or the gods get even. ♦ Chinese ♦ M-Sa lunch and dinner;

Su dinner. 720 E Las Olas Blvd (between SE Seventh and SE Eighth Aves). 761.3388 &

O'Hara's Pub A large selection of bottled beer is offered at this sidewalk jazz cafe with the requisite red and white tablecloths. ♦ M-F 11:30AM-2AM; Sa 11:30AM-3AM; Su noon-2AM. 724 E Las Olas Blvd (between SE Seventh and SE Eighth Aves). 524.1764 &

Cafe Europa ★$ Let your hair down at this unstuffy alternative to some of the trendier Las Olas eateries. Order pizza, deli sandwiches, salads, espresso, cappuccino, or desserts, then find a seat at an outdoor table to watch the world go by. ♦ Eclectic ♦ Daily lunch and dinner. 726 E Las Olas Blvd (between SE Seventh and SE Eighth Aves). 763.6600 &

Las Olas Horse and Carriage Bring your own Champagne and take a custom-tailored carriage ride through the city. Or take a prearranged tour, perhaps the 20-minute "New River" excursion or the hour-and-20-minute "Royal Palm" ride. The "Colee Hammock" tour travels through a beautiful old section of the city, past the **French Quarter** restaurant. Prices range from $8 to $90. ♦ Tu-Su 7PM-midnight. Departs from SE Eighth Ave and E Las Olas Blvd. 763.7393, beeper 357.1950

Maus & Hoffman This family-owned store sells traditional men's clothing and anything needed for a black-tie affair. Founded in the 1930s, it has branches in Palm Beach, Naples, Boca Raton, and Bal Harbour. The guiding principle here is good customer relations, with ties formed and nurtured over generations. Owner John Maus prides himself on the type of personal service that includes keeping track of clients' anniversaries and measurements. ♦ M-Sa. 800 E Las Olas Blvd (at SE Eighth Ave). 463.1472 &

Gamblers Anonymous

Florida's constitution prohibits high-stakes casino gambling, and voters several times have rejected measures that would lift the ban. But several loopholes allow wagering in other forms. Because casino gambling is allowed in international waters, a lucrative industry of oceanbound "cruises to nowhere" has sprung up on both the east and west coasts of Florida.

Gaming is also permitted on Federal Indian

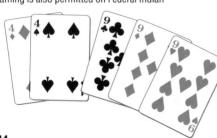

reservations, and the Seminole and Miccosukee tribes have built massive bingo halls that award cash prizes.

Finally, wagering is permitted at certain pari-mutuel establishments, such as horse and greyhound tracks and jai-alai frontons. The state sets the pari-mutuel calendar each year, so that horse tracks within the same area don't compete against each other.

Meanwhile, casino forces defeated in the recent election have vowed to try again.

Call of Africa's Native Visions Gallery
Displayed at this fine art gallery are canvases and prints by the world's best wildlife artists. A percentage of the proceeds that the establishment collects goes toward preserving wild black rhinos. ♦ M-W 10:30AM-9PM; Th 10:30AM-10PM; F-Sa 10:30AM-11PM; Su noon-9PM. 807 E Las Olas Blvd (between SE Eighth and SE Ninth Aves). 767.8737; fax 767.4729 ♿

Country Collection This homey store sells lace table settings and hand-stitched quilts and pillows, as well as unique straw baskets, embroidery, and teapots. There are plenty of crocheted items, too. ♦ M-Sa. 808 E Las Olas Blvd (between SE Eighth and SE Ninth Aves). 462.6205 ♿

Aerobic Centre of South Florida This outlet may present the oddest combination you'll ever see: In back is a highly specialized aerobics/free weights studio, while the tiny shop in front sells dresses and jewelry, plus other goodies, to show off that fit body. ♦ 814 E Las Olas Blvd (between SE Eighth and SE Ninth Ave). 523.3488 ♿

The Chemist Shop Founded in 1956, this family-owned business has been called Florida's most unusual drugstore. On the premises is a quaint restaurant with a soda fountain and a gift shop; the pharmacy definitely appears to be a sideline. ♦ M-Sa. 817 E Las Olas Blvd (between SE Eighth and SE Ninth Aves). 462.6587 ♿

Zola Keller

Zola Keller If you didn't know that Leanza Cornett, Miss America 1993, bought her winning gown at this elite apparel shop, just read the sign on the door. Important people buy important gowns here. ♦ 818 E Las Olas Blvd (between SE Eighth and SE Ninth Aves). 462.3222 ♿

Vieille Provence This breathtaking country French store draws the person who has the wherewithal to lavish on home decorating accessories, as well as the mere aesthete. ♦ M-Sa. 819 E Las Olas Blvd (between SE Eighth and SE Ninth Aves). 761.1881 ♿

Janet Marcus Catering & Cuisine ★$
Scones, anyone? Delicious cookies, tortes, cappuccino, and some of the prettiest cakes ever are the signatures of this refined spot, the perfect place for a leisurely coffee break. ♦ Eclectic ♦ Tu-W; Th 10AM-5PM, 7-11PM; F-Sa 10AM-5PM, 7PM-midnight. 821 E Las Olas Blvd (between SE Eighth and SE Ninth Aves). 463.1133; fax 463.0708 ♿

South by Southwest On a boulevard lined with many beautiful shops, this store is by far one of the most striking. The unusual Southwestern designs include Native American pots, cacti, rugs, jade, and the ubiquitous howling coyote. ♦ M-Th 10AM-9PM; F-Sa 10:15AM-11PM; Su noon-6PM. 833 E Las Olas Blvd (between SE Eighth and SE Ninth Aves). 761.1196

Mangos ★$$ Airy and tropical, this outdoor cafe is named for the exotic fruit that grows so prolifically in these parts. Choose from Caesar salad, grilled chicken, home-made soups, and other fare, and listen to live music daily. ♦ Eclectic ♦ Daily lunch and dinner. 904 E Las Olas Blvd (at SE Ninth Ave). 523.5001 ♿

You may see a roach while on vacation in South Florida, maybe even a *big* roach. But don't be alarmed, and don't call the health department. Just about everyone in Florida has roaches, and they're harmless critters. Locals call them palmetto bugs.

Restaurants/Clubs: Red	Hotels: Blue
Shops/♟ Outdoors: Green	Sights/Culture: Black

M. Sterling Isadore "Pop" Sterling, a Russian immigrant and traveling salesman, opened this men's store in 1935, making it one of the city's oldest retailers. It sells casual and business clothing by Hart Schaffner Marx, Tommy Hilfiger, Polo, Nautica, and Burberry, plus Bass and Bruno Magli shoes to accompany the togs. ♦ M, F 10AM-9PM; Tu-Th, Sa 10AM-6PM. 910 E Las Olas Blvd (between SE Ninth and SE 10th Aves). 467.7321 ♿

Carroll's A chandelier lights this fine store, which was named for pioneer Carroll Segher. With jewelry, china, and wall-to-wall crystal, the place shows up on lots of bridal registries. ♦ M-Sa. 915 E Las Olas Blvd (between SE Ninth and SE 10th Aves). 463.3711 ♿. Also at: 365 Miracle Mile (at Le Jeune Rd), Coral Gables. 446.1611 ♿

Goodebodies Take home the scent of rain, gardenia, peach nectar, or moss in the form of bath gels, perfumes, soaps, and room sprays from this pretty and oh-so-politically-correct shop. Everything is all-natural, hypo-allergenic, biodegradable, ozone-safe, and made without animal products or animal testing. ♦ Daily. 920 E Las Olas Blvd (between SE Ninth and SE 10th Aves). 462.2551; fax 467.9258 ♿

J Miles Clothing Co. Not just another T-shirt shop, this store sells unusual clothing for the artsy crowd. ♦ M-Sa 10AM-7PM; Su noon-5PM. 1023 E Las Olas Blvd (between SE 10th and SE 11th Aves). 462.2710 ♿

Mark's Las Olas ★★★★$$$$ New Orleans has Paul Prudhomme; Florida has Mark Militello, who owns **Mark's Place** in North Miami and recently branched out to open this sophisticated dining room. You've never tasted anything like the acclaimed creations of this star chef, whose status is such that Paul Bocuse once stood and applauded him. Rare, seared, and pepper-corn-crusted tuna with root vegetable mash, foie gras, and veal *jus* is one example of the many delicious offerings on the daily-changing menu. The elegantly contemporary setting does justice to the food, with lighting provided by what looks like icicles dripping from the ceiling, a patterned tile, stone, and wood floor, and a hunter green–tiled open kitchen. The outdoor seats overlook Las Olas Boulevard. ♦ Eclectic ♦ M-F lunch and dinner; Sa-Su dinner. Reservations recommended. 1032 E Las Olas Blvd (between SE 10th and SE 11th Aves). 463.1000 ♿

Anything in Chocolate The operative word here is "anything"—the confectioners will even make erotic chocolate creations. You can buy sweets off the shelf or place a custom order for a gift. ♦ M 11AM-7PM; W, F-Sa 11AM-8PM; Tu, Th noon-10PM. 1221 E Las Olas Blvd (at SE 12th Ave). 467.8844 ♿

R. Sines Antiques Established in 1955, this tiny store features only 18th-century furnishings: grandfather clocks, vases, porcelain figurines, paintings, and Oriental rugs. ♦ Call for hours. 1233 E Las Olas Blvd (at SE 13th Ave). 463.2489

Mario's East ★$$ This pink and white hot spot offers Italian specialties, garden dining, and live entertainment nightly (except for Sundays). ♦ Italian ♦ M-F lunch and dinner; Sa dinner. 1313 E Las Olas Blvd (at SE 15th Ave). 523.4990 ♿

Floridian ★$ Big breakfasts, buffalo burgers, meat loaf, mashed potatoes, and hash browns are the specialties of this old-fashioned, Southern-style deli. Don't miss the homemade conch chowder or the tuna melt sandwich (not for dieters). ♦ American ♦ Daily breakfast, lunch, and dinner. 1410 E Las Olas Blvd (at SE 15th Ave). 463.4041 ♿

Grant's Flowers If it's cute, it's here. Gifts such as teddy bears, pelicans, straw baskets, wooden cows, and orchids and plants fill the shelves. There's also flower delivery. ♦ M-F 9AM-6PM; Sa 9AM-5PM; open Sunday in winter. 1509 E Las Olas Blvd (at SE 16th Ave). 467.9035 ♿

Andrea's This high-end, family-owned linen store (formerly **Gattle's**) handles special-order monogramming and customizing with a vacationer's schedule in mind. Gifts and sachets also are available. ♦ M-Sa. 2426 E Las Olas Blvd (at SW 25th Ave). 467.7396 ♿

30 French Quarter ★★$$$$ The mayor's office and the local Red Cross once occupied this 1925 Mediterranean-style villa, which today houses one of Ft. Lauderdale's most important restaurants. The food has a New Orleans slant, and a pianist plays in the upstairs lounge on Friday and Saturday evenings. ♦ French ♦ M-Sa lunch and dinner. Reservations recommended. 215 SE Eighth Ave (north of Las Olas Blvd). 463.8000 &

31 Holiday Park Stretching south of East Sunrise Boulevard, this large park is home to the city's largest public tennis complex (with 18 Har-Tru and three asphalt courts). Chris Evert got her start here as a child, and lessons for kids are still available from her dad, James Evert. ♦ Fee for courts. Courts: M-F 8AM-9:15PM; Sa-Su 8AM-7PM. 701 NE 12th Ave (at E Sunrise Blvd). 761.5378

Within Holiday Park:

War Memorial Auditorium This 2,000-seat auditorium hosts sporting events and special shows. ♦ 800 NE Eighth St. 761.5380 &

Parker Playhouse Louis Parker, one of the inventors of television, donated this property to the city of Ft. Lauderdale. Now it showcases many performing arts presentations. ♦ 707 NE Eighth St. 764.0700 &

32 Trader Tom's With 12,000 styles, this is the largest bathing suit store in South Florida. ♦ M-Sa 9AM-10PM; Su 10AM-8PM. 914 N Federal Hwy (just south of E Sunrise Blvd). 763.4630 &

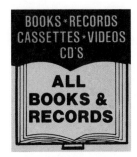

33 All Books & Records Time flies at this bargain buy/sell/trade shop with approximately 300,000 books, 200,000 records, 20,000 compact disks, 30,000 cassettes, 75,000 comics, 3,500 videos, and Sega Genesis and Nintendo. Both new and used merchandise are sold. Ask to see the rarer LPs—usually in the back room. ♦ Daily. 917 N Federal Hwy (south of E Sunrise Blvd). 761.8857 &. Also at: 420 E Oakland Park Blvd (east of Sixth Ave), Wilton Manors, just north of Ft. Lauderdale. 537.4899

34 Musicians Exchange Big-name blues acts that you'd expect to find in Chicago, including John Mayall, Koko Taylor, Buddy Guy, Matt Guitar Murphy, and local boy-made-good Tinsley Ellis, play at this dark, smoky, no-frills club. Jazz, reggae, and blast-from-the-past rock bands are also booked in the intimate room, where there's no such thing as a bad seat. This is actually a small music complex. You can buy instruments and sheet music downstairs, or take lessons or practice playing in the bays out back. This is located in a seedy neighborhood, but a guard watches cars on concert nights. ♦ Cover. Call for schedule. National acts usually play Friday and Saturday nights, but big weekday shows aren't unusual in winter. 729 W Sunrise Blvd (at NW Seventh Ave). 764.1912

35 Galleria Mall What was once an ordinary shopping center has become one of South Florida's most deluxe malls. The three-level structure, with a central court and glass-enclosed elevators, is dotted with original sculpture. Among its 150 shops are **Lord & Taylor, Saks Fifth Avenue, Neiman Marcus,** and such specialty stores as **Laura Ashley, Brooks Brothers,** and **Bally of Switzerland.** Valet parking is available. ♦ M-Sa 10AM-9PM; Su noon-5:30PM. 2414 E Sunrise Blvd (between NE 26th Ave and Middle River Dr). 564.1015 &

36 Guest Quarters Suite Hotel $$ This high-rise offers views of the Intracoastal, plus 228 one- and two-bedroom suites, all decorated in contemporary American style with washers and dryers and fully equipped kitchens (there's also a restaurant). One big draw here is the private beach; another is the frequency of celebrity sightings (Joan Rivers, Marlo Thomas, and Gregory Hines, for instance, have all been spotted here). ♦ 2670 E Sunrise Blvd (at NE 26th Ave). 565.3800; fax 561.0387 &

A 50-year-old building can be considered historic in land-boom Florida. There once was a drive to save the oldest house in Plantation—a hunting shack, circa 1947. From Miami to Palm Beach, more than 170 sites are on the National Registry of Historic Places, at least a dozen of them in Broward County. To see the first permanent school in the Everglades, go to Davie School (6650 Griffin Road, in Davie).

Ft. Lauderdale Strip

In 1935, Ft. Lauderdale sponsored its first Collegiate Aquatic Forum, a swimming competition held during the Christmas holidays that drew college kids from around the country. It was the impetus for the annual Spring Break pilgrimage, to which Ft. Lauderdale owes its image as the place to have boozy fun in the sun.

After the 1960 film *Where the Boys Are,* starring Connie Francis, about 50,000 college students showed up on Ft. Lauderdale's beach, later known as **The Strip.** This student pilgrimage evolved into an annual event that peaked in 1985, when 350,000 kids arrived, guzzling beer, diving off balconies into swimming pools (sometimes with fatal results), and crowding into hotel rooms by the dozen. The students spent an estimated $140 million, but city officials decided the aggravation and loss of much family and European business wasn't worth it. Collegians were encouraged to spend their time elsewhere (via a police crackdown and "The Wall," a concrete barricade that prevented **A1A Highway** cruising); they complied for the most part by relocating farther north to Daytona Beach.

Today, "The Strip" has undergone a $25-million face-lift, which has drawn families, joggers, strollers, and all kinds of people soaking up the rays. Europeans and locals took the place of the college students. The **Harbor Beach** area at the southernmost end is clustered with mom-and-pop motels and upscale hotel chains catering to the business traveler. The **Southeast 17th Street Causeway** area, between **Highway 1** and A1A, boasts gleaming shopping centers filled with eclectic shops, upscale restaurants and meeting places, and a $48-million convention center. Connie Francis wouldn't recognize the place.

37 Burt & Jacks ★★★★$$$$ The drive to this restaurant winds through a working port past Panamax ship cranes, military ships, towering grain silos, and cruise terminals, but it's well worth the trip. Beyond a forbidding chain-link fence is a pretty, Mediterranean-style villa landscaped with bougainvillea, hibiscus, and winding brick paths. It affords a panoramic view of the ship basin, Ft. Lauderdale, and the Intracoastal. Burt Reynolds is one of the owners, but he's not around much. The emphasis is on seafood, prime rib, steak, lobster, and Caesar salad.

The piano player in the lounge takes requests. ♦ American ♦ Daily dinner. Reservations recommended; jacket required. Berth 23, Port Everglades (at Eisenhower Blvd). 522.5225 &

38 Ft. Lauderdale Motel $ This 90-room urban motel offers easy access to downtown, the cruise port, the beach, and the city's marinas. Conference space for 10 to 50 people is available, and the bar, **Benjamin's,** is a popular watering hole. There's a dining room as well. ♦ 501 SE 17th St (at Hwy 1). 525.5194 &

39 Sagami ★★$$$ Graduate from chopsticks to tatami seating at this authentic, no-shortcuts spot for sushi, sashimi, tempura, and teriyaki. ♦ Japanese ♦ M-F lunch and dinner; Sa-Su dinner. 1005 SE 17th St (in the Imperial Point Shopping Center). 764.7874 &

相 模

40 Crown Sterling Suites $$$ Formerly the **Embassy Suites,** this 400-room, Mediterranean-inspired hotel resembles a cross between a fortress and a pink birthday cake. The lushly landscaped atrium is 12 stories high; it's hard to believe you're indoors. Complimentary breakfast and an airport shuttle are among the perks. ♦ 1100 SE 17th St (between SE 10th Ave and Cordova Rd). 527.2700 &

Within Crown Sterling Suites:

Salute ★$$ Sit outside by the waterfall and enjoy a varied menu—dolphin sautéed in lemon, crusted black-pepper New York strip steak, pasta, grilled salmon, and more. The candlelit tables are pretty at night. ♦ Italian ♦ Daily lunch and dinner. 527.2700 &

41 Chuck's Steak House ★$$$ Partner Chuck Rolles claims to have invented the salad bar in Waikiki in 1959, and maybe he did. But what his casual eatery is known for is beef—burgers and big steaks. A folk singer performs Wednesday through Saturday evenings. ♦ American ♦ M-F lunch and dinner; Sa-Su dinner. 1207 SE 17th St (between SE 10th Ave and Cordova Rd). 764.3333 &

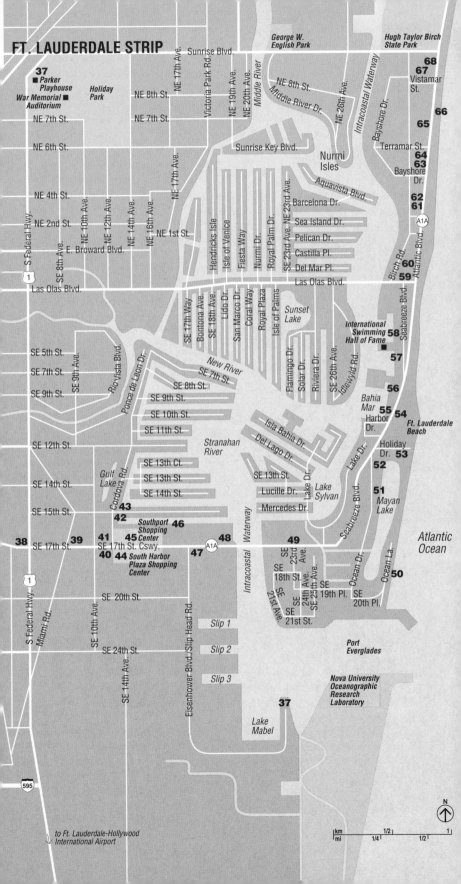

42 15th Street Fisheries ★★★$$$ Here is the seafood you came to Florida to eat. Especially famous are the thick-cut tuna, "smoking Florida stew," and sautéed snapper with fresh ginger and scallions. This award-winning restaurant is housed in an old wood-frame building overlooking a busy marina and yacht basin. It's informal downstairs in the **Boathouse,** formal upstairs. Take a Water Taxi back to your hotel. ♦ American ♦ Daily lunch and dinner. Reservations recommended. 1900 SE 15th St (east of Hwy 1). 763.2777 ᓚ

43 Southport Raw Bar ★$ This noisy neighborhood bar is known the world over because of its bumper stickers, which read: "The fish makes you live longer, the oysters make you love longer, and the clams make you last longer." ♦ Seafood ♦ Daily lunch and dinner. 1536 Cordova Rd (at SE 15th St). 525.2526 ᓚ

44 South Harbor Plaza Shopping Center This sprawling complex has an intimate feel and a woodsy decor. ♦ 1300 SE 17th St (at Cordova Rd) ᓚ

Within South Harbor Plaza Shopping Center:

Carlos & Pepe's ★$ Serapes and paper flowers brighten the spirits of diners at this cheerful Mexican place. But if the ambience doesn't do it, the margaritas will. ♦ Mexican ♦ Daily lunch and dinner. 467.7192 ᓚ

Book Rack After you've finished those paperbacks you bought at the airport, trade them in at this used-paperback bookstore, which has a huge selection. ♦ M-F 10AM-6PM; Sa 10AM-5PM. 764.8199 ᓚ

Hip Pocket This family-run store is jammed with brand-name swimwear (Catalina, Hobie, Ocean Pacific), Izod shirts, Reebok sneakers, Levis, flip-flops, and sun visors. ♦ M-F 9AM-8PM; Sa 9AM-7PM; Su 9AM-5PM. 761.7677 ᓚ

Cloud 9 Clothing If you've made it all the way to Florida and somehow forgot your bathing suit, come here for better-than-department-store prices. ♦ M-W, Sa 9AM-6PM; Th-F 9AM-8PM; Su 10AM-4PM. 463.1961 ᓚ

Nautical Emporium Walk over a tiny wooden bridge and you'll find resort clothes, hand-carved tropical fish, handmade paper art, and novelty boating items. Reef Riders boating sandals ensure you won't slip on your yacht. ♦ M-Sa 9:30AM-5:30PM; Su 10AM-4PM in winter. 761.7678 ᓚ

Siam House ★$$ Dim sum lovers can satisfy their cravings at this combination Thai/Chinese restaurant, whose decor is lovely. ♦ Thai/Chinese ♦ M-Sa lunch and dinner; Su dinner. 763.1701 ᓚ

Restaurants/Clubs: Red   Hotels: Blue
Shops/ ♥ Outdoors: Green   **Sights/Culture: Black**

Lauderdale Diver Everything you need to explore the deep, from tanks to swimsuits, is sold at this huge dive shop. Scuba and snorkeling instruction is offered, as are daily reef trips on a 42-foot dive boat. ♦ M-F 9AM-6PM; Sa 8AM-6PM; Su 9AM-1PM. 467.2822, 800/654.2073 ᓚ

Porcelain Collection Particularly tenacious collectors have extended their vacations to stop in here, one of the top 10 Bradford Exchange porcelain dealers in the nation. Why? Cathy and Greg Schulkers offer a complete collection of Bing & Grondahl and Royal Copenhagen plates, and they will hunt down missing pieces. On the wall is a $5,500 B&G plate made in 1895. ♦ M-Sa. 764.1185 ᓚ

Bobby Rubino's Place for Ribs $$ Beef, beef, and more beef, especially barbecue, is the specialty at this casual eatery. Shrimp, trout, and salad are also popular. ♦ American ♦ Daily lunch and dinner. 522.3006 ᓚ. Also at: 4100 N Federal Hwy (north of NE 38th St). 561.5305; 6001 Kimberly Blvd (at US 441), North Lauderdale. 971.4740; 4520 W Hallandale Beach Blvd (just west of SW 44th Ave), Pembroke Park. 987.5500

45 Southport Shopping Center Let's get this straight: The **Southport** shopping complex is on the north side of 17th Street; the **Northport** complex is on the south side. At the former, you'll find a big **Publix** supermarket, a 24-hour **Eckerd** pharmacy, and lots of specialty stores. ♦ 1489 SE 17th St (at Cordova Rd) ᓚ

Within the Southport Shopping Center:

Carriage Clothiers This store sells men's clothing, including Christian Dior, and formalwear. If the slacks you buy here don't fit, they'll hem them on the spot—in less than an hour. ♦ Daily. 523.3545 ᓚ

Bluewater Books & Charts For the sailor who needs help staying on course, here are atlases, maps, and more than 35,000 hard-to-come-by government boating charts and nautical books from around the world. The selection is the finest in the area, perhaps anywhere. (They have waterproof covers, too.) Pick up boating necessities such as ship journals and diaries, plotters, courtesy flags from various countries, and navigation computers. The navigational charts are updated frequently and come from the official government chart publishers in the US, Great Britain, France, Canada, Cuba, Australia, and New Zealand, as well as private publishers. ♦ M-Sa 9AM-6PM. 763.6533, 800/942.BLUE; fax 522.2278, 24-hour quick fax information line 522.2628 &

Seldom Seen Gallery The owners of this gallery travel all over the country in search of contemporary American crafts. They've amassed an impressive assortment of giftware, including candy dishes, clocks, fine jewelry, jewelry boxes, kaleidoscopes, vases, and chimes. ♦ M-Sa 10AM-9PM; Su noon-9PM. 522.7556 &

Charlie's Locker Running away to sea? Everything you'll need is here. There are two locations in the same shopping center: One is a gift shop/marine store/hardware store with specialties like nonskid tableware; the other is a clothing store. ♦ M-Sa 9:30AM-6PM; Su 10AM-4PM. 523.3350 &

☘ KELLY'S LANDING ☘

Kelly's Landing ★★$$ If you're home-sick for New England, then the stuffed quahog (pronounced *quo*-hog), Ipswich clams, Boston baked beans, and Maine lobster at this friendly and casual place will be like a call from Mom. Don't miss the clam chowder. ♦ Seafood ♦ Daily lunch and dinner. 760.7009 &

46 17th Street Quay You can't miss this Mediterranean-style stucco shopping center—it's pink and turquoise. ♦ SE 17th St (between SE 15th Ave and Eisenhower Blvd) &

Within 17th Street Quay:

International Gourmet Market You'll find espresso, imported beer, champagne, caviar, chocolates, a bakery, and a deli at this European-style convenience store. And they deliver. ♦ M-Sa 9AM-8PM. 763.3769; fax 763.6170 &

Bimini Boatyard Bar & Grill ★★★$$ A Ft. Lauderdale landmark, this is one of the most popular places in Broward. It's jammed at lunch with both the yuppie business crowd and tourists, and Friday night's Happy Hour is SRO. With its New England widow's walk, tin cupola, wood floors, and tropical ambience, this spot defies architectural classification. Big wicker chairs and ceiling fans give a space that might otherwise be cavernous a bright island charm; French doors open onto a waterside patio. Pizza is cooked in the wood-burning oven. ♦ American ♦ Daily lunch and dinner. 525.7400 &

47 Greater Ft. Lauderdale/Broward County Convention Center The focal point of this 17-acre convention center is a three-story glass atrium overlooking the Intracoastal Waterway and a fountain plaza. The signature artwork, one of the world's largest modern-day cast-bronze sculptures, is a 36-foot leaping marlin created by Kent Ullberg. With 370,000 square feet of meeting and exhibition space, the state-of-the art center is the first structure in a complex that eventually may include a hotel, restaurants, and retail shops. It is connected by a skywalk to a 2,500-space parking garage. ♦ SE 17th St (at Eisenhower Blvd). 765.5900 &

48 Ft. Lauderdale Marina Marriott $$$ This enormous self-contained resort overlooking the Intracoastal tries to be all things to all people, especially a convention site. In addition to 580 rooms, there's tennis, a health club with Universal equipment, and a pool. ♦ 1881 SE 17th St (just west of the Intracoastal). 463.4000, 800/228.9290; fax 527.6705 &

Within the Ft. Lauderdale Marina Marriott:

Riverwatch ★★$$$ Known for its Sunday brunch, this lounge and restaurant with an Intracoastal view attracts a lively weekend crowd. Arrive by car or boat (dock near the *Gallant Lady*, the yacht of a very prosperous car tycoon). In the lounge, you can dance to Top 40 music on Friday and Saturday nights. ♦ American ♦ M-Sa breakfast, lunch, and dinner; Su brunch and dinner. 527.6756 &

49 Hyatt Regency Pier 66 $$$ Not only does this mammoth resort/marina draw conventioneers and visitors such as the Malcolm Forbes heirs (their yacht, the *Highlander,* docks here part of the year), but local up-and-comers drink, dine, and mingle at its **California Cafe** (see below), and Broward County society meets here for annual galas. Overlooking one of the county's premier marinas (with 142 boat slips), the resort hosted the 1990 and 1994 **Whitbread Round the World** yachting races, run every four years—and interest has been expressed for a return in 1998. This 22-acre resort has come a long, luxurious way from its 1950s beginnings as an executive retreat. Most of the 388 rooms are located in a 17-story tower, crowned by **Pier Top,** a revolving lounge with the only 360-degree view in town (it takes 66 minutes to make a full turn). There's a

European health spa, a 40-person Jacuzzi, and a special pool for water polo. ◆ 2301 SE 17th St (east side of the Intracoastal). 525.6666, 800/327.3796; fax 728.3541 ⓑ

Within the Hyatt Regency Pier 66:

California Cafe ★$$$ Part of a trendy and upscale California chain, this eatery offers brick-oven pizza, steaks, seafood, pasta, an extensive wine list—and unbeatable views of the marina and the Intracoastal. ◆ American ◆ Daily lunch and dinner. 728.3500 ⓑ

50 Lago Mar $$$ Recently renovated at a cost of $6 million, this 177-room hotel is one of the city's most established. The resort and club are tucked away between Mayan Lake and the ocean, sprawling over 10 acres with Key West–style charm. Execs finishing meetings at the five-story conference center (popular with Fortune 500 companies) can play tennis on the four waterfront courts or swim in the two pools. The beach is spectacular—and private. Don't forget your swimsuit—there's a new swimming lagoon with an outside promenade bar. ◆ 1700 Ocean La (at Grace Dr). 523.6511, 800/255.5246 ⓑ

51 Best Western Oceanside Inn $$ This 100-room beachfront hotel—the beach is only 100 yards away—throws in a free breakfast buffet with the room rate. On the premises is a restaurant. ◆ 1180 Seabreeze Blvd (at Holiday Dr). 525.8115, 800/367.1007 ⓑ

52 Sheraton Yankee Clipper Beach Resort $$ One of the handful of Ft. Lauderdale hotels actually on the beach, this resort sprawls across Seabreeze Boulevard to the Intracoastal. All 502 rooms afford ocean or waterway views. There are three pools, water sports, a health center, a restaurant, and the **Wreck Bar,** a celebrity hangout back in the 1970s. ◆ 1140 Seabreeze Blvd (between Harbor Beach Pkwy and Holiday Dr). 524.5551, 800/958.5551; fax 523.5376 ⓑ

53 Marriott's Harbor Beach $$$$ Overlooking the ocean and the Intracoastal, this big-as-Texas beachside resort has 624 rooms and 35 suites. Forget about a mere Olympic-size pool; this one measures 8,000 square feet and is surrounded by cascading waterfalls. The resort sprawls over 16 acres, with extensive meeting facilities, three gift shops, five restaurants, and a quarter mile of beach. Included are the requisite tennis courts, water sports, and a shuttle to the **Bonaventure Golf Course.** Children's programs are on the agenda as well.

When Ft. Lauderdale became a city in 1911, it had only 300 residents.

◆ 3030 Holiday Dr (east of Seabreeze Blvd). 525.4000, 800/222.6543; fax 766.6165 ⓑ

Within Marriott's Harbor Beach:

Sheffield's

Sheffield's ★★$$$$ Breaking the sometimes oppressive tropical mold, this Tudor-style restaurant is intimate and formal, with dark paneling and a beamed ceiling. The equally traditional menu features chateaubriand, beef Wellington, salmon, Long Island duck, and veal medallions. ◆ Eclectic ◆ Daily dinner. Reservations recommended. 525.4000 ⓑ

Kinoko ★★$$$ Scallops, steak, and chicken are cooked with flair right at your table, while the tempura and appetizers are concocted back in the kitchen. A children's menu is available. ◆ Japanese ◆ Daily dinner. Reservations recommended. 525.4000 ⓑ

Surf Watersports Tired of sitting on the beach? Rent a Windsurfer, catamaran, sailboat, or waverunner. ◆ Daily. On the beach in front of Marriott's Harbor Beach. 462.SAIL

54 Ft. Lauderdale Beach This public beach stretches along A1A from the Harbor Drive area past Sunrise Boulevard. Chairs and umbrellas can be rented, and at the south end are restrooms, barbecue grills, picnic tables, and shade trees. No RVs, trailers, or buses are permitted in the parking lot on A1A near the **Radisson Bahia Mar Beach Resort** (see below). Metered parking is strictly enforced along the beach. Lifeguards are on duty daily. ◆ No parking 9PM-5AM. 468.1595

55 Bahia Cabana Beach Resort $$ You don't have to be a chain to be successful, as proven by this mom-and-pop operation, which has grown from one small motel to a complex of five. The hotel's laid-back, Keys-style **Dockside Patio Bar** was named one of the world's 10 best waterfront bars by a national boating magazine (there's also a restaurant). The 112 island-style rooms have refrigerators and safes. Bring your bathing suit; there are three heated pools, plus a

Jacuzzi. ♦ 3001 Harbor Dr (at Seabreeze Blvd). 524.1555 &

ℬahia Mar

56 Radisson Bahia Mar Beach Resort $$
It isn't immediately apparent today, but this is one of Ft. Lauderdale's most historic sites. Since 1875, when it was a shelter for shipwreck survivors, mariners have found comfort and protection here. During Prohibition, the Coast Guard used the site as a base from which to chase rum-runners. Its 350-slip marina—Florida's largest—remains the property's central attraction, offering charter fishing, powerboat and sailboat rentals, and diving excursions (see below). Benefiting from new ownership and a $7-million renovation, all 295 rooms have a new look, and regulars will marvel at the spruced-up landscaping. Among the other amenities are two dining rooms, a pool, tennis courts, a conference center, access to Ft. Lauderdale Beach, and views of the Intracoastal and the ocean. ♦ 601 Seabreeze Blvd (between Harbor Dr and SE Fifth St). 764.2233 &

Within the Radisson Bahia Mar Beach Resort:

Jungle Queen Earl and Margie Faber bought the *Jungle Queen* in 1958 as a stage for their song-and-dance act, and vaudeville is still what makes this boat an international attraction. The hokey, yet endearing, three-hour riverboat-style tour has plied the Intracoastal for more than 40 years. The dinner trip winds up at a private island with all-you-can-eat shrimp and barbecued ribs; entertainers last seen on "The Ed Sullivan Show" spin plates on sticks and exhort the audience to sing along to standards your grandmother would remember. All this, plus you'll see the homes along Millionaire's Row. ♦ Daily sight-seeing cruises depart at 10AM, 1PM, and 7PM. 462.5596 &

Radisson Bahia Mar Marina A wide array of boating activities is offered at the resort's sportfishing marina: drift fishing with Captain Bill, glass-bottom–boat tours, bottom fishing aboard the *Dragon II,* and snorkeling trips. Ships take scuba divers offshore to beautiful underwater reefs. Best-selling author John D. MacDonald made the marina home to his character Travis McGee. Glass-bottom–boat rides are offered Tuesday through Saturday at 9:30AM; Sunday at 2PM. ♦ 467.6000, bottom fishing 522.FISH, drift fishing 467.3855, scuba 761.3414, yachting 463.6302 &

Wreck of the Mercedes Dive 60 to 100 feet into the Atlantic to see the 197-foot German freighter that beached on Palm Beach socialite Mollie Wilmot's pool terrace after a violent storm a decade ago. Just a mile off Ft. Lauderdale Beach, the *Mercedes* is one of many local dive sites; others include wrecks of the *Rebel* and *Jay Scutti,* Osborne Reef, and more. ♦ 761.3413

57 RJs Landing ★$$$ Too bad the food isn't as good as the view—but oh, what a view of the **Radisson Bahia Mar Marina.** Dine indoors or out on steak, pasta, or chicken. ♦ American ♦ Daily lunch and dinner. 515 Seabreeze Blvd (at SE Fifth St). 763.5502 &

57 International Swimming Hall of Fame The world's leading swimmers' museum has inducted the likes of Johnny Weissmuller, Buster Crabbe, Esther Williams, and Mark Spitz. It had its origins in the **Casino Pool,** built by the city after the 1926 hurricane to attract business. One of Florida's first Olympic-size pools, the **Casino** (a term used back then to mean a swimming club and dressing room) was demolished to make way for today's museum, where international swim meets are often held. Also on the premises: a 50-meter warm-up pool and a library. ♦ Admission; discount for American Automobile Association members. M-Sa 9AM-7PM; Su 11AM-4PM. 501 Seabreeze Blvd (at SE Fifth St). 462.6536 &

58 Coconuts ★$$ The menu at this casual waterfront eatery includes seafood, prime rib, teriyaki chicken, and choice steaks. And there's live musical entertainment nightly. ♦ Eclectic ♦ Daily lunch and dinner. 429 Seabreeze Blvd (south of Las Olas Blvd). 467.6788 &

59 Elbo Room Spring Breakers used to line up for a 7AM opening time to drink 25-cent beer and pretend to surf to the "Hawaii 5-0" theme song blaring from the jukebox. Now, the bar's a bit toned down, with specialty pizza, salads, and sidewalk tables to lure European tourists. This breezy spot is open-air on two sides. ♦ M-F, Su until 2AM; Sa until 3AM. 241 S Atlantic Blvd (at Las Olas Blvd). 463.4615

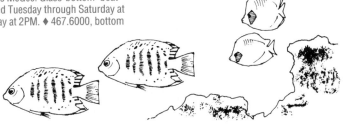

60 Carell's Swimwear Be brave and try on a thong bathing suit; after all, you're in Florida. ♦ M, F-Su 10AM-9:30PM; Tu-Th 10AM-5PM. 235 S Atlantic Blvd (between Las Olas Blvd and Poinsettia St). 462.1922. ♿ Also at: 3301 N Ocean Blvd (north of Oakland Park Blvd). 566.8740 ♿

60 Lauderdale Beach Hotel $ Constructed in the Art Deco style, this hotel has 185 rooms and a new bistro with an ocean view. ♦ 101 S Atlantic Blvd (at Poinsettia St). 764.0088, 800/327.7600 ♿

61 Motel Row Just a couple of blocks from the beach around the Bayshore Drive/Birch Road area are dozens of quiet, family-run motels. Many offer efficiencies and small apartments at weekly or monthly rates. Always look over the accommodations to decide whether they are suitable, or consult the *Superior Small Lodging* rating guide (call 765.4466 for a free copy), in which **Nova University** hospitality experts have judged cleanliness, safety, and overall quality.

On Motel Row:

Sea View Resort Motel $ Roger and Gerry Adams manage this property, which features a pool, plus cable TV in each of the 21 units (no restaurant, though). It's situated near the beach, bus stops, and restaurants; free off-street parking is a major perk. ♦ 550 N Birch Rd (at Windamar Ave). 564.3151, 800/356.2326; fax 561.9147

Sea Chateau
resort

Sea Chateau Resort $ Relax amid antiques, duvets, and in-room tea sets at host Marylyn Springer's 19-unit motel, which feels more like an inn. *Parlez-vous français?* So does the staff, who speak English, German, Italian, and Spanish as well. There's no restaurant. ♦ 555 N Birch Rd (at Terramar St). 566.8331; fax 527.1934

62 Sheraton Yankee Trader Beach Resort $$ The 465 rooms in this resort overlooking the Strip and the ocean are housed in two buildings connected by an above-street bridge. Two restaurants, two pools, three tennis courts, a health center, and all the essentials for business meetings are among the amenities. Guests can use the facilities at the **Sheraton Yankee Clipper Beach Resort** (see above), one mile south. ♦ 303 N Atlantic Blvd (between Granada St and Bayshore Dr). 467.1111, 800/325.3535; fax 462.2342 ♿

Restaurants/Clubs: Red   Hotels: Blue
Shops/ ♦ Outdoors: Green   **Sights/Culture: Black**

63 Bahama Hotel $ Life at this low-rise 70-room motel revolves around the street-side pool and **The Deck,** the outdoor bar/grill, which serves breakfast, lunch, and dinner daily. Efficiencies can be rented, too. ♦ 401 N Atlantic Blvd (at Bayshore Dr). 467.7315 ♿

63 Days Inn Oceanside $ Renovated in 1992, this chain motel offers 60 rooms and efficiencies, plus a large pool and a restaurant. ♦ 435 N Atlantic Blvd (at Rio Mar St). 462.0444, 800/243.3550

64 Surf and Sun Hotel $ This small hotel with 20 rooms and apartments is right on the beach. Each unit has a refrigerator—a real boon here, since there's no dining room. ♦ 521 N Atlantic Blvd (at Auramar St). 564.4341, 800/248.0463

64 Merrimac Beach Resort Hotel $ If you can't live without a barbecue grill, this hotel will provide one. Many of the 65 rooms have fully equipped kitchens (including microwaves); a pool and a sundeck with shuffleboard are other pluses. There's no restaurant. ♦ 551 N Atlantic Blvd (at Terramar St). 564.2345

65 Sea Club $ Europeans like this hotel with a shiplike prow overlooking the ocean. There's a swimming pool, and most of the 96 rooms have outdoor patios. Two restaurants complete the picture. ♦ 609 N Atlantic Blvd (at Bel Mar St). 564.3211

65 Beach Plaza Hotel $ The sundeck overlooks the Atlantic at this 43-room hotel, where your host is Sandra St. Cyr. There's a tropical garden, fully equipped kitchens, and free parking, but no restaurant. ♦ 625 N Atlantic Blvd (at Bel Mar St). 566.7631, 800/451.4711; fax 537.9358 ♿

66 Howard Johnson Oceans Edge Resort $$ Every balcony at this 144-room high rise overlooks a private beach and the ocean. Guests enjoy the heated pool and cocktail lounge; other amenities include a dining room, in-room fridges, cable TV, and room safes. ♦ 700 N Atlantic Blvd (near Vistamar St). 563.2451, 800/327.8578 ♿

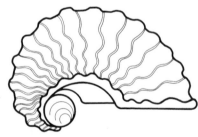

67 Bonnet House Listed on the National Registry of Historic Places, this 30-room, plantation-style home was the tropical retreat of Frederic and Evelyn Fortune Bartlett. (The property was originally owned by Hugh Taylor Birch, who gave the land to his daughter Helen Birch and Frederic Bartlett in 1919 as a wedding gift. She died six years later.)

The lush 35-acre estate, one of the last undeveloped tracts fronting the ocean, was deeded by Mrs. Bartlett to the Florida Trust for Historic Preservation (the largest land bequest in state history). Unlike the Palm Beach wealthy, the Bartletts eschewed traditional furnishings and formality, decorating their home with art and the things they loved. Native materials such as cypress and coral were used throughout. The estate derives its name from the bonnet water lilies that root in the surrounding ponds. Today, a colony of squirrel monkeys are among the creatures that make the estate their home. ♦ Admission. Tours: Tu-F 10AM, 1PM; Su 1PM, 2PM May-Nov. Reservations recommended. 900 N Birch Rd (just west of A1A, south of Sunrise Blvd). 563.5393 &

68 Parrot Lounge At this popular bar with a casual "Cheers" atmosphere and photos lining the walls, beer is served in 20-ounce pilsners (Norm would love it). Happy Hour and weekly food specials are offered, too. ♦ No cover. M-F, Su until 2AM; Sa until 3AM. 911 Sunrise La (one block from the beach). 563.1493 &

68 Holiday Inn–Beach Galleria $$ Here are 240 rooms with unbeatable views of the ocean, the **Bonnet House**, the Intracoastal, and **Hugh Taylor Birch State Park**. Room service, a pool, tennis, and a restaurant make this hotel a bargain. Guests enjoy easy access to the Strip and the Sunrise Boulevard shopping district. ♦ 999 N Atlantic Blvd (at Sunrise Blvd). 563.5961, 800/HOLIDAY; fax 564.5261 &

Bests

Jim Naugle
Mayor, City of Ft. Lauderdale

Las Olas Shopping District World-class shopping with European ambience. Dining at one of the many fine restaurants and strolling along the boulevard in shirtsleeves in January. A fun place to sip cappuccino while watching the world walk by. Look for the **Museum of Art** just west of the shops.

Museum of Discovery and Science and **Broward Center for the Performing Arts** Located in **Riverwalk**'s historical district, **MODS,** with its interactive displays and awesome five-story-high **Blockbuster IMAX Theater,** has been called a playground for the mind. Quite an experience! Across the street is the magnificent **Performing Arts Center,** the cultural destination for concerts, theater, and dance.

Ft. Lauderdale Beach The beach transformation is astounding. The streetscape comprises a coordinated look; the new wave wall, softly curved columns, and the waver paver promenade complement the rolling ocean currents. Dine in one of the many European outdoor cafes, or just sink your toes into our soft warm sand. It's too beautiful to miss!

Water Taxi Water Taxi on the Venice of America! To see **Riverwalk** and the splendor of **Ft. Lauderdale** from the famous **Intracoastal** and our many canals, take a ride on the Water Taxi to shops, hotels, clubs, and beaches, as well as the museums and other attractions.

H. Wayne Huizenga
Former Chairman/CEO, Blockbuster Entertainment Corp.

Burt & Jacks, Port Everglades, Ft. Lauderdale—the best beef and hash browns in town.

Sheffield's at the **Marriott Harbor Beach Resort,** Ft. Lauderdale—quiet elegance and fine wine.

Eating at one of Miami's great Cuban restaurants before attending a **Miami Heat** basketball game.

Watching the **Miami Dolphins** play on a perfect Sunday afternoon at **Joe Robbie Stadium.**

Attending a performance at the new **Broward Center for the Performing Arts** in Ft. Lauderdale.

Cruising the **New River** and **Intracoastal** on the unique **Water Taxi**—a great way to show visitors the city of Ft. Lauderdale.

Taking friends to the **Pier 66** revolving lounge to watch the ships depart **Port Everglades** under the glowing city lights at dusk.

Strolling along Ft. Lauderdale's beautiful **Las Olas Boulevard** in the evening.

Pat Jordan
Writer

The **Gold Coast Gym** on Dixie Highway, Ft. Lauderdale. Talking at 7AM between bouts of weight lifting with Johnny Alua, who runs the gym, about his life in pre-Castro Cuba.

Napoli Ristorante in Pompano, where Guy, the owner, will always prepare any special request and allow me to smoke my cigar.

Mark Tiki Lounge on Ft. Lauderdale Beach, where all the strippers, male and female, work on their perfect tans in G-strings and no one cares.

Shooters on the Intracoastal, Ft. Lauderdale, where there are still a few "wise guys" left from the heady 1980s drug days, and the women still dress out of Frederick's of Hollywood.

Ft. Lauderdale Beach—The Strip—which the foreign tourists are making the American Riviera.

Anywhere in Ft. Lauderdale, where people still have a Southern friendliness and a Northern savvy.

Hollywood/Dania/Hallandale

With its vaguely European flavor—a hybrid of the French Riviera and Atlantic City—**Broward County** yearly attracts as many as 380,000 Canadians, most of them flocking to the seaside towns of Hollywood, Dania (pronounced *Dane*-ya), and Hallandale, south of **Ft. Lauderdale–Hollywood International Airport.** Canadians particularly favor Hollywood, usually staying until well after other snowbirds have headed home. Every winter, the town's parking lots are full of cars bearing license plates from Saskatchewan, Ontario, and Quebec, and the lilt of French-rolled *r*s can be heard on the beach, especially at a shoreside stand called Frenchie's, which sells *poutine*, a sticky mixture of cheese curds and french fries relished by some Quebecois.

Tourism first became big business here in the 1920s, when the three cities were known as **Hollywood-by-the-Sea.** Visitors came by bus, train, and ship, drawn by ads placed in Northern newspapers by Joseph Young, the 300-pound real estate huckster who founded Hollywood. Young treated prospective lot buyers to free lunches, then sat them down in "sweat" rooms with hard-sell salespeople (a sales tactic still used by some of those who push condos and time-share vacations).

nspired by the great city of Paris, Young laid out Hollywood with wide akes, broad boulevards, and palm-fringed traffic circles. On the ocean at **Hollywood Boulevard,** the city's main drag, he put up the grand **Hollywood Beach Hotel.** He also built the **Municipal Casino,** a huge public swimming pool on **Johnson Street.** Thanks to Young's efforts, Hollywood-by-the-Sea quickly became Broward's biggest city—but not for long. In 1926, a deadly hurricane flattened much of it, and three years later, a worse blow struck: the Great Depression. Young lost everything except his large mansion, and he died in 1934 of a heart attack while plotting a new real estate scheme.

Dania and Hallandale, once quiet tomato-farming communities, broke away from Hollywood-by-the-Sea years ago. Named after its Danish settlers, Dania developed an antiques district on **Federal Highway.** It also is home to the **Design Center of the Americas (DCOTA),** an exclusive mall for interior decorators, and the **Dania Jai-alai Fronton,** home of the sport with the fastest-moving ball in the world. Hallandale, settled by Swedish farmers, is a retirement enclave with towering condominiums on A1A. The people here love their sports—particularly thoroughbred racing at **Gulfstream Park** and dog racing at the **Hollywood Greyhound Track.**

The city of Hollywood, however, is still trying to establish its own identity. It seems torn between remaining a simple seaside vacation spot and becoming a chic business-and-arts center. But perhaps a decision has already been made: The aging downtown, in the midst of a face-lift, is trying to nurture a new artists' colony and develop a vital shopping district; farther west, a spectacular glass-and-neon tower called **Presidential Circle** has sprouted—sure signs that this is a city on the move.

Area code 954 unless otherwise indicated.

1 Rustic Inn Crabhouse ★★$$$ At this casual spot, the tables are covered with newspapers, and the diners are equipped with mallets. That's because the house specialty is garlic crab, and the hammers are used to crack the claws, making quite a racket. ♦ Seafood ♦ Daily lunch and dinner. 4331 SW Ravenswood Rd (north of Griffin Rd), Ft. Lauderdale. 584.1637 &

2 Spiced Apple ★★$$$ Diners stopping at this unusual eatery encounter an eclectic menu featuring everything from fried steak and frogs' legs to gator tail and catfish. The decor is country-clutter. ♦ Regional American ♦ Daily lunch and dinner. Reservations

recommended. 3281 Griffin Rd (at SW 32nd Ave), Ft. Lauderdale. 962.0772 &

3 Tropical Acres ★$$ Prime rib, ribs, chicken, seafood, and a good variety of steaks are among the offerings at this longtime favorite for Sunday family dinners. ♦ American ♦ Daily dinner. 2500 Griffin Rd (at SW 25th Ave), Ft. Lauderdale. 989.2500 &

4 Ft. Lauderdale Airport Hilton $$ Tennis, a health club, a Jacuzzi, a sauna, a swimming pool, fishing, two restaurants, and a free airport shuttle are among the amenities at this 388-room hotel. Meeting facilities are on site for those who have to squeeze in a little work. ♦ 1870 Griffin Rd (at I-95), Dania. 920.3300, 800/654.8266 in FL, 800/445.8667; fax 920.3348 &

5 Sheraton Ft. Lauderdale Airport Hotel $$ This 251-room business hotel offers a health club, tennis and racquetball courts, a complimentary shuttle to the airport, a heated pool, and a lovely waterfall in the lobby. ♦ 1825 Griffin Rd (at I-95), Dania. 920.3500, 800/325.3535; fax 920.3571 &

The first incorporated town in Broward County was Modello, which evolved after Henry Flagler laid railroad tracks through the area in 1896. In honor of its Danish settlers, however, the city's name was changed to Dania.

Within the Sheraton Ft. Lauderdale Airport Hotel:

Moon Dance ★★$$$ You'll wonder how the chef here comes up with such unusual combinations. Guava, papaya, and plantains may be the most recognizable tropical ingredients; chicken with cornbread and chorizo stuffing is a favorite. Chase down the spicy foods with beers from around the world.
♦ Eclectic ♦ Daily lunch and dinner. 920.3500 &

Design Center of the Americas (DCOTA) Pronounced da-*ko*-ta, this mall-sized center sells everything from furniture and carpets to home design accessories, but only to the trade. If you can get in here with an accredited designer, your mind will be blown. Luckily, open-house events do occasionally take place. ♦ M-F. 1855 Griffin Rd (at I-95), Dania. 923.4622 &

6 Grand Prix Race-O-Rama In addition to miniature golf, bumper cars, and a go-cart track, there's a 24-hour arcade with 600 games. Believe it or not, this is Broward County's most popular tourist attraction.
♦ Admission. M-Th, Su until 11PM; F-Sa until 2AM. 1801 NW First St (west of Bryon St), Dania. 921.1411

7 Deli Den ★★$ At breakfast, help yourself to the basket of pastries on your table; later in the day, bowls of coleslaw and pickles take its place. Homesick New Yorkers come here for Big Apple basics like bagels, lox, and corned beef. ♦ Deli ♦ Daily breakfast, lunch, and dinner. 2889 Stirling Rd (a mile west of I-95 in Stirling Square), Hollywood. 961.4070 &

8 Beverly Hills Café ★$$ Sandwiches and 26 kinds of salads are the specialties at this chain eatery. It's all very California and very healthful, but burgers are on the menu, too.
♦ California ♦ Daily lunch and dinner.

4000 N 46th Ave (at Stirling Rd), Hollywood. 963.5220 &. Also at: 7041 Commercial Blvd (east of University Dr), Tamarac. 722.8211; 5544 S Flamingo Rd (at Stirling Rd), Cooper City. 434.2220; and 10001 Cleary Blvd (at Nob Hill Rd), Plantation. 452.2990

9 Antique Row Antiques lovers will have a field day in the 150-plus stores lining the Federal Highway. You'll find early Americana, British antiques, and estate-sale items, with quality ranging from flea market gewgaws to real rarities. Start at First Street, head south, and visit **House of Hirsch, Scintillations Antiques,** and **F&N.** Then continue past Dania Beach Boulevard and round the corner to Northeast Second Avenue to hit more places. Spend an hour or all day. ♦ Daily. Hwy 1 (between Dania Beach Blvd and Griffin Rd/ NW 10th St), Dania

10 Dania Jai-alai Fronton Florida is the jai-alai capital of the US, and this is the second-largest fronton (arena) in the state (Miami's is the largest). Bet on the ancient Basque game in which *pelotaris* (players) use *cestas* (wicker baskets) to hurl goatskin-covered *pelotas* (balls) at speeds reaching 185 mph. The object is to bounce the ball off the walls and floors in such a way that the opponent can't catch it. Clubhouse dining, cocktails, and snack bars are offered. ♦ Admission. Tu, Th, Sa noon and 7:15PM; W, F at 7:15PM. 301 E Dania Beach Blvd (east of Hwy 1), Dania. 927.2841 &

11 Barnes & Noble Grab a cup of coffee and any of 100,000 books, and plop down on a big green chair to read and relax. Enjoy discounts of 10 to 30 percent. ♦ Daily. 4170 Oakwood Blvd (at Stirling Rd, east of I-95 in Oakwood Plaza), Hollywood. 923.1738 &

12 Graves Museum of Archaeology and Natural History Local archaeologist Wilburn "Sonny" Cockrell excavated artifacts of South Florida civilizations dating as far back as 1000 BC, including pottery, ornately carved stone and antlers, and a .50-caliber musketball. In 1994, he donated to this eclectic museum 33 boxes of his discoveries from sites in or near Coral Springs. Also here is perhaps the world's most complete triceratops skull, dating back 100 million years. Three life-size dioramas depict the lifestyle of the Tequesta Indians, Broward County's original settlers. Other exhibits include an Egyptian room, African tribal art, pre-Columbian art, and fossils.
♦ Admission. Tu-W, F 10AM-4PM; Th 10AM-8PM; Sa-Su 10AM-5PM; guided tours Sa 1PM. 481 S Federal Hwy (at SE Fourth St), Dania. 925.7770 &

13 Tark's ★★$ Ssshh. Only the locals know about this roadside raw bar, which has been around since 1966. Ocean-fresh shellfish and spicy Buffalo wings are the specialties of the house. Take your purchase home, or eat in. ♦ Seafood ♦ Daily lunch and dinner. 1317 S Federal Hwy (at SE 13th St), Dania. 925.8275 ⅄. Also at: 8970 State Rd 84 (west of Pine Island Rd), Davie. 475.8275

14 Topeekeegee Yugnee Park The Seminole Indian name means "Gathering Place," but locals call this green space simply "T-Y Park." Arrive early on weekends to squeeze in a full day's use of the 40-acre lake, swimming lagoon, water slide, fishing sites, picnic pavilions, bike and boat rentals, RV and tent campsites, and trading post. Don't miss artist Kevin MacIvor's fiberglass sculpture called *Wild Dolphins,* located in the lagoon complex. ♦ Admission. Daily. 3300 N Park Rd (at Sheridan St), Hollywood. 985.1980

15 Wan's Mandarin House ★★$$ Hidden in a shopping center, this Chinese restaurant is worth hunting down for its wonderful hot-and-sour soup. ♦ Chinese ♦ Daily lunch and dinner. In Park Sheridan Plaza, 3331 Sheridan St (near N Park Rd), Hollywood. 963.6777 ⅄

16 Toojay's ★★★$ They call it a "gourmet deli," and deli diehards swear by this chain of 13 restaurants (and counting). The hardest part is deciding what to order: blintzes, nova on a bagel, the popular turkey with chopped liver on rye, or the corned beef and tongue combo ("Boca Loco"). Save room for the chocolate killer cake—the word "killer" is written on each cake. ♦ Deli ♦ Daily breakfast, lunch, and dinner. 4401 Sheridan St (at N 46th Ave), Hollywood. 962.9909 ⅄

17 Tumi ★★$$ There's live music and even livelier food at this neighborhood Peruvian restaurant. Try the *cobina a lo macho* (fish fillet topped with red sauce and seafood) or *lomo saltavo* (beef with onions and tomatoes). It's all very tangy and tasty. ♦ Peruvian ♦ Daily lunch

and dinner. 5917 Johnson St (east of Rte 441), Hollywood. 985.8358 ⅄

18 Presidential Circle Neon-trimmed towers and a 120-foot atrium have made this 1989 building designed by **Barretta & Associates** a landmark. It's the home of the *Miami Herald* and state offices. ♦ Hollywood Blvd (at N 40th Ave), Hollywood. 981.8288 ⅄

19 Hollywood Mall This is a convenient place to pick up essentials for your vacation. Stores include **Target, Woolworth's,** and **Publix** supermarket. ♦ M-Sa until 9PM; Su noon-6PM. 3251 Hollywood Blvd (at Park Rd), Hollywood. 981.1000, 962.2989 ⅄

20 Stratford's $$ Stuff yourself with all-you-can-eat shrimp and other specials, then wash it all down with an icy draft beer. ♦ American ♦ Daily lunch and dinner. 2910 Hollywood Blvd (at I-95), Hollywood. 920.6159 ⅄

21 Hollywood Library Catch up on the latest news with big-city papers like *The New York Times* and *The Wall Street Journal,* or read a book—you're on vacation. ♦ M-Th, Sa. 2600 Hollywood Blvd (at 26th Ave, on south side of circle), Hollywood. 926.2430 ⅄

22 Hemmingway $$$ Although this dining establishment is eccentric and interesting, its menu doesn't measure up. Decorated with flocked wallpaper, knickknacks, and gilded paintings, the restaurant was Hollywood's city hall and firehouse in the 1920s. The stained-glass and rococo accents are either romantic or tacky, depending on your taste. The fare, including pasta and fish, is more pedestrian. ♦ American ♦ M-F lunch and dinner; Sa dinner. Reservations recommended. 219 N 21st Ave (at Polk St), Hollywood. 926.5644 ⅄

22 Saigon Restaurant ★$ Chopsticks, not silverware, are wrapped in cloth napkins at your place setting. The unusual fare includes *pho tai* (rice noodles and beef in broth), curries, and beef and coriander soup. Ask for Vietnamese iced tea, sweetened with condensed milk. It's not on the menu, but they'll serve it if you want. ♦ Vietnamese ♦ M-F lunch and dinner; Sa-Su dinner. 2031 Hollywood Blvd (at S 20th Ave), Hollywood. 923.9256

22 Club M Admire local artists' works while listening to live jazz or rhythm-and-blues bands. Happy Hour is a misnomer here: It lasts from 1PM to 9PM daily. ♦ Cover after 10PM. Daily; live bands W-Sa 9:30PM-4AM. 2037 Hollywood Blvd (at S 20th Ave), Hollywood. 925.8396

At 120 feet wide, Hollywood Boulevard is Florida's widest paved street. To keep motorists from speeding, Joseph Young, who built the boulevard, added three traffic circles, which continue to this day to slow everyone down: Young, City Hall, and Presidential Circles.

23 Arts District To revive its moribund downtown, Hollywood planted palms in a median strip to make this area more pedestrian-friendly. This and other efforts have resulted in a bizarre mix of old and new. For a meal, check out the **Classic Dinette Co.** or **Mr. Greek.** The shuttered **Great Southern Hotel** is a Mediterranean-style landmark gone to seed. Art studios—as well as shops and parking facilities—are one block north and south of the hotel. ♦ Hollywood Blvd from Young Circle to the railroad tracks

24 Young Circle Free concerts take place in this open-air park. In the movie *Midnight Cowboy*, Ratso Rizzo (played by Dustin Hoffman) died aboard a bus tooling around the park. ♦ Hollywood Blvd (at Hwy 1)

At Young Circle:

Sushi Blues Cafe ★★$$ This tiny, funky neighborhood hot spot combines Japanese food and, yes, live blues shows Wednesday through Saturday nights. Take your pick of beer, wine, or sake. The sushi is fine, but it's really the music that draws the crowds. ♦ Japanese ♦ M-Sa dinner. 1836 S Young Circle. 929.9560

25 Hollywood Greyhound Track Dog racing enthusiasts flock here from December through April. A restaurant plus fast-food stands and cocktail bars provide refreshment. There is an on-site flea market Saturday and Sunday from 8AM to 3PM (call 454.8666). ♦ Admission. First race: M, W, F-Sa 7:30 PM; Tu, Th, Sa 12:30 PM, 7:30 PM late April-late Dec. 831 N Federal Hwy (at Pembroke Rd), Hallandale. 454.9400 &

26 Hallandale Fashion Row Also known as "Schmatte Row," this shoppers' mecca boasts more than 60 discount fashion stores, among them **Michael's** and **Sheila's.** ♦ Daily. Off Hallandale Beach Blvd at the railroad tracks

27 Gulfstream Park World-class thoroughbred racing—held here from January to mid-March —features the $500,000 **Florida Derby,** the foremost preview of the **Triple Crown.** Dine indoors at the **Clubhouse;** eat alfresco in the **Gulfdome Dining Terrace;** or visit one of the cocktail or snack bars. ♦ Admission. Post time 1PM Jan–mid-Mar. 901 S Federal Hwy (at SE Seventh St), Hallandale. 454.7000 &

28 Hallandale Beach This family-oriented beach features snack and T-shirt concessions and a picnic area. There's metered parking, but empty spots are tough to find. ♦ Daily until 10PM. Off A1A (at Hallandale Beach Blvd)

29 Driftwood on the Ocean $ In a secluded spot on Hollywood Beach, bilingual (English and French) hosts Micheline Courville and Fidel Labrecque greet guests—some of them honeymooning—at this 49-unit motel. Private balconies, in-room movies, beach-front terraces, and kitchenettes (there's no restaurant) make seclusion possible. ♦ 2101 S Surf Rd (north of Hallandale Beach Blvd), Hollywood. 923.9528; fax 922.1062 &

30 Joseph Young House The former home of Hollywood's founder, Joseph Young, is privately owned, though the city considered buying it for $1 million back in the free-spending 1980s. Built in the 1920s, it has a Mediterranean look and an ornate interior. ♦ 1055 Hollywood Blvd (between N 10th and N 11th Aves), Hollywood

31 Ocean Walk This pink hotel/condo/entertainment complex includes restaurants such as **O'Malley's** (an upscale bistro), shops, a health club, a video arcade, and bike rental facilities. Ten AMC movie theaters are across the street. ♦ Daily. 101 N Ocean Dr (at Hollywood Blvd), Hollywood. 922.3438

Within Ocean Walk:

Hollywood Beach Resort $$ Built in 1926 as the city's first hotel and the crown jewel of Joseph Young's beachside resort, this building was later shuttered for years before briefly reopening in the early 1980s as a Bible college. It's now a renovated 350-room hotel overlooking Hollywood Beach's **Broadwalk.** There's a dining room on the premises. ♦ 921.0990

32 Hollywood Beach Swim, sunbathe, or just stroll along the beach's two-and-a-half-mile **Broadwalk,** edged with palms, shops, and restaurants. Or just sit and watch the world go by. Metered parking, restrooms, showers, and a bicycle path are available, and lifeguards are on duty daily. On Johnson Street is the **Theater under the Stars** (921.3404), a band shell with free musical programs year-round and dancing on Monday evenings. ♦ A1A, from Hollywood city limits to Dania. 921.3423

33 Capone's Flicker-Lite Pizza and Raw Bar ★★$ When the Capones migrated here about 30 years ago, they brought a slice of Chicago with them. And it's still the best pizza

on the beach. ♦ Pizzeria ♦ Daily lunch and dinner. 1014 N Ocean Dr (between Michigan and Buchanan Sts), Hollywood. 922.4232 &

34 Bavarian Village ★★$$$ Hearty portions of sauerbraten, schnitzel, and wurst are heaped onto the plates of those who refuse to give up such fattening foods. Have it all with a stein of German beer. ♦ German ♦ Daily dinner. Reservations recommended. 1401 N Federal Hwy (between Cleveland and McKinley Sts), Hollywood. 922.7321 &

35 Bernard Apartments Motel $ Rina and Maurice Bernard try to make their 50-unit spread a home away from home. Quebecois enjoy a French TV channel and banter with their hosts in French, pet lovers can bring Fido or Snowball, and each apartment has a full kitchen. There's no restaurant, though. ♦ 1819 Wilson St (west of Hwy 1 and south of Sheridan St), Hollywood. 921.5190; fax 922.5297

36 West Lake Park Once swampland, downtown Hollywood was elevated with fill that was quarried here. Now the sandpit is a 1,300-acre mangrove preserve and a haven for birds and fish—and canoeists. Facilities include racquetball and tennis courts, boat and canoe rentals, picnic shelters, and a playground. Due to open at press time was the **Anne Kolb Nature Center,** with artwork by Miamian Christine Federico integrated into its design. ♦ 1200 Sheridan St (between N 14th Ave and A1A), Hollywood. 926.2410

37 Hollywood North Beach Park Here are 56 acres of lovely waterfront land with picnic tables, volleyball playing areas, bike paths, a turtle hatchery, a 60-foot viewing tower, and more than 500 species of plants. Anglers enjoy the fishing pier on the Intracoastal side. RV parking is available. ♦ 3501 N Ocean Dr (Sheridan St at A1A), Hollywood. 926.2444

38 Sea Legs IV Drift Fishing Marina Schedule a party-boat tour, a fishing charter, or even a trip to the Bahamas here. Jet Ski rentals are also available, from 9AM to 5PM daily. ♦ Daily fishing charter departures at 8AM, 1:30PM, and 7PM. 5400 N Ocean Dr (at Franklin St), Hollywood. 923.2109 &

39 Martha's on the Intracoastal ★★★$$$$ Created by the owners of **Bavarian Village** (see above), this landmark eatery serves excellent prime ribs, steaks, and pasta. With its great setting and breathtaking view, it would be hard to find a better Sunday brunch anywhere in town. Boats pull up to the restaurant's 1,000-foot dock as a jazz quartet plays at night and for Sunday brunch. The decor is tropical, with bamboo and rattan furnishings and hanging plants. ♦ American ♦ Daily lunch and dinner; Sunday brunch. Reservations recommended. 6024 N Ocean Dr (a block south of Dania Beach Blvd), Hollywood. 923.5444 &

39 Martha's Tropical Grille ★★★$$$ Rising star Scott Howard's new restaurant, which is above the more staid **Martha's on the Intracoastal** (see above), is fast becoming a destination for the younger crowd. Florida meets the Caribbean here: Try the snapper with a passion-fruit puree, or stone crab claws with a Key lime–and-wasabi dipping sauce. ♦ Eclectic ♦ Daily dinner. Reservations recommended. 6024 N Ocean Dr (a block south of Dania Beach Blvd), Hollywood. 923.5444 &

40 Bloody Mary's ★$ Casual patio dining is enhanced by a waterfront view at this lunch place. The fare is burgers, hot dogs, Buffalo wings, and such. Along with some shops, the restaurant is part of a small waterfront complex called Seafair. ♦ American ♦ Daily lunch. Seafair, 101 N Beach Rd (at A1A and Dania Beach Blvd), Dania. 922.5600 &

41 Dania Beach Showers, fishing, picnic huts, and picnic facilities are all offered here. Lifeguards are on duty daily from 9AM to 5PM, and metered parking is available at Dania Beach Boulevard and Ocean Drive. ♦ On A1A, Dania. 921.8700 ext 360

42 John U. Lloyd State Recreation Area Sheltered under shady Australian pines, this two-mile stretch of sand is one of South Florida's most beautiful, with picnic tables, a jetty for fishing, canoe rentals, boat ramps, and—naturally—swimming. Scuba divers and snorkelers can explore offshore reefs. If you're here in July, take a ranger-guided nighttime tour to watch giant sea turtles lay 100-odd eggs each right on the beach. ♦ 6503 N Ocean Dr (north of Dania Beach Blvd), Hollywood. 923.2833

Restaurants/Clubs: Red   Hotels: Blue
Shops/ ♣ Outdoors: Green   Sights/Culture: Black

West Broward County

Folks tend to shop till they drop in this part of Florida. The sprawl of retail centers, upscale malls, and housing developments is also the last frontier for civilization, because beyond developed West Broward lies only the vastness of the **Everglades**. Some of the best public parks in South Florida are in western Broward County—a paradise for anglers, sports enthusiasts, and campers. Golf courses also proliferate here.

This is the fastest-growing area in a rapidly expanding county, with city-size suburbs such as **Weston** springing up virtually overnight. New highways are excellent, particularly **Interstates 75 and 595** and the **Sawgrass Expressway**, but traffic can still be a nightmare, especially at rush hour on the east-west routes. Allow plenty of time to reach your destination, whether it is the wonderful **Brasserie Max** restaurant or **C.B. Smith Park**.

West Broward comprises many municipalities, including **Miramar** and **Pembroke Pines** on the southern end, the urban-cowboy town of **Davie**, and the bedroom communities of **Cooper City**, **Plantation**, **Sunrise**, **North Lauderdale**, **Margate**, **Lauderhill**, **Lauderdale Lakes**, **Tamarac**, **Coconut Creek**, **Coral Springs**, and **Parkland**. In truth, though, you can drive through many of these cities without knowing where one ends and the next begins.

A couple of towns sport distinct personalities: Davie has had a western atmosphere since the 1930s, when James Bright, cofounder of the **Hialeah Racetrack**, began training thoroughbreds here. Today, prosperous farmers have multi-acre spreads populated by horses. A few produce operations remain in the area, including orange groves and **Batten's Strawberry Farm**.

The town of Sunrise was developed by Norman Johnson, a sports car enthusiast, who had a peculiar brainstorm in the early 1960s. He was driving along a street in Miami when he came upon a car that was flipped over. He thought he was the witness to an accident, only to discover that the automobile was

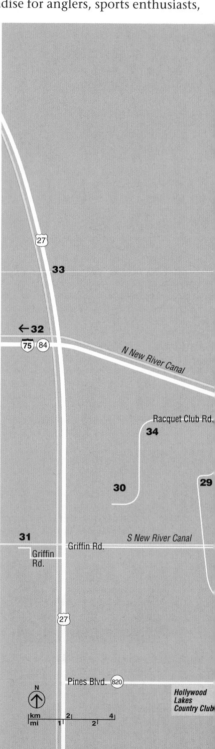

installed as a sales gimmick on a dealer's lot. Inspired by the scene, Johnson went back to Broward County and built an upside-down house in Sunrise. The house—complete with furniture bolted upside-down to the ceiling and an upside-down Pontiac convertible in the carport—was featured in *Life* magazine, and Johnson sold *many* housing lots after that.

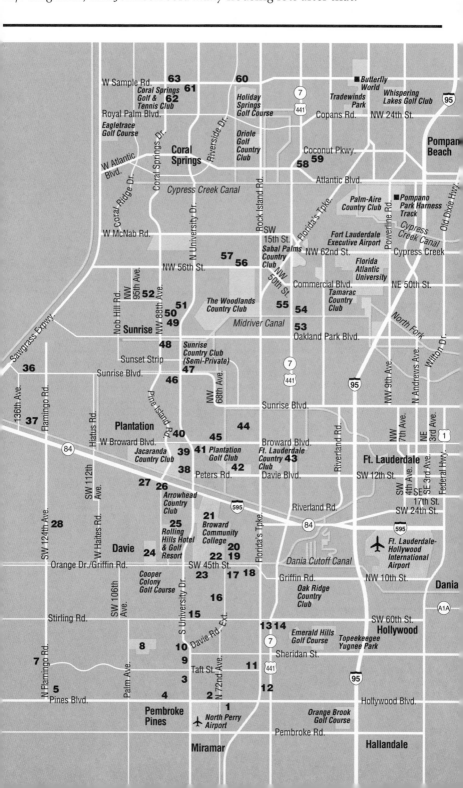

Area code 954 unless otherwise indicated.

1 Brick Oven ★★★$ This casual place sports wooden benches, while many of its patrons sport shorts. Thanks to a hickory-fired oven, the fabulous individual-size, nine-inch gourmet pizza served here has a smoky flavor. Had your fill of pizza? There's also spaghetti, hot sandwiches, and ravioli on the menu. ♦ Italian ♦ Daily lunch and dinner. 7100 Pines Blvd (at SW 72nd Ave), Pembroke Pines. 962.8822 &

2 Outback Steakhouse ★$$ *Crocodile Dundee* decor and "Strine" expressions carry out the Aussie motif at this casual chain restaurant. The bloomin' onion appetizer—a colossal deep-fried onion with tangy dip—is above average. ♦ Steak house ♦ Daily dinner. 7841 Pines Blvd (east of University Dr, in the Winn Dixie Shopping Plaza), Pembroke Pines. 981.5300 &. Also at: 1823 N Pine Island Rd (at Sunrise Blvd), Plantation. 370.9956; 6201 N Federal Hwy (at 62nd St in Prado Shopping Plaza), Ft. Lauderdale. 771.4390; 650 Riverside Dr (at Atlantic Blvd), Coral Springs. 345.5965

2 Ronieri's ★★$$$ Creative cuisine is the hallmark of this trendy place. Popular dishes include a fish sampler of snapper and salmon with light mustard glaze, crisp raspberry duck, and vegetarian meatballs served atop angel-hair pasta. ♦ Continental ♦ Tu-Sa dinner. Reservations recommended. 207 N University Dr (at Pines Blvd, in the Winn Dixie Shopping Plaza), Pembroke Pines. 966.2233 &

3 Canton 5 ★★$$ Part of the well-known Miami chain, this place serves superb Cantonese steak, and honey chicken. ♦ Chinese ♦ Daily lunch and dinner. Reservations recommended. 220 N University Dr (two blocks north of Pines Blvd), Pembroke Pines. 435.3388 &

Architectural Stew

Ever since Day One, people have come to **South Florida** from all over the world, bringing with them their particular ideas of what a home or business should look like. The result is an amazing melting pot of styles, including Oriental, Cape Cod, Colonial, Neo-Gothic, and Tahitian, among others. However, several styles dominate in South Florida. Here's a sampling, along with some tips on how to identify them:

Art Deco

Miami Beach, especially **Collins Avenue** and **Ocean Drive** in the area known as **South Beach,** exemplifies the Art Deco style. Art Deco buildings are often made from smooth concrete that has been shaped and molded into clean curves and sharp, distinct edges that sometimes give the structures a wedding cake appearance. Most of these buildings are painted white or a light pastel color—with brighter, contrasting colors used as accents around the roof, doors, and windows. (The windows, by the way, are often rounded or curved.) Overall, the Art Deco style is clean, sleek, and geometric.

Cracker

Sometimes called Florida Vernacular, this style was designed solely with function, not form, in mind. The idea was to help early settlers survive the steamy subtropical elements. The first Cracker-style buildings were constructed on stilts to avoid floodwaters during the rainy season. They had deep overhangs to shade big porches and plenty of large, rectangular screened windows to let in breezes. The characteristic tin roof was cheap, lightweight, and long-lasting.

Though today's developers don't always perch Cracker-style structures on stilts, they do include two trademark characteristics: wooden siding and smooth tin roofs. Many restaurants and homes are built in this way, and the ubiquitous tin roofs cover everything from major resorts to office complexes.

Mediterranean

You'll find this style everywhere in South Florida, particularly in such ritzy neighborhoods as **Naples, Coral Gables,** and **Palm Beach.** Historians credit its popularity here to developer **Addison Mizner,** who introduced it to Palm Beach in 1918. Mediterranean-type buildings usually have a brownish, olive, or cream-colored stucco covering. They're dotted with round arches and large windows and are typically topped with deep orange, Spanish-tile roofs.

4 Nami ★★$$ Sushi lovers, you've found your home. Casual is the theme here, where the menu lists tempura, teriyaki, and other Japanese standards. ♦ Japanese ♦ M-Sa lunch and dinner; Su dinner. 8381 Pines Blvd (one block west of University Dr), Pembroke Pines. 432.2888 ♿

5 Pembroke Lakes Mall A 17th-century Italian gazebo is the centerpiece of the county's newest mall, which has 130 shops. It's a bright, pretty place where a waterfall spills onto a rock lagoon next to the food court. Ducks sometimes swim at the lake outdoors. **J.C. Penney, Mervyn's, Burdines,** and **Sears** are the anchor stores, but **Dillards** is moving in, and there is space for one more anchor. The mall lured many businesses away from Hollywood to serve burgeoning south-western Broward County. ♦ Daily. 11401 Pines Blvd (at Flamingo Rd), Pembroke Pines. 436.3520 ♿

GRAND PALMS

6 Grand Palms Hotel $ Golfers love this spot. Newly redone, its 101 rooms and 30 suites are quite comfortable, and there's a restaurant, a pool, five tennis courts, and 27 holes of golf. ♦ 14800 Pines Blvd (at 148th Ave), Pembroke Pines. 431.8800 ♿

7 C.B. Smith Park In addition to its hiking and bike trails and an 80-acre lake, this 320-acre park has a comfortable camp-ground and myriad sports and water facilities. It's not terribly woodsy, but you'll feel as if you're getting away from it all (even though the malls are still close by). Bike rentals, miniature golf, RV sites with full hookups, canoe rentals, a water slide, tube rides, fishing, lighted tennis courts, and great picnic spots are available. ♦ 900 N Flamingo Rd (between Pines Blvd and Johnston St), Pembroke Pines. 437.2650

8 Brian Piccolo Park Named for the football star who grew up in Ft. Lauderdale and died of cancer at age 26 (his story became a film with the popular music theme "Brian's Song"), the 180-acre complex features softball, baseball, flag football, and soccer fields; tennis, racquet-ball, and basketball courts; a playground; fishing on a small lake; jogging; bicycling (velodrome); and picnicking. ♦ 9501

Sheridan St (between Palm Ave and Douglas Rd), Cooper City. 437.2600

9 Fountain Plaza Diner ★$ Home-style matzo ball soup, Greek salads, and fresh pastries are served at bargain prices. Fast service and incredible challah bread make this place worth a visit. ♦ Deli ♦ M-Th, Su 6AM-2AM; F-Sa 24 hours. 2150 N University Dr (at Pasadena Blvd), Pembroke Pines. 432.4900 ♿

10 Capriccio ★★$$$ Keep your eye on the chef—when he's in the kitchen, he prepares tempting dishes of fresh pasta, seafood, veal, and chicken. When the spirit moves him (and the kitchen quiets down), he's often found out front joining the pianist or violinist in Italian folk songs. ♦ Italian ♦ Daily dinner. 2424 N University Dr (at Sheridan St), Pembroke Pines. 432.7001 ♿

FRED HUNTER'S

11 Fred Hunter's Funeral Museum Inside the funeral home, this museum showcases antique mortician's equipment and burial clothing, hearses, an all-glass casket, and 19th-century funeral journals. ♦ Free. M-Sa, but it's best to call ahead for an appointment. 6301 Taft St (at N 63rd Ave), Hollywood. 989.1550 ♿

12 Las Vegas ★★$ The menu here features tasty and authentic Cuban fare. Try the wonderful pork dishes and black-bean soup. ♦ Cuban ♦ Daily lunch and dinner. 1212 N State Rd 7 (at Garfield St), Hollywood. 961.1001

13 Seminole Bingo and Casino Cash-only bingo can net winners big-money prizes here. This is no children's game, and the regulars are very serious. In the casino gamblers will find 36 poker tables and 290 slot machines. ♦ Daily 24 hours; bingo at noon, 2:45PM, 7:15PM, and 10:45PM. 4150 N State Rd 7 (at Stirling Rd), Hollywood. 961.3220 ♿

14 Native Village This Seminole Indian reservation sits in the middle of urban South Florida. Because the Seminole are a nation unto themselves, they may sell cigarettes tax-free. They also offer high-stakes bingo nearby at **Seminole Bingo and Casino** (see above) and put on snake shows and alligator-wrestling demonstra-tions. History buffs can learn the

story of the Seminole Indians, and anyone who is interested can see a rare, live Florida panther, bobcats, turtles, and other native animals. Or take a formal tour, then saunter through the little Indian art exhibit. Arts and crafts, gorgeous, colorful rickrack-adorned clothing, and dolls are for sale. ♦ Admission. M-Sa. 3551 N State Rd 7 (south of Stirling Rd), Hollywood. 961.4519 &

15 Shorty's ★$ Smoky Southern-style barbecue is served at informal picnic-style tables here. It's difficult to choose between the juicy barbecue chicken and ribs, both paired with great coleslaw and fries. ♦ Barbecue ♦ Daily lunch and dinner. 5989 S University Dr (at Stirling Rd), Davie. 680.9900

16 Batten's Strawberry Farm Bucolic farm country is only minutes away from the bustle of city life. Homegrown produce, flowers, and jam are for sale here, and you can pick berries by the bushel in season, January through May. ♦ Daily. 5151 SW 64th St/Davie Rd Extension (between Griffin and Stirling Rds), Davie. 792.0068

17 Armadillo Cafe ★★★$$$ This tiny, innovative cafe is tucked into a Western-style strip shopping center. Southwestern art dots the walls, and paper-covered tables invite diners to doodle with crayons, but it is the food that deserves the spotlight. Samples from the interesting menu: roasted corn and jalapeño fritters served with fresh apple sauce; marinated leg of lamb roasted with garlic and sun-dried tomatoes and served with rice pancakes; and outstanding yellowtail snapper topped with roasted peppers, garlic, tomatoes, wild mushrooms, and ginger. Sinful chocolate fritters with ice cream and a deep chocolate sauce shouldn't be missed. ♦ Southwestern ♦ Daily dinner. Reservations required (weekends sometimes are booked three weeks in advance). 4630 SW 64th Ave/Davie Rd Extension (at Griffin Rd), Davie. 791.4866, 791.5104 &

18 Bob Roth's New River Groves A basic fruit stand, this place features the ultimate tourist curiosity out front: Florida's largest (fake) orange. But real oranges are for sale, along with Key lime pie and fudge. ♦ Daily.

5660 Griffin Rd (at SW 55th Ave), Davie. 581.8630 &

19 Grif's Western Wear Urban cowhands come here to get gussied up and peruse the largest selection of boots in South Florida. ♦ Daily. 6211 SW 45th St/Orange Dr (west of SW 61st Ave), Davie. 587.9000 &

20 Fulvio's ★★$$$ This popular place may require a wait, but it's worth it for an extremely notable veal Milanese, steak *pizzaiola,* and outstanding pasta and seafood dishes. ♦ Italian ♦ Daily dinner. Reservations recommended. 4188 SW 64th Ave (at SW 41st St), Davie. 583.3666

21 Broward Community College, Central Campus Concerts and lecture programs are often held at the 1,200-seat **Bailey Concert Hall** (475.6884). The on-campus **Buehler Planetarium** presents state-of-the-art astronomy shows and crowd-pleasing special events. ♦ Admission. Planetarium shows F-Sa 7PM; family shows Sa-Su 1:30PM; laser shows F-Sa 9PM, 10:30PM, and midnight. Reservations recommended for planetarium shows. 3501 SW Davie Rd (four blocks north of 39th St, 1 mile south of I-595), Davie. 475.6680, reservations 475.6681 (until 3:30PM weekdays) &

22 Davie Arena In the heart of South Florida's horse country, this 5,000-seat covered arena hosts a monthly rodeo (January through November; call for dates). Other activities include a circus, sporting events, antiques shows, and arts festivals. ♦ 6591 SW 45th St (behind Town Hall, just west of Davie Rd Extension), Davie. 797.1166, 437.8800 &

23 Spykes Grove and Tropical Gardens

How can you come to Florida and not see a real orange grove? This one offers tram rides. Sample tree-fresh fruit and send home whatever you fancy. ♦ Daily. 7250 Griffin Rd (between University Dr and Florida's Turnpike), Davie. 583.0426; fax 583.2673

24 Tree Tops Park This was a live oak hammock, an elevated island in the middle of the **Everglades,** before much of the land was drained for development. Lots of trees remain, but picnicking, volleyball, a playground, canoe and paddleboat rentals, and horseshoe pits are what bring in the people. You'll also find nature and horse trails. Rent horses on weekends for guided rides through the park, or call ahead for weekday rides (beeper 422.4512). ◆ 3900 SW 100th Ave (off Orange Dr), Davie. 370.3750

25 Rolling Hills Hotel & Golf Resort $ *Caddyshack* was filmed at this resort set in a pretty wooded glen. It has an 18-hole golf course as well as a nine-holer and tennis courts, and its 290 rooms are furnished in soothing tropical colors. Guests have passes to the nearby ultramodern **Scandinavian Health Spa** and are close to many shopping centers and restaurants (and there's a restaurant on site). Conference facilities accommodate those combining work with pleasure. ◆ 3501 W Rolling Hills Circle (at SW 36th St, off University Dr), Davie. 475.0400 ♿

26 Garcia's ★$ Sombreros and clay pots are everywhere at this outpost of a popular chain. Start with the chimichanga and move on to the seafood *burro* (a large burrito). The Olivia sampler is for those who can't decide what to have—it combines tacos, quesadillas, and chimichangas. ◆ Mexican ◆ Daily lunch and dinner. 8800 State Rd 84 (at Pine Island Rd), Davie. 474.5226 ♿

27 Indochine ★★$$ Owner Hong Sejot is Vietnamese and her partner/husband is French, and that means you'd best forget any preconceptions you may have about Asian food. The innovative menu includes seafood "bird's nest," featuring squid and scallops. Start with a soup: Their spicy hot-and-tangy soup—made with chicken broth, pineapple, tomatoes, and bean sprouts—is memorable. ◆ Vietnamese ◆ Daily lunch and dinner. 8916 State Rd 84 (off Pine Island Rd in Pine Island Plaza), Davie. 452.8502 ♿

Flamingo Gardens

28 Flamingo Gardens See a 200-year-old live oak hammock and wander through 60 acres of gardens at this tropical wonderland. If that's not enough, there are real pink flamingos and other birds, a new free-flight aviary, ever-popular river otters and alligators, and tram rides through the Florida wetlands. ◆ Admission. Daily. 3750 Flamingo Rd (1 mile north of Griffin Rd at SW 36th Ct), Davie. 473.0010, 476.6013

29 Tutti's at Weston ★$$ The *focaccia* (Italian garlic bread served with whole roasted garlic cloves) at this Tuscan charmer is a classic. And the smoked mozzarella ravioli

and *rollatini* of spinach lure people from all over the county. ◆ Italian ◆ M-F lunch and dinner; Sa-Su dinner. 1342 SW 160th Ave (at 13th St, behind Publix), Weston. 389.5200 ♿

30 Peace Mound Park This archaeological park, one of the few in Florida open to the public, is located in an area that was home to Tequesta Indians in 3100 BC. Stand on a bridge and peer down into the excavation site, which is protected by a transparent lucite cover. ◆ Daily. 300 Three Village Rd (exit I-75 at Arvida Pkwy, turn right on Weston Rd and left on Indian Trace, then follow signs for about 2 miles). 389.2040

31 Everglades Holiday Park An airboat is a skiff mounted with an oil-derrick–like apparatus attached to a big fan. The fan puts out a deafening racket and gale-force blast as it propels you along. Here a 45-minute airboat ride lets you see nature at its purest despite the noise. It's amazing to realize so much wilderness abuts so much civilization. You also can rent a johnboat (a flat-bottom skiff). The fishing is superb, and boat ramps are available, along with picnicking, fishing guides, bait and tackle, a restaurant, a gift shop, and 100 campsites. ◆ Daily 24 hours. Airboat rides 9AM-5PM; johnboat rentals daily dawn-sunset. 21490 Griffin Rd (west of Hwy 27). 434.8111

32 Billie Swamp Safari and Eco and Adventure Tours At this Seminole Indian village, you can live as Florida's Native Americans once did. Sleep in Seminole chikee huts (with palmetto-frond roofs), and dine on alligator and fry bread. At the after-dinner campfire, you'll be entertained by Seminole story- tellers. Non- campers can take less-expensive day trips that include a guide, lunch, and a 90-minute safari. See fallow deer and antelopes on a 1,920- acre preserve. ◆ Fee for tours. Daily. Reserve at least three days ahead for camping and tours. Seminole Indian Reservation (exit I-75 at Miccosukee service plaza; go north to Seminole Reservation sign and look for park signs). 800/949.6101

Restaurants/Clubs: Red	Hotels: Blue
Shops/ Outdoors: Green	Sights/Culture: Black

33 Sawgrass Recreation Park Scratch the belly of an alligator, if you dare (its mouth is taped). A 90-minute tour includes a half-hour boat ride into the **Everglades** and visits to an 18th-century–style Seminole village and a reptile exhibit. Rent an airboat (complete with driver) or hire a fishing guide. A store sells tackle, souvenirs, and bait; the restaurant serves burgers, hot dogs, and the like. ◆ Fee. Daily; tours leave at 9AM and every 15 minutes thereafter. 1005 Hwy 27 (2 miles north of I-75). 389.0202

34 Bonaventure Resort and Spa $$ This posh hotel and spa is a favorite with the sports-minded. Tennis magazines have given its courts high marks, and two 18-hole **PGA**-managed golf courses are on the premises. Other sports facilities here include squash courts and an equestrian center. The 500 rooms are lovely, modern, and spacious, and there are three restaurants. Pamper yourself at the full-service spa (and fitness center), which has been called one of the nation's top 10. ◆ 250 Racquet Club Rd (take I-595 to Exit 1, and follow signs west to Bonaventure), Ft. Lauderdale. 389.3300, 800/327.8090 ಈ

35 Markham Park Lighted outdoor rifle/pistol ranges and skeet/trap fields make this 665-acre park unusual. But the woods also offer camping and nature trails, and there's an observatory, a model airplane field, fishing, a pool, bike and boat rentals, and tennis and racquetball courts. ◆ 16001 W State Rd 84 (at Weston Rd, west of I-75), Sunrise. 389.2000

36 Sawgrass Mills This mile-long megamall is touted as the world's largest outlet center. You'll need at least a day to see the whole place. All the discount outlets you'd expect are here, plus some you might not: **Spiegel, Guess?, Books-A-Million, Lillie Rubin, Levi Strauss, Athlete's Foot, Bugle Boy, Saks Fifth Avenue,** and more (at least 245 in all). **Ann Taylor** fans flock here from miles away. There's also the **Space Age Gallery,** which specializes in items made of titanium (such as jewelry), and a family entertainment center, two food halls, **Ruby Tuesday's,** and other restaurants. Park by the red entrance for the better clothing stores. ◆ 12801 W Sunrise Blvd (at Flamingo Rd), Sunrise. 800/FLMILLS ಈ

37 Blockbuster Golf and Games Touted as the largest complex of its kind in South Florida, this place has something for almost everybody in the family: baseball batting cages, bumper boats, a huge game room, a Disneyesque miniature golf course, and indoor miniature golf. A golf range, clubhouse, gift shop, restaurant, and training facilities also are offered. ◆ M-Th, Su 11AM-11PM; F-Sa 11AM-midnight. 151 NW 136th Ave (at I-595), Sunrise. 846.0030

38 The Fountains This shopping center is notable for the **Bookstop,** an excellent discount bookstore; **Peaches,** a music and video shop; and **Circuit City,** an electronics store. Movie theaters and restaurants are scattered throughout the property. ◆ Daily. 801 S University Dr (between Broward Blvd and Peters Rd), Plantation. 476.0018 ಈ

Within The Fountains:

Young at Art Participation and developing the imagination are stressed at this children's museum. ◆ Admission. Tu-Sa 11AM-5PM; Su noon-5PM. 424.0085 ಈ

Regas Grill ★$$ Fresh fish, ribs, and steaks are served in this upscale yet casual dining room. Watch the chefs prepare your food in the open kitchen. ◆ American ◆ Daily lunch and dinner. 452.0010 ಈ

39 Broward Mall One of the largest malls in Greater Ft. Lauderdale, this continues to be a dependable shopping mecca, despite its being eclipsed by **Sawgrass Mills** (see above). Today, **Burdines, J.C. Penney, Sears, Mervyn's,** and 126 other specialty stores attract shoppers to the place where the shopping craze that later hit West Broward started. ◆ Daily. 8000 W Broward Blvd (at S University Dr), Plantation. 473.8100 ಈ

40 Fashion Mall at Plantation One of the most attractive malls around, this one has the only **Macy's** in Broward, which is a big draw. Other highlights include **Lord & Taylor, Disney Store,** and **Barnie's Coffee & Tea,** a perfect place to sip iced cappuccino amid marble floors and sunny windows. Wheelchairs and strollers are available, and there's a centrally located post office. ◆ Daily. 321 N University Dr (north of Broward Blvd, at NW Second St), Plantation. 370.1884 ಈ

Within the Fashion Mall at Plantation:

Brasserie Max ★★★$$ One of South Florida's trendiest restaurants presents an abundant, imaginative menu featuring such specials as lightly fried chicken breast atop a Cobb salad and oak-grilled pizza. Don't miss the almond basket with raspberry sorbet and berries. The highly touted food here is served in an atmosphere that's elegant but not stuffy, with dim lighting setting the tone for dinner. Casual dress is appropriate. ◆ Californian ◆ Daily lunch and dinner. 424.8000 ಈ

40 Sheraton Suites Plantation $$ This nine-story, 264-room luxury hotel is connected to the **Fashion Mall at Plantation** (see above) and offers everything the traveler

—business or recreational—may need, such as hookups for personal computers, two TVs and a VCR in each room, and a restaurant. The lovely rooftop pool is perfect for a refreshing swim. On a clear day, you can see downtown Ft. Lauderdale. ♦ 311 N University Dr (just north of Broward Blvd), Plantation. 424.3300, 800/325.3535; fax 452.8887 &

41 Jade Garden ★$$ Traditional Asian specialties here include a honey of a honey garlic chicken. ♦ Chinese ♦ M-F lunch and dinner; Sa-Su dinner. 244 S University Dr (across from the Broward Mall in Plantation Community Plaza), Plantation. 475.3009 &

41 Baseball Card Store Thousands of baseball cards, as well as autographed plaques, bats, and shoes, are all part of Florida's largest collection of sports memorabilia. ♦ M-Sa; Su afternoon. 232 S University Dr (south of Broward Blvd in Plantation Community Plaza), Plantation. 475.4880 &

42 Plantation Heritage Park This former **University of Florida** experimentation farm still has many tropical flowering trees and a rare fruit area maintained by the park staff and the Rare Fruit and Vegetable Council. The 90-acre park offers picnic shelters, a playground, and fishing spots; bicycling, jogging, and a small nature trail also await. Rent bikes or a paddleboat. ♦ 1100 S Fig Tree La (at Peters Rd), Plantation. 791.1025

43 Dan Dowd's ★$$$ A highly seasoned gorgonzola salad has made this place a local legend. The steaks are excellent. Pick one out from the butcher shop off the anteroom to take home. There's live music on Saturday. ♦ Steak house ♦ Daily lunch and dinner. Reservations recommended. 601 S State Rd 7 (at SW Sixth St), Plantation. 584.7770 &

44 Plantation Historical Museum This museum (illustrated below) is dedicated to illuminating the history and lifestyle of the first settlers of the community. See Plantation's first fire engine as well as a display on the area's first house. ♦ Donation. Tu-Th 9:30AM-noon, 1-4:30PM; also some Saturdays. 511 N Fig Tree La (north of Broward Blvd), Plantation. 797.2722 &

45 Lord & Taylor's Clearance Center One of only three in the country (the others are both on Long Island in New York), this clearance center features rows and rows of clothes that were in malls only a few months ago. The off-season merchandise sometimes is discounted 40 to 70 percent. ♦ M, Th-F 10AM-9PM; Tu-W, Sa 10AM-6PM; Su noon-5PM. 7067 W Broward Blvd (at NW 70th Ave in Plantation Center), Plantation. 581.8205 &

45 Tuesday Morning A favorite of locals, this tastefully decorated shop sells crystal, stationery, and lots of other department-store goods at one-half—or more—off department store prices. ♦ Call for hours. 7067 W Broward Blvd (at NW 70th Ave in Plantation Center), Plantation. 792.7468 &

46 Holiday Inn Plantation $ This is your typical large Holiday Inn (more than 300 rooms), with a restaurant, exercise facilities, and space for meetings. Within walking distance are many restaurants and shops. ♦ 1711 N University Dr (at Sunrise Blvd), Plantation. 472.5600, 800/HOLIDAY; fax 370.3201 &

46 Fuddruckers ★$ Despite the unappetizing name, this is home to award-winning hamburgers. Indicate how big a burger you want or select an entrée from the long menu (basically hot dogs, fish, steak, chicken, salad), order a drink and side dishes, find a seat in the cavernous room, and wait for your number to be called. It's very informal. ♦ American ♦ Daily lunch and dinner. 1801 N University Dr (at Sunrise Blvd), Plantation. 476.8111 &. Also at: 1200 N Federal Hwy (north of Sunrise Blvd), Ft. Lauderdale. 565.0077; 1915 N University Dr (south of Royal Palm Blvd/Copans Rd), Coral Springs. 344.6110

47 Mario the Baker ★★$$ Delicious individual gourmet pizzas and top-drawer shrimp scampi are served in this noisy,

Plantation Historical Museum

unpretentious spot. ♦ Italian ♦ Daily lunch and dinner. 220 N University Dr (at Sunset Strip), Sunrise. 742.3333. Also: **Mario's East** at 1313 E Las Olas Blvd (west of SE 12th Ave), Ft. Lauderdale. 523.4990

48 Sunrise Ice Skating Center It's not Rockefeller Center, but it beats the heat. ♦ Admission. M-Th, Su until 10PM; F-Sa until midnight. 3363 Pine Island Rd (at Oakland Park Blvd), Sunrise. 741.2366

49 Hooters ★$ This is a happening place despite (or because of) the waitresses in skimpy shorts and tight T-shirts. It's sexist but draws a family crowd. Chicken wings are big sellers, and the curly fries are wonderful. ♦ American ♦ Daily lunch and dinner. 3805 N University Dr (at NW 38th St), Sunrise. 748.1000 ♿. Also at: 5975 N Federal Hwy (north of Commercial Blvd), Ft. Lauderdale. 928.1825; CocoWalk, 3000 Grand Ave (between Main Hwy and Virginia St), Coconut Grove. 442.6004 ♿

50 Play It Again Sports A paradise for weekend jocks, this small buy/sell/trade clearinghouse of sports equipment is chock-full of broken-in softball gloves, golf clubs, skates, exercise equipment, and other used goods, plus some new merchandise. Regulars swear buy it—finally, they can afford to dabble in a wide range of sports. The trick is to comb the wares for bargains, or bring in your old tennis racket or other used sports gear to trade. ♦ Daily. 4137 N Pine Island Rd (between Oakland Park and Commercial Blvds in Pines Plaza), Sunrise. 746.0055 ♿

51 Little Israel Judaica and Israeli Gift Shop Jewish religious items and art and Israeli newspapers are sold in this cluttered store. ♦ M-F, Su 10AM-5PM. 7828 NW 44th St in Lincoln West Park Shopping Plaza (south of Commercial Blvd, west of N University Dr), Sunrise. 749.7674 ♿

52 Sunrise Musical Theatre Broward County's largest theatrical venue has seating for 4,084. Natalie Cole and Diana Ross are among the performers who have graced the stage. ♦ 5555 NW 95th Ave (at Commercial Blvd), Sunrise. 741.7300, box office 523.3309 ♿

53 US 441 International Shops Get a close-up view of South Florida's ethnic salad bowl: Greek, Jamaican, Vietnamese, and other Asian cultures are represented here. The neighborhood isn't pretty, but the exotic music

playing in some of the stores is. Taste food from around the world. ♦ N State Rd 7 (north of Oakland Park Blvd), Lauderdale Lakes &

Within US 441 International Shops:

53 Sahara Mediterranean Delight Food A wonderland for cooks, this little market provides several barrels of olives for buying in bulk, plus baklava, spices, hummus, *baba ganooj* (eggplant dip), and more. ♦ Daily until 10PM. 3570 N State Rd 7 (between Oakland Park Blvd and NW 36th St), Lauderdale Lakes. 731.3033 &

54 Cooke's Goose ★$ How often do you get the chance to eat curried goat, oxtail, or akee in a restaurant that resembles a **Denny's** with a full bar? Lunch is the best bet. Try the curried goat. ♦ Jamaican ♦ Daily lunch and dinner. 3750 N State Rd 7 (north of NW 36th St), Lauderdale Lakes. 484.1566 &

55 Oriental Food Market This store's name is written in English, but it's also translated into Vietnamese **(Cho A Dong)** and rendered in Chinese calligraphy, a clue to its importance in the Asian community here. Stock up on noodles and hard-to-find spices. ♦ Daily. 4245 N State Rd 7 (one-half mile south of Commercial Blvd), Lauderdale Lakes. 485.9450 &

56 Peking ★$$ Pick your cuisine—Hunan, Mandarin, Cantonese, Szechuan, or Shanghai. This restaurant has it all, with no MSG unless requested. ♦ Chinese ♦ M-F lunch and dinner; Sa-Su dinner. 6455 W Commercial Blvd (between 66th Terr and NW 61st Ave), Tamarac. 722.0666 &

57 L'Hostaria ★★$$$ The house specialties at this very elegant restaurant—including veal sautéed in lemon sauce with mushrooms and artichokes—keep them coming back. ♦ Italian ♦ Tu-Su dinner. Reservations recommended. 6646 NW 57th St (at NW 66th Ave), Tamarac. 722.0340 &

58 Thee London Pub After you've hoisted a pint of one of the 140 beers from around the world, throw a few darts. A dart league gathers here every night. ♦ M-Th, Su 11AM-2AM; F-Sa 11AM-4AM. 5637 W Atlantic Blvd (at Hwy 441), Margate. 977.6445 &

59 Omni Auditorium, Broward Community College Everything from trade shows to basketball tournaments and operas are staged at this multi-functional, on-campus auditorium , which accommodates almost 2,000 people. ♦ 1000 Coconut Creek Blvd (at 11th Ave), Coconut Creek. 973.2249 &

60 Il Porcino ★★★$$$ Progressive preparations of *risotto ai porcini* (risotto with parmesan cheese and porcini mushrooms) and veal chops are house specialties at this cozy, romantic restaurant. So is the gracious service. ♦ Northern Italian ♦ Tu-Su dinner. Reservations recommended. 8037 W Sample Rd (at Riverside Dr), Coral Springs. 344.9446 &

61 Runyon's ★★$$$$ This New England–style steak house with a friendly, cozy atmosphere is a local hot spot. Specializing in cooking "à la heart," with an emphasis on health, it serves such entrées as blackened scallops and shrimp marinara. There's also live Maine lobster, duck breast, buffalo, and steaks. ♦ American ♦ Daily lunch and dinner. 9810 W Sample Rd (between Coral Hills Dr and NW 99th Way), Coral Springs. 752.2333 &

62 Coral Springs City Centre This multipurpose venue has a 1,500-seat theater, a gym, an outdoor plaza, and class-rooms. ♦ 2855 Coral Springs Dr (at NW 29th St), Coral Springs. 344.5990 &

63 Melting Pot ★★$$$ Diners at this Swiss chalet–style restaurant cook their own fondue in either peanut oil or a highly seasoned broth. Choose from filet mignon, seafood, cheese, and more. But make sure to save room for dessert: chocolate fondue. ♦ Swiss ♦ Daily dinner. Reservations recommended. 10374 W Sample Rd (at NW 104th Ave), Coral Springs. 755.6368 &

Bests

Joel Hirschhorn
Criminal Defense Lawyer/Internationally Known Trial Lawyer

Orange Bowl—Hurricanes football

Miami Arena—Hockey

Joe Robbie Stadium—Football and baseball

Little Palm Island—A little bit of heaven in the **Keys**

Le Festival—Good, consistent French food

Coconut Grove—Food, people watching, boutiques

South Beach—Restaurants galore!

Boating—**Biscayne Bay**

David Lawrence Jr.
Publisher and Chairman, *The Miami Herald*

Many of Greater Miami's finest attributes are free or almost so.

A visit to downtown Miami's cultural plaza, the home of the **Center for the Fine Arts,** the **Historical Museum of Southern Florida,** and the main library.

Fairchild Tropical Gardens—for serious botanists and just plain lovers of nature.

Strolling on **Miami Beach's** boardwalk.

The view of downtown at night from the **Rickenbacker Causeway.**

And the lighted tower of the **Biltmore Hotel** out of my back window.

Northeast Broward County

Northeast Broward County is **Ft. Lauderdale**'s dining and entertainment capital. In fact, many of the cities in the area, including **Hillsboro Beach, Lighthouse Point, Sea Ranch Lakes, Lauderdale-by-the-Sea, Oakland Park, Wilton Manors,** and **Deerfield Beach,** derive their fame from their wonderful seafood restaurants and their proximity to ocean and Intracoastal panoramas. It's not that the majority of the county's 3,600 restaurants are concentrated here—just more of the better establishments. In decor, they range from rustic to fabulous, but the emphasis is definitely on catering to sophisticated palates and expectations. After all, this is home to several very exclusive and cosmopolitan neighborhoods.

Nightclubs are plentiful here, too. You'll find everything from progressive slam-dancing joints (some quite upscale) to elegant singles spots for the middle-aged crowd. That's not to say that Northeast Broward lacks daytime activities or family attractions. One of the most unusual places is **Butterfly World,** where you can stand inside screened lanais and watch these "flowers of the air" alight all around—and on—you. There's also harness racing, fishing off long wooden piers, and scuba diving among exotic reefs.

Area code 954 unless otherwise indicated.

1 Crabby Jack's ★$$ Among the local spate of rustic seafood houses, this spot is definitely one of the better ones. Don't leave without trying the garlic crabs. ◆ Seafood ◆ Daily lunch and dinner. 1015 S Federal Hwy (at Hillsboro Blvd), Deerfield Beach. 429.3770 &

2 Deerfield Island Park Nature trails, a picnic shelter, a playground, volleyball, and youth group camping await at this park, which is accessible only by boat. A pontoon boat picks up visitors at no charge at 8:30AM on Wednesdays and Saturdays for nature walks. The boat also sails at 1PM on the last Saturday of the month, and free shuttles run continuously between 11AM and 1:30PM the second Sunday of each month. Those with boats of their own can visit the park any time. ◆ Daily. Riverview Rd, just north of Hillsboro Blvd at the Intracoastal (park at the shuffleboard court car lot near the dock), Deerfield Beach. 360.1320

3 Riverview ★★$$$$ What sets this restaurant apart is its great waterfront view and history—it was a gambling casino back in the 1930s. Pasta, duck, and traditional American fare are the offerings. The cozy spot is reminiscent of a lodge in the forest; its pecky cypress construction and practically room-by-room growth over the years give it a unique atmosphere. ◆ American ◆ M-F lunch and dinner; Sa dinner. 1741 Riverview Rd (west of the Intracoastal, just south of Hillsboro Blvd), Deerfield Beach. 428.3463 &

4 Deerfield Beach Resort $$$ This tropical resort offers spectacular views of the water. Each of the 244 rooms is a suite, with a living room (including sofa bed), bedroom, wet bar, and two baths. Water aerobics and children's activities are available, and Deerfield Public Beach is across the street. There's also a restaurant. ◆ 950 SE 20th Ave (at Hillsboro Blvd), Deerfield Beach. 426.0478, 800/433.4600; fax 360.0539 &

5 Brooks ★★$$$$ A formal Queen Anne setting—heavy burgundy drapes, oil paintings, and a gilt fireplace—is the backdrop for a night of Florida seafood, wines by the glass, and dessert soufflés. Don't miss the pan-roasted salmon with a sauce of lemon, dill, and capers, or rack of lamb with a mustard-rum coating and mint sauce. The southern pecan pie with banana ice cream is fabulous. ◆ American ◆ Daily dinner; closed Monday mid-May–mid-November. Reservations recommended. 500 S Federal Hwy (at SE Fourth Ct), Deerfield Beach. 427.9302 &

6 Quiet Waters Park Ever gone waterskiing without a boat? Try cable waterskiing at **Ski Rixen** (429.0215), a park concession. There's also knee-boarding, canoes, paddleboats, Windsurfers, camping (rent a tent here), a beach, miniature golf, a playground, and a biking/jogging path. ◆ 6601 N Powerline Rd (at Hillsboro Blvd), Pompano Beach. 360.1315

7 Tradewinds Park This is the place to go for horseback riding; there also are ponies and farm animals for the kids. With 571 acres, there's plenty of basic park fare: boat and bike rentals, nature trails, fishing, playgrounds, and a snack bar. But a model steam railway, a farm museum, and programs such as "Horses and the Handicapped" set this park apart.

Restaurants/Clubs: Red **Hotels:** Blue
Shops/ Outdoors: Green   **Sights/Culture:** Black

♦ Call ahead; some attractions are available only on weekends or certain dates. 3600 W Sample Rd (just west of Florida's Turnpike), Coconut Creek. 968.3880

Within Tradewinds Park:

Butterfly World At this unique spot, 2,000 varieties of colorful butterflies flit about in huge, screened aviary-type lanais and often alight on visitors. You'll also explore botanical gardens and exhibits, where park rangers explain the life cycle of butterflies and point out which plants attract these glorious insects. ♦ Admission. M-Sa; Su afternoon. 977.4400 ♿

8 Cafe Grazia! ★★★$$$ Executive chef Ace Gonzalez serves mouthwatering specialties such as grilled shrimp and calamari and a half-pound filet mignon with roasted garlic and gorgonzola. Other appetizing entrées include pasta with roast ham and spinach. The room is quiet and dimly lit, with lots of wood and greenery. ♦ Italian ♦ M-F lunch and dinner; Sa-Su dinner. Reservations recommended. 3850 N Federal Hwy (at Sample Rd), Lighthouse Point. 942.7206 ♿

9 Cafe Arugula ★★★★$$$$ Unique, award-winning cuisine is offered at this romantic landmark restaurant, where owner Dick Cingolani strives to delight diners with such dishes as pecan-crusted snapper and black-bottom pie. And don't miss the Thai shrimp taco. The eclectic decor conjures up images of the Mediterranean. ♦ American ♦ Daily dinner. Reservations recommended. 3150 N Federal Hwy (at Sample Rd), Lighthouse Point. 785.7732 ♿

10 Cap's Place ★★★$$$ Park your car at the dock by the waterway, and a boat will take you to the little island that this rustic restaurant calls home. The kitchen here is famous for praiseworthy food, such as hearts of palm salad and grouper chowder. The setting is fascinating, too: Built in 1927, this was once a speakeasy and casino that served the famous, from FDR to Marilyn Monroe. Today, it's on the National Registry of Historic Places. ♦ Seafood ♦ Daily dinner. Reservations recommended. 2765 NE 28th Ct (at NE 26th St), Lighthouse Point. 941.0418

11 Hillsboro Mile Drive down this street and glimpse some of Florida's finer homes. But a glimpse is all you'll get, thanks to private gates and skillfully hidden entrances. ♦ A1A, north of Hillsboro Inlet, Hillsboro Beach

12 Hillsboro Lighthouse Built in 1907, this iron tower still warns mariners of treacherous reefs that lie 200 feet offshore. Though not open to the public, it's a local landmark. ♦ Hillsboro Inlet (A1A), Hillsboro Beach

13 Pelican Pub ★$$ This casual eatery serves genuine (yellow, not green) Key lime pie, as

well as tasty seafood. ♦ Seafood ♦ Daily lunch and dinner. 2635 N Riverside (A1A, south of the lighthouse), Pompano Beach. 785.8550 ♿

14 Pompano Beach Pier At 1,080 feet, this is said to be the longest fishing pier in Florida. If you don't have angling gear, there's always some available for rent. Relax at the tiki bar or restaurant. ♦ Daily. 222 N Pompano Beach Blvd (at Atlantic Blvd), Pompano Beach. 943.1488

At Pompano Beach Pier:

Fisherman's Wharf ★$$$ At the base of the **Pompano Beach Pier**, this eatery's relaxed atmosphere and early-bird dinner special are both appropriate for families. Don't miss the dolphinfish. Entertainment is provided nightly—except on football nights, when patrons watch the games on TV. ♦ Seafood ♦ Daily lunch and dinner. 941.5522 ♿

15 Cafe Maxx ★★★★$$$$ At one of South Florida's most exciting restaurants, chef and co-owner Oliver Saucy serves innovative and exquisitely presented nouvelle cuisine in a comfortable and contemporary setting, with Art Deco accents. The menu is constantly changing, so if you have your heart set on the popular swordfish with *orechietti* pasta, call ahead and they'll make it for you. Try the onion-crusted snapper, too. ♦ Eclectic ♦ Daily dinner. Reservations recommended. 601 E Atlantic Blvd (at NE 26th Ave), Pompano Beach. 782.0606 ♿

16 Chez Porky's ★$$ A silly name for a place that has great down-home cooking, including chicken wings in seven flavors (try the raspberry). The spicy chicken coconut soup is excellent. ♦ American ♦ M-F lunch and dinner; Sa-Su dinner. 105 SW Sixth St (between Atlantic Blvd and Cypress Creek Rd), Pompano Beach. 946.5590 ♿. Also at: 2246 University Dr (at Royal Palm/Copans), Coral Springs. 752.7675

17 Pompano Park Harness Track Bet on the trotters at the "Winter Harness Racing Capital of the World." ♦ Admission. Call for post times; open Oct-Aug. 1800 SW Third St/Race Track Rd (off Powerline Rd and south of Atlantic Blvd), Pompano Beach. 972.2000 ♿

18 Palm-Aire Resort Spa & Club $$$ This internationally known, first-class luxury spa offers European beauty treatments, exercise programs, five 18-hole golf courses, 37 tennis courts, squash, racquetball, a jogging track, and two outdoor pools. A calorie-controlled menu also is available. Deluxe accommodations include 160 standard rooms or suites.

For the hesitant (or cost-conscious), the resort offers summer spa samplers. ♦ 2601 N Palm-Aire Dr (at Powerline Rd), Pompano Beach. 972.3300 (phone and fax), 800/272.5624 &

19 Fern Forest Nature Center An official Designated Urban Wilderness Area, this 254-acre park has a boardwalk, nature trails, an amphitheater, and picnic tables. It's a great wildlife refuge—and soul soother. ♦ 201 Lyons Rd S (between Atlantic Blvd and Florida's Turnpike), Pompano Beach. 970.0150

20 Ronny Dee Motel $ Hosts John and Carol Grigelis have welcomed guests to this 35-room motel in English, French, and German for 17 years. A pool, cable TV, shuffleboard, and a barbecue grill provide ready entertainment. Laundry facilities and kitchenettes come with the rooms; there's no restaurant, though. ♦ 717 S Ocean Blvd (south of Atlantic Blvd), Pompano Beach. 943.3020 &

21 Best Western Beachcomber Hotel & Villas $$ European tourists find the multilingual staff here reassuring, and everyone recognizes the Best Western sign. In addition to 147 rooms, apartments are available, and there's a dining room and a private beach for swimming or strolling. ♦ 1200 S Ocean Blvd (at SE 12th St), Pompano Beach. 941.7830, 800/528.1234; fax 942.7680 &

22 Traders Ocean Resort $ This resort has 93 standard yet comfortable rooms, suites, and efficiencies on the beach, plus an American restaurant. ♦ 1600 S Ocean Blvd (north of Commercial Blvd), Pompano Beach. 941.8400; fax 941.1024 &

23 Sea Watch ★★$$$ One of the best seafood places in Broward, this place is housed in a rustic two-story building overlooking the ocean; designed by **Dan Duckham,** it was built in 1974. The menu lists New Zealand orange roughy, Bahamian conch fritters, and Cajun popcorn shrimp. No fried fisherman's platters here. ♦ Seafood ♦ Daily lunch and dinner. 6002 N Ocean Blvd (at Gate House Rd), Sea Ranch Lakes. 781.2200 &

24 Howard Johnson Beach Resort $$ Many of the 181 standard and deluxe rooms here offer ocean views. If you aren't lucky enough to snag one, take advantage of the 200 feet of

private beach. There's a restaurant on site. ♦ 4660 N Ocean Dr (at Commercial Blvd), Lauderdale-by-the-Sea. 776.5660; fax 776.4689 &

25 Peter Michael's ★★$$ After serving Westchester County, New York, for 27 years at Saparito's, the owners opened this beach-feel eatery, where Italian balsamic vinegar and olive oil sit on every table. Try the homemade gnocchi or one of the "alla Peter Michael" dishes, such as shrimp or snapper with mushrooms, prosciutto, scallions, wine, fresh tomato, and garlic. The homemade desserts are wonderful. ♦ Italian ♦ M, W-Su dinner. 4331 N Ocean Dr (north of Commercial Blvd), Lauderdale-by-the-Sea. 351.0310 &

25 Tropic Seas Resort Motel $$ Located directly on the beach, Larry and Sandy Lynch's 16-room motel overlooks a secluded tropical courtyard and offers ocean views. Though there's no restaurant, a free continental breakfast is served in the morning. Walk to nearby stores, banks, and restaurants. ♦ 4616 El Mar Dr (between Commercial Blvd and Cypress Creek Rd), Lauderdale-by-the-Sea. 772.2555, 800/952.9581; fax 771.5711

26 Anglin's Fishing Pier At one of Florida's oldest piers, pier manager Will Harty sells live or dead bait and rents rods and reels. If you come back empty-handed, he'll send you to the **Pier Restaurant** for a darn good cup of coffee and a cheeseburger to enliven your spirits. ♦ End of Commercial Blvd, Pompano Beach. 491.9403

26 Aruba Beach Cafe ★★$$ This very popular restaurant is a great place to watch the sun worshipers, and it's one of the few air-conditioned spots right on the beach. Take your pick of the great omelettes, salads, and sandwiches. ♦ American ♦ Daily lunch and dinner; Su breakfast. One Commercial Blvd (at El Mar Dr), Lauderdale-by-the-Sea. 776.0001 &

27 Days Inn Oceanfront $ The 94 standard rooms here come with a choice of poolside or ocean views and cable TV. A restaurant, nightly entertainment, sailing, snorkeling, and aquabikes are among the perks. ♦ 4240 Galt Ocean Dr (between Commercial and Oakland Park Blvds), Ft. Lauderdale. 566.8631, 800/325.2525 &

Restaurants/Clubs: Red	**Hotels:** Blue
Shops/ Outdoors: Green	**Sights/Culture:** Black

28 Ramada Beach Resort $$ This 223-room oceanfront hotel boasts a restaurant, 300 feet of private beach, a pool, sailing, and wind-surfing. The rooms have partial ocean views, and the suites face the ocean. ♦ 4060 Galt Ocean Dr (between Commercial and Oakland Park Blvds), Ft. Lauderdale. 565.6611, 800/678.9022; fax 564.7730 ⅄

29 Zuckerello's ★★$$ Designer pizza is the specialty at this casual, red-and-white-tablecloth place. Try the white pizza (no sauce) or add toppings of your choice to one of the 20 styles of individual-serving, 10-inch gourmet pies. ♦ Italian ♦ Daily dinner. 3017 E Commercial Blvd (at Bayview Dr), Ft. Lauderdale. 776.4282 ⅄

30 Confetti Dance to Top 40 tunes or take the second-level walkway to the **Reunion Room** and check out the progressive scene. Call ahead to find out what's happening—perhaps free drinks for everyone for two hours on Friday. ♦ Cover. W-F until 2AM; Sa until 3AM. 2660 E Commercial Blvd (three blocks east of Federal Hwy), Ft. Lauderdale. 776.4080

31 Punjab ★$$ Sit in a private, curtained booth or at an open table to experience a meal from any region of India. Choose from *rogan josh* (spicy lamb), tandoori, vegetarian dishes, and exotic soups. The food usually outshines the service. ♦ Indian ♦ M, Su dinner; Tu-Sa lunch and dinner. 5975 N Federal Hwy (near NE 54th St), Ft. Lauderdale. 491.6710 ⅄

Thai Spice

Exotic Thai Cuisine

32 Thai Spice ★★★$$ Some critics call this the best Thai restaurant in town, so you can expect at least a short wait for a table in the cozy, 70-seat dining room. If possible, sit under the wooden shingled temple roof. The range of appetizers is mind-boggling; recommended are "coco" shrimp (with crispy noodles flaked like coconut), soft-shell crab with Thai garlic sauce, and Bangkok lettuce roll. The entrées deliver both subtle and powerful flavors simultaneously; try the crispy yellowtail snapper with spicy chili-garlic sauce. ♦ Thai ♦ M-F lunch and dinner; Sa-Su dinner. 1514 E Commercial Blvd (between Old Dixie and Federal Hwys), Oakland Park. 771.4535 ⅄

33 Cheers This rhythm-and-blues club is one of the few in the county where the party lasts nearly all night long. ♦ Cover F-Sa. Daily until 4AM. 941 E Cypress Creek Rd (at Old Dixie Hwy), Ft. Lauderdale. 771.6337 ⅄

34 Westin Cypress Creek $$ The centerpiece of the Cypress Creek business district, this elegant, 293-room hotel caters to a business clientele with fax machines in some of the rooms and coffeemakers and honor bars in all of them. Facilities include an Olympic-size pool, jogging paths, and a health club. ♦ 400 Corporate Dr (one block east of I-95), Ft. Lauderdale. 772.1331, 800/228.3000; fax 491.9087 ⅄

Within the Westin Cypress Creek:

Cypress Room ★★★$$$$ Exquisite food is the hallmark of this award-winning restaurant, set in a formal, marble-accented dining room. Among the favored entrées, all ceremoniously presented, are Dover sole with crabmeat stuffing, shelled Maine lobster, veal chops, and rack of lamb. This is a good place for a romantic dinner. ♦ American ♦ M-F lunch and dinner; Sa dinner. 772.1331 ⅄

35 Lockhart Stadium This is the home of the Ft. Lauderdale **Strikers** professional soccer team—1989 champs of the **American Soccer League** (771.5677). ♦ Pre-season inter-national games Dec-Mar; regular season Apr-Sept. 5301 NW 12th Ave (north of Commercial Blvd, west of I-95), Ft. Lauderdale. 928.1597 ⅄

36 Chuck Rohr's Balloon Adventures Once you've tried rock-climbing, scuba diving, and spelunking, what about a ride in a hot-air balloon? There are several different launch sites; depending on how the wind is blowing, you might be able to fly over the **Everglades**. One-hour Champagne flights cost $125 per person. ♦ Daily by appointment at sunrise and sunset. 6000 NW 28th Way, Hangar F12, Ft. Lauderdale Executive Airport, Ft. Lauderdale. 491.6020 ⅄

37 Lumonics Light and Sound Theatre Electronic music is integrated with a breathtaking laser display at this intimate 60-seat theater. Technically speaking, this unusual sensory experience combines light and water sculpture, live kinetic painting, lasers, sound, and scent. ♦ Admission. Sa 8:30PM (twice a month). Reservations required. 3017 NW 60th St (at NW 31st Ave), Ft. Lauderdale. 979.3161; fax 972.5802 ⅄

38 Primavera ★★★★$$$$ Broward County's finest Northern Italian cuisine, from delicate seafood to handmade pasta, is painstakingly presented in this tasteful dining room, with its lush greenery and soothing palette. The restaurant's understated location (in a shopping plaza) and its privacy attract more than a few publicity-shy celebrities, including Frank Sinatra. But anyone would do well to sample the veal chop with wild mushrooms or lobster and sea scallops sautéed in Sherry and green-peppercorn sauce. ♦ Italian ♦ M-Sa dinner. 830 E Oakland Park Blvd (between Old Dixie Hwy and N Andrews Ave), Ft. Lauderdale. 564.6363 ⅊

39 Old Florida Seafood House ★★$$ Bring a big appetite to tackle the huge meals served here. Seafood is prepared any way you like it—broiled, fried, sautéed, with marinara sauce, spicy Cajun-style, or *à la française;* steak and ribs appease carnivores. The restaurant isn't pretty, but the food is good. ♦ Seafood ♦ M-F lunch and dinner; Sa-Su dinner. 1414 NE 26th St (west of Hwy 1), Wilton Manors. 566.1044 ⅊. Also at: 4535 Pine Island Rd (between Oakland Park and Commercial Blvds), Sunrise. 572.0444

Punta Del Este Restaurant

40 Punta Del Este ★$$ This casual, storefront stop is perfect for those who can't decide between Cuban and Mexican fare—it serves both. Ask for raw chopped onions to top the black bean soup. *Ropa vieja* (shredded beef) is a good choice. ♦ Mexican/Cuban ♦ Tu-Su lunch and dinner. 1678 E Oakland Park Blvd (between Old Dixie and Federal Hwys) in Buenos Aires Plaza, Oakland Park. 561.3382 ⅊

41 By Word of Mouth ★★★★$$$ Famous for its desserts and bakery items, this European-style cafe with tile floors and an open kitchen is a local hot spot for social and business lunches, though it seats just 42 diners. Its signature dishes include the sun-dried tomato and pesto pâté; Key West lobster with artichokes, mushrooms, and amaretto cream Sherry sauce; and basil ravioli with roasted garlic and tomato sauce. For dessert, try the "chocolate órgasm." ♦ Eclectic ♦ M-Tu lunch; W-F lunch and dinner; Sa dinner. Reservations required for dinner. 3200 NE 12th Ave (at Old Dixie Hwy), Ft. Lauderdale. 564.3663 ⅊

42 Mai-Kai ★★$$$$ The Polynesian cuisine and fancy rum drinks are pricey, but go anyway for the razzle-dazzle floor show, with flame-eaters and hula dancers. ♦ Polynesian ♦ Daily dinner. 3599 N Federal Hwy (near Oakland Park Blvd), Ft. Lauderdale. 563.3272 ⅊

42 Crocco's With half-court basketball, a batting cage, games, and billiards, this place gives new meaning to the term sports bar. At night, the basketball court becomes a dance floor (or, during special events, a boxing ring). ♦ Cover for special events. M-F, Su until 2AM; Sa until 3AM. 3339 N Federal Hwy (near Oakland Park Blvd), Ft. Lauderdale. 566.2406 ⅊

43 September's One of Broward's great dance places, this club showcases an eight-piece band after 9PM. ♦ Cover F-Sa. Tu-F, Su until 2AM; Sa until 3AM. 2975 N Federal Hwy (at Oakland Park Blvd), Ft. Lauderdale. 563.4331 ⅊

44 Baja Beach Club Despite its name, this hot club isn't on the ocean but in the **Coral Ridge Shopping Center.** But you may still find the wet T-shirt contests that made the beach popular in the old days, plus dancing, music, and pool tables. On weekends, it's largely for the 20-something crowd. ♦ Cover; Florida residents free. M-Tu until 2AM; W-F, Su until 2:30AM; Sa until 3:30AM. 3200 N Federal Hwy (at Oakland Park Blvd), Ft. Lauderdale. 561.2432 ⅊

45 Skyline Chili ★★$ Homesick for Cincinnati? This is an outpost for the Ohio-based makers of the wonderful three-way chili (chili, spaghetti, and cheese served together). ♦ American ♦ Daily lunch and dinner. 2590 N Federal Hwy (at NE 26th St), Ft. Lauderdale. 566.1541 ⅊

46 Christopher's ★$$ This popular restaurant/nightclub caters to professionals who come to dance away the week's worries. There's a buffet and a Happy Hour. Select from a wide menu of chicken dishes, steaks, seafood, and pasta. ♦ American ♦ M-F lunch and dinner; Sa dinner. 2857 E Oakland Park Blvd (at Bayview Dr), Ft. Lauderdale. 561.2136 ⅊

Restaurants/Clubs: Red	**Hotels:** Blue
Shops/ ⅋ Outdoors: Green	**Sights/Culture:** Black

46 Plum Room ★★★★$$$$ Many romantics have popped the question at this local landmark. And no wonder—with pillows for the women's feet and only 14 tables, it's an elegant and intimate place. And the food lives up to the atmosphere. Savor Santa Rosa escargots in phyllo, chateaubriand, filet mignon, lobster, and other delights as a harpist plays in the background. ♦ Continental ♦ W-Sa dinner (M-Sa in winter). Reservations recommended. 3001 E Oakland Park Blvd (at the Intracoastal Waterway), Ft. Lauderdale. 561.4400 &

47 Down Under ★★★$$$$ The decor of this elegant waterfront bistro combines the feel of California with New Orleans—a river view is framed by large picture windows, Victorian-style furnishings, and lots of hanging plants. The red snapper comes highly recommended, and the dry-aged beef is excellent. The wine list has been called one of the region's best. ♦ American ♦ M-F lunch and dinner; Sa-Su dinner. Reservations recommended. 3000 E Oakland Park Blvd (at the Intracoastal Waterway), Ft. Lauderdale. 563.4123 &

47 Shooters ★$$ On weekends, boats dock six deep here. At peak times, be prepared to grudgingly accept a seat inside, lean against the bar, or stand ready to pounce when people leave one of the coveted outside tables. Once you've found a seat, be prepared to confront a 100-item menu listing everything from steaks and burgers to chicken and broccoli angel-hair pasta. ♦ American ♦ M-F, Su until 2AM; Sa until 3AM. 3033 NE 32nd Ave (at Oakland Park Blvd, one block west of A1A), Ft. Lauderdale. 566.2855 &. Also at: 3501 NE 163rd St (at the Intracoastal), North Miami. 949.2855 &

47 Charley's Crab ★★$$$$ This beautiful spot overlooking the Intracoastal is the place to enjoy fish, fish, fish—many from outside Florida—and other entrées, either indoors in the tropical dining room or outdoors on the dockside patio. The menu changes weekly. ♦ Seafood ♦ M-Sa lunch and dinner; Su dinner. 3000 NE 32nd Ave (at Oakland Park Blvd, one block west of A1A), Ft. Lauderdale. 561.4800 &

48 Galt Ocean Mile Shoppes Blink and you'll miss these shops tucked into a quaint cul-de-sac just north of Oakland Park Boule-vard on the west side of A1A. You'll find everything here, including clothing, accessories, antiques, skin care products, and gifts. ♦ Daily. 3321 NE 32nd St (at A1A), Ft. Lauderdale &

49 Hugh Taylor Birch State Park This 80-acre park was once the home of the late Hugh Taylor Birch, a Chicago attorney who escaped his city's crowds and purchased this land in 1893; he donated it to the state in 1942. Picnic pavilions, canoe rentals for the lagoon, smooth roads for in-line skating, and a nature trail can all be found here. And there's beach access. ♦ 3109 E Sunrise Blvd (at A1A), Ft. Lauderdale. 564.4521

50 The Comic Strip Eddie Murphy, Rodney Dangerfield, Jay Leno, and Robin Williams have all performed here, at South Florida's first comedy club. A new show is scheduled every week. ♦ Cover. Daily; call for show times. Reservations recommended. 1432 N Federal Hwy (between Sunrise and Oakland Park Blvds), Ft. Lauderdale. 565.8887 &

51 Bread of Life ★$ Pile up your plate at the hot food bar here, secure in the knowledge that everything is good for you. Vegetable lasagna, green-bean casserole, veggie enchiladas, and the like are offered at this little health food market/deli/bakery. ♦ Health food ♦ Daily lunch and dinner. 2388 N Federal Hwy (between Oakland Park and Sunrise Blvds), Ft. Lauderdale. 565.7423 &

52 Ruth's Chris Steak House ★★★$$$$ The steaks are incredible, the atmosphere tasteful, and the wine list extensive. You'll be given a beeper to wear while waiting for your table. Once you're seated, service is instantaneous. The porterhouse is a good choice, but don't forget your wallet: You'll need it. ♦ Steak house ♦ Daily dinner. Reservations recommended. 2525 N Federal Hwy (just south of NE 26th St), Ft. Lauderdale. 565.2338 &

THE CAVES

52 The Caves $$$ One of the goofiest concepts in restaurant history, this place actually puts you in a private cave that accommodates up to 12. The so-so cuisine doesn't deserve any better. ♦ American ♦ Daily dinner. 2205 N Federal Hwy (between Oakland Park and Sunrise Blvds), Ft. Lauderdale. 561.4608 &

53 Houston's ★★$$ Try to arrive early to beat the lunch and dinner crowds, or you'll end up standing for 10 to 45 minutes. Even so, the huge portions of food—all kinds of burgers, ribs, filet mignon, and a selection of salads large enough to qualify as main courses—are worth waiting for. ♦ American ♦ Daily lunch and dinner. 1415 N Federal Hwy (north of Sunrise Blvd), Ft. Lauderdale. 563.2226 &

54 Original Pancake House ★★$ The best place in town for breakfast, this shopping-center restaurant is particularly crowded on weekend mornings—bring a newspaper to read in line. The plate-size Dutch Baby and apple pancakes are wonderful. ♦ American ♦ Daily breakfast, lunch, and dinner. 1101 N

Federal Hwy (at NE 11th St), Ft. Lauderdale. 564.8881 &. Also at: 270 S University Dr (south of Broward Blvd), Plantation. 473.2771

54 Croissan'Time A visit to this cafe/bakery/deli is worth the trip over and over again for take-out pâtés, pastries, and baguettes. There are a few chairs and tables for a quick bite. ♦ French ♦ Tu-Su breakfast and lunch. Sunrise Square Shopping Ctr, 1201 N Federal Hwy (between Sunrise and Oakland Park Blvds), Ft. Lauderdale. 565.8555 &

55 La Coquille ★★★$$$ Not only is this restaurant very charming and very private, but the food is artfully prepared, a feast for the eyes as well as the palate. Try duck with lingonberry sauce or the bouillabaisse, considered the best in town. There's a new garden in back with romantic lights, recorded music, and lush greenery. ♦ French ♦ M-Th, Sa-Su dinner, F lunch and dinner Dec-March; Tu-Th, Sa-Su dinner, F lunch Apr-Nov. 1619 E Sunrise Blvd (at Federal Hwy), Ft. Lauderdale. 467.3030

55 La Ferme ★★★$$$ Fine cuisine is lovingly prepared in a quaint setting by the owners, a wife-husband team, and it's worth every penny. Two standouts are the veal with chanterelle mushroom sauce and the grilled lobster tail with a garlic butter glaze. ♦ French ♦ M-Sa dinner. 1601 E Sunrise Blvd (at Federal Hwy), Ft. Lauderdale. 764.0987 &

56 Sukhothai ★★$$ One of the best Thai restaurants in the city, this sophisticated place grew so popular that it expanded into the storefront next door. Chicken *panang* (with peanut sauce) is a favorite. Squid, frogs' legs, Siamese duck, curries, and soft-shell crab also appear on the lengthy menu. ♦ Thai ♦ M-F lunch and dinner; Sa-Su dinner. Gateway Plaza, 1930 E Sunrise Blvd (at NE 19th Ave), Ft. Lauderdale. 764.0148 &

56 International Bicycle Shop Rent in-line skates or a bike to whir through **Hugh Taylor Birch State Park** (not too far away) or along the beachfront. ♦ Daily. Gateway Plaza, 1900 E Sunrise Blvd (at NE 19th Ave), Ft. Lauderdale. 764.8800 &

57 Le Dome ★★★$$$$ Get a rooftop view of Ft. Lauderdale from this chic modern restaurant in the penthouse of the Four Seasons condominium. The popular swordfish *Le Dome* features swordfish topped with lobster meat and béarnaise sauce. Stuffed? Take a Water Taxi back to your hotel. ♦ American ♦ Daily dinner. Reservations recommended. 333 Sunset Dr (at E Las Olas Blvd), Ft. Lauderdale. 463.3303

58 McGuires Hill 16 ★$ The words to the Irish National Anthem are on the wall, Murphy's Stout is on tap, and a bench by the front door is stacked with copies of the *Irish American.* A crowd of regulars claps along with the band that plays on weekends, singing in hopes of a free Ireland. A full bar menu—featuring burgers and Irish specialties—is served. Walk to the adjoining patio bar for live rhythm-and-blues ♦ Pub ♦ Daily lunch and dinner. Reservations recommended. 535 N Andrews Ave (at NE Fifth St), Ft. Lauderdale. 764.4453 &

59 Ft. Lauderdale Swap Shop It's billed as the world's largest flea market, with more than 2,000 vendors. There's also a free circus, rows of food stands, and a gameroom. At night, it's a 12-screen drive-in theater. ♦ Daily. 3501 W Sunrise Blvd (at State Rd 7/Hwy 441), Ft. Lauderdale. 791.7927 &

Bests

Allen Susser
Chef/Owner, Chef Allen's

PLACES
Broward Center for the Performing Arts: The Lincoln Center of South Florida, which brings world-class cultural performances to our area.

Coconut Grove: A little like Greenwich Village, a little like Melrose Avenue wrapped up in a lot of Miami. My favorite stops here are the **CocoWalk** and the **Mayfair House;** go in and see the **Tiffany Lounge.**

Vizcaya: Elegant and opulent, the place that serves as an icon of the crossroads that Miami has become. Vizcaya reflects an amalgam of European, Latin American, Caribbean, as well as South Florida.

The Everglades: This unique ecosystem is a wonder, worth protecting and worth a visit while in South Florida.

Aventura: Starting with **Turnberry Isle Resort** and now including **Williams Island,** this affluent development has created an exclusive destination for Miami.

SPECIAL FOOD
The **Fruit & Spice Park** in the Redland.

PASTIMES
When they play, the **Marlins,** Florida's baseball team.

UNIQUE TO SOUTH FLORIDA
I-395: The link between Miami and Miami Beach. As you drive to the beach check out the *quitar* at **Hard Rock Cafe, Fisher Island,** and the cruise ships in the **Port of Miami.**

Collins Avenue: Drive through the renovated **Art Deco District** to **Ocean Drive** and fabulous **South Beach,** our Riviera.

The Florida Keys: Route 1 from Miami to Duval Street for one of the most scenic drives in the US.

The Polo Grounds in Palm Beach: When my schedule permits, I compete.

EVENTS
The Taste of the NFL: An exciting annual gala of personalities and fine cuisine. The funds raised assist the hungry in our community through the Daily Bread Food Bank.

Palm Beach County

The northern most point of the megalopolis that stretches 75 miles south to **Miami**, Palm Beach County is a land of contrasts: In the north is the rural grandeur of **Lake Okeechobee**, the second-largest freshwater lake in the US and a popular destination for Florida's anglers; in the south is **Boca Raton**, the area's restaurant capital; and in between, like a pendant on an elegant necklace, is the emerald-green isle of **Palm Beach.** It is a place where polo seems more popular than football, where exclusive housing developments have their own airstrips and private hangars instead of garages. It is also the home of America's supermarket tabloids, *The National Enquirer, The Star,* and *The Globe.*

But the extremes also mean that there's something here for everyone—golfers, tennis players, avid shoppers, history buffs—and families will not lack for things to do. The county is different from the rest of South Florida, with greener vegetation, a heavier surf, longer beaches, a more leisurely, resort-style pace, and a recollection of northern urban elegance in a tropical setting.

If Miami is the de facto capital of South Florida, Palm Beach is where it all began.

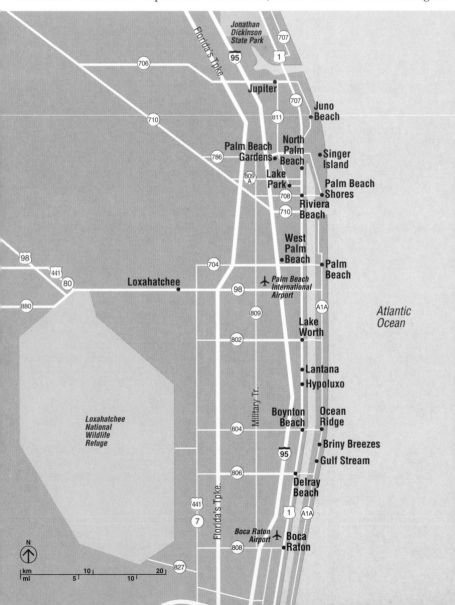

The biggest hurdle to Florida's initial development was how to attract people to the area. Even if the mangroves were uprooted, if the swamps that harbored mosquitoes the size of robins were filled in, and if the channels were dredged, getting people to move to this roadless peninsula seemed nearly impossible. Henry Morrison Flagler, however, solved that problem with his one-track obsession.

Flagler had made his fortune with Standard Oil, but at heart he was a railroad man. He originally came to Florida in 1885 out of concern for his wife, whose health demanded a warm climate. He used the railroad to transform a swamp into a paradise, spawning luxury hotels like so many rabbits from a hat. He marched south from St. Augustine, laying tracks for his **Florida East Coast Railroad,** which enabled him to lure shivering Northerners to the area with tales of balmy winters and suntans on New Year's Day.

Palm Beach began as a barrier island filled with mosquitoes and coconut palms, but Flagler, ever the visionary, saw it as the tropical equivalent of a northern yacht harbor. Sure enough, northern money chased southern sun, and industrial and merchant families—including the Vanderbilts and the Woolworths—all rode their private railway cars to the sandy shore.

Flagler also built a workers' community to support his resort construction. As the hotels rose on Palm Beach, **West Palm Beach** housed laborers and provided a commercial center for the surrounding area. The city was incorporated in 1894 and became the Palm Beach County seat in 1909. Today, Palm Beach persists as a resort community, while West Palm Beach serves as a vibrant center for banking, development, and light industry.

North Palm Beach County dramatically changes character with the seasons, as high-fashion resort living gives way to a year-round, upper-class lifestyle. In the city of **Jupiter,** actor Burt Reynolds has helped establish a thriving theater community. The **PGA (Professional Golfers Association) National Resort,** with its championship course and deluxe amenities, vies with many of the area's polo grounds for weekend attention. And as in the rest of the county, shopping is not so much a necessity as an avocation, and luxury malls dot the area.

At the southern end of the county, Boca Raton falls at a unique axis. Equidistant from Palm Beach and **Ft. Lauderdale,** the city's many excellent restaurants draw a huge urban population. Relatively speaking, Boca plays the hip youngster to matronly Palm Beach. Although IBM has closed much of its operation here, no one forgets that Boca Raton is where the PC (personal computer) was born. A number of high-technology companies continue to establish headquarters in the area, fueling a still-growing real estate market. Even the newest developments tend to echo the Mediterranean Revival style popularized by the city's principal architect, **Addison Mizner,** in the early part of the century.

Area code 407 unless otherwise indicated.

Getting to Palm Beach County

Airports

Located in **West Palm Beach, Palm Beach International Airport** (1000 Turnage Blvd, between Southern Blvd and Belvedere Rd) has been transformed in recent years from a good regional airport to one of international standing. The **Captain McCampbell Terminal,** a destination and departure point to all parts of the country, is easily accessible from **Interstate 95 (I-95).** The airport serves about 2.7 million domestic and 51,800 international travelers each year.

Airport Services

Airport Emergencies	471.7420
Business Service Center	688.9239
Customs	684.3689
Ground Transportation	233.6331
Immigration	684.1757
Information	471.7420
Lost and Found	471.7481
Parking	471.7459
Police	471.7450
Traveler's Aid	655.4483

Airlines

American	800/223.5436, 800/433.7300
Continental	832.5200,800/525.0280
Delta	655.5300, 800/221.1212
Kiwi	800/538.5494
Northwest	800/225.2525
TWA	655.3776, 800/221.2000
United	800/241.6522
USAir	233.7680, 800/428.4322
ValuJet	800/825.8538

Additionally, **Boca Raton Airport** (3700 Airport Rd, east of I-95 and north of Glades Rd, Boca Raton, 391.2202) has one 5,200-foot-long runway. Used for general aviation, the airport doesn't serve commercial airline or charter flights.

Getting to and from Palm Beach International Airport

By Car The airport is about a 10-minute drive from downtown; during weekday morning and evening rush hours the trip can take up to 20 minutes. To get to downtown **West Palm Beach** from the airport, take **Belvedere Road** east, and connect with **I-95** going north. Take the **Okeechobee Boulevard** exit eastbound, which will take you to the center of downtown. To get to the airport from downtown, head south on I-95 to Belvedere Road, and exit west. The airport is west of I-95 between Belvedere Road and **Southern Boulevard.** Long-term and short-term parking lots are near the terminal.

The following rental car companies have offices at the airport and in West Palm Beach (not all offer 24-hour service):

Alamo	684.3840, 800/327.9633
Avis	800/331.1212
Budget	683.2400, 800/527.0700
Dollar	689.7755, 800/327.7607
Hertz	686.4300, 800/654.3131
National	233.7368, 800/227.7368
Value	689.1701, 800/468.2583

By Limousine Airport Services Limo (471.7420 ex 7682) is located at the east and west ends of the airport; the fare to downtown is $8. **BBD Transportation Service** (278.4350, beeper 360.8574) offers limousine service 24 hours a day.

By Taxi Yellow Cab (689.2222) is the only taxi company authorized to provide service from the airport. To call a cab, go to the ground-transportation desk at the east or west side of the baggage claim area. Rates are $1.50 per mile; a 10-minute ride into downtown should cost about $8.

By Train There is no train service to or from the airport.

Bus Station (Long-Distance)

The **Greyhound** terminal (100 Banyan Blvd, just west of Flagler St, West Palm Beach, 833.8534, 800/231.2222) is open daily from 7AM to 12:30AM. There is a taxi stand in front of the station.

Train Station (Long-Distance)

The **Amtrak** station (201 S Tamarind Ave, between Okeechobee and Palm Beach Lakes Blvds, West Palm Beach, 832.6169, 800/872.7245) is open daily from 7:45AM to 5:15PM. Taxis line up at the station at train arrival times, which are relatively infrequent.

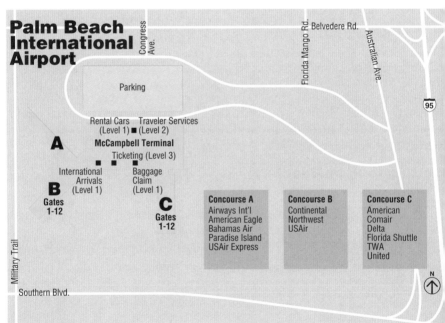

Palm Beach International Airport

Congress Ave. • Florida Mango Rd. • Belvedere Rd. • Australian Ave. • (95)

Parking

Rental Cars (Level 1) ■ Traveler Services (Level 2)

A

McCampbell Terminal
Ticketing (Level 3)

International Arrivals (Level 1) ■ Baggage Claim (Level 1)

B
Gates 1-12

C
Gates 1-12

Military Trail

Southern Blvd.

Concourse A
Airways Int'l
American Eagle
Bahamas Air
Paradise Island
USAir Express

Concourse B
Continental
Northwest
USAir

Concourse C
American
Comair
Delta
Florida Shuttle
TWA
United

N

Getting around Palm Beach County

Most of Palm Beach County's metropolitan areas hug the Atlantic shoreline, with three south-north arteries providing easy access. **Florida's Turnpike** (with a toll charged by the mile) cuts a high-speed swath to the west of most of the developed areas. About four miles east of the turnpike is **I-95,** free of charge but hectic; still, it offers the easiest access to all points in the county. **Federal Highway** (also known as **Route 1** or **US 1**) is a comfortable, somewhat sedate urban thoroughfare, and often the best link over short spans (but not recommended for long-distance journeys). In **Palm Beach** and along the strip of barrier islands, **Route A1A** is the most leisurely route.

Bicycles Several safe biking paths run along Route A1A, especially in **Boca Raton** and **Delray Beach**—but don't expect to see much of the ocean, which is blocked for the most part by high hedges. In **Palm Beach**, a bicycle trail runs along **Lake Worth**. For bicycle rentals, contact **A1A Bike Rentals** (217 E Atlantic Ave, between NE Second and NE Third Aves, Delray Beach, 243.BIKE) or **International Bicycle & Skate Shop** (17 E Palmetto Park Rd at Dixie Hwy, Boca Raton, 737.1744).

Buses CoTran (233.1111) oversees Palm Beach County's 59 municipal buses, which run from Boca Raton to **Tequesta** and west into the **Everglades.** The buses are supposed to run Monday through Saturday from 5:20AM to 7PM, arriving every half hour, but they're not always on schedule. There are 18 fixed bus routes and 10 routes that take passengers to **Tri-Rail** stations. The fare on both types of routes is $1, with a 20¢ transfer fee; monthly commuter passes cost $37 (students and seniors pay half price). The **Shopper Hopper** route **(Mall Express)**, which serves most of the regional malls near I-95, runs Saturdays.

Driving Driving is the best way to get around the county. Traffic is relatively light compared with that of **Miami** and **Ft. Lauderdale.** But if there's a bad accident on I-95 or a drawbridge is open, expect a wait.

Parking Street parking is feasible in most cities. Downtown parking is metered; watch for tow-away zones. **Allright Parking** has an outdoor lot in West Palm Beach (377 Clematis St at Dixie Hwy, 655.8640).

Shuttles Run by **CoTran** and the **Downtown Development Authority,** the free **PalmTran Shuttle** (833.8873) serves downtown **West Palm Beach,** making 30 stops. Buses (there are three) run Monday through Friday from 6:30AM to 7:30PM, and they arrive every 10 minutes. The buses begin their routes at the **Ramada Hotel** (630 Clearwater Park Rd, at Okeechobee Blvd and Australian Ave).

Taxis Most taxis require that you call for pickup. Among the major companies are **Bluefront Taxi** (832.3693), **County Cab** (274.4222, 800/899.8866), and **Yellow Cab** (689.2222).

Tours Popular tours include a look at the state-of-the-art facilities at the **Raymond F. Kravis Center for the Performing Arts** (701 Okeechobee Blvd at S Tamarind Ave, 833.3855); a walk through the historic **Northwood** district (832.4164, 800/572.8471); and the **Boca Raton Resort and Club Tour,** offered by the **Historical Society of Boca Raton** (395.6766). Among other favorites are riverboat sight-seeing tours that leave from **Phil Foster Park** on **Singer Island,** cruising past Palm Beach's elegant waterfront homes (964.4420), and tours of **Burt Reynolds Ranch, Film Studios, and Zoo** (16133 Jupiter Farms Rd, two miles west of Florida's Turnpike, Jupiter, 746.0393), which are offered daily.

Among the leading area tour operators is **Midnight Sun Tours** (1030 S Federal Hwy, between 10th and 11th Aves S, Lake Worth, 588.4446), which offers tours throughout Palm Beach. Its itineraries include a bus tour of Palm Beach, including the **Flagler Museum/ Whitehall** and **Worth Avenue;** a bus excursion to **Lion Country Safari,** with a side trip to a local orange grove; an **Intracoastal Waterway** cruise on a paddle-wheel boat; and a bus tour of **North Palm Beach County,** including **Jupiter** and the **Burt Reynolds Ranch, Film Studios, and Zoo.**

Tippett Travel (3095 S Military Trail, between Cresthaven Blvd and 10th Ave S, Lake Worth, 493.0333) will customize tours of the county to your specifications.

Trains Tri-Rail (874.7245, 800/TRIRAIL) is a commuter train that runs from Palm Beach County south through Broward County and into Miami. Stations in Palm Beach County include one in downtown West Palm Beach (201 S Tamarind Ave, between Okeechobee and Palm Beach Lakes Blvds); at **Palm Beach International Airport** (2600 Mercer Ave); at Lake Worth (1703 Lake Worth Rd, next to I-95 in Lake Worth High School parking lot); in **Boynton Beach** (2800 High Ridge Rd, south of Gateway Blvd and west of I-95); at Delray Beach (345 S Congress Ave, taking I-95 to Atlantic Blvd, west to Congress Ave, and south on Congress Ave); and in Boca Raton (601 NW 53rd St, next to Crown Sterling Suites Hotel). No subway-type transportation is available in the county.

Trolleys Lolly the Trolley (1020 Lucerne Ave, at H St in the fire department parking lot, Lake Worth, 586.1600) operates three trolleys daily from 9AM to 5PM; they run every hour. Trolley 1 runs east-west on **Lake Worth Road;** Trolley 2 runs south along **Dixie Highway** and **D Street** and also goes to the beach; and Trolley 3 runs north on Dixie Highway and south on **Federal Highway** and to the beach. The fare is $1 (seniors and kids under 18 ride for half fare).

Walking Areas best discovered on foot include **Palm Beach, Singer Island, Mizner Park** in Boca Raton, and **Atlantic Avenue** in Delray Beach.

FYI

Money Most banks are open weekdays from 9AM to 5PM. Automatic teller machines (ATMs) can be found in most banks and outside most **Publix** grocery stores. Handle currency exchange at the **Jefferson National Bank** (21302 St. Andrews Blvd, south of Verde Trail Rd, Boca Raton, 368.6900).

Personal Safety Generally safe, Palm Beach County has escaped some of the more serious crime problems apparent in other parts of Florida. But it too has its share of crack cocaine–fueled robberies and assaults. So keep your belongings safe, and avoid neighborhoods where you sense trouble. Also watch out for carjackings: Lock your doors, and keep your windows up. Leave plenty of escape space between your car and one in front when stopped at a light. If you're bumped from behind and unsure of the other driver's intentions, motion him or her to follow you to a police station, fire station, or 24-hour store.

Publications A daily newspaper, the *Palm Beach Post* publishes a section on Friday listing events and entertainment; it's available at convenience stores, news racks, and bookstores. Other publications are *Boca Raton Magazine,* a monthly city/regional magazine, and the *Palm Beach Daily News* (also called "The Shiny Sheet"), both useful to find out about events in the city of Palm Beach.

Restaurants Most highly rated restaurants recommend or require reservations, and many restaurants in **Palm Beach** require jackets and ties. It's always best to call ahead.

Shopping The best shopping can be found on Palm Beach's **Worth Avenue** (luxury goods, art galleries, and designer clothing); **The Gardens** (a huge regional mall with specialty stores and boutiques); **Town Center** in **Boca Raton** (an upscale mall); and **Mizner Park** and **Crocker Plaza,** also in Boca (both offer dining, entertainment, boutiques and specialty shops).

Street Plan Remember that the ocean is to the east, and **I-95** runs along the state's east coast. Other major north-south routes are **Florida's Turnpike, US 1, US 441, Congress Avenue,** and **Military Trail.**

Taxes Palm Beach County levies a 6 percent sales tax, plus a 4 percent bed tax (making the total tax on accommodations 10 percent). The tax on restaurant meals totals 6 percent.

Tickets Call **Ticketmaster** (966.3309), which offers phone service only.

Visitors' Information Centers Palm Beach Convention and Visitors' Bureau (1555 Palm Beach Lakes Blvd at Congress Ave, Suite 204, West Palm Beach, 471.3995) is open Monday through Friday from 8:30AM to 5PM.

Phone Book

Emergencies

AAA Emergency Road Service	800/222.4357
Ambulance/Fire/Police	911
Dental Emergency	800/733.6337

Hospitals
St. Mary's Hospital, West Palm Beach 655.6311

Boca Raton Community Hospital,
Boca Raton 395.7100

Delray Community Hospital,
Delray Beach 498.4440

JFK Medical Center, Atlantis 965.7300

Locksmith (24 hours)
A-Plus Locksmiths 795.8770
"We Key" Locksmiths............................686.7831
....beeper 650.4552

Pharmacy (24 hour)
Eckerd Drugs 965.3367
Jupiter Drugs 746.7499

Poison Control 800/282.3171

Police (non-emergency)...........................837.4000

Visitors' Information

Amtrak...800/872.7245

Better Business Bureau 682.2200

Convention and Visitors' Bureau	471.3995
Disabled Visitors' Information	355.4883
Greyhound Bus	833.0825, 800/231.2222
Metro Transit (CoTran)	233.1111
Road Conditions	684.4030
Time	832.3801
Travelers Aid	655.4483
US Customs	684.3689
US Passport Office	355.1586
Weather	832.3801

Teaching Your Kids to Snorkel

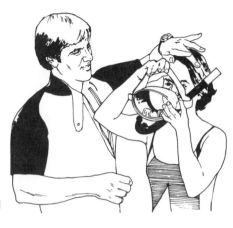

How does a parent teach a child to appreciate undersea life? First, buy a child's mask and snorkel tube at a dive shop. Steer away from the cheap (read: ill-fitting) masks available at most hotel gift shops, drug stores, and discount houses. A dive shop will help you select a mask that fits your child snugly. The mask should stay on the face without a strap when the child inhales, and the snorkel should attach to the face strap. The difference in price between a cheap mask and a "real" one is usually less than $20. You can get away with cheap flippers, or even omit them entirely.

It's also a good idea to invest in a small bottle of anti-fogging solution, which keeps the glass clear. To apply, wet the mask in seawater, then rub some of the solution around on the inside of the mask and rinse.

Standing in knee-deep water, help your children put on their masks. Show them how to sit or kneel while putting their face in the water. Tell them to breathe through their mouths. Once they get the hang of breathing with the snorkels, they can begin to swim.

Even children under four or those who don't swim well can snorkel. Use a half-inflated float ring around their waists, which will give them enough buoyancy to be comfortable face-down in the water.

Once your children start seeing fish, crabs, and other sea life, you won't be able to get them back on land.

Another tip: Children (and adults) should wear T-shirts when snorkeling. While they're admiring the sea life, the sun can be scorching their backs. And of course, no matter how proficient kids become as snorkelers, parents must provide careful supervision whenever children are around water.

Palm Beach

Glitzy Palm Beach is known around the globe as a hideaway for corporate chieftains, the rich and famous, and families whose surnames are name brands (Pulitzer, Trump, and Woolworth are just a few that come to mind). Its denizens are photographed at charity balls and polo matches, and much of the year their mansions sit shuttered behind high walls while they visit other equally renowned playgrounds.

Despite its caviar image, Palm Beach started out as a long, mosquito-infested island defining the eastern rim of **Lake Worth,** a body of water separating a string of barrier islands from Florida's mainland. Just before the turn of the century, railroad magnate Henry M. Flagler dreamed of turning the island into a playground for the rich and fortunate while making a few dollars for himself. And he succeeded: His **Florida East Coast Railroad** provided the transportation, his real estate company provided the lodging, and Florida provided the sunshine and beaches.

Today, Palm Beach remains an exclusive island community with some of South Florida's toniest shops, most expensive restaurants, and best-dressed snowbirds. Also here, overlooking the crashing Atlantic surf, is **Mar-a-Lago,** the estate that was once famous as the home of cereal heiress Marjorie Merriweather Post; Donald Trump now owns the mansion.

While Palm Beach is noticeably less populated during the hot summer than in the pleasant winter season, the city no longer closes down when the temperature climbs above 80 degrees. Still, many of the mansions along **Ocean Boulevard,** which serve as winter homes, are boarded up in summer, and from late May through late September hotel rates drop markedly. In the winter, however, it's hard just to book a table at a restaurant. Reservations are a must nearly everywhere in Palm Beach, especially for trendy spots such as **Bice,** known for its modern Italian cuisine, the traditionally elegant **Café L'Europe,** and **The Breakers,** a luxury hotel that eloquently recalls the era of Flagler's arrival.

Regardless of when you visit, don't overlook Palm Beach's fashionable and exclusive shops on **Worth Avenue**—definitely a place made for browsing on foot. Most of the rest of the city is better seen by bicycle or automobile. And if you intend to venture off the island, a car is essential: Mass transit is one of the few things *not* in abundance in Palm Beach.

Area code 407 unless otherwise indicated.

1 Ritz-Carlton Palm Beach $$$$ Palm Beach elegance is redefined in this palatial 270-room hotel, whose staff is friendly, courteous, and prompt, whether helping you arrange an intimate dinner for two or a deep-sea fishing trip. Guests are pampered throughout this pristine facility, equipped with tennis courts, a fitness center, and more. After biking on the mainland or along the South Palm Beach coast, opt for a splash in the huge pool or a massage in the spa before refueling in the restaurant, grill, cafe, or sports bar. Afternoon tea is served daily in the posh, softly lit lounge decorated with paintings and china-filled cabinets. A complete business center, kids' program, and special security options on some floors round out the amenities. ♦ 100 S Ocean Blvd (at Ocean Ave). 533.6000; fax 588.4555 &

OF THE PALM BEACHES

1 Lois Pope Theater This intimate 250-seat theater, across the street from the **Ritz-Carlton Palm Beach** (see above), was named for the widow of *National Enquirer* founder Generoso Pope and designed by architect **Ken Nash.** Home to the **Theatre Club of the Palm Beaches,** it offers contemporary plays year-round. Recent productions include *Woody Guthrie's American Song* and *The Killing of Michael Malloy.* ♦ Shows W, Sa-Su. 262 S Ocean Blvd (at Ocean Ave). 585.3433 &

2 Howard Johnson's Palm Beach $$ Even Palm Beach has a "HoJo's," this one scenically located beside Lake Worth at the foot of Lake Worth Bridge. Staying at this 98-room hostelry isn't exactly following the "When in Rome" maxim, but for those who can't afford the island's more glamorous hotels, it is an oasis. The downside? Most of the action—shopping and good restaurants—is at the center or north end of the island. Nearby, though, are Lake Worth Beach and the **Palm Beach Par 3 Golf Club** (see below), a public course down the street. And there's a restaurant on the premises. ♦ 2870 S Ocean Blvd (at Lake Ave/State Rd 802). 582.2581, 800/654.2000 &

3 Four Seasons Ocean Grand $$$$ One of Palm Beach's newest resort hotels, this place tries hard to outshine its equally lavish competitors. All 210 rooms and suites, each with two phones (including one in the large marble bathroom), overlook the Atlantic. Three tennis courts, an oceanside pool, a European-style spa, and year-round children's activities are among the offerings. You even can rent a cabana on the beach. ♦ 2800 S Ocean Blvd (north of Lake Ave). 582.2800, 800/432.2335 &

Within the Four Seasons Ocean Grand:

Ocean Bistro ★★★$$$ This is the place to experience fine dining as the natives do. The chefs use only fruits and vegetables indigenous to Florida and the Caribbean, including hearts of palm, coconut, and Key limes. Some outstanding dishes are grouper with a black-bean citrus relish, snapper in a tomato-basil sauce, and angel-hair pasta with fresh rock shrimp. The breakfasts—French toast with banana–macadamia nut stuffing, or mango and buttermilk pancakes—are substantial but worth it. ♦ South-eastern/Caribbean ♦ Daily breakfast, lunch, and dinner. Reservations recommended. 582.2800 &

The Restaurant ★★★★$$$$ Executive chef Hubert Des Marais is an accomplished networker, and on any given day his kitchen may be stocked with fresh-picked mangoes from a neighbor's tree or live soft-shell crabs plucked from nearby rivers. Highly regarded, Des Marais specializes in Floridian cuisine— a wonderful mix of local flavors with those of the Southeast, the Caribbean, and Latin America—served in an elegantly understated setting of ivory and damask. The menu might include yellowtail snapper with a relish of lemon, thyme, and melon and smoked tangelo sauce; black-eyed peas and crackling salad; or plantain snaps with blue crab. ♦ Floridian ♦ Tu-Su dinner. Reservations recommended; jacket required. 582.2800 &

4 Palm Beach Par 3 Golf Club The only public course on the island has holes situated between the Atlantic Ocean and Lake Worth. The land once was slated for condominiums, but the town of Palm Beach purchased the course through a 1973 bond issue for $4.5 million. The facility includes 18 holes, a putting green, and a clubhouse and pro shop.

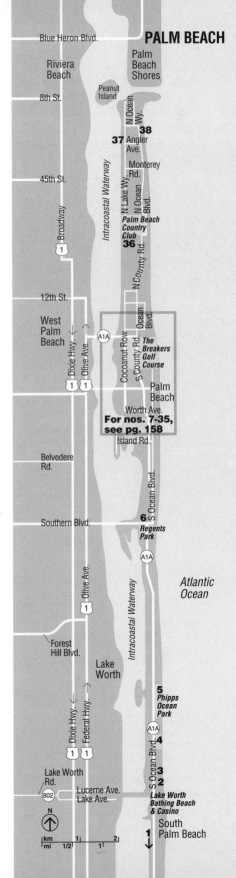

PALM BEACH

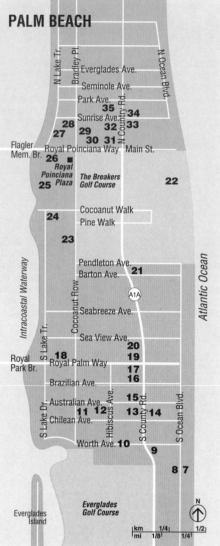

Pull and riding carts, golf clubs, and range balls are available to rent. Pros are on hand seven days a week for private lessons and group clinics. ♦ 2345 S Ocean Blvd (between Southern Blvd and Lake Worth Rd). 582.4462, Pro shop 547.0598 &

5 Phipps Ocean Park One of Palm Beach's few public beaches, this park tends to draw off-islanders and tourists, as evidenced by the preponderance of domestic and rental cars and dearth of Jaguars and Mercedes in the area parking lot (which costs a dollar an hour). It also is the site of the island's first schoolhouse (built in 1886). Most Palm Beachers stick to the public or private beaches farther north near the island's oceanfront mansions, many of which are connected by underground tunnels to the beach. Lifeguards are on duty here during the day, and barbecue and picnic areas are available. ♦ 2145 S Ocean Blvd (a mile north of Lake Worth Bridge, behind the South Palm Beach fire station). 585.9203

6 Mar-a-Lago Listed on the National Registry of Historic Places, this Moorish mansion was designed by **Marion Sims Wyeth** in 1927 to include a bomb shelter and movie theater. It was originally owned by the refined and abstemious cereal heiress Marjorie Merriweather Post. In 1926, she engaged **Wyeth** to draw plans for an elaborate mansion, whose interior would have Italian, Spanish, Dutch, and Portuguese themes, using building materials and artisans from all over the world. Post entertained friends and dignitaries like no other Palm Beacher, staging circus performances, balls, and her famous Thursday night square dance parties, which ended promptly at 10PM.

Donald Trump inherited that legacy in 1985, when he purchased the mansion for $15 million. Included were the house, a parcel of beachfront land, and many of Post's tapestries, paintings, and furnishings. He wanted to subdivide the 18-acre property into eight homesites but was unable to get permission. At press time, Trump planned to transform the estate into a swank private club. Its amenities will include a health spa; a beach club; tennis courts; a croquet lawn; a par 3, nine-hole pitch-and-putt golf course; a freshwater pool; an oceanside saltwater pool; a ballroom; and 10 guest suites. The main dining room seats 75, and the library does double duty as a bar. Should Trump go through with his plan, members would have the run of the place—all 118 rooms and 70,000 square feet of it. In keeping with his goal of creating a cultural-intellectual center, the club will offer lecture and concert series, dances, theater, and fashion shows. By the terms of an edict imposed by the Town of Palm Beach, there may be no more than 500 members, each of whom pays an initiation fee of $100,000 (though some early joiners have already paid "only" $50,000). Annual dues will be $3,000. ♦ 1100 S Ocean Blvd (corner of Southern Blvd and S County Rd). 832.2600 &

7 Public Beach Although Palm Beach is a sunbather's paradise, this Town of Palm Beach property is one of its few public strands. (Many residents have access to their own private beaches via underground tunnels that run from their homes.) Don't take a car to this one, as there's only side-street parking, and the meters require 25¢ for 15 minutes. Lifeguards are on duty during the day. ♦ Gulfstream Rd and S Ocean Blvd

charley's crab

8 Charley's Crab ★★$$$ A favorite with old-school Palm Beachers, this is one of the only oceanfront restaurants on the island. The 15-year-old establishment, paneled in pocked and weathered wood to give the feel of an Old World ship, is owned by the C.A. Muer Corporation, which runs four other South Florida restaurants. Their menus look a lot alike, full of fresh seafood and home-made pastas. There are a few options for carnivores, including roast rack of lamb and aged filet mignon. Try the owner's own Chardonnay label, Muer Cellars, and for dessert, Key lime pie, a good bet just about anywhere in the area, thanks to locally grown limes. ♦ Seafood ♦ Daily lunch and dinner. Reservations required. 456 S Ocean Blvd (one block south of Worth Ave). 659.1500 ঙ

9 The Esplanade Eugene Lawrence designed this elegant, open-air shopping mall—the only one on the island—in 1970. Its two stories are filled with fountains, colored tiles, and couture boutiques, including **Calvin Klein** and **Emanuel Ungaro.** Although most of the shops are expensive and frown on browsers without bucks, **Banana Republic** and **Chico's** offer more casual clothing with panache. The mall's flagship is **Saks Fifth Avenue,** located at the west end. Valet parking is available. ♦ M-Sa. 150 Worth Ave (at S County Rd). 833.0868 ঙ

Within The Esplanade:

Café L'Europe ★★★★$$$$ Named one of South Florida's best restaurants year after year, this is European dining at its finest. With brick walls framing leaded-glass windows and lace curtains, Oriental rugs blanketing wood-plank floors, and daisy-filled terra-cotta pots everywhere, the spacious main dining room is elegant without being stuffy. Even the tuxedoed waiters avoid robotics and chat with the customers. The painstakingly prepared fare has its origins in Western and Eastern Europe. Berlin-born and Swiss-trained chef/owner Norbert Goldner is emphasizing fish these days. A caviar bar features everything from American sturgeon to beluga and Sevruga. Light meals, such as gazpacho in crystal goblets or baked croissant sand-wiches, are served in the bistro. ♦ French/European ♦ Daily lunch and dinner. Reservations required; jacket required. 655.4020 ঙ

Wentworth Gallery Art lovers will be enchanted by this gallery, which features more than 200 original works of art, including serigraphs and sculptures by more than 40 artists. The art is gathered from all around the world, including Croatia, Germany, and South America. Part of a 37-gallery network, it has the buying power of a large chain, yet each gallery acts fairly autonomously. Traveling exhibits of major artists, such as etchings by Rembrandt, make stops here. ♦ M-Sa and by appointment. 659.5751 ঙ

10 Worth Avenue With its flower-filled *vias* (*via* is Italian for way, or road), spotless sidewalks, and fashionable boutiques, this avenue is one of the most elegant shopping thoroughfares in the world. Just a few blocks long, it is home to such boutiques as **Chanel, Krizia, Cartier,** and **Maus & Hoffman.** Most of the Mediterranean-style shops and tucked-away villas were designed by **Addison Mizner,** who, with his Spanish- and Italian-inspired architecture, turned the place into a fantasy-land. Just one of dozens of his contributions to the island, it nonetheless is the one most remembered by visitors. Not in the mood to buy? Take advantage of glittery window-shopping and people watching. Don't be surprised to see a few furs and coiffed poodles spilling out of Rolls-Royces, or a resident celebrity or two. And toward the west end, don't miss a stroll along charming Vias Bice, Mario, Roma, Mizner, and Parigi. ♦ Worth Ave from S Lake Dr to S Ocean Blvd

On Worth Avenue:

Cape Cod Cafe ★$ On and around Worth Avenue, where a quick, inexpensive bite is hard to come by, this is a find. A front wall of folding doors opens onto the street for prime people watching. Serving crisp salads and hearty sandwiches, it also makes more than 300 flavors of ice cream; you can choose from 32 varieties on any given day. ♦ American ♦ Daily breakfast, lunch, and dinner. 410 S County Rd (at Worth Ave). 659.4349 ঙ

Ta-boó
★★$$$
When the bamboo-and fern original opened in 1941, it quickly became one of the biggest draws on Worth Avenue for the wealthy and well-known. With a cozy bar small enough to see what everyone was wearing and hear what they were saying, the restaurant lured a mélange of moguls, including the Duke and Duchess of Windsor, President John F. Kennedy, Frank Sinatra, and Andy Warhol. Under a roll-away roof for dining under the stars, tales were born that are still told today, such as the one about German submariners who came ashore for a couple of drinks during World War II, or the story about Joseph P. Kennedy allegedly barricading himself and Gloria Swanson in the women's room for an entire evening. After a host of different owners, the restaurant

moved out of town in 1986, then returned in 1990. The glitz and gaiety of yesteryear are gone, but the ambience is warm and friendly. There's a piano player, and a large bay window opens onto the avenue. For something light from the eclectic menu, try the chicken Caesar salad; the menu also includes low-sodium and low-cholesterol cuisine. On Friday and Saturday, patrons dance late into the night. ♦ American ♦ Daily lunch and dinner. Reservations recommended. 221 Worth Ave (between S County Rd and Hibiscus Ave). 835.3500 ♿

Bice ★★★$$$$ Established in Milan in 1926, this restaurant group now has locations around the world. This one features fresh fish, veal dishes, and a wide selection of wines. And it twinkles constantly, either by candle-light or with sunlight pouring through the several sets of French doors. Authentic or not, most of the waiters have Italian accents and have mastered the art of dramatic obsequious-ness. No two green-marble tables are too close together. The terra-cotta tiling and a few outdoor tables under mammoth umbrellas add a light touch. ♦ Northern Italian ♦ Daily lunch and dinner. Reservations recom-mended; jacket recommended for dinner. 313½ Worth Ave (between Cocoanut Row and Hibiscus Ave). 835.1600 ♿

Privacy at All Costs?

In 1989 a resident came forward at a **Palm Beach** Town Council meeting with a crime-fighting plan: Install surveillance cameras at the four bridges leading from the mainland to the island. The cameras would record every car, biker, and pedestrian traveling from the mainland to the exclusive island of Palm Beach. Although the plan was eventually defeated, the fact that it was ever taken seriously betrays the privacy-at-all-costs mentality of the island's 19,000 permanent residents. (The popu-lation swells to 40,000 during the winter high season.)

Russian Store As the name implies, this delightful shop's bounty consists of one-of-a-kind Russian art and gifts. Browsers will find charming Matruska dolls, hand-painted furniture, lacquered boxes, rugs, amber jewelry, fairy-tale paintings, and china. The store also carries such Russian Orthodox items as incense burners, crosses, jewelry, and 19th-century icons. Some oil paintings are signed by Yuri Gorbachev, nephew of Mikhail; others, by a young, up-and-coming artist known simply as Sergei. ♦ M-Sa; Su afternoon; F-Sa evening Nov-Mar. 323 Worth Ave (between Hibiscus Ave and Cocoanut Row). 832.3090 ♿

Via Mizner The most spectacular of the five *vias* off Worth Avenue, this shopping arcade of perennially clean stucco, Spanish barrel tile, winding curves, and bougainvillea was designed by **Addison Mizner** in 1925. It offers more than the fashionable boutiques of neighboring Via Parigi. Poke around the original courtyard and you'll find the tombstone of **Mizner**'s pet, Johnnie Brown, the "human monkey." After **Mizner** completed the *via*, he and his pet moved into the four-story tower apartment he had built for himself and Johnnie, who pelted passersby with peanut shells. In 1940, Mortimer Sachs, a dead Columbia University professor famous for being able to read lips in four languages, bought the tower apartment. His wife, Rose, became known as "Queen of the Avenue" for attracting big-name tenants and visitors. In 1975, she opened their manor to the public and hosted an Old World fiesta celebrating the via's 50th anniversary. More than 3,000 turned out to see where the famous architect once lived and, to the tunes of a south-of-the-border band, to dine on 9,000 miniature hamburgers, 18 wheels of cheese, 2,000 rum drinks, and 400 quarts of Ruffino Chianti. Mrs. Sachs sold the *via* in 1985, and it has changed hands several times since. Her collie, Laddie, is buried next to Johnnie Brown. ♦ West end of Worth Ave (across from Philips Gallery). 832.6311 ♿

Hurricane This trim store is filled with hurricane lamps, dozens of candlesticks, and just about every kind of candle—scented, dripless, tapered, beeswax, imported, domestic, and more. It's the perfect stop for snapping up that eleventh-hour hostess gift or a souvenir to take home. The same folks own **Devonshire** (883.0796) across the street, which is packed with gardening-inspired items for all ages, including statues, tiles, pillows, and note cards. ♦ M-Sa. 343 Worth Ave (near Cocoanut Row). 833.6810 ♿

Restaurants/Clubs: Red   **Hotels:** Blue
Shops/ Outdoors: Green   **Sights/Culture:** Black

Everglades Club Originally intended to be a convalescent hospital for World War I veterans, this exclusive private club, with a membership of blue bloods, was designed in 1918 by architect **Addison Mizner.** Paris Singer (of the sewing machine family) commissioned **Mizner** to build it, and the magnificent structure has been called the hallmark of his Mediterranean Revival style. Nonmembers usually can be spotted in a minute, so don't try to go inside unless you know plenty of people listed in the Palm Beach social register. ♦ 356 Worth Ave (near Cocoanut Row). 655.7810 ♿

11 Chesterfield Hotel $$$ With most of the staff members sporting British accents, conversation here takes on the air of an erudite poetry reading. Nonetheless, this refined place, built in 1926, has the cozy feel of a bed-and-breakfast, plus all the accoutrements and services of a luxury hotel. The 48 rooms and five suites are decorated with Old English furniture, and the high tea is probably better than that at No. 10 Downing Street, although some muffins may cost more than a decent lunch. Many of the facilities have been spruced up, including the pink pool with a Jacuzzi and a fountain. There's a restaurant. ♦ 363 Cocoanut Row (at Australian Ave). 659.5800; fax 659.6707 ♿

12 Brazilian Court Hotel $$$$ Shrouded in foliage, this historic 134-room hotel, also built in 1926, sort of creeps up on you despite its bright yellow exterior. Two doormen greet you at the entrance, snatch up your bags, and lead you across a black-and-white tiled lobby that opens onto two spacious courtyards filled with tropical flowers and old fountains. There is a formal dining room, the **Bistro,** and the **Rio Bar,** which offers dancing most evenings to the strains of the Bobby Swiadon Trio. ♦ 301 Australian Ave (between Hibiscus Ave and Cocoanut Row). 655.7740, 800/552.0335 ♿

13 Earl E.T. Smith Preservation Park After you've walked the length of Worth Avenue, walk north two blocks to this oasis of spiritual relief—your feet will thank you. Squeezed onto a corner block, this resting spot sports a fountain, spacious stone benches (they're comfortable, believe it or not), and urns filled

with seasonal flowers in the shadow of a trellis laden with bougainvillea and scented jasmine. The style is decidedly Palm Beach, but with the comfort of a private patio. ♦ NW corner of S County Rd and Chilean Ave

13 Town Hall With a Spanish barrel-tile roof and Moorish arch details, this beloved landmark (illustrated at bottom) has been touched up many times since its construction in 1925 by **Harvey & Clarke.** The latest modification, completed in 1989, was the installation of a magnificent copper cupola; the original had disappeared from the building's tower sometime in the 1920s or 1930s. The dedication ceremony featured the gift of a two-sided clock, which had trouble ticktocking for months but now sounds churchly chimes on the hour. ♦ 360 S County Rd (at the traffic island, across from the police station). 838.5400 ♿

14 Jo's Restaurant ★★★$$$ Decisions, decisions. Look at chef Rick Kline's menu, and you may be tempted to order more than one entrée. His specials change daily, and his delectable creations are enough to turn any diner's head. Besides the fresh fish and pasta dishes, he offers roast duckling à l'orange with a Port wine–and-orange sauce, Maine lobster out of the shell with a ginger-lime sauce, Louisiana lump crab cakes in a mustard–white wine sauce, and herb-crusted rack of lamb. Dessert lovers have a choice of double-chocolate mousse cake, crème brûlée, and apple tart with crème anglaise. The mirrors and latticework give the effect of dining in a lush garden on the Riviera. A cocktail lounge is adjacent to the dining room. ♦ French/Continental ♦ Reservations recommended; jacket recommended. Daily lunch and dinner. 375 S County Rd (at Chilean Ave). 659.6776 ♿

Town Hall

15 L'Ambiance Bar and Bistro ★★★$$$

Nino Yecker (owner of the **Copenhagen Grill** in Boynton Beach) and David Duboc (owner of Boca's **Porterhouse Bar & Grill**) teamed up to open this elegant 175-seat restaurant in 1994. Appetizers include oysters Rockefeller, shrimp and lobster dip, and escargot-and-shrimp cocktail. The menu carries a wide range of delicious entrées, such as salmon, rack of lamb, roast duck, Wiener schnitzel, and chicken with asparagus and raspberry sauce; there also are daily specials. The desserts—all homemade—are hard to pass up: Danish layer cake, strawberry napoleon, apple strudel, and much more. Before and after dinner, patrons can enjoy music and dancing at the classy 35-seat bar. Valet parking is available. ◆ Continental ◆ Daily lunch and dinner until 3AM; dancing after 10PM. Reservations required for dinner. 350 S County Rd (at Australian Ave). 655.0113 ♿

16 Hamburger Heaven ★★$

To locate this 1945 diner, just look for the cow with the halo over its head. The burgers are thick, drippy, and tasty, served at a counter or in booths adorned in old Florida's loud lime green and lemon yellow. The Heavenly Bacon Burger is a favorite; the Heavenly Onion Burger is slathered with sautéed onions. For breakfast, ignore the jelly omelette in favor of the malted waffle with fruit and whipped butter. Save room for the desserts, all baked on the premises. ◆ Diner ◆ Daily breakfast, lunch, and dinner. 314 S County Rd (near Brazilian Ave). 655.5277 ♿

Plaza Inn $$ It's hard to believe, but there is a place at the heart of the island where a room can be reserved for less than $100 off-season (May through 14 December). That doesn't mean no frills, either. The island's finest bed-and-breakfast features a heated pool, a Jacuzzi, and an intimate piano bar. The 50 rooms and suites are individually decorated in 18th-century style, with four-poster beds. Discounts are offered on extended stays. ◆ 215 Brazilian Ave (at S County Rd). 832.8666, 800/233.2632 ♿

17 Amici Ristorante & Bar ★★★$$$

Chef Glen Manfra, formerly of **Bice,** and owner/maitre d' Maurizio Ciminella have teamed up to create a rustic yet chic Italian restaurant with European charm. The kitchen features a wood-burning oven, and innovative, award-winning daily specials supplement the main menu of authentic Italian dishes. The pastas are homemade, and antipasti are on display. There's valet parking. ◆ Italian ◆ M-Sa lunch and dinner; Su dinner. Reservations recommended. 288 S County Rd (at Royal Palm Way). 832.0201 ♿

18 Society of the Four Arts

In the 1930s, Palm Beachers sought a venue for promoting art, literature, music, and science. It took more than a decade to complete this building, with major contributions from four of the town's most prominent architects: **Maurice Fatio, Addison Mizner, John L. Volk,** and **Marion Sims Wyeth.** When the modified Spanish-style library became too small for the society's growing membership and acquisitions, it bought a vacant **Mizner**-designed building (intended to be used as a nightclub) across the street. Local lore has it that a supermarket chain wanted to buy the building, too, but board members held an emergency meeting and beat the grocers to the market. In 1947, **Volk** renovated the **Mizner** building (illustrated on page 163), marked by cut coral stones, raised loggias, and rectangular, arched, and octagonal windows. He enclosed a courtyard, made halls into large galleries, turned a large area into a 750-seat theater, and transformed what was supposed to have been the nightclub's bar and grill into a directors' meeting room, leaving intact its high, cypress-beamed ceilings and wrought-iron chandeliers.

The society claims some 1,500 members, who invite the public to their lectures, performances, movie classics, national and local art exhibitions, and other events.

An *American Modernism* exhibition usually caps the end of the season in April, with some of the most important exponents of that style, including Georgia O'Keeffe and John Marin. A surrounding lush botanical garden is meticulously maintained by the **Garden Club of Palm Beach,** and the sculpture garden features works from China, Italy, England, and Mexico. Check out Isamu Noguchi's 10-ton stainless steel pyramid sculpture. ♦ Admission. M-Sa; Su after 2PM. Four Arts Plaza (between Cocoanut Row and S Lake Trail, just off the Royal Park Bridge). 655.7226, library 655.2766, gardens 659.8518 &

19 Nando's ★$$$$ With fake flowers and dreary tapestries, the interior of this dark bistro leaves a little to be desired, especially considering its prices. But the restaurant has been a Palm Beach tradition for nearly a half century and continuously draws crowds. The continental cuisine—chateaubriand, rack of baby lamb for two, and the like—is generally reliable. The seafood scampi in a bath of tarragon-garlic butter is your best bet. In keeping with its expensive image, valet parking is available. ♦ Continental ♦ Daily dinner; closed in August. Reservations recommended; jacket required. 221 Royal Palm Way (between S County Rd and Hibiscus Ave). 655.3031 &

20 Phipps Plaza Designed in 1925 by **Marion Sims Wyeth** and developed by John S. Phipps, this plaza was once described in a town consultant's report as a "commercial and residential cul-de-sac... a blend of Mediterranean and Bermudian architecture... an island of calm in a sea of congestion." Although Palm Beach isn't exactly a sea of congestion, the plaza does feel like a tranquil getaway from nine-to-five reality and the cars and commerce that zip along on adjacent South County Road. Cats loll on the sidewalk, the fancifully tiled windowsills, and the flower-entwined gates; low-rise residences and offices adorned with awnings and winding staircases huddle around a small green park. Over the years, many architects and builders have relocated to the plaza, making it a mecca of creative thinkers who some say didn't always get along. Architect **John Volk** moved here in the 1940s with his wife, Jane, who still lives in the apartment her late husband remodeled (206 Phipps Plaza). ♦ West of S County Rd (between Sea View Ave and Royal Palm Way)

21 Bethesda-by-the-Sea Episcopal Church No other church in South Florida can lay claim to such a long tenure. Designed by **Hiss & Weeks,** this Gothic wonder was the brainchild of the Reverend Canon James Townsend Russell, who oversaw its construction between 1925 and 1927. The island's first Episcopal church service was held in a one-room schoolhouse at **Phipps Ocean Park** in 1889. A second church was built in 1894 beside Lake Worth, and in the early 1900s, such luminaries as President Grover Cleveland, Alfred G. Vanderbilt, and Mark Twain came by boat or ferry to attend services. The current church gets its name from John 5, the biblical story of a crippled man who was healed by Jesus at the pool of Bethesda.

Society of the Four Arts

Elegant, hand-carved figures of saints flank the main stone entrance. Upon entering the nave, glance forward to the high altar and upward to a magnificent blue stained-glass window, one of many in the stone-arched interior. The organ and Spanish trumpets contain 60 registers, 80 ranks, and 4,482 pipes. Be sure to walk through the east arcade to **Cluett Memorial Gardens.** ♦ 141 S County Rd (at Barton Ave). 655.4554 ₠

22 The Breakers Hotel $$$$ Architect **Leonard Schultze** is remembered for saying that the site of this grand old landmark and jewel of Palm Beach was worthy of an Italian palace. Inspired by the Italian Renaissance and Italy's most notable villas, he created something approximating that ideal on this site in 1926. The ceilings were painstakingly hand-painted by 75 artists imported from Europe; the walls are covered with 15th-century Flemish tapestries; bronze and crystal chandeliers fill the lobby, loggias, and dining rooms; and 20-foot-high windows overlook courtyards and fountains. Aside from the hotel's private beach area, there are 19 tennis courts, an oceanfront golf course, the **Beach Club** pool and patio, croquet lawns, and a fitness center. Not bad for a hotel that burned down twice before the current structure went up. The first fire destroyed the original **Palm Beach Inn,** built in 1896 by Henry M. Flagler, who rebuilt it in 1903. Fire raged again in 1925 (a maid's hot iron left on an ironing board was the suspected cause), and the hotel was rebuilt a year later. Today, with 525 rooms and 1,200 employees, the hotel is the island's largest employer. It's listed on the National Registry of Historic Places, and many of the world's wealthiest and most prominent people have passed through its portals. ♦ 1 S County Rd (between Royal Poinciana and Royal Palm Ways). 655.6611, 800/833.3141 ₠

Palm Beach Life magazine, once regarded as the bible of the Palm Beach social scene, ceased publication after 87 years in 1994. Falling ad revenues doomed the magazine, despite the ironic fact that the average reader's net worth was $1.5 million.

Restaurants/Clubs: Red   **Hotels:** Blue
Shops/ ♦ Outdoors: Green   **Sights/Culture:** Black

Within The Breakers Hotel:

Florentine Dining Room ★★★$$$ Those who remember the grand salons of the luxurious transatlantic ships will find the same tradition of fine cuisine and service preserved here. The decor and craftsmanship are breathtaking: In one area is a beamed ceiling patterned after Florence's Palazzo Davante; in another are paintings depicting mythological divinities. The centerpiece is a dazzling Venetian chandelier made of bronze, crystal, and mirrors. Traditional old-guard residents and younger diners make up the clientele. The menu pleases both—from meat and potatoes to fresh fish topped with nouvelle sauces, such as papaya-mango chutney. Saturdays from June through September feature a full buffet and dancing to a 10-piece big band headed by Marshall Grant, a local jazz favorite and a good entertainer with a sense of humor. ♦ Continental ♦ Daily breakfast and dinner. Reservations recommended for dinner; jackets required. 655.6611 ₠

23 Royal Poinciana Chapel Situated on the property originally known as **Brelsford Cove,** this 1895 chapel nearly adjoins Henry M. Flagler's former palatial estate, now a museum (pictured at right). Its builders included some of Palm Beach's earliest pioneers, including E.N. Dimmick, the island's first mayor. Since Flagler donated the land and contributed financially, he had much to say about the chapel. At his suggestion, it is interdenominational so that it would be "the freest pulpit in the world." Although the chapel has been moved three times, it remains very close to its original location. During its last move in 1972, the structure was entirely renovated. ♦ Sunday morning services only. 60 Cocoanut Row (at Chapel Hill Rd). 655.4212 ₠

24 Flagler Museum/Whitehall Now a museum, this pillared marble mansion beside Lake Worth was a wedding gift that Henry M. Flagler, builder of the **Florida East Coast Railroad,** presented to his bride, Mary Lily Kenan, in 1901. Sold by their heirs in 1925, it served as **Whitehall,** a luxury hotel, until 1959. The museum, with Flagler's granddaughter as president, acquired the building and, after restoring it, opened it to the public in 1960.

Today, this house looks much as it did when the Flaglers lived here. Many of the original furnishings have been returned, and rooms have been carefully restored to reflect a bygone opulence. The Louis XIV music room houses an Odell pipe organ. There are antique costumes and lavish bedrooms, and gold and silver place settings sparkle in dining areas where dukes and duchesses once supped with the Flaglers. Flagler's private yellow railroad car, the *Rambler,* built in 1886, sits restored on the south lawn of the mansion. Nearby is **Seagull Cottage,** a good example of pioneer architecture. **Whitehall** is on the National Register of Historic Places, and photographs, surveys, and floor plans have been recorded with the Historic American Buildings Survey of the Department of the Interior. ◆ Admission. Tu-Sa; Su afternoon. Whitehall Way (at Cocoanut Row). 655.2833 ♿

25 Royal Poinciana Playhouse Flanking Lake Worth, this theater is the first thing you see as you cross the island's north bridge. Open since 1959, the theater offers a Broadway series from December through April; serious drama is performed here as well. Across the parking lot is the former space of the **Palm Beach Playhouse,** which was part of the old **Royal Poinciana Hotel.** Although it enchanted visitors and residents, the **Palm Beach Playhouse,** with its leaky roof, canvas deck-chair seating, and lack of air-conditioning, was nothing like the present theater, which has a plush velvet balcony and comfortable floor seating for 878. ◆ Call for show times. 70 Royal Poinciana Plaza (at Cocoanut Row, just south of Flagler Memorial Bridge). Box office 659.3310 ♿

HIBEL MUSEUM OF ART

25 Hibel Museum of Art When Clayton and Ethelbelle Craig founded a permanent gallery for their extensive collection of Edna Hibel artworks in 1986, they had no idea they had created the first nonprofit public museum dedicated to a living artist. Here, you'll see paintings, porcelains, drawings, and stone lithographs by Hibel, famous for her work with oil glaze, gold leaf, and Asian themes and the first woman invited to exhibit in the People's Republic of China. ◆ Free. Tu-Sa; Su afternoon. 150 Royal Poinciana Plaza (at the base of Flagler Memorial Bridge near Cocoanut Row). 833.6870 ♿

26 Au Bar Boringly trendy is about as much as one can say about this private nightclub— although it has gotten a lot of publicity ever since William Kennedy Smith left the bar in 1991 with a woman who later accused him of rape. High-society types, glitterati wannabes, and those who just want to hang out in one of the Kennedys' old haunts rub elbows here. You can dine on everything from hamburgers and pasta to lobster and steak tartare. The spot was once the short-lived location of the **Palm Beach Club,** for which a local entrepreneur collected more than $600,000 in membership fees and then raised a few eyebrows when he declared bankruptcy. ◆ Cover F-Sa. Tu-Su 8PM-3AM. Reservations recommended. 336 Royal Poinciana Way (at Cocoanut Row). 832.4800 ♿

27 Bicycle Trail Either side of the Royal Poinciana Way Bridge is a good place to start cycling along the island's scenic, black-topped bicycle trail flanking Lake Worth. The

Royal Poinciana Chapel

trail extends one mile south to Worth Avenue and about three miles north to the **Sailfish Club**. Or to the east, you can start at Wells Road, along North County Road, ending up one-and-one-half-miles later at the **Palm Beach Country Club**. To the south, a trail starts at Ibis Isle and heads south for three miles to the town of Lantana.

28 The Biltmore Originally named **The Alba** for a Spanish duke, this twin-towered landmark, designed in 1926 by **Treanor & Fatio,** used to be a swank 50-room resort hotel, but it closed in 1970 and now houses condos. The Mediterranean monolith of stucco, concrete, and Key stone (oolitic limestone) originated during Palm Beach's era of magnificent hotels. ◆ 150 Bradley Pl (between Sunset and Sunrise Aves). 659.4095

29 E.R. Bradley's Saloon $ Once a gambling casino for the hoity-toity, this bistro now draws a decidedly young crowd for the free (with a two-drink minimum) Happy Hour buffet, or late-night drinking, socializing, and leering. Its origins go back to 1898, when Edward Riley Bradley opened the **Palm Beach Club** casino, where "the sky was the limit." The club was the first casino that allowed women to gamble, which may attest to its success. It was never robbed or raided by the police and survived for about 50 years. Now a bistro with a bar and loud music, it is a place where one gambles only on the food, which is mediocre, although fast and inexpensive. Grab a beer, burger, and Bahamian conch fritters and sit out on the veranda. ◆ Eclectic ◆ Daily lunch and dinner. 111 Bradley Pl (between Sunrise Ave and Royal Poinciana Way). 833.3520 ♿

30 Palm Beach Daily News Building This office building isn't known for its architecture, but for being the home of the island's premier newspaper, dubbed the "Shiny Sheet" because of the slick, nonsmudge paper it's printed on (for years, socialites who scanned the paper for their pictures didn't want to get their hands dirty, prompting the change to smudge-proof paper). Long a social tabloid with national news, over the last couple of decades the paper has shown a strong commitment to good, local journalism. As the saying goes, wherever Palm Beachers go—perhaps to their second homes in Newport, Southhampton, or even Europe—the Shiny Sheet goes. Available in the building and at local newsstands, the publication gives visitors the lowdown on what's happening in the area. ◆ 265 Royal Poinciana Way

(between N County Rd and Bradley Pl). 655.5755 ♿

31 Testa's ★$$ This is the home of one of the only neon signs in Palm Beach. What began in the 1920s at a different location as a small soda fountain has become a so-called dining tradition in Palm Beach. It's worthy of the honor for its casual, friendly ambience, thanks to the affable Testa family, and its chummy sidewalk seating. Their breakfasts—which include tasty pecan waffles—are among the best on the island. It's a beloved hangout for locals who come for its big-portion, home-style meals: steaks, a variety of pasta, fresh seafood, and famed strawberry pie. Sit outside and watch passersby and the swaying palms along Royal Poinciana Way. ◆ American ◆ Daily breakfast, lunch, and dinner. Reservations recommended. 221 Royal Poinciana Way (between N County Rd and Bradley Pl). 832.0992 ♿

31 Chuck & Harold's ★★$$$ It isn't hard to have a memorable evening at this restaurant. The beautiful people are double-thick at the bar, sipping wine and eating shellfish. Those sitting outdoors are an arm's length from sidewalk strollers. The roof in the rear **Garden Room** rolls away on clear nights for stargazing or dancing in the moonlight to the tunes of a three- or four-piece combo, usually fronted by a crooner of the Mel Torme school of singing. Salads, seafood, and homemade pasta are favorites. On busy nights, avoid sitting near the bar unless you don't mind the din. ◆ Bistro ◆ Daily breakfast, lunch, and dinner. Reservations recommended for dinner. 207 Royal Poinciana Way (between N County Rd and Bradley Pl). 659.1440 ♿

32 Chez Jean-Pierre ★★★$$$$ This artsy and comfy bistro, a showcase for unusual art, is a local favorite. The dinner and lunch entrées, such as lobster pasta and shrimp-and-scallop brochette, are innovative. ◆ French ◆ Daily lunch and dinner. Reservations recommended for dinner. 132 N County Rd (between Sunrise and Sunset Aves). 833.1171 ♿

33 Paramount Building What was once the proud, celebrity-filled **Paramount Theater** is now an eclectic hodgepodge of stores and offices, including a surf shop, children's store, TV studio, and florist. The theater began showing movies in 1927 at one or two dollars a ticket, which was considered costly back then. Black-tie was the movie-going garb, and box seats in the balcony, called the "Horse Shoe," could command $1,000 per season. The first stage benefits featured humorist Will Rogers.

The present layout sprang from the efforts of Russell Olderman, an Ohio developer who in 1985 helped turn around the neglected structure, which had been closed for six years. Some of the theater's original stonework still is visible. ◆ 139 N County Rd (at Sunrise Ave). 835.0913 ♿

34 Green's Pharmacy and Luncheonette
★★$ One of the last great soda fountains, it serves good, juicy burgers that require plenty of napkins. No one here would dispute that this is a true island landmark, established in 1937 and impervious to the passage of time. It's natural to wonder where the bobby socks and penny loafers have gone, since the lunch counter and some of the cooks haven't changed. The service is friendly and fast. Hearty breakfasts and lunches are good and cheap. Don't miss the thick, old-fashioned malted milk shakes and ice-cream sodas. There's free delivery. ♦ American ♦ Daily breakfast and lunch. 151 N County Rd (at Sunrise Ave). 832.9171 ♿

35 St. Edward's Church In a small Catholic parish of about 250 families, this church was founded in 1921 and named for Edward the Confessor, an English king who confessed (declared his belief in) the Catholic faith. The building is designed in the Spanish Renaissance style. Over the entrance, a large stained-glass window depicts St. Edward giving his ring to a beggar. Inside, the main altar of the Sacred Heart occupies a niche more than 40 feet high. In the south sanctuary is a small stained-glass window dedicated to St. Ignatius, the founder of the Jesuits, and a painting of St. Augustine, after whom the north Florida city is named. To the left of the altar is a stained-glass window of Pius V, who requested that St. Ignatius send missionaries to Florida. Each square of the nave's ceiling was hand-cast, hand-painted, and attached individually. ♦ Sunday morning services only. 144 N County Rd (between Sunrise and Park Aves). 832.0400 ♿

36 Duck's Nest The island's oldest continuously used residence was constructed from two prefabricated homes shipped here in 1890 from New York. Developer Henry Maddock ordered them from the Long Island Portable Housing Company because cut lumber was scarce locally. The sections were positioned together; the porches, a service wing, and a second floor were added later. The house's name was inspired by the ducks that swam in a nearby pond; Maddock also was known to call his wife "Duckie" sometimes. The Maddock family still owns the home, which features a seven-foot rope attached to the gable that spells out the year of its completion—1891. ♦ 561 N Lake Trail (between Sanford and Tangier Aves)

37 Sailfish Club of Florida The oldest private club in Palm Beach has grown considerably since 1914. Its first home was the **Breakers Hotel** casino, then the **Whitehall** hotel. Started by a group of enthusiastic sportsmen who wanted to promote fishing and competition, the club absorbed the **Palm Beach Anglers and Sport Club** and the **Palm Beach Anglers Club,** necessitating larger quarters. The clubhouse at the present location started out as a small structure facing the lake and dock area, and then spread north and south into seven different parcels of property. Some of the largest sailfish in the world hang on the walls of the lounge. Open to members only. ♦ 1338 N Lake Way (between Seagate Rd and Angler Ave). 844.0206 ♿

38 La Guerida The Kennedy family's sprawling oceanfront estate, practically hidden from the road, became known nationwide in the 1960s as the "Winter White House." That's because John F. Kennedy vacationed, worked weekends, and formed his cabinet in the seven-bedroom residence. The home was designed by **Addison Mizner** in 1925 for Redman Wanamaker of Philadelphia's **Wanamaker** department stores, and Joseph P. Kennedy bought it in 1933. The Mediterranean Revival–style stucco and Spanish barrel-tile residence, while perhaps historically and culturally significant, apparently doesn't carry very much architectural merit. Two attempts at landmark designation were unsuccessful. A 1980 report filed for the island's landmark commission stated that the home "is certainly Mizner at his poorest. . . . In any other place, this house would be a major architectural feature. In Palm Beach it is architecturally run-of-the-mill." And in 1990, the commission tabled the matter without a vote. New York banker John Castle purchased the property in 1995. It remains a private residence. ♦ 1095 N Ocean Blvd (north of Angler Ave)

Palm Beach Famous Faces

Many of the rich and famous call **Palm Beach County** home. Actor Burt Reynolds, raised in **West Palm,** owns a ranch in **Jupiter.** Chris Evert, Perry Como, Zsa Zsa Gabor, Estée Lauder, Dom DeLuise, Alexander Haig, F. Lee Bailey, Merv Griffin, Joe Namath, and author Pat Booth also have homes in the area.

Roxanne Pulitzer and former hubby Peter shared a home in **Palm Beach,** as did John Lennon and wife Yoko Ono. The Kennedys were known to steal away to the clan's recently sold oceanfront estate.

While blue bloods take pride in the quiet splendor of Palm Beach, some say the island just hasn't been the same since high roller Donald Trump moved in, along with Marla Maples, his second wife.

West Palm Beach

West Palm Beach has come a long way since its beginnings as a servants' community created in 1894 by Henry M. Flagler to support his dream resort, the town of **Palm Beach**, which is separated from the mainland and West Palm by **Lake Worth**. Sometimes overshadowed by the grand reputations of Palm Beach and **Boca Raton**, West Palm Beach not only is the seat of the **Palm Beach County** government, but it also is the

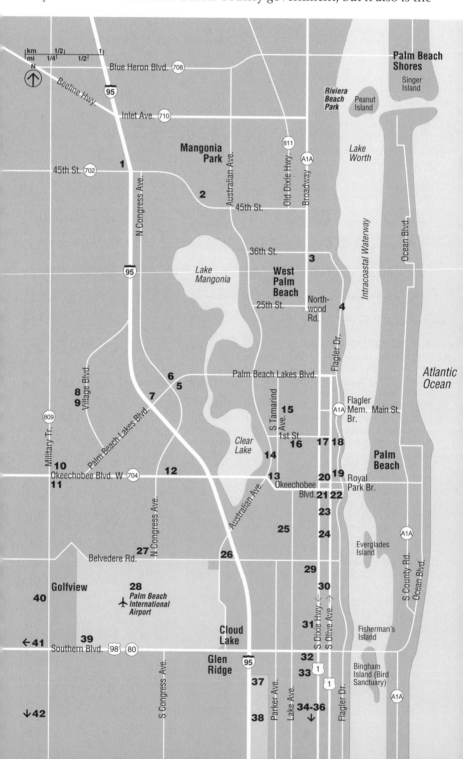

area's industrial and business center. Today, with 83,300 people, it's also the largest city in the county and one of the fastest-growing areas in the state.

Major banks and businesses have their headquarters here, lending the city a backdrop of gleaming high-rise office towers. And yet, West Palm Beach is far from losing its neighborhood feel. Many of its restaurants and bars are homey community hangouts, where almost everyone knows your name—and if they don't, they're friendly enough to ask. Bikers, in-line skaters, walkers, joggers, and anglers cruise **Flagler Drive**'s broad, paved walkway, which runs parallel to the **Intracoastal Waterway** wall. Dotted with majestic palms, the walkway extends for about one mile. The section between **First Street** and **Okeechobee Boulevard** is the city's main venue for such outdoor festivals as SunFest, perhaps the Southeast's largest. Held in May, it features live music, an arts-and-crafts marketplace, international food, rides, and fireworks.

Meanwhile, the specialty shops, restaurants, and clubs on palm-lined **Clematis Street** are helping to rejuvenate downtown. Women's boutiques, cafes, night spots, and a new gym are big draws for an area that used to close down after sunset. The city also has focused on restoring its historic neighborhoods, such as **Old Northwood.**

West Palm Beach is home to the **Norton Gallery of Art**, one of the finest small museums in the country, with works by the likes of Chagall and O'Keeffe. The $55-million **Raymond F. Kravis Center for the Performing Arts** is bustling year-round, with performances by the **Palm Beach Opera**, the **Philharmonic Orchestra of Florida**, **Ballet Florida**, the **Palm Beach Symphony**, and the **Miami City Ballet.** The enlarged **Palm Beach International Airport** provides service to the entire country via many major airlines. And, to complete the picture, the city's hotels are less expensive and more family-oriented than the oceanside resorts.

Area code 407 unless otherwise indicated.

1 Courtyard by Marriott $$ Conveniently located at an I-95 interchange, this 149-room, 12-suite hotel is not far from the **Palm Beach Mall** (see below) and the city's sports and performing arts auditorium. The many facilities—swimming pool, whirlpool, exercise room, restaurant, and lounge—keep guests happily occupied. ◆ 600 Northpoint Pkwy (at I-95 and 45th St). 640.9000, 800/321.2211 &

PALM BEACH'S BALL GAME

2 Palm Beach Jai Alai Equipped with *cestas* (wicker baskets), opponents compete in the fastest sport on foot on a walled-in court. The *pelota* (ball) barrels against the wall at about 100 miles an hour. Spectators can participate too—by wagering. ◆ M, W-Su late Nov.-Dec. 1415 45th St (six blocks east of I-95). 844.2444 &

3 Northwood By South Florida standards, this neighborhood is old: About 80 percent of its homes are more than 25 years old, and 30 percent are more than 45 years old. Northwood, declared a "model district" by the neighborhood association, contains homes dating back to the 1920s. Many of these two-story Spanish-style residences, with garage or carriage apartments, were designed by the late Palm Beach architect **John Volk**, whose work includes more than 1,000 homes and buildings, such as the Royal Poinciana Plaza in Palm Beach and the **Good Samaritan Hospital** in West Palm. Walking tours of the district are offered. Some outskirt areas have been plagued by neglect, prostitution, and other crime—problems the neighborhood is actively addressing. ◆ Bounded by N Dixie and Broadway Ave, and 26th and 36th Sts. Tours 832.4164, 800/572.8471

4 Currie Park Sandwiched between the Intracoastal Waterway and Flagler Drive, this scenic spot comprises tennis courts, a clubhouse, a playground, picnic facilities, and lots of open space for soccer, Frisbee, and kite flying. A short rock jetty, convenient for drop-line fishing, lets you walk on water without getting your feet wet. A seafood festival—with rides and games, in addition to eats—usually takes place here in November. ◆ 2400 N Flagler Dr. 835.7025

5 West Palm Beach Auditorium and Municipal Stadium Home to national theater, concerts, wrestling matches, circuses, and ice and trade shows, the tepee-shaped auditorium opened in 1967 after much controversy. Some complained the $4-million project was too expensive for a city the size of West Palm. Then after it opened, the roof leaked, causing further skepticism. The adjacent stadium is the site of spring training for the **Atlanta Braves** and **Montreal Expos.** From April through August, the **Florida State League West Palm Beach Expos** train and play here. ♦ 1610 Palm Beach Lakes Blvd (at N Congress Ave). Tickets and information 683.6012 ⑤

6 Bangkok O-cha ★★$$ Don't be fooled by the plain, storefront exterior. Authentic Thai dishes are served here in a fiery interior of red linen and carpeting. The menu can be confusing when it comes to the degree of spiciness of some entrées, so make sure the wait staff understands what you want. Fish is cooked on the bone. The shrimp dishes are delicious, but the gastronomically daring will want to try squid or frogs' leg curry. ♦ Thai ♦ Daily lunch and dinner. Reservations recommended at lunch. 1687 Forum Pl (off N Congress Ave). 471.3163 ⑤

PALM BEACH MALL

7 Palm Beach Mall Although it is now just another shopping center among South Florida's preponderance of them, this 1.4-million-square-foot, $20-million mall was the state's largest when it was completed in 1967. Its success made the DeBartolo Corporation one of the major mall builders in the country. Today, it's not as glitzy as the county's newer ones, such as **The Gardens** in Palm Beach Gardens, which has atriums, marble statuary, and a glass elevator. But it contains dependable chain stores, such as **Lord & Taylor, Burdines, J.C. Penney, Sears,** and **Mervyn's.** ♦ Daily. I-95 and Palm Beach Lakes Blvd. 683.9186 ⑤

Restaurants/Clubs: Red	**Hotels:** Blue
Shops/🍴 **Outdoors:** Green	**Sights/Culture:** Black

8 Basil's Neighborhood Cafe ★★$$ Gourmet pizza with wild mushroom, grilled chicken, basil, and garlic toppings is the standout item on the menu here. Also good are fresh pasta with peppers, and shrimp and "sprouting broccoli." The grilled tuna salad and whole grain mustard lamb chops, grilled to crusty perfection, are delicious. ♦ Continental ♦ Tu-Su lunch and dinner. 771 Village Blvd (between Palm Beach Lakes Blvd and Community Dr). 687.3801 ⑤

9 Sagami ★★★$$ Three Japanese chefs slice, dice, and create wonderful raw fish delicacies at the long sushi bar. There's table seating and two wood-framed areas with tatami mats—the traditional straw matting on which hard-core connoisseurs sit cross-legged, leaving their shoes aside. A sushi sampler offers a taste of red tuna, cobia, and crab stuffed into rolls of rice wrapped in seaweed. For those who prefer their dinner cooked, there's teriyaki and yakitori. ♦ Japanese ♦ M-F lunch and dinner; Sa-Su dinner. 871 Village Blvd (between Palm Beach Lakes Blvd and Community Dr). 683.4600 ⑤

10 Pier I Imports Like an indoor bazaar, this shop is loaded with Far Eastern, Latin American, and generally funky and unusual furniture, household goods, clothing, and jewelry. You can find anything from giant Japanese-style umbrellas and Indian beaded shoes to futons, rice mats, wicker arrangements, Art Deco wine glasses, and all kinds of chopsticks. While the prices are reasonable, milling around and browsing is just as much fun as buying. ♦ Daily. 2041 Zip Code Pl (alongside Okeechobee Blvd between Military Tr and Spafford Ave). 697.5117 ⑤

11 Cross County Mall and Movie Theater With a **Ross** discount clothing store, **Kmart, Builder's Square,** and about 40 other rather unglamorous retail outlets, this 510,300-square-foot mall caters mostly to locals. The eight-screen cinema showcases the latest flicks. ♦ Daily. Okeechobee Blvd and Military Tr. 683.8884 ⑤

THE SPORTS AUTHORITY

12 Sports Authority Stop at the city's largest sporting goods store for snorkeling, diving, or fishing equipment, as well as T-shirts, tennis clothes, and other athleticwear. Usually three or four aisles of goods are dedicated to one sport; sneakers alone take up some five or six of them. ♦ Daily. 2601 Okeechobee Blvd (in the Westward Shopping Center at N Congress Ave). 688.9501 &

13 Raymond F. Kravis Center for the Performing Arts Dubbed the "jewel" of West Palm Beach, this arts and education center with a 2,200-seat multipurpose theater is the site of performances by resident companies, including the **Palm Beach Opera**, the **Philharmonic Orchestra of Florida, Ballet Florida,** the **Palm Beach Symphony,** the **Florida Symphonic Pops of Boca Raton,** and the **Miami City Ballet.** The mammoth, sea foam green–accented facility is the corner-stone of the revitalization of downtown, a movement that began in the late 1980s to recapture the activity that suburbia and outlying malls had siphoned away. ♦ 701 Okeechobee Blvd (at S Tamarind Ave). 833.3855 &

14 Seaboard Railroad Station One of the city's finest examples of Mediterranean Revival architecture—the signature style of Palm Beach—this station was built in 1925 by the city's first African-American architectural firm, **Harvey & Clarke.** It was the flagship station of the **Seaboard** cruise line, which in the early days was used by wealthy visitors to Palm Beach—including the Duke and (airplane-phobic) Duchess of Windsor—who would take a ferry to the island. After the building fell into disrepair in the late 1980s, the city raised more than $1 million (by, among other schemes, selling personalized bricks taken from the structure) toward a major restor-ation. Listed on the National Registry of Historic Places, it is now used as an **Amtrak** passenger station and as a stop on the **Tri-Rail** commuter train, which goes from West Palm Beach to Miami. ♦ 201 S Tamarind Ave (three blocks north of the Kravis Center). 832.6169, 800/872.7245 &

15 Northwest Neighborhood This enclave was the focal point of the cultural, social, and political life of the area's black population between 1890 and 1960. During much of that period, blacks were barred from living or conducting business elsewhere in the city, after a 1929 ordinance mandated the boundaries of a black neighborhood. Before that, the area's first black businesspeople and families had settled here and had begun building the neighborhood. The area contains some 200 historic buildings, including eight churches, a school, homes, and apartments dating from 1915 to the early 1940s. By the late 1970s, the neighborhood had become riddled with drug houses, which the city is cleaning up. The district is listed on the National Registry of Historic Places. ♦ Bounded by Rosemary Ave and the Florida East Coast railroad tracks, and Third and 23rd Sts

Within the Northwest Neighborhood:

Henry Speed House This bungalow was designed and built in 1921 by the area's first black real estate agent, Henry Speed, a philanthropist who later donated land for a black high school and hospital. An excellent example of bungalow architecture, his home can easily be identified by its two dormer windows. It is a private residence. ♦ 801 Third St (at Division Ave)

Mickens House Alice Frederick Mickens, who lived out her 70-plus years promoting black education throughout the state, occupied this house. Built in 1917, it was listed on the National Registry of Historic Places in 1985. Today, it is a private residence. ♦ 801 Fourth St (at Division Ave)

Fairway Frenzy

In **Palm Beach County,** where there's a course on every corner and putting weather is prime year-round, golf is more than a game; it's a lifestyle. The county's first course—at **The Breakers**—was built in 1897. The rich and famous have been taking swings on some of the county's finest greens ever since. Jackie Gleason and Bob Hope played here, as did Presidents Taft, Eisenhower, Kennedy, Ford, and Nixon. Today, Palm Beach County has 150 golf courses—more than any other county in the nation.

The **Professional Golfers Association of America (PGA)** is based in **Palm Beach Gardens,** a northern municipality where the **PGA National** golfing community hosts several major tourna-ments, including the **PGA Championship** and the **PGA Senior's Championship.**

Although the area is known as a golfer's paradise, many of the courses here are private. Among **West Palm Beach**'s best public courses:

Palm Beach Lakes Golf Course 1100 N Congress Ave, 683.2700

Turtle Bay Golf Club 2750 Golf Club Circle, 686.0948

West Palm Beach Country Club 7001 Parker Ave, 582.2019

Tabernacle Missionary Baptist Church

Originally established in 1893 in Palm Beach, where a small settlement of black laborers first sprung up, the church was rebuilt here in 1925 in the Neo-Romanesque style. The two-toned brick used in the veneer was shipped from the Alabama home of the Reverend Coleman, a young minister who came to the parish in 1914. ◆ 801 Eighth St (at Division Ave). 832.8338 &

Payne Chapel A.M.E.

Another church that was originally established in Palm Beach in 1893, it later moved to this Neo-Gothic Revival building, which **Hazel Augustus** had designed in 1925. ◆ 801 Ninth St (at Division Ave). 832.2035 &

Sunset Cocktail Lounge

Built circa 1920, this lounge reopened in 1933 as a nightclub with an enormous dance floor. Top black entertainers, including Duke Ellington and Count Basie, played here. Today, the pink and green cocktail lounge is still worth a visit to see the architecture. ◆ Daily 4PM-closing. 609 Eighth St (at Henrietta Ave). 832.5707 &

Shotgun Homes

These narrow, gable-front buildings—each one room wide—housed Southern laborers who came to the area between 1880 and 1930. It is said that the front and back doors are so perfectly aligned that a shot can be fired straight through (hence their name). Porches extend to the street, and there's enough yard in back for a vegetable garden. They are private residences. ◆ 610-620 Douglass Ave (at Sixth St)

16 Respectable Street Cafe This "alternative" dance club is perfect for recent college grads and bohemians who enjoy live musical entertainment, ranging from blues to house music, progressive rock, and reggae. The dance area is crowned with a music video screen, and funky local art adorns the walls. Beer is the drink of choice. Local bands play Thursdays. ◆ Cover. W-Sa 9PM-4AM. 518 Clematis St (between Florida and El Campeon Aves). 832.9999 &

17 Comeau Bar and Grille ★$ Hearty burgers, sandwiches, and stews with big french fries on the side are served at back room tables or up at the brass-and-wood bar in this authentic-looking Irish pub. The place gets crowded during downtown festivals, and on Sunday afternoon football is shown on two TVs. Otherwise, a trickle of regulars comes for the casual atmosphere, bar banter, pool table, and top-notch CD jukebox with old selections like Creedence Clearwater Revival's "Midnight Special," Gene Chandler's "Duke of Earl," Duke Ellington's "Satin Doll," and Frank Sinatra crooning "Summer Wind." ◆ Pub ◆ Daily until 3AM. 323 Clematis St (between Dixie Hwy and Olive Ave). 833.2402 &

18 Robinson's Pastry Shop ★$ This downtown institution is renowned for its coconut cake and pecan logs. Jack Robinson, a baker for most of his life, insists on whipping things up the old-fashioned way—using no preservatives, mixing by hand, and baking in ovens that are several decades old. The fruit for some of his delicacies comes from his own trees. The sandwiches are good, too, and can be enjoyed at a few outdoor tables. ◆ American ◆ Daily. 215 Clematis St (between Olive and Narcissus Aves). 833.4259 &

18 West Palm Beach Library This 35,000-square-foot library, with its multicolored facade, has been threatened by ambitious developers who have lobbied the city to take over its Intracoastal-front location. The town's residents have assiduously fought such a move. The historical Florida collection housed here may be of interest to visitors. Note the three-by-five stained-glass window on the building's west side, depicting a dead soldier with an angel hovering above: Lost in 1962 when the library moved to its present location, the work of art was recovered by a local stained-glass studio owner in 1985. ◆ M-Th, Sa. 100 Clematis St (between Flagler Dr and Narcissus Ave). 659.8010 &

19 Phillips Point Locals have yet to arrive at a consensus regarding this glitzy retail and office complex. Some think the concrete Colorado quartz–pink aggregate siding is lovely; others think it smacks of tacky pink flamingo. At one point, the local Citizens Growth Management Coalition tried to halt its construction. Nonetheless, it was completed in 1986, at a time when the city was losing businesses and customers to outlying malls and suburbia, and many big-time tenants signed on. The entire top floor is occupied by the **Governor's Club**, a private dining club whose ranks are hard to break into. At sunrise and sunset, this shiny complex reflects a pink glow onto the Intracoastal Waterway across the street to the east. ◆ 777 Flagler Dr (at Lakeview Ave). 833.7337 &

Within Phillips Point:

Morton's of Chicago ★★★$$$$

Where's the beef? Right here, in this elegant dining spot with stained-glass windows, varnished mahogany, leather appointments, and wine racks built into the walls. Steak is the best reason to visit, so the meat-and-potatoes crew will feel right at home. The prime rib, New York sirloin, and Sicilian veal chop are excellent. Appetizers include fresh lump crabmeat, oysters on the half shell, and black bean soup. Those eschewing red meat can choose from lemon oregano chicken, Maine lobster, swordfish, and the fresh fish of the day. For dessert, there's chocolate, lemon, or Grand Marnier soufflé, apple pie, fudge torte, and New York cheesecake. Valet parking is available. ♦ American ♦ Daily dinner. Reservations recommended. 835.9664. &

20 Esperante Building Tall, sleek, and elegant with powder-blue embellishments, this $50-million multipurpose complex was completed in 1987. It stands at the eastern end of Okeechobee Boulevard, which city planners envision as a lavishly landscaped gateway to the city in years to come. The 20-story structure includes 214,000 square feet of office space, 27,000 square feet of retail and restaurant space, and eight tri-level town houses on the top floors, which carry $500,000-plus price tags. ♦ 222 Lakeview Ave (between Olive and Chase Aves). 650.7300 &

The Classic Collection

21 Classic Collection

"Have you hugged your gargoyle today?" asks the advertisement. Take a walk through Jeff Yansura's shop, and you'll see why. Medieval gargoyles and griffins, both menacing and playful, stare out from every wall. Yansura quit his job as a commercial property manager in 1993 to pursue his hobby of collecting Neo-Classical architectural pieces. He has since amassed all sorts of impressive interior and exterior accents and accessories, including lion's-head bookends, decorative brackets, ceiling medallions, elegant urns, planters, cherub wall friezes, pedestals, and garden statuary. The pieces are either plaster or concrete. Special orders, custom finishes, and home delivery of large pieces are available. ♦ M-Sa. 814 S Dixie Hwy (near Okeechobee Blvd). 659.6552 &

22 Palm Beach Atlantic College This four-year liberal arts institution is affiliated with the Baptist church and two Southern college and university associations. The small 21-acre campus, home to about 1,600 students, stretches from Flagler Drive to South Dixie Highway along Okeechobee Boulevard, then south to Acacia between South Dixie and South Olive Avenue. Describing itself as having a "Christian-type" atmosphere, it is one of the few colleges in the country where students voluntarily commit to outside community service work. ♦ 901 S Flagler Dr. 650.7700 &

23 Norton Gallery of Art
What began as Ralph Norton's personal art collection now makes up part of one of the finest small museums in the country. Ralph and Elizabeth Norton's gift to the museum — which included major works by Impressionist and modern masters— forms the basis of its permanent collection; Gauguin, Picasso, Cézanne, DeChirico, Brancusi, Chagall, O'Keeffe, Bellows, Hassam, Motherwell, and Hopper are represented, among other artists. The gallery is housed in a building designed in 1940 by **Marion Syms Wyeth.** In 1942 Norton acquired an impressive Asian collection, featuring archaic bronzes and jades; later gifts have broadened the museum's holdings. On site are 10 galleries, a library, a theater, and an interior garden of Chinese jade sculpture. Tours are given Saturday and Sunday afternoons. ♦ Donation. M-Sa; Su afternoon. 1451 S Olive Ave (between Pioneer Pl and Players Alley, five blocks south of Okeechobee Blvd). 832.5194 &

24 Carefree Theater This movie theater and concert venue showcases foreign films and nationally known musical groups. Also in the building is the **Comedy Corner** (833.1812), a club that attracts such big-name acts as comediennes Paula Poundstone and Elaine Boosler. The on-site **Carefree Cafe** sells coffee and dessert, and there's a sports bar as well. ♦ 2000 S Dixie Hwy (between Okeechobee Blvd and Belvedere Rd). 833.7305 &

Restaurants/Clubs: Red   **Hotels:** Blue
Shops/ ☂ Outdoors: Green   **Sights/Culture:** Black

24 Anne Norton Sculpture Gardens A tropical garden with one of the South's most extensive gathering of palms—more than 200 species—is the setting for the permanent collection of Anne Norton's monumental brick-and-stone sculptures as well as visiting exhibits. Strolling the lush three-and-a-half acres of ficus, palms, and native flowers is a calming, contemplative experience. ♦ Admission. Tu-Sa until 4PM. 253 Barcelona Rd (at Flagler Dr). 832.5328 &

⅋RMORY ⅋RT (ENTER

25 Armory Art Center This Art Deco building (pictured on page 175)—formerly an armory—features rotating exhibits of works by Florida artists. It also includes a studio art school offering ongoing classes and short-term workshops for children and adults. ♦ Free. M-F; Sa 10AM-2PM. 1703 S Lake Ave (at Park Place). 832.1776 &

26 Omni Hotel $$$ Attached to twin office towers, this 15-story hotel with its vast marble atrium lobby has a highway location just across from the **Palm Beach International Airport** (see below). Its 220 rooms include 110 suites, some with terraces and kitchenettes, and a presidential suite. The fairly upscale restaurant and the patio cafe are convenient dining options, and the lobby bar overlooks a fountain and sculpture. Additional amenities: a health club, a heated pool, and two tennis courts. There are plenty of banquet and meeting facilities, too. ♦ 1601 Belvedere Rd (between Australian Ave and Florida Mango Rd). 689.6400, 800/THE.OMNI &

PALM BEACH KENNEL CLUB

27 Palm Beach Kennel Club Greyhound racing is the sixth most popular spectator sport in the country. Here the dogs race at speeds of up to 40 miles an hour. Open year-round with matinee and evening races, the kennel club permits gambling on the races, for those hoping to return home richer for the experience. ♦ Admission. 1111 N Congress Ave (at Belvedere Rd). 683.2222 &

28 Palm Beach International Airport Visitors will find large-scale artworks throughout this airport, which was significantly expanded several years ago. The focal point of the county's Art in the Airport Project is a suspended sculpture by Larry Kirkland, an Oregon artist, that depicts two men in boats. See page 151 for more information. ♦ 1000 Turnage Blvd (off Australian Ave between Southern Blvd and Belvedere Rd). 471.7420 &

29 Cucina ★★$$$ Don't let the minimalist decor keep you from enjoying this contemporary bistro's subtle blend of flavors. Amid a lively atmosphere, the wait staff promptly answers questions and serves drinks and food with remarkable alacrity. The menu, which changes daily, offers savory Italian cuisine, although the overpriced wine list can put a damper on a budget-minded diner's plans. Be sure to focus on the desserts—they're wonderful. ♦ Italian ♦ Daily dinner. Reservations recommended. 2419 S Dixie Hwy (south of Belvedere Rd). 832.2421 &

30 Rhythm Cafe ★★★$$ As though transplanted from New York's Greenwich Village, this funky and cosmopolitan shoebox-size bistro is one of the city's best-kept secrets. The small bar, imaginative artwork, and black-and-white-tile floor are unimposing under soft, almost-too-dark lighting. The menu of innovative nouvelle dishes changes almost daily. With just 14 tables, the service is pretty good. ♦ Continental ♦ Tu-Sa dinner. 3238 S Dixie Hwy (between Greymon and Greenwood Drs). 833.3406 &

30 Pippenella's ★★★$$ You know you're in the right place when you sense the scents of garlic and parmesan. With great Italian dishes at reasonable prices and a wait staff that is quick with a smile, this casual, homey spot has been jumping ever since it opened in 1994. Maybe it's the garlic bread with melted mozzarella that keeps families and couples coming back, or the out-of-this-world eggplant parmigiana. Chicken is pre-pared five ways here: scallopini, cacciatore, *francese*, primavera (with broccoli, cauli-flower, carrots, and mushrooms and served over pasta), and Florentine (with spinach and noodles in a rich cream sauce). ♦ Italian ♦ Daily lunch and dinner. 3400 S Dixie Hwy (between Edgewood and Greymon Drs). 833.5800 &

30 Ciao ★★★$$ The decor is not especially fancy or even tasteful, but eclectic Italian cuisine has never been so good. Owner/chef Gino Rubio studied under Alfredo, Rome's fettuccine master. Portions are generous, and entrées come with a plate of pasta and salad.

With spinach that's been tenderized by soaking, the simple spinach salad appetizer scores high points. The garlicky shrimp scampi is like no other, sautéed with fresh vegetables over pasta that Gino makes daily. ♦ Italian ♦ Daily dinner. 3416 S Dixie Hwy (at Edgewood Dr). 659.2426 ₺

31 Antique Row A flurry of activity enlivens this stretch of South Dixie Highway, especially during the winter, when Palm Beachers and tourists flirt with temptation at more than 20 antiques stores. A cluster of shops that popped up in the 1980s has grown into a prime attract-ion for the fashion-conscious homeowner and anyone who likes to browse everything from chic to schlock. You'll find it all here, from jugs and country classics at the **Old Timer's Antiques Mall** to grand old pieces plundered from European castles and Palm Beach estates at the **Incurable Collector.** ♦ S Dixie Hwy (from Southern Blvd to Wenonah Place)

On Antique Row:

Peter Werner Limited Theatrical flair reigns supreme in this corner shop, where grand pieces blend comfortably with whimsical accessories. The fast-moving inventory ranges from metal sconces from a Parisian movie house to a Grosfield House 1940s console. ♦ M-Sa. 3709 S Dixie Hwy (between Walton Blvd and Lakeland Dr). 832.0428 ₺

Cashmere Buffalo Kitschy fun and thrifty finds fill this store, which is cluttered with everything from rattan magazine racks, birdhouses, and vintage Fiestaware to recycled purses, jewelry, and clothing from the 1920s through the 1950s. ♦ M-Sa. 3735 S Dixie Hwy (between Walton Blvd and Lakeland Dr). 659.5441 ₺

32 O'Donnell's Saloon ★★$ Rub elbows with locals at the bar or sit at tables crowded onto two tiers surrounded by walls plastered with black-and-white prints of major cities. Imported and domestic beers, including English Bass on draft, are a prime attraction at this jovial pub, where hefty servings of hearty fare arrive at your table almost as soon as you order. Crab cakes, chicken pot pie, and bangers and mash are tops on a menu based

on burgers, sandwiches, soups, and salads, plus daily specials. Local jazz musicians fill the air with rhythm-and-blues on Friday evenings. ♦ Pub ♦ Daily lunch and dinner. 4001 S Dixie Hwy (at Southern Blvd). 659.7506 ₺

33 Phipps Park This park has picnic areas, an exercise trail, tennis courts, a bike path, a recreation center, a clubhouse, and a swimming pool. There's plenty of space for kite flying, too. ♦ 4301 S Dixie Hwy (just south of Southern Blvd). 835.7025

34 Deco Don's Former art major/furniture restorer Don Henry crafted one of the premier tropical funk design stores in the Palm Beaches. Rattan is typically Floridian, and Henry's tiny store displays a constantly changing array of pieces—from tables to chairs to bed frames—that recall the Sunshine State's heyday. Heywood-Wakefield furniture and knickknacks from the 1920s through the 1950s round out the eclectic collection. Next door at **Real Life Antiques** (582.8064), throwaways from the 1950s fetch top dollar. ♦ M-Sa. 5107 S Dixie Hwy (near Bunker Rd). 588.2552 ₺

WATTANA
THAI RESTAURANT

35 Wattana ★★$$ Don't let its small size fool you: This is one of the better Thai restaurants in the county, thanks to chef-owner Wattana Sumonthee. And the service is friendly and quick. Choose from eight delicious soups—*tom ga kai* (chicken soup with coconut milk) and *tom yum goong* (with shrimp, mushrooms, and lime juice) are tops. For the main course, *pad thai* (rice noodles with shrimp, chicken, ground pork, egg, bean sprouts, and peanuts) is a favorite, as is chicken curry with coconut milk. Those with mild tastes can opt for the no-star version; if you can take the heat, try three stars. Sweet tooths will love the Thai iced coffee or tea. ♦ Thai ♦ M-F lunch and dinner; Sa-Su dinner. 7201 S Dixie Hwy (south of Forest Hill Blvd). 588.9383 ₺

Armory Art Center

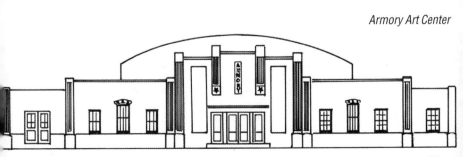

36 **GulfStream Hotel & Villas** $ Listed on the National Registry of Historic Places, this 1921 hotel is one of Lake Worth's landmarks. Rough times came in 1928, when its roof was torn off during a hurricane, and in 1988, when the six-story pink hotel was foreclosed. Then along came British entrepreneur David Giles, who bought the place and redesigned it with a European ambience. The 121 rooms and 13 villas, all of which overlook the Intracoastal, are accessible to the beach, a half mile away. The hotel's **Ocean Drive Bar & Grill** serves continental fare daily; weekend entertainment features jazz, R&B, and worldbeat music. ♦ 1 Lake Ave (west side of Lake Worth Bridge). 586.9250 &

37 **South Florida Science Museum and Planetarium** Scientific exhibits, an aquarium, a planetarium, a native plant center, and an observatory—with the largest public-use telescope in South Florida—are featured at this eclectic complex. Suzie, an elephant-size replica of a mastodon, is popular with kids, while adults prefer the Friday-evening laser shows. The aquarium is home to all sorts of regional and Caribbean sealife, including sharks. ♦ Admission. Daily; F until 10PM; planetarium shows daily. 4801 Dreher Tr N (between Parker Ave and Florida Mango Rd). 832.1988 &

38 **Dreher Park Zoo** Some 400 animals representing more than 100 native and exotic species call this 25-acre zoo home. Featured here is the only outdoor exhibit in the country of the tiny and rare goeldi monkey, all five of them leaping around and vying for the attention of visitors. Resident endangered species include the diminutive marmoset and the Florida panther. ♦ Admission. Daily. 1301 Summit Blvd (east of I-95). 533.0887

39 **391st Bomb Group** ★$$ The food here is dull, but the atmosphere is unforgettable. The restaurant occupies a re-created French farmhouse filled with gas masks, sandbags, army boots, machine guns, and other World War II memorabilia. In the bar-lounge, old movies are screened, and an old-fashioned popcorn machine spews forth scoopfuls of free munchies. Headphones at tables tune into the control tower at adjacent **Palm Beach International Airport.** All this entertainment withers when it's busy, as diners with reservations are ordered through a public address system to "report to the mess hall." The steak house–variety food is lifeless albeit plentiful, with meals served with heaps of bread, soup, and salad. ♦ American ♦ Daily lunch and dinner. Reservations recom-mended. 3989 Southern Blvd (at Kirk Ave). 683.3919 &

40 **Mounts Botanical Garden** After enduring the hurly-burly of sightseeing and beach-combing, chill out at this mini-paradise. Created in 1954, this wonderland of flowers, fruit trees, palms, herbs, and roses has blossomed into a resource much utilized by locals. Within its borders are more than a dozen display areas full of educational tips for the gardener and just plain beauty and fragrance for the traveler. A Xeriscape (Greek for "dry location") garden demonstrates growing techniques that utilize little water, while a stroll through the native plant garden reveals why Florida was named "Land of Flowers." ♦ Donation. M-Sa; Su afternoon. 531 N Military Tr (at Elizabeth St). 233.1749

World Famous LION COUNTRY SAFARI ®

41 Lion Country Safari West Palm's 500-acre wildlife preserve is the nation's first "cageless zoo." More than 1,300 animals from around the world roam free in this drive-through wilderness, and some are supposed to delight you by coming up to your car, but they rarely do. In reality, few animals can be seen, as if they're hiding; it's still a kick, though, to see an elephant lolling about. Other highlights are nature trails, boat rides, a petting zoo, a reptile exhibit, and a KOA campground. ♦ Admission. Daily; no cars allowed after 4:30PM. State Rd 80 W (west of Seminole Pratt Whitney Rd). 793.1084

42 Hoffman's Chocolate Shoppe Willie Wonka would go bonkers in this candy haven, where visitors can see chocolate made from start to finish. When all the gooey goodness gets to be overpowering, the lovely garden outside restores one's senses. Stock up on goodies, and be sure to choose truffles, coconut cashew crunch, and pan fudge from among the more than 80 products on display. Take the kids (but not when they're hungry). ♦ M-Sa; Su afternoon. 5190 Lake Worth Rd (a half-mile west of Military Tr). 967.2213. ♿ Also at: 2403 S Dixie Hwy (between Belvedere Rd and Granada St), West Palm Beach. 833.9414 ♿

Bests

Helen Muir
Journalist/Author of *The Biltmore: Beacon for Miami* and *Miami, U.S.A.*

A sunrise over water, ocean, or bay, and certainly a sunset. Give it your full attention because South Florida presents the most beautiful and exciting sunsets in the world.

A trip to the **Everglades** to experience the flight of roseate spoonbills.

Irish coffee at **JohnMartin's** in **Coral Gables** to end an Irish meal at one of the city's many fine restaurants—or high tea in the historic **Biltmore Hotel.**

Coconut Grove attracts visitors in droves because of its ambience. Take afternoon tea at the **Grand Bay Hotel,** known for its European management style. **CocoWalk,** constructed by French interests, is a kind of fair with unique shops and restaurants and an air of conviviality. Don't leave Coconut Grove without a dip into the **Coconut Grove Branch Library,** which predates the city of Miami.

Art Deco has provided a new life for **Miami Beach** in the 1990s, and no visitor should leave town without stopping by to check out the **Art Deco District.** It's becoming as well known in New York as **Joe's Stone Crab Restaurant** on **South Beach** has been for many years.

Roberto J. Arguello
Banker and Columnist

Miami Museum of Science in **Coconut Grove.** Home of the Miami Project to Cure Paralysis.

CocoWalk: Located in the heart of Coconut Grove, this shopping center is, perhaps, one of South Florida's finest. Great food, entertainment, and fun people.

Must sees: the **Miami Seaquarium,** the **Parrot Jungle and Gardens;** Miami's **Metrozoo, Fairchild Tropical Gardens,** and the **Orchid Jungle.**

Best steak in town: **Los Ranchos** restaurant and **Shula's** steak house.

Bob Hosmon
Restaurant Critic/Wine Columnist/Assistant Dean, University of Miami

South Beach—Lunch at the **Booking Table Cafe** and dinner at **Bang.**

Coconut Grove—The new Miami at Cafe Tu Tu Tango.

Best restaurant in the Sunshine State—**Mark's Place** in **North Miami.**

For understanding the Hispanic influence in South Florida—**Yuca** in **Coral Gables; Versailles** and **Casa Blanca** in **Miami.**

Native Miami—**East Coast Fisheries** in Miami, **Joe's Stone Crab Restaurant** in **South Miami Beach, Cap's Place** at **Lighthouse Point.**

Theater—**Acme Acting Company** at the **Area Stage.**

Museums—The **Museum of Art** in **Ft. Lauderdale, Norton Gallery of Art, Center for the Fine Arts,** and the **Lowe Art Museum.**

Symphony—**Florida Philharmonic Orchestra,** the **New World Symphony Orchestra.**

Best-kept secret in South Florida—The cultural program **"Cultural del Lobo"** at the **Wolfson Campus** of **Miami-Dade Community College.**

Best cultural happening—Miami Book Fair International.

Best place to look for books and culture—**Books & Books,** in Coral Gables and **Miami Beach.**

Boca Raton

The most aggressive, forward-looking community in **Palm Beach County**, Boca Raton is populated by affluent professionals, entrepreneurs, and families with a taste for the best. The median household income is about $50,000; the average age, 43. That means Boca Raton (pronounced Rah-*tone*) has a plethora of upscale options for locals and visitors alike.

Although few would draw comparisons between Boca Raton and **Palm Beach**, both towns were lucky enough to attract the genius of architect **Addison Mizner**

Inspired by the villas of the Mediterranean and Spain, **Mizner** created in the early part of the century Mediterranean Revival–style buildings that were a brilliant match for South Florida's subtropical environment. In 1925 he developed 16,000 acres along the ocean not far from **Lake Boca Raton**, naming the development **Castillo del Rey** and persuading the **Ritz-Carlton** chain to build and manage a luxury hotel by the same name on the spot. Soon, a **Biltmore** hotel was planned as well, and the development frenzy took off. **Mizner** began selling real estate to Northerners who dreamed of living in Palm Beach but couldn't afford a mansion, and a resort community was born. His legacy lives on in the preponderance of homes and buildings in the area topped with brick-orange Spanish-tile roofs.

Mizner wasn't the only one taken by the town's charms. Corporations such as IBM (which practically invented the personal computer here), Siemens, and Sony have operations in Boca Raton. And don't forget the conglomerate W.R. Grace & Co., which left the Big Apple in the late 1980s (like many of its residents) for a sunnier, easier way of life.

It's a fashionable lifestyle, too. Trendy places include **Mizner Park**, the **Boca Raton Resort and Club**, the **Royal Palm Plaza**, the **Royal Palm Polo Sports Club**, the **Boca Beach Club**, and **Max's Grille**. The **Boca Raton Museum of**

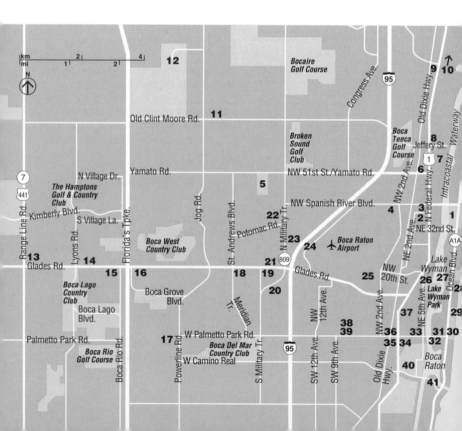

Art, featuring a wonderful Impressionist collection, is worth a stop, but most of the action in town takes place at the shopping malls, where upscale stores and clothing outlets vie for the attention of moneyed consumers.

Boca is also known for its fine restaurants, including **La Vieille Maison, Maxaluna, Baci,** and **Pete's.** In fact, the city is considered Palm Beach County's dining capital, and many restaurateurs look to Boca for culinary innovations.

Just north lies **Delray Beach**, a charming town with a slower pace and a beautiful beachfront. Quaint shops and cafes line **Atlantic Avenue,** the town's main street. To the west, the **Morikami Museum and Japanese Gardens** offer a glimpse into Japanese culture and the lives of early Japanese settlers.

In Boca, the beachfront figures less in daily life than in many other South Florida cities. Residents tend to be business-minded people who spend their leisure time enjoying the nightlife rather than pursuing suntans. Because this is a working community with an active social life, Boca Raton is less susceptible to seasonal fluctuations in the number of tourists than is Palm Beach. Hotels still reduce rates substantially in the summer (the off-season), and some restaurants close for extended vacations, but Boca Raton has the steadiest year-round pulse in the county.

Area code 407 unless otherwise indicated.

1 Spanish River Park These 70-plus award-winning acres are the pride of Boca Raton. Owned by the city and largely left in its natural state, the park comprises about 2,000 feet of beachfront, a natural hammock, and a wooded preserve. Native flora and fauna surround the park's nature trails, and covered shelters, picnic tables, grills, restrooms, and a 40-foot observation tower are available to visitors. Lifeguards are on duty daily. ♦ N Ocean Blvd, just south of NE Spanish River Blvd

2 Days Inn $ You've seen one, you've seen them all. But this 48-room inn is worth a mention because hotels in Boca aren't cheap, particularly during the six-month winter tourist season. Although prices here double in February and March, the rooms are still affordable and clean. To really save a buck, ask for an efficiency with a kitchenette. A pool, cable TV, and discounts (AAA, senior citizen, and military) are available, but there's no restaurant. ♦ 2899 N Federal Hwy (between Yamato and Glades Rds). 395.7172, 800/329.7466 ♿

3 Zuckerello's Restaurant & Pizzeria ★★$$ The big draws at this upscale 270-seat eatery are the limitless weekday lunch buffets and the Sunday brunch. Featured at the buffet are soup, salads, hot entrées that change daily (blackened dolphin, eggplant parmesan, dolphin in lobster sauce, rigatoni à la vodka), pizza, and desserts. The same goes for Sunday brunch, although an expanded menu includes eggs, bacon, bagels, cream cheese, lox, muffins, and French toast. The pace is lively at dinner, too, and the staff is friendly. House specialties include chicken *scarpariello* (boneless breast over rigatoni in a white-wine sauce). After dinner, a complimentary shot of anisette or amaretto hits the spot. ♦ Italian ♦ M-F lunch and dinner; Sa-Su dinner; Su brunch. 2700 N Federal Hwy (between Glades Rd and Spanish River Blvd). 391.9332 ♿

4 Cuban Cafe ★★$$ Everything from Cuban sandwiches to *pechuga a la plancha* (marinated boneless chicken breast) to sangría is offered at this young restaurant. ♦ Cuban ♦ M-F lunch and dinner; Sa-Su dinner. 3350 NW Boca Raton Blvd (just south of Spanish River Blvd). 750.8860 ♿

5 Patch Reef Park This is the place for any sports enthusiast who is not a member of one of Boca's country clubs. The 55-acre park has three lighted soccer fields, softball and baseball fields, basketball courts, a playground, a fitness trail, picnic areas, and a 17-court tennis complex with a clubhouse, a pro shop, locker rooms, and a lounge area. ♦ Admission. 2000 NW 51st St (1 mile west of N Military Tr). 997.0791

6 Melting Pot ★$$ Fondue freaks will be duly satisfied here. Wine-bottle lamps light the rustic, antiques-filled interior, where diners choose from cheese, meat, seafood, and various chocolate fondues. (The white-chocolate fondue is a favorite.) Meats and fish can be prepared in peanut oil or a healthy herb broth. ◆ Fondue ◆ Daily dinner. Reservations recommended; restaurant will open for lunch for parties of six or more with one day's notice. 5455 N Federal Hwy (north of Yamato Rd). 997.7472 &

7 Bagels with ★★$ Complete the name with just about any food you can think of, including seven types of cream cheese or smoked fish. The bagels alone come in more than a dozen varieties—from plain to marble or rye. ◆ Deli ◆ Daily breakfast and lunch. Kingsbridge Shopping Center (two blocks north of Yamato Rd on N Federal Hwy). 997.7108 &

8 Joe Muer Seafood ★★$$ With a chain of six popular South Florida restaurants, the C.A. Muer Corporation must be doing something right. This one's no disappointment either, although the highway location is a little bleak. The salmon and the crab cakes are favorites. ◆ American/seafood ◆ Daily dinner. 6450 N Federal Hwy (between Yamato Rd and Linton Blvd). 997.6688 &

9 Caldwell Theatre Company One of Florida's four state theaters, this one is known for presenting challenging plays. Aside from world premieres from new scripts, the repertoire includes a lineup of classics during its main season, which runs from October through May. Each spring the theater hosts Boca's annual Mizner Festival, a celebration of jazz. ◆ Performances Tu-Su. 7873 N Federal Hwy (in Levitz Plaza). Box office 241.7432 &

10 6 South ★★★$$ This trendy bar/restaurant, named for its address, would fit right in on Miami's South Beach, with its Art Deco architect-ure and "Star Trek" –like interior. Aluminum beams sprout from the sidewalk to support a blue canopy. At the bar, glasses hang from a large gator resting in midair. Neon signs, pastel floor tiles, and strip lights at the bar and deli counter contribute to the Postmodern feel of the place. But the real star here is the food. The tricolor cheese tortellini with bolognese sauce and the tricolor fusilli with fresh pesto sauce are winners. So is the grilled free-range chicken. Believe it or not, even the collard greens pass muster. If you like frozen drinks, the banana daiquiri, peaches 'n' cream, and mud slide are superlative. ◆ American ◆ Daily lunch and dinner. 6 S Ocean Blvd (at Atlantic Ave), Delray Beach. 278.7878 &

11 Royal Palm Polo Sports Club If Palm Beachers can have their polo, so can Boca. Some of the finest high-goal international polo is played here. The season runs from January through mid-April. Box seats are available. ◆ Admission. Su. 6300 Old Clint Moore Rd (at Jog Rd). 994.1876 &

The Morikami

12 Morikami Museum and Japanese Gardens Many visitors find it hard to believe, but Boca Raton has strong Japanese roots, and this museum, officially located just over the border in Delray Beach, is said to be the only one in the US devoted solely to Japanese culture. At the turn of the century, Joseph Sakai, a graduate of New York University, persuaded several farmers from Japan that Boca would provide fertile ground for pineapple and vegetable farming. By 1905 the 30-person Yamato settlement was established and thriving, where the **Boca Teeca Country Club** is located today. The community disbanded soon after the outbreak of World War II.

George Sukeji Morikami, an original Yamato settler, donated the museum's 180 acres to Palm Beach County in 1977. Surrounded by lush Japanese gardens, the building resembles a private Japanese residence. Exhibits change periodically, but a display of the Yamato settlement as it was is permanently on view. ◆ Admission. Tu-Su. 4000 Morikami Park Rd (at Carter Rd, north of Old Clint Moore Rd), Delray Beach. 495.0233 &

13 Wometco Shadowood Movie Theater With 12 screens, this theater always has a diverse lineup, including major studio releases, foreign films, classics, and animated froth for kids. Progressive-minded Boca residents call this their favorite flick spot. ◆ 9889 Glades Rd (at State Rd 441). 482.2296 &

14 Somerset Shoppes Though this is a typical suburban strip shopping center, many of the restaurants inside are worth checking out. ♦ 8903 Glades Rd (a half-mile west of Florida's Tpke) &

Within Somerset Shoppes:

Wilt Chamberlain's ★$ How about a few free throws between bites? Named after the former **Los Angeles Lakers** star player (who occasionally makes appearances) and decorated in **Lakers**' purple and gold, this sports bar and restaurant has a basketball half-court for hoop buffs, 25 televisions, and some 30 video games. The four-page menu is a hodgepodge of finger food, salads, and sandwiches. It's a fun place to take kids, and Wilt Chamberlain paraphernalia is not-so-tactfully sold near the front door. ♦ American ♦ Daily lunch and dinner. 488.8881 &

Book Stop If it's bound, it's here. Consistently stocked with well over 100,000 titles, this shop has more than 35 aisles of reading material, from the latest in nonfiction and fiction to the occult and home repair. Prices are slightly discounted. ♦ Daily until 10:30PM. 479.2114 &

15 Pete Rose Ballpark Cafe ★★$$ The fare here is American; the atmosphere, definitely sports bar. Radio talk shows are broadcast nightly, and former **Cincinnati Reds** star Pete Rose, a part owner, sometimes turns up. ♦ American ♦ Daily lunch and dinner. 8144 Glades Rd (in the Holiday Inn/West Boca just west of Florida's Tpke). 482.7070 &

16 Arvida Parkway Center This sprawling multi-use complex is full of restaurants and offices, as well as a hotel that caters to visiting businesspeople. ♦ Glades Rd (a half-mile east of Florida's Tpke).

Within Arvida Parkway Center:

Radisson Suite Hotel Boca Raton $$ Favored by business travelers and visitors looking to be near suburban amenities, this chain hotel offers 200 suites that come with fully stocked mini-bars, microwave ovens, and remote control TVs and VCRs. There's no restaurant, though. ♦ 7920 Glades Rd. 483.3600, 800/333.3333 &

Cafe Olé ★★★★$$ Come here for the best chips and salsa in town. Decorated with romantic wrought-iron candleholders, this upscale cantina offers a choice of hot green sauce or the milder red, made fresh daily. Have a sweet tooth? Wash the chips down with a to-die-for coconut margarita. For appetizers, choose from calamari, quesadillas, Mexican pizza (big enough for a meal), and spinach dip. Chef-owner Carlos Pugliese's main courses won't let you down either. Try tacos with top sirloin, shrimp, chicken, or a combination of all three. Other favorites include fajitas (with beef, chicken, shrimp, or swordfish), burritos, enchiladas, arroz con pollo, and fresh fish, blackened or grilled. Have room for dessert? Get a load of your choices: deep-fried ice cream, mud pie, chocolate brownie topped with coconut ice cream, and guava cheesecake. This restaurant is continually named the best Mexican restaurant in South Florida. ♦ Mexican ♦ M-F lunch and dinner; Sa-Su dinner. 852.8063 &

Pete's $$$$ Boca's brass rubs elbows at this clublike restaurant/lounge, which features

Boca's Big Builder: Addison Mizner

If you've noticed that **Boca Raton**'s buildings are similar to those in wealthy and exclusive **Palm Beach,** you've observed well. Both places were launched architecturally by **Addison Mizner,** who came to Palm Beach in 1918, decided the living was good there, and began designing mansions, the lavish **Everglades Club,** and much of chic **Worth Avenue.** In 1925 the self-taught architect and bon vivant made Boca Raton his object of desire. With his brother, Wilson, he began building what he envisioned as a Mediterranean-style resort city. But a year later, the real estate market plunged; by the end of the decade, **Mizner**'s development plans had fallen through. But his Spanish-influenced legacy is apparent everywhere in Boca, replete with Spanish barrel-tile roofs and ornate arches and columns. It's unlikely, though, that **Mizner** was responsible for Boca's love of the color pink, which adorns so many of the city's buildings.

a dance floor and live entertainment nightly. What's on the menu is irrelevant; people come here to meet and greet. Dress is less casual than it is at most Florida places—no jeans, shorts, or T-shirts are allowed, and you might feel out of place without a tie. American ♦ Daily lunch and dinner. Reservations required. 487.1600 &

Prezzo ★★$$ If you stick to the top-notch brick-oven pizza, the bill here is a cinch to swallow. Fresh grilled fish is a little more expensive, but still competitively priced. The booths and tables offer a lakeside view. ♦ Italian ♦ M-F lunch and dinner; Sa-Su dinner. 451.2800 &

17 Club Boca A variety of themes is featured at this spicy nightclub. Tuesday is Revival Night, a progressive evening celebrating "retro-alternative" styles; Thursday is College Night; Friday night offers classic disco with live bands; and Saturday is Ladies' Night. ♦ Cover. Tu, F 8PM-5AM; Th, Sa-Su 9PM-5AM. 7000 W Palmetto Park Rd (at Powerline Rd). 368.3333 &

18 Town Center Mall Midway between east and west Boca (hence the name), this is the only mall in the county with six anchor stores (**Bloomingdale's, Burdines, Lord & Taylor, Mervyn's, Saks Fifth Avenue,** and **Sears**). It comprises more than one million square feet of shops, all tied together by chic, Spanish Colonial–style architecture. One hundred percent of its space is leased, making it among the country's top 10 malls in terms of profitability. ♦ Daily. Glades Rd (between St. Andrews Blvd and Butts Rd). 368.6000 &

Spain once owned Florida but ransomed it to Britain in 1763 in exchange for Cuba. The British gave it back to Spain in 1783, and America bought the entire state in 1818 for $5 million.

Restaurants/Clubs: Red   **Hotels:** Blue
Shops/ ⬥ Outdoors: Green   **Sights/Culture:** Black

Within Town Center Mall:

Pampered Palate ★★$$ It's unusual to find good restaurants in malls—especially those with an ambience to match. A full-time pianist playing soft melodies provides a warm atmosphere here. Relax on your banquette and try fresh fish and homemade pasta, both house specialties. The Caesar salad topped with oak-grilled salmon or shrimp is delicious; the wheat pasta with sun-dried tomatoes, chicken, and other treats are good, too. ♦ American/nouvelle ♦ M-Sa lunch and dinner; Su dinner. 391.8211 &

19 Mario's ★★$$ If a restaurant that's packed nightly is any indication of dining valor, then this casual, family-run place wins a medal. From pizza to fish to good, well-priced Italian dishes, very little on the menu disappoints, and everything is served in a kinship-friendly way. The signature dish is *chicken scarpariello*, a boneless breast over rigatoni in a white-wine sauce with roasted peppers, black and green olives, and artichokes. ♦ Italian ♦ Daily lunch and dinner. 2200 Glades Rd at Glades Plaza (at Sheraton Way). 392.5595 &

20 Boca Center This shoppers' haven offers exclusive clothing boutiques, accessory and gift shops, restaurants, a bookstore, and a hotel. ♦ Daily. 5050 Town Center Circle (off N Military Tr). 361.9804 &

Within Boca Center:

Marriott Hotel $$$ Your basic upscale **Marriott,** it has 256 rooms, most of them spacious. The upper floors afford good views of the city, and the location is tops if you like to shop or have business at the office buildings nearby. ♦ 392.4600, 800/228.9290 &

Maxaluna ★★★$$$$ Dennis Max, South Florida's most influential restaurateur, serves nouvelle cuisine with a Tuscan influence at this local favorite. Under the 18-foot ceiling—with soffits and overhangs that make it cozy—the decor successfully juxtaposes traditional and modern elements: an exposed kitchen, old bricks, an Italian marble bar, and an oak floor. Entrées include oak-grilled veal chop stuffed with prosciutto-wrapped mozzarella, plum tomatoes, and basil; and grilled, anise-rubbed yellowfin tuna with an avocado rice roll, black-sesame-seed vinaigrette, lemon confit, and pickled ginger. The menu changes every few months. ♦ Italian ♦ M-F lunch and dinner; Sa-Su dinner. Reservations recommended. 391.7177 &

Morada Bar & Grille ★★$$$ You can't have too many restaurants serving oak-grilled fare. Guests can rest assured their cholesterol level won't budge after a meal here. Banquettes offer views through three-story-high windows. The homemade pasta prices are good, but the veal chop can be a little pricey. ♦ American/ Continental ♦ M-F lunch and dinner; Sa-Su dinner. 395.0805 ♿

Uncle Tai's ★★★$$ Boca's premier Chinese restaurant excels at nontraditional cuisine. Instead of dishes ladled from pots that have been simmering all day, this place serves freshly prepared, savory dishes such as lamb with gingerroot or shrimp with blackened red bell peppers in a spicy sauce. ♦ Chinese ♦ M-Sa lunch and dinner; Su dinner. 368.8806 ♿

21 **Houston's** ★★$$ This Midwestern-style eatery packs 'em in, especially on weekends, when waits can extend beyond two hours (count on 30 minutes at lunch). The restaurant accepts no reservations, so seating is only upon arrival. But the meal is definitely worth the wait. On the menu are salads, juicy burgers with fries, barbecued and roasted chicken, stuffed baked potatoes, fresh fish (the salmon is tops), steak, and ribs. For dessert, try the apple-walnut cobbler or five-nut brownie à la mode with Kahlua. ♦ American ♦ Daily lunch and dinner. 1900 NW Executive Center Circle (off Glades Rd, just west of N Military Tr). 998.0550 ♿

22 **Lynn University** Less attention-getting than Boca's **Florida Atlantic University,** this 123-acre college (formerly the **College of Boca Raton**) holds a special place in the hearts of locals. Established in 1962 as **Marymount** women's college by the order of the Sacred Heart of Mary, it was expanded after being sold in 1971. Benefactors since then have helped to keep it strong; the college now has more than a thousand students, many international. The **Schmidt Gallery** shows student and professional work. ♦ Gallery M-F. 3601 N Military Tr (at Potomac Rd). 994.0770 ♿

23 **Gallery Center** A must for both collectors and lovers of art, this multi-gallery retail-art mecca is one of Boca's finest. Offerings include classic and Postmodern works by nationally and regionally known artists. The latest wave of critically acclaimed Hispanic artists, including Botero and Szyszlo, can be found here. ♦ M-Sa. 608 Banyan Tr. Frietes-Revilla Gallery 241.1995 ♿; Gallery Camino Real 241.1606 ♿; Habatat Galleries 241.4544 ♿;

Jaffe Baker Gallery 241.3050 ♿; Margaret Lipworth Fine Art 241.6688 ♿

24 **Boomer's Family Recreation Center** Even if you're over 18, this place will bring out the kid in you. Nintendo junkies will be at home in the two-story gameroom, which also features air hockey and a few pool tables. Kids can have a blast in the play area and on the roller rink. Outside are two beautifully landscaped mini-golf courses, bumper boats, and go-karts. To ride on the bumper boats by themselves, kids must be at least 44 inches tall; to go it alone on the go-karts, they must be at least 10 years old and 58 inches tall. The place is perfect for kids, but don't be surprised to see quite a few adults on the go-kart course and putting mounds. ♦ Admission. M-Th, Su 10AM-11PM; F-Sa 10AM-1AM. 3100 Airport Rd (just east of I-95 at Glades Rd, next to Boca Raton Airport). 347.1888 ♿

25 **Florida Atlantic University** Officially dedicated in 1964, this school has contributed in no small way to Boca's tremendous growth during the last couple of decades. Today, the institution makes up part of the state university system. The school's auditorium/ theater offers performances throughout the year, and five to eight student and profes-sional exhibitions are mounted each year at the **Ritter Art Gallery.** ♦ Gallery Tu-F 10AM-3:30PM; Sa 11AM-4PM. 500 NW 20th St (at NW Fifth Ave). 367.3000, gallery 367.2660 ♿

26 **Haitian Art Collection** Long popular in Europe, Haitian art has made a considerable splash in South Florida, where Northeastern transplants like to decorate their new subtropical homes with bright, bold, and often playfully primitive works. Aside from original canvases, this gallery offers metal, ceramic, and papier-mâché works, as well as painted boxes and pedestals. Major artists include Yvonne-Jean Pierre, Jean Claude Legagneur, and St. Louis Blaise. ♦ M-Sa; call for Su hours. 1600 N Federal Hwy (south of NW 20th St). 338.6986 ♿

27 **Gumbo Limbo Nature Center** Snake, bee, and sea turtle exhibits await at this 15-acre nature center. On the grounds, a short walk-way with a 40-foot viewing tower overlooks a tropical hardwood hammock and mangroves. Frequent classes, workshops, and field trips are offered. ♦ Admission. M-Sa. A1A (a mile north of E Palmetto Park Rd). 338.1473

28 **Red Reef Park** Snorkelers will get a panoramic maskful at this beach and park area. Rock piers built out from the shoreline have become the hangout for the kinds of tropical fish normally seen in tanks. By comparison, the other amenities here—including gazebos, grills, and picnic tables—seem incidental. Lifeguards are on duty daily. ♦ A1A (three-quarters-of-a-mile north of E Palmetto Park Rd)

29 South Beach Park More than 2,700 feet of undeveloped ocean frontage make up this park. Spaces for 230 cars are provided, as are walkways, restrooms, and a covered shelter. Lifeguards are on duty daily. ◆ Daily until sunset. A1A (at NE Fourth St)

30 South Beach Pavilion Overlooking the Atlantic and a public beach, this tiny, covered observation deck dates back to the early 1920s. Hurricanes have taken their toll, but the pavilion has been revived each time. Parking is limited. ◆ Daily 24 hours. A1A (at E Palmetto Park Rd) ⟡

31 Kenneth Raymond Gallery Contemporary masters such as Nahle, Arlene Ehrhich, Marcel Dudouet, and Claude Schurr are featured at this well-established gallery. One wing houses abstract, contemporary, and modern works, and a bronze sculpture collection is on view. ◆ M-Sa; Tu-Sa in summer. 799 E Palmetto Park Rd (at NE Fifth Ave). 368.2940 ⟡

32 La Vieille Maison ★★★★$$$$ Literally "The Old House," Palm Beach County's favorite French restaurant makes its home in one of Boca's earliest residences, built by **Addison Mizner** in 1924. It feels like a family mansion, with many rooms connected by hallways and filled with lovely antiques. The prix-fixe menu offers such old-style entrées as flat Dover sole with pasta, brace of quail with grapes, and Midwestern rack of lamb. The chef may even import some of the fish if the local fare isn't perfectly fresh, and, in a break from tradition, he doesn't smother it in heavy sauces. You'll feel like royalty as you sip wine from Riedel crystal glasses. ◆ French ◆ Daily dinner; seatings at 6PM, 6:30PM, 9PM, and 9:30PM. Reservations recommended. 770 E Palmetto Park Rd (at NE Fifth Ave). 391.6701 ⟡

33 Wildflower With six bars and two dance floors, this club pulsates at night. Nearly every corner of the mauve- and pastel-colored interior provides an Intracoastal view, thanks to its bridge-base location. A complimentary buffet and door prizes enliven the 4PM to 8PM Happy Hour. ◆ Cover. Daily 4PM-2AM. 551 E Palmetto Park Rd (near NE Fifth Ave). 391.0000 ⟡

33 Le Trúc ★★★$$$ This is not so much a place to merely dine as it is to explore innovative gourmet Vietnamese cuisine that combines unusual textures and flavors. The chef, a culinary wizard, is a Vietnamese native who began cooking as a child, helping his mother prepare traditional dishes. A favorite is grilled marinated duck with eggplant. On the lighter side, the steamed fish with vegetables is excellent. An imperial roll features shrimp marinated in lime juice, cilantro, mint, and onion wrapped in rice paper. ◆ Vietnamese ◆ M-Sa lunch and dinner; Su dinner. 297 E Palmetto Park Rd (between A1A and Federal Hwy). 392.4568 ⟡

34 Royal Palm Plaza Known as the "Pink Plaza" to residents, this shopping center, one of Boca's earliest, looks as though it was double-dipped in Pepto-Bismol. It's a cozy place to shop and be entertained, though. The plaza includes a performance theater, restaurants, and 80 unique fashion, gift, and specialty shops. They're all located in Spanish-style pink stucco buildings, which are embellished with imported tiles, courtyards, and fountains. ◆ Daily. 303 Mizner Blvd ⟡

Within Royal Palm Plaza:

Royal Palm Dinner Theatre This theater-in-the-round has garnered several Carbonell Awards from the South Florida Entertainment Writers Association for its consistently superior present-ations of quality Broadway musicals. Executive director Jan McArt, herself a dramatic personality, is known as the "First Lady of Florida Musical Theater." On site is a dinner theater, a backstage lounge, a cafe, and an upstairs cabaret where dinners are served. The **Little Palm Theatre** offers classes and Saturday performances for children. ◆ Ticket information 392.3755 ⟡

Children's Science Explorium Each of the 35 hands-on science exhibits here is bound to either make you laugh, elicit screams, or make your hair stand on end, as the static generator here does. There's also a "face station" with masks showing every emotion, a bike that generates electricity, a lightning machine, and a plethora of computers. ◆ Nominal admission. Tu-Sa; Su afternoon. 395.8401 ⟡

35 Flanigan's Guppy's ★★$ Commonly known as simply "Guppy's," this is a popular after-work hangout. The atmosphere is tavernlike, the food is standard burgers-and-fries fare, and the wait staff is attentive. ◆ American ◆ Daily lunch and dinner. 45 S Federal Hwy (at W Palmetto Park Rd). 395.4699 ⟡

36 Boca Raton Historical Society With books, maps, old photographs, and newspaper clippings dating back to the 1920s, this is a good place to brush up on Boca's past. You'll find information about self-taught architect **Addison Mizner** and his brother, Wilson, who together built a Mediterranean-style resort town with a $1.25-million luxury hotel as its centerpiece. It's also fascinating to learn about the major role the Japanese played in Boca's development: The Japanese influence can be traced to 1905, when the first Japanese arrived and established a pineapple and vegetable plantation called Yamato, now the name of a major thoroughfare. ♦ M-F until 4PM. 71 N Federal Hwy (at W Palmetto Park Rd). 395.6766 ♿

37 Mizner Park This downtown cultural and commercial village opened as part of a major city redevelopment plan undertaken in the 1980s to replace the dilapidated **Boca Mall.** It was quite an achievement on the part of local developer Tom Crocker, who built a multi-acre oasis for visitors and locals dying to get out of traffic and shop on foot, dine on cafe fare, or sit on a shaded bench and people watch. Elegant shops, boutiques, and restaurants, as well as offices, cultural and theatrical organizations, and residences, abound here. The eight-screen movie theater is straight out of LA—clean, sleek, and reached by escalator. ♦ 400 N Federal Hwy (two blocks north of E Palmetto Park Rd). 395.9666 ♿

Within Mizner Park:

Max's Grille ★★★$$$ This hot spot, another Dennis Max (owner of **Maxaluna;** see above) establishment, consistently wins awards. Its unique bistrolike setting includes a two-story ceiling and 45-foot curtains. Diners choose from a variety of fillets, duck, seafood, and pasta. Two entrées that shouldn't be missed are the pork chops with glazed carrots and the filet mignon slathered in savory garlic. ♦ Eclectic ♦ Daily lunch and dinner. 368.0080 ♿

37 Midnight Sahara Moroccan clothing and accessories are sold here. ♦ M-W; Th-Sa until 10PM; Su noon-9PM. 395.0625 ♿

37 Baci ★★$$ One should adopt a nonchalant stance at this trendy, high-tech restaurant, which has a black marble bar, a black-and-white cement floor, and a purple-lit, metal-walled dining room. It's mellower on the outdoor patio, where diners savor tasty desserts and cappuccino. The good gourmet Italian fare includes spaghetti Fantasia, topped with scallops, shrimp, and calamari in a red sauce. Various four-slice pizzas make good appetizers or light dinners for two; other winners are the Caesar salad and the grilled tuna or salmon. ♦ Italian ♦ Daily lunch and dinner. 362.8500 ♿

37 Christy/Taylor Galleries Hand-blown glass—from bowls to sculpture—is made by artists from around the country, including Leon Applebaum. ♦ M-Th until 10PM; F-Sa until 11PM. 750.7302 ♿

37 Celebrations of Boca Discover a treasure trove of goodies, including abstract puzzles for your office desk, fluorescent clocks, and pencils in quirky shapes. This is not your run-of-the-mill gift, card, and candy store. ♦ M-Th, Su until 10PM; F-Sa until 11PM. 393.1200 ♿

37 Mieka Shoppers look here for updated women's sportswear and designer dresses and accessories. If the name sounds familiar, it's because **Mieka** has two locations on Long Island in New York State—Cedarhurst and Woodbury. ♦ M-Th, Su until 9PM; F-Sa until 10PM. 338.6559 ♿

37 Liberties Fine Books and Music A varied selection of books and music makes for a fine combination at this bibliophile's heaven, often ranked as one of the best bookstores in South Florida. Many authors from across the country stop here on their book tours and signings. ♦ M-Th, Su until midnight; F-Sa until 1AM. 368.1300 ♿

38 Old Floresta One of Boca's oldest neighborhoods was developed in 1925 by Mediterranean Revival king **Addison Mizner,** who wanted to realize his dream of a Spanish-style city. In the area are more than 25 homes, complete with Spanish barrel-tile roofs, pecky (pockmarked) cypress ceilings, decorative arches, and open spaces. ♦ Bounded by Periwinkle and Alamanda Sts, and NW 9th and Paloma Aves

39 Boca Raton Museum of Art This institution didn't truly establish itself until Dr. John and Bess Mayers of Singer Island donated 51 works by Picasso, Matisse, Degas, Bellows, Klee, Modigliani, Prendergrast, and Seurat, among other artists. Today, the museum also features year-round exhibitions and cultural activities. Well known for its art-savvy direction, it's a must stop for art lovers. ♦ Donation. Daily until 4PM. 801 W Palmetto Park Rd (at NW Ninth Ave). 392.2500 ♿

40 Boca Raton Resort & Club $$$$ Staying at this mammoth oceanfront resort is a little like entering a modern-day Camelot. The elegant pink-towered complex offers much more than 963 rooms: a majestic golf course, 22 tennis courts, pools, catamaran cruises, parasailing, a jogging trail, seven restaurants, and a bevy of shops. The lobby-level **Curzon Gallery** sells 16th- to 19th-century paintings. Come with a bloated wallet, because many amenities carry additional fees. ♦ 501 E Camino Real (east of A1A at the Intracoastal). 395.3000, gallery 394.7070, 800/327.0101; fax 391.3183 ♿

41 Radisson Bridge Resort of Boca Raton $$ A good alternative to the deluxe **Boca Raton Resort & Club** nearby, this 11-story hotel offers access to resort-style living with golf privileges, a health club and water sports, and meeting spaces. The 121 rooms, decorated in a light, airy motif, overlook either the ocean or the Intracoastal. On the premises is **Carmen's Restaurant and Lounge at the Top,** which boasts panoramic views of the water; there's also a cafe and a pool bar. ♦ 999 E Camino Real (at A1A). 368.9500, 800/333.3333 ♿

North Palm Beach County

The **Northern Palm Beaches**, which include **Mangonia Park, Riviera Beach, Lake Park, Palm Beach Shores, North Palm Beach, Palm Beach Gardens, Jupiter**, and **Juno Beach**, offer a lifestyle more relaxed and easygoing than their neighbors to the south, but development has caught up with this previously bucolic, almost rural area.

Golf is the name of the game here. Palm Beach Gardens is home to the **PGA (Professional Golfers Association) National Resort,** with its championship golf course and deluxe amenities. The **US Croquet Association** also took up residence, and there is polo, tennis, auto racing, boating, water sports, and saltwater fishing.

But don't think it's all sports. **The Gardens** mall has made a name for itself as one of the most beautiful and expansive shopping centers in South Florida. The two-story, 1.3-million-square-foot mall offers five major department stores and 185 specialty shops.

Actor Burt Reynolds is a big name in Jupiter, the oldest settlement in **Palm Beach County.** He founded the professional **Jupiter Dinner Theater,** which was originally named after him until he bowed out and let the town have the honors. Reynolds still owns a ranch in Jupiter with a mini–petting zoo and film studio.

The **Jupiter Inlet Lighthouse**, built in 1859, is the county's oldest standing structure. A small museum at its base features changing exhibits on the area's history. Jupiter's **Florida History Center and Museum** also offers a fascinating collection of celebrity mementos, shipwreck memorabilia, and photos and other documents chronicling the county's history.

More than any other part of South Florida, North Palm Beach County is a region in a nutshell, a microcosm of the South Florida experience. From chic resorts to bass fishing on **Lake Okeechobee,** it is one of those rare places that fits the cliché and truly does offer something for everyone.

Area code 407 unless otherwise indicated.

1 Murray Brothers As far as anglers are concerned, this place is an institution. The large store supplies just about everything related to fishing, even regularly updated information on angling tournaments. ♦ Daily. 207 Blue Heron Blvd E (west side of the Intracoastal), Riviera Beach. 845.1043 &

2 Crab Pot ★★$$ On the water, tucked under the Blue Heron Boulevard Bridge, this popular place is the best no-frills seafood eatery in the county. You'll find shrimp steamed in beer, broiled and fried scallops, fresh fish, a bottomless salad bowl, and Key lime pie. At night you can toss bread crumbs to the fish from the outdoor booths flanking the Intracoastal. Always expect a crowd. ♦ Seafood ♦ Daily lunch and dinner. 386 Blue Heron Blvd E (at Lake Shore Dr on the west side of the Intracoastal), Riviera Beach. 844.2722 &

3 Phil Foster Park Beside the Intracoastal Waterway, this park boasts a guarded swimming area, picnic grounds with grills, and a boat ramp. Riverboat sight-seeing tours leave here to cruise past elegant waterfront homes on the exclusive and nearby island of Palm Beach. ♦ Beneath the Blue Heron Blvd Bridge, Singer Island. 964.4420

4 Buccaneer Restaurant and Lounge ★★$$$ With a good view of the Intracoastal Waterway and the yachts docked outside, the "Buc" (as it's affectionately called) offers a pleasurable dining experience, with good fresh seafood and an even better rack of lamb. The bar, in an adjacent room, can get a little rowdy in the evening, when commercial fishermen gather round to quaff beer and tell tall tales. A dependable lunch is served at relatively low prices. ♦ American/seafood ♦ Daily lunch and dinner. 142 Lake Dr (three blocks south of Blue Heron Blvd Bridge), Palm Beach Shores. 844.3477 &

4 Sailfish Marina One of the best-known marinas in the area has a top-notch charter-fishing fleet, guest quarters, overnight dockage, a boating-equipment shop, and a

---

Restaurants/Clubs: Red	Hotels: Blue
Shops/ ♱ Outdoors: Green	**Sights/Culture:** Black

pool. The marina's restaurant, the **Galley** (848.1492), has a tropical-diner feel, with indoor counter seating and meals served on wicker-cradled paper plates. It's hemmed in by a jungle of palm trees, but you can still glimpse the Intracoastal and yachts bunking at the docks. The chowder is tops.
♦ 98 Lake Dr (south of Blue Heron Blvd Bridge), Palm Beach Shores. 844.1724 ᕀ

5 Embassy Suites Resort Hotel $$$ Many families choose to stay at this 253-unit, all-suites hotel, which has a year-round, activity-filled kids' camp program called "Fat Cat Beach Club for Kids." Parents can spend their newfound free time in the fitness room or poolside tiki-hut bar. The **Jupiter Crab Company** restaurant serves a variety of seafood, pasta, steaks, and all-American dishes. Ask about off-season (summer) rates.
♦ 181 Ocean Ave (at Bamboo Rd), Palm Beach Shores. 863.4000, 800/EMBASSY ᕀ

6 Singer Island Ocean Mall Located on a stretch of Atlantic beachfront, this is no glitzy, high-tech mall, but a small collection of swimwear boutiques and shops for the sun-and-sand enthusiast in a very beachy atmosphere. There's a take-out window for slushies, ice cream, and hot dogs. ♦ Corner of Ocean Ave and N Ocean Blvd, Singer Island ᕀ

Within Singer Island Ocean Mall:

The Greenhouse ★★$$ This popular hangout for locals and beach fanatics serves sandwiches, salads, Buffalo wings, and finger foods. Sit out on the patio and enjoy the ocean view. Beer sales here make a killing.
♦ American ♦ Daily lunch and dinner. 2401 Ocean Ave. 845.1333 ᕀ

Mother Nature's Pantry ★★$$ You won't find cheeseburgers at the home of the "giant fruit salad," just healthy sandwiches, salads, dieter's delights, fruit smoothies, juice coolers, and "energy and beauty drinks." If you want bee pollen or protein powder added to your fruit shake, it's 50 cents extra.
♦ Health food ♦ Daily breakfast, lunch, and dinner. 2411 Ocean Ave. 845.0533 ᕀ

6 Singer Island Beach Locals have dubbed this the prettiest beach in Palm Beach County, largely because the wide patch of sand is as white and smooth as silk. A couple of thatch huts near the boardwalk provide shelter for passing beachcombers. ♦ Off Ocean Ave, just behind the mall

7 Sheraton Singer Island Inn $$ Although several hotels are slapped right up next to each other here, this one, with 202 rooms, has the best-kept beachfront and some pleasant poolside views, as well as a restaurant. Its two lounges are popular with both visitors and locals. In the summer, a room here can cost less than $75. ♦ 3200 N Ocean Blvd (at Blue Heron Blvd), Singer Island. 842.6171, 800/327.0522 ᕀ

8 Cafe Du Parc ★★$$$ Set in a small house, this romantic French restaurant is known for its superb veal dishes. Candlelight and limited seating make for an intimate experience. ♦ French ♦ M-Sa dinner. Reservations required. 612 N Federal Hwy (at Park Ave), Lake Park. 845.0529 ᕀ

9 Moroso Motorsports Park Located on 200 acres of wooded land, this multi-purpose auto-racing facility has something for everyone—especially those who just can't drive at 55 mph. Speed demons will find themselves in fast-forward paradise on the two-and-one-quarter-mile, 10-turn road course and the professional quarter-mile drag strip. More than seven major drag racing and four major sports car events are held here each year, in addition to a weekly program for ages 8 to 80. "Test and tune" takes place on the drag strip on Wednesdays and Fridays for anyone with a valid driver's license. Every Saturday there's a special bracket racing program with cash and points toward track and divisional championships. Also home to the **Skip Barber Racing School,** the park is available for private rental and corporate events. ♦ Admission; children under 12 free. 17047 Beeline Hwy (13 miles west of Florida's Tpke), Palm Beach Gardens. 622.1400 ᕀ

9 Lake Okeechobee This is the place for freshwater-fishing enthusiasts. The second-largest body of freshwater in the US, it is teeming year-round with largemouth bass and other fish. The law is strictly enforced here: Legal equipment for taking freshwater fish includes rod and reel, spinner, bob, troutline with cut bait, cane pole, and line, and the maximum catch limit is five. Licenses can be obtained at most area sports shops, as well as at the **South County Courthouse** in Delray Beach. ♦ Hwy 710, 40 miles northwest of West Palm Beach

10 John D. MacArthur Beach State Park Named after the insurance mogul and South Florida land tycoon, this 8,000-foot swath of oceanfront beach affords good fishing and swimming. There are picnic areas and a nature center with guided tours and live exhibits (learn about crabs and other creatures). In summer, you can take guided evening turtle walks (reservations required). ♦ Nature center M, W-Su. 10900 State Rd 703/A1A (south of the intersection of Hwy 1 and PGA Blvd), North Palm Beach. 624.6950, Nature center 624.6952

11 Lost Tree Village Some of the area's local heroes live in this exclusive complex of lavish homes, developed by the Ecclestone Organization, which has had a hand in several upscale communities in Palm Beach County. A secured community, it is closed to the public. ♦ East of the junction of Hwy 1 and PGA Blvd, North Palm Beach. 626.2202

12 Oakbrook Square This chic shopping plaza caters to those with a taste for expensive clothing. Shoppers can visit **Mark, Fore & Strike, Jacobson's, Harold Grant,** and **Via Condotti,** among others. ♦ Most stores M-Sa. 11594 Hwy 1 (at PGA Blvd), Palm Beach Gardens. 626.3880 &

Within Oakbrook Square:

Coffee Exchange ★$ You might just walk away from this casual lunch spot with heart palpitations after sampling the wide selection of delicious domestic and imported coffees. ♦ M-Sa breakfast and lunch. 622.8950 &

Panama Hattie's ★$$ With a fireplace and a ski lodge atmosphere, this restaurant offers a delightful if incongruous view of the Intra-coastal. Some customers sail up to the dock for a meal that might include snapper or grouper piccata. Try the banana dessert, sautéed in butter and cinnamon, laced with rum and lime, and topped with ice cream. ♦ American/seafood ♦ Daily lunch and dinner. 627.1545 &

13 River House ★★$$$ Reminiscent of a Key West–style inn, this place commands a splendid view of **Soveral Marina** and its many boats. Start with the expansive salad bar and move on to the sometimes innovative sea-food, prime rib, or chicken. The shrimp dishes are wonderful. The downside is the first-come, first-served seating, though you can make reservations on Fridays and Saturdays for the upstairs dining room. If you have to wait at the bar, the variety of hors d'oeuvres will satisfy your hunger. ♦ Continental/ seafood ♦ Daily dinner. 2373 PGA Blvd (west side of the Intracoastal Waterway), Palm Beach Gardens. 694.1188 &

13 Harbour Financial Center Despite its ideal marina-front location, there has been a high turnover at this two-story, Mediterranean-style plaza of upscale stores. Check it out: You never know what new shops may have opened since your last visit. ♦ Daily. 2401 PGA Blvd (at Prosperity Farms Rd), Palm Beach Gardens. No phone &

Within the Harbour Financial Center:

Parker's Lighthouse ★★$$ With a straightforward yuppie decor of bare wood, green plants, and a two-story ceiling, this place serves a variety of top-notch grilled seafood, along with red parsley potatoes and al dente vegetables. While waiting for your entrée, gaze out onto the harbor and munch on homemade bacon-and-cheese biscuits. ♦ Seafood ♦ Daily lunch and dinner. Reservations recommended. 627.0000 &

Carmine's This gourmet food store is a delight to stroll through if you appreciate the sight of fresh fish decorated in capers and red peppers, or a grand selection of olive oils, balsamic vinegars, imported mushrooms, and about as many kinds of bottled water as there are wines in a liquor store. ♦ Daily. 775.0105 &

14 Waterway Cafe ★$$ With a circular outdoor bar floating atop the Intra-coastal and cleats for diners arriving by boat, this hub for younger folks is the place for a bird's-eye view of water activity. There's live entertainment nightly (reggae and jazz), and Happy Hour Mondays through Fridays. Crab cakes, steaks, and sandwiches make up the varied menu. ♦ American ♦ Daily lunch and dinner; Su breakfast. 2300 PGA Blvd (between the Intracoastal and Prosperity Farms Rd), Palm Beach Gardens. 694.1700 &

15 No Anchovies! ★★$$ Don't let the name fool you. The specialty at this neighborhood Italian restaurant is brick oven pizza with any topping you can imagine (including anchovies). The menu lists eight pizzas, nine types of pasta, and four sauces (marinara, pesto, Alfredo, and tomato), as well as veal, chicken, and New York strip steak. A children's menu is available, as are crayons and pizza dough to keep the little ones busy. There's a full bar and an extensive wine list.
♦ Italian ♦ M-Sa lunch and dinner; Su dinner. 2650 PGA Blvd (at Prosperity Farms Rd). 622.7855 ⓑ

16 The Gardens Ride the glass elevator for a good look at this elegant megamall, replete with marble, brass, fountains, and sculpture. The $150-million, 1.3-million-square-foot shopping mecca features 185 shops, restaurants, and services. It's anchored by **Burdines, Macy's, Sears, Saks Fifth Avenue,** and **Bloomingdale's,** where a trip to the third-floor Champagne bar is a must. Caviar, anyone? ♦ Daily. 3101 PGA Blvd (between Old Dixie Hwy and Prosperity Farms Rd), Palm Beach Gardens. 622.2115 ⓑ

Within The Gardens:

The Museum Company For sale here are stationery, jewelry, small sculptures, and reproductions of ancient pieces based on the gift collections of such fine museums as New York's Metropolitan and the Boston Museum of Fine Arts. ♦ 624.9775 ⓑ

The Nature Company This classy store delights with its nature-related books, objets d'art, games, puzzles, and jewelry, as well as its collection of astronomical goodies, including telescopes and Milky Way maps. ♦ 624.1066 ⓑ

Brooks Brothers The place to go for the old-school preppie who thrives on the status quo, broadcloth shirts, and tartan boxer shorts. This store has a long-standing tradition of outfitting both women and men in classic, no-nonsense threads that last almost as long as the wearer. ♦ 775.0383 ⓑ

White by Herratti Snow blindness is a real possibility here. All of the stylish linen, cotton, and lace women's clothing, as well as the floor and the walls, are white. It's expensive, so if you like to wear white, remember to bring along lots of green. ♦ 624.1419 ⓑ

Eddie Bauer This shop is an outdoor enthusiast's mecca for clothing, shoes, light camping and fishing gear, and sturdy watches and folding knives, all adorned with the respected store logo. ♦ 624.9801 ⓑ

FAO Schwarz This store is either for the kid who has everything or the Alice in all of us. With miniature Mercedes sports cars big enough for a six-year-old, gorilla-size stuffed animals, and life-size Raggedy Ann dolls, it truly is a wonderland. Adults may even discover a six-foot-tall wooden executive rocking horse, good for bucking the proverbial system. ♦ 624.6840 ⓑ

Mozzarella's Cafe ★★$ Looking for good food at bargain prices? You'll find it here. There's chicken pot pie just like Mom used to make, plus lots of things Mom never thought of: grilled Cajun chicken, Southwestern grilled catch of the day with tangy lime salsa, quiche, a Santa Fe burger with Monterey jack and cheddar cheese melted over barbecue sauce, and eight kinds of salads. The desserts, especially the peanut butter ice cream pie, chock-full of Reese's crumbles, are to die for. ♦ American ♦ Daily lunch and dinner. 627.0582 ⓑ

California Pizza Kitchen ★$ Wood-fired pizza is the name of the game at this outpost of a Los Angeles–based chain. Toppings include eggplant, chicken and broccoli, or pineapple (called Hawaiian-style). The sausage, pepperoni, and mushroom crowd isn't overlooked either; neither are those who've had their fill of pizza. The extensive menu includes all kinds of sandwiches and salads. White tile, yellow trim, and black chairs and tables add up to a clean, modern

Restaurants/Clubs: Red	Hotels: Blue
Shops/ 🍴 Outdoors: Green	Sights/Culture: Black

look. ♦ American ♦ Daily lunch and dinner. 625.4682 &

17 Palm Beach Gardens Marriott $$
Although not exactly a stone's throw from the beach, this 279-room hotel is a real treat, with good service, one restaurant, and a lovely marble, brass, and plant-filled atrium lobby. There's also plenty of shopping and restaurants nearby. ♦ 4000 RCA Blvd (a block south of PGA Blvd), Palm Beach Gardens. 622.8888, 800/228.9290; fax 622.0052 &

Within Palm Beach Gardens Marriott:

Club Safari This high-energy nightclub features a DJ and giant animal-like creatures and objects—such as a totem pole—that move, puff smoke, talk, and do all kinds of strange things. ♦ Tu-Th free; F-Su cover. Tu-Su 5PM-3AM. 622.8888 &

17 Loehmann's Plaza At this small shopping center with a six-screen movie theater, don't miss this famous women's clothing store, carrying designer and brand name items at discount prices. The **Backroom** offers eveningwear and leather clothing at greatly reduced prices. ♦ Daily; M-Sa until 9PM. 4100 PGA Blvd (at RCA Blvd), Palm Beach Gardens. 627.5575 &

18 Embassy Suites $$ Well known for its vast marble- and plant-filled atrium, where two swans glide about in a pond, this hostelry offers 160 single, double, and three-bedroom suites. Among the amenities are complimentary breakfast, two tennis courts, a jogging trail, a heated pool, a sauna, a Jacuzzi, an exercise room, a children's wading pool, and daily golf clinics at several courses, including the nearby **Emerald Dunes Golf Club.** Popular with golfers and business travelers, the hotel has a restaurant, plenty of conference space, and a ballroom and banquet area. ♦ 4350 PGA Blvd (at Military Tr, west of I-95), Palm Beach Gardens. 622.1000, 800/EMBASSY &

19 Cafe Chardonnay ★★★$$$ Excellent service is a trademark of this popular contemporary restaurant, whose chef whips up California nouvelle cuisine with a dash of Italian sophistication. You can't go wrong, whether you choose grilled leg of lamb, scampi *provençal* with baby artichokes, or pan-roasted veal. The reasonably priced wine list features namesake Chardonnays and California spirits. Bread fanatics will devour the scrumptious sourdough loaves before the main course arrives. Leave room for dessert, especially the fruit flans and flourless chocolate cake. ♦ American ♦ M-F lunch and dinner; Sa-Su dinner. Reservations recommended. Garden Square Shoppes, 4533 PGA Blvd (at Military Tr), Palm Beach Gardens. 627.2662 &

20 PGA National You've probably seen this upscale, thousand-plus-acre development of expensive single-family homes and condos on TV. Its 90 holes of golf have been the site of numerous national and international golf tournaments, including the **PGA** Seniors' Championship and the Ryder Cup. Golfing here is for **PGA** members and resort guests only. ♦ 100 Ave of the Champions (between Fairway Dr and PGA Blvd), Palm Beach Gardens. 626.7900 &

At PGA National:

PGA National Resort $$$$ With golf, tennis, swimming pools, a health spa, and three restaurants, this lavish hotel—which includes 336 rooms and 80 cottages—is big on amenities. If you're in town when a major tournament is scheduled on the **PGA**'s championship course, this is the place to stay. Rates for the high tourist season (December through April) are way up there, but summer and early fall rates are reduced. ♦ 400 Ave of the Champions (between Fairway Dr and PGA Blvd), Palm Beach Gardens. 627.2000, 800/633.9150 &

21 Ebisu Japanese Restaurant ★★$$$ Patrons have been flocking here ever since Akemi Takenouchi opened this sushi bar and restaurant (the area is not known for a preponderance of sushi bars). Diners can opt for Japanese-style seating, booths, or table and chairs. Sushi, tempura, and steak and chicken teriyaki are popular dishes. Try the *Ebisu bento,* a full-course dinner that includes miso soup, a salad with ginger dressing, shrimp and vegetable tempura, teriyaki fish, sushi, sashimi, and dessert. The sushi deluxe platter is perfect for sushi lovers. The desserts are sensational: banana tempura, fried ice cream, Japanese roll cake, and tempura cheesecake. ♦ Japanese ♦ M-F lunch and dinner; Sa-Su dinner. Reservations recommended. Shoppes on the Green, 7100 Fairway Dr (at PGA Blvd), Palm Beach Gardens. 622.4495 &

22 **Melting Pot** ★★$$ Did someone say fondue? That's all they serve here—seafood, poultry, and beef fondues that you cook at your table in either hot peanut oil or healthy herb broth. The rustic decor is homey, with lots of wood, brick, and old wine-bottle lamps. ♦ Fondue ♦ Daily dinner. 12189 Hwy 1 (between PGA Blvd and Donald Ross Rd), North Palm Beach. 775.9133 &

23 **Howard Johnson's** $$ Most oceanside hotels in the area charge hefty room rates, but this one is affordable—and it's only half a block from the beach. There's a small pool, and the 60 deluxe rooms—should you dare call them that—come equipped with small microwaves and refrigerators. There's no restaurant, but nearby is a 24-hour **Denny's**, which serves great pies and grits-and-bacon breakfasts. ♦ 930 Hwy 1 (at Donald Ross Rd), Juno Beach. 626.1531 (phone and fax), 800/392.9372 &

24 **Marine Life Center of Juno Beach** Get a glimpse of what Florida's coastline ecology is all about on a nature trail that winds through natural dune vegetation. There's an informative display of endangered marine turtles and hands-on exhibits for kids. Midnight sea turtle walks, when mama turtle can sometimes be spotted laying her eggs, are scheduled on Wednesdays and Saturdays in June and July. ♦ Tu-Sa 10AM-4PM; Su noon-3PM. Loggerhead Park, 1200 Hwy 1 (between Donald Ross and Marcinski Rds), Juno Beach. 627.8280

25 **Mecca Farms U-Pick** Instead of tanning on the beach, try getting some color in a tomato patch. A variety of fruits and vegetables grown in a small field can be picked and paid for by weight. The strawberries are usually as big as golf balls and as juicy as oranges. ♦ Daily Oct-June. Just east of the Donald Ross Rd interchange off I-95, Jupiter. 626.8731 &

26 **Juno Beach Park** This 300-foot beach has lifeguards, showers, and picnic areas. ♦ A1A (north of Donald Ross Rd), Juno Beach

27 **Jupiter Beach/Carlin Park** On the east side, this park includes 3,000 feet of oceanfront beach, a baseball field, and picnic areas. Across State Road A1A to the west are tennis courts and a fitness trail. ♦ Daily sunrise to sunset. A1A (south of Indiantown Rd), Jupiter

28 **Jupiter Beach Resort** $$$ Right on the beach, this 200-room high-rise, Jupiter's finest hotel, has a pool, tennis courts, and a health club. The on-site restaurant, **Sinclair's**,

serves a variety of wonderful mesquite-grilled dishes. ♦ 5 N A1A (at Indiantown Rd), Jupiter. 746.2511, 800/621.1192 &

29 **Jupiter Dinner Theater** The original and classic stage works and musicals presented here usually feature big names from Broadway or Hollywood. Your ticket also gets you dinner. Once mediocre, the food has gotten better over the years. The theater, which used to be named after its founder and hometown hero Burt Reynolds, now bears the name of the town, a change Reynolds supported. Nonetheless, his name still graces the affiliated theater-training institute, an apprentice program for promising young actors. ♦ Reservations required. 1001 E Indiantown Rd (between Hwy 1 and A1A), Jupiter. 746.5566 &

29 **Backstage** ★★$$$ Like a theater, this restaurant descends in tiers to a stage, where jazz musicians such as Copeland Davis entertain. It has a theatrical motif, with track lighting and film-star posters hanging on the wall; headliners from the **Jupiter Dinner Theater** next door (see above) often pop in. The menu puts on a good performance, too, with steaks, seafood, chicken, and pasta dishes served by an attentive staff. Although most entrées are pricey, there are some reasonable selections. Cap off your evening with a special after-dinner drink. ♦ Continental ♦ M-F lunch and dinner; Sa-Su dinner. 1061 E Indiantown Rd (between Hwy 1 and A1A), Jupiter. 747.9533 &

30 **Nick's Tomatoe Pie** ★★$$ A slice of Italy awaits those who step through the doors of this fun eatery, where the only pizza served comes in appetizer-size portions. Complete with an authentic wood-burning oven, this hot spot is respected for its tasty pastas, homemade gnocchi, and fabulous shrimp and mussels in a spicy marinara sauce served over linguine. Attention, dessert mavens: Indulge in the zabaglione, a tasty confection of Marsala wine, brandy, and strawberries topped with chocolate shavings. ♦ Italian ♦ Daily dinner. 1697 W Indiantown Rd (at Central Blvd), Jupiter. 744.8935 &

31 **Burt Reynolds Ranch, Film Studios, and Zoo** Burt's horse ranch has grown into something of a theme park. Its more than 160 acres feature a petting zoo and a variety of farm and exotic animals, including llamas, emus, deer, goats, and miniature horses. The feed store is a true-blue rancher's general store, with racks of rakes, plenty of horse soap, and mineral oil by the gallon. Tours include film studios and settings from some of Burt's movies, including *Deliverance, Smokey and the Bandit*, and *Semi-Tough*. ♦ Petting zoo daily 10AM-4:30PM; feed store daily; studio tours M-Sa 11AM-4PM; Su 11AM, 1PM, 3PM. 16133 Jupiter Farms Rd (2 miles west of Florida's Tpke), Jupiter. 746.0393 &

32 Burt Reynolds Park Surrounded by the Intracoastal, this park has a rocky and shady beach area. Boaters frequent it because of the six day-use boat slips and four boat-launching ramps; picnic areas are provided, too. ♦ 805 Hwy 1 (north of Indiantown Rd), Jupiter

Within Burt Reynolds Park:

Florida History Center and Museum
Shipwreck memorabilia, celebrity mementos, photos, documents, artifacts, and other displays that shed light on Florida's history fill this museum. The eclectic collection includes American Indian relics, tools from the Seminole Wars, and artifacts from German U-boats dating from World War II. Built in the Florida Cracker wood-frame style of architecture, it is set back from the road amid four scenic acres of lush foliage. ♦ Admission. Tu-F 10AM-4PM; Sa-Su 1-4PM. 747.6639 &

33 Blue Heron Fleet Fishing Charters The best-known fishing charter company in the county, with locations here and in Riviera Beach, takes groups out twice a day for deep-sea fishing. All equipment is provided, and mates are on hand to bait your line and remove and clean whatever you catch. Charters launch here, adjacent to **Harpoon Louie's** (see below), Tuesday through Sunday. ♦ Intersection of Hwy 1 and A1A. 747.1200 &. Also at: Southwest foot of Blue Heron Blvd Bridge, Riviera Beach, with launches M, W-Su. 844.3573

33 Harpoon Louie's ★★$$ Hovering on the edge of the Intracoastal, across from historic **Jupiter Inlet Lighthouse** (see below), this eatery has a magnificent view whether you're indoors or out on the veranda. The food is inconsistent, but the pleasant atmosphere usually makes a visit worthwhile. Many dishes from the mainly seafood menu come with the restaurant's famous string-thin curly fries. ♦ American/seafood ♦ Daily lunch and dinner; Su breakfast. Corner of Hwy 1 and A1A, Jupiter. 744.1300 &

34 Charlie's Crab ★★$$ This waterside seafood restaurant has several different dining areas, one to suit every mood. In addition to the marinaside bar and outdoor tables, there's the main dining room and a romantic upstairs veranda. Entrées include homemade pasta, chicken, and the always reliable seafood, but the place is famous for its crab cakes, which have two kinds of crabmeat and a nutty crust that magically holds up without bread crumbs. Impeccable service is another plus. ♦ Seafood ♦ Daily lunch and dinner. 1000 N Hwy 1 (north of Indiantown Rd on the Intracoastal), Jupiter. 744.4710 &

35 Jupiter Inlet Lighthouse Completed in 1859, this red lighthouse (illustrated below) is the oldest existing structure in Palm Beach County. At its base is a small museum that features artifacts and documents chronicling the history of the Jupiter-Tequesta area. In the early days, the keeper and his family were practically the town's only inhabitants. The lighthouse has survived periods of rum-running and war, and though the schedule is limited, it's definitely worth the effort. ♦ Su 1-4PM. Beside the Jupiter-Tequesta Bridge (at Hwy 1 and Alternate A1A), Jupiter. 747.6639

36 Gallery Square North This small shopping plaza is noted for its growing number of retail art galleries. ♦ Seabrook Rd and Tequesta Dr, Tequesta &

Within Gallery Square North:

Lighthouse Gallery and Museum The exhibits here, which change monthly, are usually kicked off with short evening openings at this nonprofit gallery and museum for Florida painters, sculptors, and craftspeople. Also offered is a variety of classes and seminars taught by local artists, photographers, and writers. Children's plays are periodically presented on weekends by the local **Children's Theater Group.** ♦ Free. M-Sa 9:30AM-4:30PM; M-F June and July; closed August and September. 746.3101 &

Cobblestone Cafe ★★$$$ Off the beaten track and tucked into the northwest corner of the plaza, this place, run by a couple who know fine gourmet food, is a real find. The dining room is small and intimate, and each dish looks like a work of art. Try the roast duck with raspberry sauce, grilled leg of lamb with a garlic-rosemary sauce, or fisherman's stew. The desserts are heavenly. ♦ Continental ♦ M-Sa lunch and dinner. 747.4419 &

37 Blowing Rocks This undeveloped area is quite scenic, but swimming is impossible here. The reason becomes apparent when you see the enormous rock formations and crashing surf. It's an ideal spot for fishing, though. ♦ Alternate A1A east of the intersection with Hwy 1, Jupiter (officially located on Jupiter Island)

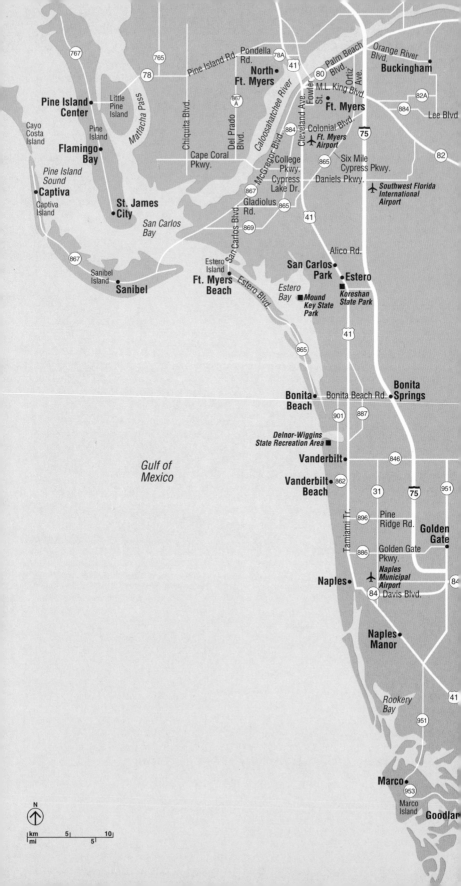

Gulf Coast

While Florida's east coast population multiplied like weeds from the 1940s to the 1970s, southern communities along the **Gulf of Mexico** sat relatively unchanged. **Ft. Myers** and **Naples** were quiet retirement and fishing towns that attracted a few token tourists who tended to avoid the beaten path. There were no major shopping malls here and very few big resorts. Espresso or parasailing? Forget it.

Then, in the early 1980s, two things changed this undisturbed enclave forever. **Southwest Florida International Airport** and the region's first freeway, **Interstate 75 (I-75)**, were constructed, allowing instant access to the area's undeveloped beaches and miles of natural reserves. Thomas Edison, who for years had come here to his winter home on the **Caloosahatchee River** near Ft. Myers, once said: "There's only one Ft. Myers, and 90 million people are going to find it."

An overstatement, yes. But in terms of growth, Southwest Florida tops just about every business-world barometer. There are more housing developments and more per-capita population gains here than anywhere else in the country. The airport that opened in 1983 has doubled in size. And today, more than half a million people call this area home.

People are drawn here for myriad reasons. In the winter, Southwest Florida is often the nation's sunniest spot. The gulf waters are known worldwide for tarpon and snook fishing. Golfers can choose from nearly 90 courses in a two-county area. **Lee County**'s lush **Barrier Islands** are sprinkled along a coastline that harbors large populations of dolphins and the West Indian manatee (or sea cow). And **Marco Island** is the perfect home base for those venturing into the **Ten Thousand Islands** or the **Everglades.**

With their crashing waves, the **Pacific** and **Atlantic Oceans** are known for their active beauty. The tranquil Gulf Coast, on the other hand, exudes a more passive charm that promotes a laid-back lifestyle. And the shelling here is unsurpassed in the US, since there are no waves to break the fragile shells.

Civilization along the Gulf Coast began with the warlike Calusa Indians. Spanish explorers, including Ponce de León, fought them for decades before the natives were killed off by smallpox and other diseases introduced by the Spaniards.

Like most of South Florida, this area remained virtually uninhabited by Europeans until after the Civil War, when ruined Confederate farmers and soldiers headed farther south to start new lives. Back then, life in the Gulf Coast subtropics was problematic, mainly due to an overabundance of mosquitoes (historically, some of the highest mosquito counts in the world have been recorded here). Today, however, **Lee County** boasts the world's largest mosquito-control district, and the insects don't pose too much of a problem anymore.

During World War II, Southwest Florida was home to two air training bases. Many recruits liked what they saw, returning after the war to start families here. Then came Social Security benefits, which allowed older Americans to migrate south for the winter. Over the years, this became a favorite sunning spot for retirees, especially from the Midwest. Nowadays the population is diversifying; younger families have discovered the low cost of living and affordable housing, and aspiring professionals are lured by new business opportunities. Tired of crowded Miami, young Anglos and Cubans are relocating to this coast, where there's less crime, fewer people, and more untouched nature. Naples seems to attract most of the area's wealthy transplants, while Greater Ft. Myers has the kind of socioeconomic mix found in larger cities.

It used to be that visitors sacrificed culture and fine cuisine in exchange for the area's natural beauty. Today some of the state's finest restaurants (many of them specializing in seafood) are in Naples and Ft. Myers. Both towns also boast performing arts halls that would fit in just fine in larger cities. If you're looking for nightlife, though, you'll find just a smattering, most of it on or near the beaches; there's a dearth of dance clubs, and younger people swear Southwest Florida still caters mainly to middle-class retirees.

Area code 941 unless otherwise indicated.

Getting to the Gulf Coast

Airports

Southwest Florida International Airport (16000 Chamberlin Pkwy, east of I-75 off exit 21, Ft. Myers), the region's main airport, sits in swampy, natural surroundings about 15 minutes southeast of **Ft. Myers** and 30 minutes north of **Naples.** At press time it was being expanded to twice its size, which should help to ease the general overcrowding and chaotic atmosphere that prevails during the tourist season. Until expansion is finished, the lines can be long, so get here at least an hour before your flight is scheduled to depart. Because the area has become so popular that it's hard to get in during high season, make flight reservations at least six months in advance.

Airport Services

Airport Emergencies	911
Currency Exchange	768.6575
Customs	768.4318
Ground Transportation	768.4457
Immigration	768.4318
Information	768.4700
Lost and Found	768.4361
Parking	768.1818
Police	768.4361
Traveler's Aid	768.4374

Airlines

Air Canada	800/422.6232
American Eagle	800/433.7300
American Trans Air	800/225.9920
Canada 3000	768.3000,
	800/993.4378 (Fiesta West)
Canadian Airlines	800/661.8881
Continental	800/525.0280
Delta	800/221.1212
LTV International	800/888.0200
Midwest Express	800/452.2022
Northwest	800/225.2525
Spirit	800/772.7117
TWA	800/221.2000
United	800/241.6522
USAir	800/428.4322
ValuJet	800/825.8538

In addition, a few commuter airlines serve **Naples Municipal Airport** (500 Terminal Dr, off Airport Pulling Rd, 643.1415). To get to this small airport, take **Highway 41** to Golden Gate Parkway eastbound. Head to Airport Pulling Road; then turn south and follow signs.

Getting to and from Southwest Florida International Airport

By Car I-75, the region's only freeway, runs north-south, with an airport exit. To get to Naples from the airport, turn south on I-75 and watch for exits about 20 miles down the highway. Those going to Ft. Myers should take **Daniels Parkway** (the road that leads out of the airport) west to **Highway 41** and turn north. To get to **Sanibel, Captiva,** and **Ft. Myers Beach** (also known as **Estero Island**), take Daniels Parkway west to **Summerlin Road.** Long- and short-term parking lots are within easy walking distance of the main terminal.

The following rental car companies have 24-hour counters at the airport:

Alamo	768.2424, 800/327.9633
Avis	768.2121, 800/831.2847
Budget	768.1500, 800/527.0700
Dollar	768.2223, 800/800.4000
General	768.1901, 800/327.7607
Hertz	768.3100, 800/654.3131
Lindo's	275.4202
National	768.1902, 800/227.7368

By Limousine Eleven transportation companies are permitted to take passengers from the airport, and the **Lee County Port Authority** sets their fares. Among the better-known agencies are **Aaron Airport Transportation, Inc.** (768.1898); **Apple Taxi & Limo Service** (463.2888); and **Majestic Limo Service** (489.4473). Sample costs: to Ft. Myers Beach (Estero Island), $26; to Naples, $46; to Marco Island, $50.

By Taxi Hail authorized taxis at a booth in the center of the terminal outside the baggage claim area. The drive to Ft. Myers costs about $20 and takes about 15 minutes; to Naples, it costs about $40 and takes about 30 minutes.

Bus Station (Long-Distance)

Located in Ft. Myers, the region's bus station (2275 Cleveland Ave/Hwy 41, at Victoria Ave)

is open daily from 6:15AM to 8PM. There isn't a taxi stand at this station. **Greyhound** (334.1011)—which is the only bus line that serves this region—links most of the cities in Southwest Florida.

Train Station (Long-Distance)

There's no **Amtrak** service to the Greater Ft. Myers area.

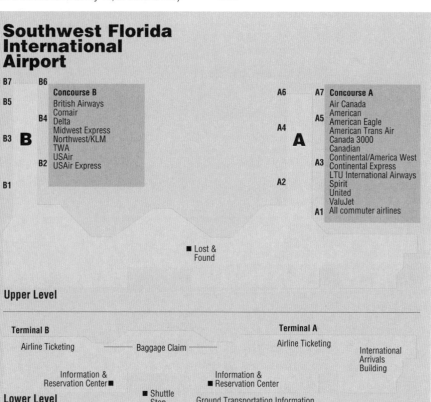

Southwest Florida International Airport

B7 B6
B5
    B4
B3 **B**
    B2
B1

Concourse B
British Airways
Comair
Delta
Midwest Express
Northwest/KLM
TWA
USAir
USAir Express

A6 A7 Concourse A
    Air Canada
A5 American
    American Eagle
A4 American Trans Air
    Canada 3000
    Canadian
    Continental/America West
A3 Continental Express
    LTU International Airways
A2 Spirit
    United
    ValuJet
A1 All commuter airlines

A

■ Lost & Found

Upper Level

Terminal B
Airline Ticketing ———— Baggage Claim ————

Information & Reservation Center ■

Lower Level

■ Shuttle Stop

Terminal A
Airline Ticketing

International Arrivals Building

Information & ■ Reservation Center

Ground Transportation Information across the street

Getting around the Gulf Coast

Mass transit in Southwest Florida is close to nonexistent. There's only one small county bus line, and it caters mainly to the carless residents of central **Ft. Myers.** Your best bet is to rent a car at the airport, or call a taxi—though here they look more like their counterparts in Central America than cabs in most other US cities: Don't be surprised if a driver shows up in a green 1970 LTD station wagon or a rusted-out 1980 Cadillac.

Bicycles Cycling is best on **Sanibel Island,** where several bike paths are located. In much of the rest of Southwest Florida, cyclists share the road with motor vehicles. Rent bikes at **Fun Rentals** (1901 Estero Blvd at Ave C, Ft. Myers Beach/Estero Island, 463.8844) or **Sanibel Cycle** (2496 Palm Ridge Rd, Sanibel Island, 395.1186).

Driving Driving is fairly easy in Southwest Florida. Remember that **Highway 41** is the main north-south artery of the region, with most other principal streets branching off at various points. Driving can be slow during the peak season: You'll often have to travel on two-lane roads that should be 10-lane freeways. Avoid morning and afternoon rush hours at all costs. And beware: Some older drivers (the region's median age hovers somewhere around 50) switch lanes with no warning.

Parking In Ft. Myers and **Naples**, street parking is metered, usually at 25¢ per hour. **Ft. Myers Beach (Estero Island)** has virtually no on-street parking. Don't park illegally, or your car may be towed. On Sanibel, beaches have automated parking systems ($3). **Captiva Island** has limited free parking at the beaches. There are no parking garages in any of the region's urban areas.

Taxis Taxis do not cruise, so it's best to call ahead for one. Some reliable cab companies are **Blue Bird Taxi** (275.8294); **Personal Touch Limousines** (549.3643); **Sanibel Island Limousine** (472.8888); and **Yellow Cab** (262.1312).

Tours The *Captain JP* (334.7474) is a big paddlewheeler that sails from mid-November to mid-April. Based at the **Ft. Myers Yacht Basin,** the ship offers a variety of guided tours—everything from three-hour excursions on the **Caloosahatchee River** to 12-hour trips up the river to **Lake Okeechobee.** Other boat-excursion operators are **Captiva Cruises** (472.5300), **Marco Island Sea Excursions** (642.6400), and **Wooten's Everglades Airboat Tours** (800/282.2781).

During the winter tourist season (December through April), visitors can explore downtown Ft. Myers on guided trolley tours, which depart from the **Thomas Edison Home** and take riders to the **Burroughs Home,** among other places. The trolleys run Tuesdays through Saturdays. For details, call the **Thomas Edison Home** (334.3614, 334.7419)

or the **Burroughs Home** (332.1229).

Rainbow Tour & Reception (9220 Bonita Beach Rd, Suite 200, Bonita Springs, 495.1557) and **Royal Palm Tours** (PO Box 06079, Ft. Myers 33906, 489.0344, 800/741.0344) are among the region's leading tour operators. For information on other such agencies in the area, contact the **Ft. Myers Chamber of Commerce** (332.3624), the **Lee County Visitor and Convention Bureau** (800/237.6444), or the **Naples Area Chamber of Commerce** (262.6141).

Trains No regional train system links the greater urban areas of **Lee** and **Collier Counties.**

Walking Walking is an option only in downtown Ft. Myers and Naples; you'll need a car to go anywhere else.

FYI

Gambling Greyhound racing is scheduled daily year-round at the **Naples–Ft. Myers Greyhound Track** (10601 Bonita Beach Rd, Bonita Beach, 992.2411), where betting is allowed.

Money Most banks are open weekdays from 9AM to 4PM; some are open Saturdays from 9AM to noon as well. Cash machines are located at banks, outside **Publix** supermarkets, and at some convenience stores. Foreign currency exchange is possible at **Thomas Cook Currency Services** (at Southwest Florida International airport, 768.6575), as well as at most major banks.

Personal Safety The Gulf Coast is generally very safe. To keep it that way, extra police are deployed during the winter tourist season. Avoid east Ft. Myers after dark.

Publications The Ft. Myers *News-Press* is a daily newspaper; its *Gulf Coasting* entertainment magazine, which lists events of interest to visitor and locals, comes out on Fridays. The *Naples Daily News* is published every day in the **Naples** and **Marco Island** area. *Gulfshore Life* magazine, which comes out 10 times a year, also is a good source of information about events that may interest tourists.

Restaurants Reservations for most eating spots are strongly recommended Christmas through Easter, but men are rarely required to don jackets or ties. Many restaurants offer so-called early-bird specials before 6PM.

Shopping Most shopping in the region is focused on malls, especially the **Edison Mall** (Hwy 41 at

Colonial Blvd, Ft. Myers), an all-purpose shopping center, and **Bell Tower Shops** (Hwy 41 at Daniels Pkwy, Ft. Myers), an upscale collection of stores featuring expensive clothing and gifts. Several small shopping centers on **Sanibel** and Marco Islands feature resortwear, art, and souvenir gifts to take home.

Street Plan Highway 41 and **I-75** are the main north-south thoroughfares. Each Gulf Coast city has its own maze of winding, twisting streets. To be sure of finding your way in the various neighborhoods, refer to a map for detailed information.

Taxes The sales tax along the Gulf Coast is 6 percent. For hotels, **Lee County** (Ft. Myers) tacks on another 3 percent, making the total accommodations tax 9 percent; **Collier County** (Naples) adds on 2 percent, bringing the accommodations tax to 8 percent.

Tickets There is a **Ticketmaster** inside **Dillard's** at the **Edison Mall** (Hwy 41 at Colonial Blvd, Ft. Myers, 334.3309).

Visitors' Information Centers Information centers are located at both **Southwest Florida International Airport** (768.4374) and **Naples Municipal Airport** (643.1415); both of these locations are open daily from 9AM to 6PM. In addition, Lee County has a **Visitor and Convention Bureau** (2180 W First St at Altamont St, Suite 100, Ft. Myers, 338.3500, 800/237.6444), which is open Mondays through Fridays from 8AM to 5PM.

Phone Book

Emergencies
AAA Emergency Road Service 939.6585
Ambulance/Fire/Police 911

Dental Emergency
  Lulu Dental 433.5858
  Dr. Jay Shartzer 433.5001

Hospitals
  Lee Memorial Hospital, Ft. Myers 332.1111
  Cape Coral Hospital, Cape Coral 574.2323
  Lee Memorial South (Health Park),
  Ft. Myers 433.7799
  Naples Community Hospital, Naples 436.5000

Locksmith (24-hour)
  Ash Safe & Lock 334.8752
  Island Locksmith 472.2394

Pharmacy (24-hour)
  Eckerd Drug 332.3050
  Walgreen's 939.1179

Poison Control 800/282.3171
Police (non-emergency) 332.3456
Visitors' Information
Better Business Bureau 334.7331

Convention and Visitors Bureaus
  Ft. Myers Chamber of Commerce 332.3624
  County Visitor and
  Convention Bureau 800/237.6444
  Naples Area Chamber of Commerce 262.6141

Disabled Visitors' Information 338.3500

Florida Marine Patrol 332.6966

Greyhound Bus 334.1011

Metro Transit
  (Lee County Transit Authority bus line) 275.8726

Time...335.8111

US Customs 433.7773, 768.4318

Weather ....332.4030, 335.8111 ex 1059

Lee County Barrier Islands

The most popular destination for visitors to Southwest Florida is the line of Lee County barrier islands scattered along the coast off **Ft. Myers.** Natural protection for the mainland from the area's violent, sometimes land-eating hurricanes, they also offer a wealth of resort areas that attract environmentalists as well as pleasure seekers.

Of the hundreds of islands, most are accessible only by boat. But to get the most out of a trip here, you need only visit five: **Sanibel, Captiva, Estero, Cayo Costa,** and **Cabbage Key.** Of all the Florida islands, these are among the most unpretentious and well preserved: Many are rich with subtropical vegetation and wildlife. Estero is the most commercial and has the island chain's only traffic light; the mood throughout is laid-back Caribbean. Expect to live in sandals and shorts—even when dining in one of the chichi restaurants.

The barrier islands were first occupied by the Calusa Indians. The 16th century saw the arrival of Spanish explorers and pirates, who hid on the islands waiting to ambush ships traveling between Tampa and Cuba. Tourism here didn't take off until the introduction in the mid-1900s of two things: air-conditioning and mosquito control.

Today, travelers are lured here for the world-class shelling opportunities; safe, gently sloping beaches (with no sudden drop-off areas); and frequent encounters with dolphins, sea turtles, and the endangered West Indian manatee (also known as the sea cow). The environmentally rich islands provide a mixture of natural beaches, boutique shopping, and fine restaurants that attract families as well as reclusive celebrities who don't want to be hassled. Nowhere else in Florida do nature and the human animal coexist more agreeably.

Area code 941 unless otherwise indicated.

Sanibel and Captiva

Connected by a bridge at **Blind Pass,** this duo is considered by locals to be one island. They have some of the most stringent zoning and land-use laws in the country; in fact, local growth-control methods are taught in universities throughout the world. Most of the more than 5,000 acres of protected refuges and preserves can be explored by canoe or bike, or on foot. A long ribbon of asphalt runs the entire length of Sanibel for bicyclists, and many visitors don't bother to drive a car.

Excluding the **South Seas Plantation** resort and a small downtown area, Captiva comprises mostly private residences. Vegetation is so thick that the main road is covered by a canopy of trees and vines, which gives drivers the impression of going through a dark-green tunnel. The island's isolation attracts high-profile people who want privacy, including artist Robert Rauschenberg and television personalities Willard Scott and Ted Koppel. Yet these two islands are very informal. Where there is elegance, it's understated. Even the poshest resorts here are minimalist in decor; many of them are low-lying and built of wood, surrounded by dense thickets of forest and vegetation.

Pirates and Spanish explorers were the first to land on Sanibel and Captiva, where they encountered the Calusa Indians. It's said that Ponce de León sailed past Sanibel after leaving Cuba, landing near the mouth of the **Caloosahatchee River** a few miles away. Local legend has it that a pirate named José Gaspar, once an admiral in the Spanish navy, set up his pillaging headquarters on Sanibel, holding his kidnapped maidens captive on Captiva Island (hence the name). In the early 20th century, farmers started to populate the islands, growing tomatoes, Key limes, and other vegetables. But powerful hurricanes in 1921 and 1926 demolished everything.

Then, in 1964, the **Lee County** government built a causeway, connecting the islands to the mainland and changing them forever. (Old-time residents romantically refer to the time before that as "BC"—"Before Causeway.") Homes and condominiums started popping up like mushrooms on the southern tip of Sanibel. And residents eventually incorporated their community and set up stringent zoning laws.

Today, Sanibel and Captiva are best known for their small, innovative restaurants, shelling on white sand beaches, and nature preserves that attract birdwatchers from around the world.

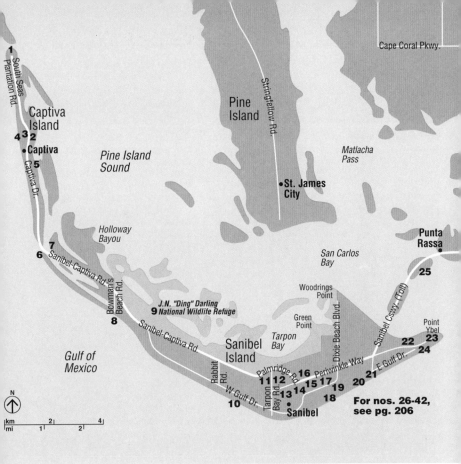

On the map:

- **1** South Seas Plantation Rd.
- Captiva Island
- **4 3 2**
- • **Captiva**
- **5**
- Captiva Dr.
- Pine Island Sound
- Cape Coral Pkwy.
- Pine Island
- Stringfellow Rd.
- Matlacha Pass
- • **St. James City**
- Holloway Bayou
- **7**
- **6** Sanibel-Captiva Rd.
- San Carlos Bay
- **Punta Rassa**
- **25**
- Bowman's Beach Rd.
- **8**
- **9** J.N. "Ding" Darling National Wildlife Refuge
- Sanibel-Captiva Rd.
- Woodrings Point
- Green Point
- Tarpon Bay
- Dixie Beach Blvd.
- Sanibel Cswy. (Toll)
- **22** **23** Point Ybel
- **24**
- Gulf of Mexico
- **Sanibel Island**
- Rabbit Rd.
- Palmridge Rd.
- **16** Periwinkle Way
- E Gulf Dr.
- **20** **21**
- W Gulf Dr.
- Tarpon Bay Rd.
- **11 12**
- **13 14 15 17**
- **18 19**
- **10**
- **Sanibel**
- For nos. 26-42, see pg. 206
- N
- km / mi 1 2 2 4

SOUTH SEAS PLANTATION

1 South Seas Plantation $$$$ This resort spreads over 330 acres, taking up the entire northern tip of Captiva Island. Exclusive yet not ostentatious, it attracts many celebrities who want to escape the public eye. World famous for its remote location and size, the resort has a full-service marina, fishing guides, a nine-hole golf course, a fitness center, 18 swimming pools, 21 tennis courts, and an expansive beach. The yacht harbor is home to **Steve Colgate's Offshore Sailing School** (454.1700). You'll find three restaurants as well, plus a pizzeria and an ice-cream parlor. The atmosphere is Tahitian: The 600 rooms are outfitted with ceiling fans and rattan furniture (though the decor does not justify the high prices), and the lush grounds are dense with palm trees and flowering plants. A caveat: Your hosts give you a credit card upon arrival, which you must use for everything purchased on the complex, making it easy to overspend. ◆ South Seas Plantation Rd, on the north end of Captiva Island. 472.5111, 800/237.3102; fax 472.7533 &

2 Bubble Room ★$$$ Visually, this is one of the oddest restaurants you'll ever visit. Decorated in a junkyard/Christmas motif, it's filled with blinking lights, aquariums, empty bottles, old photographs, and stuffed Santas. And the waiters wear Boy Scout uniforms. The

201

exterior is painted in every tropical color imaginable. Enjoy the surroundings because the food may be plentiful, but it's not great. If you like beef, order the prime rib, a house specialty. No reservations are accepted, so the wait is often an hour or more. The management here can be less than accommodating, apparently convinced the restaurant's reputation will carry it whether or not they deliver good service. It's not a good choice for a quiet, romantic meal. ♦ American/ seafood ♦ Daily lunch and dinner. 15001 Captiva Dr, Captiva. 472.5558 ♿

3 Sunshine Cafe ★★★$$$ This casual spot takes the area's two food staples—fish and fruit—and turns them into some of the most innovative dishes on the islands. Specialties include tropical fruit salsa, seafood pasta, and a spicy Cajun-style gumbo. Each paper-covered table comes with a glass of crayons, and there's a porch for dining in fine weather. ♦ American/seafood ♦ Daily lunch and dinner. Reservations recommended. No credit cards accepted. Captiva Sq, Captiva. 472.6200 ♿

4 Jungle Drums Wildlife art in all media, by artists from all over the world, fills this three-room gallery. On display are original paintings, photographs, jewelry, glass, and graphics that depict African wildlife, local birds, dolphins, and other animals. Some cost thousands of dollars, but there are a few bargains, such as a $40 pair of bronze alligator earrings. Noted Florida artists Kathleen and Jim Mazzotta run the gallery. Ask to see Jim's posters: Colorful, geometric composites of tropical plants and birds, they make good souvenirs. Also available are Caribbean Soul T-shirts, adorned with whimsical and colorful tropical designs created by the Mazzottas and local artist Dave Anderson. ♦ M-Sa. 11532 Andy Rosse La SW, Captiva. 395.2266 ♿

4 Mucky Duck ★$$ This seafood restaurant is popular because it's in a prime location for watching sunsets on the deck with beer in hand. Locals often get married outside as the sun sinks into the gulf. There's another **Mucky Duck** on Estero Island, but it is under different ownership. ♦ Seafood ♦ M-Sa lunch and dinner. 11542 Andy Rosse La SW, Captiva. 472.3434 ♿

5 'Tween Waters Inn and Marina $$ Charles and Anne Morrow Lindbergh liked to stay at this inn, which comprised spartan wooden cottages when it was built in 1926. Rooms have since been added, several with kitchenettes, but they're no better than you'd find in a roadside motel. Besides 125 rooms, facilities include boccie ball and shuffleboard courts, and the island's best tiki-hut pool bar, where live bands often play and the occasional hermit crab race is held. The frozen drinks are expensive but tasty and powerful. Across the street is a pretty but narrow beach. ♦ 15951 Captiva Dr, Captiva. 472.5161 ♿

6 Turner Beach Shell enthusiasts and fishers like this beach, located at Blind Pass, because it has several sandbars in shallow water where they can stand. Because of severe currents, however, no swimming is permitted. ♦ At the bridge connecting Sanibel and Captiva Islands

7 Lazy Flamingo ★★$$ This small, bright pink bar serves excellent steamed clams, Caesar salad, mesquite-grilled grouper sandwiches and hamburgers, and Buffalo wings, which you can order hot, extra hot, or "dead-parrot" hot. Customers include an unpretentious group of local anglers, waiters, and retired couples. The owners boast that *Playboy* magazine once wrote about the trademark T-shirts they sell to women: men's briefs turned upside down with a hole cut out for the head. The place can get packed at lunch, so try to go around 2PM. ♦ American/Seafood ♦ Daily lunch and dinner until 12:45AM. 6520-C Pine Ave, Sanibel. 472.5353 ♿. Also at: 1036 Periwinkle Wy, Sanibel. 472.6939

7 Sunset Grill ★★$$ Chef John Feagans grills just about anything you can think of, most notably beef, chicken, and exotic game. Meals are cooked to order, so don't pick this place if you're in a hurry. ♦ Steak house

♦ Daily breakfast, lunch, and dinner. 6536 Pine Ave, Sanibel. 472.2333 &

8 Bowman's Beach Sanibel's most unspoiled beach—where manta rays, dolphins, and baby sea turtles are often sighted—is never overcrowded, even during the peak season. Maybe it's the three-dollar-per-car entrance fee that keeps people away. At any rate, to get to the beach, you must cross a wooden bridge over a mangrove swamp and then walk through a pine forest. Loud radios and obnoxious sunbathers are shunned by the purists who frequent this strand. Showers and bathrooms are available. ♦ Admission for cars. Sanibel-Captiva Rd (watch for the brown road signs), Sanibel

9 J.N. "Ding" Darling National Wildlife Refuge Nearly 300 species of birds live either year-round or seasonally on the islands, and most of them can be seen in this federal preserve. J.N. Darling was a Pulitzer Prize–winning editorial cartoonist and conservationist. He spent much of his time on the island, and was instrumental in getting the US government to set aside 5,000 acres of it as a preserve. Most visitors make the mistake of driving through the refuge; it's only by canoe or bike, or on foot, that you can truly see the wildlife, which includes great blue herons, roseate spoonbills, anhingas, crabs, and alligators. Bring binoculars. Wildlife Drive, which cuts through the refuge, is closed Fridays to give the animals a rest. ♦ Admission. M-Th, Sa-Su sunrise to sunset. Sanibel-Captiva Rd, Sanibel. 472.1100

10 Best Western Jolly Roger Motel $$ Located on the beach, this hostelry boasts Sanibel's largest heated pool, on grounds peppered with coconut palms. The 45 rooms are tastefully decorated. On the beach are private grass tiki huts for shade and a washhouse to rinse off the sand and clean any shells you've gathered. There's no restaurant, though. ♦ 3287 West Gulf Dr, Sanibel. 472.1700, 800/554.5454; fax 472.5032 &

11 Jean Paul's French Corner ★★★$$ Almost every critic who comes to town, including those from The New York Times

and GQ, picks this as a Florida favorite. It's housed in a cramped, chalet-style building with terra-cotta tile floors and bright French prints on the walls. Choose from Norwegian salmon with fresh dill sauce, pâté du jour, or filet mignon in green peppercorn sauce. The chefs here have mastered sauces better than most others on the island, and there's a good wine list, too. This is French cuisine without attitude; the waiters won't make you feel intimidated by words you can't pronounce. ♦ French ♦ M-Sa dinner; closed May-October. 708 Tarpon Bay Rd, Sanibel. 472.1493 &

12 Timbers Restaurant and Fish Market ★★$$$ In local newspaper polls, Sanibel residents frequently rate this as the best fish house on the islands. There are two reasons: The fish is guaranteed fresh daily, and the cooks will prepare it any way you want. Of course, the selection depends on what was caught that day. ♦ Seafood ♦ Daily lunch and dinner. 703 Tarpon Bay Rd, Sanibel. 472.3128 &

13 Matsumoto Gallery Wildlife artist Ikki Matsumoto is known worldwide for his clean, crisp, and soothing pastel palette. His dolphin and heron prints make good, if expensive, gifts. ♦ M-Sa. 751 Tarpon Bay Rd, Sanibel. 472.6686 &

13 Bailey's General Store If you want to save money by cooking in your room, stop by Sanibel's main grocery store. The Bailey family, which still runs the store, first settled on the island as farmers in the late 1800s. Their market caters to upscale tastes, with a large supply of fresh tropical fruit, a deli that makes sandwiches to order, and a selection of esoteric magazines usually found only at well-stocked newsstands. Also available is the Sunday edition of The New York Times. ♦ Daily until 9PM. Tarpon Bay Rd and Periwinkle Wy, Sanibel. 472.1516 &

Anne Morrow Lindbergh, wife of the famous aviator, wrote her best-selling love letter, "A Gift from the Sea," without ever identifying the location as Captiva Island.

Restaurants/Clubs: Red	**Hotels:** Blue
Shops/🌴 Outdoors: Green	**Sights/Culture:** Black

13 Cheeburger Cheeburger ★$
Vegetarians, stay away! This 1950s-style hamburger shop, which is now branching out to other parts of Florida, offers just what it says: your choice of one-quarter-pound, one-third-pound, one-half-pound, or one-pound burgers. There's always a line and always a wait, but takeout is available.
♦ American ♦ Daily lunch and dinner. 2413 Periwinkle Wy, Sanibel. 472.6111 ♿

14 MacIntosh Book Shop Long days on the beach require ample reading material, and this bookstore, open since 1960, has an impressive collection of contemporary fiction, children's books, travel guides, and publications relating to Sanibel and Captiva, including history and shelling books.
♦ M-Sa; Su afternoon. 2365 Periwinkle Wy, Sanibel. 472.1447 ♿

15 Aqua Trek If you can't tell a mangrove from a sea oat or an osprey from an anhinga, then this is where to begin a Sanibel vacation. Carl Melamet, a marine biology teacher, conducts half-day excursions into aquatic habitats. He'll explain the islands' unusual tides, why there are so many shells, and what all those odd things on the beach are. If any critters fail to make a showing, you can see them in the center's touch tanks.
♦ Fee. Tours daily. Reservations recommended. 2353 Periwinkle Wy, Sanibel. 472.8680 ♿

16 Pirate Playhouse While not as intimate as the **Old Schoolhouse Theatre** (see below), this theater is air-conditioned, and the seats are more comfortable. Led by veteran directors Carrie Lund and Robert Cacioppo, the professional resident company stages high-quality productions from fall through spring. ♦ Admission. Performances M-Sa 8PM. 2200 Periwinkle Wy, Sanibel. 472.0006 ♿

The walls of Cabbage Key's historic inn are papered in more than $10,000 of autographed dollar bills. The inn serves meals to boaters at Mile Marker 60 on the Intracoastal Waterway.

A Surfeit of Shells by the Seashore

Southwest Florida, particularly **Sanibel Island,** is one of the world's best shelling spots. Only Jeffreys Bay in South Africa and the Sulu Islands in the southwest Pacific rival this area. Several hundred types of shells can be found on the **Lee County Barrier Islands,** including scallops, clams, fighting conch, coquina, left-handed whelk, and olive shells.

Why are shells so plentiful here? Partly because the **Gulf of Mexico** is calm, with no crashing waves to break the shells. There's also the gradual, sandy slant of the coastline, which for miles offshore rarely dips deeper than 40 feet. (By comparison, the ocean floor off the **Florida Keys** ranges in depth from 300 to 800 feet.) The slope off the barrier islands acts like a ramp, allowing large numbers of shells to roll onto the beach.

If you come here to take advantage of this bounty, you are likely to learn what locals call the "Sanibel Stoop"—the L-shaped posture that shell-seekers adopt as they walk the beach scanning the sand. In fact, the shells are so dense here it's sometimes hard to find the sand. Because shelling can be tough on tender feet, you're best off wearing thongs or rubber-soled shelling shoes, which you can buy in any beach store.

The optimal season for shelling is the winter, when the gulf storms break the shells loose from their beds and push them ashore. And the best time is early morning. In fact, dedicated shellers carrying flashlights are out in force before daylight to see what has washed ashore the night before. If you're a late sleeper, consider renting a boat and traveling to an undeveloped island, where there's less competition. (**Cayo Costa** is particularly rich in shells.) But remember, it's illegal to take any live shells from that island, while Sanibel allows visitors one each. You can recognize live shells by their vibrant color and by the mollusk, a brown creature, visible inside.

17 Old Schoolhouse Theatre This wooden, watermelon-colored building opened its doors in 1894 as the **Sanibel Elementary School.** Now, it's home to two local theater companies that produce plays of the same high caliber as those staged in big-city playhouses. Musicals and comedies are the specialty here. The small, black-walled venue provides an intimate theatrical experience. ♦ Admission. Performances M-Sa 8PM. 1905 Periwinkle Wy, Sanibel. 472.6862 &

18 Sanibel Inn $$$ Formerly the **Sanibel Hilton,** this property used to be tired and rundown. Then South Seas Resorts Company took over and renovated virtually everything, creating a gracious retreat just moments from the causeway. The gulf-front resort offers 96 well-appointed rooms with water views, two tennis courts, a pool with a cabana bar, and the **Portofino Restaurant,** which serves substantial Italian cuisine. ♦ 937 E Gulf Dr, Sanibel. 472.3181, 800/237.1491 &

19 Sundial Beach Resort $$$$ Considered one of the country's top resorts for families, this place has a restaurant, 16 tennis courts, and five swimming pools, as well as boat and bike rentals. Programs for the kids include shell hunting and T-shirt decorating. The 96 Tahitian-style rooms, with their bamboo furnishings, are awash in bright colors. ♦ 1451 Middle Gulf Dr, Sanibel. 472.4151, 800/237.4184 &

20 Song of the Sea $$$ While most beachfront resorts in Florida tout tropical ambience and casual wicker furnishings, this inn features a more elegant, European air. All 30 suites and studio units have a French country decor, giving them a lush yet cozy feel. The accommodations include kitchens with microwave ovens (there's no restaurant) and screened balconies; guests have access to a pool, as well as tennis and golf privileges at the nearby **Dunes Country Club.** Wedding ceremonies often are performed here. ♦ 863 E Gulf Dr, Sanibel. 472.2220, 800/231.1045; fax 472.8569 &

21 Gallery Motel $$ On an island known for pricey accommodations, this small, unassuming waterfront motel is a bargain. Each of the 32 units is comfortably outfitted, complete with balconies and wraparound porches. While there's no restaurant, there is a pool, plus wide stretches of beach right outside. ♦ 541 E Gulf Dr, Sanibel. 472.1400, 800/831.7384; fax 472.6518 &

22 Lighthouse Cafe ★$ Stop here for one of the island's best breakfasts, which is served until 3PM. The cafe incorporates seafood into its dishes, mixing shrimp and scallops in omelettes and croissant sandwiches. Take along a newspaper or book, as there's likely to be a short wait. ♦ American ♦ Daily breakfast. 362 Periwinkle Wy, Sanibel. 472.0303 &

23 Sanibel Lighthouse This brown lighthouse has been flashing warning lights to passing ships since 1884, when the US government built it to safeguard cattle and supply boats sailing from Tampa and Ft. Myers down to Key West and Cuba. Today it is listed on the National Registry of Historic Places. The design of the two cottages next door, which are part of the complex, is significant. Federal architects planned them exclusively for use in the tropics: They sit on pilings, which protect them from high tides; the hipped roofs with wide overhangs provide shade on the porch; and the numerous windows take advantage of crosswinds, the only form of air-conditioning at that time. The lighthouse is closed to the public. ♦ South end of Periwinkle Wy, Sanibel

24 Lighthouse Beach Encompassing the extreme southern tip of the island, this is a good place to spot dolphins as they swim from the bay to the gulf. Get here by 9AM, though, as parking is scarce. ♦ South end of Periwinkle Wy, Sanibel

25 Sanibel Causeway Since 1964 this stretch of bridges and man-made islands has connected Sanibel to the mainland. With good winds and a wide swath of beach, it's *the* place for Lee County windsurfers. Locals like it because they can park their cars right at the water's edge.

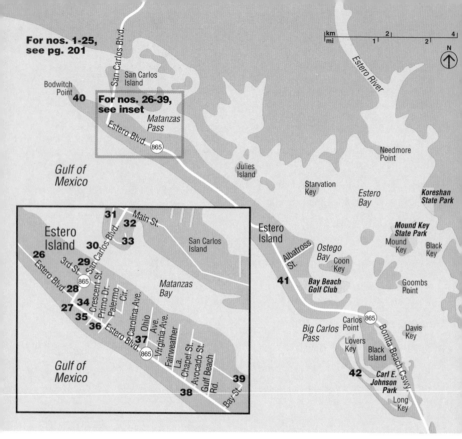

For nos. 1-25, see pg. 201

For nos. 26-39, see inset

Estero Island

Seven miles long and a skinny half-mile wide, **Estero Island** is connected to the mainland by a high, humpbacked bridge. Also known as **Ft. Myers Beach,** it's the most heavily developed of all the **Lee County** barrier islands.

Don't expect to get anywhere in a hurry by car here. The entire island has only one crowded, north-south thoroughfare—**Estero Boulevard. Molly the Trolley** continuously runs the entire length of that road, and for a small fee, you can get anywhere without walking more than a few blocks.

With its abundant cottage-type motels, outdoor restaurants, and souvenir shops, Estero has a Coney Island atmosphere that makes for prime people watching. You'll see a little bit of everything: bodybuilders, young bikini-clad women wearing boa constrictors around their necks, and retired couples holding hands as they stroll the beach.

Yet Estero has a definite small-town identity. Each year, in February or March, the Lions Club sponsors the Ft. Myers Beach Shrimp Festival, with a parade and the crowning of a new Miss Shrimp Queen. The celebration began more than 30 years ago as a solemn religious ceremony for the blessing of the shrimp fleets before they went to sea for harvest.

Most of the year, Estero Island is the ideal place for families to enjoy the subtropics without paying the higher prices on **Sanibel** and in **Naples.** The beaches here are especially safe for children because they're unusually shallow without drastic drop-offs. Yet travelers should be aware that **Ft. Myers Beach** is Southwest Florida's center for Spring Break revelers. For four weeks every March and April, some 20,000 college students from Michigan, Indiana, and Ohio fill the streets with their half-naked, sun-kissed bodies.

26 Best Western Pink Shell Resort $$$
This collection of pink-and-turquoise apartments, condominiums, and cottages sits on 12 acres at the less harried northern tip of Estero Island. The best rooms are the small, private stilt cottages, resembling tiny beach houses. Each one comes with a screened-in porch and a shaded parking spot beneath the cottage—a necessity in the hot subtropics. With rattan furnishings, the 208 renovated rooms are bright, clean, and comfortable. Outside are 1,500 feet of fine, white sand beach and a large, heated pool; inside is a dining room. ◆ 275 Estero Blvd. 463.6181, 800/237.5786; fax 463.1229 ♿

27 Ft. Myers Beach Pier Stretching 500 feet into the gulf, this pier is considered the town center, where natives come to fish and visitors to watch the sunset. It empties out into Times Square, the busiest intersection on the island. At night, the square turns into a wonderfully dizzying display of honking car horns, blaring stereos, and young pedestrians who come out to see and be seen. ◆ Estero Blvd

28 Sand Dollar Every beach town needs a shop like this. Directly across the street from the main public beach, it sells all the paraphernalia needed for a day in the surf, including suits, towels, refrigerator-size alligator rafts, and four shelves of sun-tanning (or blocking) products. It also has one of the island's best selections of kitsch, from the ubiquitous pink flamingo ashtrays to actual pickled baby sharks. The clerks here are friendly longtime residents who can tell you anything you want to know about the island. ♦ M-Sa 9AM-9PM; Su 9AM-5PM. 959 Estero Blvd. 463.6957 ♿

29 Island Motel $$ The dark and tiny rooms here are lit by those hanging lamps found in pool halls. The plus is that the 12 units form an arc around a small swimming pool, which makes it easy to meet other guests. The manager—or anyone, for that matter—might not be here when you arrive, so just sit by the pool and relax. Noise from Times Square gets loud at times, and you can hear the partying from inside your room. Cable TV and shuffleboard come with the price of a room; there's no restaurant, though. ♦ 201 San Carlos Blvd. 463.2381; fax 463.2040 ♿

30 Snug Harbor Restaurant ★$$ This is where the locals come for seafood. It sits on pilings in the bay between Estero and San Carlos Islands, so don't be surprised to see a dolphin or two swim by. Try the shrimp, blackened grouper, or scallops; the local "lobster tails," which are smaller than their New England cousins, are really crayfish but are tasty nonetheless. ♦ Seafood ♦ Daily lunch and dinner. 645 San Carlos Blvd. 463.4343, 463.8077 ♿

30 The Tall Ship Cruise the gulf on the *Island Rover*, a big-masted sailboat that offers two-hour trips throughout the day from **Snug Harbor Marina.** Though you won't go very far into the gulf, it's a good way to see dolphins and the homes along San Carlos Bay. Champagne, wine, and beer are available. ♦ Fee. Daily cruises; call for times. Reservations recommended. 645 San Carlos Blvd. 765.SHIP

31 Channel Mark ★★$$ Not only does this eatery have a great waterfront view, but it also serves fresh seafood—try the grilled tuna with kiwifruit chutney—and Italian dishes, including shrimp tortellini. Diners can sit outdoors or in. The bar offers 40-plus beers and an always-festive atmosphere. ♦ Seafood/Italian ♦ Daily lunch and dinner. 19001 San Carlos Blvd, on San Carlos Island. 463.9127 ♿

32 Europa SeaKruz The 300-passenger *Europa Star* makes six-hour voyages into the Gulf of Mexico. Casino gambling, live entertainment, dancing, and tableside meals are all available, though the food is the weakest part of the cruise. ♦ Fee. Daily cruises; call for times. Reservations recommended. 2400 Main St, on San Carlos Island. 463.5000, 800/688.PLAY

33 Ostego Bay Foundation This former fish-processing plant is now a marine-education center featuring a large touch tank and aquariums. Lectures and exhibits, plus boat and kayak tours, are offered. ♦ Admission. W-Sa 10AM-4PM; Su 1-4PM. 718 Fisher-man's Wharf, on San Carlos Island. 765.8101

34 The Plaka ★$ Located on Times Square back on Estero Island, this outdoor Greek restaurant affords diners the best view of the daily parade of swimsuits. If that doesn't interest you, focus on the souvlaki and gyros, seasoned the way they are in the motherland, and the tangy Greek salad heaped with feta cheese. ♦ Greek/American ♦ Daily lunch and dinner. 1001 Estero Blvd. 463.4707 ♿

35 Top O Mast The center of island nightlife, this club throbs with music from live Top 40 bands or DJs just about every evening. It's a dark and smoky place that smells of spilled beer, but the view of the gulf from the wooden deck outside is hard to beat. ♦ Free. Daily 10:30AM-2AM. 1028 Estero Blvd. 463.9424 ♿

36 Lani Kai Island Resort $$$ Though this 100-room, olive-green, Polynesian-style hotel tries to promote a family-atmosphere image, it caters mainly to the young, local and out-of-town party types. The grass-hut bar on the roof (and the two more on the beach) serve expensive frozen fruit drinks in plastic cups. Sometimes, two bands play outside simultaneously, within 20 yards of each other. It's raucous but unbeatable for people watching. There's a restaurant, large pool, and video arcade; plus every room has a refrigerator. ♦ 1400 Estero Blvd. 463.3111, 800/237.6133 ♿

36 Paradise Parasailing For those who are afraid of skydiving's untethered jump, this company (as well as several others located on the same beach) provides an exhilarating alternative. Harnessed to a parachute, you are pulled through the air 600 feet above the gulf for a terrific view of the barrier islands as well

Tiny Isles: Cayo Costa and Cabbage Key

Most travelers miss out on **Lee County**'s stunning natural sights simply because they can't get there by car. Hundreds of undeveloped barrier islands—some the size of a small town, others no bigger than a house—can be reached only by boat.

You could spend an entire week exploring these islands, or you could set aside a day to visit two of the more popular isles: **Cayo Costa** and **Cabbage Key,** both accessible by water taxis.

At 1,600 acres, **Cayo Costa** is one of the largest undeveloped barrier islands in Florida. Since it's a state park, it is protected from development and looks much as it might have 500 years ago, when the first Spanish explorers came ashore. With its thick palmetto brush, palm trees, and pine forests, the island has a primeval feel. Don't be surprised if you're the only one there.

Known for its spectacular displays of bird life, including ospreys, bald eagles, and pelicans,

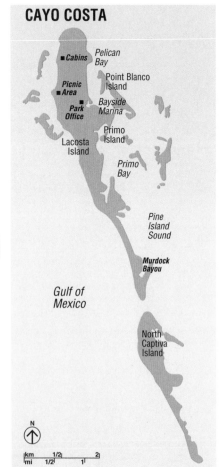

CAYO COSTA

(Map labels: Cabins; Pelican Bay; Point Blanco Island; Picnic Area; Bayside Marina; Park Office; Primo Island; Lacosta Island; Primo Bay; Pine Island Sound; Murdock Bayou; Gulf of Mexico; North Captiva Island; N; km 1/2 2; mi 1/2 1)

Cayo Costa is home to other creatures as well. On summer nights, loggerhead turtles crawl up from the sea to deposit their Ping-Pong ball–size eggs in the sand. At one time the island's many wild hogs ate most of these eggs, but in an effort to protect the dwindling turtle population, state officials relocated most of the porcine predators.

Some visitors bring a picnic and remain only a few hours. Others stay the night in one of 12 rustic cabins, available with a reservation for $20 a night (for more information, call 483.5944). There's cold-water plumbing and a restroom but no electricity. And since the state won't allow Lee County to spray for mosquitoes here, it's best to bring a bottle of repellent (or, as local fishing buffs recommend, apply Avon "Skin So Soft" bath oil, diluted with water at a one-to-one ratio). The park opens at 8AM and closes at sunset year-round. No alcohol is allowed.

If **Cayo Costa** sounds too wild, try exploring Cabbage Key. It is also undeveloped, except for the **Cabbage Key Inn** (PO Box 200, Pineland, FL 33745, 283.2278), a white, Florida-pine clapboard home built in 1938 for famous novelist and playwright Mary Roberts Rinehart. Boaters stop here for a drink and the celebrated Cabbage Key cheeseburger, which supposedly inspired Jimmy Buffett to write his song "Cheeseburger in Paradise." You can also spend the night in one of the inn's rooms, decorated in the Hemingway tradition—clean and well-lighted. Spend your days reading in a rocking chair out on the balcony and strolling through the island's 100 acres to see exotic birds, blooming ixoras, and poinciana trees with fiery red blossoms.

To find out about water taxis to Cabbage Key or **Cayo Costa,** call **Island Charter** (283.1113) on Pine Island or **Jensen's Twin Palm Resort and Marina** (472.5800) on Captiva Island.

as a chance to spot schools of fish and pods of dolphins and other creatures of the deep. ♦ Daily. Behind the Lani Kai Island Resort. 463.PARA

37 Fun Rentals Since getting around by car on the island can be aggravating, you might want to visit this shop in the pink-and-turquoise Pelican Plaza to rent a bike. A word of warning: During peak season—usually from Thanksgiving to Easter—traffic is quite heavy along Estero Boulevard, and there are no bike paths. ♦ Daily. 1901 Estero Blvd (at Ave C). 463.8844 &

38 The Mucky Duck ★ $$ What was once a beach house is now a restaurant with wooden nautical decor. The specialties here are seafood and steak, and the waiters really know their fish. The barbecued shrimp wrapped in bacon and the Key lime pie are especially popular. A children's menu is available. There's another **Mucky Duck** on Captiva Island, but it is under different ownership. ♦ Steak/seafood ♦ Daily dinner. 2500 Estero Blvd (1 mile south of the bridge). 463.5519 &

39 Matanzas Pass Wilderness Preserve Most of the island is filled with houses and hotels, save for these 40 acres set aside by the state. On bike or foot, meander along the dirt paths and wooden boardwalks, and watch the lizards and crabs scatter. The preserve is a good place to study mangroves, water-bound trees with exposed roots that look like copper pipes. Mangroves are an important part of the gulf food chain, because their submerged roots harbor hatching fish and other sea life. Stop by the local library on Bay Street for a free self-guided tour booklet put together by the local garden club. ♦ End of Bay St, behind the Ft. Myers Beach Elementary School

Bodwitch Point Regional Park This is Estero's least crowded, most unspoiled beach. Fronting both the bay and the gulf, the peaceful 17-acre park has lots of native vegetation and a wide, sandy beach. Parking is limited, but a trolley runs every 15 minutes from the Main Street Park-and-Ride Lot just north of Matanzas Pass

Bridge; look for the trolley signs. ♦ Northern end of Estero Blvd

41 Ft. Myers Beach Holiday Inn $$$ If lounging by the water is the sole purpose of your vacation, this is where you'll want to stay. The 103-room hotel offers one of the best stress cures in Southwest Florida: The island's biggest tiki bar sits right between a white sand beach and a pool surrounded by plants. Rent a beachfront efficiency with two bedrooms, a kitchen sink, a small refrigerator, and a hot plate. The only time you might want to leave is in the evening—the local entertainment is often at high volume. There's also a restaurant featuring continental cuisine. ♦ 6890 Estero Blvd. 463.5711, 800/HOLIDAY &

42 Carl E. Johnson Park This county park is made up of two islands south of Estero Island, which are connected to it by a bridge. The park features a beach bordered by Australian pines. Even if you don't feel like lying in the sun, take the tram from the park's entrance to the beach—the ride is beautiful, educational and a great way to take in the sights. Guides hand out brochures explaining the ecosystems you'll pass through and point out ospreys, mangroves, and crabs, among other wildlife. Showers and a boat ramp are available. ♦ Admission. Daily. 24340 Estero Blvd. For information, call the Lee County Visitor and Convention Bureau at 800/237.6444

Bests

Mitchell Kaplan
Co-owner, **Books & Books,** Coral Gables and Miami Beach

Listening to any of the 150 writers participating in readings, lectures, demonstrations, and panel discussions during the week-long Miami Book Fair International, held every November.

Spending a late afternoon at the beach and enjoying supper at one of the many outdoor cafes along **Ocean Drive** or more formal dining at **The Strand,** around the corner on **Washington Avenue** in **Miami Beach.**

Attending a performance by any of the artists presented by the **Miami Light Project** at the **Colony Theatre,** and then strolling leisurely down **Lincoln Road** in Miami Beach.

Sitting courtside at a **Miami Heat** basketball game.

Taking a Hobie Cat for a sail out on **Biscayne Bay** on a weekday.

Riding a bicycle down **Old Cutler Road,** with a stop at **Fairchild Tropical Gardens** in **Coral Gables.**

Attending an opening at the **Cuban Museum of Art and Culture,** followed by a late-night supper at **Versailles** on **Southwest Eighth Street** in **Little Havana.**

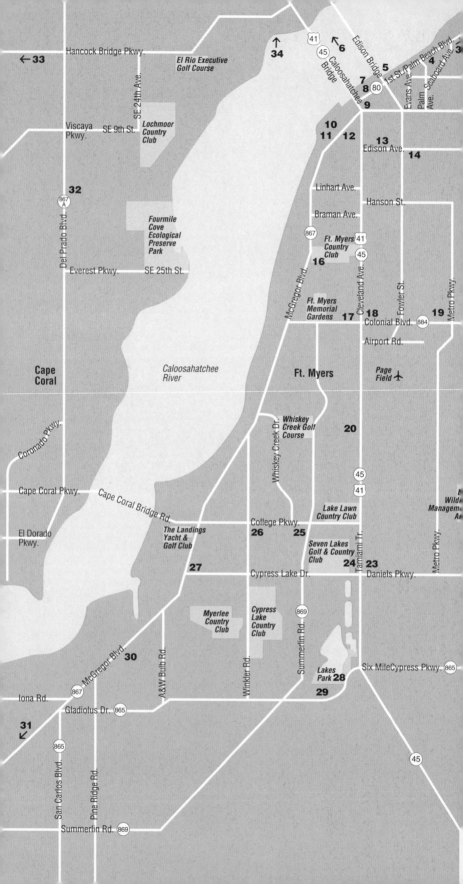

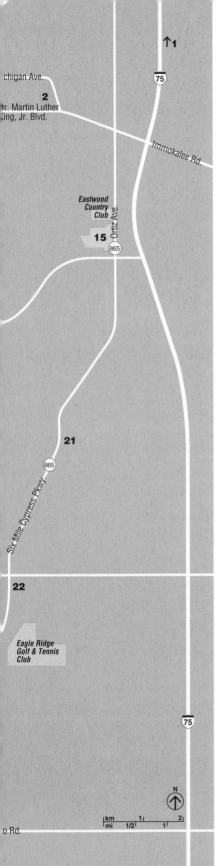

Greater Ft. Myers

The city council of Ft. Myers angered property owners a few years ago, when it forced them to inject their coconut palms with a serum to ward off disease. But local leaders felt they had no choice: After all, their community is known as the "City of Palms," and an epidemic might have resulted in a city of stumps.

Here, palms seem as omnipresent as cars, especially on **McGregor Boulevard**—a five-mile, two-lane road that slithers along the **Caloosahatchee River** and through the city, affording views of some of the most beautiful urban scenery in Florida. It's lined on both sides with thousands of majestic royal palms, their trunks as thick and straight as elephant legs. Inventor Thomas Edison, a longtime Ft. Myers winter resident, started it all by planting the trees near his home; then the city joined in. Today the palms are protected by state law.

Ft. Myers proper is small, with fewer than 50,000 of the metropolitan area's 350,000 residents. But it's being swallowed by urban sprawl, and the city is struggling to avoid becoming a center of blight and host to big-city poverty and other problems. For years, the mayor and city council have fought plans for an interstate loop that would encircle Ft. Myers—something desperately needed to clear the area's clogged roads (driving anywhere in this town requires a lot of patience and gasoline). But they fear that fly-over highways would smother Ft. Myers's small-town charm.

Across the river sits the largest city between Tampa and Miami, Cape Coral, which has grown from 100 to 85,000 residents in just 35 years. Remember all those stories you've heard about people buying patches of Florida swampland? Most likely they were buying it in the Cape. Developers traveled from city to city in the north, selling Cape Coral lots for $10 down and $10 a month. Then they brought in bulldozers, leveled the trees, and laid out neighborhoods that are still waiting to be filled—with both buildings and people. You'll see these asphalt mazes— grids of street upon street—from the window of your plane as you land at Southwest Florida International Airport.

Cape Coral is mainly a bedroom community, and most of its residents come across the bridge to Ft. Myers to find work and entertainment or to shop. In fact, nearly everything of interest to the visitor is on the Ft. Myers side of the river. But the Cape is home to a fantastic collection of family-owned ethnic restaurants, offering Italian, Greek, Thai, and German food.

Cape Coral also has Florida's largest population of burrowing owls, which (true to their name) live in holes in the ground. The threatened species has prevented construction of a freeway that would have wiped out several nests. It's worth a trip across the bridge just to see these animals, which are as commonplace in Cape neighborhoods as dogs and cats are in other towns.

The Ft. Myers/Cape Coral metropolitan area sits about 10 miles inland, on the banks of the Caloosahatchee River, in **Lee County.** For years, before tourism blossomed into the industry it is today, Lee County was known for its prolific farmers, and it produced most of the gladioli sold in the US. Today, it's the business center of Southwest Florida, where financial, federal, and state offices are based.

Area code 941 unless otherwise indicated.

1 Babcock Wilderness Adventures

For years, the Babcock family has mined phosphates and farmed on their 90,000-acre ranch in rural Charlotte County. Now they've turned a large chunk of their undeveloped property into an educational wildlife complex that's one of the state's most unusual and startling attractions. From elevated trucks painted in camouflage colors, you'll see Florida as it was before condos and concrete—nothing but pine forests and swampland so thick with vegetation that sunlight can't penetrate to the ground. Watch for bison, alligators, deer, and birds, all described by the naturalists who explain the ecosystems you're seeing. There's even a human cage from which you can see a free-roaming family of rare Florida panthers. The 90-minute tour, which has a humans-must-learn-to-live-with-animals tone, fosters a reverence for and awareness of a world that is fast dying off. Be sure to take along binoculars and insect repellent. ♦ Admission. Tours daily every half hour 9AM-3PM Jan-May; Tu-Su 9AM and 11AM June-Oct; Tu-Su 9AM, 11AM, 1PM, and 3PM Nov-Dec. Reservations required. 8000 State Rd 31, 10 miles northeast of Ft. Myers. Information 338.6367, reservations 489.3911

2 Fleamasters Southwest Florida's biggest flea market is more than just a used-goods bazaar; it's probably the best place to buy fresh produce, including locally grown peppers and tomatoes. It also features new merchandise at relatively low prices. Choose from shoes, T-shirts, souvenirs, and other assorted kitsch. ♦ Free. F-Su. 4135 Dr. Martin Luther King Jr. Blvd/State Rd 82 (west of Ortiz Ave), Ft. Myers. 334.7001 &

3 Eden Vineyards Run by the Kiser family in Alva (a small town just east of Ft. Myers), this is one of Florida's few wineries. Visits begin with a wine tasting around a bar in the winery building. Dry-wine connoisseurs will be disappointed: The products here are fairly sweet, like German wines, although the Kisers offer a carambola (star fruit) wine that's light and slightly dry, much like the yellow fruit itself. It's a homespun, unpretentious experience. ♦ Admission. Daily 11AM-4PM. 19709 Little La (off State Rd 80; exit 25 on I-75 and go 10 miles east), Alva. 728.WINE &

3 Memphis Blues Bar-B-Q ★★$ Here you'll find blues (not live, but on tape) and barbecued ribs—served wet (with sauce) or dry (well seasoned, but with no sauce). The side dishes—coleslaw, baked beans, and the like—aren't great, but the beef, chicken, and pork barbecue platters are worth the trip. Skip the garlic bread and opt for dessert instead: The Chocolate Suicide is a veritable chocolate orgy. ♦ Barbecue ♦ Daily lunch and dinner. 13908 State Rd 80, 5 miles east of I-75, East Ft. Myers. 693.2223 ♿

4 Rock Lake Motel $ This clean, friendly inn is a half-hour drive from the Ft. Myers beach. Other drawbacks: It has no restaurant, and there are no phones in the rooms. But the price is right. Owner James Moore built 18 limestone cabins around a natural lake, and his cats and Muscovy ducks have the run of the place. Be sure to take a spin down Palm Beach Boulevard: With its used-car dealers, tattoo parlors, ethnic groceries, and antiques stores, it's one of the most colorful and eclectic drives in the area. ♦ 2930 Palm Beach Blvd (at Seaboard Ave), Ft. Myers. 334.3242 ♿

5 Burroughs Home The former home of businessman Nelson T. Burroughs and his family, this restored 1901 Georgian Revival mansion is less historically noteworthy than Edison's home. The guides make it more interesting, however, by adopting the personae of the Burroughs' daughters, Mona and Jetta. Antiques enthusiasts will find much to ogle here. ♦ Admission. M-F until 4PM; tours every hour. First St (at Fowler St), Ft. Myers. 332.1229 ♿

6 Shell Factory When you see the number of shells here, you'll swear they were mass-produced; in fact, they were gathered from the coastlines of 53 countries from all over the world. Ranging in length from an inch to a foot, they fill bins like produce in a grocery store. The showroom alone occupies 65,000 square feet. The shop specializes in "specimen" shells—so perfect they could have been collected from the ocean floor instead of a beach. ♦ M-Sa; Su afternoon. 2787 N Tamiami Trail/Hwy 41 (at W Berry Ct), North Ft. Myers. 995.2141 ♿

7 Centennial Park This narrow downtown park runs parallel to the bank of the Caloosahatchee River. City-sponsored outdoor concerts, from classical to jazz, take place here year-round. Check out the park's centerpiece—a fountain/sculpture depicting Ft. Myers winter residents Thomas Edison, Henry Ford, and Harvey Firestone sitting around a campfire. ♦ Off Edwards Dr along the Caloosahatchee River (between the Edison and Caloosahatchee Bridges), Ft. Myers

8 Peter's La Cuisine ★★$$$ From the white linen tablecloths to the waiters in spotless tuxedo shirts, this is a truly first-class establishment. The menu, which changes every few weeks, features seasonal fare, pasta, and seafood—including one of the best lobster bisques you'll ever savor. Among the sinfully decadent desserts are white- and dark-chocolate mousses, both served with fresh fruit. ♦ Eclectic ♦ M-Sa lunch and dinner. 2224 Bay St (at Hendry St), Ft. Myers. 332.2228 ♿

9 The Veranda ★$$$ An institution among the old guard of Ft. Myers, this restaurant is housed in an olive-colored clapboard Victorian home. Local power brokers and members of the media meet on weekdays for Happy Hour in the bar, which, with its bookcases and padded leather chairs, resembles a dark den. Count on a good selection of seafood and beef dishes, including a succulent chateaubriand. For some reason, dinner here is much more imaginative than lunch. ♦ American ♦ M-F lunch and dinner; Sa dinner. 2122 Second St (at Broadway), Ft. Myers. 332.2065 ♿

Restaurants/Clubs: Red	**Hotels:** Blue
Shops/ ᛦ Outdoors: Green	**Sights/Culture:** Black

10 Melanie's ★$ When only the comfort of Southern fare will do, this is the place to go. You'll see lots of government types, movers and shakers, and just plain local folks hunkered over big plates of fried catfish, meat loaf, fried green tomatoes, and collard greens. Dessert lovers should try the sour cream–and-raisin pie. ♦ Southern ♦ Daily breakfast and lunch; Th-F dinner. 2158 McGregor Blvd (at Clifford St), Ft. Myers. 334.3139 ♿

11 Thomas Edison and Henry Ford Homes Edison's 14-acre riverfront estate is preserved, for the most part, as he left it. The inventor planted a botanical garden on the grounds that is unmatched in this part of the state. He also built one of Florida's first swimming pools, reinforced with bamboo. His two-story home is still lit by old Edison lightbulbs. There's a great museum as well, filled with proof of his electronic wizardry, including several phonographs and movie cameras. (What the tour guides don't tell you is that Edison's original laboratory—with all its equipment—burned to the ground in 1968.)

Next door is the second home of Henry Ford, who followed his friend Edison to Ft. Myers. But the gray clapboard house, which is open to the public, is nothing to write home about. Unless you have an architectural interest in wooden floors or large porches, you might want to pass this one up. ♦ Admission. M-Sa; Su afternoon. 2350 McGregor Blvd (south of Hwy 41/Caloosahatchee Bridge), Ft. Myers. 334.3614 ♿

12 Drum House $$ Ft. Myers's only bed-and-breakfast inn, this turn-of-the-century house contains six bedrooms, each with period furniture and a private bath. Stroll over to the Edison and Ford estates (see above), then spend part of the afternoon sipping wine in the **Music Room.** There's no restaurant. ♦ 2135 McGregor Blvd (at Clifford St), Ft. Myers. 332.5668 ♿

13 City of Palms Park The city of Ft. Myers built this $24-million stadium especially for the **Boston Red Sox,** who moved their spring-training headquarters here in 1993. The team is in residence late February through early April. At press time, the all-female **Colorado Silver Bullets** baseball team was slated to train here. The facility has 7,000 fairly comfortable seats. ♦ Admission to games. 2201 Edison Ave (at Jackson St), Ft. Myers. Main office 334.0444, Red Sox 334.4700 ♿

14 Farmer's Market ★$ No other restaurant in Lee County has such a diverse clientele. At lunchtime, attorneys, legislators, farm workers, and mothers with children all come to indulge in big helpings of Southern fare. Try the smothered steak, turnip greens, real mashed potatoes, and steamed okra with tomatoes—and don't be offended when the waitresses call you "Honey"; they really mean it. ♦ American/Southern ♦ Daily breakfast, lunch, and dinner. 2736 Edison Ave (east of Fowler St), Ft. Myers. 334.1687 ♿

15 Calusa Nature Center and Planetarium Formerly the **Nature Center of Lee County,** this environmental museum was built by the Junior League of Ft. Myers in the 1970s. With its simplified exhibits on area wildlife and fossils, it feels like a children's museum. An elevated boardwalk is the setting for a short educational walk through a cypress swamp. The planetarium features stellar shows on the heavens. ♦ Admission. Daily. 3450 Ortiz Ave (at Colonial Blvd), Ft. Myers. 275.3435 ♿

16 Tootie McGregor's Seafood Restaurant ★★$$$ This place does an admirable job with California-style cuisine. Good bets include oak-grilled salmon with grain mustard, honey, and fried leeks, and the well-aged prime rib. The setting is comfortable, with tables well spaced for privacy. ♦ American ♦ Daily lunch and dinner. 3583 McGregor Blvd (at Ft. Myers Country Club), Ft. Myers. 939.7300 ♿

17 Kartworld No matter what the kids are in the mood for, chances are they'll be happy here. There's miniature golf, bumper boats, batting cages, a video arcade, and the all-important snack bar. The amusement park, formerly **Fort Adventure,** is well maintained and supervised. ♦ Free. M-Th, Su until 10PM; F-Sa until midnight. 1915 Colonial Blvd (between Cleveland Ave and Summerlin Rd), Ft. Myers. 936.3233 ♿

18 Garden Greens ★$$ The soup-and-salad set has been keeping this place busy since it opened in 1992. It's the creation of Peter Schmid, owner of **Peter's La Cuisine** (see above) and one of the region's most innovative chefs. Here he's turned his attention to the raw vegetable, offering an extensive salad bar full of fresh ingredients. Also on the menu: a rotating trio of soups (the minestrone is a standout); hot, crusty rolls basted with garlic oil; and daily pasta and seafood specials. ♦ American ♦ Daily lunch and dinner. 4328 Cleveland Ave (at Colonial Blvd), Ft. Myers. 936.1888 ♿

19 Seminole Gulf Railway Do some sightseeing the old-fashioned way—through the windows of a slow-moving train. This railway offers afternoon tours south to Bonita Springs, and brunch, dinner, and murder-mystery excursions north to Punta Gorda. ◆ Fee. Daily. Metro Mall (at Metro Pkwy and Colonial Blvd), Ft. Myers. 275.6060 ♿

20 Miami Connection Bagel & Deli ★★$ When you simply *must* have a thick corned beef sandwich or smoked fish on a bagel, this kosher-style deli is the best spot in Southwest Florida. The sandwiches are huge, and meat and fresh fish are served with plates of crisp dill pickles and tomatoes. ◆ Deli ◆ Daily breakfast and lunch. 11506 Cleveland Ave (at Oak St), Ft. Myers. 936.3811 ♿

SIX MILE
CYPRESS
SLOUGH
PRESERVE

21 Six Mile Cypress Slough Preserve In the heart of Six Mile Cypress Swamp, the slough (pronounced *slew*) has a well-maintained boardwalk nine miles long and a third of a mile wide. It's ideal for bicycling (no rentals are available, though). Walking tours, enhanced by lectures about the preserve's natural resources, are offered. ◆ Parking fee. Daily; tours W, Sa starting at 9:30AM. Penzance Crossing on Six Mile Cypress Pkwy (between Colonial Blvd and Daniels Pkwy), Ft. Myers. 338.3300, 432.2004

22 Lee County Stadium The **Minnesota Twins** moved their spring-training headquarters from Orlando to Ft. Myers in 1991, so if you're here in the spring, it's worth getting tickets for games between the **Twins** and

other teams that train in Florida. This 7,500-seat stadium is among the most modern in the **Grapefruit League**—and it's just small enough to let you see the grimaces on the batters' faces. ◆ Six Mile Cypress Pkwy (near Daniels Pkwy), Ft. Myers. Tickets 800/33.TWINS (M-F) ♿

Bell Tower

23 Bell Tower Shops This outdoor shopping mall, designed in the Mediterranean style, is home to several upscale emporia, such as **Jacobson's** department store. ◆ M-Sa; Th-F until 9PM. Daniels Pkwy (at Hwy 41/Cleveland Ave), Ft. Myers. 489.1221 ♿

24 Carrabba's ★$$ There's no shortage of Italian eateries in Ft. Myers, but this one distinguishes itself by offering an unpredictable menu. Many entrées are grilled in an open kitchen that's visible from much of the dining room. The pizzas are good. Counteract all that garlic with a world-class dessert, such as the *sogno di cioccolata* (brownie cake with chocolate mousse and chocolate sauce). ◆ Italian ◆ Daily dinner. 12990 Cleveland Ave (one block north of Daniels Pkwy), Ft. Myers. 433.0877 ♿

Cashing in on Crime

In 1993, when criminals stepped up their targeting of visitors to **Miami** for holdups and robberies, headlines appeared all over the world. City officials acted quickly to solve the problem, establishing tourist help centers near expressway exits, founding a tourism police unit to patrol trouble spots, publishing tips on staying safe, and touring European countries to encourage visitors to come back.

But where there's trouble, there's money to be made. One entrepreneur published a tourist map indicating the areas with the highest crime rate against visitors. A national car rental agency offered a computerized car that could prevent travelers from getting lost in bad neighborhoods. More recently, a free-lance TV news photographer offered a "Miami Crime Tour": For four hours, passengers can ride with Marc Siegal on his nightly rounds of the mean streets, sniffing out malefactors and misdeeds "in one of the world's most violent and beautiful cities."

25 Barbara B. Mann Performing Arts Hall
Plagued for years by bad management, this hall is home to the **Southwest Florida Symphony;** it's also been the stage for Broadway shows such as *Les Mis* and *Jesus Christ Superstar.* ♦ 8099 College Pkwy SW (near Summerlin Rd), Ft. Myers. 489.3033, 800/440.SHOW &

26 Bolero's ★$$ Cuban restaurants have a tough time surviving in Lee County, but this one draws a sizable crowd. The menu features all the classic Cuban dishes: *boliche* (pot roast), paella, and *churrasco* (marinated and grilled flank steak), plus a selection of tapas— one of these little Spanish-style dishes can be an appetizer, and several make a meal. The flan is good, too, as is the live Spanish music. ♦ Cuban ♦ Daily lunch and dinner. 8595 College Pkwy (at Winkler Rd), Ft. Myers. 432.0033 &

27 The Prawnbroker ★$$ One of the best seafood houses in Ft. Myers, this place prepares fish to suit the customer's diet or taste buds: It can be blackened, smothered in garlicky butter, or coated in cornflakes and banana. But don't count on a relaxing meal: The restaurant is often crowded and noisy, and long lines mean they rush you in and out like cattle. ♦ Seafood ♦ Daily dinner. Reservations recommended. 13451-16 McGregor Blvd (at Cypress Lake Dr), Ft. Myers. 489.2226. & Also at: Town Center Shopping Plaza, 1051 N Collier Blvd (at Elkcam Circle), Marco Island. 394.4800 &

28 Lakes Park Don't let the name fool you, for this park has much more than lakes. Nature trails for bikers and joggers wind through forested areas, and you can rent a canoe or a paddleboat for a tour around the clear, natural lake in the center of the park. Neither pets nor alcohol are allowed. ♦ Admission; children under five free. Daily. 7730 Gladiolus Dr (between Summerlin Rd and Hwy 41), Ft. Myers. 432.2000

Cape Coral has more miles of canals than Venice, Italy.

29 Castle Golf There's no shortage of places to play miniature golf in the region, but this layout—right next to **Lakes Park** (see above)—is a top choice for its challenging course and well-landscaped grounds. Don't forget sunscreen and insect repellent. ♦ Admission. Daily until 11PM. 7400 Gladiolus Dr (between Summerlin Rd and Hwy 41), Ft. Myers. 489.1999

30 Fountain Motel $ Tim Wilson, the manager of this motel, claims that his 18 tropical-looking rooms are so immaculate that fastidious visitors have heard about them by word of mouth. Guests get a choice of rooms with sunset or sunrise views; another draw is the pool. There's no restaurant, though. ♦ No credit cards accepted over the phone. 14621 McGregor Blvd (at Kimberly La), Ft. Myers. 481.0429 &

31 Sanibel Harbour Resort & Spa $$$$ Ft. Myers's only world-class resort, this towering, tin-roof hotel sits on the mainland, right off the Sanibel Island Causeway. All 242 rooms have balconies that overlook either San Carlos Bay or mangrove forests. But the main selling point is the spa, complete with herbal wraps, massage rooms, Swiss showers, Keiser exercise equipment, aerobics classes, and a lap pool. Adjacent to the spa is a 5,000-seat tennis stadium, former venue for the Davis Cup championships. The complex also has 79 condominium units and three restaurants. ♦ 17260 Harbour Point Dr (off Summerlin Rd), Ft. Myers. 466.4000, 800/766.3782 &

32 Siam Hut ★★★$$ Perhaps the best Thai food you'll ever have the pleasure of eating is served at this restaurant. From *phad thai* (a noodle dish) to satay to crispy spring rolls, it's impossible to go wrong. Those who like a little spice in their life should order the panang or green curry medium-hot (or hotter for the hardcore); requests for mild seasoning are honored as well. You'll leave this place feeling pampered, since every detail is attended to: The linen napkins are sculpted into lotus blossoms and birds-of-paradise, and the Thai iced-tea glasses never stand empty. ♦ Thai ♦ M-Sa lunch and dinner. Coral Point Shopping Center, 1873 Del Prado Blvd (about 2 miles north of Cape Coral Pkwy), Cape Coral. 772.3131 &

35 Sun Splash Family Waterpark This water-oriented amusement park offers two dozen attractions, some wet, some dry, plus a snack bar. While it is hyped as a family place, most adults will want to pull up a lounge chair while the youngsters brave the lines and chaos for a chance to propel themselves into the variety of pools. Flotation devices, food, picnic baskets, and coolers are not permitted. ♦ Admission. Daily Apr-Oct. 400 Santa Barbara Blvd (at Lake Kennedy, about a mile south of Pine Island Rd), Cape Coral. 574.0557 &

35 Gulf Coast Kayak Co. Cindy Baer and Frank Stapleton supply the equipment and know-how, so even a first-timer can enjoy the natural sights of Pine Island Sound by way of kayak. Half-day, full-day, overnight, and even full-moon excursions can be arranged. Special trips—some overnight—head to Mound Key, North Captiva, Cayo Costa, and Cabbage Key, all nearby. ◆ Fee. 4882 Pine Island Rd (about 11 miles west of Hwy 41), Matlacha. 283.1125

34 Mariners Inn ★$$ It hardly seems possible that such an oasis of calm could exist so close to bustling Hancock Bridge Parkway and Highway 41. But this waterfront restaurant is truly serene, with a soothing view of the water and a menu that focuses on fish. Try the meaty crab cakes or the tenderloin Neptune (beef medaillons topped with shrimp and béarnaise sauce). ◆ Seafood ◆ Daily lunch and dinner. 3448 Marinatown La (a block east of Hwy 41 at Hancock Bridge Pkwy), North Ft. Myers. 997.8300 ♿

Giovanni's On-The-Water

34 Giovanni's On-The-Water ★$$ Not in the mood for fish? Right next door to **Mariners Inn** (see above), this place serves Italian food with a soupçon of Gallicism. It's small and cozy, with a screened wooden deck over-looking the marina. ◆ Italian ◆ Daily lunch and dinner. 3442 Marinatown La (a block east of Hwy 41 at Hancock Bridge Pkwy), North Ft. Myers. 656.5489 ♿

You can boat straight across the state of Florida from Ft. Myers to Palm Beach—via the Caloosahatchee River and the Okeechobee Waterway.

Bests

Arva Moore Parks
Historian/Publisher/Author of *Miami the Magic City*

Most of my favorite things are never found in a guidebook, and many of them are free. Start with the quality of light and then look up at the sky. Does anyone have bluer, more picturesque skies than we do? Don't forget to notice that in **Miami,** nature wears a year-round coat of green, and water is rarely out of sight.

Go out on a boat in the bay at sunset, preferably in February or March, and watch the western sky put on a show. Stay until the Magic City lights up and **Bayside**'s laser show begins. If you can't get a boat, catch the magnificent view from a balcony, a causeway, or from the car ferry to **Fisher Island.**

Visit **Simpson Park** after a rain and smell the natural hammock, our name for a subtropical hardwood forest. Look for spider webs that sparkle like crystal when strips of sun shoot through the jungle cover. Ask Ralph Beaudry, the affable director, for a personal tour.

Experience **The Barnacle** in **Coconut Grove**—the one place where you can almost re-enter the era of the Bay before there was a Miami. Ask to see the fingerprints on the upstairs porch.

While you are in the Grove, which is full of history, drive down **Charles Avenue,** the first black (mostly Bahamian) settlement in South Florida. Visit the **Kampong** and learn about David Fairchild and the world of tropical fruits that "grows 'round his door." Discover the area's first school-house, which is tucked in the gardens of **Plymouth Congregational Church,** and **Ransom Everglades School**'s pagoda. Finish up by having lunch (and people watching) at a sidewalk cafe in the village center.

Give yourself a South Florida geology lesson. Travel down **South Bayshore Drive** and look for the **Silver Bluff** (an outcropping of Miami oolite commonly called "coral rock"). Next, drive to **Coral Gables House** and see the beautiful building constructed from this native stone. While you are in the neighborhood, check out the entran-ces and plazas, the **Venetian Pool** (a former rock quarry), and the **Country Club Historic District.** Complete your tour with lunch at the **Omni Colonnade Hotel**'s **Doc Dammers** bar and learn some **Coral Gables** history. Enjoy afternoon tea at the beautiful **Biltmore Hotel,** and don't miss the pool (it's the largest hotel swimming pool in the world).

Visit the **Art Deco District** day or night. It is always wonderful.

Go to an event at the **Maurice Gusman Center for the Performing Arts,** formerly the **Olympia** theater. The historic theater is worth the price of a ticket.

Have dinner at a Cuban restaurant on **Calle Ocho** (Eighth Street) and order pork, *moros* (black beans and rice), yuca, flan, sangría, and Cuban coffee. Bring your children along.

End the day at **Bayside Marketplace,** sitting by a dock on the bay listening to a variety of local music. If you are lucky, you will see a "Moon over Miami."

Naples

One of the fastest-growing communities in Florida, Naples is more devoted to aesthetics than most. **US Highway 41** (also known as the **Tamiami Trail**), which runs through town, is divided by medians filled with gardens of grass, palm trees, and flowers; the **Collier County Government Complex** looks like a modern art gallery; and even the suburban-style **Coastland Center** mall displays original Rodin sculptures. In terms of average household income, **Collier County** (whose seat is Naples) vies with **Palm Beach County** as the state's most affluent region. For the visitor, that translates into a solid selection of world-class restaurants, resorts, and other attractions. But if you visit off-season (summertime), you'll find much of Naples peaceful and quiet.

Though relatively young, Naples's arts community is one of the most active in Florida. The **Philharmonic Center for the Arts** is considered an outstanding museum and performance hall. And every year, companies and private donors in the city sponsor a town hall lecture series, bringing in speakers such as **Jean Kirkpatrick**, **Tom Wolfe**, and **William F. Buckley**.

Naples wasn't always this ritzy. The town was first settled in 1876 by two brothers, **John** and **Madison Weeks**. A group of Tallahassee businessmen came south in the 1880s to develop 4,000 acres of real estate here. Meanwhile, a Ft. Myers developer compared the coastal town to Naples, Italy—and the name was born.

Naples began to take off in the early 1900s, when millionaire advertising executive Barron Collier moved here and started laying out the Tamiami Trail, opening Southwest Florida to **Miami** and the world. Even today, the Collier family owns much of the land in Collier County and continues to plan and build developments. In fact, the Collier name can be seen on everything from schools to office buildings.

Naples does boast seven miles of white-sand beaches, with several points of access along **Gulf Shore Boulevard.** So if you like the water, there are dozens of ways to enjoy it—from renting sailboats, Jet Skis, or Windsurfers to chartering fishing boats or just swimming in the ocean.

Area code 941 unless otherwise indicated.

1 Corkscrew Swamp Sanctuary A nearly pristine ecosystem, this 11,000-acre preserve is owned by the National Audubon Society. A two-mile boardwalk trail leads through the cathedral-like setting of primeval tropical trees, including strands of 500-year-old bald cypress. Pools covered with swamp lettuce (a plant similar to the water lily) are interspersed with shallow flowing water. The preserve is home to alligators, turtles, frogs, egrets, and blue herons. Nearly 200 species of birds have been recorded here—the nation's largest population of endangered wood storks nests here from November through March. The best time to see the birds is early in the day—bring cameras and binoculars. ♦ Admission. Daily Dec-Apr from 7AM; daily May-Nov from 8AM. 375 Sanctuary Rd (about 15 miles east of I-75 on Rte 846/Immokalee Hwy). 657.3771

2 Plum's Cafe ★★$$$ Warm, soothing plum tones are the setting for this casual yet upscale cafe. Baked havarti with raspberry sauce is a rich but exquisite starter. Try the grilled beef in pita bread with tomatoes, onions, and gorgonzola cheese for lunch, or the chicken carbonara with linguine, prosciutto, pancetta, garlic, and parmesan cheese for dinner. The Midnight Seduction fudge cake caps a dining experience many describe as memorable. Everything is available for takeout or delivery. ♦ American/Italian ♦ Daily lunch and dinner. 8920 Tamiami Trail N (at Vanderbilt Beach Rd), Vanderbilt Beach. 262.7076, 597.8119 &

2 Villa Pescatore ★★$$$ It may stand along busy Highway 41, but this is no truck stop. Inside, gracious but casual Italian-style dining is comple-mented by a first-class wine list. Among the anti-pasti are escargots, calamari, and grilled Tuscan *bruschetta* (toasted bread). Oak-grilled tilefish or fettuccine with rosemary chicken and pancetta sate even the largest appetites. ♦ Seafood/Italian ♦ Daily dinner. Reser-

---

Restaurants/Clubs: Red   **Hotels:** Blue
Shops/ ♈ Outdoors: Green   **Sights/Culture:** Black

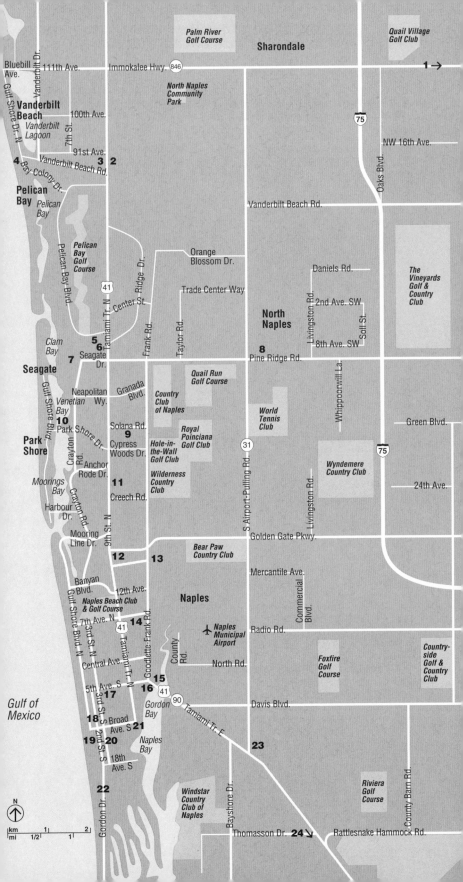

vations recommended. 8920 Tamiami Trail N (at Vanderbilt Beach Rd), Vanderbilt Beach. 597.8119 &

3 China Pavilion ★★$$$ Locals consider this the best Chinese restaurant in town, and for good reason: It's one of the few in Southwest Florida that knows what spicy means. The dark beams and earth tones seem out of place, but it's a soothing change from all that tropical decor. Try the Hunan crispy fish, lobster Cantonese, or walnut shrimp. ♦ Chinese ♦ Daily lunch and dinner. Pavilion Shopping Plaza, 8955 Tamiami Trail N (at Vanderbilt Beach Rd), Vanderbilt Beach. 566.3388 &

4 Ritz-Carlton at Naples $$$$ This world-class resort rises from the coastline like a Mediterranean castle. Even if you can't afford to "put on the Ritz," it's worth a visit to gawk at the chandeliered lobby or partake of high tea. Museum-quality paintings hang in the public spaces, which are graced with antique Persian carpets and 18th-century French tapestries. The 450-plus oversized guest rooms live up to the setting, with elegant appointments that almost make you forget about the fabulous views from the balconies. ♦ 280 Vanderbilt Beach Rd (at N Gulf Shore Dr), Vanderbilt Beach. 598.3300, 800/241.3333; fax 598.6690 &

Within the Ritz-Carlton at Naples:

The Dining Room ★★★★$$$$ The name is mundane, but this restaurant is everything you'd expect from the **Ritz.** With floor-to-ceiling windows and silk wall coverings, the room is opulent, and the food is always inventive and surprising. Typical are such dishes as stone crab tortellini in saffron and fennel sauce, and sautéed smoked sea scallops in black bean and *poblano* (a hot pepper) sauce. Live music is delivered on the ivories of a Steinway. ♦ Nouvelle American ♦ M-Sa dinner. Reservations required; jackets required. 598.3300 ext 6644 &

5 Philharmonic Center for the Arts Since its 1990 opening, the "Phil" has been Florida's west coast home to the **Miami City Ballet** and the **Naples Philharmonic Orchestra.** Christopher Seaman, the well-known English conductor, is the resident director/conductor; Erich Kunzel, of the Cincinnati Philharmonic, fills the chair of principal pops conductor. Their talents, which have impressed both musicians and the lay public, have helped this center achieve international stature. With help from affluent donors, programmers have lured such big names as the **Moscow**

Philharmonic, Wynton Marsalis, the **Alvin Ailey American Dance Theater,** and Itzhak Perlman. A cross between Neo-Gothic and Florida's Cracker style, the building houses seven art galleries in addition to the large performance hall. The center is definitely worthy of attention, even if that means only touring the building. ♦ 5833 Pelican Bay Blvd (at Ridgewood Dr). 597.1111, box office 597.1900; fax 597.8163 &

6 Waterside Shops This upscale shopping center is ideally suited for those seeking the grandest and costliest of merchandise, but window-shoppers can have fun, too. Among the nearly 30 shops are **Saks Fifth Avenue, Talbots, Williams-Sonoma,** and **Jacobson's.** Paddle fans stir the air on broad verandas, while lakes and a stream meander through the center. ♦ Daily. 5415 Tamiami Trail N (at Seagate Dr). 598.1605 &

Within Waterside Shops:

Pelicatessen Fine Foods ★★$$ Whether you need a tasty sandwich or salad to fortify you for the next round of shopping or just want lunch to take out, owner Oliver Kirrane fills the bill with assorted pâtés, smoked salmon platters, *spanakopita,* rumaki hors d'oeuvres, and a variety of desserts. ♦ Deli ♦ Daily lunch. 597.3003; fax 597.3087 &

7 Registry Resort $$$ Sensitive to its ecologically fragile environs, this resort has carefully conserved its natural setting of beach, marshes, and wetlands. But guests at the 475-room hotel go first class. Oak-paneled walls and Italian marble grace the entry hall, and the decor throughout the hotel is low key—comfortable but elegant. Facilities include 27 holes of golf, tennis courts, three swimming pools, and exercise equipment. A boardwalk tram takes visitors through a mangrove jungle to the beach. Three restaurants, ranging from casual to elegant, offer diverse menus. ♦ 475 Seagate Dr (west of Tamiami Trail N). 597.3232, 800/247.9810; fax 597.3147 &

8 Teddy Bear Museum of Naples When Frances Pew Hayes's young grandson gave her a teddy bear for Christmas, she began collecting. Today 3,000 snuggly bears are on display at this unusual museum, where visitors may see antique and limited edition bears, as well as mechanical and audiovisual bear displays of such ursine events as a bear wedding, a teddy bear's picnic, and a life-size "bear-d of directors" meeting. Bear-making classes are offered, and storytelling sessions are occasionally held in the "li-beary." ◆ Admission. M-Sa, Su afternoon Oct-May. 2511 Pine Ridge Rd (at Airport-Pulling Rd). 598.2711; fax 598.9239 ♿

9 Sign of the Vine ★★★$$$$ This small house-turned-restaurant is a gourmet's dream. Antiques, wrought-iron chandeliers, fresh flowers, and flickering candlelight lend charm to each of three rooms and a veranda. The innovative culinary skills of Nancy and Jack Christiansen delight diners, who choose from an ever-changing chalkboard menu. One recent offering was lobster hash with artichokes and scallions in herbed cream, with homemade lemon ice cream for dessert. Meals are accompanied by hors d'oeuvres, relish, salad, French bread, mulled cider sorbet, Ohio tomato pudding, and homemade popovers with tangerine butter. ◆ Eclectic ◆ Reservations recommended. American Express only. M-Sa dinner. 980 Solana Rd (at Tamiami Trail N). 261.6745 ♿

The Village
ON VENETIAN BAY

10 Village on Venetian Bay More than 50 eclectic shops, galleries, and restaurants are clustered here. Stroll past such boutiques as **Wildflower, Terruzzi's,** and **Beth Moné** for men's, women's, and children's clothing. Sip an aperitif at a waterside bistro, or dine at a restaurant overlooking the peaceful bay. ◆ 4200 Gulf Shore Blvd (at Park Shore Dr). 261.0030 ♿

Within the Village on Venetian Bay:

Artichoke & Company ★★$ Margaret and Alexander Neumann run the finest gourmet deli and specialty grocery store in Naples. Each day they prepare as many as 40 fresh salads, such as tabbouleh (a Middle Eastern dish of bulgur wheat, tomato, scallions, and mint). Another favorite is chicken breast salad with pineapple and grapes. Succulent sandwiches on fresh-baked bread are filled with unusual German cold cuts. Eat outdoors, or take out (there are no tables inside). ◆ Deli ◆ Daily breakfast and lunch. 263.6979; fax 263.2136 ♿

Bayside, A Seafood Grill & Bar ★★$$$ The casual waterfront bar downstairs is a pleasant place to sample grilled salmon with wilted lettuce and warm pancetta. Heartier—and pricier—fare is served in the Mediterranean-style restaurant upstairs. Stone crab spring rolls with plum sauce or crisp fried calamari with a spicy Portuguese sauce make good starters. Then try a veal rib chop with wild mushrooms or black sesame seed–encrusted tuna, both oak-grilled—the restaurant's signature cooking technique. ◆ Seafood ◆ Daily lunch and dinner. Reservations recommended. 649.5552 ♿

Maxwell's on the Bay ★★★$$$ For well-prepared fresh seafood and an outstanding view, this restaurant is hard to top. Massive windows open onto a panorama of Venetian Bay. The lunch menu lists baked brie with apples and raspberry sauce, grouper fingers, sandwiches, and salads. Dinnertime favorites are sautéed veal or shrimp in a cream sauce laced with Marsala; New England lobster; and Norwegian salmon. Valet parking is available. ◆ Seafood ◆ M-Sa lunch and dinner; Su brunch. Reservations recommended. 263.1662; fax 263.4421 ♿

Margaux's
COUNTRY FRENCH FARE

11 Margaux's Country French Fare ★★★ $$$ Inviting sidewalk tables mark the location of this cozy French restaurant. Inside, Monet prints and a peach decor set a continental tone. For lunch, order the blue-crab bisque and the seafood crepe. For dinner, start with the bouillabaisse *à la marseillaise* or pâté *de maison* (of the house); favorite entrées include snapper *française* and veal stuffed with lobster and spinach with cognac sauce. ◆ Country French ◆ Daily dinner; M-F lunch. 3080 Tamiami Trail N (at Rosemary La). 434.2773 ♿

Restaurants/Clubs: Red		**Hotels:** Blue
Shops/ ⏆ Outdoors: Green		**Sights/Culture:** Black

Coastland Center

12 Coastland Center This regional shopping center is the most complete in Naples, with **Burdines, Dillard's, J.C. Penney,** and **Sears** anchoring 110 fine specialty stores. A major expansion scheduled for the near future will double its size, adding second floors to the corner department stores. ◆ Daily. 1900 Tamiami Trail N (at Golden Gate Pkwy). 262.7100 &

13 Caribbean Gardens Formerly **Jungle Larry's Zoological Park at Caribbean Gardens,** this botanist's paradise–cum-zoo is crisscrossed by wood chip–covered paths that meander through 52 acres of lush tropical vegetation, including banyan trees, palms, bamboo, and hundreds of blooming plants. You can also visit the park's collection of birds, caged tigers, elephants, and an anteater, as well as a petting zoo with goats and pigs. In most cases, only a chain-link fence keeps the beasts at bay. An animal show permits kids to handle snakes and unusual critters, and boats cruise to Safari Island, whose primary residents are monkeys. ◆ Admission. Daily. 1590 Goodlette-Frank Rd (at Fleischmann Blvd). 262.5409

Conservancy Nature Center Established in 1964, the Conservancy is Southwest Florida's most influential environmental group, but its major role is education. The museum here depicts native Florida birds, fish, and other animals in their natural habitats. Outside, pine-bark trails wind past wildlife rehabilitation units where wounded birds and animals are nursed back to health, most of them to be released eventually. Free boat trips take visitors along a nearby waterway. Picnic tables invite a full day's stay, and there's a gift shop on the grounds. ◆ Admission. M-Sa until 4:30PM; Su afternoon; closed May-October. 1450 Merrihue Dr (off Goodlette-Frank Rd). 262.0304; fax 262.0672 &

14 Bud's Diner ★$ Locals swear by this real 1950s diner with a checkerboard decor and lime green vinyl seats at the bar. The wait staff claims to serve the best burgers in town. "Bud's Killer All-U-Can-Eat Breakfast," the house specialty, is served until 2:30PM. Owner Bill Johnson also runs a catering service called "Fourteen Carrots." ◆ American ◆ Daily breakfast and lunch. 536 Tamiami Trail N (at Fifth Ave N). 261.7333 &

15 Comfort Inn at Naples $$ Central to **Fifth Avenue South** and the **Tin City Waterfront Shops & Restaurants** (see below for both), this affordable hotel overlooking Gordon Bay offers 100 comfortable rooms, with continental breakfast included (there's no restaurant, though). In the lobby, pink and teal cushions top wicker sofas and chairs, setting a casual, tropical mood. The beach is but a mile away. Business needs are accommodated in a small meeting room. ◆ 1221 Fifth Ave S (at Goodlette-Frank Rd). 649.5800; fax 649.0523 &

16 Tin City Waterfront Shops & Restaurants Formerly the **Old Marine Market,** "Tin City" is named for the tin warehouse that contained a clam-shelling and oyster-processing plant in the 1920s. Overlooking the docks of Naples Bay, the area retains a rustic, maritime spirit. Shop for antiques, other collectibles, clothing, and gifts at the 40 interesting boutiques; the three fine eating places offer a choice of indoor, casual boardwalk, or deli dining. The country rockers, church pews, and iron park benches nestled in cozy nooks make for ideal resting spots. In the central atrium is an old wooden water tower that's inscribed "Naples—Population 503." Was Naples ever that small? ◆ M-Sa, Su until 9PM Nov-Apr; until 6PM May-Oct. 1200 Fifth Ave S (at Goodlette-Frank Rd). 262.4200 &

Within Tin City Waterfront Shops & Restaurants:

Merriman's Wharf

Merriman's Wharf ★★★$$$ Located at the pier on Gordon River, this casual spot offers superb food in unstudied comfort. View the boat traffic from a perch at the bar or from a table, imagining days past when this building served as a marina and a clam factory. Fresh seafood—

grouper *en papillote* (cooked in paper), broiled pompano with sliced almonds, native lobster tails, and shrimp fried in beer batter—dominates the menu, and local stone crab claws are served in season (November through May). Angus beef, veal, and chicken are tasty alternatives. ♦ Sea-food ♦ Daily lunch and dinner. Reservations recommended. 261.1811 ♿

17 Fifth Avenue South This eight-block shopping street in the heart of Naples is crammed with reasonably priced shops, as well as restaurants, banks, and brokerage houses. **Pratt's Shoes, Jami's, The Song and Story Book Store,** and **Paul J. Schmitt Jewelers** are just a few of the stores that are sure to appeal to visitors. ♦ Fifth Ave S (between Tamiami Trail N and Second St S)

On Fifth Avenue South:

L'Auberge on fifth
restaurant français

L'Auberge on Fifth ★★★$$$ Now in its 10th year, this small restaurant continues to attract discriminating diners. Its peach decor and array of international art posters give it an intimate feel, just the right ambience in which to enjoy Provençal fare. Choose a bisque of scallops with saffron aioli, fillet of sole, or roasted rack of lamb in *persillade* crust. A kir royale or champagne mimosa are both elegant starters. ♦ French ♦ Daily dinner; M-F lunch Nov-Apr. Reservations required. 602 Fifth Ave S (at Sixth St S). 261.8148 ♿

Mangrove Cafe ★★$$ Florida is the theme of both the cuisine and decor at this cozy and quiet dining establishment. Nibble lightly salted plantain chips and mango chutney while perusing a menu that includes conch and alligator chowder and grilled sword-fish à la Amaral (named after the chef) with black-bean and lemon-pepper sauces. Fresh flowers grace each table, and a few well-chosen Florida prints adorn the walls. ♦ Nouvelle Floridian ♦ M-Sa lunch and dinner. Reservations recommended. 878 Fifth Ave S (between Eighth St S and Ninth St S). 262.7076 ♿

St. George and the Dragon ★★★$$$$ This landmark is one of the finest restaurants in the city. Soothingly lit, its numerous dining rooms and bar are veritable museums of unusual antique marine treasures and local historical memorabilia. Roast ribs of prime beef, tenderloin tips en brochette, and double-cut lamb chops offer variety for the meat lover, while broiled fillet of speckled sea trout, shrimp steamed in lager, and baked lobster tails satisfy the seafood fan. The chef concocts specials daily. For lunch, try an executive club sandwich of turkey, ham, bacon, Swiss cheese, and tomato, or grilled knockwurst with soup and salad. ♦ American ♦ M-Sa lunch and dinner. Reservations recommended; jackets required. 936 Fifth Ave S (between Ninth St S and 10th St S). 262.6546 ♿

15 Inn by the Sea $$ Listed on the National Registry of Historic Places, this bed-and-breakfast built in 1937 is just two blocks from the Gulf of Mexico. The tin-roofed structure is surrounded by a lush tropical garden, and a patio offers a place for quiet reflection. The three guest rooms and two suites, all with floors and ceilings of yellow heart pine, are decorated with antiques. Fine shops, galleries, and gourmet restaurants are an easy stroll to the east. ♦ 287 11th Ave S (at Third St S). 649.4124 ♿

15 Palm Cottage "Marse Henry" Watterson, erstwhile editor of the *Louisville Courier-Journal,* built this charming 12-room home out of a mixture of burned seashells called "tabby mortar" 100 years ago. Designated a National Historic Site, the house is owned and maintained by the Collier County Historical Society. ♦ Admission. M-F 1:30PM-4:30PM Oct-Apr. 137 12th Ave S (at Second St S). 261.8164 ♿

 **Naples Pier** A local landmark, this pier was built in 1888 as a freight and passenger dock. Today it is the local meeting place for fishing, bird watching, and just plain kibitzing. Hurricanes demolished the pier three times (in 1910, 1926, and 1960), but generous donors were always ready to rebuild it. The concession stand and bait shop are open 24 hours. ♦ Daily 24 hours. 12th Ave S (off S Gulf Shore Blvd). 434.4696

20 Third Street and the Avenues Naples's answer to Palm Beach's Worth Avenue features pricey clothing stores, art galleries, and specialty boutiques, such as **Gattle's, The Mole Hole, Patchington,** and **Thalheimer's Fine Jewelers.** A jazz quartet or scaled-down symphony sometimes plays on the red-brick sidewalks. This part of town used to be the hub of Naples's early social and commercial activity. ♦ Third St S (between Broad Ave S and 14th Ave S). 649.6707 ♿

Within Third Street and the Avenues:

Busghetti Ristorante ★★$$ In a shady courtyard just off Third Street South, red-decked tables welcome diners to a Chicago tradition of authentic Italian dishes at affordable prices. Favorites are prosciutto and melon, zucchini parmesan sandwiches, and *busghetti Alfredo* (pasta with Alfredo sauce). Top choices for dinner: scallops with basil and *busghetti di Mama* (pasta with a thick classic red sauce). ♦ Italian ♦ Daily dinner; M-Sa lunch. Reservations recommended. 1181 Third St S (at 12th Ave S). 263.3667 ♿

Chef's Garden ★★★$$$$ Set in a gardenlike atmosphere, this top-notch restaurant grows better each year. An enclosed, air-conditioned porch overlooks a cozy garden, and the inner dining room is elegantly appointed. The sheer number of menu choices is staggering: Try the sautéed veal tenderloin medaillons with wild mushrooms, or pistachio-encrusted snapper. The chef's daily specials promise to tempt even jaded taste buds, and the wine list is excellent. ♦ Nouvelle American ♦ Daily dinner. Reservations required; jackets required. 1300 Third St S (at 13th Ave S). 262.5000 ♿

Truffles ★★$$ This bistro adheres to the same high standards as its downstairs sibling, **Chef's Garden,** but in a more casual setting. The well-rounded menu includes lots of appetizers, fresh pasta, salads, sandwiches, and heartier entrées, plus vegetarian and healthy-for-the-heart choices. The chocolate truffles, lemon chess pie, and Tollhouse pie on display at the entrance will jump-start any appetite, so plan your meal accordingly. ♦ American ♦ Daily lunch and dinner. Reser-vations recommended. 1300 Third St S (at 13th Ave S). 262.5500 ♿

Hilde's Tea Room & Catering ★★$ Tired shoppers revive their spirits at this inviting tea shop, with its ivy-covered walls and yellow tablecloths. Choose from a comforting menu of homemade soups, chicken and shrimp salad sandwiches, and salads. The Harvey Wallbanger cakes are so tender and moist that you'll want to take a whole cake home—and you can. ♦ American ♦ M-F lunch. No credit cards. 336 13th Ave S (at Third St S). 261.7498 ♿

21 Cove Inn Resort & Marina $$$ These 100 spacious rooms, each with a private balcony, treat guests to views of Naples Bay and the many yachts coming and going from the Gulf of Mexico. With a tropical, green-and-burgundy decor, the lobby is cozy and welcoming. Three restaurants offer everything from snacks to elegant dining. Take a fishing expedition, tour the nearby shops, or relax by the pool. ♦ 1191 Eighth St S (between Ninth and Broad Aves S, next to the city docks). 262.7161, 800/255.4365 ♿

21 The Dock at Crayton Cove ★★$$ With its nautical motif, ceiling fans, and vista of the city docks and Naples Bay, this relaxed, friendly spot genuinely evokes old Naples. Come by car or boat to enjoy a wide-ranging menu that includes Bahamian conch fritters, steamed littleneck clams, jalapeño nachos, or mango-grilled salmon. A raw bar is featured daily, and a host of tropical cocktails is offered. ♦ Seafood ♦ Daily lunch and dinner. Reservations recommended. 840B 12th Ave S (at Crayton Cove). 263.4049, 263.9940; fax 261.5074 ♿

22 Gordon Drive Spend a half hour or so admiring the extravagant homes along this street, the residential showplace of Naples. Magnificent houses and gardens appear one after the other, each vying for the title of grandest. English nannies strolling with baby carriages aren't out of place here. The drive ends at Gordon Pass, the city's outlet to the gulf. Here white rows of enclosed wooden boathouses, each with its own entry door and window, extend into the bay, recalling another, more elegant era. ♦ South of the Naples Pier

23 Collier County Government Complex
You could spend a lifetime trying to find another municipal building that rivals the beauty of this Art Deco masterpiece designed by **Windsor-Faricy Architects.** If you look at it long enough, the western side of the structure seems to undulate like a streamer in the wind. Take a walk inside to see the suspended sterling-silver ceiling lamps. ♦ 3301 Tamiami Trail E/Hwy 41 (at Airport Rd)

Within the Collier County Government Complex:

Collier County Museum With support from the Collier County Historical Society, this museum is rapidly expanding. Exhibits chart Florida coastline changes, track the coastal wanderings of the Calusa Indians, and display artifacts of 16th-century Spanish conquistadores. Outside, wander through an open-sided Seminole chikee hut. The newest addition is an orchid house set in a native garden. Under construction at press time were display rooms and lecture halls to be housed in Old Florida–style buildings connected by shady veranda walkways. ♦ Free. M-F. 774.8476 ♿

24 Coral Isle Factory Stores
This outlet complex is young and still growing. Its shops carry current season overruns, discontinued styles, and seconds, as well as merchandise produced specifically for

them. **Capezio, London Fog, Etienne Aigner, Fieldcrest, Jones New York, Polly Flinders,** and **Dansk** are just a few of the stores in the complex. All offer substantial savings on quality goods found in regular stores. ♦ Daily. 1920 Isle of Capri Rd/Rte 951 (at Belle Mead). 775.8083 ♿

Collier County Museum

Bests

Robert Ludlum
Author

In Southwest Florida, specifically the **Naples/Ft. Myers** axis, where we have a home, don't miss the following:

The magnificent **Gulf beaches,** with their incomparable sunsets and the occasional storm (yes, storm). Try a contemplative sundown on the **Naples Pier;** it's wonderful. Browse in the shops and boutiques of **Fifth Avenue South,** the **Village** on **Park Shore,** and the **Waterside Shops** in **Pelican Bay.** You won't find any better in New York or Palm Beach.

There are too many superb restaurants to mention, but at my peril I'll name a few: **Chef's Garden, Bayside, Maxwell's on the Bay, Villa Pescatore,** and just about any Sunday brunch that advertises, especially at the **Registry** and the **Ritz-Carlton** hotels (leave all thoughts of diets and cholesterol in the parking lot).

Rent drive-yourself boats at many of the marinas for leisurely trips throughout the inner waterways —the flora, fauna, and the friendly manatees and dolphins are a delight, but take care not to injure them. Children love these sojourns. Or hire a larger craft with crew for some excellent deep-sea fishing, full or half days, and be prepared to do battle with the likes of 70-pound amberjacks. Food and beverages are usually included, but bring lots of suntan lotion.

Finally, the people. They're courteous, helpful, as protective of privacy as they are of welcoming you into town and social events. It's a great place to live!

Marco Island

Marco Island looks like just another luxury oasis carved out of the wilderness—a densely populated piece of real estate dotted with resorts and upscale homes, with tall hotels and condos lining its curved beach. But first impressions deceive, and the small island is more complex than it seems.

Seafaring Calusa Indians settled here thousands of years ago, harvesting clams and oysters and leaving behind huge mounds of shells. Rum runners and pirates touched these shores, as did pioneer farmers and fishermen. The first person to promote Marco's growth was millionaire advertising executive Barron Collier, who established a railway line in the 1940s to service the clam industry. Though it later failed, two sleepy fish camps, **Old Marco Village** and **Caxambas**, were left at either end of the island. Twenty years later, the Mackle brothers of the Deltona Company—armed with blueprints and dredges—set out to build a luxury community amid the scrub oaks and hills of sand.

Still relatively secluded despite those efforts, Marco is home to one of North America's largest communities of bald eagles, and it is the perfect starting point for a journey into a pair of rich and unusual ecosystems.

Just south of the island in the **Gulf of Mexico** are the **Ten Thousand Islands**, a labyrinthine archipelago of mangroves accessible only by boat. Exploring this watery jungle, you'll see a variety of birds, other animals, and perhaps even a dolphin or bald eagle. Close by, study local flora and fauna at the **Briggs Nature Center** in its 9,000-acre **Rookery Bay National Estuarine Research Reserve.**

Today, man and nature coexist here: Royal terns and snowy egrets share the shore with visitors; dolphins, jack, and mackerel jump at the water's edge; and pelicans and ospreys rest on sandbars. Inland, bald eagles raise their young in the tall pines that shade Marco's luxurious private homes.

Area code 941 unless otherwise indicated.

1 Olde Marco Inn ★★★$$$ Listed on the National Registry of Historic Places, this white plantation-style building evokes the cool, dark feel of an old lodge. A hotel since 1883, it is now an upscale restaurant where Marion Blomeier's ample German fare complements the seafood and beef dishes (all cooked to order) also offered. With its blue and green prints and wicker furniture, the sunroom invites relaxation, while the rococo, red-velvet piano bar is intimate and cozy. Live music and dancing make this one of the brightest nightspots on the island. ♦ Eclectic ♦ Daily dinner. Reservations recommended. 100 Royal Palm St (at Vernon Pl). 394.3131 ♿

2 Café de Marco ★★★$$$ Sandra Scheeler, owner of this cozy French cafe, adds a personal touch to her delicious renditions of seafood and meat dishes. Choose from oysters Rockefeller, escargots with mushrooms, mesquite-grilled swordfish, scallops and shrimp Juliette (in a pesto-cream sauce over linguine), or surf and turf—the best of land and sea. Sporty casual dress is appro-priate. ♦ Seafood/Continental ♦ Daily dinner year-round; daily lunch November-April only. Reservations recommended for dinner. Port of Marco Shopping Village, 244 Royal Palm St (between Bald Eagle Dr and Palm St). 394.6262 ♿

226

KAY'S ON THE BEACH

3 Kay's on the Beach Four display rooms offer stylish resort sportswear, swimwear, and elegant evening attire, plus fashionable accessories to match your choices. ♦ Daily. 1089 Bald Eagle Dr (north of N Barfield Dr). 394.1033 (phone and fax)

4 Jack's Lookout To rent a boat for private fishing or sight-seeing, walk along the bay and choose *Nancy, Weis Guy,* or one of the other craft moored at the dock here. Have a beer at the small bar while waiting to board. ♦ Daily. Corner of Giralda Ct and Bald Eagle Dr. 394.5944 ♿

AND SHIP STORE

4 Factory Bay Marina and Ship Store Right next to **Jack's Lookout** (see above), this marina is located on Factory Bay. Either rent a private boat or join a group tour here. And you'll find plenty of useful nautical gear and light supplies for the day in the **Ship Store.** ♦ Daily. 1079 Bald Eagle Dr (at Giralda Ct). 642.6717 ♿

A hammock (derived from the native Arawak word for "jungle") is a dense hardwood forest. Few are left in South Florida, but at one time their proliferation made the area, especially around Coconut Grove, nearly impenetrable. Early on, many South Florida pioneers recognized the beauty and value of hammocks and took steps to preserve them. One of the finest examples is at Matheson Hammock Park in South Dade.

4 Vito's ★★★$$$ Vito Frazitta's newly decorated restaurant affords spectacular views of the Marco River and Factory Bay. And the food is almost as impressive: Try the fettuc-cine with smoked salmon, light cream, and capers, or *vitello Tosca,* medaillons of veal with lemon. Locals rave about the soft-shell crabs with sour cream and horseradish sauce, and Vito's Italian gelati are legendary. ♦ Italian ♦ Daily lunch and dinner. Reservations recommended. 1079 Bald Eagle Dr (at Giralda Ct). 394.7722 ♿

5 Romancing the Home This charming shop is a treasure hidden among several businesses across from the **Marco Bay Resort.** Owners Sharon Kraft and Marilyn Rotkvich have combined their talents to collect and display unusual, often handmade home accessories, stationery, and other gifts. ♦ M-Sa or by appointment. 994 N Barfield Dr (off Bald Eagle Dr), Unit 36. 642.5300; fax 642.8100 ♿

6 Paul's Shoe Resort For comfortable sandals or dress shoes, this shop sells quality footwear at reasonable prices. Look for Mephisto, Unisa, and Enzo brands. ♦ M-Sa. Pelican Plaza, 705 Bald Eagle Dr (at Chalmer Dr). 394.2621 ♿

7 Island Cafe ★★★$$$ This cafe brims with Old World charm, from its raspberry and burgundy table settings to its continental cuisine. Owners Henri and Thérèse Janneau keep things authentic with French onion soup gratinée, *coquilles St-Jacques provençale,* and grilled sirloin steak in a béarnaise sauce. ♦ French/Continental ♦ W-Su dinner. Reservations recommended. Collier Plaza, 918 N Collier Blvd (west of Bald Eagle Dr). 394.7578 ♿

8 Breakfast Plus ★$$ Cheery morning eye-openers can be found here at any hour, for breakfast is served all day. Besides eggs and bacon, owner Christine Brodeur's chefs excel at making cheese blintzes, eggs Florentine, and fresh bread. For outstanding lunch dishes, try the crab-filled croissants, liverwurst on rye, or any of the homemade soups. ♦ American/German. ♦ Daily breakfast and lunch. No credit cards accepted. Town Center Shopping Plaza, 1035½ N Collier Blvd (at Bald Eagle Dr). 642.6900 ♿

8 My Fair Lady Nancy and Lenny Max run this upscale dress and shoe boutique with both casual and dressy selections, along with accessories. ♦ M-Sa. Town Center Shopping Plaza, 1037½ N Collier Blvd (at Bald Eagle Dr). 642.8441 ♿

8 Crazy Flamingo ★$$ With television, pinball machines, and other diversions, this casual eatery serves a little of everything from everywhere—American hamburgers, Key West conch fritters, Chinese pot stickers, and Italian fried ravioli. The specialties are fresh fish and Galveston raw oysters, shucked to order. ♦ Eclectic ♦ Daily lunch and dinner until 2AM. No credit cards accepted. Town Center Shopping Plaza, 1047½ N Collier Blvd (between Bald Eagle Dr and Elkcam Circle). 642.9000, 642.9600 ♿

8 Prawnbroker Restaurant & Fish Market ★★$$$ The fish market at the front, which is open to the public, hints at the orientation of this fine restaurant. Inside, try the smoked peppered bluefish, crunchy grouper, or deep-fried scallops. Sirloin steak is offered, too. A green-and-wine color scheme complements the fabric wall coverings and window treatments. ♦ Seafood ♦ Daily dinner. Reservations recommended. Town Center Shopping Plaza, 1051 N Collier Blvd (at Elkcam Circle). 394.4800 ♿ Also at: 13451-16 McGregor Blvd (at Cypress Lake Dr), Ft. Myers. 489.2226 ♿

9 Pelican Bend ★★$$ The news is out: Owner Mickey Cooper's newly decorated restaurant has the best grouper sandwiches in town, if not in Southwest Florida. This popular place doesn't take reservations, so get here early. The seafood chowder is a winner, too; at night, nibble on an onion bloomer (a deep-fried appetizer) while waiting for sautéed grouper or the sweet-and-sour fried fish of the day. The peanut butter pie is awesome. Beer and wine are served inside or outside at an Indian chikee hut at the water's edge, where you can view spectacular sunsets. ♦ Seafood ♦ Daily lunch and dinner. 219 Capri Blvd, Isles of Capri (off SR 951, 2 miles north of Marco Island). 394.3452 ♿

BRIGGS NATURE CENTER

9 Briggs Nature Center Deep in the Rookery Bay/Henderson Creek estuary, the trails here lead through subtropical hammocks and mangroves. Walk along a half-mile boardwalk through five different ecosystems to study native plants and wildlife. An interpretive center provides hands-on exhibits, a fish aquarium, and live snakes. The butterfly garden is home to 20 different plant species, grown specifically to attract 27 kinds of butterflies. ♦ Admission to boardwalk only. M-Sa. Shell Island Rd (off SR 951, 4 miles north of Marco Island). 775.8569

10 Favorite Finds If you like to hunt antiques, don't miss this shop overlooking Marco Lake. Two floors are packed with old and new one-of-a-kind items—fine crystal, silver, porcelain, and jewelry. In an upstairs apartment, owner/decorator Diane Chestnut has arranged antique furniture, crockery, and delightful memorabilia in room settings—and it's all for sale. ♦ Tu-Sa. 10 Marco Lake Dr (between Bald Eagle Dr and Front St). 394.0353

Restaurants/Clubs: Red	**Hotels:** Blue
Shops/ ᵀ Outdoors: Green	**Sights/Culture:** Black

11 Alan's Hideaway ★★★$$ The name aptly describes Alan Bogdan's cozy restaurant, where the dining rooms look out on the ivy-covered walls encircling the property. The steak and seafood are first-rate. Try the roast prime rib, mango chicken, or seafood strudel—a combination of shrimp, scallops, and crabmeat baked in phyllo. The desserts are sinful. For entertainment, there's a piano bar. ◆ American ◆ Daily lunch and dinner. Reservations recommended. 23 Front St (between Bald Eagle and Marco Lake Drs). 642.0770 ঙ

12 Tigertail Beach This is one of the few undeveloped spots on Marco. The parking area is carved out of dense clusters of mangroves and sea grapes, and low wooden walkways pass over the habitats of protected flora and fauna en route to the beach. A barrier island accessible by land shelters the swimming area. Pelicans, terns, skimmers, egrets, and other sea birds flock to this bountiful feeding ground. Paddleboats and windsurfing boards are available for rent, and a refreshment kiosk offers light lunch fare. ◆ Free. Western end of Hernando Dr (west of N Collier Blvd)

13 Golden China ★★★$$ Owner Anna Huang oversees this popular place, whose signature dishes are Mandarin duck, Szechuan pork, and Imperial seafood—a combination of crab, scallops, shrimp, and abalone. Pot stickers also are a favorite. Elegant black lacquer tables, ivory statues, and an interior fountain lend an appropriate atmosphere. There's live music in season, and takeout is available. ◆ Chinese ◆ Daily lunch and dinner. Shops of Marco, 1831 San Marco Dr (at S Barfield Dr). 642.6666 ঙ

13 Estate District Don't miss a drive through this area of large, well-kept homes and tropical gardens. At 51 feet above sea level, this is the highest elevation in Southwest Florida. The highest hills, near Indian Hill and Inlet Drives, are shell mounds built by Calusa Indians more than 3,000 years ago. Of the many artifacts that archaeologists have found on Marco, the most famous is the *Marco Cat;* in pristine condition, the carved and painted wooden figure now resides in the Smithsonian Institution. ◆ Bounded by Caxambas and Inlet Drs, and Caxambas Pass and Watson Rd

13 Goodland A drive down Coconut Street in this small village is a lesson in human creativity and adaptability. Goodland's residents have taken mobile homes of all sizes and shapes and crafted houses out of them, overlaying them with wood, metal, and other materials; some are even perched on stilts. There used to be a village on Roberts Bay populated by the people who worked in the local clam factories. With an eye toward developing that area, Barron Collier moved the entire village in the early 1930s from the shores of Roberts Bay to its present site. Still a fishing village, Goodland —with its distinctly rustic character— charms modern-day visitors.

In Goodland:

Little Bar Restaurant ★★$$ Owner Nicolette Bauer satisfies discriminating tastes in this eclectic and casual spot. A 100-year-old mirrored bar sets a relaxing tone, while antique pipe  organ parts separate the bar from the dining areas. The walls of the main dining area are covered with regional antiques and stained-glass windows, and two additional rooms overlook a small bay. For lunch, choose conch chowder, fried calamari, blue-crab balls, or cheesy baked grouper. The dinner menu offers soft-shell crabs, frogs' legs, prime rib, curried empanadas, and Cajun blackened tuna, served rare. Dock space for boaters is available. ◆ Floridian/ Caribbean ◆ Daily lunch and dinner. Reservations recommended. 205 Harbor Dr (at W Goodland Dr), Goodland. 394.5663 ঙ

Stan's Idle Hour ★$ This is where the moneyed Marco crowd and the down-home Goodland folk mingle. The food—grilled fish, hamburgers, and other casual fare—is good, and the country music is addictive. You'll soon be trying the club's trademark dance, the buzzard lope. At the annual Mullet Festival, the best dancers vie for the title of Princess Buzzard Lope, but you can come to watch or practice any Sunday afternoon. ♦ American ♦ Tu-Su lunch and dinner Nov-May. 221 W Goodland Dr, Goodland. 394.3041 ♿

14 Marriott's Marco Island Resort and Golf Club $$$$ The island's most complete resort has 806 rooms and suites and seven restaurants and lounges, ranging in style from swank to simple. The oversized rooms, decorated in bright tropical colors, have balconies overlooking the water. Even if you're staying elsewhere, visit **Quinn's,** a very casual restaurant and lounge on the beach with all-day dining and nightly live entertainment. With parasailing, water-skiing, and shelling to choose from, you'll never run out of things to do on the beach. Or just soak up the sun at one of three outdoor pools. Tennis courts and an 18-hole golf course are nearby. The ballrooms handle large functions with no trouble. ♦ 400 S Collier Blvd (between Maple and Spruce Aves). 394.2511, 800/438.4373; fax 642.2672 ♿

15 Marco Island Hilton Beach Resort $$$ A green dragon is woven into the elegant Oriental rug that greets guests at this pleasant hotel, whose lobby is appointed with Chinese urns and rosewood chairs. Beyond the tall windows lies the emerald Gulf of Mexico. All four penthouses and 185 guest rooms feature private balconies overlooking a tropical pool and the beach. There is an abundance of sports facilities here: Windsurfers, catamarans, fine clay tennis courts, and, nearby, two golf courses keep guests occupied. The hotel's three restaurants offer excellent seafood and steaks. For a nightcap, slip into the cozy **Sandcastle Lounge,** where there's live entertainment. ♦ 560 S Collier Blvd (north of Winterberry Dr). 394.5000, 800/443.4550; fax 394.5251 ♿

16 Konrad's Seafood & Grille Room ★★★ $$$$ With tall windows catching light from east, south, and west, this spacious restaurant serves customers in intimate dining rooms, on the garden patio, or at the counter. The California-inspired cuisine ranges from such light fare as soups, salads, and sandwiches to Alaskan king crab legs, filet mignon, and tender New Zealand lamb chops. Elaborate pastries are made on the premises, and there's a piano lounge. ♦ Californian ♦ M-Sa lunch and dinner. Reservations recommended. Mission de San Marco Plaza, 599 S Collier Blvd (at Winterberry Dr). 642.3332 ♿

17 Radisson Suite Beach Resort $$$ Decked out in bright pink and turquoise, this hotel boasts 250 one- and two-bedroom suites, each with a balcony and well-stocked kitchen (including a microwave oven, dishwasher, toaster, and coffeemaker). The two restaurants dispel thoughts of long hours in the kitchen, however: **Pineapples** offers exceptional seafood, and **Bluebeard's Beach Club and Grill,** overlooking the pool, serves sandwiches and light fare, along with a full selection of bar drinks. Cabanas line the beach, and sailing is popular. It's not a quiet place to stay if you want to relax, but it's great for social butterflies and families. ♦ 600 S Collier Blvd (north of Winterberry Dr). 394.4100, 800/333.3333; fax 394.0419 ♿

18 Bavarian Inn ★★$$ Genuine German food seems out of place in this tropical island setting, but this is the real thing. Here, Bavarian cowbells hang from the ceiling of the cozy wine cellar/bar. Try the Wiener schnitzel or the grilled Bavarian bratwurst and sauerkraut. The prime ribs and steaks are also recommended, as is the seafood. ♦ German/American. ♦ M-Sa dinner; late-night menu until 1:30AM. Reservations recommended. 961 Winterberry Dr (at S Collier Blvd). 394.7233 ♿

The Everglades

With 1.5 million acres of land and water, **Everglades National Park** is the third-largest national park in the continental US (only Death Valley and Yellowstone are larger). Also North America's biggest area of subtropical wilderness, the park is home to both alligators and crocodiles.

The **Everglades** used to cover more than one-quarter of the entire state of Florida, but much of the land was filled in to prevent flooding caused by hurricanes and, most recently, for development purposes (some 600 to 900 people move into Florida daily). What remains is a 200-mile-long, 50-mile-wide, and (on the average) six-inch-deep "river of grass." The water flows from the **Kissimmee River Valley** near **Orlando** into **Lake Okeechobee**, and on through the marshlike swamp to **Florida Bay** and the ocean. The procession is barely noticeable; it takes the water more than a year to make the slow journey.

The **Everglades** contains tree islands, mangroves, coastal prairies, and subtropical hammocks, ecosystems that are home to about 400 species of birds, dozens of reptiles, more than 20 types of native mammals, and 14 endangered species—including the Florida panther, the leatherback turtle, and the West Indian manatee.

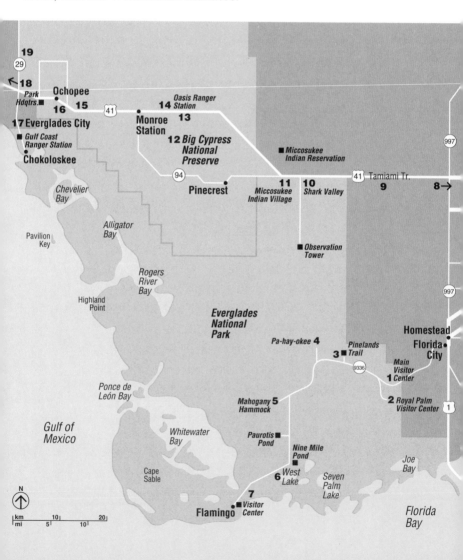

An enormous variety of flora also thrives in the **Everglades**. Pines and palmettos grow in the park's dry uplands, and nowhere else in the US can you find these temperate plants alongside such a rich selection of orchids and tropical trees. Air plants, such as Spanish moss and other bromeliads, are especially striking. If you're lucky, you can even spot the cowhorn, an orchid that weighs as much as 75 pounds, though it is increasingly rare because of plant poachers.

In addition to the continuous flow of water, the **Everglades**'s unique habitat is a result of the weather. The area has many attributes of both tropical and temperate climates, and there are only two seasons here: the warm-wet period, from May through November; and the cool-dry season, from December through April. Most visitors prefer the cool-dry period, with its more comfortable humidity and temperature levels. This is also the best time for viewing wildlife: Partly because of low water levels, the animals are forced out from the backcountry to seek water. You'll see alligators and migratory fowl, though avid bird-watchers may want to brave the summer's humidity to study the rich variety of birds congregating here—from snowy egrets and great blue herons to ospreys.

But be forewarned: Summer also fosters some of the most ferocious mosquitoes on earth. During the rainy season, they breed in abundance in the freshly filled water holes; 43 species have been identified in the park, and on warm humid afternoons and evenings when the air is still, all of them are out for blood. (Visitors who come without insect repellent can purchase it at the marina store in **Flamingo**.)

The western section of **Everglades National Park**, including the **Ten Thousand Islands**, is accessible from **Naples** via the **Tamiami Trail (Hwy 41)**. From **Miami**, you can enter the park by taking **Highway 1** to **State Route 9336**, or by heading west on Southwest Eighth Street/Highway 41. From the Tamiami Trail, visitors may enter the park at several points, from **Shark Valley** on the northeastern boundary to **Everglades City** on the west. Once inside the park you can stroll on boardwalks that provide a panoramic overview of the **Everglades**, or you can venture onto one of the park's trails on foot or by bicycle or canoe. Perhaps one of the best ways to appreciate the subtle diversity of the park is by paddling a canoe under canopies of trees toward sparkling, smooth **Florida Bay** or cacti-dotted **Pavilion Key**, where bottlenose dolphins might ride alongside you. You may still see signs of 1992's Hurricane Andrew, which snapped miles of pine trees and demolished the **Main Visitor Center** (a new one is under construction). Pick up maps at any of the ranger stations. For more information, call the park at 305/242.7700. Accommodations are scarce in the park, so check the **Homestead**-area listings or the hotels listed below.

Area code 305 unless otherwise indicated.

1 Main Visitor Center The main entrance to Everglades National Park is eight miles from Florida City and 11 miles from Homestead. Operated by park employees, the center offers informative audiovisual presentations on Everglades life cycles and information on everything from the area's history to finding the best bird-watching locations. The current center is housed in a trailer while a new building is under construction. ◆ Daily. Hwy 9336 (west of Hwy 1). 242.7700

2 Royal Palm Visitor Center Here is the starting point for the **Anhinga Trail,** one of the best vantage points for viewing wildlife in the Everglades. It is named for the anhinga, a fresh-water bird sometimes called a water turkey or snakebird because of its long, sinuous neck. The half-mile boardwalk trail—which allows visitors to see alligators in their natural habitat—leads to a freshwater slough, a wide, shallow river that slowly flows through the sawgrass. The **Gumbo-Limbo Trail** starts here, too, offering another perspective on Everglades geography. The lush vegetation changes dramatically at slightly higher elevations, with tropical hardwood trees such as gumbo-limbo mixing with oak and sumac

to create dense canopies of shady vegetation.
♦ Daily. Milepost 4. 242.7700 ♿

3 Pinelands Trail This three-quarter-mile trail through open pine forest reveals another habitat, this one created by fire. The **National Park Service** uses controlled fires to prevent overgrowth of competing vegetation, thus maintaining a natural life cycle in the pine forest and sawgrass prairie. The pine forest is a haven for animals that you won't see elsewhere in the **Everglades**—raccoon, reef geckos, and the five-lined skink, a small lizard. ♦ Milepost 7

4 Pa-hay-okee Along the park's main road, this stop got its name from the Indian word for the **Everglades,** which means "grassy waters." The short boardwalk here commands a panoramic view of the wide, grassy prairie. ♦ Milepost 13

5 Mahogany Hammock A boardwalk leads through this lush tree island, the best-known hammock in the park. By 1947, when the **Everglades** was established as a national park, logging had reduced severely the large population of these trees. What remains of them today is a dense, junglelike growth containing the tallest specimens of mahogany in the US. ♦ Milepost 20

6 West Lake One of the world's most prolific habitats can be found here, where salt water from tidal estuaries mixes with the fresh water of the **Everglades**. These conditions have created a dense wilderness of mangrove trees, whose spidery roots fill the water for hundreds of square miles and serve as a hatching ground for many marine mammals, including shrimp, tarpon, and 'coon oysters. The mangrove leaves and stems that fall into the water provide microscopic animals with nutrients; these minute critters in turn become snacks for larger animals in the food chain. A boardwalk takes visitors over the damp mangrove forest. ♦ Milepost 31

7 Flamingo Lodge Marina and Outpost Resort $ The park has only one lodge, restaurant, gas station, and grocery store, and they're all in Flamingo, at the tip of the Florida Peninsula, 38 miles from the park's main entrance. In fact, the lodge and outbuildings constitute practically the entire village of Flamingo. In addition to a 102-room motel, the compound offers 24 well-maintained cottages and suites with kitchens. Warning: Bring insect repellent, particularly in the summer, as some mosquitoes may lurk in the rooms. ♦ 253.2241, 695.3101 ♿

Within Flamingo Lodge Marina and Outpost Resort:

Flamingo Restaurant ★★$$ The highlight here is the breathtaking view of Florida Bay. The food is straightforward and well prepared: steaks and seafood, with a few Caribbean dishes thrown in for good measure. Customers can have their own catch of the day prepared for dinner. ♦ American ♦ Daily breakfast, lunch, and dinner. Reservations recommended. 253.2241 ♿

THE PIT BAR-B-Q

8 Pit Bar-B-Q ★★$ You can smell the wood smoke before you even see this small hut, with its tiny dining room and outdoor picnic area. The food is simple, down-home, and as good as barbecue gets. Try the chicken, meaty ribs, or, for those who don't like barbecue sauce, fried catfish or frogs' legs. The beans and coleslaw are good, too, but skip the fancy prefab desserts. ♦ American ♦ Daily lunch and dinner. 16400 SW Eighth St (at SW 164th Ave), about a mile east of the intersection of Hwy 997 and the Tamiami Trail. 226.2272 ♿

9 Coopertown With its population of six, calling this area a "town" may be stretching things, but there certainly is a spirit of community here. John Cooper built Coopertown in 1945, and it's been a family operation ever since. Cousin Sally Kennon, the gregarious cook at the **Coopertown Restaurant** (see below), oversees things these days. She also runs the oldest concession for airboat rides on Tamiami Trail (see below). The Coopertown Bridge has been a popular landmark since 1976, when town residents fought to prevent its demolition by the Army Corps of Engineers (who wanted to widen the canal under it). One resident went so far as to sit on the bridge for 10 days and nights to protest its destruction. ♦ Tamiami Trail (Hwy 41), 15 miles west of Rte 826

For every wading bird you see in the Everglades in the 1990s, multiply by 10; that's how many your grandparents would have seen. The bird population has been decimated by development, pollution, loss of habitat, and—
in the early 1900s—so-called plume hunters, who slaughtered thousands of birds to supply decoration for women's hats.

Restaurants/Clubs: Red   **Hotels:** Blue

Shops/ ♿ Outdoors: Green   **Sights/Culture:** Black

In Coopertown:

Coopertown Airboat Rides These exceptional tours offered by Sally and Jessie Kennon venture four miles into the **Everglades** across sawgrass prairies and hardwood hammocks, where waterfowl and alligators are visible. Some conservationists consider the 30-minute rides environmentally destructive; others feel that their informative narrative fosters an understanding of the fragility of this ecosystem, thus encouraging visitors to treat the park and its wildlife with care.
◆ Fee. Daily until dusk.
Tamiami Trail. 226.6048 &

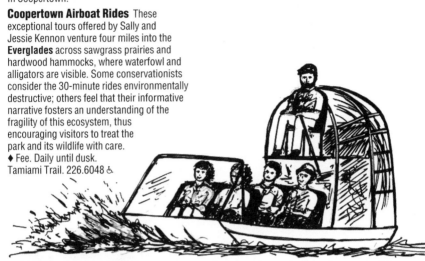

Resident Reptiles

The **Everglades** is the only place on earth where alligators and crocodiles coexist. And contrary to popular belief, the two are very different. Alligators are generally found in brackish and freshwater areas, where they feed on fish, turtles, and birds. The less common crocodile, harder to spot because of its shy nature, usually inhabits saltwater marshes and mangroves, though it has been known to venture out into **Florida Bay.** Crocodiles are sleeker and more dangerous than gators. The alligator is darker colored and has a broader head; its teeth are mostly covered when its mouth is closed, while some of the crocodile's teeth are always exposed. Both reptiles lay several dozen eggs at a time, which hatch with the help of the sun's heat.

Alligator

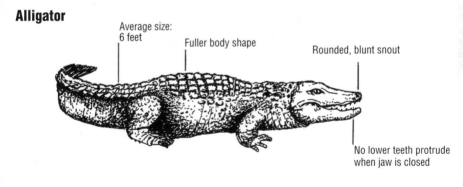

Average size: 6 feet

Fuller body shape

Rounded, blunt snout

No lower teeth protrude when jaw is closed

Crocodile

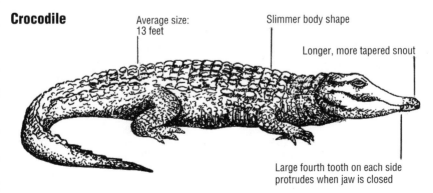

Average size: 13 feet

Slimmer body shape

Longer, more tapered snout

Large fourth tooth on each side protrudes when jaw is closed

Coopertown Restaurant ★★$$ The seemingly ubiquitous Sally Kennon, who does double duty here as the owner and the chef, offers good, basic fare. Eggs and hotcakes make up the bulk of breakfast, while burgers and grilled cheese sandwiches are the stars at lunch. Dinner includes fresh, perfectly cooked frogs' legs (her métier), various preparations of alligator tail, shrimp, catfish, and steak. ♦ American ♦ Daily breakfast, lunch, and early dinner. Tamiami Trail. 226.6048 ♿

10 Shark Valley This trail plunges about eight miles into the park. A tram covers the 15-mile loop in two hours (fee; reservations recommended; 221.8455). Cyclists (bike rentals are available at the visitor centers' in the park) can make it in three hours at a leisurely pace, with time out for a picnic at the **Observation Tower** located halfway down the trail. The route covers an important part of the park's sawgrass region, with plenty of opportunities en route to see alligators, waterfowl, and such flora as gumbo-limbo trees and willows. Educational plaques dot the trail. ♦ Daily. Tamiami Trail, 25 miles west of Rte 826. 221.8776

11 Miccosukee Indian Village

The Miccosukee, some of Florida's earliest settlers, were not officially recognized as a tribe until 1962. Also called Trail Indians, they are descendants of those who escaped the US government's efforts to round up the state's Native Americans and ship them west, as required by the 1830 Removal Act. The Miccosukee tell their story in this unabashedly tourist-oriented attraction, which includes a museum, a nature walk, and even alligator-wrestling demonstrations. Like almost everyone who lives in the **Everglades,** the Miccosukee run an airboat business. Their half-hour rides are worth a trip to the village; you'll cruise through the sawgrass trying to spot gators and birds. ♦ Admission. Daily. Tamiami Trail, 30 miles west of Rte 826. 223.8380 ♿

Within the Miccosukee Indian Village:

Miccosukee Restaurant ★$$ The atmosphere here is standard highway diner, but the menu offers more than the usual fish and fowl. Local specialties include **Everglades** catfish and frogs' legs, plus Indian tacos (fry bread smeared with a spicy meat spread and topped with lettuce, tomatoes, and so on) and burgers on fry bread. The rest of the village may be commercial, but this restaurant is sincere, and the food is quite good. ♦ Native American ♦ Daily breakfast and lunch. 223.8388 ♿

12 Big Cypress National Preserve This entire preserve, 2,400 square miles of subtropical swampland and centuries-old cypress trees, is a favorite with bird-watchers, other naturalists, and photographers. A half-mile boardwalk over the swamp allows visitors to view the fauna, including bobcats and, if you're lucky, Florida panthers. The easiest way to venture farther into the preserve is to prearrange an excursion by airboat, motorboat, or four-wheel-drive vehicle. You can then go anywhere, either in the preserve or the park itself, as do scientists, teachers, and folks filming educational videos. More adventur-ous visitors hike into the preserve; there are few trails and no facilities, but it's a wonderful oppor-tunity to take a self-guided tour of this ecosystem. ♦ Fee for tours. Daily. Everglades Institute, Loop Rd, Ochopee, FL 33943. 695.3143

13 Big Cypress Gallery Sometimes called the Ansel Adams of the **Everglades,** the burly, bespectacled, and bearded Clyde Butcher is a much-sought-after photo chronicler of Florida's wild side. Now that you've seen the **Everglades** and swampy **Big Cypress** in person, take home some huge black-and-white photographs and prints, as well as T-shirts, canvas bags, cards, and other artworks by Butcher. In an adjoining room, take a look at the artwork created by Butcher's wife, Niki: photos of beaches and more citified scenes, done in a matte finish and hand-painted in Art Deco colors. Then step out the back door of this little gallery for a four-minute stroll on a nature trail. ♦ Daily. 52388 Tamiami Trail, Ochopee, about 22 miles east of Rte 29. 695.2428 ♿

14 Oasis Ranger Station For a quick overview of **Big Cypress National Preserve,** watch the superb 15-minute audiovisual presentation offered here. Also pick up brochures and maps of hiking trails. ♦ Daily. Tamiami Trail, about 20 miles east of Rte 29. 695.4111 ♿

15 Ochopee Post Office This is the smallest—and most photographed—post office in North America. The tiny frame building with an American flag and blue box out front is often obscured from view by tour buses. ♦ Tamiami Trail, Ochopee, 3 miles east of Rte 29. 695.4131 ♿

BILL & ED'S
EXCELLENT
AIRBOAT ADVENTURES

16 Bill & Ed's Excellent Airboat Adventures Lots of folks offer airboat rides in wild southwest Florida, but this outfit also takes you on bird-watching trips, two-hour sunset tours, personalized one- to six-hour tours—and nocturnal frogging trips. Professional froggers, who wear miner-style helmets that project beams of light, can snag

Gator Holes

Despite its reputation for viciousness, the alligator is vital to the **Everglades.** During the wet season, the beast burrows with its snout and feet to create holes that store water during the dry season. These holes also serve as shelters for many other animals, such as turtles, fish, and snails, which use them to escape droughts. The alligator's hole-digging process also prevents the overgrowth of plants that could harm fish. The migrating birds and mammals that come to eat and drink at the seasonal oasis created by an alligator hole sometimes become food for the alligator.

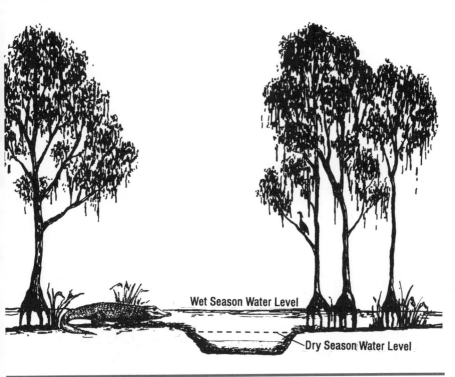

Wet Season Water Level

Dry Season Water Level

hundreds of the amphibians in one night. ♦ Fee. Daily. Call for reservations. Dona Dr (south of Tamiami Trail), Ochopee. 695.4959, 800/838.4959 ♿

17 Eden of the Everglades The biggest draw at this private concession on the edge of the park is the **Swamp Zoo,** with its many alligators. From here, you can hop on the *Jungle Queen* tour boat, which carries 30 to 40 passengers into the park for a good look at wildlife in its natural habitat, or take a 30-minute airboat ride. ♦ Admission. Daily. Rte 29, 2 miles south of Hwy 41, Everglades City. 695.2800

17 Captain's Table Resort $ This large resort—with a main lodge and outlying villas, some with decks—defines no-frills backwoods luxury. The 16 rooms are spacious, neat, and air-conditioned. Boat tours of the Ten Thousand Islands are available, as are launches to the nearest beaches. Its **Captain's Table** restaurant has a dark, super-air-conditioned

interior and also offers outdoor patio dining; the best bets here are hearty conch chowder and stone crab claws. ♦ Rte 29, Everglades City. 695.4211, 800/741.6430 ♿

17 Oyster House ★$$ What is appealingly different here is the newsprint menu, which features trivia items, anecdotes, and some whimsical house rules. The standard seafood entrées are augmented by alligator, blue crab claws, and frogs' legs; the decor is rustic diner. ♦ American ♦ Daily lunch and dinner. Rte 29, Everglades City. 695.2073 ♿

17 Gulf Coast Ranger Station At the west entrance to **Everglades National Park,** in Everglades City, you can pick up park information and camping permits without paying an entrance fee. But this side of the park is much less accessible than the east side, unless you're touring by boat. From this ranger station down the southwest coast to Flamingo at the tip of the Florida Peninsula, the coastline is dotted with small islands and keys, collectively called the Ten Thousand Islands. One of the best ways to experience this side of the **Everglades** is through the park's own boat tours (695.2591), some of which stop on various keys. Private charters venturing into the Ten Thousand Islands area include **Island Charters** (Chokoloskee Island; 695.2286); **Capt. Max** (Everglades City; 695.2420); and **Everglades National Boat Tours** (695.2591). ◆ Rte 29, Everglades City. 695.3311 ♿

RESTAURANT

17 Oar House $$ A sign next to the front door of this rustic diner reads: "Welcome fishermen and other liars." The Daffin family serves a lot of seafood here, but there's much more—from peanut butter and jelly sandwiches to T-bone steaks. The most unusual dish is the house platter of turtle, frog, and alligator. Order the eggs and grits for breakfast. American ◆ Daily breakfast, lunch, and dinner. 305 N Collier Ave (south of Tamiami Trail), Everglades City. 695.3535 ♿

17 Ivey House $ More than just a place to sleep, this single-story bed-and-breakfast offers adventure as well. Rent a canoe, a kayak, a bike, a cooler, and other equipment, or join daily guided tours: The Turner River canoe trip is offered Mondays, for instance, and the "Swamp Stomp" hike is Tuesdays. The 10 sparsely furnished, air-conditioned rooms bring to mind a college dorm; the six bathrooms are down the hall. The inn's TV is in the communal living room, as is the Trivial Pursuit game. There's a restaurant on the premises. ◆ Nov-Apr. 107 Camellia St (west of Rte 29 and south of Tamiami Trail), Everglades City. 695.3299 ♿

Restaurants/Clubs: Red   **Hotels:** Blue
Shops/ ⚘ Outdoors: Green   **Sights/Culture:** Black

17 Rod and Gun Club $ Once a private club that hosted presidents and dignitaries, this historic find is the best place around for dinner on a waterfront veranda (you can sleep at the inn and hire a fishing guide, too). The original structure was built by the founder of Everglades City, W.S. Allen, and a subsequent owner enlarged it to accommodate increasing numbers of hunters, fishermen, and yachting parties. A stuffed black bear stands on all fours atop the rustic lobby phone booth, one of several animal trophies decorating the pecky cypress–paneled first floor. Play piano or billiards next to an expansive fireplace. Among the restaurant's straightforward entrées are the popular broiled frogs' legs and lightly broiled pompano. ◆ Daily lunch and dinner. No credit cards accepted. ◆ 200 Riverside Dr (at Broadway south of Tamiami Trail), Everglades City. 695.2101 ♿

17 Wilderness Waterway Serious canoeists prefer plying the waters of western (not eastern) **Everglades National Park,** and the 99-mile Wilderness Waterway trip from Everglades City southeast to Flamingo is a legendary, well-marked trail that takes about a week by canoe (and about a day by motorized craft). It's the kind of thing some people hope to do before they die, but it takes some planning. Reserve a canoe through **North American Canoe Tours** (695.3299 or 695.4666) and request a *Back Country Trip Planner* from **Everglades National Park** (695.3311) to help you map out a few different routes—in case one turns out to be unfeasible. You'll camp along the way on raised platforms or at primitive spots with no running water and with names like **Lostman's Five Bay** and **Camp Lonesome.** Your trip can start at Turner River, Chokoloskee, or **Glades Haven** deli/store in Everglades City; they all end near the **Flamingo Visitor Center.** Bring raccoon-proof water containers; coons are notorious for biting through store-bought gallon jugs (ask rangers for advice).

HISTORIC
SMALLWOOD STORE
Ole Indian Trading Post

17 Smallwood Store
Sip a Coca-Cola from the circa 1945 Coke machine while wandering through this former store/post office/Indian trading post, in its current

incarnation a museum/gift shop. More than 90 percent of what you see was here when mustachioed pioneer Ted Smallwood traded with early settlers and Seminole Indians. It was behind this small, second-floor store (raised on pilings) that fabled outlaw Ed Watson was shot dead in 1910 by residents who, on edge after a hurricane, feared Watson would kill again. Notice the "hoopskirt" counters: The cabinets slant inward as they approach floor level so women pressing against the counter wouldn't raise their hoopskirts and reveal their lower legs. There are picnic tables outside, and the gift shop stocks books and Indian crafts.
♦ Daily Dec-Apr; M-Tu, F-Su May-Nov. Southern end of Mamie St (south of Chokoloskee Dr), Chokoloskee. 695.2989; fax 695.4454 ♿

Port of the Islands
Resort & Marina

18 Port of the Islands $ For relative luxury on the edge of the wild **Everglades,** this 500-acre, 177-room resort aims to please, with fine dining in the garden court, live nightly entertainment in the bar, heated swimming pools, a private airstrip, and trap and skeet shooting. Amenities include six tennis courts, a fitness center, croquet, volleyball and badminton courts, bicycle rentals, a waterside chikee-hut bar and grill, cable TV, children's board games, and a complete marina with boat rentals and charters. If you want nature, there's a hiking trail, a two-hour narrated boat cruise, and neighboring state parks and preserves. This place is ideal for nature lovers who want the best of both worlds: Get a good night's sleep, then start your wilderness adventure in nearby **Fakahatchee Strand State Preserve** (see below) or the Ten Thousand Islands. ♦ 25000 Hwy 41/Tamiami Trail, 20 miles southeast of Naples. 394.3101, 237.4173 ♿

18 Collier-Seminole State Park Many of the state parks here document what Florida once looked like, and this one is a good example. Threatened or endangered animals living here—and rarely seen—include Florida black bears, panthers, and crocodiles. Manatees, brown pelicans, alligators, and bald eagles are more common. Try to spot them while camping, canoeing, taking a boat tour, fishing, or hiking along the 6.5-mile nature trail. A boat ramp and basin are available in this 6,423-acre park (which provides access to the gulf).
♦ Hwy 41/Tamiami Trail, 17 miles southeast of Naples. 394.3397

19 Fakahatchee Strand State Preserve Look toward the horizon to see how the finger-like forests stand out in contrast to the flat, open terrain. This tall, dense swamp forest is home to the largest concentration and variety of epiphytic orchids in North America, not to mention the largest stand of native royal palms. Strands (elongated swamps) were formed when water cut channels into the limestone, allowing forests to sprout out of the resultant deep organic soils. One boardwalk leads to a pristine cypress strand. There's also a beautifully scenic boardwalk on Tamiami Trail, just east of Route 29. ♦ James Memorial Scenic Dr (at Rte 29). 695.4593

Bests

Robert Joffee
Political Analyst/Director of the Mason-Dixon Florida Poll

Molina's Ranch Restaurant, Hialeah—a working-class Cuban family restaurant with sublime food and 1950s prices. Try *chicharrones de pollo* (fried chicken chunks), *laconcito* (braised lamb shank), or *rabo encendido* (braised oxtail).

Osteria del Teatro, Miami Beach—great eats, high prices, lots of beautiful women, and Dino, Miami's most charming maître d'.

Lincoln Road Mall, Miami Beach—first-class people watching (spiffy retirees, ostentatious dog walkers, jogging fashion models, and Japanese tourists). Along this stretch are also the studios of Edward Villella's **Miami City Ballet** (you can look in the window and watch), the concert hall for Michael Tilson Thomas's **New World Symphony Orchestra,** legit theaters, an art-movie house, trendy galleries, and okay outdoor cafes. Go at night.

Parrot Jungle and Gardens—maybe the most beautiful man-made site in Miami, with performing, caged, and free-roaming birds in a 1920s tropical garden.

Watson Island—This man-made island, opposite downtown Miami, has breathtaking views of the city and of massive cruise ships entering and leaving **Government Cut** (the **Port of Miami**). You can catch **Chalk's** seaplanes to the Bahamas here.

Florida Keys

Gulf of Mexico

Big Torch Key

Middle Torch Key

Summer-land Key

Big Pine Key

Cudjoe Key

Bahia Honda Key

Seven Mile Brid...

14 **13** Pigeo Key

17

19

Perky

MILE MARKER 25

Ramrod Key

18

16

15 Bahia Honda State Park

Pirates Cove

Little Torch Key

Sugarloaf Key

El Chico

Boca Chica Key

Key West

Key West International Airport

With their rich natural beauty, unique coral reefs, and coastlines teeming with more than 500 varieties of fish, the Florida Keys are a popular destination for South Florida residents and visitors alike. This is the place to cast a line into the deep blue waters of the **Gulf Stream**, snorkel with barracuda and angelfish, or paddle an ocean kayak among the deserted mangrove islands. The informal, sports-oriented Keys are a long way from cosmopolitan elegance, but once you slip into shorts and flip-flops, you'll be so laid-back you won't care.

This string of hundreds of islands curves 150 miles from southern **Dade County** to **Key West**, once one of the most important ports in Florida. They were first charted in 1512 by Spanish explorer **Ponce de León**, who named them **Los Martires (The Martyrs)** because, from a distance, the islands looked like twisted and tortured men. Indeed, many men *did* suffer near the Keys, which were notorious for causing shipwrecks and harboring pirates who plundered the Spanish galleons ferrying gold from Central America to Spain.

Isolated by water, the Keys were forever changed when Henry Flagler extended his **Florida East Coast Railroad** from **Homestead** to Key West. Dubbed "Flagler's Folly," the project eventually reached Key West by linking

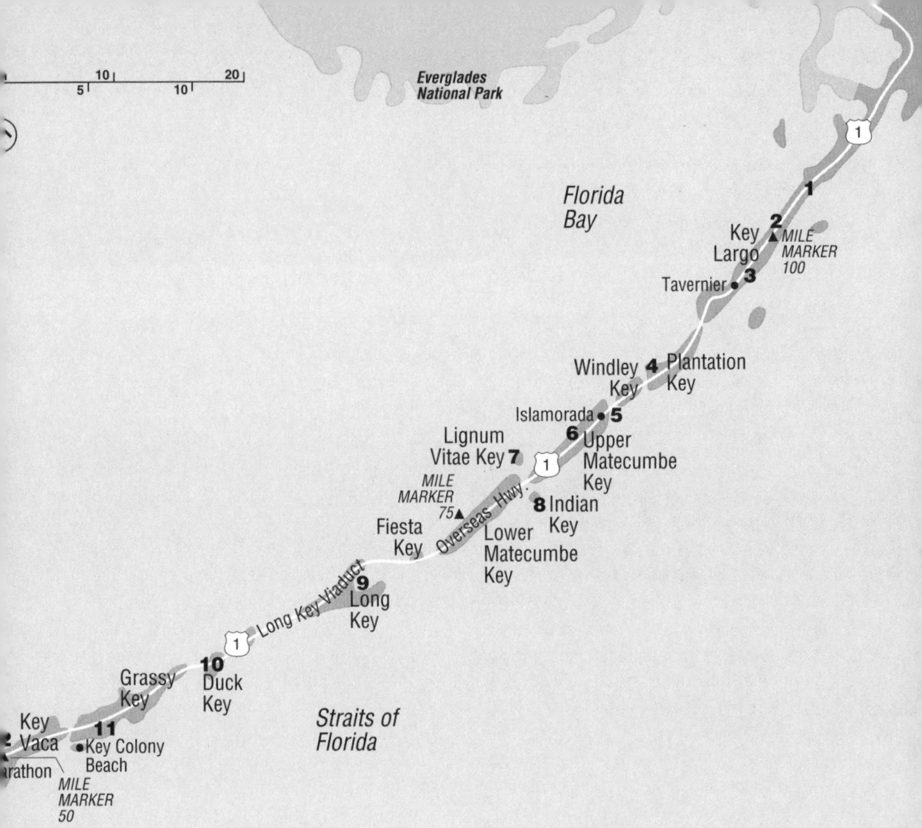

Map

Scale: 10 20 / 5 10

Everglades National Park

Florida Bay

Key Largo **1**

2 MILE MARKER 100

Tavernier **3**

Windley Key **4** Plantation Key

Islamorada **5**

6 Upper Matecumbe Key

Lignum Vitae Key **7**

MILE MARKER 75▲

Overseas Hwy.

8 Indian Key

Lower Matecumbe Key

Fiesta Key

Long Key Viaduct

9 Long Key

Grassy Key

10 Duck Key

Straits of Florida

Key Vaca

11 Key Colony Beach

Marathon

MILE MARKER 50

---

29 islands, and it provided ferry service to Havana. Yet, despite the engineering miracle of bridging so many islands, the railroad failed: A hurricane wiped out the line in 1935, leaving many Keys inhabitants with links to the mainland that were tenuous at best. In 1938 the State of Florida picked up where Flagler left off by constructing the **Overseas Highway**, which continued **US 1** south across 113 miles of road and over 37 bridges. It's one of the world's most spectacular drives, with the **Atlantic Ocean** on one side and the **Gulf of Mexico** on the other.

The uppermost island is **Key Largo**. After that, the islands are usually referred to in three groups: the **Upper Keys**, from **Islamorada** to **Long Key**; the **Middle Keys**, from **Duck Key** to **Bahia Honda Key** and including **Marathon**; and the **Lower Keys**, stretching from **Big Pine Key** to the outskirts of **Key West**. No matter in which group of the Keys you find yourself, however, you can always count on excellent food—particularly fresh fish, available everywhere—and the inimitable Key lime pie. Accommodations range from mom-and-pop motels, some with kitchenettes, to luxury resorts that boast every amenity.

Area code 305 unless otherwise indicated.

Key Largo

The first and largest of the Florida Keys, Key Largo is 42 miles south-southwest of Miami. First discovered in the 1500s by Spanish explorers, Key Largo was overlooked until a few settlers arrived in the late 1800s and the Miami–Key West railroad was completed in 1912.

Key Largo's main attraction is its underwater preserves: **John Pennekamp Coral Reef State Park** and the adjacent **Key Largo National Marine Sanctuary,** home to 500 species of fish and 55 varieties of living coral in a 188-square-mile area. Getting out on the water to see this spectacular marine life is easy; in Key Largo, it seems there's a dive shop every few yards along **US 1** offering snorkeling tours, scuba trips, and glass-bottom-boat excursions.

Key Largo also has an abundance of family-owned hotels, several upscale resorts, campgrounds, and apartments rented by the week. Restaurants are plentiful, and most menus focus on local seafood.

Because Key Largo is so close to Miami, the island can be crowded on weekends. Traffic is heaviest Friday nights and Sunday afternoons, so try to avoid traveling then.

You can take two routes to Key Largo. Following **US 1** straight out of Homestead is the shortest and quickest way, except when there's heavy traffic. Less direct is **Card Sound Road,** which connects to the island via a toll bridge.

1 **Chamber of Commerce Florida Keys Visitors Center** This center has plenty of brochures, pictures of hotels and motels, and telephones, so you can easily make reservations on the premises. Nearly half the people who stop here are bound for Key West. ♦ Daily. MM 106, Key Largo (bayside). 451.1414, 800/822.1088 ♿

1 **Italian Fisherman** ★$$$ Perched high on stilts, this spot has a large deck that offers an impressive view of the sunset over the water. That's not to say the food isn't an attraction as well. A kitschy but now legendary statue out front says it all: The plaster fisherman (who resembles a New England whaler) is a symbol of fine seafood served with Sicilian warmth and flair. Among the most popular dishes are the pastas accompanied by a variety of seafood. ♦ Italian ♦ Daily lunch and dinner. MM 104, Key Largo (bayside). 451.3726 ♿

Restaurants/Clubs: Red   Hotels: Blue
Shops/🍴 Outdoors: Green   Sights/Culture: Black

JULES' UNDERSEA LODGE

1 **Jules' Undersea Lodge** $$$$ This is about as exclusive and isolated as hotels around here get. The name pays tribute to author Jules Verne and his dream of living in the ocean; in fact, that's what guests do at this unique hostelry, the world's only underwater hotel. Located 30 feet under the sea and adjacent to **Pennekamp Park** (see below), the lodge offers numerous safeguards (good lighting, lots of windows) to calm the inevitable fears about claustrophobia in so small an environment. It can accommodate up to six people in two bedrooms and a large living room/dining area with a small kitchen. The big attraction is the ring of windows encircling the habitat, placing the "aquanaut" directly in the marine environment; a number of new dive programs put scuba divers directly into the water. Children under 12 are not allowed. ♦ MM 103.4 (at Transylvania Ave), Key Largo (oceanside). 451.2353 ♿

2 **John Pennekamp Coral Reef State Park** This park is named for a *Miami Herald* editor who was active for 40 years in efforts to set aside parkland in the state. Just under the surface of the Atlantic, it extends 21 miles along the coastline, with 178 square miles of coral reef for scuba divers, snorkelers, and glass-bottom-boat passengers to explore. Perhaps the best place in Florida for sampling the diversity of tropical marine life, the park contains 40 varieties of delicate coral reefs teeming with colorful inhabitants. On land, there are a variety of park services, including a mangrove trail, a swimming area, daily tours by glass-bottom boat, and a marina with canoe rentals. Many area outfitters arrange scuba trips into the park. One of the most popular diving sites is near *Christ of the Deep,* a nine-foot statue in 20 feet of water that symbolizes the hope for peace on earth. Arrive early on weekends; the park closes its gates when it's full. ♦ Admission. Daily. MM 102.5, Key Largo (oceanside). 451.1202

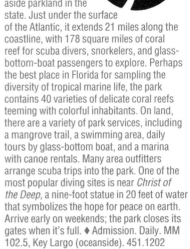

2 **Stephen Frink Photo** First-time divers and experienced "aquanauts" alike have turned to Frink to record their aquatic adventures on film or videotape. He will provide training and equipment rental for underwater photography, with advance reservations. The shop also sells some nonphotographic underwater gear and clothing for landlubbers. ♦ M-Sa, Su morning. MM 102.5, Key Largo (bayside). 451.3737 ♿

2 Maritime Museum of the Florida Keys
The history of the Keys brims with fascinating shipwrecks and the treasures they left behind. This museum displays silver and gold coins and maritime artifacts spanning 400 years. A reconstructed shipwreck is on view, and educational programs explore the underwater world. ♦ Admission. Daily. MM 102, Key Largo (bayside). 451.6444 ♿

DOLPHINS PLUS INC.

2 Dolphins Plus Allowing humans to swim with dolphins is controversial: Some experts believe it's unsafe for both the dolphin and the human. Nonetheless, several places in the Upper and Middle Keys offer visitors the chance to get in the water and hold on to a dolphin's dorsal fin for a short ride. Some entrepreneurs lure dolphins with a fish treat, but at this research and education facility, the incentives are reduced in favor of a more gradual get-acquainted experience between visitors and the sea mammals. Sessions for physically challenged patrons are available by prior arrangement. Experienced swimmers only are allowed; children must be at least 10 years old and accompanied by aparent. ♦ Admission. Daily. Reservations required. S Ocean Bay Dr, MM 100.6, Key Largo (oceanside). 451.1993 ♿

2 Ganim's Kountry Kitchen $$ Everyone loves breakfast in the islands, and this casual spot serves the most famous morning meal on Key Largo. With its smorgasbord of good, hearty American food, lunch is popular as well. This is the sort of unpretentious place where sauce is called gravy, and the coffeepot is never empty. ♦ American ♦ Daily breakfast and lunch. MM 100.5, Key Largo (bayside). 451.2895 ♿

2 Sea Dwellers Sports Center Key Largo is home to many outfitters and underwater equipment centers, and this is considered one of the best. It offers a wide range of gear for novices and experts, and the helpful staff will make your dive in nearby **Pennekamp Park** (see above) a pleasurable one. It's also a good place to receive licensed scuba instruct-ion. ♦ Daily. MM 100, Key Largo (bayside). 451.3640, 800/451.3640 ♿

2 Holiday Inn Key Largo $$$ If Key Largo had a downtown, it would be here, in the center of most of the island's hubbub. This two-story motel is on a small harbor along the Key's ocean side, and many of its 132 rooms afford views of the water. The rooms are simple and generic, but the amenities— including one restaurant and two heated pools—are good. ♦ MM 100, Key Largo (oceanside). 451.2121, 800/HOLIDAY ♿

At the Holiday Inn Key Largo:

African Queen Few so-called tourist traps match the actual thrill that comes with a voyage aboard the *African Queen* (pictured below), the 30-foot steamboat that carried Humphrey Bogart and Katharine Hepburn on their adventurous movie journey.

Built in 1912 in England, this steam launch was discovered in Africa and recruited by director John Huston to star in *The African Queen,* his 1951 film depicting the true story of a little riverboat that sank a German battle cruiser in Africa during World War I. The film was shot in Uganda and the Belgian Congo (now Zaire), and the 30-foot craft remained in Africa, serving as a supply vessel.

In 1968 the boat was brought to the US and used in charitable events to raise funds for cancer research. Before the public could be permitted to ride on the stubborn little craft, however, it took an act of Congress and President George Bush's signature to

AFRICAN QUEEN

MICHAEL BLUM

revoke the Jones Act of 1921, which forbade foreign-made vessels from engaging in coastal trade. When the *African Queen* is not in use here, it's being shown off in parades and races around the country. ◆ Admission. By appointment only. Reservations required. 451.4655 ♿

2 Key Largo Harbour Marina The waters around Key Largo are particularly rich in marine life and stunning sights. Several independently owned and operated boats are available at this marina for full- and half-day fishing and/or diving trips. ◆ Daily. Adjacent to the Holiday Inn Key Largo, 451.0045 ♿

2 Holiday Casino Cruises Despite repeated attempts by the gaming industry, Florida's constitution still bans casino gambling. But it is allowed in international waters, and several operators like this one run passengers out past the 12-mile ocean limit for casino cruises. On the 92-foot yacht *Pair-a-Dice*, which sails out of Key Largo, four-hour matinee and evening cruises include hors d'oeuvres, live entertainment, and cash bars. ◆ Daily evening cruises; W, Sa-Su matinee cruises. MM 100 (oceanside), behind the Holiday Inn Key Largo. 451.0000 ♿

2 Mrs. Mac's Kitchen ★★$ A favorite among locals, this alfresco diner offers home-style meals in a sleepy "KeyZZZ" atmosphere. Decorated with license plates from all over the country and specializing in imported beers, it wins accolades for its lunch, with great barbecue, chili, soups, burgers, pita sandwiches, fresh seafood, and Philadelphia cheese steak sandwiches. ◆ American ◆ Daily lunch and dinner. MM 99.4, Key Largo (oceanside). 451.3722 ♿

2 Sheraton–Key Largo Resort $$$$ Set well away from the road, this four-story resort with 200 rooms offers a degree of privacy uncommon on Key Largo. Amenities include shops, tennis courts, sailing and diving facilities, and a variety of water sports. There is also a hammock on the property for hiking, and easy access to the Key's 14-mile cycling

The 10 "Keymandments"

Surrounded by fragile coral reefs, crystal clear water, and mangrove rookeries, **Keys** residents (who sometimes call themselves "Bubba") are fiercely protective of their environment. So protective are they that signs went up recently listing these "10 Keymandments" for visitors:

 Don't anchor on a reef. (Reefs are alive. *Alive.* A-L-I-V-E.)

 Don't feed the animals. (They'll want to follow you home. And you can't keep them.)

 Don't trash our place. (Or we'll send Bubba to trash yours.)

 Don't touch the coral. (After all, you don't even know them.)

 Don't speed. (Especially on **Big Pine Key** where Key deer reside and tar-and-feathering is still practiced.)

 Don't catch more fish than you can eat (Better yet, let them go. Some of them support schools.)

 Don't collect conch. (This species is protected. By Bubba.)

 Don't disturb the bird nests. (They find it *very* annoying.)

 Don't damage the sea grass. (And don't even think about making a skirt of it.)

 Don't drink and drive on land or sea. (There's absolutely nothing funny about it.)

and jogging path. The resort even has a small sandy beach. ♦ MM 97, Key Largo (bayside). 852.5553, 800/826.1006 &

Within the Sheraton–Key Largo Resort:

Treetops ★★$$$ This unobtrusive restaurant maintains high standards in an area not known for fine dining. The kitchen specializes in fresh seafood, especially local snapper and pompano, and there's a lovely view of Florida Bay. ♦ American/French ♦ Daily dinner. Reservations recommended. 852.5553 &

3 Old Tavernier ★$$ Tucked away from the bustle of Key Largo, this place epitomizes Keys informality. The menu is standard Italian-American, but the skill with which the usual dishes are executed is notable. The owner, of Greek descent, adds a special flair with the excellent moussaka and other Greek dishes. Don't miss the tender, tortellini-size garlic rolls. ♦ Greek/Italian ♦ Daily lunch and dinner. MM 91.8, Tavernier (oceanside). 852.4989 &

Islamorada

The most important of the **Upper Keys, Isla-morada** (pronounced here as *Eye*-luh-mor-*ah*-da, which means "purple island" in Spanish) received its name from early explorers who, from a distance, saw light-purple shells along the shore. Though there is actually a town of **Islamorada,** the designation is officially given to 18 miles of the Overseas Highway, spanning four Keys: **Plantation, Windley, Upper Matecumbe,** and **Lower Matecumbe.**

4 Marker 88 ★★$$$ Perhaps the Keys' most famous restaurant outside Key West, this place has been wowing residents and visitors for nearly 20 years with its unusual blend of classic European cooking and simple Keys approach. German-born owner-chef Andre Mueller gives the restaurant an aura of grandeur, which it sorely needs to counterbalance the incredible din. The food is Keys elegant: everything from Everglades frogs' legs to yellowtail snapper with a sauce of mango, papaya, pineapple, and banana. If you're not feeling very exotic, opt for one of the lamb dishes. ♦ Eclectic ♦ Tu-Su dinner. Reservations required. MM 88, Islamorada (bayside). 852.9315 &

4 Plantation Yacht Harbor $$ This family-oriented, two-story lodging on Florida Bay offers 56 relatively spacious and pleasantly decorated rooms, as well as a restaurant, a playground, tennis courts, and beach access. ♦ MM 87, Islamorada (bayside). 852.2381, 800/356.3215 &

the RAIN BARREL

5 Rain Barrel Stroll through tropical gardens at this cluster of artisans' shops, where the work of more than 300 artists is for sale. You'll see unique coral coffee tables, wood sculptures, paintings, stained glass, jewelry, leather, and pottery. ♦ Daily. MM 86.7, Islamorada (bayside). 852.3084 &

5 Treasure Village Inside this castlelike building, gathered around a tree-lined courtyard, are more than a half-dozen arts-and-crafts galleries and shops selling handmade gifts and clothing. Stop at the bakery for some of the best muffins and sandwiches in the Upper Keys. ♦ Daily. MM 86.7, Islamorada (oceanside). 852.0511 &

THEATER OF THE SEA

5 Theater of the Sea Several attractions in the Keys offer dolphin rides and an introduction to aquatic life, but this is one of the oldest and most dependable. In operation since 1946, this marine park provides dolphin and sea lion shows and guided tours of coral-rock tidal pools teeming with sea life. Rides on glass-bottom boats also are available. This is a great place to take pictures, and the kids get an opportunity to observe dolphins, turtles, and sharks. ♦ Admission. Daily. MM 84.5, Islamorada (oceanside). 664.2431 &

Seven Mile Bridge is the longest segmental bridge in the world, built in 1982 parallel to the original. The old bridge starred in the climactic scene in the recent Arnold Schwarzenegger film *True Lies*. In the movie, the bridge appears to explode, but the filmmakers actually used a model they built off Sugarloaf Key.

5 Pelican Cove Resort $$$ This classic Upper Keys hostelry has 63 units decorated in tropical colors, 19 of them with kitchens. In addition to enjoying the oceanside beach amenities, including Jet Ski and boat rentals, guests can play tennis or take a plunge in a whirlpool or freshwater pool. A cabana bar serves lunch and drinks, but there's no dining room. ◆ MM 84.5, Islamorada (oceanside). 664.4435, 800/445.4690 ♿

6 H.T. Chittum & Co. Known throughout the Keys as the place for tropical preppies to purchase their islandwear, this store stocks such popular brands as Patagonia, Topsider, and Paris Blues. There also is a fully equipped tackle shop with everything for the complete angler—except the fish. ◆ Daily. MM 82.7, Islamorada (bayside). 664.4421 ♿

6 The Lor-e-lei ★★$$ The food at this popular waterfront restaurant plays second fiddle to the bar, where many Keys residents convene for a day's-end celebration. Some customers like to pull lawn chairs up to the water's edge to watch the sunset over the Gulf of Mexico. The bar is boisterous, with local musical talent, and the tavern fare—burgers, seafood, and steaks—is first-rate. ◆ American ◆ Daily dinner. MM 82, Islamorada (bayside). 664.4656 ♿

6 Cheeca Lodge $$$$ This resort (pictured below) has a reputation for being the fanciest in the Upper Keys. Guests need not leave the grounds, for everything is here: tennis courts, freshwater and saltwater pools, an ocean beach, a 545-foot pier, and programs for children and environmentalists. The complex includes 49 rooms in the main lodge and 154 villas (64 with kitchens). In addition to the wonderful **Atlantic's Edge** restaurant (see below), guests dine at the **Ocean Terrace Grill** and the **Light Tackle Bar and Grill,** both open evenings. George Bush often stayed here when he was president. ◆ MM 81.7, Islamorada (oceanside). 664.4651, 800/327.2888 ♿

Within Cheeca Lodge:

Atlantic's Edge ★★★★$$$$ When Dawn Sieber became executive chef here in 1988, she turned the resort's hit-and-miss restaurant into the preeminent dining spot in the Upper Keys. The island-themed room is a bit cavernous, but it's softened with tropical flowers and a spectacular view of the water. Sieber emphasizes tasty, nutritious food made with local ingredients and a distinctive touch; rich sauces are not her style. Try the crispy salad with scallops and a strawberry-orange vinaigrette or the Key shrimp scampi with rice and beans, done with Cuban flair. ◆ American ◆ Daily dinner. Reservations recommended. 664.4651 ♿

6 Grove Park Cafe ★★$$ Keys cuisine is primarily geared toward seafood, but this new cafe offers a change of pace with a menu of healthy Italian sandwiches and Asian, Mediterranean, and Caribbean dishes. Tucked into a quaint gingerbread house, the cafe also has an ice-cream parlor serving 16 different flavors. Boaters and beachgoers can obtain packed picnic baskets here and rent umbrellas to eat under. ◆ Eclectic ◆ M-Tu, Th-Su lunch and dinner. MM 81.6, Islamorada (oceanside, old highway). 664.0116 ♿

6 Manny and Isa's ★$ Islamorada is the last place anyone would look for a Cuban-Spanish restaurant, but Isa and Manny Ortiz set up shop here almost 30 years ago and haven't had a quiet day since. The conch chowder is a big draw, and Isa's black beans and rice and chicken with yellow rice are both crowd pleasers. But what the nine-table restaurant is *really* famous for is Manny's Key lime pie, considered by many the finest in the state. Manny makes it from tiny Key limes grown in his own orchard (he patiently squeezes enough limes to make 20 to 30 pies a day). Light and tart, the pie alone is worth a trip to

Cheeca Lodge

Islamorada. ♦ Cuban/Spanish ♦ M, W-Su lunch and dinner. MM 81.5 (between Beach and Johnson Rds), Islamorada (oceanside). 664.5019 ♿

6 Green Turtle Inn ★$$$ This is another Keys tradition, specializing in local seafood with a few beef dishes thrown in for good measure. Turtle chowder (made from fresh-water turtles, not the endangered sea turtle) is on the menu, and it's available canned across the street at the restaurant's seafood market. ♦ Seafood ♦ Tu-Su lunch and dinner. MM 81.3, Islamorada (oceanside). 664.9031 ♿

7 Lignum Vitae Key State Botanical Site This lovely, remote 280-acre island, named for the lignum vitae tree, is primarily of horti-cultural interest. Budget cuts have restricted state park tour-boat service to the island, but **Robbie's Boat Rentals** (664.8070) makes trips from Indian Key Fill (a roadbed area with space for parking and a boat ramp). There's access by private boat as well. ♦ MM 77.5, Lignum Vitae Key

8 Indian Key State Historic Site Visible from the ocean side of the highway, this wooded island was once the county seat for the southern tip of Florida. Indians lived here before the Spanish arrived, and then wreckers made their home here in the late 1700s. By 1831, it had become a prosperous town with a hotel, warehouses, and a population of 70. On 7 August 1840, the Seminoles burned the town to the ground. Archaeologists have pre-served the foundations of the settlers' build-ings. Snorkeling in the four-foot-deep waters surrounding the island is spectacular. It is accessible only by boat. Call **Robbie's Boat Rentals** (see above). ♦ MM 77.5, Indian Key

9 Long Key State Recreation Area Two hiking trails and a tropical hammock full of gumbo-limbo, poisonwood, mahogany, Jamaica dogwood, and crabwood trees are the prime attractions of this state park. Campsites are located right on an ocean beach, and picnic benches, swimming, and canoeing are available for day-trippers. ♦ Nominal admission. Daily. MM 67.5, Long Key. 664.4815

10 Hawk's Cay Resort and Marina $$$$ This resort and its affiliated condominium operation make up a small community that occupies nearly all of 60-acre Duck Key. With 177 luxurious rooms—some with kitchens—it is one of a handful of ultrafancy getaways in the otherwise low-key Keys. The island has

a cozy lagoon, and among the many resort amenities are tennis courts, a small spa, several cafes and a restaurant, organized activities for children, and all the usual sports rentals. ♦ MM 61, Duck Key (oceanside). 743.7000 ♿

Within Hawk's Cay Resort and Marina:

Portacayo ★★$$$$ Overlooking the oceanside pool, this casually elegant restaurant specializes in seafood, especially the fresh local varieties such as pompano and snapper. The menu lists nothing daring, just reliable European-influenced classics with tropical touches. The desserts are excellent; the service, professional. ♦ American ♦ Daily dinner. 743.7000 ♿

Marathon

In the center of the **Middle Keys,** on long and narrow **Key Vaca,** lies the community of **Marathon,** which was named by Henry Flagler's railroad builders. Flagler's workers decided to live here once they realized their construction project was only at the halfway point, with a huge stretch of ocean still to cross. The Middle Keys are so narrow and the water so seemingly close to the road that a trip by car is mesmerizing.

The Keys, especially the Middle and **Lower Keys,** which depend so much on tourism, are quick to respond to economic fluctuations, and Marathon has had its share of ups and downs. It is far enough away from Miami that it receives less weekend traffic than **Islamorada** and the **Upper Keys,** but it remains a center of tourist activity because of its size and its newly expanded airport, served by several airlines from Miami and Orlando.

11 Holiday Inn Resort & Marina $$ With 134 small rooms, a single swimming pool, and a dining room, this is one of the least extravagant resorts in the Keys. The price is affordable, too. ♦ MM 54, Marathon (oceanside). 289.0222, 800/HOLIDAY ♿

12 Sombrero Resort $$ Close to Sombrero Beach, this medium-size resort offers comfortable accommodations; 124 of the 154 units are suites, a few with balconies. On the grounds are a dining room, a tennis court, and a pool. ♦ 19 Sombrero Blvd (Sombrero Beach Rd at MM 50), Marathon (oceanside). 743.2250, 800/433.8660; fax 743.2998 ♿

12 Museum of Natural History of the Florida Keys Located in Crane Point Hammock, this facility was established in 1990 by the Florida Keys Land Trust, a private conservation group attempting to preserve Keys traditions. Architectural exhibits and a plant arboretum form the basis of the collection, which traces Keys history to its American Indian and Bahamian ancestors. ♦ Admission. M-Sa; Su after-noon. 5550 Overseas Hwy (55th St at MM 50.5), Marathon (bayside). 743.9100 ♿

12 Buccaneer Resort $$ Laid-back in the way of the Middle and Lower Keys, this 10-acre hostelry is both a lodge and a resort: It has plenty of resort amenities, including tennis and

boat rentals, but less of the urban boisterousness common to other resorts. There are 50 bargain-priced cottages and 26 more expensive two-bedroom condominium units with kitchens. There's no restaurant on the premises. ♦ MM 49, Marathon (bayside). 743.9071, 800/237.3329 ♿

13 Pigeon Key This four-acre island is popular with local artists who like to sketch and paint here. It's possible to go on a narrated tour of the island, which explains its history and buildings, all listed on the National Registry of Historic Places. A railroad construction camp from 1908 to 1935, the Key also served as a research center for the **University of Miami**, and it's noted for its abundant marine life. You can't drive to the island (no cars are allowed), but you can catch a shuttle bus (for a fee) at Knight Key (MM 48, bayside) and ride to the island. Or if you're in the mood for a hike, walk (or bicycle) two miles on **Seven Mile Bridge** (see below). ♦ Admission; children under eight free. Tu-Su. 289.0025

14 Seven Mile Bridge Spanning the longest stretch of water on Flagler's railroad, this bridge was one of the engineering wonders of the world when it was built in 1910. The original structure was erected in four parts, with a movable span for ships that needed more than the 23-foot clearance. A 1935 hurricane destroyed the railroad but left the bridge standing; work began in 1936 to widen and pave over the track, converting it to a highway. Narrow and disconcerting to motorists, the bridge was finally replaced in 1982 with a wider one. Spanning Moser Channel, where there used to be a draw-bridge, the new bridge is higher in order t o allow ships to pass. Still visible, the old bridge is unused now except by fishers and joggers and by visitors to Pigeon Key. ♦ From MM 47 to MM 40

In 1912, Henry M. Flagler's railroad was completed up to Knight's Key, when dredging problems halted the work. Flagler's health was failing, so two of his rail bosses asked the workers to make a "marathon" effort to extend the line to Key West before he died. Today the town that grew around the workers' camp is called Marathon.

15 Bahia Honda State Park The State of Florida has established a lovely park for swimming, camping (cabins are available for rent, too), or just a quick escape from the hectic highway. A beach with such fine sand (great for building sand castles, as the child pictured at right is doing) is rarely found in the normally rocky Lower Keys. A nature trail leads to areas of unusual

tropical plants and large bird populations. You can also get a close look at what remains of Flagler's old railroad bridge as it crosses the deep channel. ♦ Admission. Daily. MM 37, Bahia Honda Key. 872.2353

16 Little Palm Island $$$$ Because the Overseas Highway doesn't cross this island, it is the most exclusive resort in the Keys. Accessible only by private launch, it boasts the Keys' finest restaurant (see below), as well as top-flight amenities, including canoes, scuba and snorkel gear, and an exercise room. The goal here is privacy: There are no telephones or TVs in the rooms. The 30 suites have thatch roofs, and there's a tiki bar out by the lagoon pool and waterfall. Among more customary Keys diversions, numerous water sports and boats are available. A launch to the resort leaves Little Torch Key at the bottom of every hour. ♦ MM 28.5, Little Torch Key (oceanside). 872.2524, 800/343.8567 ♿

At Little Palm Island:

Little Palm Island Restaurant ★★★ $$$$ Open to the public as well as to resort guests, this is consistently the Keys' top dining spot outside Key West. True to its location, the dining room recalls the tropics, with its bamboo and rattan furnishings, bright fabrics, ceiling fans, and rough-hewn wooden frames around the French doors and windows. Chef

Michel Reymond has the resources and imagination to assemble a menu far beyond the standard fare found elsewhere in the islands. Smoked salmon with black beans and goat cheese, lamb cooked with herbs and Pinot Noir, and fresh fish grilled or delicately sauced are among his light and delightful creations. Thursday nights feature a seven-course, prix-fixe meal. The wine list is extensive, and the service is excellent. ◆ Continental ◆ Daily lunch and dinner. Reservations required. 872.2551 ♿

17 National Key Deer Refuge Key deer, a miniature subspecies of the Virginia white-tailed deer, are not found anywhere else in the world. Hunted almost to extinction and endangered by speeding cars and loss of habitat, the population now numbers about 300. They are elusive but can be spotted, chiefly in the early morning and twilight hours, in this protected area. A one-and-a-half-mile nature trail features a side trail to Blue Hole, a former rock quarry now filled with freshwater and home to several alligators. ◆ Free. Daily. Overseas Hwy (Watson Blvd at MM 28), Big Pine Key. 872.2239

18 Looe Key Reef Resort $$ Looe Key, seven miles off the coast of the Torch Keys, is not itself an island, but rather one of the most popular diving destinations in the islands. This 23-room resort/motel is an equally popular diving spot. The anchorage is just off Torch-Ramrod Channel, and plenty of dive boats, such as the HMS *Looe* at **Dolphin Marina,** are nearby. ◆ MM 27.5, Ramrod Key (oceanside). 872.2215, 800/942.5397 ♿

19 Mangrove Mama's ★★★$$ There could hardly be a less pretentious restaurant than this one. The well-worn, down-home decor and informal atmosphere make customers feel at home as soon as they enter. After the *Miami Herald* declared that it had the best Key lime pie made in the Florida Keys, the restaurant's reputation spread, and it began to lure those driving from Miami to Key West. Good food is the secret of this success, say owners Tom and Kathleen Kelly, but it helps to keep prices low (since they own the building, they don't pay the high rents that predominate in Key West). The simple menu emphasizes fresh seafood, steaks, and some vegetarian dishes, and nothing comes out of a can. Sitting to the side of the Overseas Highway, the building can be missed easily by preoccupied motorists. ◆ American ◆ Daily lunch and dinner. MM 20, Overseas Hwy (bayside). 745.3030 ♿

Bests

Millard Wells, A.W.S.
Artist/Instructor, Wells Studio-Gallery

As an artist moving into the **Florida Keys** in the late 1970s, I found a home, warm climate year-round, lush tropical foliage, and the water—the most breathtaking I'd ever seen.

Today much of that enchantment still exists. The trip down the Keys is a trip-by-the-numbers starting at **Florida City,** MM 127. I personally like salads, fruit, and fish, most of which are featured in all Keys restaurants. The view down the 18-mile uninhabited stretch is a preview off to the left of the Florida **Everglades.**

The Everglades is a "must see" . . . great lunches and motel at **Flamingo** in the national park. Bird trips at sundown about 40 miles west of Florida City.

My favorite painting locations are the state parks. The **Islamorada** area, MM 76 south to **Marathon,** has **Indian Key State Historic Site**—unspoiled and lush. **Lignum Vitae Key** is another historical site. See Park Ranger Pat Wells, most courteous and also authoritative on astronomy. The skies are best in the Keys year-round. **Long Key State Recreation Area** in Layton has the best camping on the ocean.

South through Marathon is **Bahia Honda State Park** with about two miles of natural ocean beach. The best beach on the Keys has picnic areas, across the **Seven Mile Bridge** at MM 40.

Art students ask where to paint in **Key West** (the end of our trip down the Keys). I tell them "just get out of the car"—the whole town is picturesque.

The trip to Key West from the mainland should be started about 7AM with the sun at your back—great view by car. The trip back is good at 4PM—again with the sun at your back. The view is unrivaled.

Steven Brooke
Architectural Photographer

Sunrise—standing at the water's edge, looking toward the Art Deco hotels on **Ocean Drive.**

Sunset—on **Tamiami Trail** in the **Everglades.**

Full moon rise—from the lifeguard stand at **South Beach.**

Breakfast at the **Parrot Jungle and Gardens** in **Coconut Grove.**

Coral Gables, with its beautiful fountains and entrances.

Old Cutler Road, from the traffic circle to **Fairchild Tropical Gardens; Columbus Avenue** in Coral Gables; and **Alhambra Circle** in Coral Gables.

Mimi Kelly
Director of Development & Marketing, Miami-Dade Office of Film, Television & Print

Café con leche at **Nina's** on Bird Road.

Berry picking in the Redlands.

Browsing at **Books & Books.**

Bicycling in the back roads of **South Dade County.**

Key West

The southernmost city in the continental US and the most famous of the Florida Keys, Key West is an island-city with a split personality, part Caribbean and part American. When it was established in 1822, it was the first permanent settlement in the Keys. It's separated from the mainland by a string of islands and 42 bridges along **Highway 1 (Overseas Hwy).**

Closer to Havana than to Miami, Key West really does evoke the Caribbean, with its lush foliage, flaming orange poinciana and century-old banyan trees, secluded lanes, Bahamian-style gingerbread houses, and a population that includes many with Bahamian and Cuban roots. Almost every language can be heard on a walk down **Duval Street**, the island's main commercial thoroughfare, and people watching from a sidewalk bench is a treat.

Then there's the other Key West. Duval Street, for instance, is teeming with bars and clubs blaring raucous music, dozens of T-shirt shops, hawkers, and, in winter, a sprinkling of homeless.

Hustle and bustle notwithstanding, Key West remains small-townish, a place where friends run into each other at the post office and chat on street corners. But its facade is cosmopolitan, for Key West's weather, laid-back atmosphere, and tolerant attitude make it a haven for freethinkers, struggling and successful artists, and just plain eccentrics. Its three live theaters and annual literary seminar attract noted writers. Also part of the Key West scene are a large number of gays, who have restored some of the **Old Town**'s handsomer homes. (Old Town, or the historic district, refers to Key West's older section, which occupies the west end of the island, bounded roughly by Front, South, Fort, and Frances Streets.)

Generally, Key West is expensive for tourists, since its hotel rates are as high as in most big cities. But once on the island, visitors can have a delightful time simply walking or biking. Visitors will find "Conchs" (pronounced

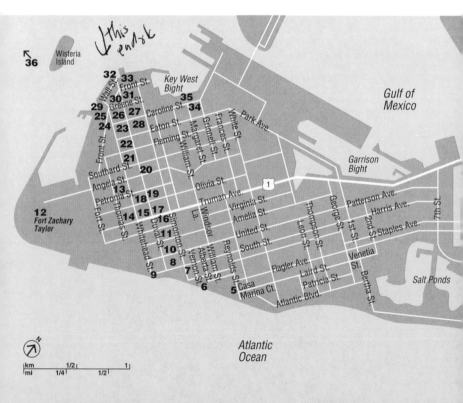

Conks)—as natives call themselves—easygoing, though they did get upset back in the early 1980s, when law enforcement officials stopped cars entering the Keys to search for drugs. That led to an "insurrection," which resulted in the tongue-in-cheek formation of the Conch Republic, which stages an annual "independence" celebration—with, in true Conch fashion, parties and more parties.

Area code 305 unless otherwise indicated.

1 Holiday Inn Beachside $$$ By Key West standards, this hotel is located impossibly far from the historic district—at least three miles. But it is the first lodging motorists encounter when they arrive on the island, and it's conveniently close to the airport. The 172 rooms are neat and comfortable, though not large. On the property are a restaurant, tennis courts, and—unlike Old Town lodgings—there's a beach nearby. ◆ 3844 N Roosevelt Blvd (near the Gulf of Mexico). 294.2571, 800/HOLIDAY; fax 296.5659 ♿

2 Casa Alante $$$ Sisters Sandy Erb and Katrina Birt, who hail from Sydney, Australia, are the owners of one of Key West's newest bed-and-breakfasts, set on an acre of tropical gardens with a large pool. Originally part of an estate belonging to the Packard Motor Company family, the seven cottages have recently been remodeled with private baths, air-conditioning, and cable TV. Guests are pampered with terrycloth robes, oversized towels, Battenburg lace bedspreads, and a complimentary continental breakfast served on the private terraces. The off-street parking is convenient, and boats can be rented nearby. ◆ 1435 S Roosevelt Blvd (between Eagle Ave and Hwy 1). 293.0702 ♿

3 Best Western Key Ambassador $$$ In addition to 100 reasonably spacious rooms, this hotel features a poolside bar and grill (for lunch only), screened balconies, and a pool. It's close to the airport and not far from Smathers Beach, one of Key West's few sandy strands. Free airport transportation is available. ◆ 3755 S Roosevelt Blvd (east of the airport entrance). 296.3500, 800/432.4315; fax 296.9961 ♿

4 Key West International Airport (EYW) Key West receives commercial flights primarily from Miami via **USAir, American Eagle, Airways Inter-national,** and **Com Air,** the **Delta** connection. (**Delta** flies in from Ft. Lauderdale.) Many charter airlines leave here for destinations throughout Florida and the Caribbean. ◆ SE corner of the island (off S Roosevelt Blvd). 296.5439 ♿

5 Marriott's Casa Marina Resort $$$$ Though near Southernmost Point (see below) and the historic district, this resort, built in 1921, appeals to those who want a self-contained retreat. The elegantly furnished lobby and intricately landscaped grounds remain an attractive reminder of the glory days, when Henry Flagler's railroad arrived in Key West. The 314 rooms are large and comfortable, and the resort offers tennis, two pools, a nearby beach, an exercise room, children's activities, and valet parking. ◆ 500 Reynolds St (at Casa Marina Ct). 296.3535, 800/235.4837 in FL, 800/626.0777 ♿

Within Marriott's Casa Marina Resort:

Flagler's ★★$$$ Key West may be one of the few locations in Florida where the experience of fine dining is enjoyed primarily at hotels, and this casual yet elegant place is a good example. Serving well-executed classics, the kitchen displays an especially deft hand with fresh pasta and local fish dishes. Nightly specials feature Florida lobster. Live music frequently accompanies dinner. ◆ American ◆ Daily breakfast, lunch, and dinner. Reservations recommended. 296.3535 ♿

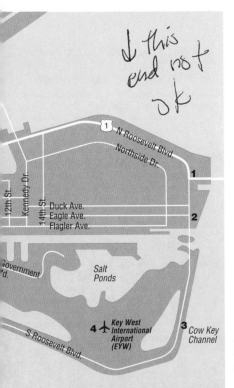

Restaurants/Clubs: Red   **Hotels:** Blue
Shops/ 🌳 Outdoors: Green   **Sights/Culture:** Black

Take the Plunge: Diving Diversions off the Florida Keys

The waters surrounding **Key West** are a prime reason for the island's popularity as a major resort; in fact, some locals call these sparkling blue-green waters their liquid asset.

Fishing and diving are as popular, if not more so, as any of the onshore activities in Key West, because the waters surrounding the island are teeming with fish, and the Keys claim to have the only coral reef in the continental US. The reef, which attracts visitors from all over the world, is a fascinating underwater home to a spectrum of beautiful and fragile marine life: brilliantly colored anemones, huge sponges, parrotfish, barracuda, bright blue damselfish, sea urchins—and coral. Reef locations commonly visited by charter boats include **Sand Key Lighthouse, Rocky Key,** and **Eastern** and **Western Dry Rocks.**

Scuba diving and snorkeling offer the most complete reef experiences. Catamarans, as well as some of the island's magnificent old schooners and powerboats, take groups of 30 to 50 people on trips. The prices of these tours vary, so make sure to shop around, and pick a captain and boat you feel at ease with. An important and comforting factor is that Key West has a good diving safety record.

Those who don't snorkel or dive can still see the beauties of the reef from a glass-bottom boat. Several boats—especially catamarans and schooners—offer sunset cruises, which evoke a sense of romance. In fact, numerous couples are married each year on late afternoon cruises, which usually feature food and drink and, often, music.

6 Louie's Backyard ★★★$$$$ Key West's most famous restaurant is set in a 1909 building that was the home of Captain James Adams, a boatbuilder and wrecker. The eatery opened in the 1960s, only to close for a time in the late 1980s; fortunately, it's back in business. Executive chef Ellen Ferry blazes new trails in island cooking, using upscale techniques to prepare simple ingredients like fresh fish, black beans, Caribbean tubers, and fiery peppers. The results are consistently pleasing, and the food is enhanced by the outdoor terrace setting. In fact, the large terrace overlooking the Atlantic is the best spot around for an oceanside nightcap. ◆ American ◆ Daily lunch and dinner. Reservations required. 700 Waddell Ave (at Alberta St). 294.1061 ﹠

7 Marriott's Reach Resort $$$$ With 150 rooms and 70 suites, this is one of Key West's most famous and posh resorts. It's also one of the biggest and, at five stories, one of the tallest. You won't find some of the amenities other resorts offer (there's no tennis court, for example), and it has lost a bit of its grace recently, but in other ways it excels—from its classic beach location to its exercise room and health club, boat rentals, and more. There is a restaurant on site. ◆ 435 Simonton St (at South St). 296.5000, 800/874.4118; fax 296.2830 ﹠

8 La Mer $$$ Managed by the same group that runs the **Southernmost Motel** (see below), this 11-unit, two-story guest house with an ocean view is geared toward families and visitors staying for several days. Some units have private balconies, others have porches, and six include kitchens. There's no restaurant. ◆ 506 South St (at Duval St). 296.5611, 800/354.4455 ﹠

8 Southernmost Motel $$ While still very close to the historic district, this motel is set in a quiet neighborhood just off the ocean. The 127 units are small, and there's no dining room; on the upside, however, the pool (with a tiki bar) is excellent, and there's a sundeck on the roof. ◆ 319 Duval St (at South St). 296.6577, 800/354.4455; fax 294.8272 ﹠

9 Southernmost Point A few short blocks south of the sign that officially designates the end of Highway 1, you'll find one of Key West's most popular attractions—the southernmost point in the continental US. It is marked by a large painted buoy, and people from around the world gather here for snapshots. No one seems to mind that the actual southernmost point is a few hundred yards away—this just happens to be where the southernmost streets end. ◆ Corner of Whitehead and South Sts

10 La Terraza di Martí $$$ In the 1890s Key West was a hotbed of activity for the Cuban Revolutionary Party, a political group seeking freedom from Spanish rule. Rumor has it that José Martí, the group's most famous leader, once gave a speech here, hence the hotel's name. "La-Te-Da," as it's known to locals, is now a popular upscale hotel catering primarily, but not exclusively, to a gay clientele. The hotel retains much of its 19th-century charm, though it has been upgraded with modern conveniences. The remodeled original building winds around the pool area like the convoluted branches of a banyan tree. Some of the 16 rooms have Jacuzzis; all are comfortable and charming. ♦ 1125 Duval St (between Catherine and Louisa Sts). 296.6706 &

Within La Terraza di Martí:

La-Te-Da ★★$$$ During the week, this is a popular upscale restaurant, and on weekends the terrace is packed for a very leisurely brunch. The menu urges customers to "take time to be out to lunch," and in fact service from the kitchen can be painfully slow. But the tables are attractively placed around the pool, and the drink service is much quicker. Once it arrives, the delightful food is worth the wait. Chef Mary Wade prepares everything from New York strip steak to innovative pasta, but her signature dish is a grilled whole yellowtail snapper. ♦ American/eclectic ♦ Daily lunch and dinner. Reservations recommended. 296.6706 &

11 Flamingo Crossing ★★$$ Dan and Eleanor McConnell, transplants from Chicago, make 100 flavors of additive-free ice cream at this place, which recalls an old-fashioned ice-cream parlor. Sit under one of the big trees (there are no indoor tables) and sample such exotic flavors as blue Curaçao, ambrosia, banana nut, guanabana, mango, and green tea (especially popular with the island's Japanese restaurants). They also serve sorbets, milk shakes, and frozen yogurt. In addition, Dan runs the **Mosquito Coast,** an organization that, among other activities, conducts five-hour nature tours of the area's small islands and mud flats where fish spawn and birds nest, and he provides kayaks and a nature guide for the trips (reservations 294.7178). ♦ Daily 11AM–midnight. 1105 Duval St (at Virginia St). 296.6124 &

12 Fort Zachary Taylor State Historic Site Construction of this fort began in 1845. Intended to guard and build up Key West's natural harbor, it was located 1,000 feet offshore and connected to the island by an L-shaped bridge. The walls of the trapezoid-shaped fortress were five feet thick and 50 feet high, dimensions guaranteed to deflect even the most powerful cannon-balls—until the invention of the rifled cannon, that is. By 1866, when the fort was completed, it had become embroiled in the Civil War. Despite Florida's decision to side with the Confederacy, the fort housed a garrison of 800 Union troops, who made sure the island was loyal to the North. After the war, the fort stood abandoned until the Spanish-American War (the Conchs still talk about the *Maine,* the ship that was blown up in Havana Harbor). Used intermittently over the years, the fort never fired another hostile

shot, and it gradually became landlocked as sand was pushed into the harbor by surging tides. The Navy took over the structure in 1947. In 1968, a naval architect excavating a building near the fort uncovered one of the finest collections of Civil War armaments ever found, many of which are on display here. Designated a National Historic Site in 1973, **Fort Zachary Taylor** today stands in ruins, but it is still an intriguing place to visit. ♦ Admission. Daily 8AM–sunset. Enter off Southard St. 292.6713 &

13 Blue Heaven Restaurant ★★$$ Tucked away in the Bahama Village section, this spot is a favorite with locals and tourists alike. The decor might best be described as Caribbean tacky. The place is informal even by Key West standards; chickens peck at the bark-chip floor as dogs wander in and out. The **Bordello Art Shop** gallery is upstairs, and a water tank —a vestige of the old overseas railroad—sits on a ledge above an outdoor stage. Owners Richard Hatch and Suann Kitchar serve tasty food at modest prices. The menu leans toward health food, with fresh fish available almost daily. Music and poetry readings are often performed on the outdoor stage on Friday nights. ♦ Eclectic ♦ W-Su breakfast, lunch, and dinner. 729 Thomas St (between Petronia and Angela Sts). 296.8666 &

14 Key West Lighthouse Museum The **Key West Lighthouse** was built in 1840, and its lantern was visible for 15 miles around the island's treacherous shoals. In 1969, when a new warning beacon was installed, the light-house was converted to the **Lighthouse Military Museum.** Its name has since changed, but it still offers a surprisingly large collection of military and historical memora-bilia and, more generally, an extensive survey of Keys history. In addition to its fine array of Civil War artifacts, don't miss the diminutive Japanese submarine captured at Pearl Harbor. Well run and continuously growing, this museum is one of the island's hidden treasures. The view of Key West from the tower is particularly good. ♦ Admission. Daily. 938 Whitehead St (at Truman Ave). 294.0012

15 Ernest Hemingway Home and Museum Hemingway discovered Key West in the 1920s and frequently returned here, seeking peace and tranquillity. In 1931 he bought this 1851 Spanish Colonial house, which he owned until his death in 1961. It is now a museum, filled with the writer's furniture and memorabilia, as well as copies of the works he wrote while on Key West, including *For Whom the Bell Tolls* and "The Snows of Kilimanjaro." Hemingway himself collected and planted much of the extensive vegetation surrounding the house. ♦ Admission. Daily. 907 Whitehead St (at Truman Ave). 294.1575 &

16 Square One ★★★★$$$ This restaurant is one of the most popular in Key West. To keep things fresh, chef Tim Reynolds and owner Michael Stewart change the menu four times a year. The key to its success is the relaxed tropical atmosphere: People can take one hour to eat—or four. Specialties are sea scallops and yellowtail, served differently each night. Also on the menu: pork scallopini, veal, and seafood. Joe Lowe and Paul Murray play mostly old, mellow tunes on the piano. ♦ Nouvelle American ♦ Daily dinner. Duval Sq, 1075 Duval St (between Truman Ave and Virginia St). 296.4300 &

17 Lucky Street Gallery Key West was once considered an artists' colony, but things have become very commercial in recent years. This is a good example of a reliable enterprise with fine island art: bright sunny paintings, intriguing sculpture, and the odd piece of furniture. Keep an eye out for hand-blown glass created by local artisans. ♦ Daily. 919 Duval St (at Truman Ave). 294.3973 &

17 Lighthouse Cafe ★★$$$ There's no lighthouse here, just a one-story house with a kitchen. The menu, which emphasizes pastas, is enlivened with brochettes (scallop or shrimp) and good seafood dishes, especially the cioppino, an Italian seafood stew. ♦ Italian ♦ Daily dinner. 917 Duval St (at Truman Ave). 296.7837 &

Croissants de France

18 Croissants de France ★★$$$ A decade ago, baker Claude Lucas and his former wife, architect Carol Eberhardt, came here from France with $4,000, fixed up a dilapidated building, and started selling croissants. Today the restaurant has an outdoor deck and serves food all day. The house specialty is couscous, served with beef, curried chicken, prime ribs, or *boeuf bourguignon*. The *gallettes* (pastries) and sweet crepes are made with chocolate, apples, bananas, and other fruits. Locals and visitors alike stop by for heavenly croissants and coffee. ♦ French ♦ Daily breakfast, lunch, and dinner. 816 Duval St (between Petronia and Olivia Sts). 294.2624 &

19 Duval House $$ A country cottage in the middle of town—that's how this elegant 1880 guest house feels. There's a small pool in the secluded courtyard in the back, and most of the 25 rooms are furnished with antiques. No children under age 15 are allowed, and there's no restaurant. ♦ 815 Duval St (between Olivia and Petronia Sts). 294.1666 &

20 Antonia's ★★$$$ Small and pretty, this place seems quietly removed from Duval Street's hustle. The menu is Northern Italian in spirit, with some island touches added to the seafood. Fettuccine with artichokes; linguine with tuna, black beans, and tomato; lamb chops with mustard and rosemary; and ravioli with fresh sage are some of the standouts. And the wine list is good. ♦ Italian ♦ Daily dinner Jan-May, Aug, Nov-Dec; M, Th-Su dinner June-July, Sept-Oct. Reservations recommended. 615 Duval St (between Southard and Angela Sts). 294.6565 &

THE GARDENS HOTEL
KEY WEST

20 Gardens Hotel $$$$ Located in the heart of the historic district on what was once the island's largest private estate, this new hotel, with 15 rooms and two suites, is the epitome of elegance. Thousands of century-old bricks once used as ship's ballast pave the graceful walkways that meander through the lush grounds; the bright and airy rooms burst with floral motifs. New Zealand artist Peter Williams's Impressionistic art adds color. The property was the home of the late Peggy Mills, a grande dame who bought a dozen or so small, dilapidated houses and tore some of them down in 1930 to make way for her walkways and gardens. The main house, carriage house, and a cottage remain from her original estate, while the two new buildings blend with the old. A breakfast buffet is served, but there's no restaurant. ♦ 526 Angela St (at Simonton St). 294.2661 (phone and fax), 800/526.2664 &

21 La Trattoria Venezia ★$$$ No gondolas ply the Key waterways, but Venetian cooking is making a big splash at this small, charming restaurant. The fresh pastas are good, and the seafood gets high praise, though the veal dishes are average. While the cuisine is predominantly Italian, a hint of Gallic influence creeps in now and then. ♦ Italian ♦ M-F lunch and dinner; Sa dinner. Reservations recommended. 524 Duval St (between Southard and Fleming Sts). 296.1075 &

↗ pick up breakfast here

21 San Carlos Institute Cuban refugees who came to Florida to plan their country's fight for independence from Spain founded this institute in a small wooden building in 1871. After having several homes, the group moved into this Baroque building in 1924. The institute —which over the years fell into decay—has been restored to its former splendor, at a cost of several million dollars. With its checkered Cuban-tile floors, marble stairways, hand-crafted mosaics, graceful curves and arches, ornate windows, and a theater with 400 bright-red plush seats, the interior has been called the most beautiful in Key West. Concerts, seminars, plays, and other events are held here, but the institute serves mainly as a cultural center for the Cuban diaspora, housing a school, museum, library, and conference center. ♦ Admission to theater. Tu-Su. 516 Duval St (between Southard and Fleming Sts). 294.3887 &

21 Jimmy Buffett's Margaritaville Cafe ★$$ The quintessential Key West poet-made-good, Jimmy Buffett sang songs about looking for the "cheeseburger in paradise" (it's on the menu here, and it's actually quite tasty) and drinking margaritas in the sun, tunes that capture one aspect of the languid Keys mentality. Festooned with pictures of the island's biggest pop star, Buffett's cafe is a comfortable place to grab a quick bite and have a margarita or other cool drink. The shop off the dining room sells T-shirts and other Margaritaville memorabilia. ♦ American ♦ Daily lunch and dinner. 500 Duval St (at Southard St). 292.1435 &

21 Fast Buck Freddie's This Key West tradition (for at least a couple of decades) is a cross between a dime store and **Bloomingdale's.** It sells beachwear and upscale poolside loungewear, toys for both children and adults, linen, table settings, and a good deal more. Service is laid-back, but the selection is upscale and contemporary. The store is located in the same complex as **Jimmy Buffett's** (see above). ♦ Daily. 500 Duval St (at Southard St). 294.2007 &

22 Holiday Inn La Concha $$$ Though it bears the name of a chain hotel, this is a Keys establishment from the ground up, based on an extensive renovation of the earlier **Hotel La Concha,** built in 1925. In the heart of the historic district, the renovated building, with its coral exterior, fits in well with the surrounding architecture. The 160 spacious, deep green rooms have brass fixtures and other quality appointments, including furniture that emphasizes its 1920s origins of the hotel. A big advantage is its location on Duval Street, close to major attractions. The hotel is not on the beach, but it has a pool; also on site are two restaurants. ♦ 430 Duval St (between Fleming and Eaton Sts). 296.2991, 800/HOLIDAY; fax 294.3283 &

23 Kelly's Caribbean Bar/Grill & Brewery ★★$$ Opened in 1993 by actress Kelly McGillis and her husband, Fred Tillman, this place adds a sparkling touch to Old Town, with its gleaming white Conch structures and surrounding picket fence. At its heart is the old PanAm Building, which was headquarters for the airline when it used to fly from Key West to Havana. With its huge old trees, the brick courtyard in the back is a pleasant spot to dine. Try the panfried fish with papaya, Delmonico steak marinated in pineapple and coconut, or spicy conch salad. On the property is a small brewery. ♦ Caribbean ♦ Daily lunch and dinner. 301 Whitehead St (at Caroline St). 293.8484 &

23 Heritage House & Robert Frost Cottage Jeane Porter, daughter of the late Jessie Porter Newton, a leader in restoring Key West's historically significant buildings, founded this complex. Among the items on display are Chinese reverse paintings donated by Henry Flagler, and Dr. Samuel Mudd's shell box, which he made for his wife while he was in prison. Many of the furnishings are from Key West's halcyon days of wrecking and salvage—activities that made the city one of Florida's richest. Admirals, politicians, artists, poets, and even fan dancers were guests of Jessie Porter Newton, and Robert Frost spent many winters in the garden cottage named in his honor. The garden is known for its unusual plants, brought back by sea captains from their voyages to India, Africa, and other exotic locales. The original cookhouse fire-place still stands in the back garden, where pirate treasure is purportedly buried. ♦ Admission. Daily. 410 Caroline St (between Duval and Whitehead Sts). 296.3573 &

23 Wrecker's Museum Also known as the "Oldest House," this white clapboard building is a textbook example of the square, solid architecture favored by the island's earliest residents. It even has a widow's walk—not surprising, since its original occupant was a sea captain, Francis Watlington. Incorporated into the house are the oldest extant outdoor kitchen in the Keys, an 1830 wall oven, a cistern to collect rainwater, and a ceiling scuttle to allow hot air to escape. Other displays trace the history of wrecking and salvage, and there also are seven model ships. What many people really come to see, however, is the dollhouse. The intricately designed house was constructed as a tribute to Watlington's nine daughters, who lived here. ♦ Admission. Daily. 322 Duval St (between Eaton and Caroline Sts). 294.9502 &

Restaurants/Clubs: Red   **Hotels:** Blue
Shops/ ♥ Outdoors: Green   **Sights/Culture:** Black

23 Banyan Resort $$ Making up one of the most charming resorts in Key West, these three buildings combine the charm of a historic home with modern amenities. A swimming pool and whirlpool are set in a secluded garden in the back courtyard. This is a time-share property, with units rented when the owners aren't in residence. Many of the 38 suites have kitchens, and lunch is served at the tiki bar. ♦ 323 Whitehead St (between Eaton and Caroline Sts). 296.7786, 800/225.0639; fax 294.1107 ♿

24 Truman Annex When the naval station here closed in 1986, the US Navy sold this 44-acre property to developer Pritam Singhs for $17.5 million. Singhs's elaborate plans included creating a residential community and commercial/entertainment complex. Some luxury homes were built, but because of financial difficulties, his plans were scaled back, and much of the land has since been deeded to the state of Florida. Several former Navy buildings, such as a foundry, remain here, but the real gem is **Truman's Little White House** (see below). ♦ Whitehead St (at Caroline St) ♿

At the Truman Annex:

Truman's Little White House The Navy had this quaint 1890 Conch house (pictured above), formerly the commandant's quarters, restored for Harry S Truman in 1948 after his surprise victory over Thomas Dewey guaranteed him a presidency. He came to Key West for working vacations nearly a dozen times over those four years—and spawned a craze for Hawaiian shirts when Miami publicist Hank Meyer brought him one. Now on the National Registry of Historic Places, the home was restored by the Little White House Company and opened in 1991 as a presidential museum, containing considerable memorabilia of Truman's time on the island. ♦ Admission. Daily. 111 Front St (at Caroline St). 294.9911 ♿

24 Fun Kruz Casino Food, drink, gambling, and other diversions are featured on seaborne excursions aboard this ship, which sails daily from the **Truman Annex.** ♦ Call ahead for reservations and times. Pier B (between Greene and Caroline Sts). 296.7529

25 Mel Fisher's Treasure Exhibit The best-known salvager in the Keys, Mel Fisher has put much of his booty on display at this fascinating museum. Gold, silver, coins, jewelry, and gemstones, many dating back to the 17th century, are all on view. ♦ Admission. Daily. 200 Greene St (at Whitehead St). 294.5413 ♿

26 Audubon House and Gardens John Geiger was a prosperous wrecker whose splendid antebellum home, built circa 1845, was later turned into a museum containing many 18th- and 19th-century furnishings and an exceptional collection of rare works by John J. Audubon, artist and ornithologist. A frequent visitor to the island, Audubon captured local birds in many of his works. He never lived here, but several trees in the garden show up in his drawings. The exhibits include Audubon's original paintings and engravings and a well-produced video on his life and work. ♦ Admission. Daily. 205 Whitehead St (at Greene St). 294.2116 ♿

26 African Arts Mary Muthoni brings a piece of Kenya to her shop in Galleon Square, next to **Mel Fisher's Treasure Exhibit** (see above). A member of the Ikuyu tribe, Muthoni gets handicrafts from her village, so the shop is full of Kenyan masks, batiks, woven baskets, paintings, jewelry, clothing, drums, and sculptures. ♦ Daily. 218 Whitehead St (between Greene and Caroline Sts). 294.0042 ♿

26 Captain Tony's Saloon ★$ As far back as most Conchs care to remember, this location housed **Sloppy Joe's,** immortalized by Hemingway in story and legend. Tony Tarracino bought it in 1958, a few years after **Sloppy Joe's** moved across the street, and he's turned his bar into its own kind of legend. Relishing his image as a grizzled, rascally curmudgeon, Tony first ran for mayor in 1985 on a no-growth platform (Jimmy Buffett was his campaign manager); he was finally elected in 1989 (but has since been voted out). The decor—a plastic shark biting a mannequin, painted graffiti on bar stools, and tacky signs pinned up on the walls—is priceless. The fare—burgers and such—is decent; the drinks are good, too. ♦ Daily. 428 Greene St (at Duval St). 294.1838 ♿

27 Sloppy Joe's Key West ★$ It is widely known that this was Ernest Hemingway's favorite bar. Originally on Greene Street, it was named after a bar in Havana and owned by Hemingway's friend Joe Russell. Today the legend is heavily commercialized, as attested to by the T-shirt store inside. But the bar itself, a huge room filled with a raucous crowd, still has a good deal of old Keys flavor. The menu stresses burgers, with pride of place given to the "original sloppy Joe." We'll never know if it's the original, but it sure is good. ♦ American ♦ Daily. 201 Duval St (at Greene St). 294.8585 ♿

27 Curry Mansion Inn $$$ William Curry used to provide wreckers with equipment and supplies—and he did it so successfully that he became Florida's first millionaire. His mansion, completed in 1899, is filled with period antiques and Tiffany glass, capturing Key West elegance at its best. Today, the award-winning inn offers 16 rooms (in a separate building) with private baths, each opening onto the backyard pool where breakfast and (later in the day) cocktails are served. Four rooms on the second floor of the mansion are available to guests, plus eight rooms in a century-old building nearby. There's no restaurant. ♦ 511 Caroline St (at Duval St). 294.5349, 800/253.3466 ♿

Within the Curry Mansion Inn:

Curry Mansion Museum All the treasures that surround guests of the inn are also on display to those visiting this mansion-cum-museum. ♦ Admission. Daily ♿

Key West Aloe Laboratory By the time anyone gets to Key West, they've seen dozens of signs for Key West Aloe, a line of skin care and sun protection products using the gel of the aloe vera plant. Known for its healing and anesthetic qualities, the gel has found a ready market among sunburned Key West visitors. The laboratory, where some products are assembled and bottled, is small but interesting. ♦ Free. Daily. 540 Greene St (at Simonton St). 294.5592 ♿

Casa Antigua

28 Casa Antigua Other buildings may claim a piece of Ernest Hemingway, but this one— often called Key West's most unusual home— was the first place in Key West that he stayed

Writers in Residence

A sleepy fishing village with a legendary history of pirates, rumrunners, and otherwise peculiar characters, **Key West** has attracted nearly a dozen Pulitzer Prize–winning writers. Some regard it as the most important literary environment in the US today—and an annual writers' seminar in January draws aspiring scribblers from all over.

John Dos Passos described his arrival in the Conch Republic aboard Flagler's train as "riding into a dream," and he recommended it to his friend Ernest Hemingway as a place to "dry out his bones." "Papa" Hemingway moved his family to a house on Whitehead Street in 1931. It was there that he wrote *For Whom the Bell Tolls, Green Hills of Africa, A Farewell to Arms, Death in the Afternoon,* and "The Snows of Kilimanjaro." He staged local boxing matches, fished in the **Gulf Stream,** and turned drinking into a sport at **Sloppy Joe's Key West** bar (see above).

Playwright Tennessee Williams led a relatively anonymous existence here marked by solitary mornings and afternoon cocktails. Other literary greats in Key West's history include Robert Frost, Elizabeth Bishop, and Wallace Stevens.

Among Key West's contemporary writers are Alison Lurie, author of *Foreign Affairs*, David Kaufelt, poet John Malcolm Brinnin, and Shel Silverstein, whose book of poems and drawings, *Where the Sidewalk Ends*, and others have been best-sellers. Annie Dillard, who won a Pulitzer Prize for her novel *A Pilgrim at Tinker Creek,* recently bought a home and plans to live here part-time. Two other well-known writers, Nancy Friday, author of *Women on Top*, and Richard Wilbur, twice winner of the Pulitzer Prize for poetry, are winter residents. As James Kirkwood, co-author of the Pulitzer Prize–winning Broadway hit *A Chorus Line,* said: "Key West is a place for lost people who are a little tilted. It's such a crazy place that the craziness helps the writing."

To learn more about Key West's literary history, read *Key West Writers and Their Houses* by Lynn Mitsouko Kaufelt (Pineapple Press, 1986).

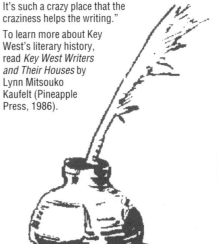

(back then, it was known as the **Coral Hotel Apartments**). It was a Ford dealership before Mary Ann and Joe Worth bought it in 1978, thus saving it from demolition. While cleaning out the building, which took two years, the Worths decided to leave the central area open, with living space on either end and walkways in between. They created a swimming pool by removing the top from one of the hotel's original water cisterns. Walking into the ultra-tropical garden, which is open for tours, is like entering another world. Also in the house is the **Pelican Poop Shoppe,** which features arts and crafts the Worths have picked up on their travels to the Caribbean and Latin America. ♦ Admission to the garden. Shop daily 10AM-6PM; garden tours on request. 314 Simonton St (between Caroline and Eaton Sts). 292.9955 &

29 Key West Aquarium This 50,000-gallon aquarium houses numerous tropical marine animals from both sides of Key West—the Atlantic and the Gulf of Mexico. Kids especially like the touch tank, where they can handle conch, starfish, and crabs. Feed-ing time at the shark tank is also quite a hit. Tours are conducted four times daily. ♦ Ad-mission. Daily. 1 Whitehead St (at Wall St). 296.2051 &

30 Clinton Square Market When developer Buck Woodruff of Atlanta decided to turn a Coast Guard building into a mini-mall, he kept its turn-of-the-century exterior. It houses some of the smarter shops in Key West, such as **America West India Co., Marine Wildlife Gallery, Blue Cat, It's You,** and **Island Jewelry.** A fudge shop and coffee bar offer respite. ♦ Daily. 291 Front St (between Whitehead and David Wolkowsky Sts). 296.6825 &

31 Key West Aloe This retail outlet carries the full and surprisingly extensive line of Key West Aloe products. ♦ Daily. 524 Front St (at Simonton St). 294.5592 &

31 Bagatelle ★★★★$$$ A grand old Conch house with wraparound porches is the setting for this elegant restaurant, which specializes in island cuisine. A fine example of classic Greek Revival architecture, the building was constructed by a sea captain in 1884 on Fleming Street and was later moved to its present site. With a splendid view of the Duval Street bustle, this popular place is famous for such dishes as Jamaican chicken, and snapper with honey-dew, cantaloupe, sliced bananas, strawberries, and kiwifruit, flamed in rum. ♦ Caribbean ♦ Daily lunch and dinner. Reservations recommended for dinner. 115 Duval St (at Front St). 296.6609 &

32 Mallory Square Sure it's touristy, but it's a tradition, and the locals join in as well to watch the sunset here each night. Sunrise and sunset times are posted in hotels and restaurants around town. The street theater changes daily, but mimes, magicians, and jugglers are invariably among the passing parade. This isn't a traditional square at all but an overgrown pier; during the day, it's a popular with anglers. ♦ Wall and Duval Sts

32 Key West Shipwreck Historeum Key West's newest museum (the name combines the words "history" and "museum") offers one of the best views in town from its **Lookout Tower.** The museum employs modern technology such as lasers to let visitors relive the days long ago when Key West was the richest city in the US. It also contains artifacts from the recently found vessel *Isaac Allerton,* which sank in 1865, and other booty from the reefs. ♦ Admission. Daily. Mallory Sq (at Wall and Duval Sts). 292.8990 &

33 Pier House $$$$ It's the rare grand hotel that fits into the Key West landscape, but this one melds perfectly. Decorated in warm pastel tones, the 120 rooms are large and comfort-able; most have private patios or balconies overlooking the water. Its beautifully land-scaped terraces, swimming pools with whirl-pools, private beach, and first-rate spa will make you want to stay in Key West forever. ♦ 1 Duval St (at Front St). 296.4600, 800/327.8340 &

Within Pier House:

Pier House Restaurant ★★★★$$$$ Tops here are the seafood and pasta, which come in such inventive combinations as lobster ravioli. The fresh fish, including grilled grouper and sautéed pompano with tart fruit butters, is outstanding, as is the wine list. The ambience is formal, with a tropical feel. You can sit indoors, or outside on a patio that affords a perfect vantage point for viewing Key West's fabled sunsets. ♦ American ♦ Daily lunch and dinner. Reservations recommended. 296.4600 &

33 Hyatt Key West $$$$ One of the Key's finest, this elegant resort has a tropical motif, with a tin-roofed bar overlooking the Gulf of Mexico to its brightly decorated rooms with ceiling fans and balconies. It offers plenty to keep guests occupied, including a large pool, a small beach, water sports, and three restaurants. Its small size (only 120 rooms) assures personalized attention from the top-flight staff. ♦ 601 Front St (at Simonton St). 296.9900, 800/233.1234; fax 292.1038 &

34 Ricco's ★$$ For years Roy Ricco sold Italian specialties from a pushcart on Stock Island (the first island north of Key West). When he opened this small place in the rear of **Maun's Market,** loyal customers followed. "If it smells like garlic, we're making money," says a sign on the wall; judging by the odor, Ricco is getting rich. He claims his meatballs are the best in the Keys, and his sausage rolls, garlic knots (a local favorite), eggplant parmigiana, and subs are equally popular. He also does a mean pizza: Among the choices are spinach, vegetarian, and Hawaiian. ◆ Italian ◆ Tu-Sat lunch and dinner. 900 Caroline St (between Margaret and Grinnell Sts). 296.5086 ఈ

35 Turtle Kraals ★$$
In the Keys, the debate over who makes the best conch chowder is ongoing, but this restaurant is high on the list of winners. It also scores points for offering good shrimp and fish dishes at reasonable prices. The setting is *very* informal—the dining

area resembles a boathouse with benches—but it's convivial, and the bar is well stocked. The name comes from some of the restaurant's residents, loggerhead turtles that weigh up to 400 pounds (the word "kraal" is Afrikaans for "pen" or "corral"). In modified pens, you can see and touch the turtles; check out the aviary that's also part of this unusual eatery. ◆ Seafood ◆ Daily lunch and dinner. Land's End Village (at the foot of Margaret St). 294.2640 ఈ

36 Fort Jefferson National Monument on the Dry Tortugas In 1513 Ponce de León discover-ed a small group of islands 70 miles west of Key West and called them Las Tortugas ("The Turtles"), after the large number of sea turtles nesting there. The islands were later named the Dry Tortugas to warn mariners that the islands had no fresh water. Pirates hauling their own water made the islands a stronghold in their raids against shipping traffic throughout the area. The US acquired the islands in 1821, and built a lighthouse here.

In 1846 the US began erecting a huge fortress completely ringing Garden Key, one of the Tortugas. **Fort Jefferson**'s eight-foot-thick walls rise 45 feet high and have a half-mile perimeter, large enough to hold 1,500 people. Technology made the fort obsolete before it was finished, however: The newly invented rifled cannon fired projectiles that penetrated stone walls (rather than bouncing off), so the fort was never completed. Instead, it was used as a federal prison both during and after the Civil War. The best-known prisoner was Dr. Samuel Mudd, the hapless physician convicted of setting the broken leg of Abraham Lincoln's assassin, John Wilkes Booth, in 1865. Continually declaring his innocence of any criminal deed, Mudd was pardoned in 1869.

Afterwards, the fort served as a quarantine station, a Navy refueling depot, a wireless station, and, during World War I, a seaplane base before being closed. In 1935 it became a National Monument administered by the **National Park Service.** Today, it is a

fascinating architectural and historical relic. Of special note is the moated entrance, which was once crossed only by a drawbridge (today, there's a permanent bridge). Also worth noting are the Tortugas' harbor light, a lighthouse built on the fort's parapet, and nearly a mile of narrow troop passageways leading to the gun rooms.

The coral reefs offshore lie in shallow, warm, and clear waters, making conditions perfect for diving. There is a park office (but still no fresh water) on the island. The **Fort Jefferson Ferry** (294.7009, 800/634.0939), sailing out of **Land's End Marina** (at the foot of Margaret St, on Key West Bight), offers full-day trips to the monument, and many charter companies provide seaplane and boat transportation from Key West. **Key West Seaplane Service** (294.6978), for instance, offers frequent flights. ◆ Key West Coast Guard 247.6211ఈ

Wright Langley
Historian, Photographer, President of Langley Press, Inc.

For the best overview of the island-city, catch the **Conch Tour Train** or **Old Town Trolley.** You can pinpoint attractions to visit later—the trolley does let you off at designated locations, and you can reboard.

Walk or bike down lanes and narrow streets, including the **City Cemetery,** with its famous epitaph, "I Told You I Was Sick." Tours are offered—check with the sexton.

View the spectacular sunset from **Mallory Square.**

So many places to eat, but a must is a Cuban restau-rant—**El Siboney** has the best variety, but if you like pork, try the Cuban Mix (sandwich on Cuban bread) at **Jose's Cantina.** For waterfront dining it's hard to beat the atmos-phere of the **Turtle Kraals** with a vestige of the island's exciting marine history in nearby historic structures.

Shops range from the touristy T-shirts to the delightful emporium of **Fast Buck Freddie's**—Key West's Bloomingdale's. Next door for all those Parrot Heads is **Jimmy Buffett's Margaritaville Cafe.**

Even though it's only seven stories, **Holiday Inn La Concha** is the highest building on the island. There's a beautiful panoramic view of the island from atop the hotel. Just a few blocks away is the **Key West Lighthouse Museum** with another bird's-eye view and the **Ernest Hemingway Home and Museum** across the street.

Other museums worth a visit—**Wrecker's Museum, Mel Fisher's Treasure Exhibit** (artifacts from the famous Spanish galleon *Atocha* and slave ship *Henrietta Marie*), **Audubon House and Gardens, Heritage House & Robert Frost Cottage, Key West Shipwreck Historeum** (animated and live interpreta-tion on the history of wrecking), **San Carlos Institute** ("Cuban Cradle of Liberty"), and the **Little White House** where Harry S. Truman spent 11 working vacations as President. There's also pre–Civil War **Fort Taylor,** with artifacts recovered from excavations and the nearby picnic and beach area—all operated as a state park.

History

8000 BC—The earliest hunters migrate into the area.

5000 BC—Florida's first permanent settlements are recorded.

1000 BC—Farming villages develop along the Miami River.

AD 500—Settlements grow and develop relatively sophisticated economic, social, and political institutions.

1400—The Indian population of Florida—about 25,000 strong—is divided into five major tribes, plus several smaller groups.

1492—Seeking trade routes to India, Christopher Columbus lands on the island of Hispañola (modern-day Haiti and the Dominican Republic).

1502—Maps are published that feature representations of the Florida peninsula, probably based on reports of voyages undertaken by British explorers John and Sebastian Cabot five years earlier.

1510—French and Spanish traders land in Florida.

1513—With a mandate from the King of Spain to find the legendary island of Bimini, its fountain of youth, and whatever gold he can discover, Juan Ponce de León sails from Puerto Rico. He lands on the Florida coast during the Easter season and names the land "La Florida," for the *Pasqua Florida* (Feast of the Flowers). Believing he has found another island, Ponce de León claims the land for the Spanish crown.

1519—Francisco de Garay explores and maps Florida's Gulf coast.

1521—Ponce de León returns to Florida to build settlements and seek gold, but he is wounded in an Indian attack, and his expedition is abandoned. He dies in Cuba, disappointed, indigent, and largely forgotten.

1525—Spanish explorers sailing up the Atlantic coast conclude that Florida is not an island but a land mass. Spanish claims encompass the entire North American continent. For the next hundred years, the Spanish use the name "La Florida" to designate all of North America.

1539—Hernando de Soto, fresh from his exploration of South America with Francisco Pizarro, organizes a major expedition to search for treasure in Florida. Unsuccessful, he dies in 1542.

1562—The French challenge Spanish claims in Florida. Several small French expeditions travel through the peninsula, building a handful of temporary settlements, including Ft. Caroline.

1565—King Philip II of Spain orders a major campaign to drive out the French interlopers, settle Florida, and convert the Indians to Catholicism. The French prove to be stubborn, the weather is miserable, and the Indians are fiercely resistant to conversion efforts. Of the settlements that have gone up, only St. Augustine survives. Meanwhile, Cuba becomes the center of Spanish power in North America.

1570—Constantly at war, the Spanish nevertheless are unsuccessful in their attempts to drive out the French or control the Indians.

1602—Having failed to discover gold in the area, Spain is unable to attract settlers to Florida. Instead of abandoning the territory, however, Spain redoubles its efforts to proselytize the native Indians. Dozens of missions are built in northern Florida, and thousands of Indians are converted, killed, or enslaved.

1670—As the British colonies expand south, the British recruit Indian allies to help them fight the Spanish.

1704—Spanish rule weakens as British raids destroy Spanish missions and devastate the native Indian population.

1708—After years of British incursions, St. Augustine is the only remaining Spanish mission.

1710—Fleeing pressure from British settlers in Georgia and Alabama and lured by the land left by departing aboriginal Indians, Creek Indians gradually move south into Florida.

1763—England and France are at war. England invades Cuba and trades it for Florida in the Treaty of Paris. Suffering from war and disease, Florida's native Indian population is reduced to fewer than 200 individuals, all of whom leave with the Spanish when Florida is turned over to the English.

1783—British Loyalists flee the US for Florida. Following the American Revolution, the British return Florida to Spain. Pro-English/anti-American sentiment on the part of Florida's British settlers runs strong.

1803—The Louisiana Purchase renders Spanish Florida totally isolated and surrounded by the ever-expanding US.

1810—Responding to popular pressure, US President James Madison annexes western Florida to Louisiana.

1818—Three years after defeating the British in the Battle of New Orleans, Andrew Jackson—now a highly regarded US Army general—moves on to Florida, where he seizes Spanish outposts, executes English subjects, and ships Spanish officials off to Cuba.

1819—By the terms of the Adams-Onis Treaty, the US obtains Florida, of which Andrew Jackson becomes provisional governor. Meanwhile, the Creek Indians—now known as Seminoles—continue to migrate south.

1820—War erupts between the Americans and the Seminoles, lasting until 1858.

1825—Florida's population reaches about 15,000, though only about 300 of its inhabitants live in the southern half of the territory.

1830—South Florida's population grows to 10,000.

1835—American troops fighting the Seminoles build roads and military posts, including Fort Dallas near Biscayne Bay.

1845—Florida is admitted to the Union, inaugurating a period of prosperity for the new state.

1861—Florida is the third state to leave the Union.

1868—A revolution in Cuba fails to overthrow the island's Spanish government. Many Cuban exiles settle in Key West, where they build a cigar industry.

1886—A fire destroys half of Key West, including the entire cigar-making industry. Most of the Cuban population moves to Tampa.

1869—William D. Brickell and Ephraim T. Sturtevant, two Cleveland businessmen, buy land near Biscayne Bay and the mouth of the Miami River, setting up an Indian trading post near the ruins of Fort Dallas.

1883—St. Augustine's warm climate and inexpensive land inspire oil magnate Henry Flagler to create a resort in the area—and to build a rail system (the Florida East Coast Railroad) to carry people to it. At around the same time, Flagler envisions a southern Newport on a small, mosquito-infested island bordering Lake Worth, which eventually will become Palm Beach.

1891—Julia Tuttle, the daughter of Ephraim Sturtevant, purchases a 600-acre tract of wilderness defined on the east by Biscayne Bay and on the south and west by the Miami River—the general boundaries of what will become downtown Miami. She appeals to Henry Flagler to extend his railroad south to Miami, but he refuses.

1894—Flagler makes West Palm Beach the focus of his building activity. William Brickell, erstwhile partner of Tuttle's father (and owner of the land both men bought in 1869), seconds Julia Tuttle in her efforts to persuade Flagler to extend the railroad to Miami, but to no avail.

1895—Henry Flagler agrees to extend the railroad to Miami.

1897—Flagler builds the lavish Royal Palm Hotel in Miami, and thousands of visitors start pouring in.

1898—Revolution breaks out in Cuba. American forces intervene, driving out Spain from Cuba. For the short duration of the Spanish-American War, 7,000 troops are stationed in Miami.

1920—George Merrick builds Coral Gables.

1925—Miami Beach is transformed into a resort for the rich and famous. The population of greater Miami reaches 150,000.

1926—A powerful hurricane hits Miami, devastating the city's economy, killing 250 people, and destroying 5,000 homes and hundreds of businesses.

1928—Another hurricane strikes, leaving even greater destruction in its wake.

1929—The stock market crashes, leading to the Great Depression.

1930—Florida's population reaches 1 million.

1950—Miami grows slowly, mainly as a retirement community.

1959—Fidel Castro leads a revolution in Cuba that overthrows the government of Fulgencio Batista.

1960—Cuban refugees begin to settle in Miami.

1961—The Bay of Pigs invasion fails, dashing hopes for a quick return to Cuba of the growing number of refugees.

1962—Miami has 1 million residents, about 100,000 of them Cuban. For the next 20 or so years, an average of about 25,000 Cubans arrive in Miami annually.

1971—Racial tensions in Liberty City—a mostly poor, mostly African-American section of Miami—escalate into confrontations between police and residents.

1979—Opening of the Florida Free Trade Zone—a designation that helps to trigger Miami's growth as an international trade center.

1980—Unrest in Cuba prompts about 125,000 Cubans to escape to the US over a few weeks in an exodus known as the Mariel boatlift. Racial tensions in Liberty City explode into massive city-wide riots.

1985—Xavier Suarez becomes Miami's first Cuban-born mayor.

1990-present—Its mild weather, low prices, Art Deco architecture, and rich Latin culture make Miami (and especially Miami Beach) a magnet for fashion photographers, models, and other glitterati. Miami is transformed from a quiet retirement town into an international jet-set vacation mecca.

1992—**Hurricane Andrew** strikes on 24 August, devastating much of South Dade County—especially the cities of Homestead and Florida City—and leaving thousands homeless.

Index

Index

Restaurants

Only restaurants with star ratings are listed below. All restaurants are listed alphabetically in the main (preceding) index. Always call in advance to ensure a restaurant has not closed, changed its hours, or booked its tables for a private party.

The restaurant price ratings are based on the average cost of an entrée for one person, excluding tax and tip.

**** An Extraordinary Experience
*** Excellent
** Very Good
* Good

$$$$ Big Bucks ($20 and up)
$$$ Expensive ($14-$20)
$$ Reasonable ($8-$14)
$ The Price Is Right (less than $8)

★★★★

Hotels

The hotels listed below are
grouped according to their
price ratings; they are also
listed in the main index. The
hotel price ratings reflect the
base price of a standard room
for two people for one night
during the peak season.

$$$$ Big Bucks ($250 andup)
$$$ Expensive ($175-$250)
$$ Reasonable ($100-$175)
$ The Price Is Right
　(less than $100)

Index